West Church Journey

Volume Two

1987 - 1998

West Church Journey

A Month by Month Record

Edited by
Rev. David Bailie

Volume Two

1987 - 1998

West Presbyterian Church
Bangor, Northern Ireland
2008

Copyright © West Presbyterian Church 2008
Published by West Presbyterian Church

All rights reserved. No part of this publication may be reproduced, stored in a retrieval system, or transmitted in any form or by any means without the prior permission in writing of the copyright owner.

ISBN: 978 0 9561826 0 9

Printed in Northern Ireland by
Dorman and Sons Limited
Unit 2, 2A Apollo Road
Belfast
BT12 6HP

"My food," said Jesus, "is to do the will of Him who sent me and to finish His work. Do you not say, 'Four months more and then the harvest'? I tell you, open your eyes and look at the fields! They are ripe for harvest".   *John 4:34*

available, many of them unsavoury and corrupting.

So a special responsibility lies with parents to seek out those that are wholesome, good and at the same time entertaining.

Derek Polley has discovered a video library with a difference. It is called 'FAMILY VIEWING', located at 9 Belmont Road, Belfast.

They refuse to stock horror, pornography or videos containing excessive bad language.

They seek to provide an alternative, videos designed for 'FAMILY VIEWING'.

'FAMILY VIEWING' now offers customers nearly 1000 titles to choose from, and a wide variety of categories.

"After two years of trading we continue to attract a large number of new members, proving that a cleaner image can also lead to new and increased business.

OUTREACH ELEMENT OF NEW HALL FUND.

The decision to give away 10% of the New Hall Fund to **outreach**, has meant that in 1986 we have been able to give well over £3000 to various causes including £800 to Leprosy work in Prantij, India.

THE BOOKSTALL,

Various books are mentioned as worthy of buying, reading and giving away at Christmas:
"WHAT EVERYONE SHOULD KNOW ABOUT HOMOSEXUALITY", written by Tim La Haye and published in 1978.

Dr Tim la Haye pulls no punches, as he draws from his extensive counselling experience.

In 1978, Tim La Haye could not have foreseen the AIDS epidemic which has spread so extensively through the gay community and greatly threatens the whole nation.

PRAYER: key to revival.
Dr Paul Yonggi Cho bases his study on one simple premise: "God has no favourite children.

What has worked for me will work for you…. If God has worked through men and women in the past, *He can also work through you."*

"YOUNG WEST CHURCH."

The beginning of the New Year heralds the beginning of a new venture in an important area of the work in West Church.

What was the BIBLE CLASS and the YOUTH SERVICE will be JOINING TOGETHER TO BECOME YOUNG WEST CHURCH.

The *YWC* service will take place each Sunday, except on FAMILY SERVICE DATES.

It will cater for those of Form one age to approximately 20 years. During part of the service there will be a time when those of Form 1 - Form 4 can be together in small groups with adult teacher/leaders.

We extend a warm welcome to all young people, whether or not they previously attended the Bible Class or the Youth Service TO BECOME PART OF THIS NEW VENTURE. We trust that the Lord will guide and lead those who attend and organise the services, and that his presence will enrich the lives of the young people.

STARTS 4th JANUARY 1987.

JANUARY WCN 1987.

Our headline for the beginning of a New Year was:
RUSSIAN-BORN JEWISH CHRISTIAN TO SPEAK AT UNITED PRAISE SERVICE

The 18th January was the date of our United Service with our Anglican and Methodist neighbours to inaugurate the annual Week of Prayer for Christian unity. It also coincided with our West Church Praise Service.

Many elements were therefore combined with a visit from ARIE BEN ISRAEL, founder and head of a ministry "CALL RO RECONCILIATION"

Sometimes our endeavours after the Unity that Christ desires for his Church can be fairly cool and academic. But not when Arie ben Israel is the guest speaker.

He was brought up in Russia in an orthodox Jewish family, raised in the spirit of the Law and of the Talmud.

His parents suffered much in concentration camps, and made every effort to emigrate to the land of their fathers. Eventually they succeeded when Arie was ten years old.

In the background of these painful experiences of his family and people **a deep hate began to grow inside him against Christians and Germans. This hatred grew even worse when his father died after just 4 years in the land of his fathers.**

And Arie was really shocked when his father told him on his deathbed that Jesus was the Saviour and Messiah of the Jews. It took him another eleven years to realise this truth in his own life, when he finally confessed: JESUS IS LORD!

From that time on his family rejected him, but his love for Jesus grew greater.

In Yad Vashem, a memorial place in Jerusalem for the victims of his people, GOD REVEALED TO HIM THE SIN OF HIS HATRED, GAVE HIM FORGIVENESS AND PLANTED A DEEP LOVE IN HIM FOR ALL HIS ENEMIES. A BURNING DESIRE TOOK HOLD OF HIM TO GIVE HIS LIFE FOR THE SAKE OF RECONCILIATION between all peoples, under the leading of the Prince of Peace.

How good for us to learn afresh the ways of reconciliation, not only between Christian denominations, but for our land so divided by poisonous animosities.

AN ADDITIONAL EVENING COMMUNION SERVICE ON 25th JANUARY.

People who were present at the Christmas Eve communion service expressed much appreciation for that beautiful, rich, devotional service.

Unhurried yet not too lengthy, enriched and deepened by sung elements in the liturgy, and given more time for silent meditation at the crucial points of receiving the bread and the wine, the service allowed us to wait upon God in a fitting manner, and receive richly from the Table.

We hope to build on what we have begun here – and maybe, by God's grace, this can become a significant service, that many will look forward to, to our spiritual nourishment and growth in grace.

CONGRATUATIONS ON C.B.E.

for Miss Doreen Hayward: Miss Hayward received one of the top New Year's honours to come to the Province for what she has accomplished as Chief Nursing Officer for the Department of Health and Social Services: in West we know her as a devoted Christian lady.

TRIBUTE TO JOHN SEAWRIGHT:

It was clearly a family of people who loved the Lord, and one another who filled the Church for the Farewell service for the Rev. John Seawright on Tuesday 6th January.

The service itself was in the form of thanksgiving and witness, praise through lovely old hymns and lively new songs, interspersed with Bible readings and telling testimonies.

HEATHER LEWIS and ELEANOR BAILLIE spoke warmly of the manner in which John taught the truth of God, with clarity and power, with reverence towards God and a sense of his holiness.

Paul, Romans 15, declared:
"In Christ Jesus, I have reason to be proud of my work for God. I have fully preached the Gospel of Christ."
We affirmed that JOHN had done this in our midst, in such a way that it had taken deep root in the hearts of our people.

Alan Stewart and **Andy Cole** related that God's Word became alive and powerful for them, as spoken through John, and had brought them to faith in Christ.

In Romans 16 we noted how warm and affectionate were the relationships of Paul with the people he had known, and everything he said in his greetings to them were designed to bless and build them up.

Two people, who had come to faith in the latter part of John's ministry in West, were **Barbara Hamilton** and Norman **Scullion**.

Barbara told how John had shared the gospel with her decisively in her own home; Norman of how he had heard and responded to the same gospel in the context of a church service, and both spoke highly of all the help they had received in the context of 'Life in the Spirit' seminars.

Two young people, **Pamela Coburn** and **Andrew Seaton** told of the change they had seen take place over recent years in the Youth Fellowship, and how they had come to know John as a real friend in the Lord.

WILLIAM McCLELLAND'S TRIBUTE.

Before asking VICTOR STEPHENS to hand over a cheque to John Seawright, which he did as a token of the affection and respect of the congregation, our Clerk of Session spoke of John's ministry among us.

He spoke of him as a man of gentleness and humility, wise in counsel, strong in faith, a man in whom the Spirit of God dwells.

"You have worked unceasingly with prayer, patience and the power that comes from God"
"You have been a builder, a listener, an encourager, teacher, leader, and healer"
"Your life and work among us has been a gift from God. You **enter upon a new dimension of ministry, but you take with you the love, prayers and deep friendship of us all.**"

THE DORES have been praying for new contacts: today Mr Sotozaki came with a 'disappointed' "love" problem. A good starting point! We plan to continue to study the Bible together!

FEBRUARY WCN 1987.

Rev. ALVIN LITTLE.

"We put our trust in God when He called our beloved John Seawright to become minister in Abbey, Monkstown, and 200 of our people were there to see him installed.

We also looked to the Lord to provide a successor. In human terms it was not an easy matter to find a fully equipped minister, prepared to serve as assistant and colleague.

We rejoice therefore, that on the night before John was installed in Abbey, **the Rev. Alvin Little intimated his readiness to join us in West Church – and that 15 minutes before John began his first service in Abbey, our Kirk Session (that had previously considered the matter) issued a CALL to him.**

We give thanks for a provision and a timing that seem to have a divine hallmark upon them!

ABOUT OUR NEW MINISTER AND HIS FAMILY.

Alvin Little grew up in Rathfriland and lived there until the age of 17 when he moved to Banbridge.

He studied at Queen's, Belfast for his B.A. degree in preparation for the Presbyterian ministry, and was an active member of the Christian Union.

As a member of the Universities' Christian Colleges' Fellowship, he had a keen sense of the need to share the gospel of Jesus in the south of Ireland.

To that end he spent two years studying in Cork (Business Studies) during which period he invested much time and energy **in establishing and nurturing study groups in the Cork colleges.**

Then he returned to Belfast for his full theological studies, and graduated B.D. from Queen's.

He became assistant minister in St. Andrew's, Cregagh, and after ordination there, served for two years as full-time assistant.

Then he went to Galway which is a joint Presbyterian/Methodist charge, with Presbyterian and Methodist ministers alternating. The previous Presbyterian minister had to retire through ill-health, and Alvin was appointed for the two remaining years of the Presbyterian period.

He comes to West with a sense of God's peace in the coming, to serve Christ's people here, and with the hope of being further equipped for his entire future ministry.

A colleague, who first told me of him, described him as a gentle, spiritual man with a deep desire to see others come to faith in Jesus. My meetings with him would confirm that estimate.

His wife LINDA did Social Studies at Queen's and Edinburgh, and worked with Dr. Barnardo's. They have a little daughter Joanna and another child is expected.

Subject to Presbytery approval, we hope for an induction service on the first Sunday evening in May.

I feel sure that we have a family here that we will find easy to welcome and love!"

A SPIRIT OF GENEROSITY:
It is good to see the spirit of generosity that prevails among our people, and for the very spontaneous way that gifts to others are given. Recent examples: £400+ to Arie ben Israel for Reconciliation work in Germany. Children giving £150 to Sycamore Club. £700 for Jim Hunter to take to Pakistan.
FEBRUARY WCN 1987 GIVES MANY OF OUR Annual Reports; organisations reporting full complements of members with dedicated personnel running them.

WEAR AND TEAR OF HALLS.

Our halls are very intensively used, so some wear and tear is inevitable. However some of it is also avoidable!
The Church Committee floated the idea that some of our retired people might keep an eye on things, especially when outsiders enter (when halls may be vacant) and abuse things.

WE HAVE 150 PEOPLE INVOLVED IN YOUTH WORK IN WEST CHURCH!
When you add up all the folk who teach in Sunday Schools and Bible Classes, and uniformed organisations, you'll find that there are more than 150 of them.
A sizeable contribution that the **Church makes to the wellbeing and health of the whole community!**

NEW FACES AT THE BUNNIES: After 10 years service, lovingly and consistently bestowed, Shelagh Gibson and Linda Curry give way to Glenda Eddis and Jenny Chambers.

HELP IS ALSO URGENTLY NEEDED FOR THE GUIDES.

Hugh **ANDERSON retires from the Bible Class after 17 years of wonderful service.**

MARGARET CONROY gives first annual report on behalf of the Sycamore Club, and acknowledges help from Helen Hanlon, Claire Hamilton, Ruth Morrow, Kathryn Derby and Moira Derby.

WEST CHURCH BOWLING CLUB continues to grow in numbers, with an enrolment of 36 members

The GB is in buoyant mood and look forward to their 8th Annual Display.

The PWA celebrate their Silver Jubilee
The YWA have 36 members with a weekly average of 27 members.

MARCH WCN 1987.

KIRK SESSION REPORT FOR 1986, presented at the Annual meeting by William McClelland.

He makes reference to 1986 as an eventful year, **and to the throbbing life of a closely-knit people, worshipping and rejoicing together in the love and goodness of the Living Lord.**
Nowhere was that deep love and unity more evident than in the Jubilee Thanksgiving Service. Led by the Rev. David Bailie, our people united in prayer and praise giving thanks for 25 years of faithful and fruitful ministry. There were few dry eyes in that memorable service as minister and people experienced in a unique way the depth of the love which binds us together, and the reality of the presence of the Holy Spirit in our worship.

As a Kirk Session we record our appreciation of the untiring service of the Rev. David and Mrs Bailie, of the joy and encouragement which they spread so infectiously among us and of the fellowship and teaching which has shaped the spiritual perception and character of this people. Mrs Bailie, with her husband, shares a very special place in the hearts of our people."

Mr McClelland went on to speak of **the immeasurable loss experienced by the congregation through the departure of the Rev. John Seawright to Abbey,**
We had another emotional service to say farewell to John, **for we felt we had experienced the breaking of a family bond."**
Our Clerk then spoke of an **inestimable gain that would come to us through our call to the Rev. Alvin Little.**
Then he added:
"The work of our two full-time ministers **is supported by the ministry of the Rev. Jim Hunter on a part-time basis.
We are indebted to Jim for the fresh challenge which his ministry brings to us as he shares with us his experience of work abroad and in many aspects of outreach in Northern Ireland. His great ability to communicate the Gospel, especially with the young, and his gentleness and wisdom as he visits in the homes of our people are greatly appreciated."**

Our Clerk of Session continues:

"In our Report last year we talked of "making disciples."

"Prophetic words, perhaps, because in the tireless energy he displays the Rev. Bailie arranged seminars on "Sharing our Faith" and "Healing" as well as "Life in the Spirit" seminars. As a Kirk Session we were privileged to hear what God has worked in the lives of those who attended these courses and how He was "making disciples."
How we long to share our faith with every family in the congregation that the dominion of darkness will be turned away and the living worship of the Risen Lord bring light, life and joy to every home."

RUSSIAN BAPTIST LEADERS RELEASED.

Last summer, two well-known ministers of the unregistered Baptist churches were released from labour camps, after serving eight and six years respectively. A third, after serving five years was released but not allowed to return to his family.

INTENSIVE TRAINING FOR EVANGELISTS.
CHINA:
In October 1985, a new scheme called 'The Field Seminar' was begun. By May 1986, more than 100 evangelists had taken the intensive 3-month course which is held in secret locations in the Chinese countryside.
For every course there are about 30 students, mostly young people. On completion of their studies the students are sent out as itinerant evangelists. 80% of the Chinese live in rural areas and this is where the evangelists carry out most of their work. **The devotion of the students is inconceivable to most Western Christians.**
Every seminar organises three courses a year, and although held in secret "Open Doors" knows of at least seven such Seminars.

FOREIGN WORKERS MUST BE SILENT.
UNITED ARAB EMIRATES;
The Pakistani Christian **Barkat Masih,** who was working in the Persian Gulf States as a foreign worker, is serving a sentence of three and a half years in prison. A colleague of his who was annoyed at his 'preaching' reported him to the police. Other colleagues have raised funds for his defence and for the support of his wife and six children in Lahore.

APRIL WCN 1987.

EARLY MORNING PRAYER IN OUR PRAYER ROOM.

A FEW WEEKS AGO, THE Rev. Derek Crumpton (a South African minister) spoke convincingly about the power of committed prayer.
He may have been 'a man of God's moment' for us!
WHERE TWO AGREE....
Two of our members have agreed together to meet in our **Prayer Room** each Wednesday morning between 6 and 7 o'clock to pray. No doubt this prayer will include adoration and praise, **as well as supplication for the coming of God's Kingdom in our church and community, in our land, and to the ends of the earth, with specific upholding of those known to us.**
If the two were to grow to seven or eight that would be wonderful. And if other 'clusters' were to develop, on other days or at other times, that would be great!
Prayer is like CULTIVATION, ploughing, sowing, fertilising, harvesting!
When the work is done, a Harvest is reaped.

Jesus has taught us to pray: 'thy Kingdom come, thy will be done.'

'And in the morning, a great while before day, he rose and went out to a lonely place and there he prayed.' Mark 1: 35.

'Pray to the Lord of the harvest to send out labourers into the harvest fields.' Matthew 9: 36.

"IT'S GREAT! – WE CAN HEAR!"

That has been the response of quite a number of our 'hard-of-hearing' members who are benefiting from the New Sound System, generously donated by some of our members, and painstakingly and lovingly installed by **Tom Hull and Peter Graham.**

And now we wonder if we could go one step further! And that is to record our services, and have them taken to our members who are no longer able to come to church.
That would mean getting equipment to record the services, and to copy the recordings in bulk.
That again would be expensive, something over a thousand pounds!

Yet how valuable that could prove!

APRIL WCN....
Expressed thanks to **IAN GIBSON** who now has West Church Directory on his word processor, so that this valuable aid to West Church fellowship, of names, addresses and telephone numbers can be immediately available to our members, as well as lots of other important congregational information.
As well Ian spent two whole days in our Church Office duplicating our annual edition of the Directory, for 1987.
THANK YOU, IAN GIBSON!

APRIL WCN also gave details of our United Holy Week Services, with the service on Wednesday evening specially adapted for young people.

ELEANOR RAINEY tells us that she is to lose her co-worker Florence, whom she will miss sorely, and asks us to pray for a suitable replacement.

THE DORES' LETTER INCLUDES THESE QUOTES FROM LITTLE SON ALASTAIR:
"DADDY, WHY DID Mr Bailie wear a kimono in the Church in Ireland and you don't in Japan. "
"Daddy, why does God send earthquakes in Japan and not in our country?"
"How did you enjoy the Japanese Church service, Alastair?" ..."It went on for years!"

JIM & MAUREEN HUNTER'S visit to Pakistan.
A tremendous privilege, including ministry to missionaries, to national ministers and church workers, and to non-Christians.
Jim and Maureen visited KUNRI which had been their base while living in Pakistan. They found the people in good heart, but experiencing weariness.

Jim says that in respect of the hospital at Kunri, a recent evaluation describes it as a **Hardship Post for Pakistani doctors and nurses,** and adds 'no one seems to have recognised it as that for missionaries yet!'

From a full and enlightening report, I pick out one paragraph:
"Bishop Bashir met with the President of Pakistan expressing concern over the new law which states that anyone who insults the Prophet Mohammed shall be given the death penalty. He was assured that this only referred to Moslems, but then the President went on to state that he considered himself and other Moslems as much better Christians than men like the Bishop of Durham. He pointed out that as Moslems they believed in Christ as the greatest prophet, they believed in his Virgin Birth, his sinlessness, his miracles, his ascension and his return. He considered himself a much better believer than many so-called Christians.
He may be right but it certainly makes it difficult to help him experience a new birth!"

"LIFT UP YOUR EYES AND SEE!"
SEE WHAT JESUS SEES – AROUND YOU!

"DO NOT SAY, 'THERE ARE YET 4 MONTHS, THEN COMES THE HARVEST'.
I tell you, "Lift up your eyes and see how the fields are already white for harvest. He who reaps receives wages, and gathers fruit for eternal life'.

Through the agency of West Church News, we were continually challenging our people to have vision to see the opportunities for Kingdom reaping all around us.

So we quote again from Frank Tillapaugh's book, 'The Church Unleashed'.

STEP ONE: SEEING THE INVISIBLE.
One of our Lord's constant frustrations was that his followers did not see what He saw.
"All they saw in Zacchaeus was a despicable little tax-collector. **But Jesus saw someone who needed a friend and, more than that, someone who needed deliverance from sin.**
At Jacob's Well, one day, Jesus' followers saw only a Samaritan woman, who looked as though she had been through the mill. **But he saw a precious, hurting human being who could be the key to spreading the gospel in Samaria. Over and over again he saw what was invisible to those around him.**"
Frank Tilapaugh continues:
"Not long ago we had a young man join our street team who was a 'delivered homosexual'.
He felt called of God to return to the homosexual bars and share his faith and deliverance. One or two nights a week he went to these bars while his wife visited lesbian bars to witness.
When we shared this ministry with the church, some remarked that they didn't even know that there were such things as 'homosexual bars' in Denver. Such places are simply not visible to our middleclass world.
A MAJOR TASK FOR THE LOCAL CHURCH BODY THEN IS TO HELP ONE ANOTHER TO SEE HITHERTO INVISIBLE SEGMENTS OF OUR SOCIETY.

.....a couple of years ago a young mother shared with me that her former church had begun a special ministry **to mothers with pre-school children.** Unless one has experienced it, one cannot fathom what it is like to be cooped up all day with one pre-schooler, let alone two or more... what can we do to minister to these mums?.... And now after two years of ministry to MOPS (mothers of pre-schoolers) **we are beginning to think of more possibilities.**

What if the Lord were to give us the leadership and show us how to target-group *a crowded apartment complex loaded with children?* In many of these complexes *the anger and despair of the tenants is obvious.* Living in such close quarters many of these people feel trapped.

The 'MOPS' target group is a ministry within the middle-class family unit. There are other middle class target groups that don't fit into the family-unit category ….singles… senior citizens.

STEP TWO: THE HOLY SPIRIT'S CALL TO MINISTRY.

Once we *see* the Target Group, *we must then wait for the Holy Spirit to lead someone into that ministry.*

Not every **need** constitutes a **call** to our Church.

The Lord can be trusted to lead us into the ministries He desires for us.

If a church sees a possible target group but no one is led to minister to it, we must learn to wait with relaxed concern. (PRAY THE Lord of the harvest to send labourers to harvest the crop). When someone shares that he feels called of the Spirit to begin a ministry to a certain group, pastors and the church as a whole, should listen seriously.

We can proceed with confidence, when we're moving into an area where God wants us, and where the leadership has God-given motivation.

STEP THREE: LEARNING FROM PARA-CHURCH MINISTRIES.

If God calls the Church to minister to a target group, it is likely that some para-church group is already working in that field- and we can learn from them. They are accustomed to think in terms of going after people.

Some may ask, "Why do we have to design a special ministry for that group? Why can't they attend our regular service like everyone else? We'll minister to anyone who will come and fit in with us."

The para-church has developed an unleashed mentality which says: 'We'll design ministries to go after those who won't come to us."

STEP FOUR: BECOMING SPECIALISTS.

The fourth step is to consider carefully the target group, **then devise a strategy to reach it for Christ. Most ministries will be built around discovering needs and meeting them….** Everyone needs to hear and understand the Gospel, and to be given foundational help in their Christian lives.

A word of caution at this point. **We don't need to wait till we have everything figured out before we begin a ministry.**

We don't need to kill a ministry by assigning a committee to study it. *LET'S START THE MINISTRY!* Let's risk making mistakes and learn in the process of ministering.

We need to see the target group first, trust the Holy Spirit to lead someone!

God will provide the home base, finances etc.

MAY WCN 1987.

This issue gives details of:-

The induction of the Rev. Alvin Little as minister in West on 3rd May.

Visit of the Rt Rev. Paul Chauhan to our Praise Service on May 17th.

A visit of nine members of the 'LIFE IN THE LAMB COMMUNITY' on the 19th May. This is a community whose members make a 3-fold promise of CHARITY, PURITY and OBEDIENCE.

The main outreach of the Community is conducting retreats, Quiet Days and Bible Studies.

So we invite members of Kirk Session and Committee, Sunday School teachers, Youth leaders, and House Group leaders – all involved or interested in the work of West Church.

OUR 'GARDENERS' are reminded that it is the season for hoeing and weeding their special allotments, to keep our grounds colourful and beautiful.

THE SYCAMORE CLUB sees an opportunity to minister to ADULTS as well as to children- and additional help will be required.

MAY WCN 1987.

REV. ALVIN LITTLE, with his family, has become quickly established in West. He will lead our Communion Services on 14th June.

PETER GRAHAM, who has played such an important part in Young West Church, in nurturing the Young People's Singing Group, and with his wife LISA in contributing to our Praise Service, has gone to take up residence in London. We give thanks to God for them, and pray his blessing upon them in England.

GRAHAM AND JANET DORE HAVE GOT TO KNOW MANY NEIGHBOURS IN A VERY SHORT TIME: LET'S KEEP ON PRAYING FOR THEM! They write:

Thank you for praying for our neighbours! Since getting married we have moved house 21 times and have never got to know so many neighbours in such a short time as here. **The granny next door is always inviting us in; the man behind is making the church signboards.** He is always inviting us in and comes to English class; the couple behind him (Kuramoto) have just bought a Bible; **the man** opposite, the children two doors down, the lady 3 doors down, a Dr's wife in the next street come to English; a lady at the end of the next street has an ex-pastor uncle. So many under our influence and prayers in such a short time!

Elizabeth's sweet, happy, outgoing nature makes new contacts daily. She's 'on duty' on the swings on fine days (i.e. most days) from after breakfast till dinner time and has an insatiable appetite for outdoors and friends. *PLEASE PRAY FOR FRUIT FROM NEIGHBOURHOOD CONTACTS ESPECIALLY KURAMOTOS who came to us quite unknown and listened intently to Isaiah 53 and Psalm 22. I felt I was in a dream- somehow they had been prepared to hear the Gospel.* We are only links in a chain. The fields are white for harvest: there must be others in Tonden, if only we can find them. *And so Graham goes on to paint a much fuller picture of opportunities and 'dreams', soliciting the partnership prayers of West Church members.*

And in West Church we have the perception that through the Dores we have a real part in reaping a harvest for Christ in faraway Japan.

OCTOBER WCN 1987.

**An unusual gap in the production of West Church News developed between a one-page issue in June and the October edition.
In writing our "West Church Journey" I have wondered why this should have been so!**

**Then of page 2, of the October issue of WCN, I found the answer under the title:
HOME GROUPS SEEK GROWTH:-**
"Our Home Groups begin their regular meetings in the second week of October **and embark on a new programme that is geared up for growth.**

Quite a number of new groups have been formed out of the Life in the Spirit Seminars of 1987, so that, with other adjustments and reorganisation, there will be almost 30 groups in all. Many meet with a high sense of expectation, because all embark on a new course, *specially prepared for our own situation, entitled:*
**OUR HOME GROUPS:
"A SUSTAINED ENDEAVOUR AFTER GROWTH-ADOPTING EVANGELISM AS A LIFESTYLE."**
The Title may intimidate some just a little, creating images of open-air meetings or door-to-door visitations. **But nothing of this kind is to be found in the practical manual that has been provided, and it is hoped that our ways of witness, while gentle and natural, will indeed be very fruitful.**

Many have experienced already in our home groups, intimacy and fellowship, reality in worship, much maturing in the Christian life, answers to prayers, healings, support, and ability to reach out and minister to others. We want to share all that with others too.

**Many of the groups have now eight or nine members to allow opportunity for growth.
Those not in Home Groups, who nonetheless have a desire to share their faith in Jesus, can gain greatly through studying this new Manual."**

When I read about that from the October 1987 WCN, it all came flooding back to me, and I realised that the summer of 1987 had been devoted to producing this Manual, which is indeed a very substantial publication, of 17 chapters, more than 60 foolscap pages in all. In addition there were provided notes for Home Group Leaders, on how to use the material and lead the group.

Each chapter had a strong biblical basis, and much illustrative material, to make it a pragmatic course, with which people could identify in the situations of everyday life.

As I read it again, after almost 20 years, I was very impressed, and realised that 'the fallow summer of 1987' had indeed been intensively used! And that there was sufficient material in each chapter to cover several meetings!

**SUBSTANTIAL CONTENT OF THIS COURSE.
One may gain a sense of what is in this Manual, by looking at the chapter headings:**

1. Offering Ourselves and our Home Groups to God.

2. First Steps in Outreach.

3. Gathering in the Wanderers and the Stragglers.

4. Learning to Sow!.

5. Leverage to overturn the World.

6. Ministering the Love of Jesus.

7. Our Attitude in Sharing the Good News.

8. Keep on Sowing your Seed, lavishly, skilfully.

9. Keep on Sowing your seeds.

10. Pointing People to Jesus.

11. Sharing the Good News, just as we happen to meet people.

12. Seeing under the crust and loving people where they are.

13. Reaching out to people in the love of God and as led by the Spirit.

14. Going out into the Harvest fields, to reap the ripe crop.

15. People are drawn to Christ, when they see his power and love among his people.

16. Robust and substantial presentation to convince the Intellect.

17. Some helpful Patterns for Sharing the Good News.

OCTOBER WCN:
On 11th October we celebrate Harvest Thanksgiving, when our Choir will enrich and enhance our worship with the special music they present; with our offerings for the United Appeal.

THREE STUDENTS AT UNION THEOLOGICAL COLLEGE.

In the late Seventies we had 3 members of our congregation who studied theology. David Knox and George Moffett became ministers of our Irish Presbyterian Church, and Ivan Warwick became a minister of the Church of Scotland
Now in the late Eighties three others are to study at Union Theological College, Belfast.
The first, the Rev. Jim Hunter, is strictly not a member of West, his home congregation being Orangefield, Belfast, but after some time of ministry with us, we lay some claim to him!

JIM HUNTER: Jim has served with BMMF for some 22 years, largely in India and Pakistan. He was ordained a minister of the Church of Pakistan.
As it has not seemed right at this time for him to return to Pakistan, Jim has made application and has been accepted as a student for the ministry of our Presbyterian Church in Ireland. This will involve a minimum of one year's study, before he could be accepted as a minister of PCI, perhaps even 2 years. Jim has enrolled for the B.D. Course at Queen's, Belfast, which could prove a useful qualification, if in a few more years he were to return to Pakistan to teach theology there.
Jim will still assist us in the pulpit ministry in West Church, though the necessity of devoting himself to a substantial course of study, will no longer allow him to do any pastoral visitation in our congregation.

ANN KENNEDY.
For a number of years, Ann Kennedy, who is a Primary School teacher, and has been one of our elders, has been giving much consideration to whether God has been calling her to fulltime service in the Church.

After much thought and prayer, pondering and praying over the matter deeply, **Ann came to feel in her heart, that indeed God was so calling her.**
Warmly supported by our Kirk Session, she made application to be accepted as a student for the ministry of our Presbyterian Church.
**After interview, and a residential Weekend at Union to consider her suitability and to validate her sense of call, she was chosen to study for the ministry of our Church.
Like Jim Hunter, she begins her studies at Union in the new academic year, October 1987.**
Our love, our prayers, our support and good wishes are with her, as she responds to this new call upon her life. Our hope and expectation is that as she has already been fruitful for God in many ways in West, so that fruitfulness will be multiplied in a wider sphere of ministry and service.

HEATHER LEWIS.
Our third student at Union, who has also felt a strong call of God upon her life, to minister in Jesus' Name and share the Good News of his Kingdom, is HEATHER LEWIS.
Heather, whose father is a retired minister of the Church of Scotland, has been a caring, effective elder in West, has been active in our Healing services, and has gained much from our various Training Seminars. She's not out of touch with studying, having fairly recently completed a Master's degree.
She will be a part-time student at Union, hoping to do the 2-year Diploma of Theology course over a three-year period.

HEATHER - PASTORAL ASSISTANT TO THE MINISTER.
Our Kirk Session, with great warmth and unanimity has appointed Heather to be part-time Pastoral Assistant to the minister in West Church.
We have now a large congregation, where the ministers are much involved in training, equipping our members and nurturing many life-generating projects.
Our Kirk Session felt that the work of ministers and elders can be profitably supplemented, especially in pastoral visitation, **and in the overseeing of pastoral visitation. This will be the PRIMARY work that Heather will be involved in. She will be fulfilling in our Church very much the role of deaconess.**
Already much loved by many who know her in West, we feel confident that she will be affectionately and positively received in the homes of our members and throughout the congregation. We rejoice in the timing and provision of God.

CHRIS RITCHIE GOES TO ISRAEL.
We see the rising tide of the Spirit's presence in our midst in many ways.
We are gratified to see young people coming to faith and growing in commitment to their Lord, with a desire to serve him and proclaim the Gospel. **We therefore rejoice that Chris Ritchie goes to Haifa, Israel for a year with Operation Mobilisation. Chris has asked for our prayers for himself and for**

the Jewish people among whom he will be serving to show that Jesus is the Messiah. He also has asked for people to write to him. That's important, to let him know that he goes out from the family of our Church.

PWA COFFEE MORNING AND CAKE SALE:
For Missions, Saturday 7 November.

REV. ALVIN LITTLE AND THE YOUTH SCENE.
Members of West have been grateful to God for the developing ministry of the Rev. Alvin Little, as pastor, preacher, teacher and man of God, identifying with young and old and all!

The Kirk Session have asked Alvin to have a special care for the whole youth scene, which is so diverse and extensive, and where there is so much to encourage and to nurture. And this Alvin is very happy to do!

THE FAMILY SERVICE.
The last Sunday of the month is FAMILY SERVICE at 11.30am. We are grateful for the team of people who meet to plan and prepare for these services- each service requires a lot of thought, preparation and prayer.

We thank God for the leadership given to this team by JANET WOOD, and thank her for the care and wisdom she has shown. We are glad that JAYNE FERGUSON has now taken up this responsibility, and pray that God will give to her and her team the wisdom and vision they require, so that the whole family, young and old, may worship God worthily and heartily, in spirit and in truth.

NEW AUTUMN SEMINARS begin:
DIVINE HEALING Tuesday 13th October; COMMUNICANTS' GROUP led by Rev. Alvin Little, Thursday 7.15; LIFE IN THE SPIRIT, THURSDAY, 8.15.

RECORDING EQUIPMENT:
an anonymous and generous gift of £1000 has been received.

HARVEST EVENING SERVICE will include THE COMMISSIONING OF HEATHER LEWIS as a Pastoral Assistant, and at the supper afterwards we shall have the opportunity of expressing good wishes to Ann Kennedy and Jim Hunter as they begin their theological studies at Union.

OCTOBER WCN tells how Dr Ian & Mrs Roberta Clarke and family plan to go to war-torn Uganda to set up the Lowero Orphan Village Enterprise, TO CARE FOR ABOUT 600 children, creating a village in 650 acres of farmland, helping to restore the infra-structure of the country.

WCN October also includes a long updating letter from the Dores in Japan.

And likewise with news from Eleanor Rainey in KENYA.

Reference is also made to GARY WILTON, a theological student from Wycliffe College, Oxford, who did a summer placement with us in West.
We found him to be a breath of fresh air. He was well pleased with his stay among us, feeling that he learned a lot about parish life, and left with a sharpened and enriched perception of what God can do within a congregational family.
From our side we gained greatly from having a young man who had the lively and fragrant anointing of the Holy Spirit upon him.

YOUNG WOMEN'S 21st.
About 125 present and former members attended a Celebration Evening on 7th September, guests including Founder-President Margaret Davidson and 7 other past presidents, all welcomed by current President, Norma Conway.
"Margaret Davidson gave an account of how she founded the Association in 1966 and talked a little about the programmes in those days. Two other past presidents, Yvonne Adams (nee Cooke) and Rhoda Montgomery also spoke of their memories during their time in office.

NOVEMBER WCN 1987.

"ON THE CONTRARY… THE PARTS OF THE BODY THAT SEEM TO BE WEAKER ARE INDISPENSABLE!

"WE ARE TRULY TAKING TO HEART THESE WORDS OF THE APOSTLE PAUL! And not just in a cosmetic, sentimental or patronising manner! *Truly we are going to count some in our midst, who may appear to be 'weaker', to be 'indispensable'.*
Many may regard the older people in our congregation, whose youthful vitality or middle-age competence and seniority in their profession or business, is now far behind them, to be the 'weaker' folk in our community.
Some of these may be 'shut in', or unable to get about with the same vigour as of yore; some may need help and support.

But, in terms of the work of the Church, many such are to be seen as 'indispensable'! Because of a very special contribution they may make.

They often have more time for quietness, meditation and prayer. And through prayer that is regular, sustained and faith-filled the most important victories are won for the Kingdom of God, breaking the power of Satan in many lives, and helping people to faith and new life in Christ. Through faithful prayer, the whole body of the Church is made vital and fruitful.

Those who achieve MOST are those who pray MOST. Often it is the older people, the retired people, those who have leisure hours at home, who are best able to pray.

"A MANUAL OF PRAYER" for West Church members, entitled "SPIRITUAL FANNER BEES" is now almost ready for publication. It can encourage and help all our members to pray, to pray more and to pray better. We invite many retired people, or those not in fulltime employment to ENLIST themselves as "spiritual fanner bees", so that the whole work of the congregation is upheld by prayer, and the energies of the Holy Spirit are released in and from this place.

When we launched our Manual to help our House Groups focus upon **growth and evangelism**, we added that such a project must be bathed in prayer -and then we made mention of "Spiritual Fanner Bees", as a way of under-girding this endeavour.

We give now the story and purpose of :-
"SPIRITUAL FANNER BEES."
This is the challenging and enlightening story of how Senior citizens in a particular congregation enlisted to pray, and saw their church transformed.

Senior members are the most populous sector in most congregations today, often attending church and giving generously.
They - and even housebound members- through regular and focussed praying, can release new life in a congregation and give power to reach out to the whole community.

ROLAND BROWN- CHICAGO PASTOR.
Sometime ago I read an absorbing book by Starr Daily, entitled **"RECOVERY." In each of 30 short chapters it tells of healings through the power of Christ, in the ministry of a Chicago pastor, Roland J. Brown. The healings were of body, mind and spirit, and ranged from cancer to epilepsy, from insomnia to alcoholism, from demon possession to healings of the soul.**

When Roland Brown became minister of the small Parkside Baptist Church in 1932, it had massive mortgage debt and unpaid bills. He inherited a church rent by divisions and bitterness. There had been a quick succession of ministers in this most difficult of pastorates..

Yet it was in this church that most of the 'miracles' described in the book took place.
Without any question, these great things became possible, because **Pastor Brown learnt to dedicate himself to God in a very deep sense, and learnt how to draw upon his infinite resources.**

Equally without question, much of the success of his work was on account of the continuous prayer support of many retired people in the congregation, and others who gave themselves, in a special way, to the work of intercession.

THE BREAK-THROUGH: - 2 FACTORS.
A CHANGE IN THE PASTOR.
One day, when Pastor Brown was praying in a great agony of soul, **that God would make him adequate for his task,** he found that words from 1 John 1: 9 burned into his soul with great intensity: **If we confess our sins, He is faithful and just to forgive our sins, and to cleanse us from ALL unrighteousness.**
Suddenly he came to understand that God meant him, so to confess each sin, as to be cleansed from ALL unrighteousness.
"Why, yes, in that very hour I had lost my patience when my little boy had got in my way, and I knew that was unrighteous. I confessed it as sin to God and asked for his forgiveness. I thought again and remembered that I had spoken in an unkindly way to my wife that very evening. I realised that that was not righteous, and that it was motivated by selfishness, so I confessed it as sin and asked for God's forgiveness. **And one by one I began to discover things in my life that were foreign to God's nature, and to confess them to him, seeking his forgiveness and promising to try to eliminate these things from my life.**

A whole flood of situations began to swarm into my memory. There was my temper, pride, conceit, resentments, self-righteousness, worry, fear and many other qualities that Christians readily experience, but are apt to tolerate and overlook, as altogether normal and natural. **But here God was telling me that if I confessed my sins to Him, he would cleanse me from ALL unrighteousness.** That was what I wanted, the complete cleansing. I knew that my repentance was sincere.

Before I had finished praying, a great peace came into my heart. It seemed as if my whole soul became flooded with the presence of the Holy Spirit. God had answered my prayer and for the first time I began to feel adequate for my ministry. *I knew that I must abide in Christ and 'Christ in me' must motivate every thought and word and deed.*
So the first change was in Pastor Brown's own heart. **One of the secrets of usefulness to God is to confess our sins and accept forgiveness; and then to go over each part of our bodies, and offer each part to God to be filled with his Holy Spirit; to offer each

thought, each memory, each feeling, each part of our hearts, minds and wills to God, to be filled by his Holy Spirit.

THE SECOND CHANGE WAS A CHANGE IN HIS CONGREGATION.

One day about this time, Pastor Brown read a little book by Professor Glenn Clark on "The Lord's Prayer."
In it he found a parable on the "Fanner Bees."
Glenn Clark suggested the need, in congregations, for what he described as an army of spiritual 'fanner bees': these were to be people, many of them retired or 'shut-ins' not able to leave home, who would be ready to devote 30 minutes a day to special prayer.

Just like the fanner bees that 'stand' near the entrance of the bee-hive, with their heads bowed and their wings constantly vibrating. This fanning circulates the air, causing fresh air to enter the hive, and stale air to leave. It's an air-conditioning system, without which the bees in the hive could not survive.

A WORK FOR OLDER MEMBERS TO DO.
Pastor Brown began to ask his senior members - retired folk, shut-ins -to take up the work of spiritual fanner-bees, and within 2 weeks more than 30 members undertook this task, so that, every hour of the day, from 5.00am to midnight, at least one member was praying every day for the church, its minister and members.

Pastor Brown relates: "We needed a new spiritual atmosphere in the church. Every person I asked to become a fanner-bee was thrilled at this opportunity for service. One lady wept, saying, 'Pastor, in all my church experience, I never before had a pastor who asked me to pray for him or for the church.

Things soon began to happen, quietly and inconspicuously. Some people who were unhappy and critical became interested in other churches, and transferred their membership from our fellowship. Some who had been indifferent to the church for years began to come back. **And a new Spirit was beginning to be felt in our midst."**

And Pastor Brown began to be used by God in a marvellously enhanced manner, many people coming to salvation, and wonderful works of healing taking place.

HOW MIGHT FANNER-BEES PRAY?

1. Become quiet before God. **Use the words of a hymn, either** to sing, or to say the words out loud to God, seeking to worship and bless him with concentration, intensity and love.

2. As in Romans 12, **offer your very self to God,** presenting every limb and organ of your body to Him, and asking him to fill your body with his Holy Spirit. **Do the same, offering your thoughts and emotions to him.**

3. Read from the Bible and pause when the Lord causes a particular verse to register with you in a special way. Then you may bring your whole life into alignment with the truth within that verse, in the way that Roland Brown did with 1 John 1:9, "If we confess......"

4. As a fanner-bee for your congregation, your aim is to pray that the Holy Spirit may invade and fill the whole Body of your Church, minister, elders, leaders, and people.

Pray in a positive and believing manner.
Envisage things as they should be through Christ, and pray positively for that.
See hearts, people, relationships, immersed and enveloped in the love of Christ.
And when you enter your church for Sunday services, pray for that, and greet people with all naturalness, in the love of Jesus, rejoicing in your heart, that God is at work within them.

5. Remember that God's purpose, through coming in Christ, is to save the world, and to bring each person to eternal life through faith in Him.
Paul, in respect of those who did not believe in Christ, said, 'Brothers, my deepest desire and my prayer to God, are for their salvation'.

TOM REES, in a book called "BREAKTHROUGH" writes:
"I believe that no one is born of God's Spirit unless somebody, somewhere, prays for him, not vaguely or generally, but personally and specifically. Whenever I lead a person to Christ, I always ask this question: 'Now, tell me, who has been praying for you?' Back comes the answer at once: 'my mother', 'my minister', 'my brother',' a Christian in our office'

TOM REES continues:
"There was a time in my life, of which I am not proud, **when I boasted that I was an agnostic.** I scoffed at the thought of God, laughed at those who went to church, and poured my contempt on those who read the Bible and prayed.
My brother Dick became deeply concerned that I should become a Christian. He tried reasoning and pleading with me, but my response was always the same, laughter and mockery.

Then one day he called together a small group of his Christian friends, and told them his problem. That night before they parted, each one had covenanted to pray for me every day until I committed my life to Jesus Christ.

I knew nothing of this conspiracy of prayer, but from that day God started working in my soul, creating a sense of inadequacy, which, by and by, led to repentance, faith and new life."

THE POWER OF CONCENTRATED PRAYER.

In the 12th chapter of the Acts of the Apostles, Luke gives us a vivid account of how a group of Christians prayed for **Peter, when he had been arrested, put in prison and condemned, by the powerful, cruel authorities of that time. Humanly speaking, Peter was lost and beyond hope, and could do nothing to save himself.**

But
But <u>prayer</u>
But prayer <u>was made</u>
But prayer was made <u>without ceasing</u>
But prayer was made without ceasing <u>of the Church,</u>
But prayer was made without ceasing of the Church <u>unto God</u>
But prayer was made without ceasing of the Church unto God <u>For him.</u>

<u>Prayer was made persistently, united with others, focussed upon God, specifically for Peter.</u>

THE POWER OF CONCENTRATED PRAYER IS IMMEASURABLE.

The bare heat of the sun rarely starts a fire, but take a magnifying glass and concentrate its rays, and in seconds you can start a major conflagration! The vague, general prayers of the average Christian are certainly better than nothing, but the man who concentrates his prayers, faith and love on an individual, kindles a flame of sacred fire, an inextinguishable blaze!

WHAT FURTHER SPECIFIC SUGGESTIONS FOR FANNER-BEE INTERCESSION?

Let each fanner-bee select not less than six and not more than twenty people, and pray for them in persistent prayer until, one by one, they come to faith, or God works a needed change in their lives.

These people should not be selected at random, but prayerfully under the guidance of the Spirit. Their names should be written - perhaps initials only! - in our Bibles, and we should purpose in our hearts to intercede for them every day. Some days we may have great liberty in prayer, but on other days we may do little more than name them in God's presence.

This is something you can do as individuals. **But there is the importance of united prayer, and once a week, for example, you may be able to join with one or two others to pray. When you do confidence and discretion are of paramount importance.**
We are encouraged to pray together, because Jesus promised:

"Again, I tell you, if two of you agree on earth about any request you have to make, that request will be granted by my heavenly Father. For where two or three are met together in my name, I am there among them."

DECEMBER WCN reports:"Our Manual of Prayer" is now ready, 500 copies printed, and available in the Vestibule.
It gives a lot of guidance and help to those who want to pray in a strong determined way, for those who want to enlist as Fanner Bees, devoting themselves, day by day, to pray.
It's of value also to those who may not be so disciplined, or have as much time to give.

DECEMBER WCN 1987.

As usual, the Christmas edition of WCN focuses upon our PCI's World Development Appeal. This enlightens us in regard to the great needs of the world and its peoples, whom God loves - loved so much, that at the first Christmas, He sent his Son into the world - the Word made flesh in our midst- to save it.

In West Church we take the opportunity to have a good look at what our Presbyterian Church in Ireland is doing in this regard. It is nourishing a whole range of projects, for example promoting better rice and grain production in Honduras and Sierre Leone, and promoting better conditions for migrant workers in Bolivia.

For example through the 1987 Appeal its theme is "THE DESERT SHALL REJOICE AND BLOSSOM" with 12 projects that bring life and hope. There's help for poor farmers in Andhra Pradesh, India; forestry project in Bihar; tree planting in Maharashtra, India; water supply in Malawi; soil conservation in Brazil; better grain production in Honduras; subsistence farming for bushmen in Namibia; tree planting in Uganda; help for migrant workers in Bolivia; Locust control in Chad; better rice production in Sierra Leone.

Obviously we cannot profitably give details of all these projects- so we have chosen one project, so that we realise just what our givings can achieve.

IT IS TO HELP FOREST-DWELLING FAMILIES BECOME FARMERS.

In a way it is tragic that it has to be so - seeking to make the best of a bad situation.
Tropical forests throughout the world are being destroyed wholesale, with disastrous consequence. This disturbs the

whole cycle of nature. Many of the great tropical forests grow on rocky lands that would otherwise be deserts. And when they are pillaged in a wholesale way, they become desert again. Large stretches of forest draw the rain in and down: droughts in many lands are linked with the wholesale destruction of the forests.

For thousands of years a community of people have inhabited the forests of southern Bihar in India. Although subsistence has never been easy, there was a delicate balance between the life of the forest and the livelihood of its inhabitants.
By shifting systems of cultivation and keeping their population low, these communities allowed the forest to regenerate. In harder years, the forests would yield enough food, growing wild, to allow for survival.
In recent times commercial lumberers, working illegally, have stripped away huge tracts of forest. **One organisation, SHRAMJEEVI UNNAYAN, HAS A PROJECT TO ENABLE 700 FAMILIES TO WORK THE LAND AND SURVIVE.**

This involves an irrigation dam, using river water, to irrigate 145 acres of land, and to allow 3 crops each year.
To cope with drought conditions a Tube Well is also being installed; a GRAIN BANK is being established; women plant fruit trees to supplement the people's diet.

It's a relatively small project but brings great hope.
The Project is being implemented by CHRISTIAN AID at a total cost of £16,000, of which PCI will give £8000.

This project will nourish 700 families in 40 hamlets.

So we can calculate that if we give £4000 this year, we would pay for one quarter of the whole project.

Breaking up the figures, we calculate that
£400 nourishes a hamlet;
£25 nourishes a family
£10 plants fruit trees -mango, olive, date etc.
£2 provides seed
£1 provides fertiliser.

AND SO THE VISION WAS PRESENTED TO WEST CHURCH CONGREGATION FOR ANOTHER YEAR!

CHRISTMAS WORSHIP:

Each year World Development has a prominent focus. But of course our prime focus is
CHRIST HIMSELF!
There is the **FESTIVAL OF CAROLS AND LESSONS.**
It is one thing to have Christmas music coming at you through loudspeakers as you trundle along the shopping mall. It is quite another thing, **and an entirely different experience,** to gather for worship with others in the House of God, and be led in living worship by a choir, that has prepared, as an act of worship, the carols in which we all can join.

A NEWER TRADITION with us is **The Christmas Eve Midnight Communion Service,** beginning at 11.00pm. This is a quiet, devotional service of reverence and beauty, of warmth and intimacy and awe, and one which many would not miss. It allows joyful worship, sacramental communion and deep participation in the mystery of Christ. On the whole traditional, but with enough that is new to make it enriching and different.
At Christmas, we cannot worship the God who gave his eternally begotten Son, too much!
Be present with us! **FIRST THINGS FIRST AT CHRISTMAS!**

Our **CHRISTMAS MORNING AT TEN** services, with an overflowing church filled with young and old, is to be expected. There's always something of a family, a carnival atmosphere, yet with joyful reverence and glad thanksgiving.
O COME ALL YOU FAITHFUL, COME AND ADORE CHRIST THE LORD!

And there will be a Social Evening for the whole family at the New Year's Eve Barn Dance!

DECEMBER WCN also tells us **that we would like to install a new piano in the church at a cost of £2000 (donations welcomed!); that EDDIE CARLETON had received two names for a Church buildings Maintenance Team- and would welcome more; That our Church Treasurer had sent £640 to Enniskillen Presbyterian Church to help the congregation respond to the Bombing needs; that our children were encouraged to make a Beautiful Christmas picture by colouring in the Scene from West Church News: "let it be the Centre Piece for your Christmas Decorations!"**

THE SYCAMORE CLUB.

It is now over a year since the girls and boys of the Sycamore Club became part of the "West Church Family."
The children love to be part of this family and are beginning to be known by many people! They love coming to church each Sunday, and two boys are regular attendees at our Evening Praise Service.

During this year we have come to understand the children more deeply, **and are learning to cater for their needs, and they in turn are getting to know us! Much of this depends on our leaders and helpers, and the dedication with which this help is given!**

Many people have expressed a great deal of interest in the Sycamore Club and are aware that many doors have yet to be

opened.
If you would like the opportunity to help to open these doors, ring Margaret Conroy.

**To sharpen our awareness and sensitivity in our dealings with the mentally handicapped, we include:
BEATITUDES FOR FRIENDS OF EXCEPTIONAL CHILDREN.**

"Blessed are you who take time to listen to difficult speech,
For you help us to know that if we persevere we can be understood.
Blessed are you who walk with us in public places and ignore the stares of strangers,
For in your companionship we find havens of relaxation.
Blessed are you who never bid us to 'hurry up'
And more blessed you who do not snatch our tasks from our hands to do them for us,
For we often need time rather than help.

Blessed are you who ask for our help,
For our greatest need is to be needed.

Blessed are you who help us with the graciousness of Christ,
Who did not bruise the reed or quench the flax,
For often we need the help we cannot ask for.

Blessed are you when, by all these things, you assure us that the thing that makes us individuals **is not in our peculiar muscles, nor in our wounded nervous systems, nor in our difficulties in learning,
but in the God-given self which no infirmity can confine.**

PAUL DECLARED:
"**CHRIST'S LOVE COMPELS US, because we are convinced that one died for all… so we regard no one from a worldly point of view… if anyone is in Christ he is a new creation**"

This is the conviction that should illumine our minds and give compassion to our hearts, through the Christ who dwelt among us in Jesus, the Word become warm flesh for us.

Christ, by his lively Spirit, lets us know that we should reach out to the mentally handicapped; that is the spur that propels us to reach out to hard-pressed and often hungry people in Bihar this Christmas.

And that is the spur that has led us, in this Christmas edition of WCN, to include a moving account of his work and experience, by the Rev. Noel Proctor, Senior Chaplain at Strangeways Prison, Manchester.

I think it may be right to include an excerpt from Noel Proctor's
"Christmas at Strangeways Prison."
"On Bible Sunday each year at the beginning of December, the **Gideons** come and share in the services and **present each man and boy with a New Testament.**

Michael was one who received a copy of God's Word. Only nineteen, he was a category A prisoner because of the severity of his offence. He was in the segregation wing and was locked up in solitary for many hours each day.
A statutory duty of the chaplain is to visit these men daily, and it was clear that Michael's enthusiastic reading of the Scriptures meant that he was searching for the Saviour. We talked about forgiveness and God's willingness to deal with our sins.

One day when I called, Michael told me that he had asked Jesus into his life as Saviour. The following day he went out on exercise. As the men walked round the yard he witnessed to another inmate who was also facing a long sentence. The man said he wanted God to lift the burden of guilt, so walking round the yard Michael prayed with him and led him to Jesus.

The officers on the segregation wing later asked, when I visited Michael, 'Well, chaplain, are you going to see Michael to get your batteries charged?'
It was like that!
Once when I visited him he quoted the whole of Romans chapter 8. Not only had he memorised the words, but he knew what they meant and was seeking the power of God's promises.

PLEASE LAY HANDS ON ME.
Just before Christmas week I called one morning. 'What are you reading today, Michael? I asked.
'Acts chapter 8, verses 14-17, he said, 'Where the disciples laid hands upon the believers and they received the Holy Spirit. **Please lay hands on me, so I'll receive the Holy Spirit**' he asked.
After I had shared the Scriptures with him, he knelt on the cell floor and I put my hands on his head and prayed for this lad who had no church connections outside, and was only allowed to come to Chapel inside (he was not permitted to attend our Bible Classes or prayer groups).
I did not know exactly what he expected. Suddenly the cell was filled with the divine presence of the Almighty as this lad kneeling in front of me began praising God in the heavenly language as the Holy Spirit came upon us both. I left that cell as if I was drunk – the joy, the victory, the blessing, the freedom.

Christmas in prison for Michael was a time of new birth and of an ever-deepening experience of the Holy Spirit. Prison walls and bars cannot contain the spirit of a soul set free by Christ."

WHY DID WE INCLUDE THIS STORY IN WEST CHURCH NEWS?

Because in our congregation we have prison officers, social workers, House Parents in Remand Homes, people in regular contact with prisoners and others requiring special care.

In our Church we should be encouraging, supporting and equipping our members who hold such positions, so that they may be used of God to see people's lives changed.
Sometimes hearts and minds, that have been moulded (and often cramped by worldly values) need to be enlarged to know just what God can do in the most unpromising situations, radically to transform lives.

And just as we have had a helpful and positive relationship with the mentally handicapped through the Sycamore Club, we should look to have a Christian input into the lives of prisoners.

THE DORES IN JAPAN – one year on!

"This month we vividly recall fond farewells in the UK in 1986; one year on, how has God's Kingdom advanced in Tonden?

WE HAVE BLITZED Tonden with 5000 church notices; personally visited 300 homes; moved to a more centrally located, prominent house which we rent for Church meetings; erected an illuminated cross and notice board and two sign boards; started English classes (45 attending); Sunday School (8) young people's group (3) cooking class (20), 2 prayer groups (3 each); private Bible studies with 7 people.

GOD has given us vision, perseverance and health to do this.
Brought the people along to meetings;
Brought Mrs Ida and Mr Arai through to faith;
Brought Mrs Tamaj from Roman Catholic background and Mrs Hoyashi and Yamgata from nominal church background to hunger for assurance;
Kept the 4 original believers together for one year;
Increased Sunday attendances from an average of 4 to 7.

YOU HAVE followed us in thought and (we hope) PRAYER. Thank you! It will take a lot more sacrifice in prayer and effort, a lot more confrontation (in Jesus' Name) of Satan before we see a God-honouring advance.
Meanwhile remember to pray for Alastair settling into OMF boarding school.

"BUT THEN YOU COME"
A poem by Harry Wakelin.

At times it is so hard to think you near… I am lonely then.
But then you come:
A smile, a child, a puppy running home,
Some indication of your love for me,
Like bursting buds are at the turn of the year,
The colour change from green to russet brown,
The season's cavalcade. At break of day,
All somersaulting trouble comes my way,
And I am lonely then. But then you come;
A word, the rime upon the apple tree,
The migrant bird sat on the window sill,
A friendly wave, a problem solved again.
But then my friends go home and all is still,
When dark, grey blinds of evening fall about,
Deep troughs of doubt engulf my questing mind
And I am lonely then. But then you come;
A line of verse, a prophet's timely word
The lacy edge of waves upon the shore,
A storm, a rainbow or a tear of dew,
A prayer, perhaps to draw you close to me,
Dear Father, can you bear to have me near,
For fears and doubts assail me through the day,
And I am lonely then. But then you come.

JANUARY WCN 1988.

"A SUSTAINED ENDEAVOUR AFTER GROWTH – ADOPTING EVANGELISM AS A LIFESTYLE."

Most people in West know about this new MANUAL that we launched for our Home Groups in the autumn of 1987, and may be asking "How is it going? Has it made any difference for those who are studying it?

There is evidence that in a lot of cases the answer is YES.

Our members are making loving and fruitful contacts with others – in church, among relatives, at the place of work; group prayers are being answered, people are being drawn to God and to his Church.

One hears of a man talking naturally, openly and effectively with a colleague at work; a mother praying with effect for her child; a daughter also praying with clear effectiveness for her father in the Name of the Christ who heals today.
There is no doubt that there is a lovely, quiet, often hidden work of witness and grace proceeding in our midst, and reaching out into our society, and for this we thank God.

And we look to God to lead us, by his Spirit, *into further outreach, so that the Name of Jesus may be lifted higher, and more and more people believe, and brought into the Church of Jesus.*

FURTHER OUTREACH STILL?

While we are convinced that the prayerful and adventurous study in our Home Groups can win a rich harvest of people – brought into the Kingdom of God and built up within the Body of the Church – we realise that there are other ways also to fulfil Christ's command to take out Good News to everyone, everywhere.

THROUGH WEST CHURCH NEWS WE HAVE BEEN INFORMING AND EDUCATING OUR MEMBERS ABOUT THE WONDERFUL EVANGELISM TAKING PLACE THROUGH THE CHURCH IN OTHER LANDS.

We have already told our people here of the fruitful Home Groups in Korea.

In this issue we give details of street evangelism in Chile.

As we look over our own history in West Church, we bear witness to the help and inspiration we have received, when others have come to us, and brought great blessing, like the Rev. Tom Smail in 1968, leading us into a new dimension of the Holy Spirit; or in this past year of ANDY ARBUTHNOT encouraging us in the ministry of Divine Healing.

From Indonesia we read of teams of people who go out from the Church in outreach work, maybe spending a weekend, or longer, on various evangelistic missions.

And might it be that the time is at hand for our members to do something similar?
Our SINGING/ DRAMA GROUP had a first, gentle foray into full public view when they sang carols at the Springhill Shopping Centre just before Christmas.
Whatever we may do, we want to be led by the Spirit of God.

HOW PAUL AND BARNABAS WERE CALLED *TO GO OUT AND SHARE THE GOOD NEWS.*

In Acts 13 we read how prophets and teachers in the church at Antioch were worshipping the Lord and fasting, when the Holy Spirit said to them "Set apart for me Barnabas and Saul for the work to which I have called them." **Then after fasting and praying they laid their hands upon them and sent them off.**

PAUL'S AMBITION TO SHARE THE GOSPEL GREW STRONGER AND STRONGER.
 In Romans 15: 17ff Paul declares:
"I glory in Christ Jesus in my service to God.
I will not venture to speak of anything *except what Christ has accomplished through me in leading the Gentiles to obey God by what I have said and done – by the power of signs and miracles, through the power of the Spirit. Thus, from Jerusalem all the way around to Ilyricum, I have fully proclaimed the gospel of Christ. It has always been my ambition to preach the gospel where Christ was not known…."*

Paul had a burning desire to see people brought to a saving faith in Christ, and was ready to sacrifice himself to attain this goal. In 1 Corinthians 9: 22ff he declares: **"To the weak I became weak, to win the weak. I have become all things to all men** *so that by all means possible* **I might save some. I do this for the sake of the gospel that I may share in its blessings."**

SOME GREAT NEWS FROM THE DORES.
One senses such a burning desire in the Dores in their missionary work in Japan, who write:
Thank you for your faithful prayers! Mr Arai, the son of the local priest, now believes. We need to pray his family to faith in the living God. Please pray for his Shinto priest father (about 73 years old). The power of darkness in the Arai home is very great. *What a witness to Tonden if a local priest were to turn to the living God.*
Mr Arai brought 5 people to the Christmas dinner – his wife, 2 children, mother and sister. *We need to see the power of darkness broken in this home.."*

The Dores speak of a Christmas dinner in a hotel, with almost 70 people present, nearly all contacts through the English and Cookery classes. Seated at round tables, eating shrimps, peppers, sushi rice, sashimi, listening to background carol music, **a 40-minute presentation on the meaning of Christmas was given, with presents of the book of Proverbs for adults and goodies for the children.**
By all means, the endeavour was being made to save some.

OUR ENDEAVOUR THROUGH WCN IS TO ENLARGE THE MINDSET OF OUR PEOPLE AND INSPIRE A VISION AND A STRATEGY FOR EFFECTIVE SHARING OF THE GOSPEL.

That is why we include accounts of what God is doing in other places in the world, in the sharing of the Gospel, so that we may come to the conclusion and conviction that **"what He is doing for others, He can do for you!."**
Many truths and principles for effective evangelistic outreach are contained in the stories we relate from the Church in Chile.
The excerpts now given are taken *from Peter Wagner's book "Spiritual Power and Church Growth."*
"If you are thinking of visiting Santiago, Chile, plan your trip over a weekend and spend Sunday afternoon and evening watching the Pentecostals in action. Their open-air meetings have become a part of Chilean local colour.
You will have no difficulty finding the 'Canutos', as Chileans have nicknamed their Pentecostals after one of their early leaders. Just take a bus and get off somewhere near the station about 5.00 in the afternoon. Begin walking in almost any

direction, and you will soon see a group of people on a street corner or in a plaza. Chances are they are Methodist Pentecostals from the big mother church called the Jotabeche church.

As you approach them you will do well to carry a large Bible. That is like an admission ticket into the circle. If you don't have one, a brother or sister will most likely try to convert you on the spot. You will hear them from a block away singing and reciting Bible verses in unison.

GUITARS WITH RIBBONS.
When you get closer, you will see maybe ten guitars with long red ribbons streaming from them, three or four accordions and a portable loudspeaker or two. The total group might number any where from 30 to a couple of hundred. After hymns and scripture, one person will take the loudspeaker and begin to preach.

The speaker might be an experienced leader or a recent convert. So deeply do Chilean Pentecostals believe in street meetings that a virtual requirement for a legitimate conversion experience is that you agree to go out on the street on the Sunday after your decision and give your testimony as to what God has done in your life. This procedure has two distinct benefits. It first helps believers cement their faith in Christ and their relationship to the body. **They may be rather inarticulate and scared half to death to speak in public, but this ultimately helps them feel like active participants in the mission of the church in the world.** As they speak their companions are praying them through, making them feel very positive towards the other members of the group.

The second benefit is that, in spite of lack of training and stuttering delivery, the message preached by the new convert gets through - possibly more than that of a polished, professional minister. The new believer's testimony carries with it a high degree of credibility, since the speaker can so readily identify with the listeners who come from the same social class, dress the same way, and understand the particular way of speaking Spanish.

COME WITH US TO CHURCH TO-NIGHT!
When the meeting on one street corner is finished, **the spectators are not simply given a piece of Christian literature and invited to come to church 'sometime' as they often are by less effective street preachers. Instead they are urged to 'come right along with us to church *tonight!*' Individuals will move out and be sure each spectator is gently persuaded to join the crowd.**

For two hours these small groups will slowly move nearer the church and stop for another brief meeting, This continues, meeting after meeting, until they have only enough time to march to the church and arrive at about 6.30, bringing the new visitors with them.
They meet others as they approach the church. More than 1000 open-air evangelists will have been working in the immediate vicinity of the Jotabeche church. **They fill the streets. Often traffic has to be detoured.** The church officers step outside to greet the street-preaching teams as they arrive and file into the sanctuary, singing loudly as they go in.

DOES STREET PREACHING WORK?
Many non-Pentecostals think street preaching is old-fashioned. Some regard it as a public spectacle that cheapens the gospel. They may not use these words, but they say, in effect,' singing and yelling out there on the street is beneath my dignity'. Some braver souls may even have tried it on occasion but failed because of inexperience or some other reason. From that they tend to generalise, claiming that 'street preaching doesn't work anyway.' **Does it really work? The members of the Jotabeche Methodist Pentecostal Church think it does. If you need proof they will simply point to their massive sanctuary. The former one on Jotabeche Street, had a seating capacity of only 5000, so after many years of overflow crowds standing out in the street, they decided to rebuild. Their new church, on the same block, but facing out on Santiago's main thoroughfare, seats 16,000 Costing over $2 million; it was fully paid for by members' contributions the day it was dedicated in 1974.**

GO!
Those who analyse what they are doing theologically will tell you they are only obeying what Jesus commands to go and preach the gospel to every creature. But they stress the word *go* in contrast to many others who expect unbelievers to *come*.
They are aggressive in their evangelism while slower growing churches are invariably more passive. **They untiringly proclaim the message of salvation to the lost, but they are not satisfied with proclamation only.** They believe in persuading their unbelieving friends to commit their lives to Christ and become responsible members of his church.

CHURCH-CENTRED EVANGELISM.
This last phrase, 'responsible members of his church' is a key concept in unlocking the secrets of Pentecostal growth.
To a very high degree, Pentecostals are church-centred, and this increases their effectiveness.
By 'church-centred' I do not mean that they are ingrown and introverted – just the opposite! They know that Christ has commanded them to '**make disciples**', and they also know that disciples are made from those out there in the world. They do not expect the people to come to the gospel; **they diligently take the gospel to the people. But at this point they do not make the mistake of others who are not so church-centred make. They are not content to see the new-born babies left out in the street. They**

need spiritual care, the milk of the Word (1 Peter 2:2), which they will not get in the street but in the church.

The lambs that are found must be brought into the fold where the shepherds can watch over them, heal their wounds and help them grow. They are not to be left in the ravines where the wild beasts will devour them.

Pentecostals are usually proud of their church. That is why they often seem uninterested in participating in city-wide or nationwide interdenominational crusades. Their seeming aloofness is not ordinarily due to any lack of love or respect for their brethren in other denominations as much as to an intuitive knowledge that the very nature of interdenominational evangelism often separates it too much from the local church.

A VITAL KEY.

Research shows that evangelistic programmes can be attractive, flamboyant, heavily financed, expertly staffed, strongly prayed for *but relatively fruitless, if they are not properly related to the local churches as an integral part of the evangelistic programme itself.*

One of Latin America's top evangelistic preachers once brought this up to me in a personal conversation.

He was concerned, he said, as to why his city-wide crusades would produce so many apparent decisions for Christ, *but that so little fruit would remain.*

He was not a Pentecostal, incidentally, although he believed in the baptism of the Holy Spirit and had received it himself.

I was equally concerned because one of my students had researched several evangelistic crusades in Cochabamba, Bolivia, where I lived at the time. His report had shown statistically that they had been surprisingly ineffective in' adding to the church such as should be saved.' (Acts 2:47)

My friend had just held the first of a week-long series of evangelistic meetings in a rented auditorium in Cochabamba. The building had been filled, and some 50 people had responded to the invitation by coming forward.

But he knew, and I knew that (apart from some believers in the group who were rededicating their lives to God), very few of those who came forward would be found in the Cochabamba churches six months hence.

COUNSELLING NEW CONVERTS.

He belonged to an evangelistic association which stressed the value of interdenominational crusades. By nature it was not church-centred. I suggested to him that this might be one of the problems. Holding the meetings in such a non-church building as this rented auditorium **did not help the new converts to associate their decision with the local church. Neither did the teaching given.**

I asked the evangelist, 'When you finished leading the people who had come forward in the sinner's prayer, **what did you counsel them to do next?**

He replied, '**Read the Bible, pray regularly, and tell someone else about your decision**'.

In my opinion there is a mistake here; **a mistake that most Pentecostals do not make. There is nothing wrong with Bible-reading, praying and witnessing - they are all beautiful Christian virtues!**

But the evangelist's instructions to the new-born babies left out another Christian virtue that *at that particular moment of their experience was as important as the other three- becoming a committed member of a local body of believers, a church.*

This cannot be overstressed. Jesus included '**baptising them**' as part of the Great Commission.

Baptism in its simplest definition is merely the rite of incorporation into the Body of Christ in its local and visible form.

When you join a church you commit yourself not only to God but to other believers, The members of the Body encourage and nourish one another. When converts are added to the church, they are likely to go on for Christ.

SPIRITUAL DELIVERY ROOM.

One of Buenos Aires' largest and most rapidly growing Pentecostal churches **stresses incorporation so much that the pastor was once suspected of holding the doctrine of 'baptismal regeneration'.**

Members of his church witness constantly and then bring those who are interested to church on Sunday evening,

After the singing, the pastor invites all to stand to receive a gift from the church. The deacons distribute New Testaments to them. **He then tells them that since they came to find out the meaning of the gospel and how to become a Christian, they should not remain in the main Sanctuary.**

'My message here will be directed to believers, not to you' he says.
He then instructs them to move into another room where some laymen will explain to them how to become Christians.

Once they are in the other room with some of the church's top evangelists one could correctly predict that the percentage of decisions for Christ will be high. But along with this, the percentage of those who become disciples, who are 'continually devoting themselves to the apostles' teaching, and to the fellowship, to the breaking of bread and prayer' is high also. Why? **Chiefly because they are immediately associated with the church. There is no difference between evangelism and follow-up.**

Three things tie them closely to the church:
1. They make their decision right there in the church. The church, in a sense, is the spiritual delivery room for their birth. Church members – not a visiting preacher from outside – are the

obstetricians.

2. without apology they are told that if they are sincere in committing themselves to Christ, they must immediately obey his command to be baptised.
To them baptism is not something optional that Christians may or may not like to do, six months, or two years, or ten years from now. Christ is Lord and his commandments must be obeyed now. They feel that if an enquirer says, 'I want to believe in Christ but I do not want to follow him in baptism' there is a real question as to the validity of the decision.

CONVERTS DO NOT GO HOME ALONE!
3. The new babes do not go home alone. A church member is assigned to each one, and accompanies him or her to their home. In the usual Latin American fashion, the visitor is often invited into the home and offered a cup of coffee and meets the family. Before leaving, the church member makes arrangements to take the new believer and other family members to church the next Sunday.
So the new believers are drawn into the warm body of the Church, where they can be nurtured in Christian life, and equipped for Christian witness and service.

FEBRUARY WCN 1988.
"OUR YOUNG PEOPLE IN BANGOR *need to be full of the Spirit.*"
Our February WCN editorial draws attention to the newly-developing and increasing prevalence of excessive drinking among the young – and sometimes very young!
"It's not a pretty sight to see people who have come under the addiction of alcohol, so that it dominates and ruins their lives. Therefore it is a matter of no small concern to see so many young people, at an early age, so freely indulging in this way.
A couple of weeks ago our local newspaper gave us the sad story of a trader on Queen's Parade who had to close a promising business because of rowdyism, assaults and damage to his premises, most of which he attributed to the influence of alcohol.
Some responsible people, I have been told, recently made a survey one night of our seafront in Bangor, counting the number of young people – mostly under age – who were involved in drinking. They counted many hundreds!
This is a matter of concern. No doubt **young people are looking for something to satisfy them inwardly, seeking company, identity, fellowship, a sense of worth.**
And it is WE who have the secret for this in Jesus, and in the Church of which he is the Head.

Many hundreds of years ago the apostle Paul, after vividly describing a society not unlike our own in its nastier elements, speaking of impurity, silly talk, bitterness, anger, malice, futility of mind and darkened understanding, alienation, greed and licentiousness, wrote:
"Look carefully then how you walk… making the most of the time, because the days are evil…do not get drunk with wine for that is debauchery: *but be filled with the Spirit, addressing one another in psalms and hymns and spiritual songs, singing and making melody to the Lord with all your heart…*" Ephesians 5:15.

OUR YOUNG PEOPLE IN WEST.
Many hundreds of young people meet each week in our premises in West Church, and we are grateful for work done in all our uniformed organisations, our youth clubs and youth fellowships, in Sunday School departments and Bible Classes.

We are particularly happy to see more than a hundred young people participating in "Young West Church" on a Sunday morning and feel that this venture, of having "A Third Morning Service" for our young people has been well worth while.

Mind you, we are far, far from satisfied that we are doing all that we should for young people in the Bangor West area.
Our concern for young people is not to be negative or critical or spoilsport, **but somehow, to be those who share with them that ABUNDANT LIFE that Jesus came to give.**

Many of our people – and of our young people – have received a fullness of the Holy Spirit; it must be our duty and joy to share it with others. We have received a commission from our Lord, and we must seek, in ways that are realistic and workable, to do so.

FEBRUARY WCN also keeps us informed of domestic developments in West:
For example **the old chairs in the Church Lounge which had become tired and tatty – and with disembowelled foam protruding from them, dangerous – are to be replaced with new purpose-built seating, creating a room of some intimacy, suitable also for Crèche on Sundays.**

EDWARD CARLETON is building up his Property Team, seeking people with tradesmen skills – Ken Macartney and Wallace Parker are the latest volunteers. Plans are afoot for interior painting of our buildings.

The Sunday service is now being relayed to the Vestibule, so that mums can hear the service there, when their children have been unsettled in Church.

A PRESBYTERY VISITATION will take place in the second half of April.

THE SYCAMORE CLUB- A

Friend Needed!
At present, we are aware of one little boy who is 13 years of age, who would benefit greatly from having a friend! **The West Church Family has already provided many friends, and if anyone feels they could respond to this need please contact Margaret Conroy.**

The Sycamore Club enjoy their fortnightly meetings with enthusiastic singing.
In June they had a Barbecue at Crawfordsburn, with lots to eat, a large area to play in, and a thoroughly enjoyable time.
In October **they were guests of the PWA. "Our evening was spent enjoying a great deal of fun, surrounded by love. We can only express our thanks to the ladies, but the children's faces that evening expressed a great deal more."**
"We have spent a Happy Year, learning God's Word, singing his praise and enjoying the company of his children. Our prayer for next year is that many 'closed doors' for both mentally handicapped children and adults will begin to open."

FEBRUARY WCN had an item from a Social Worker from the Home-finding Team, asking: "COULD YOU FOSTER A FAMILY?"

FEBRUARY WCN contains various annual reports.
THE TREASURER'S REPORT IS SUCCINCT AND CHEERFUL!
"It is indeed a pleasure to present the Financial Report. This is the first time I can remember that all our accounts are in a healthy position. Thanks are due to all those members who give, and also review their givings regularly, and I trust and pray we will all be able to continue in this manner over the next year."

IN THE YOUTH FELLOWSHIP Report, Derek Polley tells of a weekly meeting of 25-30 young people; mentions visits to other churches, 2nd Ards Presbyterian and Donegall Road Methodist; of Ards Presbytery Youth with monthly meetings of 400 young people, with the West Church group supplying the Praise leadership. He mentions Christmas Carol singing on a damp evening, and delivering of 1000 Christmas cards, raising £104.

GUIDES – NEW GUIDE LEADERS.
The start of the year saw a change in leadership. Taking over the reins are Marty Stevenson, Yvonne Monteith and Moyra McNeilly. This came after the regrettable retirement of Judy Allen and Denise Elliott who have given many years of dedicated service to our Guides.
"We, as the new Leaders, are very grateful for all their previous work for they have left us with a very good Guide Company.
Our numbers started small but over the weeks they have grown and we now have 28 very willing and enthusiastic Guides on our Roll Book.
We have prepared our Guides for enrolment – at which we also were enrolled!"
The report then goes on to give details of regular badge work, with an outing to the Swimming Pool with supper afterwards; a Badminton tournament at the Leisure Centre; A Christmas Party with the Brownies.

THE BOWLING CLUB.
"THE Bowling Club commenced the new season in the nicest possible way, by re-introducing the Annual Dinner which had not been held for several years.
Our rink evenings and friendly matches are well attended – new members will be made most welcome."
Sam Lilley, Chairman,
Reggie Scott, Secretary.

CHRIS RITCHIE from Israel writes about the body-blow loss of the ship M.V. LOGOS, praying that out of this disaster and disruption to planned ministry in South America, greater blessings in the future may yet come.

He speaks of the tense political situation in the occupied territories of the West Bank and Gaza Strip.
"Having been to the West Bank recently to sell magazines, we can all testify to the atmosphere of fear and hatred which is the real source of the problem. We can only pray for a spirit of love and forgiveness to come upon both sides, Arab and Israeli.

"As well as spiritual warfare we also need to pray for more labourers to plant the seeds which will result in a harvest….
Here in Haifa, we would appreciate prayer for more conversations and contacts with those genuinely interested in the gospel.

On a happier note we have been encouraged by recent book sales and for the times we have been able to minister to others….."

KIRK SESSION REPORT:
Mr William McClelland writes:
"as we review another year the Kirk Session is conscious of God's guidance and provision for us in 1987.
Last year the Kirk Session said a formal welcome to our new Assistant Minister, his wife and daughter. We hardly knew them then, but from our first meeting with ALVIN, we had a warm and settled conviction that God had provided the man of his choice for the growth and development of His work under Mr Bailie's direction, in this congregation.
…. Alvin's friendly and approachable personality, his joy in the Lord, the sincerity of his ministry, the dignity of worship as he leads the services, and his conscientiousness in all the work of the ministry have endeared him to the whole congregation.
ALWAYS WELCOME.
These attributes fit easily into our congregation where we have been used to – and all too often taken for

granted – the tireless devotion and service of the Rev. David Bailie and Mrs Bailie. **Mr Bailie's ministry stretches far beyond the bounds of this congregation and in this wide and effective ministry the Kirk Session gives wholehearted support.**

It does put a heavy burden upon Mr Bailie but he is a good steward of time and manages to produce sermons and teaching material of the highest order to give clear teachings in the things of the Kingdom.

It has been the mark of the congregation of Bangor West that all who come are always made welcome. Many, many people in this congregation and from elsewhere know that when they sought help from our Minister, they were immediately made to feel welcome and needed and appreciated in the body of Christ's people. To David and to Rhoda we say 'thank you'.

MARCH WCN 1988.
A VIRTUOUS CIRCLE.
'Life in the Spirit Seminars'~lead to 'Open Nights' ~~lead on to further 'Life the in Spirit Seminars.'

In 1987 we found that at the conclusion of a Life in Spirit Seminar, it was appropriate and profitable to hold an Open Night to bear testimony to what God had done.

We found that we were able to call upon our Singing Group and Drama groups to enhance the testimonies given.

And we discovered that among those who accepted the invitation to be our Guests, there were those already disposed to enrol in our next Seminars.

And so we had a *virtuous circle of Seminar, Open Night, Seminar.*

And we note that between Thursday 10th March and Tuesday 24th May, we scheduled no less than six Open Nights – with the next Seminar scheduled for Thursday 14th April.

MARCH WCN 1988 gives notice of OUR HOLY WEEK SERVICES, Monday 27th March

Friday 1st April, on "WORDS FROM THE CROSS"
'Today thou wilt be with me in Paradise.'
'Son, behold thy mother. Father, forgive them.'
'My God – why hast thou forsaken me?'
'Father, into thy hands I commend my spirit.'

Then, on Easter Evening, we will have a United Service, under the triumphant theme: 'It Is Finished.'

WCN March also gave two reports by short-term students in Nepal, and urged our own young people to pick up PCI NEWS for short-term reports and opportunities.

APRIL WCN 1988.

April was to see Ten Days of Missionary Focus and Challenge within the Ards Presbytery, with PCI missionaries involved.
This endeavour was to update us about all the missionary work of PCI and to challenge us to a greater involvement in its work.

It also tells us that already at four "Open Nights" many sampled the warmth of Christian worship and fellowship, with some planning to attend still further 'Life in the Spirit Seminars.'

WCN April also carried the news that THE NEW DIRECTOR OF PRISON FELLOWSHIP IS FRANK REA FROM OUR OWN CONGREGATION IN WEST.
"This work has been pushed forward very effectively for a number of years by JAMES McILROY. Obviously an important post and close to our Lord's heart at any time this work has clearly special **significance in the present turbulent state of our Province, with so many in prison, and with important work to do among ex-prisoners,** We wish Frank Rea and his wife Maureen well.

We plan as a congregation to offer special prayer for them on the evening of Sunday 17th April at our Praise Service, *praying that Frank may be fully endued with the wisdom and power of the Holy Spirit as he endeavours to promote and foster a liberating ministry among prisoners and ex-prisoners through Christ's Name."*

OUR SANDILANDS CARAVAN: THE FLOOR HAVING BECOME UNSAFE AND A POTENTIAL HAZARD FOR YOUNG AND OLD, THE COMMITTEE ON GROUNDS OF SAFETY HAVE DISPOSED OF IT.
Consideration about replacement is being made.

We have had further updates from the Dores in Japan and Chris Ritchie in Israel.

VARIOUS FUNCTIONS OF WEST CHURCH NEWS.

Over the years WCN has had a function to inform and inspire our members. Its purpose is to lift high the Name of Jesus, whereby people can actually reach through to freedom and wholeness.
So, in April WCN, we included an article under the title of "FREEDOM OF FORGIVENESS"
It is an extract from "CHILD SEXUAL ABUSE."
It is included so that those who have experienced the destructive and traumatic effects of such abuse **may actually gain freedom.**
And, in any congregation or readership, there will almost always be such people.
This is included that it may be read, pondered, heeded in such a way as to bring actual release and healing.

So here is "KATHY'S STORY."
Kathy is a professional woman, living with her husband and children, but with a secret pain.

"The Conference I attended was the turning point in my life. The speaker was Karen Mains and she was teaching about forgiveness. As she started talking about how our subconscious minds deal with guilt, I suddenly felt as though she was describing me – from the inside out. She explained that our subconscious minds deal with guilt, pushing it down until it finally surfaces in various ways: in erratic behaviour, in anger, in depression. I knew all too well everything she was describing.

GUILT UPON GUILT.
At the end of the session Karen **had everyone close their eyes and then she began to talk quietly to those of us who were hurt by other people. 'You may be here today carrying the wounds of another person's sin against you.'** she said.
And then she explained that there were **two kinds of guilt:** guilt that other people put upon us by hurting us, and guilt caused by things that we ourselves have done. **And I was experiencing both kinds of guilt, guilt upon guilt!**

"If you are experiencing guilt of your own, ask God to forgive you" Karen said.
That was not a hard thing for me. I was sitting there saying, "Yes, Lord, I have a lot of guilt. I ask you to forgive me now." **And I sensed he did forgive me.**

STRENGTH TO FORGIVE.
Then Karen went on, '**Now, if someone else has hurt you, I want you to ask God for strength to forgive that person**'.

I just sat there stunned. I couldn't believe what she was saying. I thought, "She can't mean this. She can't be asking me to forgive my uncle." She kept talking about giving our past with all its pain to Jesus and asking him to help us forgive the individual who had hurt us.

I sat there in my seat, and in my mind I said, 'No way. He doesn't deserve to be forgiven. There's no way I am going to let him off the hook. I can't forgive him and I won't forgive him.'
And then I realised what I was saying. Here I was, just having asked God to forgive me, but I wasn't willing to extend forgiveness, to offer my uncle what I had just asked for myself.

And Karen kept saying, 'Now forgive…. Forgive…'

My fists were clenched and I was actually gritting my teeth. I was desperately torn. But finally, reluctantly, needing God's forgiveness too much myself to hold on to this pain, I said, '**OK then, Lord, I'm willing to forgive him.**'

It was a most reluctant obedience, but God honoured it. It was as much as I was able to do at the time. I'll never forget that second as long as I live. There I sat in a room with six or seven hundred other women, and I felt as if I was alone with God. From the bottom of my feet up through my whole body, a great weight simply disappeared.

COOL CLEAN BREEZE.

The feeling was almost indescribable – like a cool, clean breeze blowing through me. And I knew that something had happened in that moment of forgiveness. I knew that I was never going to be the same. I never talked with anyone about it. I just quietly left the conference. But I went out of there knowing I was changed.
There had been a tremendous snowstorm that day and it took us hours to get home. When I got there my husband was shovelling the driveway. I said to him, 'My life's never going to be the same from this day on. I don't know what has happened, and I can't explain it yet, but I'm sure things are going to be different'.

INWARD CHANGE - FLASHBACKS CEASE.

The inward change was soon obvious. **Love, joy, peace – the very things I had longed for, but never known for more than a few minutes at a time – became real for me.** My husband said to the kids, '**I don't know what's happened to Mommy – but we have a new mommy in this house.**'
The flashbacks ceased immediately. The healing I am describing happened more than five years ago and only twice in those five years have I ever had a flashback. The above change was inexplicable, because I had struggled with those memories all through the years. It was as though God erased a painful part of my memories.

ABLE TO TELL MY HUSBAND.
At last I was able to tell my husband about my pain-filled childhood. He had no idea of it until about three months after my initial 'freeing' when I told him about it.
He was wonderful – he took it as information that would help him understand me better. What a relief to have him sharing my life fully! He had always been good to me; now my love and respect for him is simply limitless.
As for the guilt I had carried so long, there was a tremendous, immediate release. I thought then that the problem was dealt with for ever; I didn't realise that there was deeper healing still to come.

SHE COULD PICK UP THE HEAVY KEY…

At the moment Kathy realised that she could be free of the hatred and resentment that held her prisoner. **She also realised she had a choice to make…** She could pick up the key that was offered, open her prison of pain and walk out free. **Or she could reject the idea.** The key of forgiveness is, after all, a heavy one, and it is a painful struggle to turn it in its rusty locks.
Kathy chose to take the heavy key and turn it in the locks of her soul, stiff and rusted as they were. And suddenly she was wonderfully

free. Free to accept the forgiveness of God for her own sins; free from the death-clasp of the abuser on her life.

Forgiveness is a choice which each of us has the opportunity to make – not only once but many times throughout life. And each time we choose to forgive, we make a choice for freedom.

MAY WCN 1988.

JOHN WIMBER TO GO TO JAPAN?

GRAHAM DORE writes:

"Maybe, partly to spy out the land for a Wimber visit, Bob Fulton, his brother-in-law and founder of Vineyard Ministries, visited Japan in March.
We and about a hundred (mainly Japanese) people met him and his 6-member team in Sapparo.
It was quite a change from normal formality to be singing Wimber songs in Japanese, and for many it was maybe revolutionary to sing TO God, to think only of HIM, to enjoy worship etc, and to be involved in praying for healing. I don't know how common this is in Japan, *but for us it was a first, and we were sorry more people we know weren't there.*

On the 10th April **we held our first Sunday School.** We prayed for at least ten, and **twelve came!**
With the helpers (Mr Munakata, Miss Sato, Miss Schmidt and three children) that made the room look full, and we expect a couple more in future. **Most of these are new to the gospel so we must keep their interest to see them coming regularly.**
The same day **Mr Arai ("new well")** was baptised in a nearby church. A good number (11 adult Japanese) from Tondem, including his wife (first time in church) joined about 80 from that church. The singing was stirring. In my brief introduction I said I hoped Mr Arai would no longer be a "well", but a "new spring" (cf. John 4: 14-15): effortlessly yielding living water. From a Shinto priest family, his grasp of biblical truth is still confused, but he is open to instruction. He will be our **fifth** member!

JUNE/JULY WCN.

SURELY AN UNUSUAL TIME TO PLAN A VISITATION OF THE CONGREGATION?

THE SUMMER!
During the Summer from mid-June to September, we are planning, as far as we possibly can, to visit all the families of the congregation.
This visitation will involve our three theological students from Union College, Jim Hunter, Ann Kennedy, and Heather Lewis who is of course working with us as a Pastoral Assistant.

We believe we have seen God do many lovely and wonderful things in our Church, **and we want to spread the good news of this around.** For that is how the sphere of grace is extended more and more in our congregation.

"SHORTLY BEFORE YOU ARE VISITED, you will receive a leaflet to give you advance notice and to share a little of what God is doing among us.
As well, there will be a fairly comprehensive booklist. **Take a good look at it, and you will almost certainly find some book that will be of special interest to you.**

When your Visitor arrives from the church, whether he/she is a theological student or your own elder, or some other member of the congregation, take full advantage of the visit.

There's plenty of evidence in the world today that God is very much alive, and that those who seek him may find him.

Your visitor will be happy to share with you, plenty of specific illustrations of the way that God has been working in many lives in our own midst.

And he/she will have an **Invitation to you to come along and sample one of our *OPEN NIGHTS*** where you can experience for yourself a meeting in which the Holy Spirit is clearly present, in the warmth of the worship and the love and openness of the fellowship. *HAVE A GOOD VISIT!"*

TO EXPLAIN AND BUTTRESS THIS SUMMER VISITATION, a sermon was preached on Sunday evening 22nd May from 1 Thessalonians 5:8ff, on "Improving the Quality of congregational Care."

Here are some of the points made:

"**We are a large congregation where one in three families seldom attends church: where one in four communicants may not take part in the Lord's Supper.**

Yet good things are happening in our midst. People crowd into our seminars… however some of our people are ignorant of the good things God is doing right here.

Through a Summer Visitation we plan to tell them!

Our Theological Students will help though it is still the task of the whole body of believers.
We learn from Paul how to fulfil our Christian Commission:
"Therefore encourage one another and build each other up, just as in fact you are doing" 1 Thessalonians 5 11.

In our congregation many people **are encouraging others** by telling them of how people have been healed and have received eternal life through faith in Jesus: **and that this is very real for the people concerned!**

And through our Visitation Programme **we plan to encourage many more!**

In 1 Thessalonians 5: 12-13 Paul exhorts:
Now we ask you, brothers, to respect those who work hard among you, who are over you in the Lord and who admonish you. Hold them in the highest regard in love because of their work.

"It is the task of a leader to exert himself to lead, of a teacher to feed the flock, of a shepherd to lead them and tend them with all his energy by the Holy Spirit – and his congregation should respect, support and follow initiatives to build up the church and extend its frontiers.
We ministers in West are truly grateful to God for the respect and support you give us, and for the love that we experience so freely. We know, for example, that there will be a widespread endeavour, this summer, in our visitation, to gain new ground for the Kingdom of God and to build up and strengthen our congregation.

Paul continues, verse 13: **Live in peace with each other.**
An apt word, for a Christian community enjoying peace, is in sharp contrast with the world of bickering, criticism, innuendo, jealousy, unease. The seeking and maintenance of peace must be of high priority among us. A Christian people at peace draw folk from a critical and divided world.

Paul continues, verse 14:
"And we urge you, brothers, warn those who are idle, encourage the timid, help the weak, and be patient with everyone.

From this we learn, that we are not to be careless or idle, **but to work hard to build up the fellowship and to share the Gospel.
We are to arouse one another to save and to heal.**

Paul tells us to encourage the fainthearted, the timid, the sorrowful, and the dejected. **And there are many broken people out there for us to restore and heal.**
Paul says to help the weak and be patient with all.
And there are broken and exhausted people out there for us to care for.
In our congregation we need to learn to bear and forbear, not to be upset or aggrieved, or to take hurt to heart, but by waiting upon God to gain restraint and wisdom from him. We are to be **patient with them all!** The Lord is patient, not quick to judgement, and so must we be also.

Paul continues, verse 15: **Make sure that nobody pays back wrong for wrong, but always try to be kind to each other and to everyone else.**
We must be imitators of God. And we need to invite God to search our hearts to ensure that there is no residue of resentment or ill-will in them when others have hurt us. Instead we must do good and bless, so that a vital peace permeates all our relationships.

Paul continues, verse 16ff **"Be joyful always, pray continually; give thanks in all circumstances, for this is God's will for you in Christ Jesus."**
Within the church we are to learn that whatever adverse circumstances threaten, we can rejoice because God is near and he has destroyed the power of evil.
Like Paul and Silas in the dungeon at Philippi, though heavily beaten, they sing the praises of God in the midnight hour: and discover God's power to intervene, and bring great good out of evil.
When we follow this example, we will find God faithful to intervene and save.

Paul also exhorts: **Do not put out the Spirit's power; do not treat prophecies with contempt. Test everything. Hold on to the good. Avoid every kind of evil.**

How do we quench the Spirit – by withdrawing the supply of fuel from it? We must maintain the conditions of togetherness and worship and give priority to keeping the flame alive and burning. We are not to forbid speaking in tongues or prophesying. It is wonderful when God speaks a direct word as a body of Christians worship together. Jesus spoke a direct word of knowledge to the woman of Samaria, and gained her instant attention, and a change of heart.

So, through this Meditation upon Paul's words to the Church at Thessalonica, we in West Church found ourselves encouraged to be good witnesses for Jesus to those around us, and to become a tenderly close-knit community of love.

Thus knit together and infused by the Spirit we sought to launch out upon our **Summer Visitation.**

This endeavour to make our whole West Church congregation a body of love and of faith is promoted in many ways – in our Praise & Prayer meetings, in our Open Nights, at our Home Groups, at our Sunday services.
As well there are surges of love and life that come into the Body, for example through Weekend Retreats. A year ago, in May 1987, we gave an account of a Women's Weekend at Rostrevor, so much appreciated. The Report concluded with the suggestion that other groups could emulate the women, by organising such a Weekend.

AND GUESS WHAT?

A year later, we find another report from the women, again at Rostrevor. The final paragraph of their report goes as follows:
On Sunday, after attending church services, we all came together to share and to give thanks for the weekend. We had

been given the opportunity to seek the Lord and to rest in Him; to meet and to get to know people behind their masks, and to have fun and fellowship. And so we rejoiced! We gave thanks for the ministry of Cecil and Myrtle Kerr, the community at Rostrevor and also our own beloved Margaret Bailie who lovingly took the time and made the effort to arrange the weekend.

AND GUESS WHAT ELSE?

We read about THE MEN at Rostrevor for a weekend also, under the title:

"IT'S FRIDAY – BUT SUNDAY'S COMIN'!"

"The drive down to Rostrevor took an hour longer than Andy's (Cole) word-processed itinerary suggested.

A bed six foot long is too short if you measure six foot three.
It rained all day Saturday, grey clouds glowering down from the Meath hills, the wind whipping grey Carlingford Lough into sullen spume.

Immediately after being granted freedom to worship as we pleased – standing or seated – we were ordered to stand!

These were, perhaps, some practical aspects of the "Friday" for those attending the Men's Weekend. However, as the Tony Campolo video, enjoyed by all, and whose theme seemed to play a second to the Weekend's main melody – that God had prepared a Table of Good Things for us (Psalm 23:5a) – put it, they were quickly swept aside – "Sunday" come!

Andy had characterised the Weekend's central purpose as being "to meet the Lord." From the moment when we, travel-weary and somewhat disorientated, stood to the sound of the first guitar chord, that is precisely what we did! A spirit of peace, of relaxation, of oneness with each other, settled gently over us, our differences in stance, in attitude, in approach, as we sang, prayed and worshipped together, faded into proper insignificance. All knew the Lord's Presence – "Sunday" come!

And throughout the Weekend, this soul-quickening Presence continued to make himself felt, in the community-led formal session, when aspects of this bountiful - but often unclaimed - provision for us were explained; in the mealtime banter in the kitchen; in laughter; in awe-filled silence; in praise, the presence of Him who transformed Friday's despair and desolation into Sunday's ongoing victory, now made manifest to us.

"LORD, IT IS WELL THAT WE ARE HERE." Matthew 17: 4.

G.M.

LIVE LINK TO THE DORES!

Wasn't it good to be able to give the Dores live greetings and to hear their voices again last Sunday at our Family Service? And good to hear Alastair's teacher tell of her very clear call to minister to the children of missionaries.
The Dores have asked for special prayer to cover a major endeavour to reach through to men on Fathers' Day.

We count it a privilege, in Christian and in warm human terms, to be represented by this family, the Dores, as they endeavour to plant and extend Christ's Church in Japan.

FRANK REA, Director of Prison Fellowship, N. Ireland, writes:

"It is hard to realise that over seven weeks have passed since that wonderful Praise Service on Sunday 17th April, when prayer was made for me as Director of Prison Fellowship, N. Ireland.
It has been a very busy and encouraging time as I have met with Prison Governors, Chaplains and those in the Northern Ireland Office responsible for prison work.
I would particularly value your prayers for additional members for our Team going into Crumlin Road Prison on Wednesday evenings between 5 and 7 p.m.
We need men for these teams, including someone to lead the Praise.
We also need men prepared to visit someone or to write letters. If you feel the Lord speaking to you about any of these areas, please contact me.

AUGUST WCN 1988.

YES! YET MORE 'LIFE IN THE SPIRIT' SEMINARS – one for adults beginning on Wednesday 31st August, and one for YOUNG PEOPLE (16-17 YEAR AGE RANGE) to be led by Alvin, and beginning on Friday 9th September.
As well two 'Open Nights' scheduled for Thursdays 1st and 29th September.

OUR WITNESS BOX.

You will remember that when we launched our Summer Visitation of the congregation, we had the aim of sharing with the members of the congregation, some of the lovely things that God was doing in our midst. So many healing and renewing things!

Some of these life-changing episodes were known to *some* of those going out to visit – but many were not. So we sent out about forty letters to people who had come to new life and vigour in Christ requesting them, briefly, to write down their story.
Our members willingly responded, and wrote superbly,

bearing eloquent witness to what God had done for them, under a veritable anointing of the Holy Spirit.
And so our **WITNESS SHEETS** came into being.
Our elders and visitors and theological students were able to carry these with them, as well as a supply of helpful, challenging Christian books, and leave them for our members to read.

When the AUGUST WCN was published, there were already **55 of these witness sheets** – an index to a work of the Spirit, that had been bubbling up strongly in our midst.

They have been added to over the years since, and have been used in many places and situations to draw attention to the grace and dynamic of Jesus and to be a magnet to draw folk to Christ. There's no calculating the workings of grace wrought through them in a multitude of hearts! A quote from WCN:
"All over the summer, we have found it necessary, week by week, to replenish supplies. Folk have been taking them, and we trust, reading them, and often sharing them with others."

To illustrate, we printed one of them in the August edition of WCN. It was by Margaret Graham, under the title: "I COULD NOT COME TO TERMS WITH BEING ALONE, ESPECIALLY AT NIGHT"
Through bereavement she felt lonely, lost, afraid, and suffering from arthritis.
"Going to church the first Sunday and hearing the words of the chorus made me feel like crying. I knew there was something here that I wanted, as I got a great feeling of peace."
Then it tells her story, and concludes:

"Now I can lift my hands and praise the Lord for He has accepted me and forgiven my sins.

I now praise the Lord all the time no matter where I am.
'This is my testimony', Margaret Graham.

This sample illustration was given, in the stated hope, that some others might feel inspired to tell their story also!

WE NOW GIVE A FEW EXAMPLES FROM THE WITNESS SHEETS WRITTEN AT THAT TIME.

MOLLIE WATSON writes:
"I WAS CRIPPLED WITH ARTHRITIS."
"I came to be more aware of the gifts of the Spirit *through the gift of healing here in West Church*, a good number of years ago.
I was crippled with arthritis in both hip joints, and one evening the late Mrs Frazer noticed my difficulties getting up and down during the service. She mentioned the **Divine Healing meeting after the Evening Service.**
IMPRESSED, I decided to go and my husband came with me. We were greatly impressed spiritually with all the prayers that went up to God for my healing. **In a very short time my pains eased until, eventually I had no pain, and I have had no pain in my joints for a long time now. I thank God for his love and goodness to me.** Praise His most gracious Name.
[David Bailie recalls: I remember Mollie Watson, after a Mediterranean summer holiday, returning and telling us, with great wonder and enthusiasm, how she had been able to swim again. As a young person she had been a keen swimmer, but for quite a number of years her arthritic joints prevented her from doing so. But this time she was able to swim once more. She rejoiced in doing every swimming stroke – with joy she could do them *all!*
And how in the Healing service we rejoiced with her, and exulted in our Healing God!]

I WANTED SOME WORK TO DO FOR CHRIST – *AND IT CAME!*
A very short time after this blessing, in prayerful thanksgiving. I kept asking for God's guidance for some work to do, in the Church or outside it - *just as He would direct!*
To my surprise and delight, a very short time later, Mr Bailie asked me if I would like to do something for him. **I said YES – if he thought I would be capable! And so I was made responsible for the distribution of West Church News. My husband Hugh and I had great joy and satisfaction in doing this together** – work to further Christ's Kingdom here on earth.
[This was quite a formidable operation! DGB.]

YET SOMETHING STILL LACKING.
"I still found even with this, *there was something lacking!* I became interested in the Life in the Spirit seminar and began to attend it. **I found everything I needed in the Baptism of the Holy Spirit. Love, joy, peace, contentment, and life's problems more easily solved through answered prayers.**
I continued on in great faith, hoping that one day my husband would come to know and see through me in the home what a wonderful life it could be, *and wonderful it is since he also went through a Seminar and now knows more fully our Redeemer, Saviour, Healer, Comforter and the great joy of being together on the heavenly wavelength.*

I URGE ANYONE WAVERING – 'STEP FORWARD'.
And I would earnestly urge anyone who may be wavering on the brink, **to step forward boldly and get to know the great joy of salvation through our Lord Jesus Christ.** *One's life can change so dramatically when all desires for a full relationship with the Saviour of the World has been achieved through His great love.*

PRESS ON!

As Paul writes in Philippians 3: 14 'Press towards the mark for the prize of the high calling of God which is Christ Jesus.

This is the secret of the true way of life if we adhere to it, and it can be achieved through Christian fellowship and friendship in West Church."

"UNDER REPEATED BLOWS, SANDRA REJECTED GOD." Ken & Sandra Douglas.

"This is a story about Ken (that's me!) and my wife Sandra, *and more importantly, about God who has changed both our lives.*

When I first met Sandra she was a very happy young girl who enjoyed life to the full, and like many others she believed in God, attended Church regularly and was a Sunday School teacher.

Sandra's home was a happy place and very soon I became part of the family.

Her father Robert was full of life and made everyone feel welcome in their home

TRAGEDY STRUCK.

When Sandra was only eighteen tragedy struck her home and Robert was rushed to hospital where he died the next day.

Sandra's mother, Lily, struggled to bring up her daughter and two sons; Raymond, the eldest son, took on the role of "father."

Raymond took all the family problems on board and after struggling with epilepsy for a number of years, he died at the early age of twenty-seven.

You can imagine the effect that this combination of circumstances had on Sandra.

SANDRA REJECTED GOD.

She rejected God, stopped going to Church and was constantly asking why a good and loving God could allow these things to happen to her family.

They had tried to live a decent life, to be helpful to others, especially when they needed friendship, and generally to live life the way God wants everyone to live.

OUR FIRST CHILD ALMOST DIED – I KNEW GOD HEALED HER.

The year after Raymond died our first child Alison almost died after her birth. I prayed to God to heal Alison and two weeks later she was allowed out of hospital fit and well.
I knew that God had healed Alison but Sandra was still not convinced that a God of love really existed.

WE ATTENDED CHURCH FOR SOCIAL REASONS.

Two years later our son Peter was born and, as a family, we attended Church purely for social reasons. *It is not the accepted thing, 'Not to have the children baptised', we thought.*

I was still drifting along not really thinking about God's existence.
Then, in September 1985, my own father died very suddenly from cancer.
*The sort of questions Sandra had been asking for years took on a new significance for me.
What was life all about?
Where do we go when we die?
Is there really a God of love?*

It appeared that people, who lived a life opposed to God's Word, were better off in every way!

WE CONTINUED TO SEARCH FOR ANSWERS.

We both continued to search for answers. **God led Sandra to West Church in October 1987,** *and after seven weeks of questioning, God's power so changed her heart that she became a Christian.
She realised for the first time in her life that Christian Assurance was much more powerful than answers to intellectual questions.*

I WANTED WHAT SHE FOUND.

**From this point on the change in Sandra was so obvious that I wanted what she had found.
In January 1988 I joined a seminar in West Church.**
I saw the power of God at work in my group and the dramatic change in other people's lives through prayer, and I committed my life to God in May 1988.

LIVES TRANSFFORMED.

**Our lives have been transformed through the power of God's Holy Spirit and it is our prayer that your life will be too.
God has the answer to all your questions!**
And I tell you, Ask, and it will be given to you; seek and you will find; knock and it will be opened to you." Luke 11: 9.

WITNESS SHEET 20 WAS WRITTEN BY MURIEL STEPHENSON:

"MY EASY-GOING CHRISTIAN LIFE SHATTERED BY CANCER -HOW I WISH I HAD LOVED HIM SOONER."
"THAT WOMAN HAS JESUS IN HER."

"I would love people to look at me and say 'that woman has Jesus in her'. Maybe some do! – but very often we get cross, or have worries about health or families, or about what people have said to hurt us, or maybe what we have said and wish we had not!

JESUS UNDERSTANDS! *HE LIVED IN A FAMILY!*

Jesus understands he lived on earth like us, and had a family, Mark 6:3; Matthew 10: 36; John 7:5.
If I were to tell you about my dark and troubled times, you would not want to read what Jesus has done for me – **He washes away sin and gives new life.**

I GAVE MY HEART TO JESUS, BUT DID NOT FULLY WANT TO BE CHANGED.

It is just seven years since I gave my heart to him, *but I did not want to tell anyone, did not really want to be changed – some days I was all for God and some days I forgot about Him; most likely I was a Christian on Sundays!*

CANCER!
Then something happened to shatter my easy-going life; I was

told I was ill with cancer in January 1985 and needed major surgery. I was not angry, was not bitter, just numb as if it was happening to someone else; the hardest time was waking up in the morning when it hit hardest.

THE LORD SPOKE TO ME THREE TIMES THROUGH THE SCRIPTURES – *AND GAVE ME FAITH TO BELIEVE!*
I found I could not pray; that was when I wanted to tell everyone I knew Jesus, **to merit** *their* **prayers.** On the Sunday before I went into hospital, I opened my Bible at Mark 11: 20 -26.
[In this passage we read how the fig-tree that Jesus cursed has withered, and Jesus says **'have faith in God'** and **'whatever you ask for in prayer, believe that you have received it, and it will be yours'.**]
I really clung on to those promises **and the strange thing was I believed** *and had faith to hold on.*
My friend took me along to the Healing Service that night; we had just sat down when someone said they felt they had a message from the Lord for someone there and started to read Mark 11: 20 26.
My friend squeezed my hand hard
When the minister came in (he had been delayed at a Marriage Rehearsal) he came first to pray with me. My hand was nearly squeezed off when he used the same words Mark 11: 20-26.
Three times the Lord has promised me, but not only that, *He has given me the faith to believe I had received.*
I did not cry myself to sleep that night, but was rejoicing, knowing the Lord was with me.

HOME IN HALF THE TIME.
I had my operation and it was 100% successful. Not only that, I felt so well and was home in half the time stated, and all through my stay I could feel the power of prayer. **My life is changed from then – before I believed, I would not have prayed about small things - I felt there were** *so many people in trouble, in our country and in the world!* **NOW I bring EVERYTHING to the Lord in prayer, no matter how small: and He answers, not always in the way I want, but as He knows best!**

"JESUS TAKE ME AS I AM"
I was invited to a 'Life in the Spirit' seminar; I had my doubts – I am not good enough; I am too nervous! I am not like these other people! I then told myself that **Jesus had other ideas! Praise Him!**
Week after week I began to know Him better, and to love Him more, and to look forward to being in His Presence.
There is a chorus we sang often **'Jesus take me as I am, I can come no other way'** – I felt that for me this was the most important thing, **'Seek first the Kingdom of God'** then He will change what needs changing.

I LOVE MY NON-CHRISTIAN FRIENDS – AND KEEP PRAYING FOR THEM!
I pray that everyone would come to know Jesus. *I have so many non-Christian friends and I love them so, and can find no fault in them. In many ways they are much nicer than me!* **"But"** – such a small word yet says so much – 'but' they are missing so much. God's peace, God's love – *I will keep praying for them.*

HOW I WISH I HAD LOVED HIM SOONER!
1 Corinthians 13 really spoke to me about love and **loving. If we give love it comes back to us. If we love Jesus, how much more will He love us!** *How I wish I had loved him sooner!*

----

*IN OUR **WITNESS SHEETS***
IS A GREAT RANGE OF HUMAN NEED AND BROKENNESS DEPICTED – AND OF THE ANSWERING **GRACE** OF GOD.
In WITNESS 63 is a Trilogy in verse, by Colin Gillespie. We give one of these poems: **'MY TURMOIL WAS CONSTANT.'**

"In silence and darkness I lay on my bed
No silence or rest could I find in my head
My turmoil was constant, thoughts would not cease
I fought with my conscience to try to find peace.

The thoughts I turned over just raced round and round,
Not one single answer could ever be found,
I yearned for a silence elusive as dreams
But the roaring got louder and louder it seems.

Oh God! Oh God! Give me comfort tonight
Oh God if you're there will you teach me to fight,
To fight away anger, to fight away fear,
Oh God will you listen! Oh God can you hear?

I did sleep a little and wakened up sore,
I felt in my heart I can't take any more,
I talked to a friend, he said 'Won't you pray?'
God used him that morning to teach me the way.

"To ask and accept, not to fight it, give in,
Through total surrender is how you will win"
So that's what I did in the depths of despair,
I opened my eyes and found God was there!

I said "God, take over; I'm beaten, I'm through"
"Just trust me" He said, "That's all you've to do."
I couldn't believe it, the onus had shifted
The weight of my worries had suddenly lifted.

Now nothing has changed, the problems still there
The wonderful thing is, I don't have to care
This joy and this peace, you may

not understand, I know why I have it, I'm safe in His hand."

IN WITNESS SHEET 14, RENNIE NELSON WROTE: "COMING TO KNOW JESUS... A GENTLE AWAKENING."

"Coming to know Jesus was for me a gentle change in my life, knowing His love more and more each day and acknowledging Him as my Lord.

SOMETHING MISSING.
Previous to coming to Bangor, I did attend Church quite regularly which I was taught to do, from childhood, *but I got nothing really out of it* until I started attending West Church *when I realised something was 'missing' in my life.*

MY WIFE'S ILLNESS LED US TO PRAYER.
My wife took ill about this time and this led us both into prayer. In prayer we experienced God's love for us, when things got pretty rough and we were really low. What a comfort He gave us as we came before Him – to be lifted out of the darkness into the light.

GENTLY LED.
I was being gently led and I wanted to become more involved in the work of the church. I became a member of Church Committee and later Congregational Secretary. **Unfortunately my wife died and I found great difficulty in accepting this. But the Lord is a loving God and His love strengthened me and acceptance came in time. Some years later I was able to remarry and be very happy again.**

AN ELDER... AND THE BAPTISM OF THE HOLY SPIRIT.
More and more my life was changing in knowing God and loving Him. I wanted further to serve and I was made an elder of West Church and shortly after my wife and I received the Baptism of the Holy Spirit. **I was asked to lead a House Group, through which I know I have** *grown* **in my Christian life.**

A GREAT PRIVILEGE – TO SPEAK OF JESUS.
Knowing the love of God and trusting in Him has given me many blessings. Recently I had a great burden lifted off me through prayer, and something that gave me great joy was when God prompted me to visit a good friend of mine who was terminally ill, and not a Christian, and in God's perfect timing to speak to him of Jesus.

LOOKING AT PEOPLE IN GOD'S LOVE.
Being a Christian has given me much joy. I now seek to look at things and people in God's love. *My life has changed. I still fall down often but now I am quicker to get up.*
Coming to Jesus has not been for me a sudden overnight change, but a gentle awakening to God's love for me.

MARJORIE – from outside the congregation of West – wrote WITNESS 97.

"WHAT HAVE I GOT MYSELF INTO?"

"When Mr Bailie asked me to write about how *I was baptised in the Holy Spirit,* although I said I would, I didn't for a long time, *as I wondered if it would last.* I can say after a number of years that not only has it lasted *but has completely changed my life.*

It all began when I had to take my sister-in-law to *Life in the Spirit Seminars,* as she didn't drive. On the very first morning she couldn't go. However God impressed upon me that I was to go – not because of my sister-in-law, but for myself.

BAPTISM IN THE SPIRIT – FEAR!
Each week I faithfully completed our 'assignment' and never read ahead as we had been told not to. *It came as a shock to me when one day I discovered that Baptism in the Holy Spirit was going to be covered one day.*
I came from a background where the Holy Spirit was hardly ever mentioned and Baptism in the Spirit was considered wrong. My first thought was, "what have I let myself into?! I was full of fear!

I READ A BOOK – SOMETHING HAPPENED!
The week before our group was to be prayed with if we wanted to be baptised in the Holy Spirit, our leader talked with us individually and I can remember expressing to her the fear I had.
The following day I had to take our car to the garage to be serviced. As it was very cold and wet, I decided not to shop as planned **but to sit beside a heater in the car showroom and read a book – "I can Trace a Rainbow" by Sheila Millar.**
It is the story of how God led Sheila and her husband John from Londonderry out to Malaysia as missionaries. I could identify with a lot of things they experienced because my family and I had moved back to N. Ireland from the United States. **Sheila went on to tell how, although she was a missionary, she felt there was something lacking in her life. She began to hear people mention 'Baptism in the Holy Spirit' and how one day she was baptised in the Holy Spirit. As I was reading the Holy Spirit touched my life. The best way I can describe what happened is by the words of John 7: 38 - .".. out of his heart will flow rivers of living water."** 'Something' was flowing out from deep inside and I was praising God. Tears were flowing and God was very real. <u>How much God loved me was impressed upon me in a way I had never experienced before.</u>

THIS EXPERIENCE CHANGED MY LIFE. My husband could see such a difference in me that he wanted what I had and he too was baptised in the Holy Spirit.

NOT WORKED UP!
Because of my religious background I have been so thankful for the way God touched me. No one can say that it happened because of the type of service I went to or that it was worked up.

A MIRACLE.
As for my sister-in-law, she became a Christian through the seminars and since that time we have seen God work a miracle in a humanly impossible family situation. But that is another story!

J.W. HAS WRITTEN WITNESS SHEET 43, UNDER THE TITLE: "MANY, MANY BLESSINGS – AND A HUSBAND WITH TIME FOR GOD AND GOD'S PEOPLE."

FROM CHILDHOOD FAITH THROUGH TEENAGE DOUBT.
"I trusted the Lord as a young child and tried to make my life pleasing to Him. **Doubts only began to creep in when I was in my teens.** I was worried about the choice of a career, put the problem in the Lord's hands and felt peace about it.
I went to University with the definite intention of building up my faith.
Most of my friends from school were Christians and I went with them to Bible studies and Prayer meetings run by the Christian Union.
One evening I prayed for faith that I would be able to believe that the Bible was true, for I, at times, had doubts.
As I read 1 Peter chapter one faith came into my heart. I was reading the verses about faith being more precious than gold which has been refined.

A WOMAN BESIDE ME IN A HOSPITAL BED FINDS FAITH.
Two experiences stood out which showed me **the reality of God.** In hospital, several years ago, a middle-aged woman was seriously ill. She had just been through an operation for cancer. On noticing my Bible she began to tell me a bit about herself. **She did pray and read her Bible** *but because she smoked she didn't feel that she could call herself a Christian.* **Jean said that she had been reading Psalm 121 before she came into hospital: "I to the hills will lift mine eyes from whence doth come mine aid. My safety cometh from the Lord who heaven and earth hath made."**
This psalm goes on to say that the Lord will preserve his loved ones from all evil.
Her minister visited her home after she had read the psalm and before he left **he opened his Bible and read the same psalm.**
This woman desperately wanted to believe that the words were meant for her.
That evening the hospital chaplain came round **and as I was due to be operated on the next day he prayed with me.** *Then he read Psalm 121.*
When he had gone Jean said, **"Did you hear what he read?"**
In this way the Lord let this woman know that He cared for her. *She put her trust in Him!*

A DYING UNCLE'S FAITH RENEWED AND A COUSIN GIVES HIS HEART TO THE LORD.
An uncle of mine was dying from lung cancer about four years ago. He couldn't get any sleep at night because he could not breathe properly. His faith had deserted him when he needed it most and he just couldn't believe the Christian doctrine that one man would give his life willingly for others.
I came to the HEALING SERVICE very worried about him. Prayer was made. *That week there was a big change in my uncle. The Lord gave him peace and joy in his heart, so much so that he was singing hymns in his hospital ward. He was also able to sleep peacefully.*
This change meant the world to the family, and when he died we were very much aware that he had gone to the Lord.
My cousin gave his heart to the Lord as a result of the Lord's intervention in his father's life.

RHEUMATISM – AND SEEKING GOD'S KINGDOM FIRST.
Several years ago I had rheumatism which affected my knees and back. *It was painful to go upstairs.* I was very worried when I read medical books and learnt that the dividing line between rheumatism and arthritis was pretty weak.
I came to the Healing Service and everyone in the circle concentrated their prayer on me. *As a young girl prayed aloud, the stiffness and pain left my legs straight away.*
One member of the Healing Team had these words: "**Seek ye first the Kingdom of God and His righteousness and all these things shall be added unto you.**"
They prayed I would have peace and joy in my heart, and indeed I did!
WHEN I WENT HOME..... I said to my son that I intended taking a close look at my life and cutting out everything that the Lord did not want to be there..
MY SON said he felt that the Lord was saying this to him as well and he would do the same.
The following week the American preacher TERRY FULHAM visited West Church *and his teaching confirmed me in the belief that the Lord wanted more of my life.*

THE LORD RAISED MY EXPECTATIONS.
Following this I enjoyed going through a Life in the Spirit Seminar and benefited from the close fellowship and love of other Christians. **My expectations regarding what the Lord would and could do for others were raised.** *When I meet people who are ill or worried, I'm more alert to the fact that the Lord might want to do something for them.*

A HUSBAND'S WORK PATTERN ALTERED.
Around this time I experienced the truth of the words which say that if

you honour the Lord in all your ways he will give you the desires of your heart. My husband was always most conscientious about his work.
All our married life he has brought work home and gone through papers in the evening. I accepted that this was necessary and how our lives would always be.
The Lord however worked in my husband's heart and gave him such a desire for Him and for the company of other Christians, that he didn't have time to bring work home. This change brought much happiness and many friends into our lives.

POSTSCRIPT: A Witness Sheet, gives testimony to what the Lord, in grace, has done in somebody's life at a particular time. It's a significant snapshot – not the whole story! People may still experience trials as well as joys. For the most part people go on to lives of fruitful service. For example, in speaking to JW recently, she has much satisfaction in the knowledge that all three children are actively and fruitfully committed to the work of the Lord.

THE MORROWS GO TO MALTA.

John and Jacqueline Morrow had been married in West Church; John worked in Harland and Wolff's, and in 1988 they decided to go to Malta.
It was at this time that we wrote about them:
"John and Jacqueline have invested a tremendous amount of time and energy in the work of the congregation, particularly in the youth sector.
Indeed, as an elder, John's designated work was among our young people. He had two very heavy assignments: Leader of our Youth Club and Captain of our B.B. Company.

We thank him most sincerely for indefatigable labour on behalf of our young folk. The gap that jointly, they leave will be a big one. We must to fill it with a lot of thought and care."
We thank them both!

OCTOBER WCN 1988.

THERE'S A LOT BUZZING ON THE YOUTH SCENE.
SCORES OF OUR MEMBERS ARE HELPING!

There's a lot going on among our young people with scores and scores of our members helping. You will find them in the Crèche and Junior Beginners' Sunday School, through all the Sunday School departments, and on through to Young West Church, each Sunday morning.

You will find them in Squirrels and Beavers, Cub Scouts and Scouts and Venture Scouts; in Bunnies and Brownies and Guides; in all the departments of Boys' Brigade and Girls' Brigade; in Youth Club and Youth Fellowships.

All these – we take it for granted – will be usually well manned, and often growing.
IT'S AN ASSUMPTION, HOWEVER, THAT SHOULD NOT JUST BE TAKEN FOR GRANTED.
For new leaders *just don't appear! They are people who need to be motivated, cultured, and nurtured!*
And we are happy that *many, though by no means all of those undertaking new responsibilities in our midst, have been nourished and brought up within our own West Church Family*

OVERVIEW OF YOUTH SCENE REVEALS NEW INITIATIVES, AND MUCH WORK CURRENTLY BEING EXTENDED AND/OR STRENGTHENED.

For example we have now THREE Sunday evening YOUTH FELLOWSHIPS.
Our SENIOR Youth Fellowship, with a lot of people in their upper teens or early twenties (and still under the leadership of Derek Polley and Anne Logan) has become THE YOUNG ADULTS GROUP.
The JUNIOR YOUTH FELLOWSHIP, led by John Barklie, Chris Wilson and Tom Ross, has now become THE SENIOR YOUTH FELLOWSHIP – with additional help from Simone Lemon and Scott Hunter.
And a new JUNIOR YOUTH FELLOWSHIP has been formed with Alvin Little taking the lead, and currently helped along by Paul Wyeth, Barry McCroskery and Pamela Wilson.

BIBLE BUSTERS:
A new initiative for boys and girls between 7 and 11 years is a direct consequence of some of our young people meeting over the summer months to pray to God and make themselves available to Him. Called the BIBLE-BUSTERS, it will be run along the lines of a Junior Christian Endeavour, seeking to involve the lively participation of our youngsters, and to build and train them up in the ways of Christian service. Among those involved are: Pamela Coburn, Joan and Linda Cummings, Ruth Fisher, David Bates and Rodney Blackmore.

TWO HOME STUDY GROUPS FOR BOYS AND GIRLS, 14-15 YEARS.

The 'fellas' meet in the home of Alvin and Linda Little and are led by John Barklie and David Smith.
The girls meet in the home of Brian and Christine Martin, who lead this group.

YOUNG ADULTS' HOME

GROUP.
This group meets on Fridays in the Praise Room, and are studying our "Outreach Manual", led by Rennie Nelson.

And of course there's the 'Life in the Spirit' Seminar for young people, led by Alvin Little.

ALL THIS REPRESENTS BUT *ONE SECTOR OF OUR YOUTH WORK*, and similar additions to our teams, and extensions of our organisations continues right through all our uniformed organisations.

TRAINING CONFERENCE FOR SUNDAY SCHOOL TEACHERS.
This Conference will be led by the Rev. David Armstrong and a colleague, on Saturday 22nd October between 10.00am and 4.00pm.
It will cover the age range between 3- 11 years. This will be a training/refresher course for our teachers. **It will also provide an excellent opportunity for those considering Sunday School teaching as an avenue of service, to explore, before committing themselves.**
And additional teachers are currently required for P5 and P 6 children.

DEDICATION SERVICE FOR ALL OUR YOUTH LEADERS.
In past years we have often had such a service for our **Sunday School Teachers and Bible Class leaders.** This year we want to expand this to include our leaders in **Uniformed and non-Uniformed organisations.** This service will be on Sunday 23rd October at 7.00pm.

YOUNG PEOPLE IN DRAMA, MUSIC AND SINGING.
Our young people have been very active in 1988. They take an active part in our Praise Services, both instrumentally and vocally.
It's great to see and hear LOUISE WILSON on the drums. They help lead worship at Young West Church.
They have played a prominent part in the DRAMA at our Open Nights, and in various summer Outreach programmes. They are to be found in our Guitar Class, preparing for future service.
We thank God for them!

NOVEMBER WCN 1988.

SCHEDULE OF SERVICES FROM 23RD OCTOBER – 18TH DECEMBER, when David Bailie takes morning services, indicates Service Arrangements in the interim period, when the Bailies will be in India, on their long-projected visit!

November WCN informs us NOEL BOYD is to be the new BB Captain:
"At its last meeting our Kirk Session was pleased to appoint NOEL BOYD as Captain of our Boys' Brigade Company, in succession to JOHN MORROW. **Noel** has had experience as an officer in the B.B. Company at Trinity Church, and, with a strong team of officers behind him and a fine company of boys, we look forward to continued growth in every respect in our Company.
At a recent meeting of the company a presentation was made to John Morrow, with Jacqueline, for the immense amount of work John had invested in the BB in West.

THE KIRK SESSION WAS ALSO PLEASED TO APPOINT A NEW LEADER FOR OUR YOUTH CLUB.
Chris Wilson has, in earlier years, poured a tremendous amount of energy into work with our Cub Scouts and Scouts. He did a two-year Training Course with the YMCA in London, and has been active in YMCA work.
The Kirk Session was pleased to appoint him as leader, and glad that he has a strong team, with a real sense of vocation in youth work, to lead.
The team has been strengthened by the addition of Paul **Skitt**, **Christopher and Sharon McWilliams, Wallace Parker and Harry Glendinning.**

GREAT START FOR "BIBLE BUSTERS."
The leaders of the "Bible-Busters" were joyfully overwhelmed, that on the first night 61 young people, in the 7-11 age category turned up – well in excess of what was projected!
The essence of this group is participation of the members – which means MANY leaders!! Naturally the team has had to be increased – **and this has been done without diluting it! The original team has been strengthened by the advent of Nancy McNeill and David McClelland.**

A SEMINAR ON THE SACRAMENTS:
A SIX-WEEK Course on the **Sacraments of Baptism and the Lord's Supper begins on 20th October, led by Dr. John Thompson, Professor at Union College, Belfast.**

DECEMBER WCN 1988.

In the absence of the Editor in India, **DECEMBER WCN still highlighted the PCI World Development Appeal, and gave details of PCI Projects among Refugees in Thailand, in Pakistan and work being done to alleviate suffering among Palestinians on the West Bank; work in Ethiopia, refugees from Mozambique in Malawi; 60,000 displaced in El Salvador; Angolan refugees in Namibia; Burmese refugees in Thailand.**

THE REV. JIM HUNTER gives a moving Meditation on the Sickness of a Child:

"I close my eyes to pray but hear again the screams of pain. I see the eyes all filled with fear, the nostrils stretched, the writhing limbs, the panting breath, the sweat so grim.
What can I do, what can I say to calm my little four year old?
I hang my head and pray, and pray and whisper 'Steady, steady hold my hand brave heart. The pain will pass, will pass, will pass. I'd bear it child but I'm not God. I cannot enter in and take the pain and loss.'
"Daddy, stop them, stop them, I don't want the needle, not again."
And I stand by and hold her hand, 'How could a sick child ever understand that for her good, I must stand by,
And let the pain sweep on, roll on and break and die, and see her lie exhausted on the bed, her faith in fatherhood near dead,
all but a shadow of the trust which once it was.
I whisper low, 'Dear Jesus, take the pain', 'In mercy Lord, Hush, hush sweetheart, see Jesus comes, He cares and died and rose again, to bear our sicknesses and sin, He'll bear the pain.'
And yet again she screams; it seems all faith is but a dream. Where is the peace, where is the One who promised much?
When will he come and bear again, that which he bore and he alone can bear?'
"Behold I come and I will hear the prayer of Faith,
Wait on, don't go, I come, pray yet, I come but you must first beget within your heart, a shadow of the agony I feel,
For all the blinded hearts that kneel to other gods,
for they would turn to me to bear the pain, but cannot see,
Until you tell them that I live and care and share their agony and loss.
They cannot know until you go and preach and show MY CROSS."

At a time when the main World Development Appeal of the PCI focuses upon REFUGEES, it is significant that we have three illuminating contributions, from West Church people, from Jim Hunter in relation to Afghan refugees in Pakistan, Chris Ritchie's Reflections on the Palestinians of the West Bank, and Jane Richardson, on "Malawi – the warm heart of Africa." Each of them, out of their own experience, is able to stimulate our hearts to generosity for this year's PCI Appeal on behalf of Refugees.

AFGHAN REFUGEES.

"Over 3 million people from Afghanistan have been living in tents in great privation on the borders of Pakistan for some years now. At last it looks like they will be able to go back to their villages again soon, in many cases however those villages have been destroyed, the fields have been left untended and the flocks slaughtered, so they are in a most acute state of need. **There is a long history of Christians helping Muslims, and it is good that we are continuing to do so, that they might see something of the grace of Christ in us.**
While working in Pakistan we met quite a few of these people. They were mostly very hardy and humorous, fiercely independent, reluctant to accept free help except when absolutely necessary. In many cases they could speak little Urdu, and so are seen as a separate people. Most are highly educated and willing to work but work is scarce and must go to Indian or Pakistani nationals, **so they long to return to their own land and culture and language and start afresh. What we give now will help them to become self-supporting, and as we give let us pray for peace in their land and the peace of Christ in their hearts.**

ON JORDAN'S BANK:
Chris Ritchie reflects on his work with the Palestinians on the West Bank.

"**When the Partition of Palestine received approbation by the U.N. and the tiny state of Israel was declared,** *there were few who would have predicted a prosperous and peaceful future.*
Certainly the Palestinian Arab community felt an assurance from neighbouring Arabic states that the new-born nation would not survive its infancy.
For this reason some Arabs left their homes within Israel to await the coming jihad (religious war) which would throw the Jews into the sea and restore their homeland.
Others of course remained whether through mere inertia or an enlightened belief that the two peoples could co-exist in relative harmony. After all, in centuries past the Jews had always found least persecution in Arabic countries where they were regarded as perhaps a cousin people and not, as elsewhere, an accursed and inferior race.
Some of those remaining were given assurances by the new government but it must be said that stories abound of Arabs being encouraged or intimidated into leaving.
Certainly there were regrettable incidents on both sides, in the flux and panic of those times, the Jews anxious to preserve their precious new nation and the Arabs fearful of losing their lands and rights.

The Arabs who fled, the refugees, set up homes in camps on the banks of the Jordan and Gaza strip, and awaited events. The ensuing war saw their hopes defeated as Israel against all the odds fought and won the 1948 war.

What were the refugees to do?
They could not or would not return to Israel having abandoned all their property which was now in Jewish control. Their only hope seemed to be to wait and hope that the protection of Syria, Jordan, Egypt and others would amount to something.
**The sad fact is that they are still

waiting, some 40 years later. **Israel is now firmly established controlling the West Bank of the Jordan and the Gaza Strip.** Sadder still, the Palestinian leaders, the P.L.O. have not tried too hard to remedy the situation and some would say their refusal to negotiate the fate of the refugees is nothing more than an attempt to raise sympathetic support by keeping their people in a homeless scenario. **Certainly one can surmise that the wealth of the Arab nations could provide much-needed relief, for those who, for a generation have been self-exiled.**

Still, politically misused or not, the refugees are there and are without hope of a restoration of what was formerly theirs. It is not a matter for blame but compassion for those who have lived, borne children and died waiting for the materialisation of a lost hope. Such are the refugees of Palestine.

A third member of West Church, JANE RICHARDSON speaks of **MALAWI - THE WARM HEART OF AFRICA, and how it has received refugees from Mozambique.**
"The warm heart of Africa" -this is how the tourist books and holiday brochures describe Malawi, and having spent 3 years teaching there I can certainly confirm this description.
The Malawians I worked with and taught really made me feel so much at home while I was there. I found them tremendously hospitable, very generous, and extremely friendly. In fact the friendships made then still remain and two of the Malawian teachers from the school I taught in have visited West Church over the last few years. They have gone back too, impressed with the friendliness of the Irish!

Malawi is a very poor country with little in the way of natural resources except, of course, its beautiful scenery. However, since independence in 1964 Dr Banda who is still President, has encouraged the Malawians to work hard and seek to become self-sufficient in producing food. The country has certainly a much, more cultivated look than its neighbours and the Malawians take great pride in their gardens - which are used to produce food! It has also been one of the most stable African countries having had the same government since 1964. So the money it has received in aid has been used to build the country up rather than in war.

Although the Malawaians are poor they are willing to share what they have. This is seen in the care for the extended family where young brothers, sisters and cousins are often put through school by those who are earning, - and great care is taken of the old. **It has also been seen recently with the increase of refugees from Mozambique due to the fighting and famine there, this obviously stretches their already meagre resources considerably, and yet those who have little already share with those who have nothing. Surely this must challenge those of us who have much, to give out of our abundance. I know that the money which is sent will be spent wisely.**
So let us show the Malawaians that we can be described as 'the warm hearted people of Bangor!'

JANUARY/FEBRUARY WCN, 1989.

RELATIONSHIP WITH INDIA RENEWED!

"Your decision at our Silver Jubilee, to send your minister and his wife on a visit to India, to give them a good holiday, and give them the joy of retracing their steps of 30 years ago, and of meeting old friends, *has been richly validated!*

For we have had a marvellous holiday in India, a country that impresses with its vitality, colour, and diversity. We have seen great progress on many sides; have been heartened to witness the good effects of the 'green' revolution, in better seeds and the use of fertilisers and in irrigation dams and tube wells - giving more bountiful crops. India too has thriving and progressive industries, making it the world's eighth strongest industrial country. Of course there is still much poverty, but it is to be seen against the backdrop of much progress in the economy, and is all the more remarkable considering the massive increase in population.

In Gujarat we had the joy of meeting many people we had known before - boys in their teens had become married men with children of their own!
It was great to spend 3 weeks in Gujarat, to preach on four Sundays in different places, and to speak to and listen to many people.
Your decision to send us to Gujarat has been amply fulfilled!

LEARNING TO VALUE AND SHARE WHAT WE HAVE HERE!
Sometimes it is only when people leave home that they realise how much they have taken for granted.
We did not take for granted the work of God's Spirit in our own congregation, the genuine love and faith among our people, the many evidences of new life and healing mediated through Jesus' Name. We did not take these things for granted! But we came to understand that what we had entered upon and enjoyed, was not to be found everywhere! And with that the conviction that it should be shared!

AN INDIAN MINISTER IN WEST?
Over the years, ministers and students from Gujarat have come to the West to study in our theological colleges. This **has meant** a better

grasp of theology, no doubt. But sometimes such people have been isolated and lonely, not immersed in the warmth and love of a Christian fellowship, not experiencing a demonstration of the power of the Spirit in the life of the Church, in such a manner as to send them back with renewed vision.

In that context, it came to me to float the idea with Bishop Paul, to send a minister to work with us for a year in West Church. Bishop Paul was enthusiastic and introduced me to the Rev. Wilson Baria, who was pastor of a Gujarati church in Bombay. In fact we spent the whole of our last day in India in his home. He was a man enthusiastic and ardent- and we felt he could benefit from ministering with us in West, and would have a lot also to contribute.

Bishop Paul was eager to send him, but in the end it could not be arranged, as at this time he was a minister in another diocese.

However, our visit to India in 1988 opened up communications again with the Church in Gujarat; and in due course the Rev. Hemantkumar came to study in Union College, Belfast, and was often with us in West Church, and spent a lot of time in our home.

As well after my retirement, we had a major visit to Gujarat in November 2000, allowing substantial ministry there, and opening up a connection with the ministers of the Gujarati Church. In our Millennial visit, I was given the opportunity to speak at a Conference for 1300 young people; to give lectures to all the ministers of the Diocese at their Annual Conference, and to take meetings throughout the Diocese, observe vibrant church life in many places, and see the dynamic growth of the church, especially in South Gujarat and in the Panch Mahals. At the Diocesan meetings I offered to send Christian books to those ministers who had an adequate knowledge of English and could benefit from reading them. This has allowed us to send many Christian books over the years since then, and we have about fifty names on our mailing list. This has opened up a fruitful partnership in the gospel, and has brought real stimulus to at least some of these pastors.

Some of these men have since come to study in the West, in Belfast, Dublin and Birmingham.

Our Millennial Visit to Gujarat, allowed us to see the dynamic growth of the church, and to rejoice at the manner in which the Spirit is at work. Established congregations have been strengthened under dedicated young ministers, and a major work of evangelism and church planting is taking places, with scores of little groups of believers springing up, and growing!

Insight into that, and some real involvement in it also, came to us through that Silver Jubilee generosity of our congregation in West Church, with the suggestion that the travel voucher be used to return to India.

In the early pages of our "West Church Journey" mention was made of our early years in Gujarat. And it has been a great spiritual boost and bonus, to have some part in its life and development in our own 'retirement' years.

JANUARY/FEBRUARY WCN 1989.

In this issue we have a Financial Overview for 1988, with a buoyant picture, showing our New Hall debt liquidated, pointing out that many projects had been nourished through the 'Outreach' element of the Fund, and inviting those who felt able to continue with their givings in this Fund, to do so, and grasp an opportunity for a quite new dimension of outreach.

The importance of COVENANTS was again emphasised, and warm tribute given to MR CHARLES LUTTON, for ten years' work in which he had nurtured covenants within West Church, to the great benefit of our work.

This work would now be taken up by MR JOHN POOLE, who had been Treasurer of our New Hall & Outreach Fund.

SANDILANDS MOBILE HOME:

"Last year the Church Committee decided to replace our Mobile Home at Kilkeel, by a fine, newer model, since we had been advised that the old one had become unsafe. This cost £2250 from our Number 1 Account and £407 from the Benevolent Fund... It is a fine home and well furnished and we want to make the maximum use of it. We are glad to see it extensively used throughout the whole season. A good gas fire ensures that it can be used, even when the weather turns that bit chilly.

WE like to give first preference to FAMILIES DURING THE SCHOOL HOLIDAY MONTHS OF July and August.

For others there's lots of good weather during May, June and September - and even beyond that.

We suggest a range of contributions from £30 -£50 per week, according to people's circumstances. But of course, where people may be unemployed, or under particular financial constraint, **it is our privilege to offer this free.**

OUR CHURCH LOUNGE HAS NOW BEEN COMFORTABLY FURNISHED AND READY FOR FURTHER USE.

CARRYING THE WORSHIP AND FELLOWSHIP OF THE CHURCH TO THOSE WHO CAN NO LONGER ATTEND OUR SERVICES.

"It is difficult for many of us, who enjoy good health and have mobility, going out and coming in as we choose, **to realise the restrictions under which some of our older people live, now often largely confined to their homes.** No longer are they able to go out and enjoy a good walk, maybe in the company of a partner, or go for a drive, or for shopping. **These normal, everyday activities are sorely missed.**

For not a few, one of the losses most keenly felt, is the inability to go to church each Sunday for public worship, the glad and refreshing experience of active participation in worship, the warm and humanising experience of meeting and talking with others, the healing, restoring and enlivening fellowship of Christian people together.

POOR AND INADEQUATE SUBSTITUTES.
For most Christians, thus deprived and restricted, the radio or TV service are poor and inadequate substitutes. **The same can apply to the recorded service brought on cassette from one's own church.** Of course some people CAN USE these services better than others. One fine Christian lady used to make preparation for the Sunday morning broadcast service, by getting her Bible and hymnbook ready, with readings and hymns - already marked, so that she could ACTIVELY take part in the service in her own room. Excellent! And something that shut-in people would do well to emulate!

However, for most people, such services remain something of a 'spectator' activity! When you are in the midst of a congregation at worship, you are involved in singing and praying and hearing in an active, living way. You are in immediate, warm fellowship with others.
IF OUR SENIOR, SHUT-IN PEOPLE CANNOT COME TO CHURCH TO WORSHIP, WE WILL SEEK TO TAKE LIVING WORSHIP TO THEM!

Our Kirk Session have given consideration to this, and have decided, that where people would welcome this, either in their own homes, or when they live in residential homes, we should do our best, with some regularity, to take 'living worship' to them. At least once a month, or once a fortnight, we would like little groups of two or three people, as appropriate, to visit our shut-in people, to bring them warmth and friendship, news of what is happening in the church, things that need to be prayed about; also to read the Scriptures and pray; and especially to sing, whether well-known old hymns, or simple, lovely new hymns.
Thus we realise that we belong together, one Body in Christ.

We want to discover:
Those who would welcome such a visit;
And those who would like to be involved in such a ministry.
We hope, bit by bit, to make progress in this enterprise, so that we care more effectively for our senior members, and continue to enjoy partnership with them in the work of the Kingdom.

LIFE IN THE SPIRIT
SEMINARS - to indicate what an influence these seminars had in the development of our congregation, we simply make note of the fact that 2 new Seminars will begin, one on Thursday 2nd February, and the other on Wednesday 22nd February.

A STUDY ON REVELATION-
Tom Garrett, has been making over a considerable time, his own study on the Book of Revelation. This he has done, not through consulting erudite commentaries, but just through pondering the Word, seeking the help of the Holy Spirit. He has written a substantial commentary of 70,000 words.
He shares what he believes God has taught him from this Book, each Monday evening, between 7 and 8 in the Praise Room.

A KEYBOARD!
A keyboard, used and loved by the late **Muriel Thompson** has been donated to West Church. In one sense **old,** but **new** to us and useful, especially valued because of its rich and tender associations.
And by the way, if there should be any other unused Keyboards, we might possibly use them in our Home Groups or on Pastoral Visitation!

THE JUNIOR SINGING GROUP.
It was good to see, at our most recent FAMILY SERVICE, how our Junior Singing Group led the worship. **It was a good beginning, and one rejoices to see these young folks, participating in and leading the worship of God.** *Some of them have already made great strides as instrumentalists, and we trust they may grow up into a group able to lead with confidence and verve, in the love and power of the Holy Spirit.*

THE DORES RETURN TO THE U.K. - A HARD AND AGONISING DECISION!

Graham and Janet Dore, with Alastair and Elizabeth are to return to the U.K. and will probably arrive in England at the very beginning of April.

Spiritually it has been a very testing and stretching time for them, seeking to know and obey the will of God in terms of missionary calling and family needs. We know that their first love and loyalty is to the Lord and feel confident that they will discover that all things work for good to those who love Him. Our God is a living and dynamic God- the God who led Abraham through many journeyings, crises and circumstances to the Promised Land.
Return to the UK will mean a radical change for the Dores, and we will want to give them much love and support at this time.

In their Prayer Letter of 23rd December the Dores wrote: "Since the summer we have been increasingly concerned by the fact that Alastair is still not coping with the unnatural separation from home and the community living at Chefoo (Malayasia).
After much prayer and consulting with OMF leaders and friends, we eventually felt led to resign from OMF in March and return to the UK.
<u>We thought we would be here for a lifetime of service… it will be harder for us to return to the UK in 1989 than it was to leave UK in 1975.</u>
We remembered how God said to Abraham, in respect of his son Isaac, '**Do not hurt the lad**'… and he would not want us to hurt Alastair to serve him, and He can use our service elsewhere."

[NOTE: Incorporating this in our "West Church Journey" in 2006, we rejoice in the wide and fruitful ministry that God has given to Graham Dore in the intervening years with Wycliffe Bible Translators, and rejoice too that Alastair and Elizabeth, as young adults, are ardent in their service of the Lord.]

"THANK YOU, JEAN CRICHTON" FOR 16 YEARS OF WONDERFUL SERVICE!

Jean Crichton has just completed 16 years of wonderful service in the Junior Beginners' Department of the Sunday School, and we are grateful to God for such a loving, consistent ministry.
Out of her own warm faith and love for God there flowed a wise and gentle love for the youngest children in our Sunday School; an ability to enlist and encourage other teachers to help her and to form them into a loving, praying team; to enlist and likewise encourage many junior helpers and to initiate them into the same serving, praying spirit; **and a gracious receiving of mums and dads, often as they made their first appearance in West Church, and for the first time entrusted their precious wee ones to us!**

Jean has won the affection of all who worked with her, and retained the affection of many young people who had their first experience of church - and of West Church -in her department. We give sincere thanks to God for all that she has done, and for all that she means to us.

Upon the excellent foundation that she has laid, **her successor, HONOR DAVIS,** is ensuring that this department is growing from strength to strength, **where our little ones are warmly and truly led into the worship and knowledge of God.**

BIBLE VERSES TO PONDER IN CHURCH.

A WHOLE, NEW WIDE RANGE of Scripture Verses is being prepared, **and will be placed in the velvet bag to be found at the left side of the main entrance doors into the Church.
You are invited to take one of these each Sunday as you enter church for worship.
There's something of excitement and mystery in seeing what you draw out! And there's always great profit in meditating on God's Word.
And what a rich preparation for the service when numerous folk, are feeding, so richly and diversely, on the manifold truth of God's Word!
There will be thousands of God's precious promises from every book of the Bible in our velvet Bag.
Have a very SUBSTANTIAL STARTER!**

JANUARY/FEBRUARY
**WCN have substantial Annual Reports from:
Kirk Session
Treasurer, Secretary
Youth Club,
Sunday School
PWA
YWA
The Sycamore Club
The Boys' Brigade
The Bowling Club
The Badminton Club
Bible Busters
Junior Youth Fellowship
7th Bangor Scout Group
Cub Scouts - Hawks.
Scouts,
The Squirrels
The Guides.**

ALVIN LITTLE writes on **PLANS FOR YOUNG PEOPLE IN THE COMING MONTHS.**

"**Time and again I am both thrilled and amazed at the number of young people around West Church.** I always think that being a teenager is **the** most difficult thing in life - everything is **boring** and there's never anything to do!
The second most difficult thing in life **must be to work with teenagers through all their ups and downs, their mood swings and their degree of interest.** They can move from wild enthusiasm to complete apathy all in one month.
As parents we need constantly to encourage that enormous team of men and women who work with our teenagers in all the various clubs, organisations and fellowships in West.

In our society these same teenagers live under enormous peer group pressure and it is in this context that we as God's people long to help our teenagers through to a full and complete commitment of their lives to Jesus Christ as Saviour and Lord of all.
We also want to encourage them to live strong and attractive Christian lives in school environments, which can often be quite antagonistic and derisory of a real, living faith in Jesus. *Our young people need the care and prayer and influence of God's people and God's church in the*

ongoing battle for their lives.

In the context of the quiet, ongoing work which is carried on week by week in the various clubs, organizations and fellowships, **we have identified two new opportunities among our young people which I feel may well prove, in God's goodness, to be vital and important for our young people at this time.**

1. **WEST CHURCH SUMMER SCHEME.**
In August (probably 14th - 18th) we hope to have our first Summer Scheme.
It is hoped that it will be a mixture of the Holiday Bible Club and the school type summer scheme which is so popular.
It is because Jesus is Lord of all life that we feel this combination of spiritual and physical activities is right and good. The age range will be 7 - 17 year olds, so watch out for more news of this.

2. **Coffee Bar Outreach.**
We are hoping in the autumn to have a special week of Coffee Bars for young people, and we hope that this will be a venture in which the various organisations and clubs will be able to work as one. Using different combinations of music, chat shows, speakers and drama, we hope in a relevant and fresh way to challenge our young people with the claims of Jesus, and the alternative of real and new life in Him.

We are so thankful to God for all that He is doing among our young people and we really are excited by the future and all the opportunities that lie before us.
I am reminded in those words in Corinthians that **'God makes things grow'.**
Please do pray that we will see the work among our young people grow and flourish with a joyful enthusiasm that will draw many to our Lord and God.

MARCH WCN 1989.

March Edition of West Church News deals mainly with domestic congregational matters, like the purchase of a Gestetner COPY/DUPLICATOR, to improve the quality and speed of production of our formidable amount of printing in West, not only our monthly news, but our annually-produced West Church Directory, West Church Pulpit, Witness Sheets, and assorted booklets, leaflets, cards etc.

A bookcase Display is being sited in the refurbished Church Vestibule.

A new group for 'MOTHERS AND TODDLERS': Maureeen Blackmore writes:
"Every Tuesday there will be an opportunity for mothers with young children to meet together to relax, and enjoy a chat over a cup of tea or coffee, in our refurbished LOUNGE.
Mothers, who spend a lot of time with their young children, can often feel isolated, and this group should provide encouragement and fellowship.

OUR YOUTH CLUB has recently received a generous grant that has enabled them to buy two fine Table Tennis Tables; a fine television set and a video recorder.
In a video age, we do not forget that there are many fine video programmes which serve as a handmaiden to the faith and can be used in the service of Christ for the up building of His Church.

There is a 'BLANKETS appeal' for Ethiopia; and details of our Holy Week Services and our Dawn Service at Ballywalter.

APRIL WCN 1989.

THE CHURCH IS STEEPED IN THE WORLD - GOD'S ANTIDOTE- THE TEN COMMANDMENTS!

The Church is steeped in the world! Often without realising it! Christian people are largely unaware of **how many values** they take on board that **are alien to the ways and teachings of Christ, our Lord.**
We absorb so much without realising it! We are exposed to so much, so constantly, through what we watch on television, what we read in newspapers, what gets through to us in skilful and costly advertisements that we do not realise that **fundamental shifts have taken place in the values we hold, in our ways of thinking and living.**

How else do we account for the fact, for example that Christian **people are to be found, in alarmingly increasing numbers, who trample under foot their marriage vows, and fear not, it seems, to break the seventh commandment?**

We need to be grounded again, it seems, on the fundamental truths of God, that God gave to Moses in the Ten Commandments... We need also to remember that Jesus, the Truth made incarnate, said **that he had not come to abolish the Law and the Prophets,** *but to fulfil them.*
And that it is Satan, the great Deceiver who comes to blind and bind people, to kill, to hurt and to destroy.
We need to study to take to heart *all* the commandments, as exemplified and fully revealed in Jesus.
And so, on 23rd April, we shall begin a new series on the Commandments, Sunday by Sunday, often in the morning and sometimes in the evening services.
We shall print some copies of these sermons that will be available for some HOME GROUPS to study.
We must realise that it is not enough to deplore the breaking of

God's commandments.
We want to build our families on God's truth, and thus offer the true life that Jesus came to give.

OUR BOOKSTALL.

We have placed on our bookstall a range of books designed to nurture our relationship with God, and with one another, also that offer help for Marriage and Family life.

'How to REALLY love your child' Dr Ross Campbell.
'The Creative use of Conflict', by Joyce Hogget.
'Love Life for every Married Couple'. Ed Wheat.
About this book Charles Swindoll says:
'I read everything I can get my hands on regarding marriage, the home and family relationships. But in all my reading, I know of nothing better than Dr. Ed Wheat's book. When it comes to the subject of intimacy between husbands and wives **it is biblical, practical, specific, easily understood, and filled with hope'.**

There are GUIDES for parents with children in the 5-11 category, and 12-16 category.

And a number of other relevant books!

In our West Church News we aim to make people aware of personal and social problems, and to be given Christian insight into how these may be resolved, and people helped into positive living.
In this issue there is an extract from OSWALD SANDERS' book, 'FACING LONELINESS'. "THE DEATH OF A LOVED ONE DOES NOT MEAN THE END OF ALL THINGS, AND SOMEHOW, SOONER OR LATER, REALITY MUST BE FACED."

It deals with the plight of the widow and the widower, and highlights both Old Testament and New Testament concern and care. It deals with practical problems.

To read this book gives insight, and promotes concern, so that there may be true fellowship within the Body of Christ's people.

APRIL WCN points forward to two Weekends at Rostrevor, one for men and the other for women.

It points forward also to the BB's Annual Display;
To the fact that Jim Hunter and Ann Kennedy move into their final theological year, where they will be doing placements, Jim at Kilmakee, Dunmurry and Ann at Harmony Hill, Lisburn.

It also informs us that another Wycliffe College, Oxford student, Keith Elford will be doing a placement with us in West Church.

It informs us too that GRAHAM KENDRICK WILL LEAD AN October Conference in Belfast on "True Worshippers."

JUNE WCN 1989.

IN WEST, ONE KEY TO ADVANCE IS *PERSONNEL!*

In West Church we are **RICH** in many ways- that we have scores and scores of men and women involved in Sunday School teaching, in 'Young West Church', in uniformed organisations, in Youth Club, in Youth Fellowships, and the like!
Our elders and Church Visitors and House Group leaders also run into scores! We have Choir, Singing Group, Drama Group; PWA and YWA and various recreation clubs; and Healing Service!
WE ARE RICH!!! Much work *is being done* in the Kingdom of God.
In recent times folk have told me of the tremendous support and encouragement they have received - in times of crisis or difficulty- from their Home Groups - practical love and faithful prayer carried them through.

MUCH IS BEING DONE because we have so many loving, experienced and committed Christian people!
Many of these have come through our Seminars and been nurtured in our Home Groups.

YET, WE HAVE A LARGE CONGREGATION AND *MUCH MORE WAITS TO BE DONE!*

<u>We have half as many families in our congregation as are to be found in some of our sparser Presbyteries, like Strabane, Donegal or Monaghan.</u>

We have much need of better pastoral care within our congregation,
and of outreach into our community round about us, where many have no living church connection.
This will be done through the lively love and witness of all our members,
But our members need to be encouraged, nurtured, trained, motivated for this work - *just as Jesus trained and equipped the Twelve, and the Seventy, and sent them out. Jesus chose Twelve to be with him constantly,*
And he taught and equipped them to reap the fields and the over-ripe crops.
Jesus DID and taught others TO DO.
WE SEEK TO FOLLOW THE SAME PATTERN!

Seven things we need to do and plan to do!

(1) BETTER PASTORAL CARE.
Beginning in September our KIRK SESSION plans to make a

SPECIAL VISITATION of our congregation, **district by district.**
WE shall seek carefully to scrutinise each district, to see how we can best care for each family, each person.
We'll seek to share the Good News, with those who have not yet received it, and encourage those who have.
We'll seek to take living worship to the old and shut-in.
We'll seek to draw upon the resource of our members to promote the work of Jesus.
We want each elder's district to be as a well-ploughed and cultivated field, producing much fruit. We want none of it to remain fallow or overgrown with thorns and briars.

(2) "OPEN NIGHTS" and "GUEST SERVICES."
In connection with this VISITATION we hope to have "Open Nights" and "Guest Services" to which people may be personally invited. This would be done in connection with our Home Groups, and enlisting the aid of our Drama and Singing Groups.

(3) AN ENLARGED "LENDING LIBRARY."
In our Summer Visitation for the congregation in 1988, we made a supply of books available to our elders, who offered these, as they felt appropriate to our members.

An interesting feature of this has been that members of the congregation *have kept coming to sample the books on that table in* the Approach Room, so that there has been a regular turn-over of books.
We hope to enlarge the stock of books there, for elders and church Visitors to use in their Visitation, and for members of the congregation to come and borrow.

(4). AN ENLARGED RANGE OF SEMINARS.
We have seen the tremendous advantage of holding 'LIFE IN THE SPIRIT' seminars and we naturally plan to continue with these life-changing life-enriching and life-equipping Seminars.
But we hope to enlarge the range of Seminars available.
We plan to have seminars that **will assist parents in caring for their children with Christian insight, whether the children are young children or adolescents.**

In the light of the high incidence of **marriage breakdown IN OUR SOCIETY, WE FEEL THERE NEEDS TO BE MORE 'INPUT' for young people planning to get married in West Church.**

In addition we may have some lecture courses available.
We may well seek out and use good material available on video. A few years ago we used Dr. James Dobson's material on the Family, on Sunday evenings. That material is now readily available on video.

(5). INCREASED TRAINING AND NURTURE OF OUR ELDERS AND CHURCH VISITORS.
The disciples of Jesus became effective because He taught them so well and imparted his Spirit to them, and because he had such a close and warm contact with them. **Likewise we need to provide in-service training for our pastoral workers, so that they may be wise, loving, skilful and fruitful for the Lord. This we hope to do at our Kirk Session meetings.**

(6) FURTHER NURTURING OF HOME GROUPS.
The Home Groups have accomplished much by way of giving encouragement, support and vision to their members.
But we believe that there is a much fuller potential to be realised in terms of spiritual growth and outreach.
This requires a lot more nurturing, which must receive priority.

(7). OUR SUNDAY SERVICES.
This is the "meeting-place" for the whole body of the congregation to be refreshed and renewed. **Here we are nourished by the Word of God. We must do our best to see that the whole people is served with substantial and appetising fare, whether it be from the Book of Ecclesiastes, or the Letter to the Philippians or the Ten Commandments.**

It is the place where we ALL have an opportunity to meet together, to pray, to praise and to worship. It is a place where we can love and encourage one another. THE SCRIPTURE TELLS US NOT TO NEGLECT THIS.

THE DORES BACK IN ENGLAND.....

and living temporarily next door to Graham's mother, who is far from well.
A telling quote from Graham:
"Being uncertain whether to pursue "Christian" or "secular" work opportunities I'm a bit like an aimless runner, inquiring in all directions, ears open to any suggestions or advice.
The idea of full-time study for the ministry is daunting, expensive, and I don't know if I have the gift or calling.
The idea of earning one's own living, and no longer living off the generosity of other people, is attractive, but is this the same as Peter after the Resurrection going back to fishing?"

Graham, grateful for faithful supports, enlists our prayers for guidance in respect of his future.

NEW LEADERS REQUIRED FOR SQUIRRELS.

GWEN DODDS and JEAN SAVAGE, WHO HAVE GIVEN SUCH EXCELLENT LEADERSHIP TO THE Squirrels for quite a number of years now desire to hand this organisation, for boys aged 4-6 years, to others.

We thank them for the outstanding work they have done, and for the gracious spirit of their leadership. They have made friendships with these wee lads that will remain in many cases as they grow up. They have enriched the boys' lives and will, themselves, have gained much from this experience of adventurous service!

AUGUST WCN 1989.

New 'Life in the Spirit Seminar' begins on 24th August.

In our "West Church Journey" it could seem a little tiresome to draw attention to yet another Seminar! Yet the Seminars continued to draw people to them where spiritual blessings abounded. We introduced this Seminar as follows:
 "Many in West Church have come to spiritual life through "Life in the Spirit Seminars." Many already mature in the Christian way, have entered into a deeper dimension of life in the Spirit, experiencing a new reality in worship, in fellowship, in ministering and serving in the love of God.
Not a few have come in the context of personal crisis, and have found in the love of the Lord, and of his people, renewal and deliverance, and what it can mean to be rooted and grounded in Christ.

The Seminars do not demand an impossible high-jump from people, into the place of Christian commitment. **Instead the grace and promises of God are so placed before us that the 'broken reed' is not snapped off and 'the dimly burning wick' is not extinguished.** In the context of the infinite Love of God and of his immeasurable grace, we become free to acknowledge our sins and shortcomings, and are encouraged to believe that the Blood of Christ cleanses us from all sin.
The ethos of the Seminar is one of firm but gentle progression, where no one is ever pushed or hurried. It has been a place, so often, where heaven touches earth, where the Spirit of God broods, and is released in the lives of many. It is a place where people have found:

"There's wideness in God's mercy,
Like the wideness of the sea,
There's a kindness in his justice,
Which is more than liberty.

There is no place where earth's sorrows,
Are more felt than up in heaven:
There is no place where earth's failings
Have such kindly judgement given.

For the love of God is broader
Than the measures of man's mind;
And the heart of the eternal
Is most wonderfully kind.

There is plenteous redemption
In the blood that has been shed;
There is joy for all the members
In the sorrows of the Head."

**Many come to a Seminar because there's still an ache or a hunger in the heart, not yet satisfied. Some have seen a change in others, or sensed the love of God in their lives in such a way, that they desire to enter into that secret also.
GOD INTENDS FULLNESS OF LIFE IN THE HOLY SPIRIT FOR ALL!
You will be made most welcome at the Seminar, whether you come on your own or with friends. Come, and welcome!**

AN URGE TO WRITE, A PROMPTING TO BE A WITNESS TO THE LOVE AND POWER OF GOD?

Psalm 107 begins:

"O give thanks to the Lord for He is good; for his steadfast love endures for ever!
<u>Let the redeemed of the Lord say so, whom He has redeemed from trouble, and gathered in from the lands, from the east and from the west, from the north and from the south."</u>

A personal witness to the lovely and mighty things that God has done, brings due glory to God, and can be a witness of hope, to people who need to experience that same love and power of God.

In our Vestibule we have more than 50 TESTIMONIES (1989) to the grace and love of God.

In this August edition of WCN we give the testimony of Heather Ennis who suffered from Anorexia Nervosa, and trust it may be used of God.
When you read such stories, pause to give thanks to God, and pray God's continued blessing upon those who have written their story, that they may continue to be enveloped in the Light of Christ.

"ANOREXIA NERVOSA AND ME."

"Ten years ago I had my first son and at the same time my husband left a 9am to 4.30pm job to join the RUC (police). **Thus followed the onset of depression.**
I did have friends in Newtownards where we lived, but the motto was always "Look after Number one", especially if there was any trouble.

HE CRIED 22 HOURS A DAY - NO TIME TO EAT.
I, like most young mothers, had a vision of a beautiful baby, who slept most of the time, when in fact I got the complete opposite. Keith cried for a minimum of 22 hours per day, the other two hours would be taken up with feeding, being sick and changing nappies. **I was never so alone in my life and I had no time to eat.**

MY FAVOURITE FOODS … ENDED UP IN THE BIN.
My mum and Dad came down twice a week and brought me my favourite foods which I would

nibble at, when they were there, but always "kept some for later on"; - they always ended up in the bin. My excuse for myself for not eating "later on" was that I was too tired or the baby was crying again.

William (my husband) worked for 5 months in County Fermanagh, and then a further five months in Enniskillen town.
During this period Keith had been in hospital four times for short stays to try to make me rest.
By now my weight had gone from 9 stone 12 lbs to 6stone 3 lbs, **but I did not think that I was thin!** I thought everyone was crazy bringing me food and trying to make me eat - apart from feeling very tired, all the time I thought there was nothing wrong with me..

VERY ILL - SUSPECTED MENINGITIS - ANOREXIA NERVOSA.
Then I became very ill, I was very sick, I lost the power down one half of my body and the pains in my head were awful. **I was rushed into hospital with suspected meningitis.**
I was in Purdysburn Hospital, had lumbar punctures and various other tests were carried out, but the doctors found no physical illness, and diagnosed Anorexia Nervosa, a mental illness.
I did not believe them nor did I accept it. It took me a full eight years, before I could face this major problem in my life.
In hospital my excuse for not eating very much was 'hospital food'; then Mum began to bring me food from home. I passed myself by eating small amounts and "keeping some for later."

VERY DEVIOUS.
I packed all my food scraps into my soap bag and pushed it to the back of my locker. No one found it. Anyone who has Anorexia Nervosa is very devious and brilliant at hiding food.
I DID NOT THINK I WAS THIN!
For a further 3 years I stayed under 6 and a half stones, and survived by drinking coke and smoking about 40 cigarettes a day. **I still did not think that I was thin.** William used to get home at weekends so on Friday I did shopping for the family, and I did eat very small quantities at the weekend.

On Mondays I bought baby food, coke and cigarettes and that did me until Friday came round again.

SO LOST… SO VERY LONELY.
I can feel the pain right now of those times which have passed. I was so lost and so very lonely, but I did not realise then that all I needed was to be truly loved. If only I had turned to the Lord sooner - so much needless pain I bore!

When Keith was five years old I became pregnant with Mark. I had to pull my socks up now or I could lose my baby. I tried to eat properly but found it very difficult until I started to drink Guinness, and after ten days of drinking just one small bottle per day, my craving for food began.
I gave birth to Mark who was a very good baby. I had no post-natal depression and little loss of appetite.

A MENTAL ILLNESS - SELF-IMPOSED.

Anorexia Nervosa is without doubt a recurring illness and its prospects are frightening, even yet I am aware of just how easy it is to stop eating. This is a mental illness which is self-inflicted, but unfortunately you are completely unaware of this fact during the critical stages.

It is only when one admits and recognises that he/she has the illness that one can begin slowly to try to beat it.

THE LORD LOVES ME!
Four years ago I joined West Church. I love the Lord, but what is more important is that I am very aware of how much the Lord loves me!!

If the Lord had been in my life ten years ago I know I would never have been ill. I just needed the love of a big family and the beautiful security that comes from being a Christian!

A LOVELY P.S.
Sometime later, William Ennis, Heather's husband joined a "Life in the Spirit Seminar."
During the first session of it, I asked those who had enrolled what it was that drew them to the Seminar. Among those who had a ready answer to give was William.
"What has drawn me is the change I have seen in my wife. I am sort of jealous for what she has got!"

KEITH ELFORD COMES FROM OXFORD.

Another theological student from Wycliffe Hall, Oxford, is to join us on the 26th August. He is Keith Elford, who will be entering his final theological year in September. Keith spent a few days with us last year, on the occasion of Mary's marriage. Among other things he loves to sing and lead in worship. We know that, as with **Gary Wilton**, the congregation will take this fine young man to their hearts and into their homes.
Gary, by the way, is now curate in a town outside Bristol, CLEVEDON. And there's so much happening there, of the Lord that he can hardly bear to go away on holiday!

**AUGUST WCN informs Children and Young People of the Summer Scheme beginning on 14th August; Gives us cheering accounts of the Men's and Women's Weekends in Rostrevor;
Tells us that the SANDILANDS Mobile Home was fully booked throughout the summer; and gives latest news from the DORES:**

They have now been back in England from the end of March and have ceased being under the care of OMF from the end of June….."**200 letters of enquiry, numerous applications, and several interviews have not yet brought a job…."**

They make this plea:

"Please pray that God will **soon lead us into the light of the certainty that we are in his will, which includes an income, a more settled home, and a ministry for him."**

SEPTEMBER WCN 1989.

Celebration of Discipline - STUDY PROGRAMME FOR HOME GROUPS 1989-90.

'CELEBRATION' and 'DISCIPLINE' may **not seem to go very well together!**
'Celebration' conveys released and exuberant **joy.**
'Discipline' speaks to us of hard work, **and sticking resolutely and perhaps painfully to a programme.**
Sometimes, especially with children and young people, the discipline may be monitored, even enforced, by parents and teachers. And, of course, there are other situations also, where, in sports' training, or in business, the discipline is also there, as a team works and trains together, under supervision.

While **Celebration** and **Discipline** may be thought of as **Opposites**, in reality, they are often just the opposite sides of the same coin! We may speak of the **virtuoso performance** of a pianist, or a great singer or performer, be enthralled by the skills of ice dancers: there is always the **appearance** of such grace and power and spontaneity and competence, such a sense of sheer **celebration**.
But we all know that behind the **celebration** lies the **discipline** -the hours and days and weeks and years of study, of practice, of discipline.

In our relationship with God we are meant to have joy, wonderful communion, to be able to draw upon his wisdom, power and grace, for ourselves and others! We are meant to have celebration! But behind such an outpouring of his Spirit in our lives, there has also to be discipline.

In our HOME GROUPS, during the coming year, we plan to study Richard Foster's book 'Celebration of Discipline'.

This book is a Study of the 'Spiritual Disciplines' of the Christian life, **and a practical Manual, that aims to help us to proficiency, in our relationship with God.**

WHAT ARE THESE SPIRITUAL DISCIPLINES?
Well PRAYER is a 'spiritual discipline'.
In **prayer** we worship God, listen to God, allow God to work in our lives.
Often our praying is of poor quality, fitful, haphazard, ineffective, with our relationship to God obstructed. **Yet prayer can bring us into deep communion, and allow God to work powerfully, in and through our lives.**

When the disciples saw **the quality - end effects- of the way Jesus prayed, they requested: 'Lord, teach us to pray'.**
So PRAYER **is an art, a discipline that can be learnt, so that we come into a deep and fruitful communion and partnership with God.**

THUS Richard Foster shows us, in this book, that there are many other 'disciplines', that we can become skilled and proficient in, through which we can know and serve God better.
He focuses on a dozen of these 'disciplines', but declares that this list is not exhaustive.
We may study, from his book:

MEDITATION PRAYER FASTING STUDY SIMPLICITY SOLITUDE SUBMISSION SERVICE CONFESSION WORSHIP GUIDANCE CELEBRATION.

DOES ALL THIS FRIGHTEN YOU A BIT? Well, don't let it! Just remember how the disciples said to Jesus. 'Lord, teach us to pray'. And he did!
And how those fishermen learnt to pray!
Throughout the gospels we find the things that Jesus taught them about prayer. And, after Pentecost we see ordinary Christians gathering together, with such power released from their prayers that the sick are healed, works of power are accomplished, and many are brought to faith in Christ.
And He is able to teach us still- ordinary people, office-workers and housewives, production- workers and teachers, young and old, men and women.

WE MAY NEVER BECOME SPIRITUAL GIANTS, But we all may learn something more! That's better than stagnation! That's progress!

Further on in this edition of West Church News is a lovely testimony from **Lorraine Barklie** about the way they prayed for their 6-year old son John when he took ill in Spain- and how prayer in Jesus' Name brought healing.
Five years ago the Barklies would not have known how to pray like this- but faith in Jesus, the reality of the Holy Spirit, and what they have learnt about prayer, enabled them to do so.

Also further on, you will read about **'LISTENING POST', A CONFIDENTIAL SERVICE** and **SENSITIVE MINISTRY, for individuals to talk, to listen and to pray.**

We make a simple point: *we can*

all learn something more! And each new thing we learn - and learn to put into practice- helps us to grow up into maturity in Christ.

During the coming year we may *not* learn, to absorb and put into practice *all* we read about in 'Celebration of Discipline'. Yet everyone will learn *something new*, and some will learn *a lot!*

Over the year, let our attitude be:
"Lord, teach us to *pray*…."
"Lord, teach us to *meditate*…
"Lord, teach us to *serve*…
"Lord, teach us to *worship*…."

HOME GROUPS will meet in the New Hall on Tuesday 5th September at 8.00pm
For PRAISE & PRAYER
And for an Introduction to "Celebration of Discipline."
RICHARD FOSTER- its author- WILL SPEAK TO US ON VIDEO!

LISTENING POST.

This is a confidential service for individuals to talk, to listen and to pray.

A 'DROP-IN' SERVICE.

It is proposed to start a 'drop-in' service for those who feel the need to talk through a problem or a stressful situation whether it is due to loneliness, fear, loss of partner or relationships in the home or at work.

In the first instance the service will run for 12 weeks to assess need and to plan how best to meet the need in 1990.

From 10th September to 8th December 1989, Miss Doreen Hayward will be in the Prayer Room in West Church on the following days and times:
**Monday afternoons 2.30 -4.30.
Friday mornings 10.30 - noon.**
To talk with, to listen to and to pray with people who 'drop-in' for this purpose.

Would you like someone to listen to you?
Would you like someone to listen to you, to help you think through a course of action or just to meet with you to share your need and to pray with you in privacy and confidence?

If so 'drop in' to West Church, and meet Miss Hayward in the Prayer Room.
Alternatively, if you would prefer to make an arrangement for a visit to your home or to meet in the Church on a different day or another time **leave a message in the box in the Church Vestibule labelled "Listening Post" -messages for Miss Hayward.** Leave a note stating your name, address, telephone number and suggested dates and times to meet.
If you are in need of a listening ear you are welcome to 'drop-in'.

MISS DOREEN HAYWARD is a retired professional lady of wide experience, and of sensitive Christian spirit, trained to listen to people, and to listen to God, well able to give wise counsel.
[DGB]

A HOLIDAY EXPERIENCE OF SICKNESS - AND HEALING!

"While on holiday this summer in Salou (Spain) our son John aged 6 years developed severe vomiting and diarrhoea. Despite giving him medicines he was still being violently sick and having severe stomach pains.
It started on the Monday and by Tuesday lunchtime we were really worried as we had to go home the next day which meant we had to vacate our room at 10.00am, and as we were not leaving the apartments until 5.00pm that night he would be very uncomfortable with no room to stay in when he was still being sick. Also we had a one and a half hour journey to the airport by coach which would probably have no toilet facilities.
**After another attack of diarrhoea and being sick again, I just didn't know what to do - the medicines were just not working.
John was lying on the bed settee and I said, "John what about saying a wee prayer to Jesus and see if he can help you - I can do nothing for you."
He immediately agreed and we said a short prayer together - he repeating it after me, thanking Jesus for loving and caring for us even when we are on holidays, and asking Him to help John keep his medicines down and to stop the diarrhoea.

Within one hour John wanted his lunch -I was wary to give him anything in case he'd bring it up again, but my husband John said to give him something, so he had a piece of bread and some chips! I kept looking at him waiting for him to rush to the bathroom again but he didn't.
An hour later I was having a cup of coffee and a sandwich and John asked if he could have a sandwich also. Again I was wary of giving him anything but let him have one and he kept this down also. A little later we were able to take him down to sit by the swimming pool.
Our hearts were just full of thanks and praise to Jesus for making our son better again and for strengthening our son's faith and our own that He is always with us - we are never alone - a strange country- language difficulties -but he is still beside us, looking after us -THANK YOU, LORD!**
Lorraine Barklie.

SEPTEMBER WCN gives an account of two weeks spent by COLIN WILKINSON with a Youth for Christ outreach team in France; of how BRIAN WEIMANN had a great family holiday with relatives in Germany.

"HOW TO RAISE A

CHATTERBOX"

"GOOD COMMUNICATION BETWEEN THE GENERATIONS depends a lot on your ability -and willingness - **to listen to what your youngsters have to say. Try this simple 'hearing aid'.**

Alvin and Linda Little plan to run a "LIFE IN THE FAMILY SEMINAR" for 4 weeks, to provide a Discussion and Support group for Parents of pre-School children, mid-October to mid-November.

OUR HEALING SERVICE.

Our Healing Service goes on, after the Sunday evening Service, normally 52 Sundays a year. And week by week we see the good things that God does in the lives of those who come to it.
Tell people of the good things God is doing in our midst, and let your compassion go out to those who need the healing ministry of Christ, in body or soul!

HAVE YOU A 'WITNESS' TO MAKE?

Our 'Witness' sheets have been reprinted and will soon be suitably displayed. We are happy to have additional 'Witness' material from those who feel a prompting to write. **It can be a way of stretching out a hand of help and encouragement to others, in the love of Jesus.** *So don't let false modesty hold you back. When you write, you seek to exalt, not yourself, but God.*

FAREWELL TO REV. JIM HUNTER.

"It's coming up on five years since the Rev. Jim Hunter came to share with us in the ministry in West Church, and during that time he has gained a place of real affection in the hearts of our members **for the warmth of heart and readiness of spirit, that have so characterised him.**
Since July he has been assisting Rev. Ruth Patterson in Kilmakee church, Dunmurry, having been assigned there in the final year of his B.D. theological course at Union.

We do not want him to leave West Church without recognition of our regard for him and we hope to have the opportunity of showing our affection within the next few weeks."

That opportunity was taken at the Evening Service of Harvest Sunday. A little later your minister received this letter from Jim:
"Dear David, I would like to thank you and the congregation of West Church for the lovely 'Farewell' they gave me some weeks ago.
It was a great blessing to Maureen and me. We were especially grateful for the very generous cheque which you gave me. It really thrilled my heart to receive it along with the love and good wishes of the congregation. Please convey my warmest gratitude to them, to the Committee and to the Session.
I can truly say that *I have spent some of the happiest years of my life in fellowship with you and pray that God will richly bless you and the congregation for all you have done for me. Without you we would not have a home to live in at the moment, and I probably wouldn't have had the vision to follow the long pathway to Presbyterian ordination.*"

And there was also a warm letter of thanks from ANN KENNEDY FOR "THIS GENEREOUS AND UNEXPECTED GIFT", received on the night of Jim's Farewell, as an expression of encouragement as she enters upon her final year at Union Theological College.

SEPTEMBER WCN GIVES FULL DETAILS OF ALL OUR ORGANISATIONS AND GROUPS THAT RESUME FOR THE AUTUMN TERM.

OCTOBER WCN 1989.

A LETTER FROM HARRY GRAHAM.

In the last week before he died, knowing that he would soon be with his Lord, HARRY GRAHAM -beloved and much loving husband of Lyla Graham, felt a strong compulsion to use his fast-dwindling energy - and decaying fingers, to write to a number of people, including his minister. I give in full the letter he wrote.

First of all, a word about Harry! The Graham family were linked with West from the very outset of the congregation, and Lyla, a devoted member, became one of our elders. Harry was a devoted husband and father, and he always made Sunday lunch while the others were at church. He was a most caring man- but he never attended church! He had his questions! About a year before his death, he was diagnosed with the illness which was to take his life away. At that point, I encouraged him to join one of our 'Life in the Spirit Seminars' and that was to bring him to faith, and to a profound change in his life. In that context you will read his letter.

19 Strathearn Park,
Bangor BT19 1 DE,
24 August, 1989.

Dear David,
I am writing to you now as I feel the time allocated to me in this life is less than I require for doing the many things I should already have attended to. However, our Lord will decide the time and place when I leave. You and I have formed a very close relationship so far as my spiritual life is concerned, but it is more the outcome of that relationship, than the formation of it, that I wish to speak of.

As you know, David, I have been endowed with a very happy married life and could not have been blest with a more loving and devoted wife or with two more lovable sons. Over the past eighteen months, with your help, I have had to pose certain questions to myself, such as:-

DO I BELIEVE IN A CREATOR?

DO I BELIEVE IN A LIFE AFTER THIS?

DO I BELIEVE IN THE FORGIVENESS OF SINS?

DO I ACCEPT THE WORD OF GOD?

After these decisions had been made, two further questions arose:-

HOW DOES ONE MAKE CONTACT WITH GOD?

HOW DO WE KNOW WHEN GOD IS NEAR?

The answer to the first question, I found, was simply **'talk to him'**, Recognising that He is Lord and Master of all, but yet simply just **'talk to Him'**, discuss your problems, and seeking his help for those about us who really need help, and not forgetting to ask his help for one's own problems.

It is so wonderful that the more you ask and pray for help, the lighter your load becomes, but relief does not always come as you expect it to come.

In regard to knowing when God is close to us: this proved to be more difficult to understand at first, but became less so, the more one began to search.

God's hand can be seen in the morning with the rising of the sun, the blue sky, the white clouds, the rain gently falling.
His hand can be seen in the forests, the trees and shrubs, the green grass, the fruit on the trees, flowers in the garden or wild flowers, and each and every thing that grows.
His voice can be heard in the singing of the birds, in the crying of the sea birds on the shores of Belfast Lough, in the sighing of the wind, the rustle of leaves on the trees, the lapping of the waves on the seashore, and in the delightful shrill voices of children enjoying God's freely given gifts.

The most satisfying aspect of all is to be able to see our Lord all around us.

I can see God in the people around me. He appears with every single thought and kindness expressed to me; with the genuine smile from a friend, each and every offer of help, every thought and consideration, every expression of love and affection, every embrace or clasp of hands.

He is always there when people pray for each other, giving that warmth and satisfying glow within, which always makes me feel God's presence so close.

Love for one's fellow man is always available, but we must make the effort to use it. What a wonderful society we would have if we were all to make the effort.

Dear David, You can now see how I listen to God and how I can see the love He has for us, but which can mostly be portrayed to us through others.

I have written this letter to you because you may have a use for it when trying to help others in a similar situation to me, but, of course, only with the grace of God, do I offer this.

All my Love, David to you, Rhoda and your family.
Harry.

"I heard a voice from heaven saying to me,
'Blessed are the dead who die in the Lord from henceforth: Yea, saith the Spirit that they may rest from their labours; and their works do follow them.'"

OCTOBER WCN also tells us that new bookstalls have been sited in the Church Vestibule and adjacent to the Lounge, allowing us to stock and display more books, and that this has resulted in many more books being bought.
It also asks:
"HAVE YOU NOTICED THE MASSIVE DOUBLE BOOKSTALL IN THE APPROACH ROOM?"
If you have, you will have noticed that it is empty and many have wondered about its purpose.
THE PURPOSE is *to have a much more extensive Lending Library, and also to have a RESOURCE CENTRE, PROVIDING VIDEO TAPES THAT MAY BE BORROWED, and may be used by elders, Church Visitors, Home Group Leaders, and others as appropriate.*

They were installed in the hope that they could be stocked.
They were not there more than a few days, when a very generous gift, in memory of our late dear brother Harry Graham, <u>is enabling us to begin a substantial stocking with books and video tapes, which we feel to be a very fitting memorial to Harry.</u>

We are delighted that Harry's wife, **LYLA,** has consented to be in charge of the Lending Library and Resource Centre. Make her job easier by ensuring that books and videos are returned as soon as possible.
This demonstrates a right courtesy and grace towards others who may want to borrow also.

We have suggested that this new facility might be called
"Memorial Lending Library and Resource Centre."
For there may be others who may want to give even a modest gift on behalf of a loved one, to provide our church family with a few books or videos.
This can be of great value in up-building Christ's Kingdom in our midst.

USED BOOKS: Members may also want to donate fine books that have blessed them, to our Lending Library, that still others may be blessed!
Good quality books - not old junk, please!

EXPANDING OUR MINISTRY IN WEST.

In the beginning of 1989 we held out the hope that the Rev. Wilson Baria, a minister of the CNI in Bombay might come to serve with us for a year. In the end this has proved not to be possible, to the deep disappointment of all involved.
One door has closed, but another one has opened. (See page 393)
<u>DON AND HELEN RITCHIE have felt an increasing call of God upon their lives for fulltime ministry, at home or abroad, wherever the Lord might call them.</u>
Our Kirk Session felt, that wherever their future might be, it could be beneficial for them, for a time, to gain experience in their own congregation. So the Kirk Session has given an invitation to Don -assisted by Helen- to serve with us in West from the beginning of November, for a year. We shall explore the main spheres of work in which they will be involved.

OCTOBER WCN ALSO PUBLICISES A HUNGARIAN APPEAL FOR CLOTHES, SHOES AND BLANKETS FOR Romanian refugees fleeing from an oppressive Communist regime, where whole villages are being destroyed and rural communities forcibly resettled in soulless urban developments.

DAVID BATES and CHRISTINA GILBERT were part of a 'Youth for Christ' team that left Belfast in August to work in LIMERICK with "Child Evangelism Fellowship."
They travelled down to Limerick in the **Tea Trawler,** an unmistakable bright red bus with blue waves along the side!
They did "Five-day Clubs with the children - six clubs each day on the streets of various housing estates in the area. -'we sang choruses, taught memory verses and told Bible stories.'

SINCE THEN DAVID BATES AND CHRISTINA GILBERT HAVE BECOME ENGAGED TO BE MARRIED!

NOVEMBER WCN 1989.

A SUNDAY PICNIC AT LAODICEA - and much more!   DGB writes:

"I suppose that had it not been for a visit of RON GEORGE of 'People International', we would not recently have paid a holiday visit to Turkey!
RON GEORGE, who took part in this year's Worldwide Missionary Convention, spoke one Sunday evening at the end of August in West Church and told us of "People International's concern for 180 million people of Muslim faith, who scarcely have a Bible or a viable Christian witness or congregation among them, stretching from Albania in the west to Mongolia in the east.

A LAND WHERE JOHN, PETER AND PAUL LABOURED IN THE GOSPEL.

And this is pre-eminently so in the land of TURKEY, a country larger than the British Isles and France added together, **and a region where many of the events recorded in the Bible, both Old Testament and New Testament took place.**
In the Revelation of John, Christ sends messages to seven churches from Ephesus to Laodicea - all of them found in the western part of present-day Turkey.

PAUL'S missionary journeys also largely featured Turkey, perhaps naturally enough, since his birth place TARSUS, is near to Turkey's southern Mediterranean coast.
When PETER wrote his First Letter to Christians during 'the fiery trials', he addressed it to those who lived in the provinces of Pontus, Galatia, Cappodocia, Asia and Bithynia - all of them part of modern Turkey.
SO THE FOREMOST OF THE APOSTLES, JOHN, PAUL AND PETER HAD MINISTRIES THAT DEEPLY INVOLVED THEM IN THE LAND OF TURKEY.

PICNIC LUNCH AT LAODICEA.

So, on Sunday 15th October, about noon, Rhoda and I sat down on the scant ruins of an ancient building, and under the shade of a solitary tree, to eat our picnic lunch, on the vast and empty site, where the city of Laodicea had once stood. As we ate the delicious white Turkish bread - akin to French bread- and drank some cherry juice and crunched upon the large, red and flavoursome Turkish apples, we could look all around us, from atop the gentle eminence of this ancient site, and see on every side the grandeur of great mountain ranges.

SITE NOW WELL NIGH EMPTY.

The extensive site, on which the proud and prosperous city of Laodicea once stood, is now well nigh empty. There is a large area littered with broken marble, tops of stone masonry walls, and here and there the remains of some public buildings, the overall impression is emptiness. a vast field with bits of rubble here and there. There are a few remains of some public buildings, two theatres, a large stadium, a water tower and the truncated conduits that were part of the water system of the city.

THE DESIRE TO GO BACK.

As we sat on such an empty site there was the desire to go back, if

that had been possible and to envisage the city, its grand streets and markets and buildings and people, at the time of its ancient glory, and to witness the church at the time of the apostles.
It was strange to realise that here was once a flourishing church, and now, as far as we could know, no one in this area that loved and revered the name of Jesus.

A City at the Crossroads.
There was a time when Laodicea was at the intersection of the main trade routes running from Ephesus in the West and Syria in the East, with the north-south route between Perga and Sardis.
It had been a great banking and financial centre, **so rich that when devastated by an earthquake in A.D. 61, its independent citizens refused outside help from Rome for the rebuilding of their city.**
Its sheep were famous for their soft, violet-black, glossy wool. It was a great clothing manufacturing centre that mass-produced cheap outer garments.
It was a famous medical centre, renowned for its medicines of eye and ear.
Like the city of Hierapolis nearby, it had a large Jewish population.
It had prospered as a city and **there was a considerable Christian Church established there.** In the Book of Revelation, **the church here is condemned for being neither hot nor cold, and so distasteful to the Lord.**

When Christ speaks to the Church at Laodicea, he tells them that their riches have blunted their devotion, made them self-satisfied and proud, indifferent and apathetic, and so distasteful to him.
Yet He yearns for their devotion and allegiance, and draws near to them as a lover that knocks upon the door of the beloved, seeking admission.

NO TRACE OF CHURCH AT COLOSSE.
In his letter to the Church at Colosse, nearby - and of which there is now no trace- Paul says in chapter 4: 16,
"And when this letter has been read among you, have it also read in the church of the Laodiceans, and see that you also read the letter from Laodicea. **And say to Archippus, 'see that you fulfil the ministry received from the Lord'.**

Archippus was the bishop or leader of the Church at Laodicea - a sharp word here that he lead the Church with zeal and energy. Perhaps in these early days the rot had already set in.

EARLY CHURCH LARGE AND POPULOUS.
One of the impressions we gained from our visits to some of the cities, like Ephesus, in which the early church was established, **has been that the church did not consist of a few minor pockets of believers - RATHER THAT THE CHURCH WAS LARGE AND POPULOUS.**

Therefore all the sadder <u>to see no trace of Christianity in Laodicea and to realise how very few people in the whole land acknowledge the Name of Jesus.</u>

BUT THE CHURCH IN THE WORLD CAN GROW AGAIN - LIKE A MUSTARD SEED.

On Sunday past, I mentioned that the Evangelical Church in Latin America has grown from 50,000 in 1900 to around 50 million at present, with a growth rate that could carry it to 100 million by the year 2000.

At the present time we are seeing the break-up of what seemed the impervious and invincible structures of Communism in Eastern Europe and Asia.
The Lord's Commission is to take the Good News to the whole creation. Spiritual warfare is involved.
Some battles we have lost, as when the Church was wiped out in North Africa and Turkey and regions of the Middle East, through the sword of Islam.

But the War, to win the world for Christ, still remains to be won. Millions live in a spiritual vacuum, or in spiritual darkness. THE LIGHT OF CHRIST MUST BE CARRIED TO THEM, AND THE SPIRIT WILL ENABLE AND SHOW THE WAY!

THE DORES CONTINUE TO BE INVOLVED IN THIS WORLD MISSION!

Graham Dore writes:
"**We had a sense of loss and waste as we left a full ministry in Japan and found none here (UK). We struggled with outer rejection and inner questionings as we tried to find our feet in this strangely familiar culture!**

We realise how right it was to return: Alastair needed home security to develop normally....

... I worked with Wycliffe Bible Translators for a week in August... and they offered me a job..... We're really pleased at the prospect of involvement in the enormous missionary task again... I'm impressed with the extent, dedication, and expertise of WBT.
<u>AND GOOD NEWS FROM JAPAN.</u>
Yoko Munakata (daughter), Mrs Hasegawa, Akita and Mizoguchi, for whom you prayed, and the Schmidt's son, **were all baptised in the sea at Tonden - great excitement! Praise the Lord for breakthrough of resistance, especially on the part of Mrs Mizoguchi's husband.** Until early this year she seemed terrified to talk to him about church!
Mr & Mrs Munakata, church members **are each teaching the Bible to one person, a great step forward. And there are now two women's meetings.**
ALL ARE REJOICING!

SERVICE WITH WYCLIFFE:

About half of our members are involved in linguistics, translation and literacy work among the ethnic and minority groups of the world, for which training is provided.
The other half of the team serve as teachers, secretaries, accountants, nurses, artists and in dozens of other support roles.
Both long-term and short-term options are available, though long-term service is available for actual translation work.

FINANCIAL POLICY:

Wycliffe Bible Translators does not pay a salary; members look to God to provide for their needs through his people - usually through home churches and other Christian friends.

THE JOB OFFERED TO GRAHAM DORE involves writing (for which he has clear gift and ability), and correspondence etc in the Communications' Department.

YOUNG WEST WEEKEND, Guysmere Report by Don Ritchie.

In the old days we always said that the best report of a weekend was as follows: "We went away. We are back. Aren't you pleased to see us?"
Alan said that was not enough! He told me I would make new friends. I would meet lots of young people. I would enjoy it!
He didn't say that I would be greatly blessed. I would learn to cook for 70. I would be accused of snoring!
It started in the back of a mini bus with 9 girls and me. **Billy and Rosie Mullan** were driving. I looked out of the window and they talked, sang and played games. They then drew me into the action; we had a great time and quickly arrived at Guysmere!
Joan had to organise the food and cooking arrangements. The gas oven crouched in the middle of the kitchen and malevolently hissed at us. It reluctantly disgorged the sausages for supper and Joan gave it one of her 'looks'!

Saturday morning found us praising, and listening to **John Kilpatrick** who showed us that we must look to God to make us grow, and that we are either for or against God - we cannot sit on the fence.

It is just amazing how much time is spent preparing to eat, eating and then clearing up after! And clearing up the Centre took some time - how did all that sand get where it did? Everyone enjoyed the experience, and the question was "when are we going again?"

DECEMBER WCN 1989.
AGAIN WE MOBILISE AND INSPIRE OUR PEOPLE TO SUPPORT PCI APPEAL FOR CHILDREN:
Saving children from contagious diseases in HAITI.
Supporting a HOME for unwanted boys in Cape Town.
Setting 'bonded labourers', virtual slaves, free in India.
Helping a Rehabilitation Centre in Burkino Faso- since 1966, 3000 people have been assisted.
We may never witness the good our gifts accomplish, but maybe one day we may hear a voice that says: "As you did it to one of the least of these my brothers, you did it to me."

LATE NIGHT FILM OR LATE NIGHT PRAYER?

When it comes to the growth of the Church and the extension of the Kingdom of God *we need to recognise that we have a battle on our hands!*

When Paul wrote his first letter to Thessalonica, he told them that he prayed for them constantly, and with thanksgiving. He rejoiced in the vitality of their fellowship, the warmth of their love, and their great zeal in sharing the Gospel.

Yet, separated from them, he had anxiety, for he knew the pressures they were enduring, and had a fear that the Tempter might undermine them. When greatly desiring to visit them, he was frustrated - "Satan hindered us."

In West we rejoice at the many good and lovely things God has been doing in our midst.

But we have anxiety too, lest Satan undermine the work of God in this place.

We have anxiety when we see people who were at the centre of God's purpose in this congregation, retreating to the sidelines. Or those who would never have missed a service, somewhat negligently at home! Sometimes our best soldiers, who have been in the forefront of the battle, seem to have been picked off, one by one, so that they are no longer in the positions they once occupied with glowing Christian faith.
Paul spoke of the way **'Satan hindered us'. He has many ways of attempting to do so.**
Sometimes it is overwhelming us with other concerns; pressures from business; stress; distress within the family; Sometimes people get discouraged or 'hurt'. Sometimes they have prayed and not got answers to their problems or needs. Often Satan accuses and presses guilt strongly upon our members.

We rejoice in good initiatives taken in 1989 and not a few lives changed during this year.
AND YET!
AND YET there is not the full dynamic of the Spirit that we can and should have in our midst. Spiritual obstacles have to be overcome by spiritual weapons.

(Some) PRAYER DOES NOT WORK!
Sometimes we may complain that prayer does not work, when in truth it is only the pathetic, weak praying that we make, that does not reach through to the heart of God. We need much more concentrated prayer.
Paul speaks of **'praying with all**

prayer and supplication in the Spirit, and watching thereunto with all perseverance and supplication for all saints.'

In our Lending Library, we have placed a book by Colin Whittaker entitled 'Korea Miracle'. It has a chapter entitled 'The Miracle of a Praying People'

THEY BELIEVE IN PRAYING: Some prayer does work!

"In the West we believe in prayer: **in Korea they believe in praying!"** There the level of praying is inspiring.
They all pray, they are always doing so, and they intercede in every possible way. They pray alone and they pray in twos; they pray in small groups and in their homes; they pray in their churches and in their mountains; they pray in their own language and 'in the Spirit', in other tongues; they pray silently and loudly; they pray with tears and with holy laughter; they sing their prayers and sometimes they groan their prayers as they intercede and get under the burdens which the Holy Spirit lays upon them; they pray in the morning and in the evening; they pray at midday and at midnight; they pray with fasting and they pray over their meals; they pray for their friends and for their enemies; they pray for their neighbour and for their nation; they pray for the church and for the world; **they pray for everyone and about everything"**

YONGGI CHO IS EMPHATIC THAT FOR REVIVAL YOU HAVE TO ORGANISE MASSIVE PRAYER IF YOU ARE TO EXPERIENCE A GREAT OUTPOURING OF THE HOLY SPIRIT.

Colin Whittaker says:
"It is a tremendous tonic to visit **Korea** where prayer meetings are not measured in handfuls of mainly women and elderly people, but in thousands of men and women and of vast numbers of young people, and the frequency and duration of the prayer meeting is daily and for many hours, instead of just weekly and for a few minutes."
"It is a Western pastor's dream come true to find people queuing to get into the all-night prayer meeting and to see them struggling to find a seat in a beautiful, circular auditorium, much larger and more modern than London's Royal Albert Hall. **Such is the experience every Friday night in the Yoida Gospel Church.**

THE WHOLE CONGREGATION PRAYING TOGETHER.

Colin Whittaker goes on to give a picture of a Night of Prayer. The services are remarkably 'structured' and led, and include praise, sometimes testimony and teaching. But there is much praying. The praying may be led by one of the pastors, the congregation joining in hearty 'Amens', or the congregation may be given topics and concerns to pray about, and then every member of the congregation begins to pray aloud, so that a vast symphony of voiced intercession ascends to the throne of God.

In this context the power of Satan is broken; the power of God is released!
Through such united, intense, sustained prayer, many mighty things are done. *Such prayer works!*

IN ROTA
Different sectors of the church are responsible in rota for the Friday Night Prayer Meeting. Few people may be there each week, but many are there once a month.

LENDING LIBRARY:

Among new books in our expanding Lending Library you will find, both ancient classics and those recently written.
You'll find one written by Justin Dennison about a Church Growth Conference he attended in Korea, under the title:
'Six reasons why the Korean Church grows.' This supplements the article we have already written on Prayer.
You'll find John Bunyan's 'Pilgrim's Progress.'
'Partly Right'
by Tony Campolo.
'God's Answer for **THE UNEQAULLY YOKED'**, written to encourage and strengthen by William Dell.
REBUILDING YOUR BROKEN WORLD by Gordon McDonald.
YOUR CHURCH AND THE THIRD WAVE by Peter Wagner.

And many others!

DECEMBER WCN also gives details about our Christmas services;
That our New Hall has been finally paid for leaving us a balance of £5108, providing a very necessary cushion for our Outreach Fund;
That our *monthly* Development Fund envelopes are being replaced with *weekly* envelopes

JANUARY WCN 1990. Prayer Mobilisation.
In December we saw how the Church in Korea mobilised itself for 'massive' prayer, so that the resistance of Satan was broken down, and the kingdom of Christ established.
We are seeking to increase the amount of praying that goes on in our midst, especially at our Sunday Evening pre-service prayer meeting.
We seek to mobilise our districts on a rota basis to be on duty from 6.20pm for one month of the year. For example Districts A and B would be on duty in January, Districts C and D in February, etc.
Of course any others are invited to come also as they are able, but the Districts on duty would provide the stable, core group each week.
We pray that the glory of God may more and more brood over

FRIDAY MORNING MEN'S GROUP
WALTER McALLISTER has led this group from its inception.
Starting with a handful it has now a normal weekly attendance of more than one hundred!

DAVID AND RHODA BAILIE WHO TOTALLY SHARED THE ACTIVE MINISTRY IN WEST CHURCH OVER ALMOST 37 YEARS. (1988)

ASSISTANT AND ASSOCIATE MINISTERS WHO HAVE SERVED IN WEST.
John Seawright.
Jim Hunter with Maureen; Alvin Little with Linda.
Terry Laverty with Sandra.
Bobby Liddle with Ann.   See Index for more details.

Many SINGING GROUPS have flourished in West over the years.
YOUTH groups led by Robert Sinclair and Roger Cooke.
The Singing groups led by Alan Stewart, Carol Moorhead, Andrew Seaton; and by Paul & Beulah Shields, Noel & Janet Johnston and Tom Eddis.

THE CHURCH COMMITTEE.
Ken Macartney, Derick Riddell. Alan Logan, Cecil Stewart, Noel Maitland, Ethel Anderson, James Smith, Reggie Scott, Geoff Alcorn.
Seated: Victor Stephens, William McClelland, Brian Wilson, John Poole.
Ronnie McDowell polishing the Burning Bush; George Stevenson who has been cutting our lawns for a quarter of a century!   And Ken Macartney, who with James Smith seem incessantly at work, inside and outside!

FORMAL OPENING AND DEDICATION OF THE '91' COMPLEX, by Rt.Rev. Dr. John Dunlop. Keys were handed over by Mr Ken Macartney, November 1992.

CHURCH CHOIR AND BELCANTO, with Maurice McKenzie.
See Index.

MARGARET CATHCART for many years co-ordinated CHRISTIAN AID collections in Bangor West, and paid a visit to India, p 406.
DON & PAT McNUTT served in retirement in Malawi. See Index.

ABBA TRUST, for local philanthropy established in May 1991. See Index.
Ken Mottram, Renee Robinson, Margaret Mottram, Margaret Bailie, Elaine Ward, Derick Riddell and John McCroskery.

our sanctuary and our services.

LIVELY UPDATE from Don and Helen Ritchie.

"We thank you for the wonderful welcome you have extended to us. We are greatly humbled by the way you all have received us into your homes and groups. God has guided us to our present station in life. Pray that we may be an encouragement and blessing to all."

"YOUNG PEOPLE ON TUESDAY NIGHTS.
Tuesday Nights at 7.00 sees an answer to prayer - 25 to 35 young people come to our church and meet in a relaxed manner. We sit and talk, listen to a little music, play softball and get to know one another. Questions get asked and I answer them, and so, perhaps young people who never come to church may learn of the love that Jesus so freely gives. Pray!

HELEN INVOLVED WITH YOUNG PEOPLE ON FRIDAY NIGHTS.
Friday night sees 2 youth groups, folk who meet as young Christians to pray, to learn about growing in the Lord, to reach out to others and enjoy one another's company. The age range is from 13 to 20+. **Pray for Alvin, Helen, Billy Mullin and Joan Cochrane.**

YOUTH DRAMA GROUP.
One thing leads to another and opportunities open up in a lovely manner.
Out of the Summer Scheme, where Alvin expected 30 and got 120+, we now have a very active Youth Drama Group, which meets on Monday Nights with Joan Cochrane and Helen.
They are really enthusiastic youngsters and so talented! Already they have been used in the Sunday School, and outside in the Ards' Presbytery's BB Outreach.

WE ARE AMAZED at the number of groups there are in the Church.

We have been so warmly welcomed by all we have met, and look forward to meeting you again and again. Please ask us, at any time, if we can be of help or encouragement to you!"

REV. JOHN SCOTT:
Our warm and prayerful good wishes go with the Rev. John Scott, our neighbour and friend over the past 9 years in St. Gall's. We've always had an excellent relationship with St. Gall's and we shall miss the Scotts most sincerely.

FEBRUARY WCN 1990.

As usual the February edition of WCN gives overviews from our annual Kirk Session and Committee reports and from many of our organisations. We can but touch on a very few of these!

Mothers & Toddlers.
"Tuesday 7th March 1989 saw the beginning of our Mothers & Toddlers' Group. The kettles were boiled, the scones buttered and we waited. Eight mothers and small children arrived. We grew and grew, until there are now 42 mothers and 53 children on the register. We average about 25-30 mothers and their children at any one Tuesday morning. Mothers enjoy the relaxed and friendly atmosphere in which they partake of refreshments while their children play happily within their view….. My sincere thanks go to Isobel Coburn, Elizabeth McClelland, Jenny Robinson, Janet Johnston, Susan Wyeth and Alison Beatty for all their help and to Roslyn Wilson who helps us to keep up a good supply of tray bakes.

Note: in 2006 **Maureen Blackmore** -who started it all- is still to be found every Tuesday at the Mothers & Toddlers!

THE DORES - AND MISSIONARY ENDEAVOUR!

Over several years, we in West have been given insight into hard missionary work, through following Graham and Janet Dore, with Alistair and Elizabeth, who began a missionary project in Tonden, Japan. They started from scratch, and began to see a little church grow. And we rejoice that, after their departure, it is still growing.
It was anguish for them to leave it!
But now Graham has become established with WYCLIFFE BIBLE TRANSLATORS -*AND THAT HAS OPENED UP A WIDE, WIDE FIELD FOR MISSIONARY WORK IN WHICH WE CAN ALL SHARE!*
Graham Dore writes:
"It came as news to me that for 300 million people **the words of Jesus are unintelligible, or don't speak to their hearts, because they are only available in a foreign or acquired language, and they can't read! It seems unfair to deprive masses of people from the only thing that can set them free!"**
Graham Dore adds:
"We were helping to bring the Word of God to sophisticated, literate, self-sufficient people **in Japan, who have the Bible.** Yet the task continues - to bring the Word to the underprivileged, often illiterate, often very earnest people on the fringe **who haven't the Bible.**
Jesus had time for *haves* **and** *have-nots!*

ADOPT A PROVINCE IN TURKEY.
Recently we have spoken of the fact that the apostles Peter, Paul and John laboured fruitfully in the area now covered by modern-day TURKEY.
Ron George of 'People International' declares that *Turkey remains the largest unreached nation on earth - and yet many Turks are open to the Gospel.*
"I would like to put before you a strategy that may well tip the

balance and make long-lasting results for both Turkey and your own fellowship.

Quite simply put, we believe that a Church, a Bible College, a Christian Union or a Fellowship, *by adopting a province of Turkey, and concentrating its efforts on that province in the years to come, could well result in the Church being re-established in every one of the 71 provinces of Turkey.*

And a map with Turkey's 71 provinces is included.
Geographically Turkey is larger than the British Isles and France combined, and with a population of 55 million. And it is difficult to find more than 5 viable New Testament churches in the whole country!

"FOR THE LOVE I LOST, I NO LONGER WEEP.."

In a recent PRAISE SERVICE the Holy Spirit did something powerful and lovely in the life of someone present that has been expressed in a poem:

"Now I'm delivered from sorrow and pain,
The new life I've found washes it away like rain,
My heart is in ecstasy, my soul is in heaven,
The gentle Lord Jesus has given me leaven,
He died on the cross to deliver me from sin,
Now I am content and joyful within,
For the love I lost I no longer weep,
Because the love I have found is strong and deep,
Oh gentle Jesus stay in my heart,
Nothing on earth will tear us apart,
You've stripped me from bitterness, heartache and strife,
For you are the way, the truth and the life,
With your Holy Spirit you have cascaded my heart,
Now you are the horse and I am the cart,
In infinite glory your love cleanses me,
And your death in Jerusalem sets my spirit free."

OUR GUIDING ORGANISATIONS WILL BE ATTENDING OUR 'FAMILY SERVICE' ON 25TH February.
MARCH WCN 1990.

WE ARE PRAYING MORE- and it's showing!

Over many years the **WEDNESDAY NIGHT PRAYER MEETING**, led by **Willie Hall**, has been a place of fruitful prayer and fellowship.
More recently the Sunday Evening prayer time in the Praise Room has been developing and growing.
**As well, there is much praying and ministry in our Home Groups.
We would like to saturate our parish with many groups in twos or threes meeting to inundate the whole work of our congregation in prayer.**

LATE-NIGHT PRAYER TIMES ON FRIDAYS, 10.15 -12.15.

This will not be a heavy affair with time passing at a snail's pace. Those who have been present at the Sunday Evening Half-hour of Prayer, know that the time passes quickly - with never enough time to complete our prayer assignments.

In our Late-Night Prayer times we will not abandon people or leave them without guidance. There will be enough time for Praise to lift our hearts together to God; enough of God's Word to give us guidance and inspiration for prayer; yet the bulk of the time will be spent in structured praying. There will be variety and richness in our praying.

We have 13 Pastoral Districts in our congregation, from A to M, and 13 Friday nights in each quarter! All members are invited, but we would like each district to provide a core group for each Friday night.

THE ULTIMATE PROMOTION FOR

MARGARET GIBSON.

Seldom have we felt with such intensity the emotions of sorrow and joy, the sense of loss and the sense of gratitude, than in the passing and at the promotion of our beloved friend and elder, dear Margaret Gibson.

Jesus has told us that it is those who are most conscious of grace and mercy for themselves, who most lavishly exude the grace and love of God. This truth has been magnificently demonstrated in the life of Margaret Gibson.

We have already included in our *"WEST CHURCH JOURNEY"* Witness Sheet 33, where she relates the circumstances in which she came to faith in Christ and was filled by the Holy Spirit.

Her whole life came to glow and flow with the fullness of the love of Jesus.
She touched with blessing the lives of hundreds!
How many say, 'She was the first to speak to me in West Church'; 'she brought me along to the Healing Service''; 'she encouraged me to come to a Seminar''; 'she prayed with me…and I was helped..healed blessed.. comforted'.

She had a holy boldness and it was saturated with the love of God.

Margaret truly had a heart like her Lord, always seeking out EVERYONE for her Lord, but with a heart especially for the weak, the hurt, the broken, the bruised, and all in the confident faith that Jesus heals, restores, gives a brand new life.
She was a true 'fisher of men', persuading people, like Paul, that ' *now is the day of salvation'.*

She had an insatiable thirst for God in prayer and praise, and it was her 'meat and drink' to bring home the sheaves for harvest.

Margaret was herself a Good Shepherd with a 'servant' heart, and with faith and love she was often involved in the *heavy work of the Kingdom,* as she prayed at night, interceding, wrestling in costly petition.

On her sideboard, she had a little card that said: 'Jesus in me loves you'.

And how many of us have felt the love of Jesus in Margaret's greeting, encouragement, gifts, lavish love and prayers!!!
HOW MUCH WE WILL MISS HER - YET HOW WE BLESS GOD FOR HER, AND THAT HE IS RAISING UP OTHERS LIKE HER.

RECENT VISIT BY TOM SMAIL.

"A few weeks ago we had the very special pleasure of a visit from Tom and Truda Smail, when Tom was speaking at the Christian Renewal Centre in Rostrevor.
In truth we have seen very little of the Smails since they left Whiteabbey and Northern Ireland in 1972
In Witness Sheet 1 I have spoken of his visit to West in February 1968, and its impact, through the Spirit upon West Church's minister - and congregation.
From 1972 he spent several years with the Fountain Trust when he was also Editor of the Renewal magazine. Then he was Professor at St. John's Theological College in Nottingham, and currently a Team Vicar in a large South London Anglican Church.

SOME QUOTES THAT REACH HOME!

Under the Spirit of God, Tom made an impact upon us way back in 1968.
There are some extracts from his Editorials in Renewal Magazine that it might not be amiss to quote. Tom can be both trenchant and tender!
"**Better to be sick in the arms of Jesus than healed in any other name. I was rebuked recently for saying that, but anybody who jibs at it had better ask himself where, amid all his exciting experiences and releases, he stands with the Word of God.
The renewal will become the opposite of what God meant it to be, if we allow ourselves to be seduced from the Word."**

"I find in my own ministry that the way to lose vision and become a mere fulfiller of engagements and a trudger from this conference to that, is to talk endlessly about spiritual things when you yourself are not giving the Spirit opportunity to touch you deeply and show you afresh the reality and power of what you are talking about."

Then there are a couple of books that he commends that might pique our curiosity, and consequently bless us!

JOYCE HUGGETT: 'OPEN TO GOD'.

Her book shows the reader the 'way to biblical meditation and contemplative prayer. The first half is a general overview of the subject with many helpful suggestions.
The second half comprises 28 Meditations. The whole is beautifully presented with quotations, line-drawings and colour photographs.
This is not a book to flip through. It is a book that can be used to lead the reader into contemplation; to stop, to ponder and to cogitate. And so a couple of pages may well take half an hour. This is the book's purpose and value.
The real heart of the book lies in the 28 meditations... I am finding that they give depth in my prayer life and have led me to contemplate Jesus more meaningfully. It is helpful that the biblical text is fully printed out. I can thoroughly recommend this book.

The other book is very different. It is the compelling biography of Billy Bray entitled **"GLORY" BY F.W. BOURNE.**
Tom writes:
"The publishers are to be congratulated on reprinting this classic biography and enabling a new generation to make the acquaintance of the captivating character of Cornish Methodism, Billy Bray.
Since it was first published in 1877 it has gone through thirty editions and his name has become famous around the world.
**Prior to his outstanding conversion Billy Bray was a drunkard, and 'the wildest and most reckless of men'.
He had a natural sense of humour which he used in the alehouses to 'turn sacred subjects into ridicule and fun'; but when he was 'born again' and delivered from drink his ready wit and humour were sanctified and turned to telling account in the service of his Saviour. Billy enjoyed his Christianity and wanted everybody else to enjoy Jesus with him.**
Billy's faith was of the praying and praising kind. 'I cannot help praising the Lord', he said. 'As I go along the street I lift one foot up and it seems to say 'Glory!' and I lift up the other, and it seems to say 'Amen!', and so they keep on like that as I walk.
'And unless I am very much mistaken, you will find yourself shouting your glories and amens too as you turn the pages and read Billy's exploits of faith and his stories of the power of God in action.
His narrative of the salvation and healing of an old lady, Florence Hoskin, who had been crippled for over seven years, is guaranteed to prise a 'glory' from the lips of the most silent of saints. Not to mention the story of how God answered prayer for the pilchard fishermen at St. Ives and filled their nets to overflowing at a time when the fishing had been very poor.
Billy's last word on his deathbed was 'Glory!'
If you have never read this book

then buy your copy now, And if you have never uttered an 'Amen' or a 'glory' in your life, I defy you to get to the end of this book without breaking silence.

APRIL WCN 1990.

"DEVELOPMENT."

In the beginning of 1990 we gave our members *weekly* DEVELOPMENT Fund envelopes instead of the *monthly* ones previously issued. This has resulted in a considerable increase in this Fund, comparable to the corresponding period in 1989.

The Development Fund aims primarily to enable us to have further personnel for pastoral care, and the promotion of the Kingdom of God at our home base.

On this basis we have been able to enlist DON AND HELEN RITCHIE TO HELP US.

AND NOW JULIE HAMILTON IS TO JOIN US ALSO.

In the second half of 1989 Julie Hamilton joined in one of our Seminars, and has subsequently been leading the group formed from it. **She is a trained deaconess of our Presbyterian Church, a young woman who had her first stint of service in Greenwell Presbyterian Church in Newtownards.**

I suppose one might say that a spiritual crisis led her to give up that work for a time. Her goal is now to return to it. In the interim period we believe that Julie can very profitably work with us, to our mutual benefit. So our Kirk Session has unanimously invited her to do so, and our Church Committee made the necessary arrangements. So Julie will be serving with us from the beginning of April for the rest of 1990. I should say that this arrangement has the warmest possible blessing from Miss Betty Morrow of Church House, who oversees the work of our deaconesses.

THERE IS A CONNECTION BETWEEN FINANCIAL RESOURCES AND CHURCH GROWTH!

In 1 Corinthians 3: 6 Paul writes: "**I planted. Apollos watered, but God gave the growth."**
Yes, of course we know that except by the living breath of God's Spirit, we can accomplish nothing. Only by his Spirit do men become alive. Only by his Spirit do healings take place, are miracles performed.
AND YET WE HAVE OUR WORK THAT WE MUST DO, THAT GOD EXPECTS US TO DO. Paul continues:
"He who plants and he who waters are equal, and each will receive his wages according to his labour. **For we are God's fellow workers! You are God's field, God's building."**

GOD CHOOSES TO USE US AND OUR RESOURCES TO HARVEST HIS CROP.

This means that we are to work hard - and *trust God!*
We are to use our resources for the work of God.

Already we have spoken of the great work of witness, prayer and evangelism in Korea, by which hundreds of thousands of people have been harvested into the Kingdom of God. We have read of care and ardent prayer.
But there is a financial element too that speeds the work!
Most of the Christians in Korea tithe their givings. This enables churches to be built and many people harnessed for full-time service. They have a strong team to lead their church in its work of witness.

AND THAT'S WHY AS A CONGREGATION WE SHOULD GRASP THE OPPORTUNITY TO INCREASE THE VALUE OF OUR GIFTS BY ONE THIRD, THROUGH COVENANTING!

AN EXPANDING BUSINESS IN THE KINGDOM OF GOD, with Vocation Opportunities in the Sycamore Club!

MARGARET CONROY reminds us that the Sycamore Club, a Sunday School for mentally handicapped people, has been meeting in West Church for some years.
"We began with a small group of children from Barnardo's, most of whom are still with us. It is a natural progression in life that at different stages we become too old for one group and should progress to another.. **This has led us into a second Sycamore Club for mentally handicapped adults.** Indeed some of our original members have gained promotion to this group.
We have always asked and trusted the Lord to lead us as we seek to share a simple understanding of his love and of his Word and we have been richly blessed, both in our 'teaching' and in our helpers. Now we would also seek your prayerful support.

LOVING AND CARING PEOPLE TO REACH OUT:

Our **experience** has increased over the years. The Lord has **provided** us with many loving and caring people to help us in this work **and this now enables us to reach out further, seeking out more children with special learning difficulties.**
We would very much welcome your prayers **that the Lord will open many doors** that we will be ready and able to meet the needs of those children **and that he will guide us**

as we seek to expand our outreach and increase our numbers! PLEASE REMEMBER US IN YOUR PRAYERS!

TWO EXPERIENCES!
We would like to share two experiences we have had within the 'Sycamore Club', one from the children and one from the adults.

Prior to Christmas we were asking the children **to make out a list of things they would like.** In no time our list was completed.
The next stage of the lesson was **to ask the children to compile a second list: of things we had already been given.**
We were hoping **to have the second list longer than the first!**
When the question was given to commence the second list **Gregory had no hesitation in replying,** "GOD GAVE US HIS SON, JESUS"
No second list was necessary! I wonder how many (normal) children would have given the same reply.

ADULTS: Theme - The Lord's Prayer.
The adults had been learning the Lord's Prayer over a number of weeks. February 8th brought the section dealing with
"**Lead us not into temptation, but deliver us from evil.**"

KIERON'S INSIGHTS:
The illustrations of this were concentrated around 'The Temptations of Jesus' in the wilderness.
The first two temptations had been covered in a simple way and the fact that even though Jesus was tempted, **he resisted by quoting Scripture, because he knew he had a very special job to do for God, in God's way, and the devil was only trying to stop Jesus from doing it.**
When the third temptation was reached, **Tanya asked the question:**
"Why do you think Jesus would not take all the rich things the devil was offering Him?"
Kieron answered:
"Jesus knew that God wanted him to die on the Cross and come to life again so that we could be his friends. He knew that what the devil wanted him to do was wrong, and so he said 'Go away, I will not do what you want me to do. I will not follow you'"

Tanya asked:
"What should we do when we are tempted to do wrong things; to be rude, or unfriendly or unhelpful?"

Kieron answered with great conviction:
"We should say 'Go away' to the devil. I am Jesus' friend and not yours. I will not do what you want'!"
Tanya felt humbled.
Yes indeed, we have been richly blessed.

APRIL WCN 1990 tells that THE MISSIONARY INTEREST GROUP MEETS on the first Sunday morning of each month.
APRIL WCN tells that PATRICIA FERGIE takes up a teaching post in July at Woodstock School, India.

Our services will be video-recorded on Palm Sunday.

GB Display 19 & 20th April.

United Holy Week Services, Monday- Friday at 8.00pm.

BB Display 5 & 6th April.

Many new books in our Lending Library.

Life in Spirit Seminars begin on Tuesday 24th April at 8.00pm and Thursday 26th at 10.30 am.

Dawn Service at Ballywalter.

Open Night, Thursday 19th April.

SUNDAY EVENING PRAYERTIME. Don Ritchie writes:
"You know we began a Prayer Meeting earlier in the year to pray for the evening services. At first just a few, and then more and more people discovered the blessing of praying together for others. The most wonderful things began to happen, we were blessed; and our church services were filled with love, and notable changes happened to our people.

We see answers to prayer again and again in our Healing Service, and I know that every time I attend I am wonderfully blessed."

NEW BOOKS: One new book is:

"AFTER THE WEDDING" - Philip Yancy and his wife belonged to a Young Marrieds' group. This book candidly reveals real people in real situations, giving insight and reassurance.

MAY WCN 1990.
"THE NORTHERN IRELAND SITUATION."
OPTIMIST OR PESSIMIST?

"The Northern Ireland Situation" has been the backdrop against which our "West Church Journey" has been - often violently- lived out, and pain, trauma and despair have often gripped the hearts of our people

Our May WCN editorial asked the question, "Optimist or Pessimist?"

"I was more a listener and observer, than a participant, as I sat at table where two able men fluently discussed the prospects for our Northern Ireland community. Neither of them were committed and active church members, so that dimension did not bear in a personal way on the conclusions to which they came.
One of them would have described himself as an **optimist**, believing that as in Eastern Europe people had become tired of a sterile and

negative philosophy, so also in Northern Ireland many have become tired of negative politics that bring destruction **and are ready to opt for more co-operative ways.**
The other did not share this viewpoint, but rather believed we were locked into a situation **from which we could not easily find a fruitful way out.**

The one hoped that perhaps a new attitude would break open in the hearts of the majority of people - the other felt that the resentments that our history had bequeathed us, **would keep on breeding conflict, discord and violence, and that there was no likely way of breaking the vicious circle of prejudice and hatred.**

….I found myself in a somewhat different position from each of them- I neither believed in the optimism of the optimist, nor in the pessimism of the pessimist!
First, **I felt the optimism that sees a new society emerging because people have become tired of old, sterile, destructive ways, and thus able to embrace more positive attitudes - while having some commonsense validity - to be somewhat fragile.**

Likewise, **as one who sees Christ work radical changes in the hearts and minds of many people -taking hatred and bitterness out of hearts, and giving new hearts that love and bless - I could not believe in the pessimism of the pessimist either.**

I myself would be slow to make any prediction or prophecy as to the changes that may take place in our society in Ireland, north or south, during the next 5, 10, or 20 years.
Nonetheless, as I shared with the optimist, **the Lord is doing wonderful things in many lands. I shared a few examples of what Jesus is doing in the lives of individuals, churches and peoples today!**

AN UNEXPECTED BONUS!
And I was given an unexpected bonus when the optimist told me that he had recently been at a marriage service, where a whole congregation of people had accompanied one of the partners. He spoke of the great joy, love and vibrant worship of this group, and how Jesus was so real and central to them.
Perhaps unknown to himself, this was an undisclosed element behind his optimism!"

MAY WCN gives us lively accounts, both of the BB and GB Annual Displays; and -by a reluctant early-riser for the Dawn Service at Ballywalter!
It invites young men between 13 - 23 years to a wonderful holiday at the "Share Centre", Lisnaskea with the BB, led by Don Ritchie.

And gives a raft of new books added to our Library - and much more besides!

SOMETHING WORTHWHILE
OUTSIDE OF CHURCH ACTIVITIES.
HEATHER EVES WRITES:

"I had been a Christian for a number of years and while I was involved in church life as much as my nursing shifts would allow, I felt I wanted to be doing something worthwhile beyond church activities. Jesus told me I was to be salt in the world, and yet I was hardly exposed to the world.
It was so easy to be in Christian circles in my free time - not intentionally, but that's just the way life was. So it was at this time of wondering what I could do that I read an article in my Church Magazine.
It was about "LIFE - care of the unborn."
A group seeking to provide help for women facing an unplanned/unwanted pregnancy, perhaps thinking about abortion as the solution to their problems.

I contacted the number given and there started my involvement with "Life, N.I."

AND SO HEATHER GOES ON, AT LENGTH, TO SPEAK OF THIS ORGANISATION, AND OF HER INVOLVEMENT WITH IT.

THE STORY OF JAMES - A HOME FOR A PROFOUNDLY HANDICAPPED CHILD.
Told by Doris Galbraith.

"ASKING GOD TO SHOW ME WHERE HE NEEDED ME."

"A few years ago I had reached a stage in my life where my children had become more independent and I was beginning to feel that I needed some way to use whatever talents I possessed. I remember walking the dogs one lovely sunny day and asking God to show me where He needed me that I could help someone. **It was a real cry from the heart as I felt a great longing to serve Him in whatever way he asked.** A short time later I read in West Church News about a family with a little handicapped boy who was embarking on a programme of exercises to help him and they needed volunteers to help. I knew very little about mental handicap and, in fact, like many people I was a bit afraid of it, but something urged me to help.

MY FIRST FALTERING STEPS.
That was to be my first faltering steps into God's plan for me. I lost my fear almost immediately and began to learn a little about handicapped children and to admire the reserves of strength that these parents seemed to have.

AN APPEAL - I NEEDED A

LITTLE PUSH.

My next command came one Sunday morning in church. Margaret Conroy made an appeal for someone to be a 'friend' to a little mentally handicapped boy. I thought about it during the service but dismissed it. However, on my way out, my daughter **Julie volunteered us - a family- to help. God decided that I needed a little push!!**

VISIT TO CARRAIGFOYLE PAEDIATRIC UNIT - AND A VISION OF JESUS.

A few days later I received a phone-call from Margaret McKeown, a Social Worker at Carraigfolyle Paediatric Support Unit asking me to come up, see the Unit and meet some of the children. I was still hesitant but I agreed to go.
Well -words can never describe my feelings when I first entered that place, and was introduced to some children and staff. *I had this instant vision of Jesus sitting in the room with these little ones in his arms surrounded by others reaching up to Him for love.* Suddenly my blinkered eyes could see that this was not a group of mentally handicapped children - this was a room full of little individuals each special and beautiful in their own way.

MARGARET McKEOWN TALKED TO ME ABOUT 'BEFRIENDING'.

Margaret then took me to her office and talked to me about 'befriending'. She showed me videos and talked about how much support the parents need. She asked me if I would like to help with their crèche one afternoon per week, just to learn more about the children. I jumped at the chance and so I continued to go every Tuesday. **In time I met Gary and his family and became their 'befriender'. With the help of my husband Maurice we took Gary out for two hours every week. After a few months I also befriended a little Downs Syndrome Matthew and both friendships brought great** joy and a lot more experience for me. *Let me strongly recommend 'befriending' - the rewards are indeed 3-fold and, even if you can offer only a little time, it is well worth doing. The need in the Bangor area is great.*

I MET JAMES - I KNEW IT WAS DIFFERENT!

During this time I continued to help with the creche and there I met this little boy called James whom we brought down from the Ulster Hospital every Tuesday afternoon. **James has cerebral palsy and is profoundly handicapped. He is unable to walk, talk, sit or even lift his head and he needs help with everything. James is five years old but only weighs about 13 lbs. He has lived in hospital since he was born and when I first worked with him at Carraigfoyle** *I knew he was special.*
Although I loved all the children there, this little one was different - he had never known the constant love of a family and so I felt drawn to him.

APPOINTED TO NIGHT RESPITE UNIT.

Carraigfoyle also has a Night Respite Unit where parents can leave their child with trained staff who will care for them overnight. A job became vacant here and, anxious for more experience, I applied and was appointed. Through this job I encountered many of the difficulties that parents face, e.g. sleep problems, feeding and behaviour problems. Looking back now I see that I was being trained for another job, but at that time I was unaware of that.

I LOVED THIS LITTLE 'BROKEN' BOY DEEPLY.

During all this time there had been vague discussions about trying to get James fostered but nothing ever materialised. Then, one day during our Summer Scheme, it was nearly home time and he had fallen asleep in my arms. I just knew that day that I loved this little 'broken' boy deeply, and that everything must be done to get him discharged from hospital and into my care. **I thought about my family and was really nervous about their reactions. I told our Project Leader May Anderson of my wishes, and so the long hard battle began.**

GOD'S POWER - OBSTACLES FIRMLY REMOVED.

It was during this time that God's power was evident. Obstacles that seemed insurmountable were gently but firmly removed. He used so many people who were all in the right place at exactly the right time. He taught me the long hard lesson of **patience.** He dealt with my fears about the family - they had a long time to get used to the idea and to meet James and to think about how our lives would change. **I will just say here that they have been quite wonderful - supporting me in every way.**

My thanks go to my husband Maurice, daughter Julie and son Chris for all their help. I would also like to thank Tracey and, of course, Mr Bailie for their support through prayer. Thinking back I see that God's way is indeed perfect, for He prepared everyone for the idea - even James' natural mother.

JAMES' NATURAL MOTHER WANTED ME TO FOSTER HIM.

She was re-united with James at Carraigfoyle, saw how he was responding to all the love and attention and she expressed her desire that I should foster him. This helped our position tremendously and Social Services decided to proceed with our assessment. This also involved a time of preparation and attendance at some training nights. We received maximum help and support and have met some wonderful people.

JAMES COMES TO US.

Just before Christmas 1989 James' long-term placement with us began. The first few weeks were pretty harrowing and I was quite nervous and seemed to have no time to do anything except care for James. I was trying too hard to get everything right all by myself, **but now I have learned not to rely on my own strength, for God will provide all my needs.**

James has settled beautifully and on 26th March he started at Clifton Special Care School. This means that I now have some time for myself again - I can now care for James *and* my family *and* still enjoy walking the dogs!

MY HEART OVERFLOWS!

My heart overflows with love and thankfulness for my new task. James has brought a new joy into our home. Psalm 145: 13 "The Lord is faithful in all his promises and loving towards all He has made."

Please pray that James will be spared to enjoy his new life, full of loving care, and if you see us at church come and say "Hello"!

I would like to share this little prayer/poem about James with you:

To: JAMES With: LOVE.

"Gentle James so sweet, so mild
-Lovely, tiny, trusting child,
Beautiful words you long to say,
I know your meaning anyway-
"Love me, cherish me, every day"

Fleeting smiles that come and go;
Quiet stories from you flow,
Eyes that search and plead for love,
"Love is what I have to give
For as long as you shall live."

Music is a joy for you
A language of colours - yellow, red, blue
Special sounds beckoning from on high
Follow them and your soul will fly-
"Love is everywhere hovering nigh."

"Thank You God for the life of this child-
Gentle, gracious, guileless and mild,
Bless him with love and the joy it brings
Surround him with care till his little heart sings,
And the eyes dance with magic as if they had wings."

DORIS GALBRAITH

JUNE WCN 1990.

ANALYSIS OF OUR FINANCES
Shows that we only claim a fraction of what is available to us from Revenue repayments on Covenanted givings, with strong encouragement to our members to use this facility to the full, and so release resources for Kingdom work. We could readily draw upon an additional £14,000!

CALLING THOSE WITH A HEART FOR OUTREACH TO MEET, THINK AND PRAY TOGETHER ON THURSDAY 14TH June.
Here were 'starter' ideas:
Worship/Drama/Witnessing Group that might visit other congregations or go out into the community, a ministry to the unchurched, in the workplace.

Specialist group to witness to and minister to those with special needs, for example alcohol problems.

A different kind of Worship Group might minister to the elderly in our Nursing and Residential Homes.

Survey Groups to visit homes in our area to discover what kind of initiatives and ministries are required to reach to the hearts of our people

Our members may be aware of the gifts that they have, that could be used for service in Jesus' Name - *and so far they have had little opportunity to use them!*

We want to release and encourage initiatives of every kind that the Holy Spirit may be inspiring among our people.

IN THE EVENT, JULY

WCN tells is, we had a 'marvellous response' to the invitation to meet, to share ideas, to wait upon God, to allow the Holy Spirit to 'hatch out' and germinate new ideas in our minds. More than 50 members came. And there were ideas in plenty -some of them [in 2006] waiting full implementation!

An "OPEN DOOR" in our Church Lounge where people could come into a warm, welcoming and friendly environment, to meet or bring friends or neighbours to enjoy a 'cuppa'.
To go through the "Open Door" of entry into our Residential Homes, with pastoral care and worship so that the elderly are not neglected in our midst. And to expand that care to people in their own homes, so that we may bless them - *and their neighbours!*

Further initiatives - beyond what we have in the multifarious youth ministries in West- to the youth constituency in the community, with growing problems of drunkenness and drugs.

Wider use of our WITNESS SHEETS, Audio tapes of Praise Services, a Baby Sitters' Bureau, where old people could render service to the younger, etc, etc.

"MARCH FOR JESUS":
"The bus left Bangor at 8.40 am with just a few and then filled up at Oxford Street with happy people who wanted to witness that Jesus lives in Ireland today.
What a joy to sing his praises most of the way to Dublin, and with 10,000 others walk the main streets

of **DUBLIN** with radiant faces, uplifted voices and dancing feet! Nine folk from West were part of the happy throng, and look forward with many more to taking part in the **BELFAST 'MARCH FOR JESUS' ON 15TH** September, 1990.

June WCN also brought us the news that **ELEANOR RAINEY'S WORK IN** Kenya was coming to an end and that she would return home in July.

It also brought the news that an Irish/Kenyan family would follow in August, Declan and Peres Bowers and their six children aged 3 - 16 years, with Eleanor providing initial residence at her seaside cottage in Donaghadee.

To Eleanor we say: "Well done, good and faithful - *and generous and hospitable*- servant!."

VISIT OF BISHOP PAUL.

Bishop Paul from Gujarat came to take part in the 150th Anniversary Celebrations of our Presbyterian Church in Ireland, whose first act had been to send 2 missionary families to Gujarat. We were delighted to have him in our home and to stay an additional two weeks that allowed him to meet former missionaries to Gujarat, and also to be immersed in West Church life. He attended our Seminars on 'Divine healing' and 'Life in the Spirit', and the Special meeting we had on 15th June, to consider new initiatives for Outreach.

All these things made a deep impact upon him.

He explained to us why Rev. Wilson Baria of Bombay had been unable to come to us, but hoped that another young pastor, the Rev. Hemantkumar might be able to do so."

"PROVE TO ME THAT JESUS EXISTED".....BY ALAN COWIE

"How many times has the above question been asked by those who don't believe, don't want to believe and don't want anyone else to believe. I used to ask it myself!

In my previous life as an agnostic I was quite dismissive of the whole subject of Christianity. My favourite statements on the subject used to be that 'The Bible had been written approximately 2000 years ago by some unknown Greek "hack" trying to earn a crust for himself' and that 'only the front page was missing, the one that said that the characters and events depicted were totally fictitious…'

I had heard these statements bandied about by others, no doubt thought that they sounded "real cool" and parroted them.

So what changed my opinion and how was it proved to me that Jesus Christ had indeed existed? THE EVIDENCE fell into my possession (at a time when I was struggling with belief) IN THE FORM OF A VIDEO, "MESSAGES FROM THE MEMORY BANKS."

The video wasn't dramatic and didn't put forward anything revolutionary, **only well-researched facts,** the basis of which I will now attempt to pass on in the rest of this article, in what I hope is a logical fashion, by first examining the rationale for accepting the documentation available, then looking at the content of the documentation itself..

THE DOCUMENTATION.

It is accepted by historians that the reliability of a historical document depends on two factors, **namely, the number of good copies in existence, and the time gap between the oldest copy and the date of the original.**
Historians believe evidence to be acceptable *if this time gap is in the order of 1000 -1200 years,* hence they have no difficulty in accepting Julius Caesar's accounts of his victories <u>with ten copies</u>, or the works of Plato <u>with only 7 copies.</u> In the period OF THE NEW TESTAMENT, <u>parts of the manuscript date only 60 -70 years after the death of</u> Christ <u>with a full manuscript having 13000 attributable copies within 750 years.</u>

By the standards of the "learned men" of our age, seemingly ample proof.

Indeed Sir Frederick Kenyon, a former director of the British Museum no less, stated:

"No other ancient book has anything like such early and plentiful testimony to its text and no unbiased scholar would deny that the text that has come down to us is substantially sound."

Note: This is but part of the evidence that **Alan Cowie** adduces from "MESSAGES FROM THE MEMORY BANKS" to confirm the reliability of the New Testament, and to provide other material from **The Talmud** and from **The History of the Jewish Nation, by Josephus** a Jewish scholar, to the fact that Jesus was a historical person, who was put to death by the Jews.

Note also how Alan tells that "Messages from the Memory Banks" fell into his possession '*at a time when I was struggling with belief*'.

LET ME PUT IN CONTEXT HOW THIS 'AGNOSTIC' CAME TO BE STRUGGLING WITH BELIEF!

"IS IT ALL RIGHT IF…..?"

As people were being farewelled one Sunday after a morning service, one bright-faced young woman, Pauline Allen asked me "Is it all right if I asked some of my neighbours to come to my home, to sing some of the new songs that we sing at our Praise Services?"

"Of course, Pauline it's all right. That's a great idea! You don't have to ask."

For we had been encouraging our members to be innovative and adventurous in natural and friendly outreach.

So Pauline invited some of her neighbours to her home. One of those invited was ALISON COWIE, wife of Alan Cowie. Now Alison was a totally convinced atheist. She accepted the invitation because she was curious about what made other people 'tick'.

Some years later **ALISON COWIE** was to write one of our West Church WITNESS SHEETS - actually Number 100! Let me quote:

HAPPY AS AN ATHEIST - RELIGION A CRUTCH!

"People here at West are familiar with the 'question and answer routine' that Mr Bailie sometimes uses with a member of the congregation. My husband, Alan, was in this situation a few years back, when Mr Bailie stated, 'You were an agnostic, your wife was an atheist?'. Alan's reply was, 'Yes, I didn't have enough faith to be an atheist!'. In a manner of speaking, Alan was right. You have to know for sure that there is no 'God' out there to be an atheist.

AND THAT WAS ME!

I had a very simple philosophy for living - you are born, you live, then you die. End of life.

Throughout life you have various decisions to make, right from school where you have to choose your 'O' level and 'A' level subjects, University or not, what career, marriage or not, children or not etc, and no matter what happens to you, even the unpleasant things, you had two options left open to you - **to sink or swim, and I was determined to be one of life's swimmers!**

Truthfully, I was very happy as an atheist, I didn't think or feel there could be anything more. I felt that any religion was a crutch, rather the way that alcohol and drugs, prescribed or otherwise can be, though obviously not as sad.

I have always been interested in people's way of life and their beliefs, whatever they are, whether it is a tribe up the Amazon or a 'religious' neighbour. And that's what happened! My daughter started in a playgroup alongside a neighbour's child and we started to become friendly - though a good friend of mind did 'kindly' warn me to watch myself as she thought that this girl was 'good living'. **My immediate response was that it might provide some interesting discussion, for my curiosity was aroused as to what she actually believed and why.** We did graze on the subject a few times and then I was asked to a **Praise Service.** I went, simply because it would have been impolite to say no. **West was different to any of the few churches I had been in - I actually saw happy people.** I went to another Praise Service where one of the announcements was of a new 'Seminar' starting in the New Year. I asked my friend about this, and being curious of course, I decided to go for the first night. **I asked Alan to take me, and knowing that I would not go alone, he agreed to come.** I need to give you a bit of background at this point, for in many ways, my husband's and my own testimony are linked.

ALAN TOOK MUMPS - THEN M.E.

Two years previous to the January when the Seminar started, Alan began a new job with a new employer. That April he took mumps out of which he contracted M.E. At that time, not only was there not much known about M.E., but some doctors were rather sceptical about its existence. Fortunately for Alan, blood tests taken by a specialist in the July showed his blood to be very inflamed -**so he obviously was ill!** At that time, Alan was at his worst - he was confined to his bed, he had to be helped to the bathroom and was having 3 or 4 hot baths every day to help with the pain in his muscles. Certain noises would go through him, one being crying babies, which was unfortunate as our children were approaching one and three years, so with teething problems it was hard for a while. With a lot of rest and a commonsense approach, he very slowly got better, and with pressure from his employers and knowing how much his job was needed, Alan returned to work nine months later, though still far from well.

With his illness **there had come a personality change part of which was that he had no confidence in himself,** and the attitude of his boss, who didn't believe in such an illness, made him worse. Most nights he didn't sleep and we talked, and when he came in from work, if he didn't go to his bed, he rested on the settee. Weekends were also rest times for him - all so he could hold on to his job. **This was the pattern for the following year which takes us up to the January of the Seminar and makes me very appreciative that he came that night.**

GOD.... WOULD 'ZAP' ME!

The first night we went to the Seminar I was so sure that if there was a God he would 'zap' me or do something so that I would know of his existence. He didn't, and being very disappointed as well as feeling that I had been right all along, **I knew I wouldn't be back. But God had other plans.**

On the way out Mr Bailie stood at the door shaking hands. It came our turn and Alan, shaking his hand, told him that he had been ill but tonight he felt really well and looked forward to next week. Well, I looked at Alan and thought he was only being polite. But no, he wasn't. That night Alan prayed for the first time in his life, he read the little Seminar book faithfully every night, he bought a Bible, and went to church the following Sunday. **He hadn't felt as well as this since before he became ill. Meanwhile,**

I felt nothing and only went back the following week because Alan pointed out that he went with me when I asked and obviously wanted me to do likewise.

We both continued with the Seminar, Alan enjoying it, me, having my moments but on the whole, it certainly wasn't the highlight of my week. **On reflection, I can see that I continued to go only because I could see the change that was taking place in Alan. But I wanted FACTUAL as well as PHYSICAL proof. So I looked at the Bible as a purely historical book. With the help of other books, a video, much debate with Alan, I found out what a really *factual* book it is. *I also found that a man named Jesus had lived and had been crucified. BUT WAS HE THE SON OF GOD?*** I looked at the Bible from a science point of view. I found it amazing what men knew then - things that man is only now realising! But how did they know such things? Obviously they did not have the technology then that we have nowadays. Was it possible that there was a God who told them these things?

I NEEDED TO *FEEL* GOD - I CAME TO FEEL THE SHEER MAGNITUDE OF HIS LOVE.

There were now times that I could have been called *agnostic* rather than *atheist*. **But I wanted and needed to feel God - after all, if He exists I should be able to feel him, especially now that I was 'sort of' searching for him!**

At the Seminar we had reached 'The Baptism in the Holy Spirit' week. Alan was now no longer an agnostic. He believed in the Christ who died for his sins. I no longer knew what I believed and for somebody as opinionated as me *that was not a good feeling! I was also worried about going to the Seminar on that night - worried if there was a God that He wouldn't want me after all the times I had denounced Him. I went, deciding that if there was still nothing, I wouldn't be back.*

"MY CHILD!"

At the Seminar we sat on our chairs in a circle, praying. I remember praying, "If you are there, God, let me know, let me feel you." Mr Bailie was singing in tongues. As he sang I had this picture of a man singing to a baby girl in a cradle - his daughter. The style of dress and surroundings were of Biblical times. It stayed, then it changed. Now the baby girl was a young woman and she was sitting in a chair, sewing and singing to her now older father. It was a picture of the special love between a father and his child. Mr Bailie was making his way round each of us to pray with us. He came to me, prayed over me, and then spoke - "My Child!." At that instant *I KNEW - THERE WAS A GOD! He had touched me, and the way that He continued to touch me over the next week is the most beautiful experience of my life. I was very fortunate, for I have always known love, I came from a loving and affectionate home. I married a very loving and caring man, and everyone knows the total love that small children have for their parents, AND YET, I KNEW THAT IF ALL THAT LOVE WAS PUT TOGETHER, IT WAS NOWHERE NEAR THE SAME MAGNITUDE OF THE LOVE THAT GOD WAS NOW POURING INTO ME, BUT ALSO SURROUNDING ME WITH.*

It was like I was surrounded by a force field of pure love. God's love wasn't only in me, it was in front of me, behind me, and at both sides of me. I actually felt that I couldn't possibly physically bump into anything because it moved with me. God was letting me know, not only that He existed, *but how much He loved me!*

I feel very blessed for the way He chose to do it, but I'm also aware of how blessed are the people whose love for God is so strong and faith so powerful that they do not have to physically feel Him.

ALAN HAS CONSTANTLY GROWN IN HIS CHRISTIAN LIFE .... I ASKED GOD TO SHOW ME WHAT WAS HOLDING ME BACK.

Since becoming a Christian, Alan has constantly grown in his Christian life. However, the same could not be said for me. My problem was, yes, I knew God existed, I had been baptised in the Holy Spirit, **but I was still very much in the driving seat.** I had spent so many years running and controlling my own life that I found it hard to give over or to share any of my problems with God. So God's will did not come anywhere into my life - it was still my will at times which I tried to force upon God. Yet for a few years I was happy standing still and was unconcerned at the spiritual growth that was taking place in Alan's life. Eventually, as I didn't grow, for how could I have, I went through a very bad time spiritually. **I got as far away from God as it is possible for a Christian to be, but when you have felt God in your life you will always want him there.**

So, through listening to someone sharing, I started to pray differently for I knew that God was still there, that it was I that had moved away. **I asked God to show me what was holding me back as a Christian, what were the sins and hurts that still troubled me and to get to the root of the problems. It really is wonderful the way God answers prayers.** Through and during prayer, God showed me that whilst he had forgiven me for a sin in my past, I had not forgiven myself. I was still carrying round the guilt which I had to hand over to Him. He showed me that something I joked about was something that I actually felt a lot of guilt about, and when this hurt was handed over to God, I really felt for the first time this 'freedom' that Christians talk about. *It really is such a feeling of release.*

God wants me to be obedient, which I'm trying to be, *and then*

God told me of a very deep hurt, which over the past twenty years has stopped me from growing as a person, let alone as a Christian. He took that pain from me and such a burden has been lifted from me. I had known that God would forgive me all my sins when I truly repented, but I had never, as the song says, given Him 'all my years of pain'.

I thank God that He is in my life, for the amazing love He has for me, as He has for each one of us, *and for the enrichment He has brought to this atheist's life.*

AN AGNOSTIC FINDS FAITH - THROUGH A REVELATION GIVEN BY JESUS.
ALAN COWIE'S STORY.

"As I write, it is just over one year since the 24th January 1990, the date that I first set foot in West Church. It is from this date that I count the length of my new life. I didn't come to the 'Life in the Spirit Seminar' that started that evening in search of God or Jesus. I was (I thought) quite happy being an agnostic.
I came only because my wife, Alison, wanted to come but was too shy to go by herself. My words to her were 'I'll come along with you for the first night until you get to know some of the people there'.
God, however, had other plans!

I FELT REALLY ALIVE … A HEAVY WEIGHT HAD BEEN LIFTED.

I don't really remember very much about the first night of the Seminar itself, rather, it was the way I felt going home that sticks in my mind. *I felt really alive and well and about ten feet tall. I felt as if I was walking on air, and as if a heavy weight had been lifted off my chest. I know now that it was because I had experienced my first 'touch' of the Holy Spirit.* I had a pretty good idea even then that it was something to do with the Seminar.

This feeling of well-being was all the more remarkable in my eyes as I had for the previous year been fighting off the after-effects of M.E., a terribly debilitating illness which had kept me off work for nine months, and which continued to hang on, dragging me down with excessive tiredness, depressing me and affecting my ability and confidence at work, depriving me of my powers of concentration and the dogged tenacity that had typified my career to that time. Added to these problems were the 'personality' problems that I and those I was working with were having with our senior officer (she was, I think, a graduate of the Attilla the Hun School of Man Management). As you can guess, I wasn't exactly feeling at my brightest up to that point.

FOR THE FIRST TIME IN MY ADULT LIFE I PRAYED.

When we got home that night I said to Alison 'I've got to get back to see if I can get this feeling again'. That night for the first time in my adult life, I prayed. I prayed to God, not to Jesus. I didn't at that time believe that Jesus ever existed, let alone accept that he was the Son of God."

EDITOR'S NOTE. How Alan's convictions were changed has already been told, a few pages back in his article "Prove to me that Jesus existed."

There Alan concluded: "I was forced to accept that it was indisputable that Jesus Christ had existed as a man and had indeed been crucified. What the video of course couldn't do was to prove that he was the Son of God. Still I had two parts of the jigsaw with only the third and most important part missing.
Alan continues:

'I continued to pray. I continued to attend the Seminar (where I will be the first to admit no pressure was put on me. I was gently taught and had my questions answered objectively, without being made to feel that I was being foolish).
I started reading the Bible (I had to buy one!) This in itself caused some amusement when I related how I had gone into the Bethel bookshop and asked for a 'Good News Bible', only to be told rather pointedly that 'We don't do that here'.

A REVELATION - I KNEW INSTANTLY IT WAS JESUS.

One night, about four or five weeks into the Seminar I was praying (downstairs, in the dark, practically hiding. I didn't even have the confidence to pray in front of my wife at that time) when I saw a picture of green hills and a blue sky.
In front of my eyes the picture started to come apart, as if slivers were being stripped off it, until, eventually, I was left looking at a simple shaped brown hill, against a bright red sky. On the hill were three crosses and around the base of the hill were people.
Suddenly, I 'zoomed in' to one of the figures on the cross. I knew instantly it was Jesus and that I was looking into his eyes.
It was only some weeks later when I recounted my experience to the Rev. Bailie that I realised that Jesus turned his head to look at me. The figure on the cross was not that of the usual representation of Jesus, with a long, sad face and beard. Instead I was looking at an ordinary looking Jewish man with no obvious facial hair. (I later found out that prior to crucifixion it was normal to pull a man's beard out).
It was the eyes, however, that drew and held me. The eyes contained so much pain and hurt, and said to me 'How can you doubt that I am doing this for you?'
I was startled.

The power of what I had seen shook me so much that the picture disappeared.
I continued to kneel for a while wondering if I was going mad.
I ran upstairs and woke Alison and told her what had happened. She didn't think I had 'cracked' but suggested that I spoke to Mr Bailie about it.
As usual, with my wife's good advice, it took me some time to get around to it.
When I did, however, he didn't think me mad either. In fact he used a word I had never thought of, *'a revelation'*.

THE POWER OF WHAT I SAW HAS STAYED WITH ME.

The power of what I saw has stayed with me. The picture itself is more elusive. I cannot call up the picture as I want, but it has occasionally re-occurred to me in flashes, usually when I'm under some pressure. It has an instant calming effect, for I know then that I am not alone, that Jesus is always by my side, and that when times are tough I can lean upon his shoulder.
Jesus has become the cornerstone of my life and the Rock on which I stand. His love for me is so strong that He suffered pain beyond belief to pay for my sins. In return all He asks is that I believe.
I DO BELIEVE!

AUGUST WCN 1990.

PATRICIA FERGIE GOES TO INDIA. The needed residence visa appears to be on its way, and Woodstock School Mussoorie would like her to be there by mid-August! Patricia will be taking up a 3-year post, and we feel that she has the warm Christian qualities to make a vital contribution in a key missionary institution. We plan to have a Commissioning service for her on Sunday morning 5th August, with a supper and reception at the conclusion of the Praise Service on the Sunday evening.

OTHERS WORKING OVERSEAS: Paddy Brow is working with TEAR Fund building a Children's Home for street children in Sao Paulo, Brazil; Chris Ritchie is in the USA working with emotionally handicapped children with the YM; Barry McCroskery is in France with OM and Stephen McWatters with YFC; and many of our young people will be involved in our own SUMMER SCHEME here in West, 13-17th August.

FESTIVAL OF HARVEST CELEBRATION - **VENTURE INTO DONEGAL.**
In May of this year your minister spoke to the elders of Donegal Presbytery on the subject of RENEWAL.
From this has come an invitation from the minister of Donoughmore and Stranorlar, and their Kirk Session to lead a Festival of Harvest Celebration from Sunday 7th to Sunday 14th October.
The idea is that at the Sunday services, and each evening from Monday to Friday we have special services, hosted during the week by various groups from within our congregation, women's, men's youth groups etc, and that we would have major input from Worship, Drama and Witness groups from within West.
"So undergird this outreach, and the Rev. Elinor Henning and her elders, with prayer, that in everything we may be led by the Holy Spirit."

GRAHAM DORE has now been formally appointed to Wycliffe Bible Translators which is a great honour.
However this appointment carries no salary. Those appointed must find Christian churches and friends to support them. That is why; in this issue of WCN we enclose an envelope to facilitate their support.

900 million people can't read the Bible because it hasn't been translated for them. How can they be saved if they haven't heard properly?

Last year eleven more New Testament translations were completed, so millions more people have the opportunity to receive God's Word into their hearts.

Amazingly, God is opening doors into hitherto 'closed' countries of Mongolia, USSR, China and Iran.
IN AUGUST WCN 1990, INGEBORG JAMESON BEARS WITNESS:

"I SUFFERED FROM MIGRAINE ATTACKS FOR 30 YEARS."

GOD'S GREAT MERCY IN HEALING AILING BODIES.

"Today I join my brothers and sisters who have written about God's great mercy to them in healing their ailing bodies. I suffered from migraine attacks for over 30 years, sometimes having only one or two days of rest before a new attack would start.
Working in a hospital, I had doctors and medical care right when I needed it, but without any relief from the pain. I either reacted to the medicine with an allergy to it, so that taking that particular drug was forbidden, or it would show no relief whatsoever, having tried whatever drug was available without success. **I had to face each attack for the last eight years, just living through it.**

ANYTHING… WOULD END IN A MIGRAINE ATTACK.
Anything out of the normal daily routine, a busy day at work, a shopping trip, a visit from my children or grandchildren, a leisurely day at the swimming pool, a walk in the country, just anything

I was looking forward to, would end in a migraine attack, as well as eating cheese, drinking coffee or tea.

TRIP TO NORTHERN IRELAND.
The day came when I had to join my husband on his trip to Northern Ireland to talk to our solicitor, and by the time we set out on the journey I was well on the way to living through another attack. We stayed with friends, and when, the following evening this important meeting was over, **I gladly gave in to my husband's and friend's advice, to just lie down and forget the world around me.**

NO EARTHLY REMEDY … ONLY GOD'S HEALING POWER.

Little did I know that while I was dozing the hours away, Rosalind, our friend, and Brian, my husband were talking about my condition **and my husband was telling Rosalind he firmly believed that no earthly remedy could help me, only God's healing power. This jolted Rosalind's mind: years ago somebody had been healed like this.** *The next four hours Rosalind spent on the telephone talking to friends from past teaching days to get the name and phone number of the one man she knew had been used by God for a healing ministry.* Eventually she spoke to him, but he was miles away from where we stayed, and it was impossible for us to see him, but he passed Rev. D.G. Bailie's 'phone number to her, saying he probably would help us.

At breakfast next morning, feeling a little better, Rosalind asked me (both had said nothing of the activity the night before), **what did I think about the healing ministry? It took my breath away, for I had known for quite some time that this was the only way to be healed from those horrible attacks, but did not think Rosalind would be the link.**

But that is how God works!

BETWEEN WEDDING CEREMONY AND RECEPTION.
Although the Rev. D.G. Bailie was fully booked up that Saturday morning, he agreed to see me between a Wedding Ceremony and the Reception.
Rosalind, Brian and I set off to be in plenty of time at West Church. We even found baby-sitters at the last minute for Rosalind's three children so that we all could go into church.

"IT'S JESUS."
Rev. D.G. Bailie asked us into a room, and, after introducing each other, we sat down and he asked me about the attacks: How long I had them, how did it start, did I know the reason why etc??? **"You know it's not me who heals you. It's Jesus"**, and with these words he came over to my chair to pray with me.

"I KNEW JESUS WAS THERE."
The Rev. D.G. Bailie put his hands on my back and on my head (I remember thinking that is exactly the spot in my back where it so often hurts as well). And while he was praying softly in his own words, and then in tongues, I knew Jesus was there. Jesus was healing me. Warmth and peace flowed through me from head to toe; a joy to praise God, thank Jesus and his Holy Spirit, started to well up inside me which broke out in the afternoon when everybody had left to go to the Park and I was alone in the house, singing to God in adoration for his great mercy.

I knew I was healed. **Today well over a year has passed and I have not had another attack.**

"Thank You my heavenly Father for setting me free, through your Son Jesus Christ and your Holy Spirit -Three in One -Almighty God, our Loving Father."

Ingeborg Jameson,
Glasgow June 20th, 1990.

"LIFE IN THE SPIRIT."
In every such Seminar, eminent and releasing works of grace were done in many lives, bringing joy, freedom and solid peace.
COLIN GILLESPIE expresses his experience in a little poem:

"I searched for a sign in the stones on the beach,
If I found the *right shell* I'd know!
**How foolish to think that a stone or a shell
Could ever affect your life's flow!**

Your love's like the ocean that covers the earth,
But it won't ebb and flow like the tide;
**It's shown by the print of the nails in your hands
And the hole of the spear in your side!**

You poured out your life's blood to ransom my soul,
You wiped out my sin with your pain,
And *I* looked for a sign in material things -
Through faith I won't need to again!"

SEPTEMBER WCN 1990.

PRAYER MOUNTAIN.

OUR HEALING SERVICE IN WEST - over a period of years, *every Sunday Night without fail, we gathered in the Praise Room after the evening service, usually for a period of up to two hours* to pray for the sick, and for people with problems and needs of whatever kind. Folk came to realise that there would be people there to minister in an unhurried manner, and that they would be greeted with tenderness and faith in Jesus' Name.

At this time, in 1990, we were also seeking to build up a regular two-hour Prayer time on Friday nights, and to get our people, in rota fashion, to make this our "PRAYER MOUNTAIN." What, you may well ask, is the significance of that phrase? "PRAYER MOUNTAINS" is the title of a book written by Colin Whittaker which we placed in our Lending Library to quicken a vision for sustained prayer in our own congregation in West.

In the early Seventies, Yoida Full Gospel Church in Seoul, Korea, now with a membership of 600,000, purchased a section of mountain for a cemetery. The church's pastor was Yonggi Cho. His mother-in-law Jashil Choi was a remarkable woman of prayer, and God gave her a vision for the purchased mountain to be, not just a cemetery, but a place set aside to pray to God.

PRAYING THERE IN A TENT.
For three years Jashil Choi prayed there every night in a tent until the first Prayer Buildings were erected. So, from a simple beginning **with one woman praying,** this has become a place **where there are prayer meetings every day of the year, with great numbers of people who have come with one purpose - to pray.**

Furthermore the prayer is constant not casual. You can guarantee you will find there between 2000 and 3000 people praying.
In addition a large percentage of them will be fasting. At weekends numbers regularly swell to more than 10,000, and on special occasions crowds of around 20,000 throng the site.
Yonggi Cho is a convinced believer in the power of organised prayer by great numbers. You cannot be in his presence very long before you will hear him declare with great conviction. *'If you don't involve your churches in mass prayer, you will never see revival. Prayer is the key to revival and church growth. You can have all kinds of gimmickry, but none of it will work if you do not pay the price. You must have massive organised prayer in your churches if you are to experience the miracle of church growth'.*

COLIN WHITTAKER writes: "If you want to see massive organised prayer being practised, then International Prayer Mountain is the place to visit.
At the same time it must be stressed that the praying there is additional to the Full Gospel Church's regular intensive prayer programme at Yoido. That consists of all-night prayer meetings every night of the week, with at least 2000 people each evening, and at the big one on Friday night **they regularly exceed the 25,000 attendance figure. Furthermore, prayer is an integral and main part of the more than 50,000 house groups which meet every week.
There is a regular full-time staff of ministers and helpers who man Prayer Mountain around the clock and throughout the whole year. They have no problem in understanding Paul's exhortation to 'pray without ceasing'. Their biggest problem is stopping people once they have started praying, whereas ours is getting people to start.**

PRAYER WITH FASTING.
"JASHIL Choi does not mince matters when preaching on the subject of fasting.
She will tell you that if you fast for just one day and spend lots of time 'eating' or 'devouring' or 'feeding' upon the Word of God as well as praying, then you are giving your stomach a vacation, and the heart and liver and other organs also benefit. Your thinking becomes clear and your heart is filled with forgiveness. However she believes that if you fast for two or three days there is no one you can hate but if you fast for 30 days (as she has done a number of times) then you take pity on others who are sick. Furthermore you are rejuvenated and filled with joy. **She was seventy-three years of age when she told me this and she said that she had been examined by her doctor who told her that she had the body of a 40-year old. When I met her she had preached every day for 130 days. The previous day she had been to a small village in the country and had preached for four hours!**

There are many thousands of authenticated testimonies of miracles of healings of all kinds that have occurred at Prayer Mountain.
'A Christian lady had suffered for 28 years with a disease that was gradually paralysing her. She had medical treatment, including acupuncture for three months, without any improvement. Her family wanted her to go to hospital but instead she chose to go to Prayer Mountain to pray and fast for ten days. She was completely healed. When her backslidden daughter (who had married an unbeliever) saw what God had done for her, they both yielded their lives to Christ. It was not long before her son-in-law went to Bible College and became a pastor.'

**LESSONS FOR US TO LEARN ... THINGS TO DO.
There are great lessons for us to learn from all of this:**

The great value of unhurried, extensive, focussed praying!

The importance of organised praying, with large numbers taking part.

The need to have such prayer times with an agenda and well-led.

The new dimension that fasting can give.

The hope that our FRIDAY NIGHT PRAYER TIMES may grow into something robust and fruitful.

The awareness of things that seem to happen almost spontaneously in the context of Spirit-filled prayer, like the experiences of Alan and Alison Cowie, or the healing of Ingeborg Jameson.

SEPTMEBER WCN 1990: Alvin Little tells of JOY and LIFE among our Young People, released during the Summer Scheme.

In the mornings West Church was overrun with **secret agents** who investigated Jesus, worshipped Jesus and got involved in all kinds of outdoor and indoor activities.
It was marvellous to see more than 120 children (7 - 11 years) so full of life and joy.

In the evening we had a scheme for teenagers. We took our lives in our hands and tackled an Assault course at Palace Barracks. Every night a fella called **Terry Laverty** challenged us with a brilliant talk about Jesus.
We must have had about 40 young people helping in the Scheme this year.

For the first time ever **we ran a Junior Life in the Spirit for 9 -11 year olds**, from the Summer Scheme, who wished to go and learn what it really means to follow Jesus, and how the Holy Spirit helps us day by day. There was a lovely gentle working of God's Spirit in the little group that met each morning.

A TEENS & TWENTIES SEMINAR HAS HAD A BRILLIANT RESPONSE with around 38-40 young people getting together.

Thrills & Spills are offered to our young people by everybody these days.
J oy & Life are things that only Jesus can give **and these he gives generously.**

OCTOBER WCN 1990.

DON & HELEN RITCHIE
INVITED TO STAY ON IN OUR WEST CHURCH TEAM.

It does not seem like a year since our Kirk Session invited Don Ritchie to work with us on a full-time basis for one year with Helen helping on a part-time basis. This was funded for one year from our Outreach Fund.
Since then Kirk Session has been aware of valuable work done by the Ritchies. Recently two Men's Weekends have been up building and fruitful for all concerned. Over the year we have seen relationships develop in a frank and caring fashion with the young folk who come around our premises on a Tuesday evening. The young people recognise the warmth and integrity of our leaders and many have come to the point where they are ready to listen to authentic Christian testimony. For example, last night (2/10/90), while the 'Praise & Prayer' meeting was going on in the New Hall, about 20 of these young people were listening to Christian testimony in the Praise Room. That, one feels, is something that wouldn't easily have happened a year ago. If we support this with our love and .prayers a harvest will be reaped Helen has been involved with the Young People's Seminars and Drama Groups.

So the Ritchies have been invited to continue to serve with us. The Church Committee feel that it is now appropriate to fund this from our Development Fund.

PATRICIA FERGIE
WRITES FROM WOODSTOCK SCHOOL, INDIA.

"Thank you for all the support and encouragement you gave me as I was preparing to come here….Dr. Barton met me in Delhi and eventually we made it up through the clouds to Woodstock School, having been delayed for 9 hours until a landslide on the road had been cleared.
I arrived on Tuesday Night straight into an Orientation Session - it was all a bit of a blur, many names, faces, and the rolling of lumps of dough to make chapattis. I started teaching on Thursday, and I thought **'Lord I'm really in at the deep end here!'** - A week to organise my class, to do a one hour presentation on Japan - **I've just left Ireland, arrived in India, to think about Japan!**
Then I read in Isaiah 51: 5 'on my arm they will trust'.

I'm teaching a Grade 4 class. There are 22 children from many nationalities, 14 of them are boarders. I'm enjoying the class and they had all made me welcome cards. One read: 'Welcome to Grade 4 - we were waiting for you and *at last* you have come. I am the only person in my class who wears glasses'.
Patricia concludes: 'I feel God has given me a real sense of responsibility for the children, not only to teach them, but really to love them, and to seek to share with them a living God! I pray for wisdom as I seek to do this.'

RESIDENTIAL HOMES
FOR THE ELDERLY.
October WCN reports the opening of 'Crestacare' on the Crawfordsburn Road with West Church plans to hold services there.
It also reports that BETTY JACKSON, and Hugh and Margaret Fergie have already begun to hold services at The Richmond Home, where Mrs Sharon Bryans is Matron.
MARCH FOR JESUS.
October WCN quotes from "The Irish News" which relates how the Belfast 'MARCH FOR JESUS' brought the city to a standstill as 'ten thousand people sang and danced their way through the city on Saturday. These marchers weren't likely to go on the rampage, looting shops and smashing up cars. Instead they shouted **'Hallelujah'** and **'Praise the Lord'.**
'Jesus is Peace, Love, Light, Alive' their banners proclaimed.
Led by twenty Christian Rock and folk bands the parade set off from Botanic Gardens, winding its way

along the Lagan embankment and down the nationalist lower Ormeau Road, drawing scores of people on to the streets to watch.

'It's **a welcome change to see something like this,**' said Patricia Breen of Dromara Street. 'We are usually barricaded in by the police when the Orangemen are marching. It's a pity the Orangemen couldn't behave like this on the Twelfth.' **Taking the organiser's advice to dress colourfully was Don Ritchie the lead vocalist on float 7 from West Church, Bangor, rigged out in yellow and blue Bermuda shorts and a crocodile hat. Flanked by 3 backing singers he shook, rattled and rolled in a spirited routine that would have left even Diana Ross and the Supremes green with envy.**

Outside the City Hall, singer-songwriter GRAHAM KENDRICK set hands clapping and feet tapping to his repertoire of heavenly music.

NOVEMBER WCN 1990

OUR DONEGAL MISSION
"THE 70 RETURNED WITH JOY."

It wasn't exactly Seventy that went to Donegal - in fact, over the nine days involved, the number was in excess of one hundred! But each evening, as groups returned home to Bangor after the long trip and in 'the wee hours', there was little doubt that the dominant emotion was one of joy, a sense of deep fulfilment and exhilaration.

A COMPLETE TRANSFORMATION IN ALT!
On the two Sunday mornings we led the services in **Alt, Stranorlar and Donoughmore.**
ALT is an altogether beautiful little church with just about 30 families. A year ago the church building was dark, dirty and decrepit. **In September it was reopened, completely renewed and refurbished in the most tasteful manner. This had been accomplished almost completely through the voluntary labour of the members,** *two of whom gave 12-14 hours a day over a period of 8 months. There was great pride in this little community over what they had accomplished.* **We sensed this in the church services, and also when, as a congregation, they invited the West Church team for lunch on the Wednesday.** We encouraged them to believe that God was wanting to work *a similar transformation on the 'Body of Christ'* in Alt and we believe that some were quickened by a new vision and experienced the touch of the Lord in healing and blessing.

STRANORLAR.
The second congregation was the town church of Stranorlar which has quite a lot of its members living in the surrounding countryside. Here our second service on the final Sunday evening was held. **I think it is no exaggeration to say that a deep impact was made upon the lives of quite a number of people there and that we left a congregation quietly buzzing with new heart and hope.**

DONOUGHMORE OUR HOST BASE.
Donoughmore was our host base for our services during the week. It is a congregation drawn from a prosperous farming **area** and we received warm hospitality in many homes.
We don't believe in counting our chickens before they are hatched **but we believe overall, that a quite powerful witness to God's call and grace was made throughout the week and many became aware of the presence and mighty working of God.**
We had a sense that the Word was shared, crisply and convincingly, so that the message was clear and challenging, that the quality of the worship and the songs had a compelling Spirit-filled quality, and that the testimonies made by so many of our members, declared, movingly, tenderly, powerfully, that a God of grace, can, by his Spirit, bring life and hope to one and all!

THINGS WE CAN LEARN!
No doubt there are things we can learn from this our first major outreach as a congregation. Overall we feel it was great and we thank God for those who invited and received us, and we give glory to God.

SOME OF THE LESSONS *WE* MAY BE LEARNING FROM OUR EXPEDITION TO DONEGAL.

THE FRESHNESS OF DOING SOMETHING NEW.
There is always that special excitement in doing something for the first time! There's the *newness*, going somewhere unknown, the sense of adventure. However behind that lie deeper and more lasting emotions, the sense of joy in bearing honest witness to the Lord, and **the camaraderie** of doing so in company with others. Many of our members got to know and appreciate one another more deeply as they travelled up and down from Donegal. **Some were even introduced to one another there! In the Donoughmore Manse, on the first Sunday afternoon, as the house bulged with West Church members, Jayne Ferguson introduced herself to a couple she did not know, to the utter astonishment of the minister, the Rev. Elinor Henning, who at first thought she was making fun!** In a smaller, country congregation, where everyone knows everyone (at least on a certain level), it was almost inconceivable that people should travel up on a team from West and *not* know all the others! However, even people who did know one another (like members of the Singing Group who meet for practice every week) found out a lot more about one another, where they worked, what they did, etc, etc - and that was good!

WHEN *STRETCHED* WE DISCOVER NEW RESOURCES.

We found that it was good for us to be stretched as a congregation. For example, **with the necessity of leading the praise each evening, we asked Pamela Dobbin to help,** *and she trained two different Singing Groups, for the Monday and Wednesday evenings,* who led the worship in a lovely manner. *When the bulk of our Praise Team was away in Donegal we discovered that we still had the resources back home to continue with a YOUTH PRAISE SERVICE in a refreshing and exciting manner.*

ALL THIS HELPS US TO BECOME AWARE OF THE GIFTS AND RESOURCES WE HAVE IN OUR MIDST AND THE IMPORTANCE TO HARNESS THEM FULLY IN THE WORK OF THE KINGDOM.

A WORD FROM THE LORD!
During our week in Donegal one of our members received 'a word from the Lord' fairly early in the week. It was to the effect that in weakness the Lord would make us strong; that while there was not yet an appetite for the message we were speaking, *that appetite would grow* if we made our witness with honesty; and that, by the end of the week the hunger would be there with opportunities for healing and ministry.
That's exactly how it turned out to be!

HOW MAY WE APPLY THIS KNOWLEDGE AT HOME?
In Donegal we were able to see a hunger for God emerge and grow! A truth to be applied back home?! How, here, can we bring those with little spiritual appetite to a place where they are awakened? In Donegal we saw the effect of honest testimony and of our Witness Sheets- **they had great power to convince!**

LOVE REVEALS JESUS!
People in Donegal sometimes expressed their awareness of the love that seemed to exist among our members, with openness and sincerity. Of course Jesus had promised **"by this shall all men know you are my disciples, if you have love for one another.**

WE PRAYED FOR DONEGAL.
We did a lot of praying before we went to Donegal especially at our Friday Late Night Prayer Times. That was a key to the measure of success and fruitfulness that we witnessed.
That's a lesson for us to take to heart in our endeavours at home. Elders and Church Visitors, week by week, are offered the special opportunity to pray for their districts, and this opportunity should be fully grasped.

NOT JUST ONE EVANGELIST -MANY INVOLVED.
In Donegal, not just one minister or evangelist, but *many* people were involved.
As well, in the ministry of song and music, we had the traditional and the new. There were familiar hymns and songs; there were newer devotional songs, and 'meaty' new songs like those of Graham Kendrick.
And how much we were indebted throughout to our own organist, **MAURICE McKENZIE**, for his presence, zeal and constant helpfulness.

On the Friday Night when our Youth Team was present, with the Donegal Presbytery Youth Choir, we saw the importance also of drama, and how it can be potent in the proclamation of the Gospel
Like Paul, it must be our desire *by all means to save some! Back at home in Bangor West or wherever God chooses to send us!*

PATRICIA FERGIE- SNIPPETS FROM WOODSTOCK!
"Yesterday we (Ruby Gamble and Patricia) walked to the bazaar and back. It took us about four hours: up hill/ down hill… and I thought it was a hill up past Glenview Manor!"
"The wee class is fine. There are 22 children from about 10 different nationalities. They're very good - no discipline problems, no raising of voice - quite a novelty!"
"I've started going to Indian cookery classes, which is fun. My nose runs every week with the effect of all the spices. I feel my tongue will burst into flames."
"I killed a scorpion last night; I'm nearly scared to open cupboard doors wondering what will leap out!"
"Outside there are monkeys… swinging and leaping about. And the noise they make fighting and pulling each other"!
"I've had a few wee cards from West Church Really it is a great comfort and encouragement to know I'm being remembered in your prayers. I just couldn't have coped in my own strength, but when we cast our burden on the Lord He does indeed sustain us."

ASIA MISSIONS CONGRESS 90.
This was held in Choog Hyun Presbyterian Church, Korea in August 1990, and attended by 2000 Asian Christian leaders. It told of growing churches and gave Mission strategies for world Evangelism.

"On December 2, 1945, a group of 27 Christian refugees from Communist persecution in North Korea got together for prayer and worship. Now, 45 years later, the Lord has blessed the church to **have five worship services each Sunday. They have 860 church school teachers and about 6000 students. Missionary work is one of the essential qualities of the church. They send out missionaries to ten overseas nations. These Korean Christians attempt a daily practical living for the Lord.
They express caring love for others through their Widows'**

Home, Babies' School, Orphanage, Deaf-and-Dumb church and Prayer Retreat Centre.

The Choon Hyun Presbyterian Church, where the Asia Missions Conference was held, is a church of dynamic outreach. With only 18 members in 1953, this church has now more than 25,000 members distributed in 14 districts throughout Seoul

AND ALL OF THIS UNDERGIRDED BY AMAZING, EXTENSIVE, INTENSIVE PRAYER!

NOVEMBER WCN 1990 tells how our Senior Sunday School supports EMILIO an 8-year old boy in Guatemala, through TEAR Fund; how West members can provide goods and help to PRISON FELLOWSHIP'S Christmas benevolence; a letter from a believer in repressive Communist Albania who is refreshed and sustained through listening to Christian broadcasts; Pamela Brow's account of the LADIES' WEEKEND in Ballycastle; news of BB and GB Enrolment services, and much else besides!

DECEMBER WCN 1990.

As usual our front page news in the December edition relates to PCI's World Development Appeal. This year it is for a LITERACY PROGRAMME FOR WOMEN IN PERU- OUR AIM IS TO SEND £4500.

Perhaps an endeavour to increase the level of literacy may seem **less glamorous and appealing than an urgent call to save children from starvation or immunise them against killer diseases.**
Yet for many communities a higher level of literacy can, in the long run, save from sickness and poverty, and promote health and prosperity.

A PICTURE OF LITERACY IN A BANGALADESHI VILLAGE.

"A Bangladeshi village is already shrouded in darkness by 6.30 in the evening. Tiny flickering lamps silhouette the pattern of the wattle walls of the villagers' huts. **From one hut shines the brighter light of a hurricane lamp. Inside twenty people are crowded around the lamp, each with a slate and a chalk and a small book called 'The Shining Path' open in front of them.** One of the literacy classes is in progress. Within nine months most of the students will have learned enough to read a popular newspaper. In Bangladesh only one person in twenty is able to do this.

Many of the literacy groups stay together and develop into credit unions and co-operatives.
Women's groups are particularly interested in developing small businesses. **Through the classes vulnerable people are gaining confidence and taking control of their lives.** *In one area, a large group of disinherited farmers have even been able to repossess their land.*

PEOPLE ALSO ABLE TO READ THE WORD OF GOD.

In our services of LESSONS & CAROLS at Christmas, the last lesson read is traditionally from John's Gospel, where we read that the WORD, through whom everything came into being, BECAME FLESH AND DWELT AMONG US FULL OF GRACE AND TRUTH.
Peter, James and John, and everyone else, were able to see clearly, in Jesus, an exact image of the Father.
And the supreme benefit of being able to read is to gain an exact picture of the Eternal God that is not blurred and distorted. People are able to have a full picture of Jesus, to hear the exact words He spoke and read of the wonderful things He did. This brings freedom and this brings life.

OUR CHRISTMAS GIFTS will promote literacy projects in Peru, to raise women - and the whole society- to a new dignity and fruitfulness.

And of course, we still have Graham Dore, now of Wycliffe Bible Translators, to remind us how disadvantaged people are when they do not have the opportunity to read, or to read the Word of God, in their own language.

YOUTH CLUB 'MANIA' STRIKES WEST CHURCH.

Yes, each Saturday night the doors of the church are opened to admit 130 eager and often boisterous members (aged 10+) to play football, hockey, badminton, snooker, pool, watch a video, talk, dance or listen to music for three hours.

DO YOUR CHILDREN COME TO THE YOUTH CLUB ON A SATURDAY NIGHT?
Why do you let them come? Presumably because you feel they are safe, supervised and happy in the Youth Club environment, **and are removed from the evils of drugs, magic mushrooms and under-age drinking which unfortunately are so prevalent in our society today.**
As far as I know West Church Youth Club is one of the few facilities available to the youth of Bangor on a Saturday night where the evils of under-age drinking and drugs are not on the agenda. Accordingly we have members joining from all arts and parts of Bangor.
SO WHAT'S THE PROBLEM?
Quite simply, given our catchment area we attract members who have been subject to the influences already mentioned (particularly alcohol). They have, and still do on occasions, turn up having consumed alcohol and disrupt normal activities. Thankfully they

are a minority. However the disruption caused can be considerable.

As a result we now operate a policy of no admittance to the club when alcohol has been consumed. Additionally, the doors are locked from 7.30 until closing time and no member (once admitted) is permitted to leave without a verifiable reason or unless collected by a responsible adult.

The need for discipline in the form of simple rules, has created certain tensions within the Club, and, more worryingly, outside the Club (when admission is refused) to the extent that the current leadership is severely stretched in not only supervising the various activities inside the club, but at the same time keeping an eye for trouble outside the Club.

ASK YOURSELF THE FOLLOWING QUESTIONS?

Do you fully support and recognise the work of the Youth Club?

Have you recently demonstrated your support in any shape or form?

Are you as a parent sure your child attends the Youth Club after leaving home and is not down the Glen drinking?

Do you spend your Saturday night productively?

A negative answer to any of these questions should give you cause for concern and may suggest that you should join the dedicated team who are currently trying to keep the Club running.

A failure to recognise this call may result in the eventual closing of the Club with potentially dire consequences for the current membership.

What is the requirement?

A minimum of 6 new leaders is urgently required.

All you have to do is to turn up on a Saturday night when you will be guaranteed a warm welcome.

AN OPEN DOOR…

A door being opened to us, is to visit our Residential Homes, where we have the opportunity to lead in worship and provide pastoral care and love- 3 teams visit Carnalea Clinic on Thursday mornings at 11.00, led by Janet Wood and PWA members, Margaret Bailie and the Thursday Morning Ladies' Group, and Julie Hamilton with a team from a recent Seminar.

We also plan to extend our care to those members of our congregation who used to worship regularly with us in church but are no longer able to be present and, we are aware, sorely miss the fellowship and vitality of live worship.
This will be achieved by provision, on request, of a recording of each Sunday's morning service, made and willingly delivered, during the current week, by David **Baillie**.

JUNIOR DRAMA GROUP
Many of our members were impressed, at the Sunday evening Praise Service, by the quality and spiritual vitality of the drama presented by our Junior Drama Group.
There are about 16 of these young people, aged between 13 - 15 years. It is good to see their devotion to the Lord and their desire to glorify him.
On Monday past they had a visit from representatives of the Comber Romanian Appeal, when they handed over £160 they had raised through a Sponsored Bicycle Ride to Donagahadee in the summer and through the sale of Andrew McCroskery's book of Poems. The first edition of fifty copies sold out quickly and no doubt a second edition will soon be forthcoming.

The Comber Romanian Appeal has adopted two Orphanages. Helen Ritchie and Don, have been invited to join a team visiting Romania.

AND BY THE WAY!
ANDREW McCROSKERY is now a minister of the Church of Ireland!

B.B. BUGLES.
Our BB Bugle Band spent an enjoyable day at Omagh with the Regimental Band of the 1st Batallion the Worcestershire and Sherwood Foresters.
During the course of the day we received tuition on our instruments, and of course improved our marching. A new tune was learnt and a great experience was had by all when we played along with the regimental band.
Two brothers in our Company won awards in a competition arranged by the bandmaster for inexperienced drummers and buglers. Take a bow David and Richard Polley. They were each presented with a commemorative plaque of the Regiment for their playing and all of us came home with a Regimental Medallion to remind us of our visit.

WHAT'S IN STORE IN 1991?

At the moment of actual writing:

TALKS ON THE GULF at GENEVA, have come to nought, prospects of peace seem bleak.

1991 has begun WITH FURTHER MURDER AND VERY WIDESPREAD DESTRUCTION IN OUR PROVINCE.

THROUGHOUT EASTERN EUROPE AND ALL ASIA THERE IS MUCH UNREST, THE UGLY SIDE OF NATIONALISM, THE FANATICAL SIDE OF

RELIGIOUS FUNDAMENTALISM IS VERY APPARENT.

We ask: DO WE *COUNT* IN THE MIDST OF SUCH VAST MOVEMENTS?
Some despair about having any influence in the midst of such mighty tumults

but, in Jesus' Name we have a FATHER who counts the hairs upon our heads and who hears the prayers we make.
THESE PRAYERS
can protect the individual from evil
and can be a FULCRUM upon which larger events may turn.

That's why our prayer projects in West, faithfully implemented, are so important!

WHAT'S IN STORE FOR 1991?
For ANN KENNEDY it means ORDINATION in Cregagh Presbyterian Church on 27th January.

A NEW YEAR'S PRAYER by Julie Hamilton.

"O God our Father, I come now in prayer to You as I reflect on the old year and welcome the new year.
For all the happy memories of the past twelve months I bring You my thanks.
There have been many wonderful times:
When new life joined my family;
When I've found new friends which have added to my life;
When I've known a new depth in my relationship with your Son Jesus;
When I've proved your grace to be all-sufficient in my times of need.
O Lord, there have been some things I would like to forget, mistakes I've made and deliberate sins causing you grief.
I am not proud of the mistakes I have made last year, and would not want any of them to slip from me unforgiven.
May your Holy Spirit now in the quietness reveal areas where I need forgiveness.
Father, during this last year I have known much pain and grief. I hurt inside even as I remember those times. I have known loss at such a deep level, I have felt rejection.
I have been let down by friends, I have felt lost, abandoned and far from You. I have even doubted my faith in You.
Help me now in your strength to face those memories so that I may allow your Spirit to begin to bring me inner healing.

I thank You, O Lord for the fresh, strong wind of your Spirit which comes to bring me refreshment, cleansing and perfect peace thus enabling me to enter this new year, free, obedient and eager.

Strengthen my witness during this year, in the home where I live, in the place where I work, among those with whom I worship. And let the lovely everlasting things for which Jesus Christ lived and died and triumphed become more and more real in my life this year.

IN JESUS' NAME WE PRAY!

EVELYN'S STORY.

This is a story that leads through stunned grief and anger against God to eventual peace and patience and expectation of glory. Roberta Corbridge, her daughter, felt led to write this story - no doubt for the encouragement of all who read it.

EVELYN'S STORY.
"Evelyn looked down at the quiet still body of her husband of 26 years. She glanced at the clock. Seven thirty on a cold dark February morning. The room felt strangely peaceful now, after the long and difficult struggle of the night during which Jim lost the final battle of this life and succumbed to the long sleep of death. *She could not accept this. She would not accept it.*

The next few days seemed to pass in a daze. Sedated, and mechanically going through the motions, she was unable to give vent to the myriad of emotions and feelings which ebbed and flowed within her heart and mind.

It felt strangely unreal to be sitting in the lounge of the home she had shared with Jim, talking to people about 'old times' and even smiling occasionally at some amusing story from their younger days. Looking at the sea of faces that streamed endlessly through the house, her mind refused to face the reality that she had said 'good-bye' to her husband for the last time, at the funeral service.

MOUNTING ANGER.
Reverend David Bailie had been a tower of strength, quietly listening as the family talked through their memories. But deep inside, Evelyn could not stem this mounting anger at a God who could cruelly rob her of her purpose for living. She had never been a regular churchgoer but had never denied God's existence. Now the only way she could make sense of her pain and anguish was to conclude that either there was no God, or if there was, then He could not be a God of love and compassion. *She wanted nothing to do with Him.*

CHANGES WITHIN HERSELF.
In the weeks that followed Evelyn began to notice changes in herself. Always a forceful and dominant character, herself well organised, she tended to organise others as well. *Now she found that life seemed to be out of control.* She had lost her sense of purpose and direction. Depression descended and enveloped her like a cloak

which she could not throw off. She felt physically exhausted. Sleep eluded her and yet she longed for the oblivion that would anaesthetise the nagging, gnawing pain which threatened to eat her away. *She could not be comforted. She would not be comforted. Her anger against God increased daily.*

In desperation the family sought help from the G.P. who tried hard to break through to Evelyn, but after many months became discouraged and advised the family that Evelyn could not be helped because she did not want to be helped.

Around this time Evelyn became aware of other changes, this time more tangible, physical changes. During Jim's illness she had noticed that she had occasional **blurred vision** in one eye. This was not only persisting but becoming a real problem. Eventually she agreed to consult her G.P. once more.

The day after this consultation, Evelyn found herself in the Out Patients' Department waiting to see a 'specialist'. She had undertaken to make this visit alone. **She was not prepared for the news she would receive. Without much ado the consultant announced at the conclusion of his examination, that Evelyn had a malignant tumour in her eye and the eye would have to be removed immediately.**

WRAPPED IN HER CLOAK OF DEPRESSION.

Still wrapped in her cloak of depression and withdrawal, Evelyn felt the familiar unreality of this situation but consented to the operation. **Eight months after Jim's death from cancer, Evelyn lost her eye to the same insidious disease.** But the prognosis was not all bleak. Apparently the surgeon was almost 100% certain that all the malignant tissue had been contained in the eye itself and had not spread to the socket. All should be well.

REBUILDING…

Painfully, slowly and fitfully, Evelyn began the harrowing process of rebuilding her life. The Reverend Bailie continued to call and even invited Evelyn to a 'Life in the Spirit Seminar'. To everyone's surprise, including her own, she agreed. But she did not finish the Course and over the next months continued to try to piece together her shattered life. But the pieces did not fit securely. They kept falling apart. **What could be wrong?** Evelyn was making the supreme effort - that's what was wrong!

SOMETHING WONDERFUL HAPPENED.

After an interlude, Mr Bailie once again suggested the Seminar. This time Evelyn not only agreed to go, but finished the course. During this time something wonderful happened to Evelyn. She met this God to whom all her anger was directed. And in his presence she found comfort and love bathing the still raw wounds which had stubbornly refused to heal. She watched her wounds, irrigated and cleansed by the water of life, begin to heal. For the first time in almost three years she began to feel whole, loved and accepted for what she was. *She had been spiritually and emotionally healed and freed by God's Holy Spirit.*

It seemed such a long time since Evelyn had felt purpose and direction in her life. The family welcomed the change in her, even though some did not share her new-found faith in Christ. **In the weeks and months that followed Evelyn found that her 'family' was much extended as she was accepted and welcomed into the fellowship of West Church.**

A HEALING SEMINAR.

Evelyn had trouble with the false eye, fitted after her surgery. It proved most uncomfortable, and she was very conscious of the change in her physical appearance. Plastic surgery did help a little but several visits to the Healing Service were necessary before she finally felt comfortable about the whole thing.

Because of her own experience, Evelyn's interest in the ministry of healing was kindled and she later decided to enrol in a Healing Seminar, hoping she might be able to help others.

AND SO ALMOST SEVEN YEARS FROM THE BEGINNING OF OUR STORY, WE SEE EVELYN HAS COME FULL CIRCLE. A HAPPY ENDING? NOT QUITE.

During the duration of this Seminar, Evelyn felt the recurrence of an old 'gall bladder problem'. This time, however, things did not settle down and after several months investigations were ordered. The gall bladder would have to be removed.

On a bright May morning, Evelyn entered hospital for the routine surgery. She appeared to recover well but the family remained uneasy. Something about Evelyn made them feel this way. Enquiries to the staff produced no concrete evidence for their uneasiness but it remained all the same.

DEVASTATED.

On her release from hospital, Evelyn went to spend a week or so with one of her daughters. She was strangely quiet and appeared more anxious than one would expect. Eventually Evelyn's daughters decided to contact the consultant. They were devastated by the result of their visit. **Evelyn had cancer of the liver. Somehow, malignant cells from the original tumour had migrated to and multiplied in the liver. She had an estimated three months to live.**

SHOULD EVELYN BE TOLD?

Should Evelyn be told? If so, when? By whom? How would she cope? All these questions were addressed in turn and it was decided that the girls would accompany Evelyn for her check-up and she would be given the facts by the consultant.

The next ten days were difficult for the family. Eventually the day

dawned and the journey to hospital was made by three falsely cheerful people. Evelyn listened intently as her condition was described. She asked pertinent questions and seemed unnaturally calm. She made the decision not to have the treatment as the chances of keeping the cancer at bay were very remote and the treatment itself would make her ill.

Evelyn did not wish everyone to know of her illness straight away. Some members of the family were not informed at this stage, but some friends and some of the 'family' at West were. **In the following months much prayer ascended to the Father's throne, prayers for strength, and prayers for healing, prayers for pain relief. Many of her brothers and sisters at West Church committed her faithfully to God in daily prayer.**

Initially Evelyn felt very positive and was sure physical healing would come. She was well enough to return to her own apartment and insisted on being independent to the frustration of the family. However she did not appear to be suffering greatly, and the three month period since diagnosis had twice expired. The hospital was amazed.

Perhaps Evelyn would be healed after all. During the seventh month after diagnosis she began to deteriorate. Her energy was easily sapped. She was becoming more uncomfortable. **One of her daughters who had spent much time in prayer, could not shake off the feeling that Evelyn would soon die. But this seemed to fly in the face of all those who believed beyond doubt that Evelyn was being healed.**
Once again the Rev. Bailie provided a listening ear as the fears and hopes were aired. God has given him much wisdom and he was a faithful servant and friend in the weeks that were to come.

CHRISTMAS EVE.

On Christmas Eve, Evelyn's daughter arrived to transport her to her home for the holiday. Evelyn was in pain, severe pain. Once settled at her daughter's the doctor was summoned. He felt she had suffered 'a bleed' from the surface of the liver causing referred pain in the shoulder. He was concerned.

This was to be the last Christmas Evelyn would share with her family on earth. God granted her the strength to enjoy and participate in the celebrations. When Evelyn returned to her apartment she was not to leave it again. Now confined to her room and her strength failing daily, *she began to accept with great grace that death was not far off.*

SHE GLOWED.
During the last few weeks of her life, God's grace and peace were much in evidence in Evelyn's life. *SHE GLOWED! She had never experienced peace like this before.* Throughout the ten months of her illness **Evelyn had felt inspired to write some verses expressing her love and joy in the Lord.** She had never written anything in her life before. She did not think she had it in her.
Her last piece, **written shortly before her death encourages us to commune with our Lord in everything, in hope, in despair, in sadness, in joy and always with thanksgiving.**

"When we are hurt and in despair, what is the first thing we do?
Get on our knees and pray to God to help us in our needs.
But we also have to remember to thank Him every day, for all,
The many blessings He has given us along the way.
So don't just call when in despair,
Call also in your joy,
And sing your praises to his Name, Lord Jesus Christ on high."

"NINE O'CLOCK IN THE MORNING."
Evelyn died at 9.00 a.m. on February 26th 1987. I remember looking at the clock and thinking "Nine o'clock in the Morning." (An allusion here to Dennis Bennett's well-known book on how renewal came into his life and church).
The beginning of a new day.
A brighter day illumined by the presence of her Lord. I recalled one of her favourite songs, "Set my Spirit free" and realised that now at last her spirit was free.

A GLORIOUS CONTRAST.
Much had happened since the beginning of our story.
We began with a situation in which death meant a life destroyed, blighted and without hope. We end with a situation where life in Christ meant wholeness, joy, peace and purpose.
Even in the midst of death, the peace endures, the joy endures, and in the Lord's presence, freed from our ailing, disease-ridden bodies, *we are made whole!"*

DAUGHTER ROBERTA CONCLUDES:
"Perhaps you are wondering why I have chosen to share this, now three years after my mother's death. For no other reason than I felt prompted to do so.
I hope that any of you facing difficulties that seem insurmountable, will take heart in the knowledge that with Christ nothing is impossible, and when we are grafted into him, nothing can separate us from his love.
DEATH IS MERELY A GATEWAY INTO HIS PRESENCE."

[And if any of you should wonder why this story has been included in our "WEST CHURCH JOURNEY" IT IS FOR EXACTLY THE SAME REASON!].

FEBRUARY WCN 1991.

Front page exhortation was:

"LOVE ONE ANOTHER WITH BROTHERLY AFFECTION; OUTDO ONE ANOTHER IN SHOWING HONOUR."

"At a service just before Christmas, **Alvin Little** was teaching us, so often sated and blasé in our affluent ways, **not to take things for granted and not to take people for granted!**
If we are opening shoals of Christmas cards, we should do more, in our own minds than just acknowledge the names of those they have come from. He taught us in opening the cards to give thanks for the donors and quickly to pray a blessing on them.

I realise that it is easy for us, in the large congregation of West Church, to take one another for granted. Our congregation is a very large organism indeed, with its many limbs and organs and its many organisations.
It is important for us not only to acknowledge one another in a cerebral manner, but also to value one another, to honour one another and to count others better than ourselves.
Better still if in our hearts we pray a blessing on others.

HOLDING OTHERS IN HIGH RESPECT!
As I edit West Church News and edit the material that comes in, **it is important for me to thank God for all who write the reports and acknowledge the work that is done, so well and so willingly.**
In receiving the financial reports, one thinks of our Treasurer, **VICTOR STEPHENS**, and the massive amount he does so cheerfully through the year - and there's **ALLAN LOGAN** with the Development Fund, **JOHN POOLE** with Outreach Fund and Covenants; there are the Counting Teams etc.

AND IT'S THE SAME WITH EVERY REPORT!
Behind BB or GB or Scouts or Guides or Sunday School - or whatever organisation, *there's a lot of workers involved.*
One wants to give thanks for all that is done - even the production of West Church News means **CHRISTINE CARLETON** available to type, Billy Richardson ready to spend hours and hours on duplicating, **MAUREEN BLACKMORE** collating the magazine, **ELIZABETH McCLELLAND** preparing it for a team of Distributors; ALAN STEWART who does all the inscribing to give WCN its special character. And not forgetting BETTY CRAWFORD who keeps our buildings clean.... And ALL who give their service in Jesus' Name.

JILL YOUNG writes about "TUESDAY EVENINGS AT WEST."
Care of the Wayward!

"Although not an official organisation, we nevertheless felt it appropriate to write a short report on what happens on Tuesday Evenings.

For over a year now we have been offering a welcome to the youth of the area, a cup of tea, friendship and a witness about Christ and his love.
We have over 50 young folk, mostly boys, who drop in, some every week and others only occasionally. I think a feeling of 'belonging' has developed and certainly we have become very fond of these rather rowdy and unruly young folk. They range in age from 10 up to 20+, and are all very different, with varying needs and problems. **They have caused more than a little grief at times by their behaviour, and have managed to annoy and upset quite a cross section of the congregation, but we cannot give up on them and** *do see an improvement.*

They have heard many wonderful testimonies of God's grace and have shown tremendous interest in the changes that have taken place in other people's lives.
**DAVID HAMILTON (formerly of Prison Fellowship) has been with us a few times and brought a film one night to show them.
CHRIS KILLEN,** a young man from Lisburn has been with us a few times and brought others who were also able to testify to God's saving power. We are very grateful for the help of these people and for the Lord for prompting them to come and to care.

A CHRISTMAS PARTY.
We had a Christmas Party **which was a step of faith** for we had no idea how it would go.. I think they enjoyed it in spite of themselves, and most of them joined in to some degree.

TEA TRAWLER - PLEASE PRAY.
Just last week we had our first visit (Every 2nd Tuesday for 3 months) of the **Youth for Christ 'Tea Trawler' which is a bus fitted out with seating areas and serving tea and biscuits.**
Please pray that some of the seeds we have planted in their hearts would now be developed by the Team on the Bus and that God's Holy Spirit would move in their hearts. Pray that we would see the strongholds of Satan broken down and the Light of Christ poured into their lives. **Christ loves us all and none are beyond his reach as Don, Alan Cowie and I can testify- so let us all join together and pray these young people into the Kingdom of the King!**
1 Timothy 1: 15-17.

SYCAMORE CLUB-
As this report is being written all of us in the Sycamore Club are preparing for a 'Post Christmas Party' for almost forty of our members, both adult and children.
In September we felt strongly that we needed to reach out to more people by way of special invitation.

This resulted in a large harvest and within a week our membership had doubled!

Since then much time has been spent learning both old and new songs, listening to Bible stories and getting to know and understand all our friends. In February we are hoping to learn about **Joseph and his family**.

There is a great amount of love freely shared in our group, and often, we who are leaders, feel humbled by the love we receive.

Many people within and out with WEST have been drawn into the warmth and love of this group and we are indebted to them for their help……
Margaret Conroy.

FEBRUARY WCN gives many other annual reports, all enlightening and encouraging, for which unhappily we do not have space!

MARCH WCN 1991.
This edition highlights our united Holy Week services and concludes with EASTER EVENING UNITED COMMUNION SERVICE.

"On Easter Evening we have the culmination of our Holy Week services in a United Communion service in West.
This will be a **culmination** not only for those who have attended the services throughout the week but also for some at least, **of those who are currently attending our Communicants' Class.**
On Easter morning they will be given the opportunity to confess their faith in Christ, and then, in the evening, of coming forward to the Lord's Supper.
The service is in West Church, and we hope it will have some of the characteristics of our last, informal communion service, **in which the singing of old and new songs, figured so helpfully.**
We hope again, at this service, that our Praise will be led *by a United Choir + Singing Group.*

Perhaps it was in respect of the afore-mentioned informal Communion Service that PAMELA BROW wrote, *in appreciation,* **under the title:**

"WERE YOU THERE?"
"I would love you to share my feelings as I sit quietly in West Church, or listen to an uplifting tape of a service, at home or in my car.
I would love you to share my joy and anticipation of what the Lord might have next for me, as I drive nearer and nearer to West Church for a service, or a meeting nearby where God's people are gathering. And so I say *"were you there?"*

I am so glad that I was there, at West Church, last Sunday evening, 10th February for the very special and beautiful Communion Service. Its presentation was unusual and many hearts were touched, and full, at the gentle invoking of God's presence among us, through all the beautiful songs and hymns of Communion, Rev. David Bailie's prayers and his insights around a story of Jesus, gave us a great awareness of what God offers us as He draws us closer.

We are greatly blessed in West Church that God's Spirit has been poured out upon so many, who can now share amongst us their inspired talents and thoughts for our encouragement, and to the glory of God.

We have wonderful leaders and teachers in music and Word, and thus, God reaches out to us *continually* **to help us, and so to help us** *shine* **for him.
He did more for us, each one of us, than we can ever repay, when He gave us his Son,** *yet so often all He asks is for our Presence.*
"WILL YOU BE THERE?"

DARK RED SPLASHES

ON THE GROUND –
SURELY IT COULDN'T BE BLOOD? Anne Anderson.

"I felt quite cheerful as I stepped out briskly one cold morning a few months ago, heading for Bangor Market. I was thinking about my shopping and preparations for Christmas as I battled against the cold wind, watching out for icy patches on the pavement.
Suddenly I became aware of some dark red splashes on the ground - my heart missed a beat- surely it couldn't be blood?
There seemed to be quite a lot of it- where could it have come from? There was now a steady track of the red splashes along the pavement before me. Perhaps someone had had a nose bleed - yes, I was sure there was nothing to worry about. I tried to ignore it, but there it was, still ahead, and now I realised there were unmistakable large red pawmarks among the drops - a dog with a bad injury - it must be, every few yards there was a larger patch of blood, then more of the erratic paw prints weaving along in a drunken line. My mind raced over the implications - the dog must have been so weak that it had to keep stopping. I wondered where the dog was now - had its owner been with it? Had it been in a fight?
After about 150 yards the blood trail suddenly left the pavement and went into the road. I found myself following it, now totally preoccupied with thoughts of the poor dog. The marks did not appear to continue on the other side of the road. I suddenly realised what must have happened - the dog had been hit by a car and injured. The tracks I had been following had led me to the scene of the accident. I actually felt tears pricking my eyes as I envisaged the scene. I told myself to stop being ridiculous and forget it - "after all it's only a dog" and you aren't a great dog lover anyway. It may have caused a bad accident- perhaps there was an injured

driver with a damaged car - I wonder if he stopped? More likely 'hit and run' - had the dog been too weak to reach home? What if it collapsed in a garden at the place I had first noticed the blood!"

MY MIND KEPT RETURNING TO THESE QUESTIONS.

My mind kept returning to these questions all morning as I did my shopping, as I walked home passing the trail of blood again, I felt quite miserable at the thought of the pain the animal must have suffered. I wondered if the dog was being well cared for, perhaps it was dead - maybe the owners were still looking for it...

FOR MANY DAYS...

For many days after this incident I kept thinking back to the picture of those blood-stained paw prints. I asked my children and their friends if they had heard of an accident involving a dog, but none had heard anything. The evidence remained for some days with the red marks surviving several showers of rain and the footprints of many passers-by. Each time I walked up that road in the following weeks, I could not help remembering sadly the pain and distress of the unknown dog.

A COMMUNION SERVICE.

One Sunday, two or three weeks later, we had a Communion Service at church. As I prepared myself to receive the bread and wine, I closed my eyes as usual and thought about the broken body of Christ and his blood shed for me - suddenly I was confronted by a new truth about myself - I saw the blood of Christ splashed on the ground beneath the cross *just as clearly as the dog's blood on the pavement. In a new way the reality of his pain and suffering was clear to me.*

I remembered my tears and anxiety for the injured dog and realised with shame that I had never felt moved to tears in that way about the Blood of Jesus - I had never felt distressed about Him as I had about the dog.

THE PAINFUL TRUTH.

The painful truth about my mixed-up priorities came home to me as I realised how many times in recent weeks my thoughts had turned to the fate of that dumb animal, and how little time I had spent thinking of my Saviour and his suffering and spilt blood - *caused by the wilful disobedience of sinners, including me. My guilt is worse by far than that of any hit and run driver - my sin includes blindness to the enormity of my guilt and failure to understand the depth of Christ's forgiveness and love for me.*

"THANK YOU LORD FOR SHOWING ME SOME MORE OF MYSELF AND SOME MORE OF YOUR LOVE AND SACRIFICE FOR ME."

"I ATTENDED, ENJOYED CHURCH, *BUT I STILL HARBOURED MY BITTERNESS.*" Beulah Shields.

"I became a Christian, to my surprise, in September 1981. I had always known about the need for salvation, but I avoided what I thought would be the end of all the fun. However, Christianity proved to be exciting - at first. **Then routine set in.**
1982 was an eventful year and one which left me disillusioned and embittered, the only good part being my marriage. During the next few years my husband Paul and I attended and enjoyed church, but I still harboured my bitterness.

OUR WORLD SEEMED TO FALL APART - OUR FIRST SON STILLBORN.

In July 1986 our world seemed to fall apart when our first son was stillborn. **Since that time I felt an emptiness which physically hurt. Why had God taken my son? How could he love me? My faith crumbled around me. I couldn't read my Bible. I couldn't pray; and yet through the prayers of others, and having the Bible read to me, I realised I was lifted up.** Although my husband was devastated, his faith remained strong and he had the assurance our child was with Jesus - an assurance I didn't have.

I COULDN'T FORGIVE GOD.

When John was born in September 1987, after an anxious pregnancy which included hospitalisation, **I couldn't believe he was mine.** I couldn't sleep in the hospital with having to check every hour that he was real. And even after his brother Andrew was born in May 1989 **it was as if I couldn't forgive God for causing me such hurt and pain, as I thought.**

THE REALITY OF GOD'S LOVE ENABLED ME TO FORGIVE SOMEONE...

In the summer of 1988 we decided to leave the Presbyterian Church we had belonged to, something that was not easy since four generations of Paul's family had been connected with that church. We had decided to try a few different churches, Presbyterian or otherwise. But we got no further than the first church we tried - 'West'.
We were pleasantly surprised by the homeliness and the emphasis on Family (however noisy that may have proved!) and the spirituality and love.
We settled in quickly and during a visit by Mr Bailie were asked if we would be interested in joining a 'Life in the Spirit' seminar.
I went first, rather hesitantly, I must admit, in September 1989, but after the first days' reading from Jeremiah 31: 3 **"I have loved you with an everlasting love, so I am constant in my affection for you."**
The reality of God's love and forgiveness **enabled me to forgive someone, and the resentment and bitterness against that person that I had built up since 1982 was finally gone. What a relief!**
SAFE IN THE ARMS OF JESUS.

The following week, with the prayerful help of Mr Bailie, **the assurance I needed was given to me through a revelation of God -** which our first child was safe in the arms of Jesus, and the barrier which I had built up and reinforced was broken down. Since being baptised with the Holy Spirit I feel closer to the Father, and I know that even in my weakness He can use me to help others."

APRIL WCN 1991.

IMPROVING OUR PASTORAL CARE.
Jesus told Peter to tend the lambs and feed the flock with a willing spirit.
We too must learn to look after our committed members, look after those with special needs, or who may have strayed from the warmth of our fellowship; and to seek 'other sheep' who are to be brought in.
Since we have more staff than formerly in West we have been able to enlarge the range of our services, seminars and classes, and to improve the quality and extent of our visiting in the homes, and are taking steps to improve the communication between our Team members and our elders/church visitors.

HELEN RITCHIE WRITES WITH WARMTH AND APPRECIATION OF THE YOUTH DRAMA GROUP WHO WENT TO Harmony Hill, Lisburn, in the new BB bus to take part in a Gospel Concert to aid the **Romanian Orphanage Appeal, where they did two mimes and a worship dance with the Lord's Anointing upon them.**

DON RITCHIE IS DOING A COURSE AT THE Belfast Bible College on the Book of Psalms, 1 & 2 Thessalonians, and the Gospel of John.
HE WILL SHARE WHAT HE LEARNS with members of our congregation, each Monday night from 7 - 8 o'clock.
And Don will no doubt discover that the best way of learning and assimilating *is to share what you have been given.*

OUR YOUNG PEOPLE LEARN TO REACH OUT...

For 3 weeks, the Friday Night Youth group are to learn about OUTREACH from members of the AGAPE FELLOWSHIP, Belfast, who will teach out of their own experience at Cornmarket and the Golden Mile in Belfast. The first 2 weeks will be on teaching- the third week on putting it into practice!

JOAN COCHRANE IN FALKLANDS.
"I am really enjoying the work here and I know that I am where the Lord wants me to be. Although we work quite long hours it is very rewarding. We open '**The Oasis**' seven days per week It is basically a **Coffee Shop where the service personnel can get a bite to eat, play board games or simply sit quietly and write letters home. Without it they have only their rooms or the many bars in which to sit, and many of the lads have told us it is an absolute 'Godsend'** to them.
We have also seen the Lord working in the lives of many of them and about 5 or 6 have come to know Him since Christmas, while several others are showing an interest."

APRIL WCN gives many vibrant reports on the ongoing work of our organisations.

There are reports from the BB and GB with notices of forthcoming annual Displays.

Details of '**VARIED PROGRAMME**' for the 7th Scouts and '**ANOTHER GOOD YEAR**' for the Hawks and a 'TRIP TO DUBLIN' BY THE Beavers.

THE JUNIOR BADMINTON CLUB reports that they won Division 5 of the North Down League.

THE CHURCH COMMITTEE reports on extensive, ongoing repairs and improvements throughout our suite of buildings.

MAY WCN 1991.

THE ABBA TRUST IS BORN.

"**Great oak trees from little acorns grow**" - the Thursday morning Women's Group planted their little acorn when, in response to a plea for needy families, they decided to put 1 John 3: 18 into practice: *My children, our love should not be just words and talk, it must be true love, which shows itself in action.*
Much prayer surrounded the whole venture and we felt that God was gently urging us to follow this leading. And so the '**ABBA TRUST**' was born out of our concern for those in need. A Committee was quickly elected, and at our first meeting the following aims were agreed:
To help those in need.
To show love in a practical way.
To further God's Kingdom through our help.

Margaret Bailie and Ken Mottram then took the whole venture to the Kirk Session, where it was decided that in the meantime, the Trust would remain under the charity umbrella of West Church.

Specific Needs made Known!
We will have a notice board in the Vestibule, where specific needs can be notified. **It must be remembered that the people we want to help have fallen on hard times, mostly through**

circumstances beyond their control. All our 'possessions' are really the Lord's, given to us in trust for Him, so we must be sure not to use this scheme for dumping worn-out unusable items. Rather, let us give what we can with love.

Carol Aspinall was Secretary of the Abba Trust and Margaret Bailie Treasurer.

A PROPHECY FINDING FILFILMENT?

A COUPLE OF YEARS AGO WE HAD A VISIT FROM THE Rev. Andy Arbuthnot of the London Healing Mission.
He told us that when he was conducting worship at our Sunday Service in the church **he had a clear vision of an EXPLOSION in which the walls of the church were blown out! But it was an explosion of love from within, so that the love of God was being carried out into the community and country!**

Is the formation of the ABBA TRUST one expression of that explosion of love?

"SHAKEN BUT NOT STIRRED."

A potent factor in spreading the "renewal" throughout the Church and the land, in these years, was national, provincial and local conferences. GEOFF McELWAINE, a frequent and articulate contributor to West Church News, gives his impressions of the 'Spring Harvest' Conference in Ayr 1991.

"It is probably unwise to attempt to categorise or articulate the tide of impressions, experiences and memories swirling around my head and heart after five days spent on the 'mountain-top', in Butlin's Wonder west World, Ayr.. **My heart is too full of God's unmerited yet unstinting** goodness to me, and six thousand others from all over the British Isles, who gathered on a blustery Tuesday afternoon to seek His face. Nonetheless, I am 'bursting' to share at least something of what He did and which our children rightly describe as "brill."

A CAGED DOVE BREAKING FREE.
The week's theme, symbolised by a caged dove breaking free, referred to the fact that, although the Holy Spirit's work, in "shaking" Christians to fulfil their God-given potential, has become widely accepted, *it has often failed to "stir" them to reach out to the hurting world around them.*
Bible-readings, seminars and celebratory evening worship-times bore upon aspects of this central topic. I was particularly impressed by the strong emphasis placed on God's Word and the need, in the midst of a bustling schedule, to spend time with Him.

The Conference provided for young people of various age groupings, as well as adults. In the mornings there were Bible studies on a wide range of subjects, and on varying levels.. In the afternoons **there were more than twenty optional seminars.**

On a personal note Geoff, 'typically' notes: **'I was amused to note the usual linkage between inadequate bedding and blessings applied! Our bed's narrowness required a joint decision before either turned over; we were usually so tired it did not matter.'**

STIFF PRESBYTERIAN… HANDS RAISED.
"For me the evening 'Celebration' constituted the days' highlight. Led by Ian Trayner and what my more knowledgeable daughter tells me was the Mannifest Band, the two and-a-half hours of worship and teaching on the Acts-based theme "The Church in action", all mixed with humour (in the 'warp' of doing serious business with God, laughter formed the 'woof'), was pure joy. *This stiff Presbyterian was even spotted raising his hands in a gesture of adoration and praise to his God.* The presence of two thousand fellow-believers joining in this praise in the unlikely setting of what, in normal usage, is a "Ball-room of Romance" lent the evenings a memorable quality.

Having been graciously 'stirred', our natural sadness on leaving, to return to the 'nitty-gritty' of normal life, was mixed with the fearful excitement at the prospect of God using us to help fulfil His purpose."

MAY WCN 1991
ALSO ADVERTISES A
PENTECOST CELEBRATION
In the National Stadium Dublin, On Saturday 18th May, with "Sharings" from Rev. Cecil Kerr, Michael Cullen, Rev. Des Bain, and Fr Pat Collins C.M.

BRIGHTON CONFERENCE:
This very much an **INTERNATIONAL CONFERENCE** scheduled from 8th-14th July.

DR IAN CLARKE WRITES FROM UGANDA.

[For a time some members of the "Bangor Fellowship" made their congregational home in West prior to forming their own organisations, which developed into "Kings" in Bangor, and CFC in Belfast.
So we came to have cordial and affectionate links with Ian & Roberta Clarke, and family.

The Clarkes proved to be among those who were both "Shaken" and "Stirred"!
In Uganda Ian Clarke writes movingly about the scourge of AIDS and develops a heart, not only to empathise with people in

their needs, but to take action.

"We built a MATERNITY CENTRE to help the village girls have safe deliveries, yet Margaret, from only a few miles away, didn't come.
Her boyfriend didn't bring her and she had no money herself, so perhaps she was afraid to come. Perhaps she felt that the old hag she was taken to would do a better job, who knows? **But the consequence will stay with her for life. A dead baby, a chronic infection and a hole in her bladder that will make her incontinent every time she stands up. What did she do to deserve it? Nothing that every other girl in the village hasn't done - she got pregnant.**"

"Robbie talked to a young man from the TB ward. He was having treatment for TB, **but he was also HIV POSITIVE. Robbie has had the thankless job of telling scores of people that they have Aids. It is a faith-draining occupation - trying to give people hope, and holding on to hope yourself. The young man took the news very badly and said it was all over for him, he would commit suicide.** Robbie continued to talk with him and he appeared to change. She promised she would return with a Bible in the afternoon and came home and marked passages of hope and comfort. In the afternoon he had gone. The warden had written across his notes "ran away." **Ran away to what? - to suicide? - to despair? Had he received any hope?**"

Ian Clarke continues: "We don't even speak the language. We live a Western lifestyle that bears no relation to most of the people here. We are from a world apart, *yet these people touch us at a deeper place than I have ever been touched before. We are not worthy of them. We do not suffer, we identify only superficially with their pain. It amazes me, but doesn't surprise me that Jesus didn't stop at anything less than death, in his entering into their suffering, He gave his all.*"

WELCOME VISITORS TO "OPEN NIGHT."

ALAN COWIE about whom we have written earlier, might also be described as one who was both 'shaken' and 'stirred'.
He asks: "How many people looked round at the end of last Tuesday's 'Open night', and noticed, sitting at the back, a group of between six and ten young people dressed in various assorted clothing with haircuts to match? If you were surprised to see them there, then so was I!

Alan writes: "These young people are part of the usual "Tuesday Night Group" that Don, Jill, Carol and I look after while attempting to put a little Christian input into their lives.
It is not always easy to maintain a Christian attitude when dealing with them. They can often be 'a bit of a handful' but occasionally a conversation can lead to the chance to witness to them about Jesus' love, how it has affected our lives and how it can affect theirs. **It was uplifting to see these young people (none of whom would claim to be Christian - quite the reverse in fact in most cases) sitting in at an ' Open Night' and behaving, even singing in some of the choruses. I don't kid myself for one minute that they were there for any other purpose than to get at the tea and buns afterwards, but just to get them there in the presence of the Holy Spirit, listening to Christian testimony, choruses and prayer, and to see them reading Witness Sheets afterwards, encouraged me at least, no end.**

I hope and pray that this will not be the last such opportunity we get and thank all of those who kindly fed our young visitors and made them feel welcome, in the best tradition of West Church."

JUNE WCN 1991.

A 'SPECIAL' FOR PROPERTY REPAIRS.

Very extensive repairs, involving the outside and inside of our church building, and of our whole suite of buildings, have transformed and beautified our premises - but severely dented our finances! So our 'special' offering on Children's Day will be devoted to this purpose, with a 10% increase to our Number One Account sought.
To complete our overall scheme EDWARD CARLETON and KEN MACARTNEY ARE PLANNING A PAINTING BLITZ on our church halls in the second week in June when evenings are bright and buildings largely unoccupied. Squads of Ten are sought for four evenings.

OUTREACH MINISTRY CONTINUES!
When Bankers' Orders for the Building and Outreach Fund expired, the new building having been paid for, - members were invited to continue, so that we might foster our OUTREACH MINISTRY. John Poole tells us that members continue at 88% of their previous level. We give thanks for this generosity and vision.

WITNESSING ON QUEEN'S PARADE.
Helen Ritchie reports:
"On Friday 17th May, about a dozen of our young people, plus Alvin, Billy, Jill, Trevor, Barry, Sharon, Don and I met in our Praise Room - in some fear and trepidation, but also with anticipation and trust in God - *to have a time of prayer and praise, with our friends from the Agape Fellowship, prior to going down to Queen's Parade to talk to people about the Lord Jesus.*"
Helen adds: "I personally was far more nervous than our young people, who were an inspiration

to us all. The Rev. David Bailie also joined us to encourage and pray with us.

Ian Carroll and his wife Rachel (Agape Fellowship) and their marvellous young people had joined us for the previous 3 Friday nights and given us some inspiring and practical teaching on Evangelistic Outreach…… we went off in pairs as we had been taught. We had prayed especially for *compassion* for those we spoke to, and also for *encouragement* for our young ones, and also for *good weather, and the Lord answered all these prayers!*

HE TOOK AWAY OUR FEAR.
He also took away our fear, so that when we all met up again, **we all felt so encouraged and blessed!** There had been many good conversations, many invitations made and excellent tracts given out; **we were all exhilarated and greatly encouraged.**
We went over to the Cloisters (The Christian Pub), where some of our young ones carried on conversations with people they met - as well as on the street outside. Many of them said: '**When are we going to go out again?**'
Helen concludes: "I really thank and praise the Lord for all his grace and mercy, and would ask you to pray for all those who were spoken to, that the seeds sown may grow in their hearts!"

DON'S BIBLE STUDY.

We have mentioned that Don Ritchie planned to share, on a Monday Evening Bible Hour, what he was learning at the Belfast Bible College.
For Pamela Brow, who had longed to study there herself, this was a real answer to prayer, for she is gaining so much from Don's 'relayed' teaching, with his own enthusiasm and personal insights giving additional blessing.
Pamela says: "**Each time I now hear Psalm 23, I can see a picture for each line…**"

Likewise, in respect of 1 Thessalonians: "**As Don paints a picture of the people of Thessalonica a gap of almost 2000 years is bridged!**"

JUNE WCN 1991 tells of lectures by the Rev. Ruth Patterson under the auspices of RESTORATION MINISTRIES, under the themes of "Our Inheritance"; "Our Reactive sin to Bondage"; "Jesus loves me and needs me Free"; "How this Freedom is possible."

Some of our members attended these classes by Ruth who had left parish ministry for this counselling work. As a schoolgirl Ruth had been a member of West and we followed her innovative ministry with affectionate interest.

JULY WCN 1991.

**The leader in July WCN encourages us to make good use of holidays to be refreshed for work ahead. It points out that God gave a 'Sabbath' to his people for refreshment and recuperation and to focus upon worship.
In West we rejoiced that, with increased staff, we were able to maintain a substantial programme over the summer months. For example, to maintain a Healing service every Sunday evening, to have a weekly 'Praise and Prayer' meeting, to begin a new 'Life in the Spirit' seminar.**

DRAMATIC RECOVERY.
We had a letter of thanks from Valerie and Leslie Gawn, former members of West who had gone to live in England, appreciative of help and support given during the illness of their daughter Ashleigh.
Valerie writes: "I believe you met for prayer on a Friday night, and that Ashleigh was prayed for. I'm sure that it will encourage you to know that on the Saturday morning she made a dramatic recovery. She had spent the Friday lying listlessly on the settee, and hadn't eaten for ten days -and on the Saturday morning she ate a large breakfast and went out to play."

GULF WAR FEAR LED TO CHRIST.

In our July WCN we have two WITNESS stories. They are by two sisters, Beverley Graham and Debbie Shaw, and they indicate how fear, engendered within them by the Gulf War, led them to faith in Christ.

Beverley writes about a Fear she could not get out of her mind:

"In August 1990, war, fear, doom, death and hell filled my life as I heard about the Gulf War.
Until this point in my life, I always prayed to God for help and went to church now and again - that's as far as it went. I had heard somewhere that the Third World War would be in the Middle East, and now I was sure this was it. From August to January I got on with life as best I could - **but I could not get this fear out of my mind.** It was always on the News. At Christmas time I was very depressed, thinking of my husband and children and how I was going to hell. *So I said 'right, as soon as the fighting starts I will go to church and see if that does me any good'.*

"I'LL GO AT NIGHT; THE SERVICE IS NOT SO LONG."
"Well, sure enough, the first weekend fighting started *I didn't feel like going to church*, but I had told myself from August that this is what I would do, so I thought 'I'll go at night, the service is not so long'.
Well, it was a Praise Service. I had never been to one before and was surprised to see so many men and women lifting their hands and praising the Lord in a sincere and loving manner. *I left feeling it would be great to know God in that way."*
"*On Monday I went back to the News and worry.* On Tuesday, **Heather Thompson from the church called. I was pleased to see**

her. We talked. I told her of my fear about the Gulf War. She told me about 'Life in the Spirit Seminars'. She invited me to one the next morning. I went with my mother and sister who like me were not Christians at that time. We were made to feel very welcome- my initial feeling of embarrassment quickly left me.

'OPEN NIGHT' IN FEBRUARY.
I went to the Open Night in February and after that night asked the Lord into my life. As the Seminar went on, I found that I was able to take part, relax and enjoy the talks. I learnt a lot from other Christians. The Lord has changed me.
John 14: 1 is now a personal verse for me who used to fear everything: "Do not let your hearts be troubled. Trust in God, trust also in me."
God is good…. I went to a Ladies' Weekend in Rostrevor, where I had a very uplifting and fulfilling time. I got to know other members of West and came home knowing that there is nothing to compare with God's goodness. *THANK YOU, LORD!*

And now, Beverley's sister, **DEBBIE SHAW** tells her story. We also find FEAR in Debbie's life. She relates:
"Five years ago my niece Stephanie was christened in West Church. The sermon was all about keeping promises to God and how serious it is to break them. **I sat bolt upright in my chair and was frightened for I knew I had definitely broken promises to God. I knew there and then I was going to hell.** I told myself I would not make any more promises as I was unlikely to be able to keep them - **but the fear had set in.**
I was not a church attendee and did not belong to a church. **I had felt close to God as a child, and said my prayers out of habit, but was aware that I was no longer close to God."

"HELEN RITCHIE - I just wished I could have been like her."
"Four years ago Blayne my little boy was born and I decided that if I was going to hell, at least he might have a chance of being saved, if I brought him up in the church. I decided to go to West Church as my sister had already joined and there seemed to be a lot going on. **It was about this time that I met Helen Ritchie through work. She invited me and two other young mums with children around to her house for coffee.** *We knew she was a Christian and were all worried in case she started preaching to us. She didn't. I remember leaving her house and thinking 'so that's what it's all about, she's definitely going to heaven. Helen and her home were full of love and warmth and I just wished I could have been like her.'*

PRESSURE TO HAVE HIM CHRISTENED.
When Blayne was 9 months old I could no longer hold out to the pressure I was under to have him christened. I thought 'well it's not going to make any difference now, I'm going to hell anyway - it's too late!' Rev. Bailie came round to see me and I was able to talk to him, he knew something was wrong. I told him I knew I was going to hell but didn't want to change; I was very happily married and apart from this fear was otherwise happy. He told me when I prayed to ask God to help me want to change.

FRIGHTENED.
"I ATTENDED West Church a couple of times but it frightened me, there was so much in the sermons that was relevant today! *On the day that Blayne was christened, the Rev. Bailie touched me and a strong sensation shot through me - which I now realise was the Holy Spirit. I looked at my husband Philip to see if he had experienced it too but he just looked normal. 'I decided there and then I'm not coming back here. If I keep coming here I'll have to become a Christian.'*

I KEPT MYSELF BUSY.
"For the next couple of years I kept myself busy. I became pregnant with my little girl Kirsty and during that time was very content. Now and then past sins would haunt me and I'd pray the prayer the Rev. Bailie taught me. I'd also ask God to make Philip my husband a Christian as I felt I needed someone to lead me. **On the whole I had everything - 2 lovely children, a happy marriage, my husband's career was going well and I had started my own business, working from home, which I loved. I had started going to another church so as Blayne could attend Sunday School.**

GULF WAR… TOO LATE.
Then War broke out in the Gulf and I thought 'this is it - the end. I've left it too late!' My sister and I discussed it and tried to accept our fate, neither of us wanted to change and I told her about the prayer the Rev. Bailie had taught me. We had never discussed these things before, and we were terribly frightened. I remember going to my Aerobics Class and everyone seemed normal. My husband was glued to the War on the TV and I kept saying to him 'can't you see what really is happening?' and he said to me "Debbie, a little knowledge is a dangerous thing." And I knew he was right but wasn't sure what to do about it.

THE PRODIGAL SON … PERHAPS I COULD BE SAVED.
"I thought about calling round to see Helen Ritchie - but couldn't pluck up the courage. I knew nothing about the Bible, but God was giving me some encouragement. I'd picked up a book to read to Blayne- it turned out to be the Prodigal Son and the words at the end of the story really hit me '**Jesus wanted to teach the people that God loves everyone - no matter what she or he may have done**'. *I read them over and over again and thought perhaps I could be saved.*

MY SISTER PHONED.
"Philip and I were watching TV one evening - the Gulf War, when suddenly, without explanation the TV went off. I froze. I though 'this .is it, Jesus is here and I've had it.' I was terrified.
The next night my sister phoned to say that someone from West Church had called, and she was going to a meeting the next morning to find out about becoming a Christian, and asked if I'd like to go too. I said 'no, I don't think so' but Philip's words were ringing in my ears, "A little knowledge is a dangerous thing." I went - amazingly or maybe not so amazingly - and I kept saying to myself 'what am I doing here?'

GOD ANSWERED MY PRAYER.
God had answered my prayer. He had given me someone to lead me and my sister Beverley - Don Ritchie, Helen's husband, whom I had never met took my seminar, and I was delighted about this and felt it to be a positive sign. Don answered all my questions that first morning without me having to ask a single one, and *as I drove to work that evening I was filled with a wonderful peace that has stayed with me. God answered my prayer that I'd been praying, sometimes half-heartedly, 'please make me want to change!'*
It's taken me five years to get this far. I thank God for his patience and pray I'll make better progress in the next five years.

"I love the Lord, for he heard my voice;
He heard my cry for mercy.
Because he turned his ear to me,
I will call on him as long as I live." Psalm 116.

NOTE: In our 'West Church Journey', we have seen God at work in many lives, in diverse situations, and we have been happy to include these two testimonies where people have been newly enlightened and lifted out of fear, into peace in Christ.

AUGUST WCN 1991.

SAINTS FOR HEALING.
This is an autumn study for our Home Groups, a course of 9 weeks, which involves members in some daily Bible Study and prayer at home each day, so that the weekly meeting together can be especially profitable. It has been produced by Anglican Renewal Ministries.
The course is by no means 'heavy' yet it is not light or trivial. Believers can embark upon this course with profit and gain a great deal from it in terms of personal up building and devotion.

ABBA TRUST work grows!

Little did the Thursday Morning Group realise when they planted 'their little acorn' in love and faith, back in February, just how much the Lord would make the venture flourish.

MORE THAN 50 FAMILIES HELPED.
Each week the numbers of those in need contacting us is increasing. To date we have helped in excess of 50 families - with furniture, groceries, coal, clothes etc. **Our eyes have been opened to the desperate needs in our community; those needs include** *everything* **-FROM BEDS AND WARDROBES DOWN TO KITCHEN UTENSILS AND CROCKERY.**
It suddenly dawned on Margaret Bailie, when delivering to one family, that they didn't even have a knife or fork - we hadn't even thought of cutlery, and yet such a necessity. **So Margaret approached Oneida who were most generous with their help. And we must also thank Hugh Anderson and Spence Bryson for their generosity.**
As we have been meeting these needs, we have realised just how very heavy the work-load is, the organisation and the collection and delivery of all the furniture and others items.

WE need strong men to help….
And good quality furniture!

THE FOURTH DECADE OF OUR WEST CHURCH JOURNEY.

OCTOBER WCN 1991.

WELCOME TO THE REV. HEMANT PARMAR.
The Rev. Hemant Parmar of Maninagar Church, Ahmedabad, India joined us in the first week of September, coming to study for a year in Union College and to have inter-change of pastoral experience with us in West.
This has meant separation from his wife Urvashi son Jackson and daughter Jaqueena and from his flourishing congregation. Members of West were encouraged to receive him to heart and home-and Hemant was to spend much of his time with us in the Manse.
We got Hemant, through "West Church News" to give us a picture of his lively, growing congregation of three hundred families.
In addition to Sunday services, Sunday School and prayer meetings in church and homes, **there were nine 'cottage meetings', Retired People's fellowship, a weekly Nurses' Fellowship for nurses from different parts of Gujarat, a Women's Fellowship, a Youth Fellowship, 9 different church committees, and an Evangelistic Committee to foster evangelism. In a new industrial zone Maninagar Church fostered a mission, born out of much prayer, and involving the giving of Gospel tracts to fifteen thousand families. Before embarking on this they had half-nights of prayer, a whole night of prayer and a whole day of prayer.**
ONE SIGNIFICANT POINT: the people, Hindu and Muslim, gladly

received these gospels-THERE WAS NO OPPOSITION!

WE CAN LEARN FROM ONE ANOTHER!
It is good for us in West to note the innovative ways in which others share the Good News of Jesus.

AT THE TIME OF BEREAVEMENT.
"In our Gujarati newspapers we find Death Notices of Hindus and Muslims with their addresses. We use these to send Gospel packets to the bereaved families. *In these we send the Gospel of Luke, some tracts and a letter. We have done this for 3000 families up to date. And we get letters back!*
In India, father, mother and their married children live together, and so we reach a very large number of people in this way. Two of our senior leaders (60+ years) are involved in this work.

ADVERTISEMENTS ON CITY BUSES.
We have put Bible verses on the advertisement boards of 50 Ahmedabad City buses for a period of 6 months. Each bus takes 60 passengers and does 10 trips per day - so 30,000 people have the opportunity of seeing these Scriptures every day! Our Maninagar church has paid for this!

BAPTISM OF A BRAHMIN GIRL.
Miss Rina S. Chakravarti comes from a high caste Hindu family. Her parents are from West Bengal. She is a Brahmin - the priestly caste within Hinduism. **Rina attended our Sunday services for a period of five years.**
In 1988 I (Rev. Hemant) was transferred to Maninagar. Rina came to know my family and other committed Christian families. In this way she came to know Jesus.
In 1991 she attended our training class for preparation for Christian baptism. Before her baptism *she shared her testimony during a Sunday worship service.* During the 1991 summer vacation she married a young Christian man. Both are happy. Mrs Rina Maxwell Christian has joined our choir. Pray for Rina and her husband and for their family life.

ABOUT HEMANT PARMAR: UPDATE -Hemant is currently minister of the big city-centre church in Ahmedabad. We met him during our visit to India in 2000 and letters from him indicate that he continues to have a ministry, not only to his own urban congregation, but to other ethnic Christian groups, and to many non-Christians, reaching out to villages way beyond Ahmedabad.

REACHING THE OUTSIDERS, and warmly receiving them into the Body of the Church.

I (DGB) remember one Sunday morning, in the narrow space between our two morning services, greeting a young woman whom I had not seen before, asking where she came from, and how she happened to be with us that morning, getting this reply: "Well, it is a really a family tragedy that has brought me along"
I give her story below.

SHARON McWILLIAMS writes: "A BRUTAL TRAGEDY SET ME SEARCHING."

"We had always thought of ourselves as Christians - simply because we believed in God. We didn't think there was a need for anything else. But how wrong we were!

BRUTALLY MURDERED.
On Sunday October 4th 1987 we received the tragic news that my eldest sister Carol, aged 22, had been brutally murdered in her East Belfast home. *We didn't know it then, but the events of the next few days were to change our lives.*

ONE PERSON A TOWER OF STRENGTH -our lives empty by comparison.
How can you describe the sadness of a family after such a loss, and yet throughout that ordeal, one person stood out as a tower of strength to us all. **My mum, although heartbroken, somehow displayed an inner strength, together with a quiet dignified sort of peace, which carried the family through.** It was not only the immediate family that was aware of this quite extraordinary gift. People, including ministers who came to the family home to give comfort, went away comforted. Such were the qualities of this lady, who gave herself to the Lord when she was still in her teens and by her life since then has been an example to many. Mum had something in her life which made ours empty by comparison, *and it was something we both longed for.*

THE SEARCH BROUGHT US TO WEST CHURCH.

The search brought me to West Church one Sunday and to the Rev. Bailie, who when told I was searching, said that I would find. David called at our home a few days later and told us about the 'Life in the Spirit Seminars' and invited my husband Christopher and me to go. *We went along and did indeed find a new life in the Spirit which has taken us from being simply "believers", to having a real deep personal relationship with the one true living God- and how our lives have changed!*

THE LORD IS NOW WITH US.
We still meet every Wednesday, and through the fellowship of the rest of the group, we are strengthened and encouraged. *We have asked the Lord to take charge of our lives, and he is now with us in all that we do, and our family is all the richer for it.*

I SOUGHT HIM BECAUSE HE FIRST SOUGHT ME.
I SOUGHT THE Lord, and afterwards I knew He moved my soul to seek him, seeking me!

"It was not I that found, O Saviour true - I was found by Thee!"

Like many others who come to faith in Christ and a fullness of the Spirit through our Seminars, Christopher and Sharon McWilliams were to discover that this was not the conclusion and culmination of a new life, but the beginning, and that through the fellowship, teaching and ministry of the Church they would grow into richer maturity and fuller ministry. For example, through **A WEEKEND FOR COUPLES in September 1991.**

THE McWilliams write about this Weekend of teaching, sharing and ministry for married couples under the heading:

…TILL DEATH DO US PART!

Christopher writes: "No, not the title of an old television sitcom, **but the final line in a list of solemn vows exchanged by two people when joined together in marriage!**

Those of you who can remember that particular television series will recall that the story each week revolved around **the constant marital strife of its two main characters, Alf Garnet and his long suffering wife- the silly moo!** Not exactly recommended viewing for the serious Christian, but I'm sure it must come close to portraying what a marriage can be reduced to **if God has no part in it.** For the Christian, marriage is much more than choosing a partner and raising a family. A Christian partnership *where both persons put God first in their lives is a sacred alliance blessed and guided by God. Such a team can be used mightily by the Lord.*

WITH TEN OTHER COUPLES
at Childhaven, Millisle.

It was with that desire in our hearts that we, together with ten other Christian couples from various denominational backgrounds made our way on Friday 13th September 1991 to the Childhaven Centre.

Childhaven is a magnificent Dutch Barn-style property owned and managed by the Belfast Central Mission of the Methodist Church. Built in 1938 and recently modernised and decorated throughout, its tranquil and peaceful setting high above the Donaghadee Road, just outside Millisle, made it the perfect venue for a weekend of praise, worship and some very special ministering to 11 couples seeking spiritual refreshment and God's blessing on their marriages. A prompting from the Lord, a lot of prayer and not a little effort on the part of **Don and Helen Ritchie** brought us all together on that weekend. The prayers were answered - and how!

WEEKEND LED BY NIALL AND GERRY GRIFFIN,

Our weekend was led by Niall and Gerry (Geraldine) Griffin who together share a healing ministry called Colann Ministries. Colann is an old Irish word meaning 'whole body'.

This was to be significant for us all as during the weekend our denominational Christianity gave way to the power of the wholeness of Jesus. They were the perfect choice for our needs. Niall is an ordained minister of the Church of Ireland, and both had lived and worked at the Christian Renewal Centre at Rostrevor before starting Colann Ministries - and of course they were a married couple themselves.

ALAN STEWART LEADS PRAISE.

Alan Stewart (how he is gifted!) led the praise and worship and throughout it was truly uplifting; at times ecstatic. At one point we were all on our knees before the Lord. The Holy Spirit was on the move! On another occasion the gift of tongues filled the air with beautiful heavenly sounds. There was praise and teaching of quite a different kind when Brian and Carol Moorhead shared their gifts of mime and song. They certainly provoked some spiritual lateral thinking!

TAUGHT ABOUT GRACE.

We were taught about grace - that we get right with God not by religious laws but by God's saving grace through faith in Jesus Christ who has set us free from sin. We learnt that marriage is a gift from God and how a Christian partnership can be a powerful witness for God. There was private counselling where couples and individuals were ministered to and obtained answers, advice and release from troubles, problems and anxieties. But, just as the head steward discovered at the marriage feast in Cana that the best wine was kept to the last, so it was with our weekend.

A VERY SPECIAL SUNDAY MORNING.

We believe that Sunday morning was specially set aside by the Lord just for us. After breakfast we assembled as a body on the front lawn of Childhaven where we praised and worshipped the Lord in prayer and song. Standing there at one with God's creation - the sunshine like his grace pouring down upon us, the sound of the sea lapping the shingle, the birdsong and the rustle of autumn leaves as a gentle breeze moved through the trees which stood all around us - **prayer came easily on that morning!**
Inside, the 23rd psalm was brought alive in a hitherto unimaginable way. Next time you turn to it, try reading it as if it were written by a sheep!!

MARRIAGE VOWS RENEWED.

A little later in an atmosphere of intimacy and real love, each of us hand in hand with our partner, **renewed our marriage vows.** I am sure that for many of us, the first time we made those vows, the Lord had little part in them, **but for those few moments on Sunday morning in Childhaven,** *the Lord stood right there with us as we rededicated our lives to each other, and in so doing also dedicated our marriages to him. We will never forget the love that was shared in that room. There were tears of happiness as Niall and Gerry prayed with each couple in turn and then anointed us all with oil. This gave way to more tears and embraces. What a joy-filled occasion it was!*

MORE THAN WE DARED TO HOPE FOR.
For us the weekend was all and more than we ever dared to hope for. We came away spiritually renewed, invigorated, ready as a team blessed by God, to go boldly forward in our Christian walk prepared and eager to do whatever He should ask of us. *Anyone can have a tolerably good marriage without Jesus but it falls sadly short of what God intends for those who truly know Him and walk with Him.*
"The land has produced its harvest, God, our God has blessed us. God has blessed us, May all people everywhere honour Him." Psalm 67.

EARLY MORNING PRAYER IN WEST-
SOME THOUGHTS FROM PAMELA BROW.
"The Lord put in my heart the desire to see West Church open for prayer in the early morning…when I heard BRIAN MARTIN sharing with us in church, that the Lord had given him some verses urging early morning prayer for a specific cause, the Young People's Summer Scheme in West, my heart leapt!
So we met for five mornings in the Praise Room between 6 and 7 a.m. **Brian led the meetings and Paul Shields chose the songs of worship.** Both these men have a great sensitivity and love for the Lord, so goodness flowed and prayers were answered amazingly - the Summer Scheme was truly blessed in every way with the Lord's touch and encouragement. **There were other important needs for urgent prayer and these were accommodated also, with joy in our hearts."**

ROSTREVOR YOUTH WEEK - DON RITCHIE.

We have close links with the Christian Renewal Centre in Rostrevor and Helen and I were delighted when we were asked to be house-parents at the Kilbroney Centre. We were to be responsible for 130 teenagers between 11.00pm and 9.00am. The 'crack' as they say, was 'mighty'.

We were ably assisted in the organising of sleeping arrangements, breakfast and late supper by a team of really super young Christians **from across the divided community.
Ireland's youth are just fabulous and we found that the mix of Bible teaching and sharing really got everybody talking.** The sharing groups were a little like our own house groups- we were able to discuss freely on a number of different subjects of concern to us. After lunch we joined a workshop of our choice **for music, drama, dance, prayer, leading youth groups, New Age, Marriage Partners and how to find one!!**

The evening meal started at 5.30pm and the big marquee was a cacophony of sound as we all met together and ate, discussed the day and made new friends.

The evening session of Praise, Worship and Teaching was always a time of learning as Fr Jim Burke, a missionary Bible Teacher led us on the theme of the week, **"Who do you say I am?"**

10.30 - TO LATE. This saw us enjoying "Late Night Extra" which developed into a wonderful time of interviews, songs, poetry, drama, comedy and testimonies. The stories of what had happened to people and how they were growing in Jesus were just marvellous.

We met a really alive group of 50 young Christians, from Poleglass in West Belfast. Their leader, Ed Conlon is a most dedicated youngish American, whose team we are meeting soon to arrange a sharing of talent with our Young West.

I can assure you that the next generation is alive and vibrant, and with the Lord's help, Ireland could well survive the current disaster.

BELCANTO.
BELCANTO is a group, that has been formed under the leadership of our organist Mr Maurice McKenzie, that aims to sing the gospel of Jesus Christ, and to carry it beyond the confines of our own congregation. Many of the songs will be to settings composed by Maurice. These settings so often combine sheer inspiration and prodigious hard labour! Let us pray that this group will flourish and be fruitful in the Gospel.

NOVEMBER WCN 1991.

CELEBRATING 30 YEARS.
We celebrate 30 years in West Church by a Weekend with Canon Tom Smail and his wife Truda. In February 1968 Tom sowed seeds with us that have yielded fruit many hundred-fold. He's still a dynamic preacher, a superb teacher, a warm-hearted man who can be both tender, and when required, pungent and robust. He brought us into a new dimension of the Spirit in 1968,

and is the author of 2 books "The Forgotten Father," and "Reflected Glory" which focuses on the Son, Jesus Christ. He is well qualified for his subject for the Weekend, which will be **TRINITARIAN RENEWAL.**

SETTING THE AGENDA FOR YEARS AHEAD.
As we celebrate 30 years in West we believe that this visit can help us set our agenda for years ahead. Our ambition in Christ is for radical advance.
AND THIS IS NEEDED!
In my sermon on Sunday past I quoted the following statistics:
*** "More than half the people who have ever lived are now alive! The world's population is climbing past 5 billion.
***If we don't have an awakening in this generation, more people will go into an eternity without knowledge of Christ, than in all the past generations put together!
In that context 'Business as Usual' is not enough! Let us pray that, under God, this visit from the Smails will form part of that launching pad that will thrust us into that orbit that God has ordained for us in the Nineties and beyond!

HOW TO HELP YOUR CHILD SAY NO TO SEXUAL PRESSURE.
Whether your child is 7 or 19 they face tremendous pressure in this permissive age.
Josh McDowell and Rob Parsons, in a Belfast Conference, will help parents to discover how children are under tremendous pressure to be sexually active and "to learn how to create moral convictions in your child without sounding as though you are from another planet!" They aim to help parents create a positive view of sex for their children, and yet find ways to compete with the combined offensive of raging hormones, peer pressure and media manipulation.

IN NOVEMBER 1991, **KEN SYMINGTON** WROTE WITNESS SHEET 86.

"TO BELIEVE IN JESUS, IS TO ACCEPT THE WHOLE JESUS - I WISH I HAD REALISED THIS TRUTH YEARS AGO."

"I had everything and suddenly knew I had nothing.
I went to church for ten years in the belief that I was a Christian. I rarely missed a Sunday service. I took communion. I tithed, covenanted, prayed at the side of my bed every night. Our home even hosted a **Share & Prayer Group** every fortnight. I did 'good **works**' many a time in prayer I had asked Jesus into my life. **I understood and believed the gospel** (*though much, if not all of the Old Testament was a mystery, and seemed in total conflict to the God of love that was taught.*)

SO WHAT WAS MISSING?
It took ten years and a Mission Praise chorus to bring me to the point where *I began to have an uncomfortable feeling that something was wrong.* The simple chorus '**In my life be glorified**' and '**In my work be glorified**' *began to convict me that I was a fake.*
For as I sang it (with great gusto!) I began to see that in no part of my life was Christ glorified. At Church I 'behaved' like a Christian. In the House Group I 'behaved' like a Christian, and when I prayed I 'behaved' like a Christian. *But yet I never told anyone about Jesus. Never even owned up to going to Church, because I knew what my colleagues and friends thought about Christians. In no way had I the right to stand there and sing 'In my life be glorified' when that was the very part of my life I kept to myself!*

WEIGHING SCALES.
I was also aware that when safely away from the people I 'behaved' in front of, *my life was anything but glorifying to Christ.* (I justified my *weaknesses* as I called them, using the good old scales: my good points outweighed my bad points. Therefore I was overall a 'good' person and fit to call myself a Christian.)

CONFUSED... CRIED OUT!
This realisation confused me to the point that I began to feel very uncomfortable with Christians. *I began to argue with them over difficult Scriptures.* Over theology. And yet I found myself requesting them to sing this chorus over and over again.
One Sunday at Communion I mentally cried out to God from the heart *"If you're there and you care, help me, help me!"*

A few days later I was debating theology again, with a Christian in work. "**If God is love**" I argued, "Why is it every time I open the Old Testament, He's always asking for bulls and goats and sheep and lambs to be killed? Where is the love in that?"
"Can you not see?" the Christian replied, "Can you honestly not see?" "No, I can't see and I wish someone would show me!" I shouted in total frustration. At this point the young Christian beat a hasty retreat.
A MIME REVEALS ALL!
That night, that very night, my wife got a phone call to ask her if she would take part in a mime, because one of the original members was ill. She said she would if the other three members would teach her the part. Later that night the girls arrived at our home to rehearse and later they asked me into the kitchen to see the mime It was called '**Where is the Lamb?**' and explained perfectly, and beautifully my afternoon's question.
WOW!
No words can explain how this hit me. Not so much the explanation, which was wonderful, but the fact that God had personally spoken to me. My theological, doctrinal God

had answered my question. **He had been with me when I shouted my frustration. He had brought this mime to my house that night. He was in my home watching my reaction. Wow!**

AGLOW.
For three weeks I was aglow with this 'experience' but didn't know what to do about it, and so the memory gradually faded, and I slid back further than ever. I was even on the verge of quitting Church. **I had accepted now that something was missing, but I didn't know what it was. I thought I had done everything I could to be a Christian. I didn't know what else to do.**

A SUCCESS... BUT THE POOREST MAN THERE!
A month or two later we decided to go to the Methodist Annual Holiday Week. I had no intention of going there but that's exactly where God intended me to be, and in a story that is amazing (but too long to tell here) that's where I ended up. **I was locked away from the world for a whole week, and it changed my life.**
I owned three successful businesses. Drove a Porsche, and a Volvo Estate. Had a lovely family. A room full of business and sporting trophies. Worked in a glamorous, high profile industry with 'lovely' people. I knew the right people, holidayed in the right places. I counted myself a success. And yet as the week went on, and I really got to know the people I was camping with, **I began to see that all my jewellery was on the outside of me,** *while their jewellery was on the inside.*
Then on Thursday, the Speaker Rob Frost spoke on Philippians 3: 4-12. *'If any man thinks he has reason for confidence in the flesh, I have more'.* Here he described how Paul had achieved everything in the world that the 'flesh' could want *'but whatever I had, I count as loss because of the surpassing worth of knowing Christ!'* This from a man in prison!

In a moment I saw that my 'treasures and pleasures' were worthless. I was the poorest man there!

WORTH ABSOLUTELY NOTHING!
In a moment I saw that everything I had done was in the flesh. And could now see clearly that the praise of men, and wealth and position were worth nothing, absolutely nothing. I was Lord of my life, and had stuck Jesus and 'Christianity' on the outside of my life. **My invitations to Jesus to come into my life had been invitations from my head, and not my heart. I ran life my way, and thought I could invite Jesus to come into my life to sit on the passenger seat while I drove.**

I STILL DIDN'T KNOW WHAT TO DO!
..... Until next day when Rob Frost asked anyone who wanted to make a commitment to Jesus to come and kneel at the front. **I squirmed as he said this.** My head filled with different arguments. Confusion reigned. Then he said **"Come now"**, **and I leapt up and went to the front. There I truly gave my life, lock, stock and barrel to Jesus and the relief was** *immense. I surrendered. I wanted him to have all of me, for ever. I surrendered. I asked him to take this empty life and do something of real value with it.*
And praise the Lord, who was kneeling next to me, but my wife!

NEXT DAY.
The next day the 'Lord' entered my heart in dramatic style, leaving me in no doubt that my invitation had been faithfully accepted. Faith gripped my heart like a vice. *The Bible came alive. Praising Jesus brought a lump to my throat. And I literally could not stop telling everyone and anyone about him. The Holy Spirit shone his light on the Old Testament and I revelled in its dramatic beauty. It seemed that there were never enough hours in the day to feed the new spiritual hunger within.*

A 'HIGH'.
For six months I was on a 'high', and then for a year the Lord 'allowed' Satan to throw everything at me but the kitchen sink. With the Lord's help I came through it, with many branches pruned off, and my faith deeper than ever in the Lord and the Scriptures.

LED TO WEST CHURCH IN OCTOBER 1990
where, during a Life in the Spirit Seminar we received the Baptism of the Spirit and the lovely gift of tongues (Mark 16: 17).

What I realise as I look back, is that I thought I could have a divided Jesus. **Have Him as Saviour and me as Lord. One foot with Adam. And just to be safe one foot with Jesus. The Bible makes it abundantly clear that if you don't have Christ's Spirit in you, you don't have Christ (John 4: 13), and if you don't have Christ's Spirit you aren't born again, and if you aren't born again you remain under God's condemnation.**
If Christ isn't Lord He isn't Saviour and yet sadly I recognise others in the position I remained in all those years. The hardest ones to reach are those who believe they're saved through what they 'do'.
To believe in Jesus is to accept the whole Jesus. "My Lord and my God!" I wish I had realised this truth years ago.
Ken Symington, November 1991.

"YOU WILL NEVER KNOW TRUE SOBRIETY UNTIL......" TERRY ALLEN CAME TO A 'LIFE IN THE SPIRIT SEMINAR' IN JANUARY 1990.

David Bailie writes: "In October 2006 I met with **TERRY ALLEN**, and he told me of the dark pit in which he had lived for many years, in which he had hurt many people, even stole from his own mother, and walked out on

his young wife and did many things of which he was ashamed in his heart.
He belonged to Alcoholics Anonymous, Narcotics Anonymous and Gambling Anonymous, being hopelessly addicted in all three categories. Through Alcoholics Anonymous he came off all alcoholic drugs in 1979.
To keep off he needed to attend AA two or three times a week and relate his story to others. He dare not miss, for the desire was still there - though the body was sober, the spirit was still drunk!

TRUE SOBRIETY.
Terry had a brother Wesley, who lived in Enniskillen, was partially paralysed and registered blind, who had been 'saved' for 21 years. In a rare conversation with him, Wesley said to him, 'you *will never know true sobriety until you receive Jesus into your heart'*. Terry thought that this was nonsense for; after all, he had got off alcohol through the help of AA.

A NERVOUS BREAKDOWN.
Eventually in 1986 he had a nervous breakdown. He couldn't live with the guilt of his past life, of walking out on his marriage, hurting every member of his family network and his friends - *he never could get this out of his head!*
His GP referred him to the PNU at Ards Hospital where he was a patient under the care of Dr. Kernaghan for a year. This was good in that he was encouraged to *talk* about his past, from his teenage years. **Things were brought out!**

A YEAR IN NORWAY, THEN TO YMCA IN BANGOR.
Terry was then to spend a year in Norway in a situation that ministered to people who were total addicts.
In 1989 he returned to Bangor to the YMCA desiring to help young people
Two ladies, Rosie Mullan, a member of West, and Valerie Dunn were helpful towards him.

They always had prayer in the YMCA before the young people arrived and this brought him into a dimension from which he had been absent for many years. **By this stage Terry was questioning, searching, and aware of a great need.** Rosie suggested a Seminar in West.
So, very nervously Terry proceeded to West, but was welcomed and reassured by the presence of Don and Helen Ritchie, whom he knew.
Terry did not talk in the Seminar but listened attentively, and came to realise the truth of what his brother Wesley had said *'you will never know true sobriety until you receive Jesus into your heart'.*

STUMBLING BLOCKS.
~But there were stumbling blocks. **In Terry's estimation the sins of his past were too great to be forgiven!** Walking out on his young wife, in the context of the gambling that undermined all trust and grievously hurt his wife. *God could not forgive that!*

Yet in the context of the Seminar he came to see, through the help of the Spirit, that Jesus had died in his place, his blood had been shed for him, Jesus came under the guilt of all his sin.

AN APPOINTMENT.
In that context Terry made an appointment to see me. He was helped to accept and receive in his heart the Saviour Christ, **realising that all his sins, all his guilt, had been borne by Jesus on the cross. And as he did this, prayer was also made for him to be filled with the Holy Spirit.**
Terry says: 'I remember the tears, the warmth, wishing that my mum was with me! A great weight, as of a heavy anvil, was lifted from my shoulders. *All, all, all was forgiven!'*

TWO LADIES WATCHING!
Terry tells: *'I went down and parked my car on the Queen's Parade opposite the YMCA. As I crossed the road I saw that two ladies were watching, waiting for my return. I waved and smiled and the pair ran down the stairs to meet me. Rosie said "You have asked Jesus into your heart!'*

THE NEXT MORNING!
Each morning I said the Serenity Prayer. Next morning, for that day, I said **'Come into my heart, Lord Jesus, Come in today, come in to stay, come into my heart, Lord Jesus!'**
That morning, 7th February 1990, there was no desire for drink, and there has never been ever since and each day begins with a renewed invitation for the Spirit to fill his life.

Terry does not feel the need to keep going over the painful things of the past which Jesus has fully dealt with.
One of the first things he did was to go round to his mum's and tell her - she embraced him with love and deepest gratitude to God, *declaring that her prayers were answered!*

He phoned his brother Wesley, greeting him with a question, **'How are you, brother?'** Wesley did not miss the significance of the last word, *and broke down in tears.* Terry reminded him of that conversation of years before and said, *'Tonight I know true sobriety!'*

BLESSED. AND A BLESSING!
God has greatly blessed and used Terry in the years since then.
Ten years ago he and Barbara married (his first wife remarried years previously) in a marriage 'absolutely of the Lord!'; Terry is a fulltime lay worker in the Methodist Church in Bangor; and currently is involved every Friday in helping to run an Alpha Course for 'lifers' in the Maghaberry Prison.

JANUARY WCN 1992.

POLYCULTURE -MEN IN NEW DIMESNION!

David Bailie writes:
"We had parked our bicycles under the shade of a welcome tree beside a disused church, were having our picnic, and had got into conversation with a local farmer who was depressed by the drought from which the Loire Valley had suffered for two or three years and by a general gloomy prospect about farming. 'What kind of farming are you involved in?' we asked. 'Polyculture' he replied, an expressive word that seemed richer than our 'mixed farming'. At the time, it registered in my mind and heart that I could have given the same answer in respect of the work of Christ's Church! POLYCULTURE! Many forms of cultivation are required to bring in the full, rich harvest that Christ seeks from us. And that's why we hope to open up a new field for cultivation in 1992.

MORE WOMEN THAN MEN IN CHURCH.

That is a fact! We are happy to have all the women we have! In the Church we have women's groups and mixed groups, but few men's groups. We feel that there may be a place for some MEN'S GROUPS. **And so we plan an 'OPEN NIGHT' for men on Tuesday 4th February. We are convinced that we have good news for everybody,** *men included.*
There will be plenty of sincere, straightforward testimony to the fact that people's lives have been changed for the better and greatly strengthened and enriched *through faith in Christ- over the whole range of situations that affect the everyday, workaday life of MEN!*

Sometimes, like **John McCroskery,** men may have the conviction that the Christian life is dull, burdensome, boring! John tells us about that in his Witness Sheet. Not long ago in one of our Seminars, a man shared his concern for three men he knew **whose lives and homes were being destroyed through addiction to alcohol.** Read what **Desmond Perry** has written in an article entitled **"Beyond Reasonable Doubt."** Sometimes a man is brought to the place of faith, like **Ken Douglas** whose wife Sandra had rejected God under repeated blows from life. When he saw a great change in her life, he wanted what she had found. He writes: 'I joined a Seminar… I saw the power of God at work in my group, the dramatic change in other people's lives through prayer, and so I committed my life to God.' **Several other examples are mentioned in January WCN.**

We realise that many men are kept away from the life that is in Christ and the vitality that is in the Church, through *fear!*

THE TWILIGHT ZONE.

An outreach towards young people will take place through a Young People's Coffee Bar between Thursday 30th January and Sunday 2nd February.
Its aim is to challenge and win young people for Jesus, in our district and in our schools.
And it is to train, equip and release young people into sharing their faith with a whole new confidence and effectiveness.
The speaker will be Steve Stockman- the meeting for teens and early-Twenties. There will be bands, speakers, videos and interviews.

Mention has already been made in January WCN of Desmond Perry and his Witness also appears in it. We give it now, under his heading of:

BEYOND REASONABLE DOUBT.

"All of us like sheep were lost, each of us going his own way." Isaiah 53: 6.

"HELL-BENT ON DESTROYING MYSELF."

"**Two years ago I was such a sheep and the way I was going was leading to destruction, self-destruction.** 1989 was, for me, **a year of deaths -** my mother died at the beginning of January, a close friend in May, the 21-year old daughter of other friends in June; by the autumn I had been to seven funerals and with each one, I sank lower and lower and with no spiritual anchor, it was a matter of time before I was going to be the main feature at an eighth. **It was apparent to everyone who knew me, that I was intent, even hell-bent, on destroying myself.**

INTRODUCED TO A CHRISTIAN GIRL.

Then, in November, I was introduced to a Christian girl. I was told that she wouldn't preach at me and she didn't - she talked to me about heaven and the fact that I wouldn't get in, which I rather resented, because I didn't think I was such a bad person - I didn't lie or cheat or steal, or do any of the bad things we sadly see around us. **But I didn't believe in Christ, so the pearly gates would be firmly shut in my face. What made matters worse was the fact that some of the villains that I deal with in my work would get in, if they truly repented, even if it was at the last moment - that wasn't fair, thought I and said so.**
But it made me think. I also thought about the girl, there was an aura of peace and happiness about her.
Then she invited me to go with her to West Church - an irony was that I had gone to West when it was in Carnalea House. I warned her that there was a considerable risk of the place falling about our ears if I crossed the threshold - it didn't and at the end of the service I met Mr Bailie again for the first time in 25 years - he recognised me! **I went back twice more and on those three occasions it was as if David was preaching to me - I cannot recall the actual sermons but it was about searching.**

I DEAL IN PROOF BEYOND REASONABLE DOUBT.
My searching had resulted in one tangible thing - I had met the woman I wanted to spend the rest of my life with. But what of the after-life? By that stage, I was prepared to accept the probability of God, but I need more - **I deal in proof beyond reasonable doubt and I didn't know where I would get that.**

THE END OF MY SEARCH - JESUS CHRIST.
I went to see David and he prayed with me. A 'Life in the Spirit' seminar was starting, and I enrolled, not knowing what to expect. The first meeting was Wednesday 24th January 1990 and there were no huge revelations, no flashing lights, blasts of trumpets - it was 'interesting'.
Then, the next day, driving down the Bangor Road in the rush hour, which would normally have me up to 'high doh', **I got this amazing feeling of tranquillity - I didn't realise it, but I had arrived at the end of my search - Jesus Christ. I had unwittingly issued an invitation to Him to come into my heart - so simple in retrospect, and proof beyond reasonable (no, any) doubt!**

THE INEXORABLE SPIRAL INTO OBLIVION - HALTED, REVERSED.
The second tangible result was life, everlasting. *No more was there the desire to destroy myself, the inexorable spiral into oblivion had been halted, reversed.*
The girl, Carmel, and I married on my 40th birthday. One of the hymns at the wedding contained that wonderful piece - *"On Christ, the solid rock I stand, all other ground is sinking sand."*
I suppose I have slipped off it a couple of times, but Jesus is always there to help you back up."

DESMOND PERRY, November 1991.

Another person who, also in November 1991, wrote her WITNESS **story of how, eventually, she came to know God and gain freedom from a longstanding depression was PAT HAWTHORNE**, under the title:

14 YEARS LONG ENOUGH TO BE ON DRUGS - THE SLOW SLIDE INTO MENTAL AND EMOTIONAL MISERY BEGAN AGAIN.

"I first became ill with depression about a year after my fourth child was born. It was kept at bay with drugs and I lived a normal family life but misery was just below the surface ready to break out. I was always nervous and anxious, and though everything in my life looked normal, I was always on edge, not really enjoying all the good gifts the Lord gave me. My husband was always supportive and encouraging but could not understand, as I could not, what was wrong and why I could not enjoy my life.

I HAD TURNED MY BACK ON THE LORD.
When my doctor decided that 14 years was long enough to be on drugs, the slow slide into mental and emotional misery began again. I looked and acted normally and most people did not realise anything was wrong. After a few glasses of wine I was lively and cheerful, **but afterwards I was in despair again. Often I wished my life could be over but the Lord held on to me and never let me go.** I had turned my back on him at fifteen about a year after I had been confirmed in the Church of Ireland. Even though I said I did not believe in Him any more, there was always the feeling of something missing, something not right in my life.
I sought to fill this void by finding out about other religions like Buddhism, Islam, Hinduism, and even the occult fringe like Tarot, palmistry, horoscopes etc, seeking for some meaning in something other than the material world, but nothing was sure and lasting.
I felt alone for nobody else I knew seemed to feel that way, they all seemed to enjoy their lives except when there was obvious trouble. I had studied a course called 'Man's Religious Quest' and the text books were still in the house, when about five years ago in 1986 I remembered the words of Jesus, 'Ask and it shall be given to you, seek and you will find, knock and the door will be opened to you'. *With great intensity I prayed, "Lord, you said these words and I am asking, I'm seeking and I'm knocking. I don't know what it is I'm asking for, but there must be more to life than this; please open the door to me."*

I FELT I WOULD LIKE TO READ THE BIBLE.
Not long after I was in the house alone when I felt I would like to read the Bible. Not being familiar with the Scriptures, and not knowing where to start, I used one of the textbooks that had selected passages of Scripture in it. **The book opened easily at the Sermon on the Mount and I settled down to read it. After reading only a few lines the words seemed to come alive for me** *and I had the overwhelming sensation of Jesus speaking directly to me from the page. My eyes seemed to fill up and by the end of the piece I was weeping and knew the Lord was with me. I knelt down on the floor and told him I was sorry I had turned away from Him and that I would turn to Him now and put my foot on the road that would bring me nearer to him.* At this time I attended church only occasionally, and didn't know to read the Bible regularly.

OCCULT INVOLVEMENT.
It was a couple of years later that a friend suggested my going to West Church where the music at the Praise Services was lively and enjoyable. so I went occasionally. **A colleague at work suggested starting a 'Life in the Spirit' seminar,** *and it was there I learned to love the Scriptures, to meet with*

other Christians on a regular basis and to attend services more regularly.

I learned to trust the Lord more fully, and learned of his love and power to change lives. Now there was hope and meaning in my life and a new direction *but still I did not feel fully well. I knew the Lord's presence with me often but there was still something not right.* We used to sing a chorus with the words. "You have set this captive free" but I knew I was not free yet. In faith I prayed that I *will* be free.

It was some months later, one evening in church that someone spoke of a girl needing ministry that did not seem to be successful until it was discovered that she had some occult involvement in her past. When this was confessed she was healed and became a Christian.

READY TO TAKE COMMUNION FOR THE FIRST TIME IN 30 YEARS.

This struck me forcibly, and I decided to go after the main service to the Healing Service where two people prayed with me. This was a great relief, but I didn't feel any different.

A couple of weeks later a friend invited me to attend a Day of Prayer at Rostrevor Christian Renewal Centre, **and again I prayed that the lingering traces of past occult involvement be taken away from me, and that the Holy Spirit would cleanse me and fill me.** *There was a deep sense of peace about this. The following Sunday was a Communion Service and I felt ready to take communion for the first time in about thirty years. The service was very special. Two days later I was walking into work when I realised I was singing very happily to myself, and realised that I felt wonderful and that the depression had entirely gone. I was full of joy and almost euphoric for several weeks.*

I GIVE HIM ALL THE GLORY.

That was two years ago and though I do, sometimes, not feel really well, it is only temporary, and lasts only a few days, **whereas before the depression, it never lifted and I thought this would have to be endured for the rest of my life. He continues to show me wrong attitudes in my life and my dependence on his goodness and mercy increases.**

I give Him all the glory and honour and thanks, for He has brought me from darkness into his wonderful light.

BRIAN SCOTT relates:
"I FELT A MOVEMENT IN MY INJURED BACK, LIKE A VENETIAN BLIND CLOSSING."

MY BACK INJURED IN 1958.
"In 1958, while in the Merchant Navy, I injured my back, and spent some time in hospital. Following my discharge from hospital I returned to work, but thereafter I had trouble with my back, having spells of back pain, lasting for weeks at a time. Between these attacks I was well, and had no pain at all. However over the years the attacks became more frequent, and often I would not only have pain, but also a 'twist' in my back, which pulled me over to one side. I was advised to put a board under my mattress, but usually I had most ease when lying on the floor.

TREATMENT AT R.V.H.
Over the past 20 years, I attended the late Dr George Gregg in the Royal Victoria Hospital on many occasions. Dr Gregg died about 5 years ago, and I was concerned as to whom I should see if the problem arose again.. However, about that time my wife was asked to a **'Prayer & Praise meeting' in West Church, which she very much enjoyed, and eventually we started to go to the Praise services on a Sunday evening.**

CONTINUOUS PAIN.

In 1983 we moved from Gilnahirk to Dundonald, and we needed a new path in the garden. Feeling fairly fit at that time, I decided to do the job myself, with the help of a friend. However, shortly afterwards I again developed back pain, **with severe pain radiating down my left leg to the foot.** I tried lying in bed for a few days, but had no ease from this, and so I decided to go back to work with the aid of a walking stick. I went to see my own doctor, and received pain-relieving tablets, and anti-inflammatory tablets, but unfortunately these didn't help. **Weeks went past and I was in continuous pain.**

I JUST PROPPED MYSELF AGAINST THE WALL, AS I COULDN'T SIT DOWN.
One Sunday evening my wife wanted to take her mother to the Praise Service in West. **My back was extremely painful, but I felt I wanted to go to the service with them. When we got into the church I found it very difficult to sit on the wooden chairs and Anne asked me if I would like to go home. However, I felt I wanted to stay.** I had to pull myself up out of the chair by holding on to the chair in front of me when we had to stand for the hymns. When Mr Bailie made the announcements he mentioned **The Healing Service, and my wife asked me if I wouldn't like to go to that service.** I felt it would be rather long for my wife, mother-in-law, and son to hang around, **but they persuaded me.** I was very thankful when the main service ended as I was very sore indeed, **and on entering the Praise Room, where the Healing Service is held,** *I just propped myself against the wall, as I couldn't possibly sit down again.*

LIKE A VENETIAN BLIND CLOSING.
Mr Bailie came over to speak to me and William Hall was with him. Mr Bailie put his hand on my shoulder and William prayed. **I felt movement in my back, which I can only describe as like a Venetian blind closing, or a row of dominoes toppling over. The pain was disappearing, and I was able to raise my left foot from the floor quite easily. By the time the prayer was over I was completely

free of pain.
FREE FROM PAIN.
It was a wonderful feeling to be free of pain, and I thanked God for healing me, and then spoke to Mr Bailie and William. Following this I was able to drive my mother-in-law across town, without any pain whatsoever. Since that day, now 3 years ago, I have never had pain in my back or down my leg. *The great Physician had healed me, and I now know from personal experience that miracles do still happen today, just as they did 2000 years ago."*

POST-SCRIPT August 2003.
"Following my healing I asked God to show me what He wanted me to do for Him. I continued to pray for guidance as I did not feel led in any particular direction, but sometimes the answer is so simple we just don't see it. I was a technical representative and travelled all over Northern Ireland, *and I often found myself telling people about my healing. One day I realised that God was using me and I just hadn't been aware of it.* I had called to see an engineer who was having a problem with a machine in a big engineering company. During the course of our conversation he mentioned that he had a 'bad back' and was in considerable pain. I asked him if he had had prayer for his condition, and he said it was the only thing he hadn't tried. I then told him of my healing which he thought was an amazing experience. I then opened my briefcase and gave him one of my testimony sheets, which I always carried for just such a situation. *This made me realise just how God was using me, in my everyday business, to glorify His Name.*

When I look back over my life I see how God has been with me all the way, and I want to continue serving Him. *Because of this healing I am particularly thrilled to be able to assist the Special Care Group with the disabled children - something I most certainly could not have done before the Lord healed me.*

FEBRUARY WCN 1992.

The February edition of West Church News is normally bulging with annual reports from all our groups and organisations - and an opportunity to look back and to look forward.
VICTOR STEPHENS, OUR CHURCH TREASURER helps steer a very large financial ship, and year by year does a prodigious amount of work. He writes:"Our Church accounts this year are very satisfactory. Considering that we had an outlay of £13,596 for building and repairs we ended the year just £4,488 overspent. Our FWO receipts increased by 11% and we had a wonderful response to the Christmas World Development project for water for Somalia of £5,794.
Our Number 5 account was overspent by £2,771, but as this account is steadily increasing in congregational givings, I would forecast at least a break-even point at the end of 1991.
Our Number 6 or Outreach account remains in a healthy position even with our generous allocation of Annual Donations.
In all a good year and our thanks are due to those who give so generously to all our Church Finances.

WILLIAN LYNN gave his last report as congregational Secretary. We thank him for work steadily and effectively done, and wish him well as he has taken up duties as Organist in St. Andrew's, Bangor.

**MAKE AN EXPERIMENT AND SAY 'THANK YOU' TO BILLY RICHARDSON.
The Experiment:**
Count the number of pages in West Church News and in the Financial Statement, and **multiply by 1100+
Then calculate the time that it has taken him to print all this for us.**

And similar calculations could be made for Maureen Blackmore and her collating team, and for Elizabeth McClelland as she prepares all the bundles for our distributors.
I am sure that you miss the beautiful graphics that ALAN STEWART has done for us for so long. A Word Processor is not quite the same, but under pressure of time one submits to the temptation of what is immediately available!

KIRK SESSION REPORT.
This is a substantial one as we have completed 30 years and gives us a mini-review of our thirty years.
The Kirk Session report:
30th ANNIVERSARY SERVICES:
"…that harvest and the challenge still before us were the twin reasons for our Anniversary Services conducted by the Rev. Canon Tom Smail, who was accompanied by his wife Truda. In these unforgettable services we rejoiced in God's goodness to us and were reminded of the unconditional love and provision of God for us as Canon Smail in one of his sermons used these words, *"in the midst of the mess there is a ladder to God (Genesis 28:12).*
As we listened there was a convincing, encouraging and welcome message which we can take to those who are all too aware of the pressures of life, the despair of their particular situation or seemingly insurmountable problems, but who feel they have no ladder to climb, no faith in a good and loving God, and who might ask, "what has the church achieved in 30 years?"

Mr William McClelland, our Clerk of Session gives this answer to those in the community who ask to know what God is really like, and what the Church has achieved, as follows   the evidence of those who come to enquire is there in plenty. Read our Witness sheets and you will find the real life accounts of people who were fearful, oppressed or unbelieving and who found faith in the living Christ to be all that He claimed to be. *They have found the answer to their questions. Our 'Life in the Spirit Seminars' are open to all who wish to ask these questions seriously or who are in any trouble or despair and need somehow to find the ladder to God.*

GRIEF OVER SINCLAIR SHOOTINGS.

One of the events that brought profound shock and sadness to the whole West Church congregation and Bangor community were the tragic deaths, by gunshot of the parents of Robert, Samuel and Jayne Sinclair, and of Jacqueline (married to Paul Wilkinson). This evoked a deep response from the congregation, which involved substantial work on the home to make it warm, bright and welcoming. Members of the congregation also provided meals, from time to time.

February WCN gave news of this, and also included a poem of 20 verses, entitled "Friends" by ROBERT (well-known among our young people for his outstanding musical talents). This poem appeared in "THE TREE MONKEY" a new publication produced by our young people in West, that allowed Robert to articulate his feelings through the time of trial, and his gratitude for love received. Here are some verses:

"The times I've had this year alone,
Bring a smile upon my face
This year has seemed like four-year long
But I can keep the pace.

But this year ended sadly,
I lost my loving Mum,
She really meant the most to me
And I was her Number One.

I still cannot believe she's gone,
I don't think I ever will,
There's an empty place in my life
That no-one else can fill.

She taught me how to love people
And treat them with respect,
Don't be angry or cruel to them
And love you can expect.

But I love the truth in thinking
I will see my mum again,
I haven't seen the last of her,
For she was 'born again'.
I don't know where my Dad has gone,
It's all in God's hands now,
I feel so very sorry for him,
Some people don't know how.

I don't feel bitter against him,
He was a very lonely man,
He never went out with friends at all
And had a money saving plan.

I don't understand what God has done
But I trust Him all the way,
For He helps me build my happy life
Every single day.

My friends are more precious than anything else
For they help me and I help them,
Naturally, God comes first
But I know He works through them.

Thank you each and everyone
Of my beautiful, loving friends,
I love you all for what you are
And the love through you God sends."
Robert Sinclair.

THE FRIENDSHIP GROUP IS FORMED- OUT OF THE 'YOUNG WOMEN'S ASSOCIATION'.

LINDA WILSON reports that the YWA celebrated its 25th Anniversary in September 1991, when some 120 members and guests attended, Margaret Davidson, and its first President reminiscing. The name of the organisation was changed to THE FRIENDSHIP GROUP, which meet on the first and third Mondays of the month.

OUR DEAR, DEAR WALTER BURRELL"

February WCN gives an update from WALTER BURRELL who has won a place of affection in the hearts of West Church members through his annual visits to our congregation. We are always impressed by this man of small stature but of immense heart and courage, who with his wife Mary, has given himself sacrificially to the seamen who come in a variety of ships and from a multitude of nations, to Cork Harbour.

A one-time alcoholic, he was saved from destructive addiction for life-giving service to a multitude of men over many years and for caring for women -many with broken lives and enmeshed in prostitution- who went on to these ships.

Walter left a good job, with company staff under him, to join a Mission where the finances were at very low ebb. In so doing, he also gave up a lovely home for two little rooms and where the very food on the table was scant.

"My first morning on the dockside, fear gripping my heart, home and security gone, going up the gangway of the weather-beaten Cairngorm, my first ship. A lone seaman at 9.00am, a crate of beer at his side, a bottle on his lips, grunted 'Who are you?' Hearing I was from a Mission, he grabbed my hand, urging me to sit by his side, showing me the loneliness of these men.

23 years later, hundreds and hundreds of gangways, leading me on board super-tankers in Bantry Bay, timber boats from Africa, Russian cargo ships, fishing factory ships from Romania and Bulgaria…….and Scripture Gift Mission supplying us with Bible tracts in all languages."

The stories that Walter tells, his compassion in Christ for so many, the utter giving of himself to so many in need, reminds one of the spirit and labour of Paul who has written: *as servants of God we commend ourselves in every way: in great endurance; in troubles, hardships and distresses… in hard work, sleepless nights; in the Holy Spirit and in sincere love; in truthful speech and in the power of God; sorrowful, yet always rejoicing; poor yet making many rich; having nothing, yet possessing everything."*

In Walter, we in West salute a man, who always brought us encouragement and challenge, who by his word and example ever urged us to keep going forward in the Lord's ministry.

WHAT A CHANGE!
Carol Aspinall and 'Life in the Spirit'.

"I was forty-five years old when I came to true faith in the Lord. My birthday is on Christmas Day and I always felt it was special to share Christ's birthday - yet I almost never went to church.
I prayed to God and my prayers were answered - so much I can hardly believe it, looking back - but I didn't really love or worship Him, because I hadn't given my life to Him.
I joined the **Church of Ireland**- wanting my children to have the upbringing I had missed. I rather like the kneeling and ritual and became a communicant- but nothing spiritual happened to me. Gradually, I fell away and virtually stopped going to church.
I became ill in 1974 and was diagnosed as having Multiple Sclerosis. My husband lived with this knowledge for a year, until I found out for myself in 1975. This was a devastating blow for our family and, I must confess, I found it hard to come to terms with.
For five or six years I was not too badly affected - I could walk and look normal- although I was always in pain... I started to deteriorate and, very suddenly, in March 1983, I could no longer walk and the dreaded wheelchair became a part of me.

I STARTED TO PRAY THAT I WOULD DIE!
Gradually I became depressed. Then some really horrendous symptoms of the MS started to occur and I sank further and further into depression. I was at the bottom of a black pit and I could see no light. I was still praying, desperately, for help - *then I started praying that I would die!*
'When you reach rock bottom, then God takes over'- this is what happened to me.
I was just home from hospital when a friend came to see me and said, 'Come with me to West Church'. She'd been to a 'Life in the Spirit Seminar' and gained so much, she was going to another.

FROM THAT FIRST NIGHT, I WAS HOOKED!
I didn't know what to expect but, from that first night I was hooked! I could see such joy on the faces of those I knew to be Christians- I wanted that joy. I loved the seminar, and gradually realised that the lovely feeling I had there was staying with me.
What had been words to me before - that Jesus had died for me - **at last I understood, I knew!** I opened my heart to Him, the Holy Spirit took my hand - I really did feel that one night - and He has never let me go!

What a change in my life! I joined West Church and go every Sunday. I am in a house group and I go to the Thursday Morning Young Women's Get Together. I value so much the fellowship and love I meet in these groups.

My physical condition has got worse, but my depression is cured completely, so I can cope with my difficulties because I know the Lord is with me all the time. I had hardly ever read the Bible, but now I read it every day and love it more and more.
I go regularly to the Healing Service, in faith I will be helped. I can witness to His presence in my life - even though I am still in a wheelchair - and I do! I love and worship my Lord with all my being. He has done wonderful things for me!

GRAHAM DORE-
WYCLIFFE BIBLE TRANSLATORS.
Over the years it has been ever refreshing for us to hear from Graham Dore, to delight in his use of language and the inventive and compelling manner in which he communicates the Gospel that has laid hold of his own life.
In January 1992 he writes:
"The old problems of 1991 frown upon us, but we look forward to the new things God will do in us, for us and through us. *As you support the work of Bible translation along with us, this will include bringing many people worldwide out of darkness into light as the Gospel enters their hearts for the first time in their own language.*
"It was refreshing to meet a couple just returned from Indonesia, where they had been distributing copies of the newly translated Mark's Gospel. **For many this was their first book.** *For most people there, religious things are a performance, having no meaning. Important things are done in their own language.* So when one of the Indonesian translators led a church service entirely in the local language, they were all ears, and for once no one was gazing out of the window!
It was also great to hear from a couple we know in Mongolia. They translated the New Testament and introduced it to the fledgling church for the first time in 1991. **It had an immediate powerful effect."**

DGB writes in 2006: **We take opportunity also to salute Graham Dore, and his wife Janet, and to rejoice that their children Alasdair and Elizabeth have become also ardent emissaries of the Good News of Jesus.**

DIED FROM AIDS - BUT DIED AS A CHRISTIAN.

February WCN also brought tidings from Dr Ian Clarke and his wife Robbie from Uganda. His letter begins:

"This Christmas, our hearts are heavy, as a dear friend of ours has died. ANDO was very quiet, a man of few words - but so steadfast and reliable that we had come to depend on him. He had the keys to the stores in the hospital, and was general site foreman for the workers. If there was ever a somewhat awkward or difficult job to be done, Ando could do it. Ando had a sweet spirit; he was the kind of person who thought of others before he thought of himself. **Three years ago, we had the privilege of helping Ando to come to faith in Jesus Christ as Lord. It was a faith that he very much needed as 6 months later I had to tell him that he had AIDS."**

Ian Clarke goes on to paint a picture of a marvellous Christian man, and then of his death.

An equally moving story is shared when a woman for whom Robbie cared also died, leaving four children orphaned., a great cause of grief for the Clarkes and their children. When Sean Clarke (son\) heard that Ando had died he summed up our feelings: **'We are surrounded by death on this holiday, why do all the good people have to die?'** and he wept quietly.

DGB- When we read such stories, much abbreviated, of people in whom Christ's compassion burns strongly; **we in West also salute them in Jesus Name!**
EARLY MARCH WCN.

MAJOR EXPANSION.

"At our best attended ever **ANNUAL MEETING OF THE CONGREGATION ON 11TH March 1992, it was warmly resolved to purchase two adjacent properties, 91 and 93 Crawfordsburn Road. The resolutions were brought before the Annual Meeting with the unanimous recommendation of both Church Committee and Kirk Session.**

OUR PRESENT SITE RESTRICTED.
As our present site is severely restricted, these purchases, which almost double our land area, will help secure the future for further development as may be required.
91 is a commodious house that we can begin to use for a variety of purposes right away. A house provides an ideal setting for smaller group meetings, for seminars and for youth work, providing a community atmosphere and environment.
93 is a modern bungalow that can be developed upstairs, that may probably be let in the shorter term to help pay off our substantial debt.
The extensive grounds may help to provide much needed additional car parking.

A 'ONCE-IN-A-LIFETIME' OPPORTUNITY - *NOT TO BE MISSED!*
It is to be emphasised that this is probably a 'once-in-a-lifetime' chance to buy these two properties that have come on the market at the same time. **Planning permission had already been sought to build another house in the extensive grounds of 93. Should this have happened the opportunity to buy the property in the present way would have gone completely.** *The timing of this matter has not been of our choosing - and yet the timing may have been altogether right!* **In any case we have felt it to be an opportunity to be grasped without hesitation!**

A WORD OF COMFORT - AND A STRETCHING CHALLENGE.
Mr John Poole, who has been the Treasurer of our Number 6 'Building and Outreach Fund' over the past 9 years, informs us that during that time £195,000 has been raised, which paid for our New Hall and allowed us also to give £36,000 for various Outreach Projects. *That's encouragement from the past.*

However, when we launched that Fund our target was not much in excess of £100,000 and we had the opportunity to build up a substantial balance before work actually began, *and at no point had we to borrow much more than £40,000.*
This time the target is nearly double and we could therefore have to borrow up to £150,000. *This is why it will be imperative for us to raise a substantial sum with the utmost speed to defray crippling interest charges.*

The plan laid before the congregation was to secure as many lump-sum gifts as possible, (by Giftaid for sums over £600) AND to get 300 families making monthly payments (preferably by Banker's Orders) over a 4-year period, and COVENANTED.

Various illustrative tables were presented to indicate how we might reach our goal
NOTE: The magnitude of the task of raising £170,000 is such that we invite our members to give, as far as possible <u>both</u> lump sum gifts <u>and monthly</u> contributions.

TO HELP US MAKE OUR RESPONSE: OUR TREASURERS WILL HOLD 2 SATURDAY CLINICS.

This is a time of opportunity and a moment of testing for West Church and in faith and generosity we want to rise to the occasion.

We have done our utmost to present clearly the ways in which our members may respond, both by *lump sum donations,* and by *monthly Banker's Orders,* <u>and the importance of covenanting both.</u>

We know that several pages of closely written material *can be daunting, however, with experts personally present to advise and clarify, things appear much simpler.*
So our Covenants' Secretary, who is also our Property & Outreach Treasurer, Mr John Poole, with a team of others will be present on Saturday 29th February and on Saturday 7th March, *to advise, to witness signatures and to help you update and complete your transactions for West Church at this important time.*
Do come, at any time between 10.00am and 12 noon.
SATURDAY CLINICS, 29TH FEBRUARY AND 7TH MARCH.

APRIL WCN 1992.
ALLELUIA! GOD HAS BEEN IN *THIS* GIVING!
AND WE ARE GRATEFUL AND GIVE THE GLORY TO HIM!

In the March edition of WCN we placed before the congregation our plan for purchasing 2 additional properties, 91 and 93 Crawfordsburn Road at a total cost of £170,000. Then we said: *"This is a time of opportunity and a moment of testing for West Church, and in faith and generosity we want to rise to the occasion."*

THE WHOLE FINANCIAL PACKAGE NOW IN PLACE: WONDERFUL!

The Lord has given to our people a remarkable single-minded spirit and a great and cheerful generosity. The result of this is, that through Giftaid donations, lump sum gifts, and monthly banker's orders, with covenants **we now have enough money to pay off the total amount, including the interest on the money we must borrow. And all this within a period of 4 years!** This is a wonderful response, a generosity inspired by God's own Spirit. We are glad, and grateful and deeply happy. **At the beginning of 1992 we did not even envisage such a venture, and now, at the end of the first quarter, the whole financial package is in place.**

OUR GRATITUDE TO OUR TREASURERS FOR THEIR 'SATURDAY CLINICS'.

Just over a month ago we were struggling to present a coherent and comprehensive financial package to our members, and found that it took several closely-typed pages to cover all aspects of our proposals. It was in that context that **Brian McQuitty** suggested a **"CLINIC" to which people might come, with our treasurers in attendance to offer help.** It was a great idea, to which our members responded warmly. **We planned 2 Saturday Morning Clinics. In the end we found it necessary to have 5!**
We are most grateful for our Property&Outreach Treasurer John Poole, who was in attendance each week, assisted by our Treasurer Victor Stephens and our new Church Secretary Brian Wilson and our supportive and encouraging, 'coffee-making' Clerk of Session, William McClellland.
We are most grateful to all these men for the time they gave and for the work that they put in. YOUR Response was such that there was always a smile to be seen on their faces! Again, we thank you!

BEHIND THIS RESPONSE, A VISION FOR THE FUTURE?

Our people were aware that, through the purchase of these buildings and their extensive grounds, we were doing something important in securing the future for coming generations in West. There was a realisation that God had lined up many things for us to do in Jesus' Name. Again we reminded ourselves of Andy Arbuthnot's prophetic picture of an explosion of love flowing out from our Church into the community, near and far.

We feel that this is already happening, more and more intensively.

'LIFE IN THE SPIRIT SEMINARS' - record numbers already enlisting in 1992.

Not only are our own members enlisting in these Seminars, *but more and more people are crowding in from beyond our own membership.*
In January we started 2 Seminars, a morning one led by Heather Thompson, and an evening one led by myself (DGB) assisted by Julie Hamilton. Between these 2 Seminars about 50 people are in attendance.
Then there's a MEN'S SEMINAR led by Alvin with a dozen people in it, and another one led by Julie with more than 2 dozen in it.
Alvin also leads a YOUNG PEOPLE'S Seminar on a Saturday morning with 20+ members.
And our next scheduled new Seminar will begin on Thursday 23rd April at 8.00pm.

All this shows a spiritual hunger and that it is being satisfied in the meetings we hold. It is a joy to see people being released into life and wholeness in the Spirit, for there are so many people who need to know God and to be saved, healed and empowered by Him.

OUR NEW HOUSES GIVE US OPPORTUNITY FOR ENLARGED MINISTRY.

WE NEED TO BE IN TUNE WITH GOD AND GET OUR AGENDA FROM HIM.

At a recent Late Night Prayer Meeting and at one of our Seminars, having studied the passage in John 4, where Jesus gave 'the living water' to the Samaritan Woman at the Well and then told his astonished disciples to *'lift up your eyes, for the fields are already white for harvest',* I nvited people to be silent before God for a period, asking Him to show us where the harvest is ripe in our midst, and

<u>**to show us how to reap it,
and to show us how our new
houses might be used in all of this.**</u>

The things that came into people's minds were interesting and illuminating and may be pointers to future ministry lying ahead for us.

HERE ARE SOME OF THE IDEAS THAT CAME:

Especially in respect of <u>91</u> - that it might be 'An Open House', 'A Counselling Centre', 'A Christian Helpline' - an alive home, where the bell could be rung, always someone there to welcome, with understanding and ability to help; a Light in the community, a place of Ministry, a place, easier for some to come to than a formal church building.
A place where praying is nurtured.
A Centre that makes available to our members and others the vast, untapped reservoir of expertise that we have within our congregation, where people could get advice privately.
A Centre point for social matters, like co-ordinating transport to hospitals etc. A Study Centre, for Bible Study, to help Christians to grow spiritually.
Weekend Courses.
An Oasis in the desert, a place of 'refuge' for the alcoholic, the abused, the dispirited.
A place for the up-building of Family Life, bringing healing and reconciliation.
A place to address the needs of lonely old age.
A place to run 'Retreat' days.
A place with the function of a Confessional.
A place to provide a 'Common Room' for local residents. A place for Seminars to promote Christian Nurture of our young people.
A place having the function of 'the cities of refuge'

One person, in praying about the use of these houses, and God's place and purpose for us in West Church, seemed to be aware of a command **"Aim High."** It came in such a way that she raised her head to look up. **The command was repeated "Aim higher!" and then "Still higher!", and with that there were the words "Attempt Great Things!"**

All these ideas have been given, just as they came into people's minds, as they waited together in the Presence of God.
*The Scriptures tell us not to dismiss any such thoughts, as it were 'out of hand'.
Maybe they seem impractical - maybe they are 'off target'.
But they are to be considered.
We are to ponder and to sift, and keep what is good. We wait before God and we attempt to gain insight into the way in which He wants to lead us.*

CENTRAL TO THIS VISION TO SHARE THE GOOD NEWS OF JESUS.
We want to share Good News in the grace and compassion of Christ, with a servant heart, to not a few who may be troubled or without hope.

NEW MINISTRIES NEED TO BE STEEPED IN PRAYER.

Our Thursday 'Early Morning Prayer' and our Friday 'Late Night Prayer' have not been altogether crowded **but are nevertheless necessary and fruitful. It is doubtful that anyone comes and on leaving feels, 'Well, that was a waste of time'!** *Normally, people feel just the opposite - not only has the Spirit of God brooded over the matters prayed about, <u>but also over those who have been doing the praying,</u> so that they themselves leave refreshed!*

Therefore such praying needs to be nurtured further - people may pray in our Prayer Room at more convenient and less sociable hours. And people may be helped to pray better! In this regard **HEATHER THOMPSON** will lead a six-week Seminar to give such help and encouragement.
We would like to see our little PRAYER ROOM extensively and intensively used! Perhaps in this way we may *aim higher and attempt great things!*

DON'T FEEL LEFT OUT OF IT! THERE IS SOMETHING *YOU* CAN DO!

There has been a great sense of joy and buzz of fulfilment in our success in raising finance for the purchase of our new properties. But not all families have been able to participate in this way - and for some of them there may be some sense of disappointment or even hurt.
**BUT THERE IS SOMETHING THAT MOST CAN DO!
Our 'Development Fund' provides the finance for us to pay for our personnel- Assistant minister and various Pastoral Assistants, all of whom contribute powerfully to the growth of the congregation and to bring many to faith.
The Fund needs to be strengthened to maintain this growth.**

Here's how 300 families, unable to participate in buying our new property, *can nonetheless help further the growth of the Body of Christ's people.*

ONE EXTRA COIN A WEEK WOULD ACHIEVE THIS!

100 families giving an extra 20 pence a week;
100 families giving and extra 50 pence a week;
100 families giving £1 extra per week;
ALL THIS WOULD CREATE £8840 A YEAR!

JOHN POOLE - "A TREASURER'S TALE."

"Here we go again!" was my first reaction.
Just as the Number 6 Account for which I am Treasurer was

looking healthy, we wanted to spend £60,000 on property! I recovered quickly - after all we already had £16,000 in the account, and if the congregation supported the project, it could be done!

I went on a business course for a few days. When I got back the project had trebled. We would like to spend £170,000. My personal reaction was "how will we ever do it?"
As an accountant, I knew that with high interest rates one could be talking about needing a quarter of a million pounds. If the appeal did not go well we might have a very long time of debt on our hands - maybe ten years of struggling, or more.

Someone said we could pay it off over 4 years - an unrealistic target I thought. The first indication that I was wrong came at the series of meetings - Committee, Kirk Session and the Congregational A.G.M. The project was fully approved with wholehearted enthusiasm.

COULD I BE WRONG? The second hint that I should not doubt came at the Saturday Morning Clinics with my colleagues (**a brilliant idea!**) We were to have 2 Clinics. Maybe we would have a few callers! We had 3 Treasurers with queues of people! *So much generosity was overwhelming.*

COULD I BE WRONG? The third thing that should have convinced me was the speed with which the total of new money given and promises grew.
First Week £36,277. Second Week, another £42,950. Total £79,136.

COULD I BE WRONG? I still thought "there's a long way to go." We decided to have 2 more Clinics. **Still the people came.** Members giving large and small amounts. The post at home was eagerly opened - money and promises arrived every day. The telephone calls asking for clarification came nearly every night. After three weeks we had been promised over £100,000. I was staggered.

I STILL HAD DOUBTS. But still the money came in. One evening I opened some envelopes with small amounts in them. Every contribution was most warmly welcome but I wondered if the flood of contributions was about to dry up. As if in answer the very next envelope I opened contained a single gift of £3000.

HAVE NO MORE DOUBTS. What I feared was going to be the work of attrition, chipping away at a huge mountain of debt, turned out to be a joy, not just for your treasurers, but for the whole congregation and for future congregations.

I suppose that doubting is natural but it must not stop one from stepping out in faith.

RITCHIE HOME BURNT DOWN.
People in West Church were shocked and distressed when they heard the news that the Ritchie home had been largely destroyed by fire, but were grateful that all the members of the family were safe.
Sympathy and love were readily forthcoming on all sides and for this the Ritchies express their thanks..
"In the days following the fire we received tremendous love and care from our church… we are so thankful to God for many blessings. We are grateful for our lovely temporary home and for the strength and grace that God has given."

MAY WCN 1992.

**CONCEIVING
…ENVISAGING
……..REALISING
……………ALL PARTS OF A COMPLETE PROCESS.**

"Two hundred years ago, in Japan, lived a famous painter named HOKUSAI. A patron came to see him, asking for a painting of a cockerel in all its glory. Hokusia agreed.
Some time later the patron sent a servant, asking if the painting was ready. "Not yet" said the painter. Again, after some time the same thing happened. **A year went by and then the patron came himself.** "Is my painting still not ready?" he asked. The painter took him into his studio. He stretched a piece of silk, prepared his paints and brushes and in a few minutes produced a magnificent painting. His patron was overjoyed, *but then began to get angry. "If you could paint that picture in ten minutes," he asked, "Why did you keep me waiting so long for it?" Hosukai led him into the next room. There, all over the floor were stacks of drawings, sketches, studies of cockerels. Some of a whole bird, others of a head, or claw, or a feather.
The reason he could paint the ten-minute masterpiece was the year's work he had spent in preparation."*

WEST CHURCH: CONCEIVING, ENVISAGING AND REALISING!

The last 2 issues of West Church News provided substantial reading: the March issue presented the case for the major acquisition of adjacent properties; the April issue rejoiced in the success of that project and began to *envisage* the possible uses of these properties in enlarged and new ministries.

We are now in what may seem to be a fallow period, though in truth it is a period of '*conceiving and envisaging*' that we trust in due course will lead to *realising*.

A SERVICE OF THANKSGIVING ON TUESDAY 5TH MAY.

We will join together to thank God for his goodness and mercy in respect of our purchase of 91 and 93 Crawfordsburn Road

WAITING UPON GOD.
But as well we shall wait in silence before God, asking him to put his ideas into our mind, in respect of the ministries He may want us to foster.
As well OUR KIRK SESSION will meet for a whole morning on Saturday 9th May at 9.30 to deliberate further on these matters.
So it is a time for "conceiving, envisaging, realising" in which we seek that the whole Body will be listening to the Head.
Before the famous Japanese painter quickly produced his masterpiece there was much time spent in preparation.

In that context we have been intensifying the practice of prayer within our congregation.

MAY WCN 1992 also gives us a report by Beth Myatt and Heather Ennis on THE GUITAR GROUP.
Years earlier MAUREEN KENNEDY had formed a group to teach the Guitar to West Church members and this created a pool of competent guitarists able to help in the worship of many of our Home Groups. This work continued over the years and widened in its scope and purpose.
Beth and Heather relate:
"Over the past 2 years we have led the Guitar Group, a really rewarding experience for pupils and teachers alike. We have rejoiced in the presence of the Holy Spirit and in the tremendous love shared within the group. This love has been carried out to many different churches in our area where people are singing and praising the Lord, with their guitars in tow.
One girl over the first year learned to play well and now plays for a large group of mentally and physically handicapped children in her own church.
Several people have come from the Baptist Church, first year women, second year their husbands…the women have been singing and playing in groups in their church, and the men did 'a turn' at a special Men's Night!
Last year we had five children, two of whom went on to play at a Children's Seminar in our own church.
Barbara, reserved at first has attended our Group for two years; has also joined a Morning Seminar, been filled with the Spirit, and herself receives beautiful songs and music from the Lord!
"Let there be love shared among us."   Beth and Heather.

BELCANTO- ON THE FIFTH SUNDAY OF THE MONTH - occurring every quarter- Belcanto will lead an Alternative Praise Service. We look forward to 31st May at 7.00pm.

MEN'S GROUP AT MAGHABERRY PRISON.
"Remember those who are in prison as though you were in prison with them." Hebrews 13:3.
FRANK REA writes:
"Some months ago as I was coming out of church, Robert Crawford asked me if there could be an opportunity for some of the Men's Fellowship to go into one of the prisons to share with the men there what God had been doing in their lives.
After making a request to the Governor and Security Department at Maghaberry Prison to bring a group in and getting a very positive YES, the above verse became a reality for eight members of the fellowship on Friday 21st February.
There was naturally a little apprehension among the group on their first visit to a prison, but this soon evaporated as they began to sing praise and worship the Lord. The prisoners who had come to the meeting were soon singing heartily, some songs that were new to them, even joining in the actions of "From the Rising of the Sun."
The Theme of the Evening was "Reach out and Touch the Lord", and right at the beginning Robert Crawford encouraged all present to do just that.
Testimonies were shared very sensitively and very powerfully by Alan Cowie, Ronnie Baird and Ken Douglas. Alan Stewart ministered to all present through a beautiful song given to him by the Lord.
There was time at the end for the Bangor group to speak personally with the prisoners and some received ministry. After an hour and a half all the apprehension was gone and I was being asked 'will you have us back again?'
The Holy Spirit has really anointed this group of men from West Church and is using them very powerfully to bring good news to those who need to hear it and to encourage Christians to move on in their lives in the power of the Holy Spirit.
As Director of Prison Fellowship, Northern Ireland, I want to express my appreciation to Robert Crawford, Ronnie Baird, Alan Cowie, Ken Douglas, Jim Neill, Paul Shields and Alan Stewart for giving us their time to come and be a blessing to some of the men in Maghaberry Prison. **May God continue to use them in the days ahead.**

JUNE/JULY WCN 1992. THE KIRK SESSION CONSIDER….
On Saturday 10th May 1992 the Kirk Session gave consideration to the ways in which we should be ministering to the needs of our congregation and community. The acquisition of our new properties sharpened this consideration for us, as we felt that enlarged premises invited enlarged ministries. Already, through waiting upon God, we felt that we had a number of

matters to ponder and how our new premises might be used.

A. A Place of Counselling, Healing, a Helpline.
In West much <u>Counselling</u> already takes place in the context of Seminars, or through the individual ministries of our Team members and others.
Likewise much <u>Healing</u> takes place at our established Sunday Evening Healing Services, or through the ministry in Home Groups. And many find within the family of West Church a very real <u>Helpline</u> in time of need.

But could this be expanded through the use of <u>91</u>?
There are many people in our society who are hurting or in need, sick or troubled, people who could do with comfort or good counsel. There are unemployed people, anxious young people, those who have been abused, with alcohol or drug problems, those who feel crushed or failures, or who carry within them bitterness or guilt. Is there need for a place where, confessional-like, people may come and share their troubles in complete confidence?

B. A Place for Nurturing Prayer.
In terms of nurturing and under girding many ministries, *there is need for people to grow in ability to pray in an enlightened and disciplined manner.* In a large measure this already happens in our Life in the Spirit Seminars, and in our different Seminars on Prayer, in our various Prayer meetings
Might it be helpful to be able to offer prayer to people who come, at certain fixed times? Or to run **Retreat** days to facilitate and nurture prayer? Or to enlist people for praying in our '**fanner-bee style**'?

C. The Establishment of a Study-Centre or Bible-School.
Eventually, to develop such a Centre to operate one or two mornings, or evenings a week- with opportunities to study different books of the Bible. This could build up new Christians in the Word of God or enable mature Christians to deepen their knowledge of God's Word.
It could be a place to train and send out lay-witness teams; to help train and equip our own elders and church Visitors etc. etc.
Is there need for such a Centre to grow and develop?

D. Special Courses/Conferences for the whole Church Family and the Wider Community.

We can have a ministry, not only for West Church but far beyond it. Many now attend our Life in the Spirit Seminars from beyond West Church. Recently many from outside profited from the meeting led here by Canon Tom Smail. Occasional Weekend Conferences, using West Church resources and hospitality, could strengthen and enliven the wider church. In times past, members from many congregations went to York where David Watson was minister to their great spiritual uplift. And there could be conferences to challenge and inspire in various fields.
A possibility, an opportunity to be grasped?

E. A Place of Social Fellowship.
There is much loneliness, not only among those who are retired and live alone, but also among those who work all day and return to an empty home, the 'singles' of our society.
Many frequent the club, or play bingo, while some just sit at home, feeling empty.
It is suggested that as the kitchen is the heart of the home, so one of our houses needs to have a live kitchen, where people can come for a cuppa and chat with one another, old or young.
It is suggested that this might be a 'common room' for local residents.
A place where people can talk - about what matters, or be involved in some useful activity with others.

Ideas here worth pursuing and realising??

F. A Ministry of Restoration or Re-Instatement.
In our society many people get into trouble and need to be reinstated. In the church some people, even those in church leadership, 'fall from grace' and need to be restored. We have the classic example of Simon Peter, who denied His Lord, and then was so carefully, lovingly, tenderly and firmly reinstated by Jesus.
And there are those whose spiritual ills are so deep rooted that 'normal' ministry will not reach them. Something more intensive is required. What a shame, for example, if people are left to fester in addicted ways, *when a ministry of restoration and steadfast love might fully restore them.*
One of the significant revelations given to one of our members was that there should be a ministry to fulfil the function of the *'cities of refuge'* in the Old Testament, Numbers 35.
Such a provision and ministry needed in our day when so many are being outlawed???

G. A Resource Centre/ Training Centre.

The Resource Centre could be well-managed and well-stocked with books, cassettes and videos and used in a whole variety of ways e.g. in pastoral care and marriage counselling, teaching, evangelism, etc...
Adjacent small rooms could be made available for discussion, training etc.. and these facilities

not solely for West Church members!

All these matters were discussed by the Kirk Session.

The Japanese painter, in the story alluded to earlier, took a whole year before he was able to produce a masterpiece picture of a cock!
And we have the realisation that some things need to be long thought about and prayed through, before they can be fully realised.

JUNE/JULY WCN gives details of:
The Summer Scheme August 17-21;
The Men's Weekend at Childhaven;
G.B. party's visit to London to receive Duke of Edinburgh gold brooch awards;
Wycliffe news from the Dores;
Patricia Fergie's letter from India,
And much else besides.

DESPONDENCY - OR A NEW OPPORTUNITY.
AN EXCERPT FROM HERBERT WEIMANN'S Witness Sheet.

"Almost a year ago I started to get really excited about the prospect of going back to my native country, (seeing my family, especially my mother, who was 87 years of age, and freely travel in both halves of Germany for the first time since the war, and to visit Berlin for a stroll "unter den Linden", the wide street leading up to the "Brandenburg Gate."
Then 2 days before setting off by car for the long haul Larne - Stranraer - Dover - Calais - Lille - Aachen - Koblenz - Stuttgart - came the bombshell: Redundancy!

First of all I was shocked by the prospect of having to go down to the 'Buro' in about 3 months time, after over 28 years in steady employment, and secondly by the fact that it would mean a drop from a proper salary to about £40 a week and the spectre of losing one's home hovering in the background.

However, after a very short time, *and following a visit by Roslyn Wilson, our elder, ending in a lovely prayer, my outlook seemed to change very quickly, starting off with a conscious decision not to allow matters to spoil our holiday (I had not been 'home' for almost five years) and tackle the situation after coming back."*

Herbert goes on to speak of his holiday in Germany, and how it came to him that he could use his technical knowledge and his knowledge of English to allow him to facilitate foreign firms who wanted to do business in the UK, and how he was able to carve out a new career for himself, working at home.
Herbert was able to obtain membership of two professional bodies, and these qualifications indicated to potential clients that they would get value for money.
Herbert concludes:

"So it is true, after all, that when one door closes another door opens and I do think that attending church *and a visit by Alvin have helped to shape my outlook and to see things in perspective. I have tasted the freedom that comes with being one's own boss (on the days my wife is out working!) and so controlling one's own time.*
Now I know what the slogan 'job satisfaction' really means: "Doing what one likes best and getting paid for it into the bargain!"

I do thank the Lord for having provided me with the opportunity of being able to look after my family once again, and having lifted my spirits from almost despair to looking forward with anticipation to the challenges of the future."

SEPTEMBER WCN 1992.

In September and October editions of West Church News we read of the integration of '91' Crawfordsburn Road into our West Church Complex. It was necessary to remove the boundary hedge, and to paint, re-wire, upgrade and furnish the house for our use.
A new passageway from our inner church vestibule was made through the area previously occupied by the Men's toilets, and a new toilet block for men and women constructed in the area previously occupied by the Ladies' toilets.
The old 'tin' garage of '91' was demolished, to give a much more open aspect upon our rear lawns, and to make this an attractive area with real potential.
The Moderator of the General Assembly, Rev. Dr. John Dunlop will speak at both morning services and at Young West on Harvest Sunday, 9th October, and will also formally open '91' on that day.

NOT JUST DEDICATION BUT INAUGURATION.
The visit of the Moderator will mean much more to us than a ceremony that opens a door and dedicates a building. It is not just a destination representing property acquired and made ready for use.
Rather it is a public sign that a whole new expansion of our work in the Kingdom of God is about to begin, and upon that, most of all, we will be seeking the blessing of God *and an ability to venture where He guides.*

We have just completed a wonderful week among our young people that has been greatly blessed. We have been seeing the build-up of this work over a period of years, and at a much more intensified level over the last year or two. It is now bearing fruit, and we expect sill more

fruit.
It was great, for example, that on Tuesday evening, 19 of our young people told, in simple, eloquent terms, the difference that faith in Christ had meant in their lives. One has no doubt that this will have a powerful effect upon all the groups that heard this sincere and unpretentious testimony.

CECIL GRANT'S ACCOUNT of the summer visit of 47 of our young people to Capernwray, also indicates the extent of input into our young people's work.

One is able to see that all such endeavours in Jesus' Name, bear fruit.
A verse from Ecclesiastes 11: 4 encourages us to press on:
"If you wait for perfect conditions, you will never get anything done. God's ways are as mysterious as the pathway of the wind; and as the manner in which a human spirit is infused into the little body of a baby while it is still in its mother's womb. **Keep on sowing your seed, for you never know which will grow- perhaps it all will!**"

PLANS THAT WE ALREADY ARE GETTING INTO PLACE!

We plan a whole series of Seminars directed at particular sectors and needs.

A six-week Seminar on "Coping with loss and Bereavement" to be helpful for those who have experienced these things, and for our Elders and Church Visitors who have pastoral care for our people.

A twelve-week Bible Study for Widows. And an equivalent Seminar for Widowers.

We plan to have a short Seminar on 'Visiting the Terminally Ill', calling in some expert help.

There will be a 6-week Seminar on 'Sexual Abuse'.
And a Seminar with the help of EYM on 'How to be Encouragers'.

We plan to continue Seminars on 'Teaching People to Pray'

Doreen Hayward will lead a 4-week Seminar on 'Contemplative Prayer'.

WE plan to have a Seminar on 'Marriage Preparation' - we already have ten marriages booked for 1993. In addition to the personal meetings that couples have with the minister, this will help couples to give thought to the whole matter of marriage, something truly necessary, since marriage is under such pressure in our society.

We plan also to have a Seminar to strengthen **FAMILY LIFE**. We want to build **QUALITY** into our families. **BRIAN MARTIN** will lead a Seminar for parents with 7-11 year-old children.

HELEN RITCHIE will do a similar one for parents of teenage children. And yet another Seminar on **NEW AGE** philosophy and practices.

We live in a troubled Province, into which we need to inject a Christian influence. **JEAN McCormick** will lead a Seminar with material provided by ECONI which aims to get inspiration and help from the Scriptures, so that as Christians we may have a right and effective input into our community.

ARTHUR YOUNG - A CALL TO MINISTRY- IN LEEDS!

"Seven years ago, I experienced over a period of time, *God's call on my life to enter the service of fulltime Christian ministry.*
At that time I was sure that that call was in the direction of ministry within the Presbyterian Church in Ireland. But after a period of secular study which was necessary to obtain a degree for entry into Union College, I discovered this was not to be.
From that point on I felt very discouraged and depressed, still believing I was to enter into Christian ministry. Yet things were not working out the way that I had planned.. *There was my problem- the root cause of my failure - it was because I was doing all the planning...* During that period I was striving and straining against God's ways and will. *I was pushing doors that were not to be opened, going up avenues which had no openings, and having to swallow pride and come back down again!*

I SURRENDER MY WILL - DOORS BEGAN TO OPEN.

But things began to change as I surrendered my will, and let the Holy Spirit implant God's will into my life and future - doors began to open, barriers were pulled down, resentments and hurts healed, and my faith in God restored and strengthened..

THREE YEARS STUDY - WITH A FULLTIME JOB.

After some time of seeking God's will for what the next step was to be, I moved to Bangor Congregational Church where I became involved in the life of that congregation. Still experiencing God's call upon my life for the ministry, and having a greater peace than ever before, I applied to Belfast Bible College to do a day release course. At the same time I was encouraged to apply to Trinity Theological Seminary, U.S.A. to do a degree in Theology. **To my amazement I was accepted by both colleges and embarked upon both courses in 1989.**
At the same time I was holding down a full time job as manager of D.I. Y. shop.
During the past 3 years it has been hard work, discipline, late nights and no spare time. But the study, though demanding, has been rewarding and I also have learned that I could glorify God through the

printed page of my essays and research papers, **this giving me a whole new meaning to study.**

SUMMER WORK IN LEEDS - ESTATE OF 80,000 PEOPLE.
During a period of my summer holidays I had a chance to work alongside the Rev. John Semper of Seacroft Congregational Church in Leeds, in a huge estate of 80,000 people where there is much apathy and indifference to the gospel of Jesus Christ.
As I began to meet people and visit around the estate I became aware of the great needs of people there, materially and spiritually. An area that is filled with so much bad news **became a burden to my heart so that I prayed for direction to serve in that place. Again to my amazement I received the call from Seacroft Congregational Church to become the assistant minister for two years. This summer I accepted that call and will take up my ministry at the end of September.**

I rejoice and praise God for his goodness, love and encouragement over the past years, for all that has taken place, far more than I could ever have imagined. I have enjoyed going to the Ten O'clock Service at West Church, where I have profited from the ministry of the Rev. David Bailie and the Rev. Alvin Little. Also going to the Healing Service has made me able to pray with people in a way I never knew before, and seeing God at work in the healing of many lives has been a great and glorious thing. -something I hope to carry on in my ministry in Leeds.

I VALUE YOUR PRAYERS.
I do value your prayers very much as I go to Leeds and enter into a new way of life and a new culture. Please pray that I may be able to have new contacts as I visit from door to door, also that I would get involved with many of the young people and teenagers of that estate. I praise God that in the congregation there is openness for new things to happen, a freedom for God's Holy Spirit to work. Pray for the Rev. John Semper and Mrs Semper that some of the pressures would be taken off them, and that we will enjoy ministering with each other.
I would like to finish by thanking my brothers and sisters in West Church for their love, support and prayers over the past number of years.

THE AFRICAN CHILDREN'S CHOIR- A DEEP IMPRESSION WAS MADE UPON AN OVERFLOWING CONGREGATION IN WEST ON THE 8TH NOVEMBER, through the joyful released singing and demeanour of these African children.

"There is usually an idea, a person, and an inspiration *behind every brilliant initiative!*
And this is true of the African Children's Choir.
The person to whom the idea came was Ray Barnett. A book has been written about this man under the title "Where the Brave Dare not go."
Rarely will you read a more dramatic chronicle of one man, used by God, to go where few would dare and to do what seems impossible. From the hostages in Beirut to the Siberian Seven in Moscow, *God has used Ray Barnett to help free imprisoned believers.*
Born in early October 1936 as a weak and fragile infant thought unlikely to survive, he was adopted into a family near Coleraine, where Lavinia, a mother with seven children of her own, *lavished love and care upon him.*

At a time when dyslexia was not yet understood and the words 'learning disability' had not yet entered the English language, school for the young Ray, was, for the most part, *torment. But he was able to read, wonderfully!*

The story of his coming to faith in Christ, the cure of his stutter through the baptism in the Holy Spirit, and the deep urge of his heart to share Christ, are graphically told in "Where the Brave Dare not go."

Ray has, in Christ's Name, dared to go many places and believe for impossible things, in the compassion of Christ. **Just one of them was the formation of the African Children's Choir. The need originally was the desperate plight of starving children in Uganda.** *There was the basic thought that these joyful faith-filled children of Africa, who could sing with such fervour and vitality, could sing in the West, to inspire and kindle faith, and that in return we could send help to ease the clamant, urgent material needs of starving children.*

In West Church the faith of many was kindled by their visit, and compassion and generosity evoked, so that the dual purpose that Ray Barnett envisaged, was amply fulfilled.

HOW DO YOU FEEL ON SATURDAY MORNING?

"Isn't it lovely just to think that people might wake up on Saturday morning feeling different because they were prayed for on Friday night?"

That was a comment made by **Paul Shields,** at our late-night Friday Prayer meeting.
We link that with two other quotations.
"Healing is Jesus meeting us at our point of need." Bishop Morris Maddocks.
"There is no pit so deep that Jesus is not deeper still." Corrie ten Boom.

West church members are asked: "Are you aware that you are prayed for by name, at least 4 times a year? In many cases this quite probably happens after you have gone to sleep."

"I am referring to the Late Night Prayer Sessions which take place in the Praise Room every Friday starting at 10.15pm.
Many things and many situations are prayed for in our local community and around the world, **but at about 11.30 pm those present begin to pray for a specific church district, street by street and family by family. With 13 districts to cover, it becomes your turn four times a year.**

What a shame that more people do not attend more often. It is a great pity because knowledge of a person's particular needs can **put direction into our praying. Our prayers can then be specific rather than general.**
But this does not mean that people are gossiped about. On the contrary they are prayed for lovingly and with a great desire that Jesus will meet their every need and lift them out of their deepest pit...
The attitude of those praying was put very well by Paul Shields not long ago when he gave us that lovely thought quoted above.

**People feeling different on Saturday morning!
People feeling different any morning!
More confident! Less depressed! Stronger! More able to cope!
Just because we prayed!
And Jesus answered!**

Do come along and join us on a Friday night, especially when you hear your district announced. If you think you don't know how to pray, then you and I have something in common and we are no different from Jesus' disciples. Read what Jesus taught them in Luke ll: 1-13. Then come!

Our God is very much alive!
In prayer we are able to talk to him as a child to a loving Father.
"Ask and you will receive;
Seek and you will find;
Knock and the door will be opened to you." Jesus Christ.

JRB.

WHAT IS IT LIKE TO LIVE IN A CHRISTIAN COMMUNITY? ONE YEAR ON, JILL YOUNG WRITES FROM ROSTREVOR.

DIFFICULT, "GROWTHFUL"!

Greetings to everyone at West Church, from Jill and Lindsay Young and **may God bless you all!**

We have now been at the Renewal Centre for one year and what a year it has been! I cannot say that it has been an easy year, far from it. It has probably been one of the most difficult and yet most "growthful" years of my life. **There have been many times of struggling to adjust to community life and despairing that I would never learn to cope with this rather strange way of life.**
One cannot begin to explain what living in a community is like, especially one like this with such a variety of people, **from so many different backgrounds, cultures and denominations.**
It is certainly a community working for reconciliation, usually amongst ourselves! We are constantly being challenged by God to examine our relationships, and always find them wanting. I have become so aware of the fact that we, as Christians **are the Body of Christ and that the Body is sick!**

PROSTRATE ON THE FLOOR!
This is, of course, reflected time and again in this country of ours, **so torn apart by conflict and violence.** At the same time it has become vary apparent that we cannot be reconciled to one another without the manifold grace of God working in our lives.
Many times, when relationships here are difficult I find myself prostrate on the floor asking God to please help me to understand the other person, or people, and most of all to help me to love them. *God in his mercy hears our prayers and I have found that in spite of our differences He does give us the ability to love, to be committed to and to be supportive of each other, even if we do not fully understand each other.*

GOD'S PROVISION.
I have been thrilled to see God's provision for us, both as a community and as an individual. **Often we think we will not have the money to pay our bills but God always supplies just in time.** It is interesting that when things get really "tight", and we take time to pray about it (often at 6.30am) **God always takes us back to relationships and commitment to Him. Allowing the money to "dry up" seems to be His way of drawing our attention to our failings, and when you think it may be your fault that there is going to be no oil for the central heating, it certainly makes you seek the Lord and put right whatever it is that He is putting his finger on!** It is certainly a faith builder when everything we have is provided by God's people under his prompting, and also a confirmation that the Centre is "on target."

EVERYTHING DECIDED BY 16 PEOPLE!
Patience has never been my strong point, but I can tell you, when everything you do has to be decided by 16 people, *patience begins to develop.* I am an activist in the extreme and when others are more contemplative types it can be very frustrating, but God uses us all to balance and complement one another, and we must remember that we all hear God and serve God in different ways.

REPENTANCE, FREEDOM, HEALING.
A deeper call to repentance, both on a personal and collective level is **a significant factor as I look back on the year.** We have, many times, been led to repent for the sins within the Body. On a more personal note **God has worked**

within my heart concerning things which I had virtually forgotten. He brings them to light so that they can no longer have any hold over us, as we bring them to Him for forgiveness and healing.

One of the main thrusts of the community has been a call to prayer and repentance for our land. God must weep when He sees our land divided and torn apart by violence, and when He sees people turn away from his truths and precepts to New Age practices and occult activities., with consequent suffering and sickness.

MY WORK HERE…

My work here continues to be challenging. I am still involved heavily in the catering end and also with bits and pieces of mending and upholstery as well. And now I do a little gardening as well.

Leading prayer times has become less of an ordeal - thank you for praying for me in this. The Worship Team has been growing in courage and ability, and I have taken my turn in leading the worship a few times.

A new area has been allocated to me - the Youth work has been handed over to me and to Greg. **We would value your prayers as we plan the Youth Alive Camp and weekends.**

Lindsay did well at school last year and continues to do so. She has progressed well on her flute and plays with the Worship Team quite often.

I miss you all very much but have learnt to look more to God and lean on Him, and I have kept in touch with the progress at West through the Church News and letters some of you have sent me….. I will leave you now and urge you to read Romans 12, the recipe for a healthy Body!

FAMILY SEMINARS, using VIDEO PRESENTATIONS BY DR. JAMES DOBSON WILL TAKE PLACE EACH

WEDNESDAY FROM 7TH OCTOBER TO 25TH NOVEMBER.
This acclaimed series, with one-hour video, followed by informal discussion, will be led by Brian and Christine Martin.

OCTOBER WCN 1992 contains many other articles, reports and news items, including a report from Stephen Innis, doing Final Year Theology at Bangor, North Wales, who went to Kenya with a TEAR Fund Team to build a Water Tank in a very poor village about one and half hours from Nairobi. The cost was borne, one third by African Inland Church, one third by TEAR Fund and one third by the local community.

The tank will hold 20,600 gallons of water, and will provide a constant supply of drinking water for 500 families.

Hard work! Well done, Stephen!

A VERY MERRY SINNER.

Don Ritchie relates how he gave his heart to Christ as a little child and felt a deep repentance at eighteen years at Capernwray Hall, making a more mature commitment. However, coming to believe you couldn't have a good time **and** be a Christian, he became **a very merry sinner**, a ringleader among his friends, pursued a downhill and wilful way in a wasteful and unproductive life. He relied upon his wife Helen's prayers for protection.

Over a time he became dissatisfied and realised he must have Christ in his life. Waiting for an appointment with David Bailie, he read **"without faith it is impossible to please God." "**Well, I just wept with David, asked the Lord Jesus into my life and was immediately rewarded with the peace of the Holy Spirit."

DIVINE HEALING

TODAY- a 12 week Seminar led by Reggie Bates, based mainly on POWER HEALING by John Wimber, begins Friday 16th October in '91'. Each session 90 minutes.

NOVEMBER WCN 1992.

'91' FULLY INTEGRATED!

DR JOHN DUNLOP, Moderator of the General Assemby dedicated '91' and declared it open on Harvest Sunday. The task of preparing '91' for integration was carried out with cheerful expertise and has added greatly to the brightness of our whole Church complex with its hub in our Vestibule area.

"We want to thank all who helped us to open on schedule. Our thanks go especially to **Ken Macartney, one of our Property Conveners who works tirelessly, cheerfully and self-effacingly the year round on our church property. He also co-ordinated, planned and coaxed many different people, so that the work was completed on schedule.** We thank **Geoffrey Alcorn**, one of our own members who was responsible for all the building work and procured for us the necessary sub-contractors. **Jim Neill** did the beautiful tiling in the new toilet block. **Edward Carleton** extended our Church Wall at the front, **George Stevenson and James Smyth** did all the gardening work, and quite a number helped with painting and other work. **Anne Anderson and Liz Baird chose our colour schemes** and helped us with the choice of furniture. **And Julie Hamilton, resident, managed to survive in the midst of it all!**

And a whole raft of Seminars is now taking place in '91'.

THE 7th BANGOR SCOUT GROUP - FAREWELL AND 'THANK YOU' TO GEORGE STEVENSON and WELCOME TO CHRIS MILLER.

George Stevenson has made a faithful, substantial, cheerful and worthwhile contribution to scouting in West Church for which we thank him most heartily. His enthusiasm, warmth and readiness to help one and all, have made a deep impression, and we thank him for what he has done for boys in Bangor West. Many other pressures conspire to lead him to stand down at this point.

Chris Miller, who has already done much with Heather his wife for Scouting in West, takes over and we are confident that his enthusiasm, diligence and forthright, cheerful spirit, with his care for the boys, will enable him to make a first-class contribution. It's a time of re-grouping and pushing forward, and we look ahead to a new, buoyant chapter in scouting in West under his leadership.

HOLDING THAT EXQUISITELY BEAUTIFUL TREASURE IN OUR UNWORTHY HANDS!

We quote from Graham Dore at Wycliffe Bible Translators:

"Last year I met Uche and Marianne Aaron from Nigeria *who translated the New Testament into their own Obolo language,* and were here for the typesetting process. They have just received a printed copy of the New Testament and write:

"We had the pleasure of holding that exquisitely beautiful, priceless, precious treasure in our unworthy hands. We felt it over to make sure it was real. After a brief, emotive moment, and a prayer of thanksgiving, we opened it and read from it.

I listened as Marianne read, and the words stung my heart.
All of a sudden I realised that for the first time in my life I was digesting God's Words <u>directly from the source to my heart without having to translate it first.</u>
<u>Yes, I had previously worked through every word in it and had read through the trial editions several times, but then they were on sheets of paper and I was in search of errors. This time it was different. I am reading from the Book, and in search of meaning. It is wonderful to use it in my devotions.</u>

[DGB COMMENT: In West Church, we have treasured our relationship with Graham Dore, with his wife Janet, and with Elizabeth and Alastair, over many years. We rejoice in the key position that Graham has with WBT, and for the tender, articulate and compelling manner in which he presents to the wider church membership the WBT work of making the Scriptures known in more and more languages!

Thank you, Graham, for the excerpt we have just chosen from your most recent letter!]

IMPROVING OUR PASTORAL CARE.

"We are always seeking to improve our pastoral care, yet while there is a constant stream of people coming to new spiritual life, and thus, in due course, with the ability to minister and serve in various ways, *the supply never quite seems to match the opportunities,* <u>and so we are always stretched!</u>

It is a *bonus*, therefore, when people join us with rich pastoral experience!

SACRAMENT of the Lord's Supper to those who are SHUT-IN:

We are glad that **The Rev. Joe McAteer,** Senior minister of Armoy is happy to assist us with some Home Communions, so that we are able to minister more regularly in this way to those who are largely confined to their homes.
Another person who has joined us is **Miss Lily Hogg. A retired deaconess,** who has a warm, pastoral heart, and much experience, who will also be visiting, on a regular basis quite a number of our older people who are largely confined to their homes.
We thank both for this work being readily and warmly undertaken.

REBUILDING OUR CHURCH CHOIR-

Of late, insufficient numbers in each section of the choir has limited the range of material that can be attempted - so this is a time for rebuilding! Already we have a number of new members who are planning to join, and are seeking to enlist still more, to bring it to full strength. Our choir is a body of warmth and welcome, and this is a good time to explore entry! A real welcome is assured!

MANY ENCOURAGING THINGS HAPPENING AMONG OUR YOUNG PEOPLE.

Helen Ritchie tells how, since the visit to Capernwray Hall many teenagers have been growing in Christian maturity, and many of them helped as leaders in our own Summer Scheme.
Many of our older teenagers have gone off to College where they have been encouraged in Christian life and witness.. And it is good to see how some of our young teenagers have been writing to them - **a gift of letter writing, regularly and often!**

Helen also tells of a wonderful weekend at Guysmere.

"On Sunday last, 1st November, about 50 young people, including almost 20 of Don's Tuesday Night group, went to Rostrevor Christian Renewal Centre for a special Youth Day. We thank God for his protection as we travelled down in various cars. We did **one drama and two mimes and three of our group shared what Christ means in their lives today.**"

WHAT IF YOU MARRIED THE WRONG PERSON?

The increasing divorce rate in our country emphatically declares that many have come to the conclusion that they married the wrong person!
"If I'd only known what I was getting into…! Some, at times, feel 'sad and cheated'…expectations not fulfilled!." See page 410.
From time to time we use West Church News as a medium for encouraging, strengthening, counselling, so that folk may realise 'there is no perfect spouse', and come to know that "**even when we marry someone who in retrospect seems 'wrong', God can redeem our unwise choice.**
And so we have included an article by Janis Long Harris, with the sub-title, "**What to do if your choice of spouse suddenly seems less than heaven-made."**

DECEMBER WCN 1992.

A £6000 GRINDING MILL FOR TANZANIA???

Each year, we choose out a particular project from the PCI's World Development Appeal. Projects run by Christian Aid or TEAR Fund are particularly effective because often linked with indigenous churches, and tend to be free from corruption in a way that big international programmes are not.

In West Church we highlight a project in Tanzania administered through the Africa Inland Church, which has a membership of 300,000, with 200 pastors and 1500 evangelists. It is to provide one of the 5 Grinding Mills for which its Projects' Department will be responsible. The Grinding Mill will be powered by Lister water-cooled, diesel engines.

WHY SO URGENTLY NEEDED?
Because the area is full of malnourished children. The women can make porridge for their children only by grinding the grain on a grinding stone or in a wooden mortar. Or else they have to carry the loads of grain on their heads over long distances (sometimes with a baby on their backs).
The Lister mills, where they have been installed, greatly **improve the nutritional condition of the people and promote agricultural interest in the area. They give some youth employment, increase income and provide more time for literacy classes.**
The Church, with membership throughout the rural areas, and with workers and leaders who have respect for the rural population, is in an ideal position to administer this project in an efficient and honest manner.

SO LET US LOOK AT WHAT THIS PROJECT SHOULD ACHIEVE.

1. Present methods of grinding mean malnourished children and adults. A Grinding Mill will enable them to have adequate food for themselves and to sell to others.
2. There will be time for Literacy and Educational Classes organised under the auspices of the Africa Inland Church that will make for a general uplift in development.
3. Better agricultural methods will be taught.
4. Additional employment.

THE PROJECT will generate Income- to buy more mills.
to buy water pumps.

If West Church were to raise £6000, for a village of 450 families, it would mean 3000 well fed and healthy people, with better agriculture, literacy, clean water from a new water pump and better health all round

So £6000 would greatly help 3000, not with a once-off hand-out, *but in a sustained way, year by year! So £2 gives a new quality of life to one person; £15 transforms the life of a whole family; £45 sees 3 households transformed; £100 will put new life into 7 families, 50 people.*

CAN WE INSTALL THIS GRINDING MILL?

Yes, we can!

ANGLICAN VICAR TO VISIT US IN JANUARY.

REV. MICHAEL WOODERSON TELLS OF EVANGELISM THROUGH THE MEMBERS OF THE LOCAL CHURCH.

Over the past number of years we have laid emphasis on Evangelism. We have studied this in our Home Groups and have seen many people come to faith in our Life in the Spirit Seminars. And some individuals have had that special joy of bringing people to faith in Jesus.
In our congregation there is a warm, healing influence that reaches out to touch and bless others.

GOOD NEWS.
Recently I read the story of a minister who encouraged the ordinary, faithful members of his congregation to share their faith with others in a way that is not threatening. Rev. Michael Wooderson has written 2 books, "The Church Down the Street" and "Good News down the Street."

I quote from a Book Review: "Michael Wooderson's booklet '**Good News down the Street**' has pulled thousands of Christians out of their pews to share the Gospel of Christ. '**The Church down the Street**' brings Michael's account up to date and helps us grasp his vision for down-to-earth local evangelism.

I have been impressed as I have read Michael Wooderson's books and have been pondering their message for some time. **I believe that in West Church we have a large pool of warm-hearted, spiritual people of kindness, gentleness and love and with a**

desire to see others come into the Kingdom.
And I have a conviction that Michael Wooderson, by relating what he has encouraged his people to do over many years, *may be an important person, in the providence of God, to pay a visit to us.*

Last week I phoned him and asked him if his programme was still alive!

He said that just recently his congregation had sent out 15 teams of 3 members each, into homes in the parish, to share a simple, prepared course with people who were prepared to receive them.

We talked! And the upshot is that he will be coming over to visit us for a weekend in much the same way that Tom Smail did last year. The weekend is from Friday 15th to Sunday 17th January.
I believe it may indeed be significant for us.

Last night I asked one of our members, who herself has been the warm and vital link that has directly encouraged a number of people to come to our Life in the Spirit Seminars where they have entered into new life, **whether she had ever been used, herself, to lead people into faith in Christ.**
The answer was 'No'. In response to the further question, '**Would this be something you would like to be able to do?**', the answer, *assuming it was possible,* was a very emphatic '**YES**'. -and one could already see *eyes glistening with joyful anticipation.*

If it were possible! That's the big question!

Michael Wooderson will be telling us that it is possible!

MUCH SINGING!
Choir rebuilding is in progress with 3 additional ladies and 2 men already in place!
THE SINGING GROUP who lead our Praise Services and share in morning service worship, is also being strengthened.

CERTAINLY, DO IT!
When our Choirmaster Maurice explored the possibility of BELCANTO leading the service in Ballygilbert, I said, 'Certainly; do it! We will turn our loss into an opportunity to do something different and worthwhile!'
And so we did!
Our Junior Singing Group led us in a YOUTH WITNESS SERVICE.
And they will be leading us again at our Praise Service <u>at which 18 of our members will be confessing their faith in Christ, prior to coming to the Lord's Table.</u>
At the moment our Junior Singing Group lead one in three of our Praise Services.
December WCN also gives notice of our Service of Carols and Lessons where we will have a full complement of traditional Christmas carols, as well as some lovely new ones.
It gives notice of all our Christmas Services, including the Christmas Eve Communion service, and the now traditional service on the Sunday evening after Christmas when Alvin Little will welcome students back home for Christmas, and invite some of them to take part in the service.

PAMELA BROW WRITES TO THE PRINCESS OF WALES.

"For quite some time I had felt I wanted to write to the Princess of Wales to encourage her in many different aspects of her life, writing as a friend would.
When I read Romans 12, I can see so much of her in it, so I know God already has his hand on her, *but I'm also aware that she is open to so much temptation, if the media can be believed even one little bit.*
Early in November at a Ten O'clock service, I heard Rev. David Bailie pray lovely words for God's guidance for our Royal family in their present troubles. Julie Hamilton then prayed tenderly for those relationships which begin in hope and confidence - relationships now strained or damaged -that the Lord would grant time and His healing love to those hurting, that those relationships might be restored.

David preached on forgiveness, as Jesus teaches us in Matthew 18, and of how important it is to forgive again and again, so that we ourselves are truly forgiven, and receive blessing and freedom in our spirits, *as we truly forgive.*

That morning I heard God speaking to the Princess of Wales and so I ordered a tape of the service so that she might know of our prayers and God's hope for her and her family in their difficult times.

At the early morning Prayer meeting, Pat and the others prayed that the Holy Spirit would guide me.
I told Princess Diana something of our increasing awareness and experience of the Holy Spirit in this place, and that I desired for her a fullness of life, only found through Jesus' Name. I also sent three little Scripture cards.
As I finished the letter, the terrible fire at Windsor Castle was raging, so I took the opportunity to speak for us all, to convey to her Majesty, the Queen, our heartfelt sympathy and understanding, with a prayer that God will provide experts and an available workforce, to restore and renew in this situation also.
I received a prompt reply from St. James' Palace, probably one of hundreds efficiently posted that day to many more letters like mine.
Now I ask for your prayers, that by the power of God's Holy Spirit, who enables, that **all** the words of the tape, the letter and the scripture cards, will fall on fertile ground, to

comfort, encourage and guide.
We can do so little but God can do *so much more*!

JANUARY WCN 1993.

VISIT OF THE REVS. MICHAEL & ANNE WOODERSON, FRIDAY- SUNDAY 15-17th.

We are glad that on his visit to us in West Church, Michael Wooderson will be accompanied by his wife who is also an ordained deacon in the Church of England.
We shall, therefore, have a double input into what promises to be a significant weekend.

On the Friday Night Michael Wooderson will deal **with the principles behind 'Good News down the Street'.**
This shows how members of a congregation, in small groups of three, may visit in a friendly and effective manner **those who are ready to learn something more about Jesus in a simple and straightforward way.** *The approach is not to be heavy or domineering, not pressurising or manipulative, but to have a lighter, warmer touch.*
On the Saturday morning the Woodersons will deal with the materials used in the 6-week course, and how to use them. The whole format will be open for questions, comment and discussion.
The main thing is that in the Woodersons we have people who have used these methods with great fruitfulness over a period of 20 years. And we listen with attention when people speak out of experience!
On the Saturday afternoon, the Woodersons will deal **with the nurture of those who have come new to faith.**
Michael will preach at our First Sunday Morning service - and after that it's a quick dash to the City Airport to catch the noon flight to Birmingham.

And now let us dip into February WCN for a moment to gain impressions on the Wooderson Weekend.

RUN-DOWN ESTATE OF 8000.
"I was impressed when Anne Wooderson told us how, in a run-down, desolate estate of 8000 people, with no civic amenities and no church, and with every conceivable social problem, she was to see, within a couple of years, a little congregation of 50 believers come into being - *and that through the witness of ordinary Christians, in their little 3-member Good News teams.*

EVERY MEMBER HAS TAKEN PART.
I was impressed to hear Michael Wooderson tell how, in his present congregation, *every member has been part of such a Good News team.*

As I heard him speak, and as I read his book, *I became quite convinced that what he has seen God do in his congregations can happen here! And richly so!*
I have great confidence in the quality of dedication and love among our members
Time will tell! But we have to grasp the opportunities!

A NECESSARY KEY TO THE SUCCESS OF THIS METHOD IS THAT WE HAVE HOMES WILLING TO RECEIVE THOSE WHO COME TO THEM IN FRIENDSHIP, AND OVER A PERIOD OF SIX WEEKS, SHARE WITH THEM A FEW BIBLE PASSAGES FROM A MODERN VERSION OF THE BIBLE.

Our own Pastoral Team, with elders and church Visitors, should be able to approach likely people. What has happened in England, should happen in Ireland also!

No doubt we have sufficient homes for us to make a worthwhile experiment!

AND NOW, BACK TO JANUARY WCN, AN ISSUE THAT MAJORS ON *OUTREACH.*

In this issue we have an important article by CHARLES COLSON, President Nixon's minister, who went to prison over the Watergate scandal - and became a Christian, has inspired Prison Fellowship worldwide and much else besides.
In an article **'Being Light in the Darkness'**, he has much to say that is pertinent, challenging and salutary to us *about the manner in which we should seek to share our faith with others.* The Wooderson visit aims to inspire us to share the Good News of Jesus in our own community.
We quote from Colson's article:
"My friend Charlie tells of an evening when he and several others, armed with copies of the "Four Spiritual Laws", set out to witness in a Charlottesville, Virginia bar.

WISDOM IN WITNESSING.
Charlie struck up a conversation with a well-dressed young professional **who soon admitted his own spiritual emptiness.** As Charlie told the man of his own experience with Christ the rapport between them deepened.. *Sensing that the man was not ready for commitment*, Charlie got his phone number and made plans to contact him later.
After they left the bar, one of Charlie's companions queried him excitedly. **'Did you go through the book with him?'**
'No', Charlie replied. 'He wasn't ready. We're going to talk again later'.
The young man was furious. 'I can't believe it!' he exploded.
'Here we are trying to witness and you didn't even go through the book!'
Six months later the same young man had a nervous breakdown.
While there are many occasions

to witness, as God's Spirit leads, Jesus' charge is to be <u>a</u> witness. To understand this - that we don't always have to bombard people with tracts and gospel plans - **is wonderfully liberating.** But it is also intensely demanding. For **being Christ's witness** involves every aspect of what we are and what we do, individually and collectively, as the community of faith.

HOW ARE WE TO BE CHRIST'S WITNESSES? Both by word and deed?
This involves responsiveness to the Holy Spirit, our best judgement, and sensitivity to other people. *Often we miss the balance by tilting to one extreme or the other.*

SENSITIVITY AND BOLDNESS.
ON THE ONE EXTREME *are those who say plenty <u>about</u> God, but don't live out their faith with the same vigour. Their lives lack love, purity, hope.*
Sadly they are the ones the world stereotypes <u>as the Church</u>: the worker who sips coffee from a Jesus Mug and showers co-workers with Christian platitudes *but does the shoddiest work in the office;* the businessman who prays before every meeting *and then cheats his customers;* the neighbour who invites her neighbours to Bible coffee mornings **but constantly complains about her husband;** the pro-life activist who wears a 'God loves you' button *while hurling hateful invectives at women entering abortion clinics.*
For the watching world it is difficult to separate the message from the messengers.
AT THE OTHER EXTREME there are those who earnestly live their faith, but never articulate the reason for the hope that is in them.
While people may look at us and see a reflection of Christ - and even admire the reflection - 'You're such a good person' - *unless we tell them about Him, they may never know the source of the goodness.*

God uses ordinary people, empowered by his Spirit, to proclaim his Gospel. People in every walk of life, people who thrill to tell about Christ, and even people who do so while dragging their feet.
In the Great Commission Jesus says '*as you go share the Good News', something that flows naturally out of the context of your everyday living - not a set of formulas, techniques or memorised scenarios."*

OUTREACH:
Today we in West Church are giving serious consideration to sharing the Good News of Jesus in the wider community. That's why we've had a visit from the Woodersons.

FINDING COMMON GROUND.

CHARLES COLSON tells us that we've got to make real and sympathetic contact with people, to find common ground with them.
In the thirties and forties and even the sixties a majority may have believed the Bible to be the true and trustworthy Word of God, so one could say to people '**The Bible says..**' and gain attention! Today the majority may find the Bible to be an interesting collection of ancient legends and stories that **they don't believe.**
Today people **deny the existence of absolute truth**- some people believe one thing, some another- it's all relative, all your preference! So if you say '**Jesus changed my life'**, the response may be '**if Christianity works for you, that's great, but I don't believe in Jesus'.**
If you seek to emphasise eternal life, the afterlife, which should make us think of how we conduct our lives now, they may say, '**I don't believe in the afterlife - when you die you turn into dust'.**

WE NEED HELP OF HOLY SPIRIT.
Yet the truth is that the knowledge of God, *conscience,* **resides in each person, and through the power of the Holy Spirit the Word of God can penetrate even the toughest human heart.**
We are not to abandon our personal testimony, or a direct telling of gospel truth, but we need the help of the Holy Spirit to understand and overcome the mindset of secular people today.
Pre-packaged God-talk won't do. Before we tell them what the Bible says we have to tell them why they should believe the Bible - and for this a great case can be made. We need to have a love for those we talk to, and touch chords deep within them. We need to translate the gospel for those we speak to.
Charles Colson gives an example from Odessa Moore, a Prison Fellowship volunteer:
"Eight years ago when Odessa was visiting a juvenile jail, she met a teenager waiting to be tried as an adult for first-degree murder. **His eyes chilled her; they were so full of anger and hate.**
'I don't care about anything', he said defiantly, 'I don't feel no shame'.
A familiar story emerged as they talked: **father a drug user; mother an alcoholic; both parents abusive. They would beat the boy and tie him up in the closet for hours. All his life he had been told he was nothing. No one cared about him, but that was all right,** he said.
' I DON'T CARE ABOUT NOBODY'.
'There is someone who loves you' Odessa told him.
'No way' he responded 'nobody'.
'You're in here for murder, right?' asked Odessa.
'Yes, and I'd do it again', he said.
'How would you like it if someone came in here tonight, and said 'I know you committed the murder, and they are going to give you the death penalty, but I am going to take your place for you'. How would you like that?'
For the first time the boy showed a spark of life. 'Are you kidding? That would be great!'

Odessa went on to tell the boy about Jesus, the Prisoner, who did take his place, who had already paid the price for his wrongdoing. Using word pictures the young man could understand - he had obviously never heard anything about the gospel, she walked him through the steps to a growing understanding of sin, repentance, forgiveness and freedom - true freedom- in Christ.

STONE-COLD TEENAGER HAD MELTED.
By the end of the evening the stone-cold teenager had melted, weeping tears of repentance. He committed his life to Christ that night.'
CHARLES COLSON declares:
"I have experienced the same thing on hundreds of occasions. Salvation seems remote to prisoners; but when I talk about the historic Jesus who was executed for a crime He didn't commit, on a cross between two thieves, their eyes light up. This they can relate to."

THE APOSTLE PAUL says that he is not ashamed of the Good News of Jesus, because, when he has declared it, the very worst of people, the off-scourings of humanity, have been transformed, gaining new life and dignity and fruitfulness.

And we in West, often in the context of our Seminars, have found that when people ponder the true words of God and put trust in the Risen Christ, they are transformed.
Yes, people receive the seed of new life, and in the context of the Christian fellowship, grow up into maturity and usefulness.

DISCIPLE-MAKING within the context of the local congregation.

Charles Colson says:
"It is a great disservice to unsaved people - as well as an impediment to the cause of Christ -**to get them excited, lead them into some kind** of *emotional response and then dump them on the doorstep. Unless evangelism brings converts into the visible Body of Christ, it is like assisting in a baby's birth and then leaving the infant out in the cold alone.*
New converts should be nurtured within the fellowship of the Church.

"J.C. Harris is pastor of a Baptist church as well as chaplain in a North Carolina prison. In prison he is constantly seeking to bring inmates to Christ. But when a prisoner does make a profession of faith, this wise pastor counsels the new convert about *choosing and joining a local church - even though he's still in prison!*
'In prison we don't baptise new converts. We want them to be baptised into a fellowship in their hometown, and *then to become a long-distance part of that particular congregation, just as if he were in the Army or something.* Then, when he gets out, he goes back home and his church family is waiting there for him, with food, clothes, a job, accountability. Discipleship takes place within that fellowship.'"

So in West, when we think of outreach and church growth, and of fulfilling Christ's Commission to go out into the world in its lostness and darkness, we want to make sympathetic contact with unbelievers, to bring them to life and carefully to nurture them in that life. We are not to be satisfied to scoop church hoppers from other congregations by our more lively services! That's not genuine growth at all, that's not the kind of addition to our membership that makes the angels in heaven rejoice."

CHRISTIAN NATIONALS-
THROUGH WHICH WE CAN PROMOTE GROWTH IN OTHER PARTS OF THE WORLD.

There are 2000 million people who have heard nothing about Jesus. We know that an obligation lies with us that they should hear that liberating news. But how, but how can this be done??
In the past folk attempted to do that by sending missionaries abroad, where they learnt the language of the people among whom they settled, and learned, often with real difficulty to adapt to a very different culture and lifestyle. This was often painstaking work, requiring many years before even a meagre harvest was reaped.
Now the gospel has been proclaimed over all the earth, and the church established in most lands. Obviously it is better if the Gospel be communicated by indigenous people, who already know the language and already share the culture and lifestyle. In that way communication is more direct and effective.

THIS IS WHERE 'CHRISTIAN NATIONALS' COME IN.
Their aim is to train indigenous Christians to be pastors and evangelists among their own people. In poor countries finance can be an obstacle to the provision of such training.
A sum of £300 per year enables Christian Colleges or Bible Schools to train eager Christian nationals for the work of evangelism or church planting. Their newest Partner-Ministry is the St. Petersburg Christian College. where 29 students await sponsorship, with 300 students worldwide.

IT IS AMAZING!
Christian Nationals tell us that over the past 6 years, the Lord has used Sponsorship Programmes to begin, on average, *one new church every day!*

In 1993 our Church Committee has decided to contribute £600 from our Outreach Fund, to sponsor 2 people in this programme.

Who can tell what harvest this may gather into the Kingdom of our Christ in a distant land!

PASTORAL TEAM:
AN OVERVIEW OF THE WORK THEY UNDERTAKE.

When we read through our West Church Directory we become aware of the large number of folk who *do not come to church and are not actively involved in the practice of the faith.*
In other words we have a whole 'Mission Field' within our membership!
In short we have *much fallow ground that needs ploughing and cultivating, for sowing and watering and fertilising, so that we may gain a harvest from it.*
AND WHERE WE DO THIS DILIGENTLY, RELYING ON THE HELP OF THE HOLY SPIRIT <u>WE DO GAIN A HARVEST FROM IT.</u>

WE HAVE SEEN ALVIN LITTLE do this in the <u>YOUTH SECTOR</u> of our congregation. While he does much else besides, *he has been set free to concentrate on this sector of our constituency.*

ALVIN is involved regularly with **Young West Church** and been able to build up a relationship with the **100+ congregation of young people,** nurturing and encouraging, building up and sustaining **a team there.**
Often he meets with **small groups of young people**, drawing them on to faith and building them up when they have come to faith.
When he's not present at the 11.30 service, that's what he's doing!

On Tuesday evening he has the **J-Troop and recently a Communicants' Class for young people.**

In the summer there has been **the Summer Scheme,** *and Life in the Spirit Seminars, flowing from that.*

In the autumn there has been all the work of **the Twilight Zone, an outreach endeavour,** where our young people are trained in praying for others, and reaching out to them.

He has wide contacts with another sector of our young people in **the GB Bible Class on a Wednesday Night,** and that's followed later by a meeting to nurture and encourage our young people **in their Twenties.**

As well there is the contact kept **with our young people who have gone off to college.**

Then there's a whole plethora of activities among young people on **Friday Nights** and encouragement for groups of various ages, **the most recent being the Lasers.**

Shortly Alvin also hopes to be involved with 'Don's Young people' on a Thursday night, to endeavour to reap a harvest there also.
To further useful contact with young people, he often now teaches a couple of classes in **Gransha Boys' High School,** as well, of course, as being involved in **Grange Park Primary School.**

And so that he is not completely **locked in'** to young people's work, he has currently embarked on an adult **Life in the Spirit Seminar** on a Tuesday night

And normally he is with us in the Church on one **Sunday morning a month, so that we do not lose sight of him there!**

There's naturally a lot of pastoral work and counselling, and nurturing of people in leadership, as well as visitation in the congregation.

ALL THIS - and much more goes into the cultivation of our patch - and yet there's so much more that needs to be done.

HEATHER THOMPSON.
Heather Thompson plays her full part in the pastoral care and nurture of the congregation., diligently, faithfully and effectively putting in a very full week's work.

She leads two Bible Study groups, an Old Testament one on a Monday Night, a New Testament one on a Thursday morning.

Heather has led various Seminars on **Prayer/Counselling** and seeks to nurture a **Prayer Network** in the congregation

She is currently leading and nurturing **two Life in the Spirit Seminars,** that meet on mornings.

She is very actively involved in **the Healing Service and gives much time to counselling/healing work.**

She visits in the congregation assiduously, and extensively and does quite a bit of work in pastoral care/administration.

She is currently involved in preparing our new West Church Directory for publication. The preparation for that seems ongoing and never-ending, as additions, deletions and alterations never cease! Like the reputed painting of the Forth Bridge that never ceased - by the time the painters got to the end of it, *it was time to start again at the other end!*

It is a substantial task to obtain Church Visitors and install them in their duties - and Heather is having quite a share in that overall administration. For some time now she has been working with us on an almost fulltime basis.

JULIE HAMILTON.
Julie Hamilton's sphere of work and interest differs somewhat from Heather's and is complementary to it.
She has made a real impact with **her almost weekly work at Carnalea Clinic,** among the elderly, with whom she communicates with skill and ease.

She also works alongside Betty Jackson in our Tuesday together meetings.
She leads one of our Home groups, and a Life in the Spirit Seminar that she started in early 1992 seems in process of graduating into a Home Group.

In the autumn she led Seminars on Sexual Abuse; Bereavement; and helped in a Seminar on how to be an Encourager.
She is gaining in confidence and effectiveness in pulpit ministry, in the prayers that she often leads so reverently and beautifully, and in sermons that have the hallmark of sound preparation and sincerity.
She is also involved in the work of visitation and counselling.

HELEN RITCHIE.
Helen has a very special empathy with young people and a ministry of warm, supportive love towards them, yet in a way that is not flabby but challenging.
With Don she has been taking large groups of our young people to Capernwray in the summer, and sometimes also to Rostrevor, and even to Poleglass.
It is clear that these times away together have had an up building, and often life-changing, impact upon the lives of our young people

Helen has a considerable influence upon our young people **through drama, and especially upon the populous Monday Night Junior Drama Group.**

She is also much involved in the growing work among our young people on Friday Nights *and shares with them her heart for outreach, and a desire to bring them to maturity in Christ.*

She is well acquainted with the Youth Scene and in respect of many of the forces that try to gain the allegiance of young people in the world today.
This qualified her to lead an autumn seminar on NEW AGE, and the ability likewise to lead a seminar, for the parents of teenage children, which was well attended and helpful to those who came.
Helen also leads a **Home Group** and is involved with Alvin with the Tuesday night Life in the Spirit seminar.
Helen has a special gift of getting alongside women in the congregation, to encourage and lead them into the Christian way.

DON RITCHIE, though much younger in the faith than Helen, **is a great support to her in dealing with the young people, especially in respect of the various camps and outings.**
In West Don is best known for his work among a sector of young people who meet on a Tuesday night - and more recently also on a Thursday night- for informal conversations and discussions. **Don has a very extensive knowledge of a wide range of young people,** *who have not found their way into our other organisations or groupings, and it is good to see the rapport he has established with them.*
Don also leads a Home Group on a Wednesday Night and in recent months has been given responsibility for leading the **Late Night Friday Prayer meeting. He is also involved in visitation.**

So this is our Pastoral Team, all having a share in the total outreach endeavour and in facilitating the whole membership in loving, faith-filled outreach.

FEBRUARY WCN gives the Kirk Session report for 1992 as well as the annual reports from many of our organisations, giving a buoyant picture of life within the congregation; and many other articles and contributions from members.

MARCH WCN 1993.

JULIE HAMILTON TO BE INSTALLED AS DEACONESS IN WEST.

"**Julie is now well known in West through her pulpit ministry, the seminars she conducts and the counselling she does.**
A native of Kilkeel… she studied at St.Colm's, Edinburgh for deaconess work… and took up work in Greenwell Street, Newtownards in September 1984. She served there until December 1987, when for emotional and spiritual reasons of a personal nature, she felt led to resign from the work of deaconess.
After some time she began to attend West Church and in August 1989 she attended one of our Life in the Spirit Seminars that for her began a restoring, healing and up-building process.

In April 1990, when she found herself unemployed, she began work in West. This was designed to meet an immediate need on her part and prompted by the conviction that it might be a way in which, in due course, she could find her way back, into full deaconess work. From the beginning we made it clear to the PWA in Belfast that we were in no sense laying claim to Julie as a deaconess for West -our personnel commitments left us already stretched financially, and Julie was paid only a very low salary by us.

DEACONESS IN WEST ON AN INTERIM BASIS.

Since that time we have kept in touch with the PWA through its officers responsible for our deaconesses, first Miss Betty Morrow and more recently Miss Dibbie McCaughan.
In the period since 1990 the possibility of Julie's taking up deaconess work in other congregations has been actively considered, but each time, in the end, it has seemed best that she remain with us and the time spent here has meant - before our eyes!-

such a strengthening, restoration and development in her, which has left us the blessed beneficiaries, as she has led in public worship prayer, or taught God's Word, or nurtured a seminar group.

In November 1992- after a lapse of almost a year (how time flies!) in terms of contact with Church House PWA, a conversation with Miss Dibbie McCaughan, seemed to indicate a possibility of Julie's serving as deaconess in West Church. This was on the basis of West Church's current salary to Julie, *central funds making up the balance. Our Kirk Session expressed its happiness to issue a call on this understanding. This was of course subject to in-depth interviews with Julie on the part of the PWA personnel, to reinstate her as deaconess.*

These procedures have been happily negotiated, and subject to the approval of the Ards Presbytery, a Commission of the Presbytery will install Julie as deaconess in West on Sunday 14th March at 7.00pm.

OPPORTUNITIES FOR 'INREACH'.

In these days there is an amazing amount of intensive pastoral work to do in a congregation of our size **and the opportunities of claiming new ground for the Kingdom of God are abundant.**

At the moment we are thrilled at many of the developments within the congregation **which indicate real outreach, and, to coin a word 'inreach'.** We trust that Julie will have a full and growing part in all this work."

LIGHT IN DARK PLACES.

Julie writes: "Following on from our 'Seminar on Loss and Bereavement', we are beginning a new 'Seminar for Widows'.

The Seminar will take the form of a Bible Study with opportunity for sharing and caring for one another. The series is called '**Light in Dark Places**' and will commence on Tuesday 9th March at 10.30am in '91' Crawfordsburn Road.

MARRIAGE PREPARATION-
"LOOKING UP THE AISLE"
With Jeremy and Heather Eves.
Part of our 'Inreach' as a congregation, *is to build strength into our marriages.*

In our Marriage Service we say, of marriage, 'unless the Lord build the house, they labour in vain who build it'.

In our land and society **many marriage houses are jerry-built so that they collapse speedily. It's hard to shore up and save any house that has been built on deficient foundations. It's a much better policy to ensure that good, strong foundations are laid down in the first instance.**

This is what our MARRIAGE PREPARATION COURSE is all about! We want to build strength into our marriages.

MARRIAGE MATTERS!

In the autumn term we had 5 **Marriage Preparation evenings for 8 couples who plan to marry in 1993.
On the last 2 evenings they were joined** *by 8 married couples from the congregation to watch a CARE VIDEO, entitled 'Marriage Matters'.*
AND THAT WAS AN EXCELLENT IDEA FOR ALL CONCERNED!

JEREMY AND HEATHER EVES, who have attended a Weekend Course on Marriage Preparation at a Conference Centre near London, have already met a number of our couples who had been unable to attend the Autumn course, and plan now for all getting married in 1993 to join together for another short course of four weeks, beginning on Tuesday 9th March at 8.30pm in '91' Crawfordsburn Road. **And we would like the married couples to join them on the fifth week, for** supper, after attending the Holy Week service in West, on Tuesday 6th April.

[2006 NOTE: We find here the beginning of a ministry by Jeremy and Heather Eves that has continued year by year since then, right down to the present time. It is impossible to estimate the blessings that have flowed out to and rested upon the couples married in West as a consequence. We are grateful to God for the grace, the wit and the wisdom that this couple have evinced. Many young couples who came to this Course with trepidation on the first evening left with a lightness of spirit. The wisdom imparted must have prevented many a heartache and added value to the quality of the marriage.
JEREMY, HEATHER, MANY THANK YOU FOR A WONDERFUL MINISTRY WITHIN OUR CONGREGATION!]

WORSHIP AND PRAISE IN WEST.
"We are delighted over the last few months to see the build-up in our Church Choir, and to see it restored to be a formidable singing force - and there's still room for a few more!

It was a real blessing on 21/2/93 to be led in worship by our **Youth Praise Group** and to have such a large Choir of young people - reverent, worshipful and released - leading us.

At the Praise Service on Sunday 7th March, we hope to have the participation of **Brian and Carol Moorhead**, who are gifted in mime and song, with the Senior Praise Group."

PATRICIA FERGIE RETURNS TO INDIA.
"The flight from Amsterdam to Delhi was very plush. Since the

flight was fully booked we got Business Class and received a bag of 'goodies', toothbrush, toothpaste, cologne etc.
Having got to Mussoorie we organised a jeep to take us and our luggage to Oakville. However we could only get part of the way as the road had been dug up.. We carried our backpacks and found a coolie to carry the rest. On his back he had our two suitcases, the suitcase with the books, and our two small backpacks - quite a sight! I felt a bit guilty seeing him so burdened…..
Now I'm back here again I'm happy in knowing I'm in the right place where the Lord wants me to be.

ARTHUR YOUNG ORDAINED IN LEEDS.

We were thrilled to see Arthur Young at Christmas. He is now working in a large housing estate in Leeds. He wrote after his return to thank us for the gift we gave him, and to tell us that **the Rev. John Seawright had preached the sermon at his ordination service in early February.**

HARVESTING IN THE STORM. VISIT OF SAMUEL CHIANG.

In the last issue of WCN we gave details of our support for CHRISTIAN NATIONALS.
At our morning services on 14th March we shall have a visit from Samuel Chiang, from Hong Kong, where he is Coordinator of the fast-growing East Asia Ministries.

In spite of fierce persecution and difficulties the underground church in China is growing in a phenomenal manner, and there is an urgent need for new believers to receive Bible teaching and training.

INTENSE HUNGER TO LEARN.

"In addition to long hours and formidable schedules **TRAINERS** are invariably overwhelmed by the hunger of the new believers. Everywhere we found people eager to hear the Lord's Word.
The trainers teach both leaders and new Christians, although in China the line between the two groups is often sketchy. With the country's explosive church growth, there is no time for new Christians to spend years in theology school….. Lack of sound biblical training is the perfect ground for breeding **heresy, a problem that already exists in China in growing proportions.**
…. Three years ago a church in the eastern part of China sent several hundred missionaries to unreached areas in the west and northwest. They could not remain because they were forbidden to evangelise outside their own provinces. **But they did a wonderful work and many came to know Christ. Today there are 40 meeting places and house churches. Now they need leadership for these new believers."**

One can therefore readily see the crucial work that Christian Nationals do in providing trained evangelists and teachers who give leveraged growth and stability to the fast-growing church. Remember how Jesus said '**Feed my Sheep**'.

ABSTINENCE - RADICAL CHOICE FOR SEX EDUCATION.

We have included in WCN a lengthy article on Abstinence, because the prevailing philosophy of our times is entirely permissive.
The teaching of Jesus shows us the way of the God who created us, and the robust, frank teaching of the apostles that confronted, head-on, the seductive promiscuity of their times.
We must do no less, lest we allow our people to fall, unwarned, into destructive and thorny ways.

APRIL WCN 1993.

REV. ALVIN LITTLE, CALLED TO DONAGHADEE.

Emotions in West were strongly mixed when news broke that the congregation of Shore Street, Donaghadee had made out a call to Alvin to be their new minister.

For many the emotion that dominated at first **was a deep sense of loss, that someone so deeply loved and respected would no longer be with us.**
And this was no doubt followed **by an emotion of gratitude and goodwill, the awareness that we would be releasing a mature and fruitful minister for service and leadership in a large congregation with many opportunities.**
'In truth, Alvin, we release you with much affection, and the prayer that, as you have been fruitful for the Lord here, you will increase in effective work in the Kingdom of God, in Donaghadee.
And our good wishes and affection go out to Linda, and to Joanna, Kerry and Christine.'

In the May Edition of WCN we pondered the truth that "here we have no continuing city", but like Abraham we are pilgrims on life's journey, that we are called to journey on, and often called to move out of our 'comfort zones'. The main thing is that we are responsive to God's call with a readiness to listen to Him and obey him.

VISION AND STRATEGY.

Alvin has steadfastly followed the leading of God, 'has shown himself to be a person who receives both vision and strategy from the Lord, with a diligent heart, ready to work hard in the fulfilling of God's plans.'
"A person can also be responsive to God *by staying in one place and allowing things to develop and grow. We have been fortunate in West that our two ministers who came to help us have stayed long enough to make a real impact - John Seawright for 7 years and Alvin for six years."*

The JUNE EDITION OF WCN gave us words of wisdom from our departing minister.

"DO NOT UNDERESTIMATE IT - *AND DO NOT WASTE IT!*"

Alvin spoke of *something special he had found in the West Church fellowship that had brought him healing for some of the bruises with which he came, and brought him into a fuller and more fruitful ministry.*
'Do not underestimate it and do not waste it!'
He spoke of a danger- that those who have known a deep communion with the Lord and joy in worship should begin to take it *for granted.*
It is easy to grow a bit careless and become apathetic and less diligent in attendance:
Do not underestimate what you have got- and do not waste it!

On a number of occasions when that quality of worship was present in full vigour at our Praise Services, the church was but 'loosely filled' rather than packed as of yore.

In a service, brimming with the sense of the presence of God, an important ingredient is the presence of people *who come in a regular and disciplined way, intent upon giving worship. Unnecessary absence undermines.*
To illustrate: not long ago, a member from a Seminar I had been leading joined our Singing Group. After his first Practice Night, he returned to the Seminar full of joy, *saying that he had never experienced such love as in that fellowship, nor such a sense of the presence of God.*

A danger! Alvin warned, not to underestimate, nor to waste!

But we had a full and glorious farewell service for Alvin and his family, and sent him forth in the richness of God's love and power.

ELECTION FOR 15 NEW ELDERS - 2ND MAY 1993.

It has been quite a number of years since our last election of elders and this election is perhaps a little overdue.
As has been done at every such election, we set out in West Church News the technical details involved in such an election, a procedure to be undertaken with special care, and a process that takes about 3 months. A picture is given of the spiritual calibre of the men and women we require, and the manner in which we seek God's guidance, so that the corporate will of the congregation is inspired by the mind of the Holy Spirit.

CHRISTIAN NATIONALS- OUR FIRST STUDENT IS Fyodor Dzyba, St Petersburg.

In the wake of the collapse of the former USSR, Russia remains by far the largest republic, stretching from Scandinavia in the North West to China and Mongolia in the south east, **a vast area encompassing almost every terrain and climate.**

The collapse of communism has opened up the way to new freedoms, but this is fraught with all kinds of difficulties and hardships. Industrial pollution threatens not only the environment but the health of many people.
St. Petersburg is one of Russia's major and famous cities. It is often thought of as Russia's version of Venice with impressive waterways and architecture.

It is in St Petersburg that Fyodor Dzyba, whom we in West support, studies. He writes:
"Through your support we get an education and learn how to preach. We have good teachers at the Bible College. I am married and my wife Helen also studies here. The town in which we live has 120,000 citizens. Our church consists of 250 members.
We visit prisons, hospitals and tell people about God's love. Some have accepted God.
Continue to pray for us please. God will bless you. We will also pray for you."

APRIL WCN ALSO GIVES DETAILS OF; the United Holy Week Services; the Dawn Service in Ballywalter with Paul Shields leading the worship. Breakfast was provided by Alvin and Vicky Wallwin and team; Janet Wood expressing thanks to the Church Committee for providing chairs in the church helpful to those with 'bad backs'; the forthcoming Men's Weekend at Glenada; Irene McGucken demitting her charge of West Church Anchor Boys through leaving Bangor and positive reports from all the Scouting organisations, including the Beavers who have carried off the Cup at the District Beaver Sports.

CHRISTIAN NATIONALS.

Our second West Church Sponsored Student is MARIVIC FETIZANAN attending The Philippine Missionary Institute.
All students at this Institute are Filopino Christians who are dedicated to serving God among their own people.
95% are actively engaged in pioneer evangelism, mainly working in remote village and island areas where the need is greatest. **The students are also active in evangelism and Christian service as a part of their training.**

Marivic Fetizanan writes:
"Formerly my parents were devoted Catholics. In the year 1980 my mother accepted the Lord as her Saviour. Although my father attends church on Sundays he has not a right relationship with Jesus. Until now he is a churchgoer.
My two brothers are Christians. From the time my mother accepted Christ, she often brought me to

Sunday School where I learned a lot about Christ.

I really praise and thank God for enlightening my dark paths. In the year 1987 I accepted him as my Lord and Saviour.

I have decided to enter PMI to answer God's calling and be prepared for His ministry. I have gifts in arts, lettering and card making."

AT HOME AND ABROAD.

It is right that we intensively cultivate the church in our own parish and land as we endeavour to do.

It is also right that we share in the worldwide mission of the church, as, for example, we seek to do through Christian Nationals.

It is a bonus that we are encouraged and inspired by learning of the vibrant way in which the church is growing in far-off lands whether it be in Asia or South America.

We will receive a blessing on Tuesday 18th May when Dr. CHRIS MARANTIKE, Principal of the Evangelical Theological Seminary in Indonesia will pay us a visit, accompanied by the College 'Men of Vision Choir'.

Dr Marantike is associated with 'Vision 111'.

VISION 111
Aims to plant a Christian congregation *in every village in Indonesia, all within one generation.*

The programme began in 1968 *and already 600 new churches have been planted.*
(Of course one knows that when such a work gets thoroughly under way, the rate of growth can increase dramatically.)

Before he is allowed to graduate, each student at the Seminary must plant a new congregation with at least 30 new converts.

And PLEASE NOTE that all this is taking place in a predominantly Muslim country.

CHRISTIAN AID WEEK.

In May each year, the 3 congregations in Bangor West unite to hold a Christian Aid Week Service.

This year it will be held in West Church on Sunday 16th May, in the context of a Praise Service, when the speaker will be the Rev. Peter Murray of Carnalea Methodist Church.

The three congregations provide a team to do a house-to-house collection for Christian Aid..This is an unpretentious endeavour that requires an unsung faithfulness, yet with awareness that needy, distant people will experience the compassionate touch of Christ upon their lives because of it.

MARGARET CATHCART,
a member of West, has coordinated this work of collecting, over many years. Appropriate then, that Margaret was one of ten, *chosen to visit South India* **to look at development work funded by Christian Aid. After her visit she produced this excellent article for West Church News to give us all a fresh insight into what is accomplished through Christian Aid.**

"Last October I set off with nine other Christian Aid supporters to visit the South of India to look at Development work funded by Christian Aid. The group was made up of five men and five women, all strangers to one another, but united by a deep interest in third world development and relief work. **It was part of Christian Aid's public awareness campaign, and we were all expected, of course, to fund ourselves.** For many months I had been concerned about whether I would be able to raise the necessary amount, so it was with some relief that I actually set off, although I wasn't sure what lay ahead of me.

19 DAYS - EXTENSIVE TRAVEL.
We were to travel in and around the **Madras** area and then south to **Madurai** and north to **Hyderabad**. The tour was to take 19 days. We were to travel extensively, **mostly through rural communities, where the landless poor** try to survive in an area of low and erratic employment on land owned mostly by absentee landlords **and where there is a high level of bonded labour.**

First impressions were of heat, noise, colour, crowds of people clamouring to carry our luggage, beggars without limbs, beautiful young girls giving us garlands, sandalwood oil and sugar crystals - **and lovely Indian smiles.**

MILLIONS BORN INTO DISEASE.
The poorest people in India are the Harjans, the people who are known and treated as 'the untouchables'. Millions are born into disease and despair, trapped in poverty by the religious and social injustice of the **caste system. They have no means by which to improve their lives, having no voice or status.**
Development agencies, funded by Christian Aid **have been working in the villages of Tamil Nadu, acting as catalysts to enable the rural poor to help themselves.**

We visited six development projects **where the aim is to create village self-sufficiency** and thereby also to stem the flow of unemployed villagers moving to larger towns and cities, **creating even more slum settlements with the inevitable disease and deprivation.**

MONEY GOES DIRECT TO THE PROJECTS.
Christian Aid's policy of using the country's own expertise to solve its problems in the most efficient way is extremely effective.
**The NGO's (non-government

organisations) send their officers into the needy areas to assess the situation. They then forward their proposals for long-term development to the funding agencies. In this way the money goes direct to the project and is used by the people who know exactly where it can best be used. **We were greatly impressed by the development organisations we visited - by their dedication, intellect and knowledge of sensitive environmental issues.**

LAFTI - WILL STAY IN OUR MEMORIES.

The first project we visited will stay in our memories. It was LAFTI, **Land For The Tillers' Freedom,** who are a Gandhian-led organisation, negotiating peacefully with landlords, government and industrial banks to try to gain an acre of land per family for the landless poor. Once land is gained, **the villagers all work together on a co-operative basis, sowing and reaping their crops for the good of the whole village.** The first village we visited had just been given 52 acres for 52 families and had been waiting in the heat of the sun for us to come and bless their first rice transplants before planting. **We were greatly moved and humbled by their welcome and were honoured to be able to witness the obvious joy and pride felt as they proceeded to plant on their own land for the first time.**

WORKING DIRECTLY THROUGH THE WOMEN!

All the agencies concerned were working directly through the women. In India women are doubly oppressed. They work long and hard for very low wages and they are entirely responsible for all the homemaking and childcare, preparing and cooking the food, *always eating least and last,* and the fetching and carrying of all the water and firewood, walking long distances to do so. **They are given no status and no say in the running of village affairs.** They are apathetic, with no self-esteem. *However development organisations are motivating the women and helping them to overcome their hopelessness and to learn new skills and literacy.* We were continually astounded by the dignity and grace with which the women bore the brunt of their hard daily chores, early and multiple childbirth (they often marry at the age of 12 or 13) ill-nourishment and bad health *and yet still attend the evening classes. Their progress was rapid and the whole village soon improved by their organisation and management.*

'BAREFOOT EXPERTS'.

The other projects we visited were sending officers into the villages to create 'barefoot experts' to use their term, among the villagers. **They were being taught irrigation methods, horticulture, agriculture, animal husbandry, forestry and crafts like artificial gem polishing, mat weaving and rope making, to help create other employment.** Additionally there were non-formal education classes and training given to young women to help start kindergartens. We were very impressed at the progress some villages had made in quite short periods. **Everyone is so keen to learn and put their knowledge into practice.**

We all felt a tremendous sense of hope having seen for ourselves just what long-term development means to previously poor villages.

SQUALOR OF THE SLUMS.

None of us were prepared for the squalor and deprivation of the slums in Madras. **We were moved by the welcoming smiles, even in that grey dismal place, without proper sanitation.** But even in the slums there was hope. 'The Madras Christian Council for Social Services', **funded by Christian Aid, is providing building materials to help provide secure homes, vocational training and health care classes.** *Again we were aware of the innate dignity of the Indian people*

TRAVELLING HUNDREDS OF MILES.

We travelled hundreds and hundreds of miles on long overnight train journeys (on very hard bunks, more like foldaway shelves really, *very public and very noisy; on minibuses over dusty roads or sometimes tracks, always very hot and without enough rest. Some of the groups became ill. We had colourful, close encounters with the insect world in some unexpected places. Nevertheless, we would not have missed the experience for the world. All of us came away with feelings of hope and the overwhelming sense that something was really happening to alleviate the suffering. We are confident that Christian Aid funds are being used in the best way possible and we feel very privileged to have been able to see all this for ourselves.*

ALL THINNER!

We were all thinner and united in the feeling that we would NOT have an Indian take-away for some time, but also united by a unique experience of a country which you hate and love at the same time **and which beckons your return.**

As Christian Aid week approaches, please remember to give generously - a little help from us means an enormous amount to someone who has nothing. Please also try to take time to read the leaflet delivered with the envelope.

JUNE WCN 1993.

WELCOME TO THOMAS MULHOLLAND- AND LORRAINE.

Alvin and Linda and their family have just left us, and now we are prepared to bid welcome to Thomas Mulholland- and Lorraine.

A native of Kilrea, educated at Coleraine Academical Institution and at Preston Polytechnic, he is entering his final theological year at Union, Belfast, has an interest in leading praise/worship and in counselling, feeling also a strong commitment to conservation and environmental issues. In mid-June **he plans to marry Lorraine, who has just completed her first year in Theology at Union.**

They hope to move into our accommodation at '91' which we are making into a self-contained flat, but with access to the kitchen below.
Thomas will not be starting work with us in West until October. As a final-year student at Union, he is permitted to do only 6 hours work per week with our congregation, so in no sense does he replace Alvin.

A CONSIDERABLE PROBLEM FOR US!
It is hard to quantify all the sectors of work in which Alvin was involved - Young West Church, Friday Nights, Bible Busters, Sunday School interests, Summer Schemes, Twilight Zones, Seminars for Young People, Communicants' Classes - **and hard to quantify the vision and encouragement imparted to leaders, and to young people;** *the way he nurtured the infra-structure of youth work; his interest in and love for individuals and groups.* **ALL THAT AND SO MUCH MORE WILL BE SORELY MISSED!**

OUR NEW ELDERS -
EACH GIVES A PERSONAL PROFILE IN WCN.

JOHN ELLIOTT
BILLY RICHARDSON
PHIL & MOLLY DORMAN
J W RUSSELL
ROBERT ADRAIN
PAUL SHIELDS
MAUREEN BLACKMORE
HUGH FERGIE
REG WILSON
BRIAN MARTIN

HELEN RITCHIE
REG BATES
BRIAN McQUITTY
DEREK POLLEY.

A Service of Ordination and Installation of our Elders-elect will be conducted by a Commission of the Presbytery of Ards at 7.00pm on Sunday 13th June.

FAMILY SERVICES
THROUGHOUT THE SUMMER AT 11.30 AM.

A LONG, UNINTERRUPTED YEAR FOR OUR Sunday School Departments comes to a climax on Sunday 20th June with our YOUNG PEOPLE'S SERVICE AT 11.30AM. Paul Cameron of Scripture Union will be our Guest Speaker. In this service we will have the participation of the children *from all our SundaySchool Departments.* **This also is an opportunity to say 'Thank you' to all those who have taught our children so faithfully and lovingly throughout the year.**

This year the 11.30 Service will be a Family Service over the two summer months, so that parents and children may come together and remain together throughout the service, hopefully enhancing the sense of *Family* within the congregation.

Those desiring a more traditional and quiet service should make a point of coming to the Ten O'clock service!

RALLY OUTSIDE GPO, DUBLIN - WEST CHURCH MEMBER ON PLATFORM PARTY!
ROBERTA CORBRIDGE TELLS OF "PUTTING YOUR MONEY WHERE YOUR MOUTH IS!"

"The awful devastation of the City of London last weekend serves as one more reminder that the men of violence in our society remain seemingly ever present with us. They appear to be able to move about with little hindrance, leaving mayhem, suffering, and distress in their wake. *All this in spite of the fact that most people in Ireland, North and South, would want to see an end to this destruction which is laying waste our land.*

SUSAN McHUGH, A DUBLIN HOUSEWIFE.
The Warrington bombing and in particular the deaths of the two young children, outraged many people throughout the British Isles.
One of these was a Dublin housewife called Susan McHugh. Listening to the reports of the bombing, Susan was particularly affected as she gazed at her own young daughter, Emma, the same age as the youngest victim. How would she cope if it had been Emma who had lost her life in such tragic and altogether avoidable circumstances?

THE ENNISKILLEN BOMB ON POPPY DAY had also affected Susan profoundly and at that time she organised a Book of Condolences from the people of Dublin and took it to Enniskillen herself. Now she felt anger and despair that these atrocities were continuing in the name of the Irish people.
Susan McHugh, an Irish Catholic, did not feel that the IRA represented her and she felt that there must be many other Irish people who were sickened and weary of this campaign of violence. *LISTENING TO A LOCAL RADIO BROADCAST, SHE FELT STRONGLY ENOUGH TO PHONE IN AND SAY SO. NOT FOR ONE MOMENT DID SHE REALISE THE CONSEQUENCES OF HER ACTIONS!*

SWAMPED WITH CALLS!
The radio station was swamped with calls of support for Susan's

stance. Within a few days she found herself a national figure. A meeting in Trinity College was organised for 24th March, in an effort to give the people of Dublin an opportunity to express their abhorrence of the acts carried out by the IRA in their name. The response exceeded everyone's expectations and it became clear that the need for ordinary people to show their solidarity against the men of violence was growing daily. **Consequently, an open-air meeting was to be held in Dublin on Sunday 28th March. Ironically, the venue was to be outside the GPO in O'Connell Street."**

Roberta Corbridge continues:
"Having seen Susan's broadcast on TV on Friday 26th I felt compelled to contact her with a word of encouragement. Many of us, I'm sure, have shared Susan's views, but few are prepared to make the stand she did, bringing herself and her family under public and media scrutiny. **I first spoke to Susan at RTE studios after her broadcast and she was both encouraged and delighted with the call.**
As we talked she told me she was a practising Catholic and had felt prompted by God to continue her campaign after the initial phone-in. **She said she had been praying for contact with a Protestant mother from the North.** At this point I had not made Susan aware of my religious denomination! **As our chat progressed, Susan suggested that I should come to Dublin for the weekend and take a stand with her on the platform on Sunday. Talk about putting your money where your mouth is! My first reaction was to recoil in horror. This was totally out of character for me. I am not usually an "up front" sort of person. I was hesitant,** *but after a great deal of prayer, self-examination and encouragement from Susan, I finally agreed at 11.00pm on the Friday evening.*

ARRANGEMENTS MADE.
Arrangements were made for me to travel to Dublin by train on Saturday afternoon and to be met at the Station by friends of Arthur and Susan McHugh. They would also provide accommodation and take me under their wing.
During the train journey, I talked myself in and out of the situation a dozen times, but suddenly there I was on O'Connell Street Station being greeted by a family with my name on a card.

LATE NIGHT PRAYER SESSION.
Saturday evening was spent getting to know each other and eventually in a late night prayer session about the rally next day. Susan had received some negative calls and this had discouraged her a little. She was also very tired after four days of media saturation.

SUNDAY MORNING CHAOTIC.
Sunday morning in the McHugh household was chaotic to say the least. Reporters and camera crews seemed to be crawling out of the woodwork. Susan had initially invited me to address the rally but I was beginning to feel less comfortable about this. **Eventually we decided that I would probably be most use to Susan as a prayer partner, praying for her as she spoke.**

ALL WITH ONE COMMON DESIRE.

During the couple of hours before the rally, I had an opportunity to meet and talk to many people of different, political and social backgrounds but all with one common desire- *to see an end to this cancer corrupting our society.* Each of us had an opportunity to explain the circumstances leading to our presence in Dublin that day **and for me it was a chance to state my position as a Christian and tell a little about our congregation here at West.**

MORE THAN 15,000!

The rally was an unqualified success and an attendance of 15,000 plus, certainly far exceeded the estimate of 5000 hoped for. **Looking from the platform in either direction a sea of faces united in singing the prayer chosen by Peace INITIATIVE '93,** *"make me a channel of your peace…." was indeed an encouraging sight."*

Roberta concludes: "I reflected on the strange events of the weekend as my train sped North, returning to Bangor feeling a little less hopeless about Northern Ireland than I had done for some time.

Pray for God's Spirit to continue to stir the hearts of our people and convict the hardened hearts of the men of terror. Pray also for Susan as she continues to urge the people of Ireland to denounce violence by word and deed.

But be careful when you cry to the Lord about the state of our country and your feeling of helplessness, about being able to do anything to bring about change. *You never know what surprises may be in store for you!"*

**JUNE WCN has many other items of news and enlightening articles.
From Patricia Fergie's Letter from India - how about this excerpt?**
"Our Senior Class had a 'skip day' when they had a day off school for an excursion. The School bus and a truck were in a collision, but happily, the only damage was a broken bus windscreen, so praise the Lord for looking after everyone. **By the way - the truck driver had no insurance, so the bus driver took a wheel off the truck, to pay for a new windscreen!
JUNE WCN also carries comprehensive news from all our Scouting groups, beautifully illustrated and presented under the title of "Scouting News."**

WCN continues to INFORM our people of all that goes on within the congregation; and also to INSPIRE - to encourage and educate our members in the Christian way, and to let folk know where they may gain help and information to cope with the problems of life and be built up in Christian character and godliness.

FOR EXAMPLE-
THERE IS A FOUR-PART VIDEO SERIES ENTITLED:

THE ADAM AND EVE FACTOR -
EXPLORING FOUR AREAS OF COMMITMENT, CONFLICT, INTIMACY, SERVANTHOOD

In one of these PHILIP HACKING declares "The Goalposts have moved"…
'Six out of eight couples coming to me for marriage are already living together. Most are sublimely unaware that this might be a problem for me. I think it's an inevitable follow-through of a generation which threw overboard Christian doctrine *but thought they could keep the Christian ethic. Now blissfully unaware of the origin of such values, today's youth have rejected the very values themselves. Doing what is right in their own eyes is leading to a breakdown in society in general, as well as in marriage.*'

MISMATCHED:
CHRISTIAN WIFE/ UNBELIEVING HUSBAND.

Young Christian 'singles' are often warned not to be 'unequally yoked'- a hard message to teach or to receive!
I remember a young woman who attended one of our Seminars and came to vital faith in Christ. With her children she had for a short period separated from her husband and was living with her mother. She said to me - *'Now I won't have to return to my husband for the Bible says 'do not be unequally yoked'.*
My reply was 'the Bible also says *'Wives, fit in with your husbands' plans; for then if they refuse to listen when you talk to them about the Lord, they will be won over by your respectful, pure behaviour. Your godly lives will speak to them better than any words.'"*

You may read the outcome of these words on pages 231ff of "WEST CHURCH JOURNEY."

Often Christian truth gets through - to people struggling and under pressure- most effectively, through giving an actual account of people in the very circumstances where they are '**mismatched**'.

A MISMATCHED MARRIAGE.
Lee Strobel knows firsthand the tensions that arise when a Christian is married to a non-Christian.
Fourteen years ago when his wife, Leslie became a believer, Strobel reacted with anger, alienation and fear.
In his book "Inside the Mind of Unchurched Harry and Mary" he shares how Leslie discovered four simple- yet powerful- ways to live out her faith in their spiritually mismatched marriage - without alienating him.

GOD JUST WASN'T ON OUR AGENDA.

"Six words sum up the role God played during the early years of my marriage. *He just wasn't on our agenda.* After we were married in 1972, our lives became packed with far more pressing matters. We were both busy with our careers, we were starting our family, and we had finally bought a house. **Frankly there was no room for God - even if he did exist!** Leslie and I were best friends and for the most part didn't have any worries.
I pictured our lives together as though we were driving a convertible with the top down, laughing, joking, waving at people as we zoomed by, "Look at the Strobels", they'd say "Aren't they happy? Aren't they doing great?" And we were, at least on a superficial level.

ON THE SKIDS.
Our happiness went into a skid in the fall of 1979, when Leslie told me of her choice to follow Jesus Christ. She had been introduced to Him through the gentle witness and friendship of a woman whose daughter was the same age as ours.
Leslie's decision initiated the most tumultuous era of our relationship.
Most Christians can't appreciate the emotional state of a nonbelieving spouse - or what motivates his behaviour. I felt hurt and suddenly devalued in Leslie's eyes.
Leslie was meeting all sorts of new people at church and seemed so enthused by their spirituality **that I felt she was looking down at me.** Of course she wasn't, but that didn't stop me from worrying that Leslie's respect for me would dwindle because I wasn't committed to God.

One Sunday morning as I lay in bed, Leslie dressed for church and pleasantly asked me if I'd like to come along. **The truth was, going to church was the last thing on my mind.** I wanted to roll over and try to sleep off my hangover from the night before. But I felt Leslie was being pulled into a new sphere of relationships -```**and I didn't want to lose her.**
So I snapped, "Yeah, okay, I'll go." I stomped around the house, slammed some doors, refused her offer to fix me breakfast, and got dressed. It was raining as we left the house, and we got wet as we tried to get into the car. I was in an ' 'ornery' mood, driving much too fast on the slick roads. Every once in a while I'd swear at the weather. Finally, Leslie broke down in tears. "Look, I'm not twisting your arm." she said. "If you don't want to go, don't. Just let me go in peace."

I had made matters worse. I felt obligated to go to church because I thought I was losing her - yet I ended up pushing her further away.

BAIT AND SWITCH.
I was afraid Leslie was turning into a wild-eyed religious fanatic. Would she embarrass me in front of my buddies? Would she shame me every time I drank too much? Would she spill details of our private life in her prayer group? Would she reject all of our old friends? Would her church friends poke fun at me behind my back?

FRUSTRATION.
Another emotion I felt was frustration. For the first time in our relationship our **values were at odds. For instance we had always agreed how we would spend our money.** Now Leslie wanted to give money to the church and I blew my top. She felt so strongly about giving that she got a part-time job just so she could contribute. **I thought of all the fun we could have with that extra cash - and it grated on me.**
To me it was a clear case of bait and switch: I married one Leslie, and now she was changing into someone I hadn't bargained for. **I wanted the old Leslie back!**
Looking back now, I realise that the more Leslie tried to live out the Christian life - with purity, integrity, honesty, tolerance and forgiveness -**the more obvious it became that my life was corroded with cynicism, bitterness, superficiality, and self-centredness. It was as though Leslie was unwittingly holding up a mirror and I could see who I really was.**
The Bible calls this being convicted of sin. It made me angry because I didn't want to face my sin. I wanted to maintain the illusion that I was a wonderful guy and everything in my life was great.
While I professed tolerance for Leslie's newfound faith, my unspoken attitude towards her was, *What's wrong with you? Why do you need that kind of crutch?*
It hurt her that I could be so open-minded about most things, but when it came to Christianity my mind was slammed shut.
Emotions boiled inside me like a cauldron. Arguments erupted. Disagreements broke out. I'd stomp out of the house instead of trying to work things out. I couldn't diagnose what was going on, but I felt our marriage was headed downhill - fast!

SURVIVAL STRATEGY.
Nonbelieving spouses can't believe why their decision to remain 'spiritually neutral' sends such damaging tremors through their marriage- *but it does*. And for the Christian spouse, *every time he or she sees a Christian couple whose marriage has a joyful Christian dimension, there's grief over what is missing in his or her marriage. A spiritual mismatch ignites a powerful keg of emotion in both spouses. And when you add the tendency for some believers <u>to go overboard to win their spouse for Christ, the marriage can become increasingly rocky.</u>*

If you are married to a non-Christian, it is important to understand the feelings that may haunt him. Some of these emotions - as difficult as they are to endure- **can actually be a part of the process of his coming to God.** But as tough as it is to be a spiritual mismatch, **there's hope.** God won't abandon you. He will offer you wisdom to survive. During that tumultuous time in our marriage, **Leslie followed four basis pieces of biblical advice that saved our relationship and paved the way for my coming to Christ. If you need help in getting through turbulent times, here's some counsel.**

HARNESS THE SUPPORT OF OTHERS.
The Old Testament says, "Two are better than one, because they have a good return for their work: If one falls down, his friend can help him up. But pity the man who falls, and has no one to help him up! (Ecclesiastes 4: 9).
Leslie realised from the outset that she couldn't get through this situation alone. So she cultivated her friendship with Linda, the woman who had led her to Christ. Linda offered godly advice, consistent prayers, and a shoulder to cry on. She made sure Leslie didn't get mired in self-pity or become negative towards me. Leslie easily could have developed an attitude that said, "It's God and me against Lee." *That mindset would have poisoned our relationship.* **Instead Linda insisted that Leslie focus on the good aspects of my character. She made sure that Leslie didn't start blaming every little problem in our marriage on the fact that I wasn't a Christian.**

If you're married to an unbeliever it is easy to say, "If only he would become a Christian, everything would be perfect. He'd help around the house without complaining, he'd always control his temper, he'd always put my interests first, and he'd automatically stop working so much at the office." **That's not reality. Christian marriages are not perfect - no matter what image people try to project.** It's important to keep from idealizing marriage to a believer. **Not all of a spouse's shortcomings can be attributed to his spiritual condition.**
What Leslie's spiritual mentor did was to keep Leslie focussed upon God - not on her situation. She encouraged Leslie to keep building on the common ground we shared, so that we wouldn't drift apart.
If you're married to an unbeliever, do you have a confidante like Linda? Are you friends with a mature Christian who can give you support, guidance and encouragement? It's critically important to link up with someone you can consistently pour out your heart to and pray with.

EXERCISE RESTRAINT.
Believe me, Leslie's ability to restrain herself from trying to stuff Christianity down my throat

was a major reason why I eventually came to Christ. Even though there were times when she wanted to whack me over the head with a Bible, tie me up and force me to listen to a sermon tape, or to drag me to church by the hair, **she gave me space.**

If she had taped bible verses to my mirror in the morning, stuffed tracts into my socks when I was packing for a trip, kept resetting my car radio to a Christian station, or hung crosses all over the house, it certainly would only have heightened the tension.
Leslie also restrained herself from getting too deeply involved with church. I didn't mind if she went to church on Sundays, but if she had been out several nights a week at prayer meetings, seminars or small groups, I would have said **"Time out! Something's got to change! This is controlling your life!" She accommodated me.**
Perhaps the most important way that Leslie exercised restraint was that she didn't heap guilt on me every time I had a few drinks or let loose with some bad language. She didn't refuse to go to parties or movies where the language might be a little offensive. While she did hold her ground on important issues, she didn't elevate everything into a spiritual battle.
Many spiritually mismatched Christians struggle with how far to push because they feel so impassioned about wanting to reach their partner with the Gospel. **They can inadvertently inflame their partner's emotions or prompt him to stubbornly dig in his heels.**

LIVE OUT YOUR FAITH.

As a new believer, Leslie wasn't ready to answer my sceptical and often hostile questions about Christianity. If she had tried to debate with me about God, the conversation would have degenerated into a fruitless argument. If she had started quoting Scripture to me I would have walked out of the room.

But Leslie did something more effective: **she let God change her character, attitude and outlook. She yielded herself as fully as she could so that God could mould her into a more Christ-like person.**

I WATCHED AS SHE INCREASINGLY BECAME A PERSON OF HUMILITY, INTEGRITY, LOVE AND SELF-SACRIFICE. And, in the end, the main reason I was willing to take an open-minded look at her faith was because I was astonished by how Leslie was being transformed into a better person.

PRAY, PRAY, PRAY.

When you're feeling hurt, frustrated, angry and afraid, **who but God can really help?**
Leslie often focused her prayers on this Old Testament verse: "**I will give you a new heart, and put a new spirit in you; I will remove from you your heart of stone and give you a heart of flesh." (Ezekiel 36:26).**
She often told God: "Lord, Lee's heart is like granite - I can't crack it open. But I know you have the power to do a spiritual heart transplant. Lord, please, give him a new heart and spirit because only You can do it."

She also prayed, "**Your Word promises that if I ask for wisdom, You'll give it. Lord, give me the wisdom to know how far to push and when to back off. I don't want to alienate Lee; I want to cooperate with You in reaching him."** When I was especially obnoxious, she obtained God's power to keep loving me when, frankly I wasn't very lovable.
Do you know what happened? **God used this difficult time to mould Leslie into someone she never would have become without it. She learned how to pour herself out in heartfelt prayer. Formula praying didn't cut it; she needed to express her deepest feelings - anger, frustration and pain - to God, and that meant her prayers weren't always polite or fancy. Sometimes they were messy and tear-stained.**

Throughout this time, Leslie learned to wait on God's timing, even when she wanted desperately to take matters into her own hands.
She learnt how to forgive someone who was hard to forgive, and she was taught lessons of perseverance and hope.
God can take your heart-breaking experience of living with an unbeliever *and mould you into someone whose faith has a depth, character, and quality it might never have had otherwise.*

A WONDERFUL ENDING.
Our spiritual mismatch has a wonderful ending. Two years later, after much searching and investigation, **I accepted Christ.** Leslie and I have discovered the heights a relationship can take when Christ is at its centre. *But not every husband and wife end up together in God's Kingdom.* I know a woman who has been married to an unbeliever for 16 years, and he only recently agreed to come to church with her for the first time. *That single step was the culmination of 16 long years of praying, hoping and dreaming.*

REMEMBER, YOU ARE NOT HELD ACCOUNTABLE TO God if your spouse rejects Christ. **Husbands and wives are responsible for their own choices. Don't let misplaced guilt wear you down. Don't let your actions be driven by an inappropriate sense of responsibility for your spouse's spiritual state, because, inevitably, that will cause you to cross the bounds and push too hard.**

In the end, your responsibility is to live out your life, as best you can, in a Christ-honouring way. As a fellow-pastor says, "If you honour God with your everyday life, He'll honour you for a lifetime" even in the midst of a spiritual mismatch.

AUGUST/SEPTEMBER WCN 1993.

AMBITIOUS PROGRAMME
FOR ELDERS AND CHURCH VISITORS, 1993-4.

We have now a very large team of Elders and Church Visitors, *many of them embarking on Pastoral Service for the first time.*
The meetings for Elders and Church Visitors will be on the second Monday of each month beginning on 13th September at 7.30 for Kirk Session, to conduct business and at
8.15 joined by Church Visitors.

From 8.15 -8.30 there will be a time of worship, introducing the programme for the evening.

Each evening the programme will be designed to train and stimulate our pastoral team of Elders and Church Visitors; and to allow them, in groups, to discuss, plan and pray together, for those allotted to their care.

Each evening, we may receive reports from groups within the congregation, so that we may be more fully informed about activities and endeavours within West Church. We will consider things that encourage us, and things that require attention.

From time to time we may review challenging books or have a glimpse into helpful videos, so that we prosecute our work in an enlightened manner.

LAYOUT FOR EACH EVENING:
7.15 Pre-meeting Prayer.
7.30 -8.15 Kirk Session Business.
8.15- 8.30 Worship as Kirk Session is joined by Church Visitors.
8.30 - 8.50 Reports from organisations/ reviews books/ videos.
8.50 - 9.20 CORE TEACHING.
9.20 - 10.00 Discussion/ Prayer in groups.

CORE SUBJECTS:
September.
Reports from elders and Visitors in GOOD NEWS teams to enable us to assess what is happening and how to capitalise on what we have learnt.
October.
The Rev. Ian Hart will help us to gain a Biblical perspective on our secular life as the sphere for Christian ministry.

November.
Ministering in the HOME - gossiping the Gospel, Devotions in the homes we visit; under girding this work by prayer, personal and corporate.
Led by Heather Thompson.

December.
Ministering to Special groups - Birth and Baptism of Children; Preparation for Marriage.
Experience of Good News teams. Jeremy and Heather Eves on Marriage Preparation.

January.
Ministering to the Senior section - special visitation, tape ministry, Tuesday Together, bereavement, Communion in home etc.

February.
Ministering to a wide range of needs, personal, spiritual, social, family. Seminars, Sycamore Club, Abba Trust; broken families, single parents, unemployed. Fostering hospitality. Our social and recreation groups etc.

March.
Release of gifts of the Spirit for the up building of the whole body - Church Committee, Home Groups. Choir/Singing groups.

April.
Updating ourselves on the whole work of the PCI at home, overseas, summer outreach for young people etc.

May.
A Weekend away??

This gives a bare skeleton awareness of material to be studied by our elders and church Visitors in 1993-4.

GOOD NEWS - RIGHT IN YOUR OWN HOME!

In January 1993 the Rev. Michael Wooderson and his wife Anne paid a visit to us in West Church. They told us how, over a period of almost twenty years, little teams of 3 people, have visited homes in their parishes, and shared 'Good News' with them.

NOT SPECIALLY TRAINED.
The people sent out *had not been specially trained for this work, and had not been taught to apply salesmen's techniques.*
They were ordinary, loving, believing members of the congregation, meeting people in their homes with warmth and friendliness.

NOT GOING FROM DOOR TO DOOR.
Nor had these little groups of three gone from door to door seeking admission. **They went only to homes that had invited them! They went as invited guests!** It was normally through the minister that these invitations came. He knew the homes where there was an interest - the homes that could specially benefit from such a visit. **So, with a little encouragement and reassurance, people came, sometimes a bit nervously, to issue their invitations for people to come.**

SOME HAD DOUBTS!
When we in West heard this story from the Wooldersons, many had questions, some had doubts.

YET 20 HOMES RECEIVED!
And yet the facts are that by the

summer of 1993, almost 20 homes have received 'Good News Teams', *and about 50 of our members have already taken part in these teams!*

A WIDE RANGE OF HOMES.

A wide range of homes have been involved, from young couples giving thought to the baptism of their children, to mature people giving further thought to the spiritual significance of life, to older people unable easily to leave their homes.

WHAT DOES A TEAM 'DO' WHEN IT COMES INTO A HOME?

It comes each week for six weeks. The first week is largely spent in getting to know one another! Then, each week, people read from the New Testament in the simple language of the Good News Bible - which is provided by the Team. *This helps all to understand who Jesus is, what He has done for us, and how we may know Him.*

Already in the congregation there are those who are filled with gratitude and happiness on account of receiving the Good News Teams into their homes. The members of the teams also have benefited enormously in every way.

Should you wish to enquire about a Good News Team, speak to the ministers, elders or Church Visitors.

PAUL SHIELDS LEADS A 'GOOD NEWS' TEAM.

This was rather remarkable because Paul had had grave doubts about the appropriateness of this approach for our Irish situation. As well he was suffering much pain through many months of 1993, and his son John was also ill at this time. Paul tells the story. (Written 2006)

WHO WOULD WANT THREE 'BIBLE THUMPERS' IN THEIR HOME?

"West Church had had a visit from Michael Wooderson and his wife, who told us of their experiences **in leading others to faith through conducting team-led Bible Studies in local homes.** They had entitled this extremely successful venture **"Good News down the Street."** I had enjoyed the Woodersons' visit very much, but had decided that the Good News Team concept was a nice idea that happened to have worked for the Woodersons and their parish. *My experience of Northern Ireland families was that they would have been unwilling to invite a team of 'Bible-thumpers' into their homes!.* The fact that the Good News Team comprised 3 people meant that a husband and wife in the home would always be outnumbered! The reason for the three was: a man and a woman should be present; husband and wife teams were not encouraged; and a man and woman who were not married to each other should be accompanied by another person. After the concept had been launched by the Reverend David Bailie in West, **I was approached by Pauline Allen who was sure that I was the right person to lead a Team in the home of a couple who lived close to her.** I was less enthusiastic, but soon weakened to David Bailie's approach.

1993 A CHALLENGING YEAR!
1993 had already been a challenging year. I had been aware of breathing in the icy cold air as I left John Rea's house around midnight on the first Saturday evening of the New Year. *Within 24 hours I had completely lost my voice.* I continued to talk in a hoarse whisper for 6 weeks. *At several points I despaired that I would ever sing again. Some feared that I would!*
Additionally **the back pain** I had suffered from during much of 1992 had re-emerged as a referred pain in my left leg, *a pain that was exacerbated by the seating position dictated by an aircraft passenger seat.* I had taken on a new role in work that involved me in increased travelling.

By the time the Good News Team was launched on the Wednesday after the May Day holiday, I had already been to both California and Montreal twice each, to France and Germany [it is true no birds sing at Auschwitz!] numerous times. I had already done the usual UK mainland trips and **I was in permanent physical discomfort. In addition our son John had shocked us when he described his urine as being "like red juice."** Hospitalisation was inevitable as the medical people puzzled over John's haematuria. It only complicated matters that I had been 'volunteered' to lead this, one of a number of Good News teams. *I was convinced it was doomed to failure and that is why I wanted no part in it.*

NOEL & JANET JOHNSTON.

The proposed venue of the Good News Team was 11 Rosemary Avenue (close to Pauline Allen's house), the home of Noel and Janet Johnston. Janet had made a profession of faith in Jesus Christ the previous year, but her husband, despite having attended an evangelistic evening for men in West Church, remained unconvinced. **He had been out of work for some time having been a typesetter in a local newspaper office, a role that had been rendered redundant by the computerisation of the industry.** The couple had two children of primary school age and a young baby who proved to be a distraction during our studies. However we persevered. **My team comprised myself, Roberta Corbridge and Ian Kyle.** I knew Roberta slightly but I didn't know Ian at all. We had agreed we should meet the Tuesday before our first visit to the Johnston home for introductions and discussion. **I was at one of my life's all time low periods that evening, having left my wife Beulah at John's bedside in the Children's Ward of the Ulster Hospital.** *Thankfully Don Ritchie, who was serving on West's*

Pastoral Team at the time, took us aside and suggested he 'make a wee prayer' [in the words of Margaret Gibson, a late friend and continuing source of encouragement].

PRAISE FROM A HURTING HEART.

That evening as we prayed and began to bring praise to God in anticipation of what He was going to do in the Johnston home, **I experienced** as I had done several times previously, **something of the power that there is in praise,** *particularly the praise that emanates from a hurting heart.*
The book of Hebrews speaks about offering up the sacrifice of praise. This reminds me of the account of an incident in the latter part of David's life when he was compelled by the Lord through the prophet Gad to offer up a sacrifice on the threshing floor of Arunah the Jebusite.

As David approached the owner to purchase both the threshing floor and the oxen to be used in the burnt offering, Arunah stated that he was prepared to give it all over to him, free of charge; after all, he was the KING of Israel. **However David was not prepared to make an offering to the Lord that had cost him nothing.** *For me, praising God appeared to be a costly sacrifice that night, but it brought great reward.*

A LIFE-CHANGING CHOICE.

It was to be a 6-week course, but in typical West Church fashion it was still continuing 12 weeks later. **The purpose of the Course was to study what the Bible claimed about the Christian faith** *and in particular, the person, words and work of Jesus,* to let the participants decide how reliable its claims are and then to encourage them **to make a life-changing choice based upon personal belief in the Bible's claims**
There is a song by a popular American singer/songwriter **Billy Joel, called "HONESTY."** Its words go like this:

"If you search for tenderness
It isn't hard to find;
You can have the love you need to live.
But if you look for truthfulness
You might just as well be blind,
It always seems to be so hard to give.

Honesty is such a lonely word,
  Everyone is so untrue.
Honesty is hardly ever heard,
But mostly what I need from you.

THIS SONG USED TO ILLUSTRATE.
I happened to use this song on one of our evenings together to illustrate our goal for the Good News Team; not to force anyone's religious opinions on someone else, **but to be honest about the Bible with a view to discovering the truth. Noel and Janet both played in pop bands and knew the song well.** My seeming knowledge of music relaxed the situation for all of us, *and music was to play a large part in our evolving relationship.*

THE TEAM WENT ON TO EXPLAIN that the author of the Bible was the Holy Spirit, *and if we wanted to know the truth of the Bible where it seemed ambiguous, we could ask that same Holy Spirit to tell us what He had meant.*

Paul Shields continues: "The inclusion of this, in that evening's discussion, together with the Johnstons' interest in music inspired me to write and record a song: "Into the Truth."

"Why don't you ask Him what He meant
When He said those words so long ago?
So many questions to be asked:
So many answers you need to know
The One who wrote the Book can tell you today;
So many things that He wants to say.

Let God's Spirit guide you into the truth,
Let God's spirit guide you into the truth,
Let God's Spirit guide you into the truth
into the truth.

What was the relationship the Son had with the Father
Before time began?
How could He love the world so much to leave His throne
to become a man?
The Holy Spirit can tell you why Jesus came to earth to die."

THE SECOND VERSE WAS PROMPTED by the fact that, unknown to the Team, *each Thursday evening a team of JEHOVAH'S WITNESSES, was conducting with the Johnstons a study similarly structured to ours.*

There were inevitable, irreconcilable differences that emerged as discussions began to concentrate on the person and work of Jesus Christ.

Often when Thursday evening's study contradicted Wednesday evening's study, **rather than waiting almost a full week for an explanation,** Noel would call with his brother Billy to question him!

BROTHER BILLY.
Billy, by his own admission, had come to a stage where he was going through the motions in his Christian faith. **The possibility of another family member coming to living faith excited Billy. These questions forced him to search the Scriptures for answers, which he found and shared.** *This set Billy's faith on fire again.*
What Noel and Janet both marvelled at was how Billy's explanation regarding any question was always the same as the one given by the Team on the following Wednesday. They concluded that we were all reading from the same **"Question & Answer" Manual, which in a sense was true, but later they had the revelation that we were each relying on the same Holy Spirit,** *the writer of the Book and our present-day Guide.*

NOEL KNEELS, CONTENDS FOR TRUTH, DEVOURS THE

WORD OF GOD.

By the time the end of the course was in sight, Janet had become firm in her faith and Noel had shared with us how some weeks previously he had knelt in the bedroom and committed his life to Jesus Christ.
When God's Holy Spirit is permitted to lead individuals into the truth, *He will lead them into all truth.*
Noel's situation of being out of work *had been dealt a further blow by his application to join the RUC having been turned down.* <u>However he recognised and seized the opportunity to read the Word for at least three hours each day.</u>

HE SKILFULLY ARGUED WITH THE JEHOVAH'S WITNESSES each Thursday evening from his newly-gained knowledge of the Bible until they wheeled in reinforcements from Belfast. *They were not able to contend with his Spirit-led understanding and eventually withdrew!*
Book after book was studied on subjects such as the inerrancy of the Bible, the literal nature of the biblical account of creation and the last days; also biographies of great Christians such as Charles Finney.
Noel's appetite for knowledge of the Christian faith seemed insatiable *and Janet's desire was to invite friends and neighbours into their house to tell what great things the Lord had done.*

THE THINGS OF THE SPIRIT.
Because of the reputation West Church has with regard to the things of the Holy Spirit, it seemed reasonable to tag a 'bonus pack' on to the Woodersons' original study material, concerning the fullness and gifts of the Holy Spirit, a sort of a mini "Life in the Spirit Seminar."
This introduced Noel and Janet to the power by which an authentic Christian life can be lived and also served to launch them on a journey of earnestly desiring spiritual gifts, gifts such as tongues, the interpretation of tongues, prophecy, words of knowledge and healing. It led them to crave the fullness of the Spirit, a journey that is continuing until this day. **When Janet returned from the Centenary Celebration of Azusa Street revival in Los Angeles earlier this year (2006) she had received an obvious and infectious infilling.**

JANET SINGS WHILE NOEL GIVES TESTIMONY IN

In those years we had Praise & Prayer meetings during the summer months, when the House Groups didn't meet, in the New Hall.
I was responsible for one of the evenings and **I asked Janet to sing and Noel to give his testimony. What a joy that meeting was!** This introduced the family to the West Church congregation although there was a problem with Sunday church attendance for the Johnstons.
Noel still played in a show band on both Friday and Saturday nights. That meant that Sunday morning services were well nigh impossible, and because of the baby, Sunday evenings were awkward too. However, because neither of the couple had a job, the income from entertainment was welcome. *But soon Christian conviction was to overcome the need for money, money that is usually paid in cash and taken on an undeclared, tax-free basis.*

NOEL CONCLUDED that he didn't believe in the sentiments of the songs he was playing, AND JANET PLEDGED she would sing for the Lord and write songs extolling Him.

Her response to my song "Into the Truth" was her song "He is There":

"If your worries are too hard to bear,
Or if your loved ones can't be there,
Maybe you're wondering 'Does anyone care'?
Ask and you'll find that Jesus is there.

If you're searching for one who's heard
Or if you're waiting for God's true word
Maybe you're listening to someone's prayer
Ask and you'll find that Jesus is there.

*He is there when you need Him
He is there when you call.
He is there when you want Him,
He is there, for He is Lord of all."*

18 FURTHER MONTHS OF UNEMPLOYMENT..... BUT.

In the following 18 months of unemployment during which another Johnston baby was born, Janet told me that it was not unusual for mysterious packages of groceries and baby goods to arrive on the doorstep of 11 Rosemary Avenue, as the people of West exhibited a typical generosity. I remember hearing that after Noel had decorated a room for the non-Christian mother of a member of West, he refused payment stating: **"The Lord takes care of my needs."**
It was not unusual in those days for my wife Beulah and me to leave Noel and Janet home from the morning service and stay until the evening service. The time would be spent singing, praying and discussing theological issues emanating from the books Noel had most recently read.

A PRAISE BAND.
In 1994 several of us had been praying and praising informally in the Praise Room on Friday nights and Saturdays. Noel and Janet and Beulah and I were often present. Eventually we began playing together as a band in church services and soon became a permanent fixture at the 11.30 Service.
Noel was a sensitive drummer who could play quietly and loudly. As Maurice McKenzie used to say: *"Noel doesn't play the*

drums, he plays the song"
During that time we learned the benefit of drums in spiritual warfare. It was an enthusiastic musical and spiritual association that God was to bless for nearly six years.

LIKE A BEREAVEMENT.
In the summer of 2000 Noel and Janet told us they were leaving West to join a smaller and seemingly more progressive Pentecostal fellowship where they would be worship leaders. *The event was like bereavement to us For five years Noel had drummed behind me every Sunday, with the exception of one when he was suffering from a hand injury. We read each other musically, and Beulah and I almost gave up as worship leaders in West at that time.* Thankfully we now recognise that one of the enemy's ploys is to lead us to depend too much not only upon ourselves, but upon other Christians.
We have maintained contact with the Johnstons, whilst Roberta Corbridge and Ian Kyle seem to have disappeared over our horizon. Noel and Janet both fulfil leadership roles in the church they now attend and Noel regularly preaches. Billy Johnston, Noel's brother and his family joined West soon after Noel and Janet joined and is presently in charge of the audio-visual recordings.

OUR GOOD NEWS TEAM-
On the night of our first meeting in the Johnstons' home, I returned home just ahead of a visit from our minister, David Bailie.

He had been to visit John in hospital. He had prayed over him and was confident of his future wellbeing. A Christian friend at work had assured me John would make a full recovery, through what could only have been a word of knowledge. **John's condition appeared to be the result of an allergic reaction to the anti-bodies created through his anti-immune system fighting the streptococcal** virus. He steadily improved to regain his full health. He is presently studying mechanical engineering at the University of Newcastle-upon-Tyne.

PAUL'S RECOVERY.
I had to wait until October of 1993 before my leg pain abated. It was during the first visit of REVEREND JIMMY SMITH from Georgia, USA. He had performed a concert in West, and David Bailie formally closed the meeting. However he invited those who would like to stay to hear *'words of knowledge'* that Jimmy had received during the concert. *There followed a time of great blessing and healing. I had gone up to the front for a healing touch. I did not feel much relief that night, but as the subsequent days went by the pain eased. By the time my November trip to California came around I was able to enjoy a pain-free eleven-hour flight from London to Los Angeles.*

JIMMY SMITH'S SECOND VISIT TO WEST- prayer for boldness!
On Jimmy Smith's second visit to West he called to the front **all those who were due to take part in the second phase of GOOD NEWS TEAMS SO THAT HE COULD PRAY FOR BOLDNESS!**
My wife Beulah was one of those who went up. Whilst her Good News Team venture was subsequently cancelled, *she received boldness!*
Until that time she had never sung, spoken or played in public. Her testimony had previously only been given 'second hand' by Helen Ritchie.
Since receiving that prayer from Jimmy she has sung, spoken and played guitar, tin-whistle and tambourine with boldness.

ANOTHER SIGNIFICANT EVENT.
It is interesting to note that on the Sunday prior to Jimmy coming to West Church, he had conducted a service in the Stormont Hotel organised by Shalom Christian Fellowship. During the course of the evening Jimmy had stopped preaching mid-sentence, as he was prone to do, and called a lady up from the back. He told this lady, Margaret Hawkins, not to worry any longer about her daughter as she was in God's hand and sent her back to her seat.
Several weeks after Jimmy' visit to West, a group of younger ladies felt led to come together, each of whom Jimmy had prayed with for boldness. *They felt led to start an evangelistic meeting in one of their homes. This comprised Bible Study and Praise. The first morning that they met, one of the invited guests, Pamela Priestly, returned to faith after a long period of rebellion. Pamela is the daughter of Margaret Hawkins!*

GOOD NEWS TEAMS - BY REG BATES.

"The good news of God's love for us!
The Good news of Jesus!
Who He was and what He did!
The gospel story!

The purpose of the "Good News" teams was to take the good news of Jesus, his life, his death and all that it meant for us, into the homes of anyone searching for a meaning to life or simply in need of a top-up to their faith. The teams were active in the months just before the arrival of the Alpha course and, looking back **to that time, I suppose Good News was rather equivalent to a small and much personalised Alpha held in the comfortable surroundings of one's own home.**

As someone who had the opportunity to lead a number of these courses, my main memories are those of enthusiasm and happiness, of friendship, and of awakening and re-awakening to the love of God and the gospel story.

"GOOD NEWS" was a course, which was simple both in content and presentation. **But that made it very flexible and very adaptable to any family situation.** It would be wrong to give too many personal details by way of examples, but I remember the contrast between the two men:

One was young and not long married.

The other much older and living alone.

The young man knew little about Jesus and nothing about the Bible. I remember having to explain to him how it contained the Old and New Testaments and that, as well as letters and books of history, there were four short accounts of Jesus' life, as seen by four friends.

He listened to us and asked questions. He took in everything we had to offer. Towards the end of the course he accepted Jesus and his wife proclaimed, "I didn't think I would ever hear you say that!"

By contrast, the old man was quiet. He didn't say a lot. There were few questions. But we knew he had 'always been' a Christian. We knew that he prayed. We knew that he understood the meaning of salvation. And we knew on each occasion that we met that he was happy with our company. **He was happy to listen to our proclamation of the gospel story in his home. And for us to pray with him!**

God works in his own rather mysterious ways.

It is difficult for any of us fully to understand His reasons or His timing.

The young man was soon to experience the break-up of his marriage.

The old man is now in Heaven.

The good news of God's love for us!

The good news of Jesus!

God's timing is perfect. His love is beyond understanding."

DGB NOTE: "GOOD NEWS" TRIPLET TEAMS were flexible and adaptable to visit a whole variety of homes, occasionally with radical and dramatic outcomes, often with the effect of embracing, including and strengthening our members, so that they were more regularly to be seen in church and with a deeper sense of belonging and worship.

HILARY GUEST writes: "At Mr Bailie's request I was one of a team of three who were invited into the home of a retired couple who attended West. We were cordially received and commenced weekly sessions where we discussed Luke's Gospel. This led to times of discussion where there was freedom to share our opinions. It was amazing how this led us to gain an understanding of God's Word and to share our different viewpoints and experiences. At times we learned to accept that our views differed, and we were always conscious that we had been invited into their home as their guests. We were privileged to be able to continue these studies for the set period. It was perhaps difficult to gauge the impact of these sessions shared in the home, yet a closer bond was established which has continued with this couple's ongoing involvement in church life.

REV. IAN HART TO HELP US.

The Rev. Ian Hart, who has served as a missionary of our Church in Singapore for seven years, and was previously minister of Ballyhenry Church, will be giving us some help over the next few months in West. As he waits for a congregation to serve, he will be working part-time in Newtownbreda Presbyterian Church, and will also help us. **This will be partly in our pulpit ministry; he will be giving a course of Bible Studies on the Minor Prophets, and will be having special input into our Home Groups.**

The theme for our Home Groups in the autumn session will be 'Glorifying God in our Daily Work'. Ian will prepare a course for us, in this subject in which he has made a special study.

LINK WITH THE SOUTH CHURCH, GIRVAN.

Some time back our Kirk Session welcomed the idea that had been proposed to us, that we form a link with a Church of Scotland congregation in Girvan - very conveniently across the North Channel and just a few miles up the road from Stranaer.

Rhoda and I paid a visit to the Rev. Ian McNie and his wife Anthea in the early summer and found them to be a warm-hearted, lively couple, most welcoming and hospitable. Now Ian plans to be with us for our Communion Sunday, 12th September, as a first step in establishing our relationship. His wife Anthea is undertaking a Lay Training Course that precludes her from being with us on that occasion. Such links can be fruitful and stimulating and we pray that it may be so in this case.

PRACTISE HOSPITALITY, GIVE ENCOURAGEMENT.

PEOPLE WHO SERVE BEHIND THE SCENES CAN HAVE TREMENDOUS IMPACT FOR THE KINGDOM!

Just this week, at very short notice I was asked if we could help with hospitality for 2 people from 'WORLD IN NEED' coming to the Missionary Convention.

And so A YOUNG MAN FROM CROATIA *will be staying with Alan & Jean Crichton and then with Phil and Molly Dorman. Likewise a lady from China will be staying with Ken & Pamela Dobbin and then with Hugh & Anne Anderson.*

No doubt this will be for the mutual enrichment of all!

Paul exhorted people to practise hospitality. He himself who endured hardship and suffered much, was grateful for the hospitality he received.

When Paul first arrived in Corinth, having been hounded out of Macedonia, it was **in weakness and fear.** It was in this context that he met up with **Aquila and Priscilla, who were tentmakers like himself, and was invited into their home, becoming partners in business and in the gospel.**
This brought huge encouragement to Paul and much spiritual benefit to Aquila and Priscilla. Of this couple Paul was to say that **they risked their very necks for him.**
When Paul moved on to **Ephesus** he took this couple with him - and when he left Ephesus, he left Aquila and Priscilla with responsibility for the work.
Hospitality and Encouragement may mean investing time in someone; encouraging a hurting friend; lending a hand to your pastor; making yourself available, reaching out to newcomers, serving in a supporting role, *as Aquila and Priscilla were accustomed to do.*

Every act of kindness or of hospitality warms strengthens and enriches the whole body. And sometimes *one act* **may lead into** *a life-giving ministry.*

ANN & MAUREEN KENNEDY.

Every Sunday, after the first morning service, the home of Ann & Maureen Kennedy is an open house for tea/coffee for as many as come to enjoy vivacious company and warm fellowship. I imagine it may have begun with an invitation to someone *'Come round now for a cuppa and a chat'!* **And then this was extended gradually to others, until it became a ministry!**
This is hospitality that gives and blesses! Whether it is done every week, or for many; or occasionally, or just for one or two, matters not!
It's a way of embracing those who live alone and after a church service return to a lonely house. And sometimes it is the person who lives alone who can issue the invitation! Two or three 'lone' persons can make lively and fruitful company! Dare to try it and see!

AUGUST/SEPTEMBER WCN GIVES NEWS OF ALL THE GROUPS, ORGANISATIONS AND SEMINARS THAT RESUME FOR THE AUTUMN TERM.

OCTOBER WCN 1993.

PROLIFIC YOUTH OUTREACH - MANY TESTIFY!
In October WCN many of our young people bear eloquent and extensive testimony about what they experienced, mainly over the summer months.

ALISON LOGAN speaks of her time with Summerserve as terrifying and fantastic!
She was nervous about joining a team, in Willowfield Parish where she knew no one, involved in an Outreach in East Belfast.
But she was to learn a lot about God's power - and Satan's opposition- and the wonderful, awesome power of prayer. She speaks of a Prayer Meeting where 'the sense of the sovereignty of God hit me so strongly, that words cannot describe it.'… God's Spirit filled us that night and bound us together with a unity that remains among the team even now that Summerserve is over…. From that point on we went from strength to strength. The coffee bars and children's clubs began with fantastic results. **All in all fourteen people were saved and many more were made aware of God's love for them. We also held a Karaoke Night, open-air evangelism on the Woodstock Road and a barbecue.**
We learnt: **'I can do everything God asks me with the help of Christ.'**

DAVID WILSON reports on the Summer Scheme, conducted by St. Gall's, Carnalea Methodist and West.
The morning Summer Scheme for primary age children was held in the New Hall in West and in the Methodist Centre.
An amazingly varied programme is described, giving enjoyment and education, and teaching about Jesus, and leading in worship.
The evening session for the older young people drew 'an incredible number of people' to a varied programme.

ROBERT SINCLAIR gives a vivid account of Summer Madness, and we have independent reports on the PCI Outreach to Cork, given both by DAVID POLLEY and VICTORIA STEWART.

GAVIN MACARTNEY makes his first trip to Capernwray and is super-enthusiastic about this experience.

Don & Helen Ritchie went to "Love Europe 1993" at Offenberg, Germany, run by 'Operation Mobilisation', and attended by 2500 young people.
'We had powerful Bible teaching every morning, and then we were taught a skill - sketch board, drama, music, visuals, prayer, spiritual warfare, reaching out to children, Muslims, ethnic communities etc.
Each afternoon we had further training about our campaign orientation, and meeting with our fellowship groups.
The evening meeting involved enthusiastic praising of the Lord; there were speakers from all over the world. George Verver commissioned us to reach out in

Jesus' Name.

IN POLITICAL AND PERSONAL TERMS IS FORGIVENESS A SOFT OPTION?

A few months ago in our 'West Church Journey' we read how Roberta Corbridge was led to Dublin to join in a protest against the violence and murder that scarred our land.
At this time we were much aware of the political unrest and terrorism which were the background to our lives for more than twenty years. At the same time this was compounded by the manner in which ancient enmities had exploded into ugly life in the Balkans, bringing widespread murder and ethnic cleansing. It was important for us in the Church to know the mind and way of Christ in this situation.

To give us insight and to raise issues in a sharp and personal manner, we included material in WCN by Philip Yancy, under the title

'CAN FORGIVENESS OVERCOME THE HORROR?'

Yancy writes:
"In the midst of this year's deluge of news from Bosnia, I picked up a book I had read at least ten years before: **"The Sunflower" by Simon Wiesenthal.**
It recounts a small incident that took place during this century's most successful 'ethnic cleansing' campaign, an incident that does much to explain what propelled Wiesenthal to become the world's foremost Nazi hunter and the most relentless public voice **against contemporary hate crimes.**
The book centres on forgiveness, and I turned to it for insight into what role forgiveness might play in the moral quagmire that once was Yugoslavia."

[And we look to it for insight into our Northern Ireland situation].

WIESENTHAL - POLISH PRISONER.
"In 1944 Wiesenthal was a young, Polish prisoner on his way to the concentration camps. He had looked on helpless, as Nazi soldiers forced his mother into a freight car crammed with elderly Jewish women and as they shot his grandmother to death on the stairway of her home. **Altogether 89 of his Jewish relatives would die at the hands of the Nazis.**
Wiesenthal himself had tried unsuccessfully to commit suicide when he was first captured.

ARE YOU A JEW?
One bright, sunny morning as Wiesenthal's prison detail was cleaning rubbish out of a hospital for German casualties, a nurse approached him, "Are you a Jew?" she asked hesitantly, then signalled him to follow her. Apprehensively Wiesenthal followed her up a stairway and down a hall until they reached a dark, musty room where a lone soldier lay, swathed in bandages. White gauze covered the man's face, with openings cut out for mouth, nose and ears.
The nurse disappeared, closing the door behind her to **leave the young Jew alone with the spectral figure.** The wounded man was an SS officer, **and he had summoned Wiesenthal for a confession. 'My name is Karl'** said a strained voice from somewhere within the bandages. **'I must tell you of this horrible deed - tell you because you are a Jew.'**

Karl began his story by reminiscing about his Catholic upbringing and his childhood faith, which he had lost when he was in the Hitler Youth Corps. He later volunteered for the SS, served with distinction, and had recently returned, severely wounded, from the Russian front.
Three times as Karl tried to tell his story in his weakened raspy voice, Wiesenthal pulled away as if to go. Each time the soldier reached out to grab his arm with a white, nearly bloodless hand and begged him to stay. He wanted to talk about something that had happened in Ukrainian territory.

BOOBY TRAPS KILLED 30 SOLDIERS.
In the town of Dnyepropetrovsk, abandoned by the retreating Russians, booby traps killed 30 soldiers of Karl's unit. As an act of revenge, **the SS rounded up 300 Jews, herded them into a three-story house, doused it with gasoline, and fired grenades into it. Karl and his men encircled the house, their guns drawn to shoot anyone who tried to escape.**

"The screams from the house were horrible," he said. "I saw a man with a small child in his arms. His clothes were alight. By his side stood a woman, doubtless the mother of the child. With his free hand the man covered the child's eyes - then he jumped into the street. Seconds later the mother followed. Then from the other windows fell burning bodies. We shot...."

BESEECHING FORGIVENESS.
All this time Wiesenthal sat in silence, letting the German speak. Karl went on to describe other atrocities, but he kept circling back to the image of that young boy with black hair and dark eyes falling from the building, target practice for SS rifles. **"I am left here with my guilt",** he concluded at last. **"In the last hour of my life you are with me. I do not know who you are. I know only that you are a Jew and that is enough.
I know that what I have told you is terrible. In the long nights when I have been waiting for death, time and time again I have longed to talk about it with a Jew and beg forgiveness from him. Only I didn't know whether there were any Jews left... I know what I am asking is almost too much for you,** *but without your answer I cannot die in peace."*

Simon Wiesenthal, an architect in

his early twenties, now a prisoner dressed in a shabby uniform marked with the yellow Star of David, felt the entire weight of his race bearing down upon him. He stared out of the window at the sunlit courtyard. He looked at the eyeless heap of bandages lying on the bed. "<u>At last I made up my mind,</u>" *he writes,* "<u>and without a word I left the room.</u>"

WIESENTHAL'S DILEMMA - 'DID I DO RIGHT?'

The SS officer Karl, unforgiven by a Jew, died, but Wiesenthal, liberated from a death camp by American troops lived on, haunted by the scene in the hospital room, and asking himself and others: **'Did I do right?'**
In due course he enquired of rabbis and priests. Finally he wrote his story and sent it to the brightest ethical minds he knew, asking them **'Did I do right?'**

Of the thirty-two men and women who responded only six said Wiesentahl had done wrong in *not forgiving* the German. Many thought he had done right. A few of the Jewish respondents said that the enormity of the Nazi crimes exceeded all possibility of forgiveness. Novelist Cynthia Ozick said bluntly 'Let the SS man die unshriven. Let him go to hell'.

Some said that forgiveness had no place in a world of genocide. *Forgive and the whole business might repeat itself.*
In a world of unspeakable atrocity, forgiveness seems unjust, unfair, and irrational.

AN EQUAL AND OPPOSITE ATROCITY.
Yet where unforgiveness reigns, a Newtonian law comes into play: for every atrocity there must be an equal and opposite atrocity.

Philip Yancy points out that today the Serbs are everybody's whipping boy and everybody is utterly repulsed by the ethnic cleansing of the Serbs.

Yancy points out that the Nazis - who murdered 89 of Wiesenthal's relatives, during World War Two directed an 'ethnic cleansing' *against* the Serbs.
The Serbs had now killed tens of thousands of Croats - but under the Nazis the Croats had killed hundreds of thousands of Serbs. This is the logic of unforgiveness. The law of revenge never *settles the score.*

Forgiveness may be unfair - it is by definition, but at least it provides a way to halt the juggernaut of 'justice'. Only forgiveness frees us from the injustice of others.

We began this article by asking whether, in political or personal terms, FORGIVENESS IS A SOFT OPTION.

Yancy asks whether there is a place for forgiveness *in the arena of nations.*
Yancy points out that as a nation Germany repented of the very abominations that prompted Simon Wiesenthal's confrontation.

WE FEEL SORROW AND SHAME.
"Before unification West Germany paid out $30 billion in compensation to Jews. East Germany denied any moral responsibility for 45 years, but after the cords of communism began to loosen, and East Germany elected a free parliament, *that body made its first order of business an act of contrition.* "We feel sorrow and shame, and acknowledge this burden of German history", said the deputies, using language rarely heard in international affairs. "We ask all the Jews of the world to forgive us."
<u>The fact that a relationship exists at all between Germany and Israel is a stunning demonstration of transnational forgiveness.</u>

WE FORGIVE YOU! WE FORGIVE YOU! WE FORGIVE YOU! POPE JOHN PAUL 11 VISITS POLAND.

In 1983, before the Iron Curtain fell, Pope John Paul II came to Poland during a period of Martial Law and conducted an open-air Mass.
Hour after hour, throngs of people streamed across the Poniatowski Bridge to the designated stadium. Organised by parishes, they marched in orderly rows on a route <u>that passed in front of the Communist Party's Central Committee Building. All afternoon the marchers chanted in unison, "We forgive you. We forgive you. We forgive you!!!"</u>
And today, all over Eastern Europe, dramas of forgiveness, large and small are being played out.

No doubt, through this, something dynamic happened in the heavenly places that brought about the widespread collapse of cruel, totalitarian regimes, without force and without bloodshed.

[We included this article with its insights in our West Church News in 1993 to help our people to understand, that in both personal and political senses, the forgiveness that Jesus teaches, and the blessing of enemies that He inculcates, is right and powerful and transforming.]

NOVEMBER WCN 1993.

ULSTER TURMOIL AND TERRORISM.
Most of the first 30 years of West Church' history was against the background of turmoil and terrorism in Northern Ireland and consequential widespread crime in society.
In respect of people caught up in all this, there was a desire for effective action to be taken. The sentiment of not a few was:

"PUT THEM IN PRISON AND THROW AWAY THE KEY." That was the headline of November WCN. - With the added words: "We'll build more prisons!"

- Yet Jesus says:
"The Spirit of the Lord is upon me, because he has anointed me, to preach good news to the poor. *He has sent me to proclaim release for the prisoners, and recovery of sight for the blind, to release the oppressed, to proclaim the year of the Lord's favour,"*

"It is said of the first Christians that they not only **outlived the pagans** but that they *out-thought* them also. There are times when Christians, seriously, need to put on their 'thinking caps'.
We need to gain insight and understanding in respect of the times in which we live.
We need to understand why there is such an explosion of crime and violence, and why, although we spend vast sums on security and policing, and incur the huge expense of committing more and more people to prison, yet we have less and less security"!

HIGH INCREASE IN PRISON NUMBERS.
I therefore invite you to read the article written by **Charles Colson**, entitled **Crime and Morality**. In it he cites current statistics, as follows:
'In 1973 there were 98 people, in each 100,000 of the population, in prison in the United States. Today there are 512! However, even today, the state of Minnesota has only 73 in prison for each 100,000.'
Thought-provoking enough, one hoped, to make people read and study Charles Colson's article; and gain from it insight from the Lord!

CHARLES COLSON ON 'CRIME AND MORALITY'.
For any who may not know, **Charles Colson was right-hand man to President Nixon**, when he had to resign as President of the United States in connection with the Watergate Scandal. Charles Colson was to serve a prison sentence, and so came to know conditions in prison from the inside. He came to a vital encounter with God, and in due course was to set up 'Prison Fellowship'.
He was to win the Templeton Prize for Progress in Religion, and invited to address the National Press Club. Below we give a few excerpts from that address.

LEADING THE WORLD BY A WIDE MARGIN.
The United States leads the world in the high percentage of its citizens imprisoned - way beyond the Soviet Union or South Africa.
"In spite of the huge number of criminals imprisoned, **our crime rate has continued to rise. In 20 years violent crime rate has climbed over 75%.** *Each year the people who commit these bloody crimes are younger. 20% of high school students carry weapons to class.*

PRISON TALK - GETTING EVEN!
"Statistics can leave us cold, but I have seen the dreadful cost of this system in the faces of thousands of human beings trapped in it. **When I was a prisoner**, I watched men spend their days lying on their bunks doing nothing, staring into emptiness - bodies atrophying, souls corroding. **Prison talk centred on how they would get even with those who had wronged them or with society in general.** I have never been in a place so filled with anger, bitterness, despair and dejection.
It is no wonder to me that after being released, between 66 and 74 per cent commit new crimes within 4 years. *The wonder is that 25% do not! The prison experience is brutal, dehumanising and counterproductive.*

FAILED PHILOSOPHIES AND POLICIES.
COLSON declares:
"The blame for the mess we are in rests squarely on the shoulders of politicians - whether liberal or conservative, each holding myths... The liberal approach is that **crime is caused by poverty, racism, oppression and lack of opportunity.** Thus, following widespread looting during an infamous 24-hour blackout in New York, President Jimmy Carter said the rioting and looting was caused by poverty. Yet studies afterwards showed that most looters were employed and stole things they didn't need or have any use for. **The conservatives believe that the way to deal with crime is to lock the criminals in prison and throw away the key** but this deterrent theory doesn't work either."
Colson sums up:
"**If prisons did rehabilitate, or if the threat of prison did deter crime, surely we would be living in utopian peace.** *But the stark fact is this: Though we have thrown more people in prison than at any other time in human history, few sensible people would be willing to take a walk in this city's combat zone after dark. One out of four American households will be victims of crime this year. Crime and the fear of crime disrupt our lives and haunt our nights."*

WHY HAVE THESE APPROACHES FAILED?
'Because each has ignored our *moral life, has passed over our character and forgotten our soul!'*

In the 1950's, a psychologist, Stanton Samehow and a psychiatrist, Samuel Yochelson, **sharing the conventional wisdom that crime is caused by environment, began an experiment to prove the point.**
They began a 17-year study, involving thousands of hours of clinical testing of 250 inmates in the District of Columbia.
To their astonishment, they discovered that the cause of crime cannot be traced to environment, poverty or oppression. Instead crime is the result of individuals making wrong moral choices.

They concluded that the answer to crime is a "conversion of the wrong-doer to a more responsible lifestyle."

In 1987, Harvard professors James Q. Wilson and Richard J. Herrnstein **came to similar conclusions in their book,** 'Crime and Human Nature'.
They determined that the cause of crime is a lack of proper moral training among young people during the morally formative years, particularly ages one to six.

THE EVIDENCE OF HISTORY.
In the early 1980's James Q. Wilson surveyed American history *to find some trend or cycle that would correlate with crime data. He noted a startling pattern.*
Crime did not correlate with poverty.
During the Great Depression, for example, there was widespread poverty - 34 million people unemployed - *and yet crime dropped.*
Nor did it correlate to factors like urbanization. The middle of the nineteenth century was a period of rapid urbanization, **yet the level of crime actually fell. Why? During that same period a great spiritual awakening took place.**

Conversely, during the good economic years of the 1920's crime rose. Why? Because, Wilson concluded, "the educated classes began to repudiate moral uplift and Freud's psychological theories came into vogue." People no longer believed in restraining a child's sinful impulses; they wanted to develop his 'naturally good' personality. **The weaker emphasis on moral training led to an increase in criminal behaviour.**

IF CRIME STEMS FROM MORAL FACTORS, THEN THE SOLUTION TO CRIME MUST BE MORAL AS WELL.

Charles Colson declares: first, **We need committed Christian people who will transmit to prison inmates a message of hope and redemption.**
'At this moment Prison Fellowship has 50,000 volunteers going into prisons, holding seminars, conducting Bible Studies, mentoring inmates as they are released from prison, visiting their families and bringing gifts to their children.'
"Does it work? Emphatically yes", declares Colson, who mentions that for himself it was through faith in Jesus Christ that a lasting change took place in his life.
Second, *to deal with the crime crisis, we need a balanced criminal justice policy, one that offers both real punishment and real redemption.*
That means abandoning altogether the idea that prisons either rehabilitate or deter. Prisons succeed in keeping violent and dangerous criminals off the streets. **Beyond that they accomplish little.**
Yet 50% of those admitted to prison each year have committed nonviolent offenses.
We could solve the prison overcrowding problem overnight if we had the political courage to take nonviolent, non-dangerous inmates out of prison, **put them in work-camps or in community-based treatment centres or in home incarceration and make them work.**
In this way they could recompense their victims rather than sit in a prison cell at a cost of $20,000 a year to the taxpayers. **It is redemptive for the individual, teaching responsibility for his actions; and it is redemptive for society, restoring the victims of crime.**

RESTITUTION - Biblical Principle.
Restitution is a Biblical Principle that works.
In 1973, Minnesota revised its corrections system, coupling alternatives to incarceration with sentencing reform. The results are impressive - an incarceration rate of 73 per 100,000 residents. **The numbers do prove that alternatives to incarceration do succeed.**

Third,
IF THE SOLUTION TO CRIME INVOLVES A MORAL RESPONSE,
We must deal with our culture's crumbling moral consensus. Crime stems from a failure in moral training.
Any culture requires a **moral consensus** of shared beliefs about right and wrong, i.e. a common standard of truth. **This motivates self-sacrifice, undergirds law and permits freedom without anarchy.**
The problem is that our moral consensus has been shattered. How do we restore it?
Colson declares:
"Virtue is something that grows from within, not something enforced from above. The law does have a role in moral instruction. But the roots of our moral life go deeper than laws and bills. Government programmes can feed the body; they cannot touch the soul. They can punish behaviour; they cannot transform hearts.
This points directly to the essential role of religious values and religious hope in our common life. *Religion is the only way to reach into the darkest corners of every community, into the darkest corners of every mind.*
Religion provides a moral impulse to do good.
It has sent legions of Christians into battle against disease and oppression and bigotry. It ended the slave trade, built hospitals and orphanages, tamed the brutality of mental wards and prisons. It motivated marches for civil rights. It has provided a voice for the weak and a hope for the hopeless.

Religion also provides the power to BE good. It subdues an obstinate will. It provides new values to old sinners - even to people like a White House hatchet man.

The great paradox of our age is this: in the interest of tolerance we are aggressively seeking to scrub religious values, and even reminders of our religious heritage, out of our public life. Yet it is that religious heritage that is essential for the recovery of character.

COMMENT: In November 1993 WCN, we invited our West Church readership to give serious thought to crime and imprisonment, and to read the contribution included by Charles Colson.

At the time of now writing our "West Church Journey" in 2006, these issues are no less pertinent. Charles Colson has emphasised the moral/spiritual aspects and declared that the work of 'Prison Fellowship' was effective.

He could have given startling confirmation of this by mentioning an article by Juan Zuccarelli, a Pentecostal pastor and evangelist in Argentina, entitled "God's Kingdom in Olmos Prison" to be found in a book "The Rising Revival" edited by C. Peter Wagner & Pablo Deiros.

Zuccarelli was called by God into the high security Olmos Prison in 1984. **It is an amazing, enthralling story that tells how, by 1995, 45% of the population of more than 3000 had become Christian.**

One can read similar stories of lives transformed in prison through Alpha courses today.

As Christians we need to lift up our heads in the knowledge that in Christ there remains the power to transform lives and make the foulest clean.

OUR STUDENT IN THE PHILIPPINES.

Our student, Marivac Fetizann attends the Philippine Missionary Institute, seeking to train Filipino Christians for work in remote and rural areas. She is now in her second year of study. She writes: "Greetings in the precious Name of our Lord and Saviour, Jesus Christ, his unspeakable gift to us.
**I am so grateful for what the Lord has done, especially in my Christian service.
I STARTED TEACHING FIVE CHILDREN.**
"I patiently taught them how to worship the Lord through prayer by singing songs, by reading God's Word... **At first I was discouraged but the Lord patiently encouraged me, and taught me to be patient in all the things I do.**
I continued teaching them and as the days went by **fifteen children have been added.** I'm so happy for what the Lord has done. These children wanted to have more discussion about the Lord, and I show them how to accept Christ Jesus. I have taught them how to find verses in the Bible, how to use the Bible and to memorise verses. When I ask them "for whom are you doing this?" they reply "For Jesus." The attendance is now 25 and I ask for your prayers that these children remain true to God and abide in Him 'till He comes'.
May these children become active members of Christ's Body. I want to thank you for your prayer and support."

NORTH INDIA 3:9:3.

CHRISTIAN NATIONALS have an ambitious work based in Rajasthan, India at Jaipur. Its students have discovered that villagers long to learn to read. By teaching literacy classes they have found an open door for the Gospel.

So far, 1124 literacy centres have been operated, resulting in 23,000 learning to read; 3400 people accepting Christ and 406 new village fellowships started.

Now the pace is accelerating! The "3:9:3" programme for literary evangelism is under way.
This enables each student to spend one month at the Institute, followed by 3 months working in a village. In the period of field experience, one new literacy centre must be started by the student.

This 4-month cycle is repeated 3 times in the year.

It costs £35 per month to establish and run a Literacy Centre.

FOCUS ON THE FAMILY.

**We live in an age of increasing social disintegration in which it is estimated that 10 million people in the UK are now from fractured families.
Therefore there is concern that plans for more general SUNDAY TRADING will mean less time spent together by children and parents and by husbands and wives.
Research and common sense alike point to a consequent weakening of family life.
It will also affect attendances of families at Sunday worship and make it hard for Family businesses to survive.**
In 1986 Sir Peter Mills wrote:
"I fear for family life. Sunday trading would create a lot more part-time working. This would inevitably mean children with parents who work part-time **not having a day together. Family life could be seriously affected. There are enough attacks on family life at the moment."**

DECEMBER WCN 1993.

**West Church Christmas World Development goal is to bring uplift to four Indian villages and 2500 people.
West Church focus will be upon the SEVAI PROJECT STARTED IN 1984 IN A DROUGHT-PRONE AREA OF SOUTH INDIA.**
500 acres of land are being developed for farming, with 35 acres already developed.
FORESTRY is being developed on a community basis, growing different types of trees - for fuel,

fruit trees, and trees for sale as timber.
This forestry prevents erosion and creates a microclimate.
Major benefits will be for the poorest people. SEVAI's programme includes education and skills development, Youth and Women's leadership training, building of low cost housing, health and sanitation.

Those who have already read MARGARET CATHCART'S account of such projects will be convinced that this is a project well worth supporting.

DECEMBER 'WEST CHURCH NEWS' GIVES US ALSO:

Jottings from Church Committee, with designated gifts from the Outreach Fund in 1993;

tells us that we need a small team to polish our wooden floors;
brings us greetings from Romania from Jane McNutt;

a letter from Patricia Fergie in India;

news of Eleanor Rainey's visit to KENYA.

PERSECUTION OF CHRISTIANS IN ETHIOPIA AND NIGERIA;

West participation in a Belfast Prayer-Walk for peace with one hundred others, starting from St. Anne's cathedral;

News from the Dores at Wycliffe Bible Translators who tell of an 'explosion of joy' among Jamamadi Indians in Brazil who have received the Scriptures in their own language; and of a translator in Papua, New Guinea who was killed when the New Testament translation in the Nabak language was almost completed;

ST. PETERSBURG CHRISTIAN COLLEGE.
reports a visit to West of Dr Peter Penner, President of the St. Petersburg Christian College, who told us of the burgeoning work of this institution, and of the great need for theological books for the Library there, so that the students may be properly trained and equipped. Bible Commentaries and inspirational books are alike needed and welcome. A lorry to Russia is ready to take these books directly to St. Petersburg for us. Arrangements have been set in place for us to give books- and money, knowing that £5 purchases a good quality theological book.

JANUARY WCN 1994.

DEATH DEALS US HEAVY BLOWS!

During the last few weeks DEATH has dealt quite a number of heavy blows to us, and we have in our midst those who mourn, bearing the loss of loved ones, husbands and wives left alone, parents grieving over the loss of children, children the loss of parents, brothers and sisters grieving for loved ones.

The apostle Paul speaks of DEATH as the last ENEMY to be destroyed by God.

LIVES INTERTWINED.
How deeply our lives are intertwined with others, how much we are part of them, and they with us, how deep the chasm left by their departure.
We can know the reality of the comfort of loving friends, especially when those friends have a love and strength that comes from God Himself.

If Death should mean extinction, dust to dust only, then all life would be meaningless. It is here that the story of Jesus, His words and deeds, death and resurrection, and the promise of everlasting life for those who believe in him, *has the ring of truth in our hearts,* and the Scriptures convincingly answer many vexing questions. *And when prayers for healing are NOT answered, we may still know His presence, his Spirit, as Heather Ennis relates in her Diary.*

WE SHALL ALL DIE.
Life is fragile and transient: we shall all die. We need to put our faith in Jesus Christ that at the point of death He will be there to escort us into the heavenly home He has prepared for those who believe in Him.

HEATHER ENNIS: A DIARY KEPT DURING WILLIAM'S ILLNESS.

"At the present moment in time my Husband is in Hospital seriously ill. He was hurried in on Friday 30th July having been ill for seven weeks. There are several things wrong at the moment, problems with gallbladder, liver and heart. He also has had a lung drained.
We are waiting today for more blood tests and x-rays to be done; consequently we are unsure of the future. We are both very aware of all the prayers which are being said for us. At the moment I find it hard to pray, so I am relying on our friends.

PRAISE SERVICE.
Last night I was at a Praise Service and what I really want to share more than anything else *is the amazing way the Lord just lifted me through the praise and worship songs. My spirit soared and sheer joy that went through my body just lifted all my cares away. Praise the Lord!*

TWO WEEKS LATER.
We didn't expect everything to be plain sailing, but who thinks it would be quite this hard! We really were shocked when cancer was diagnosed. I pray that what I am saying will perhaps some day help someone else. Always remember

there is power in the Blood of Jesus.

TWO WEEKS LATER.
William has had a very rough time with lung drains, minor operations and now a bone marrow biopsy. He is very weak physically but spiritually he is strong. As for myself, I would be probably known to my friends as the world's worst worrier. I guess I could pass an 'A' Level in this subject. *I almost always remember to hand my worries over to the Lord, and then five minutes later take them back again!*
The situation is different altogether. We both feel the Lord is totally in control and neither of us is worried about the cancer nor the outlook. It never ceases to amaze me how the Lord works. I often find myself thinking "how am I so in control of this situation?" Then I realise with complete clarity I am not in control at all, but God is. AMAZING!

5th SEPTEMBER 1993.
I have now been told by the consultant that William has 4 weeks to live. The tumour is very large. William's total belief is that he will be healed of this cancer and it will never kill him. He is strong in the Lord's presence.
For me, my song would be, **"The Battle belongs to the Lord"**, my trust should be the same as his, but maybe I've watched him suffer so much, watched him try to hold on to his independence, watched him trying to breathe, watched him getting so thin. **It's very hard to trust for healing on earth. Surely perfect healing is when we come face to face with our Father in heaven.**

William's cancer is on the outside of his windpipe which makes it inoperable. We were told by the Radiotherapy Department that the only course of treatment was one dose of radiotherapy which would shrink the tumour and give him temporary relief, but then last Friday the Consultant started him on a course of Chemo. This has given him a good deal of relief. Thank the Lord!
Again we don't know what's ahead but we live in the knowledge that our heavenly Father is always one step ahead of us and he'll carry us through.

22nd OCTOBER.
William died on Monday 27th September, he had been in hospital for 8 days. Dr. Nelson had been on holiday for the first seven days. William's breathing had been difficult but not too bad. I was still able to bath him, in hospital - William was adamant that no nurse should bath him. He really was brilliant - I know he's my husband, but he was so brave, I was really proud of him.

Dr. Nelson came back to the hospital on 27th and spoke to William before I arrived. His words to William were "We shall never beat this cancer because it's growing so fast." William told the doctor he was not willing to give up the fight for life and he wanted to know if the Doctor was going to give up fighting for him. Dr. Nelson said he would fight with every piece of knowledge he had and that he wouldn't give up.

PRECIOUS TIME TO TALK.
WE had time that Monday to talk and it was a precious time - in fact all times we had in hospital were very precious. *We laughed and cried and talked about our times together. I will always remember him saying when I asked him what he thought about our lives together, his answer was (with a big grin) - "Well, Heather it was never boring!"*

I was with him almost all day on Monday but on Monday evening I had a sore throat. William had gone to sleep after a big injection of Chemo (the start of his second course), so I left him at 8.15pm. I had an uneasy feeling that evening so I phoned the hospital at 9.00pm to enquire if he was all right. The nurse checked on him and said he was sleeping. I dosed myself with Vit C to try to combat the throat infection so I would be OK for Tuesday.
At 9.25pm the Hospital phoned to say William was having some breathing problems and could I come up? Well this happened before, so I was not unduly worried but arrived at the hospital at 9.37pm to find William had died four minutes before I arrived.
When the picture of life is completed we will see the whole. If we have trusted in God rather than faith or an experience, we may find that there is a purpose for what happened. WE MUST BELIEVE HE IS LORD EVEN WHEN WE CAN'T UNDERSTAND."

DGB writes:
"I well remember a long conversation with William Ennis, one evening we bumped into each other at the Maxol Filling Station. William was a policeman, and not, as far as I remember, a regular churchgoer.
He told me that in his work he was involved in dealing with child abuse cases. This greatly distressed and angered him that young people should be so cruelly treated.
We talked and talked. In the end I suggested that he come to a 'Life in the Spirit Course'. This, in due course, he did, declaring that he had been brought along through seeing the change that had taken place in his wife, Heather.
In the Seminar, the anger in his heart was confronted and dealt with, without diluting his tenderness and care for the abused. He came to a lively faith in Christ, and experienced the indwelling presence of the Holy Spirit.
His passing was a deep grief and blow to us, but our consolation was in Him who is the resurrection and the Life.

JANUARY WCN 1994 mentioned that DEATH had dealt us many blows, and with and for each we

grieved.
In the Kirk Session report for 1993, our clerk has written:

"The year has seen many families suffer the loss of a loved one. To them we express our sincere sympathy.

MRS HEATHER ARMSTRONG'S DEATH. This *was a great loss to our congregation. Heather's gifts as a singer, her work with the choir, her marvellous caring personality, friendliness and her special gift of making others laugh will have a lasting effect in West."*

Yes, her voice was clear as a bell, was sweet, expressive, and beautiful, often with a haunting quality as when, at our Carol Services she would solo sing:
'In the bleak mid-winter
 Frosty wind made moan,
 Earth stood hard as iron,
 Water like a stone...'
The song that came from her lips seemed effortlessly perfect, but was the fruit of a professional who prepared for every solo piece in a meticulous and God-honouring way.
We felt that when Heather was in the choir, the choir would lead the worship beautifully and without faltering!

So many people have enriched our West Church soul and psyche, made us the body of people we became - *and not least Heather Armstrong!*

'How bright these glorious spirits shine!
Whence all their white array?
How came they to the blissful seats
Of everlasting day?
Lo! these are they, from sufferings great
Who came to realms of light,
And in the blood of Christ have washed
Those robes which shine so bright'.

THE "YEO" ISSUE.
Mr Yeo has resigned as a Minister of Her Majesty's Government.
PRIVATE MORALITY/ PUBLIC SERVICE.
For quite some time now it has been widely held that private morality and public service are quite separate from each other. And in many countries, and down through history, the leaders of nations have often been sexually promiscuous.

Now it is being declared again that a person who does not keep vows to a marriage partner is less likely to be trustworthy and honest in public and political life.
And this has been sharpened because the nation is becoming aware of the cost to the treasury of begetting children outside the framework of a stable home, and of other destructive social by-products.

PRE-MARITAL ABSTINENCE?
But has a nation that has largely renounced the Ten Commandments and the active worship of God any good justification for condemning public servants for their sexual behaviour? The current 'condom philosophy', that declares it is natural for young people to be 'sexually **active**' - and quite puritanical, preachy and unreasonable to suggest pre-marital abstinence and marital fidelity that the Bible teaches -**is surely not in a strong position to condemn adult promiscuity.**
If we teach young people in their teens that they may be 'sexually active' - with proper precautions of course! - can we be surprised to find this mode of life continuing into adult years?

We include in January WCN an excellent article by Michael Harper on 'The Family in Crisis', and give here some suggestions from a PCI pamphlet on "HOW WE CAN ACTUALLY BEGIN TO RESTORE THE FAMILY."

"We cannot escape the fact that the Church today needs to recover that powerful family unity which was so characteristic of both Old Testament and New Testament times, and which has always been bound up in the religious training based on the home.

THE CHRISTIAN FAMILY.
I have a few simple suggestions to offer as to how the family bond can be strengthened in such a way that parental nurture of children becomes integral to family life, and is a pleasure rather than a chore.

BEDTIME.
From a child's earliest days there should be an evening prayer time.
The word **time** is the key.
Too often nowadays because parents **are absorbed in watching television the children are ordered to bed (too late at that!) and are expected to attend to themselves and even switch off the light. More, many children have their own televisions and fall asleep viewing some film or show.**

The domination of television must be challenged and firmly ended.
Parents must see the half hour with their children before the light goes out as family time, *when love for each other and for God is shared together. There are many books that can be used to make bedtime a learning time about God.*

FAMILY DEVOTIONS.
There should also be family worship. In my own home, Bible Reading Notes were used at breakfast every morning. (I know that early morning may be a difficult time, but the family timetable can be arranged to include ten minutes for a morning reading and prayer, if such family worship has a high priority. Then parents will make sure the family rise early enough to allow sufficient time for those vital minutes of quietness together right at the start of the day (and the secret of early rising is to be found in the time the lights go out the night before!)

VISIT OF JIMMY SMITH, U.S.A.

Reference was made to an Evening Concert led by Jimmy Smith to West in October - an evening that few will forget, and some testify to long-term benefits received. Jimmy Smith is a man attuned to the Word of Knowledge, and through whom not a few experienced the phenomenon of 'being slain in the Spirit'.

A further visit is scheduled for Sunday -Tuesday 6th - 8th February, with emphasis on Praise/Teaching/ Ministry.

JANUARY WCN 1994 tells us that so far nine marriages in West are scheduled for 1994, that Jeremy & Heather Eves will run a Seminar course for couples, and that 12 books on Marriage have been added to our Church Library in the Approach Room.

It also tells us that our redundant spectacles may find a use in India;

brings us news from Astrit in Croatia;
speaks of an industry that:
kills more than a third of its long-term customers;
kills, every year, another 53,000 *involuntary* users of its product;
paves the way to marijuana and cocaine addiction;
spends $500,000 an hour hawking its deadly merchandise
gets 90% of its new customers from children;
and then goes on to give testimony from one of our West Church members who, set free from smoking addiction, now desires to minister healing to others, in Jesus' Name.

January WCN also reports that BARRY McCROSKERY sets off to spend one year with "Operation Mobilisation" in France.
It also tells us that a new group for MEN is scheduled to start on Friday 21st January at 10.30am.

"It aims to provide a meeting place for men who may be retired or otherwise at leisure during the day, who would appreciate the opportunity to chat together over a cuppa. There will be some programme week by week to add some element of interest to the coming together.
Walter McAllister will lead this, with Billy Hanlon to assist and Willie Hall to give a little coaching from the wings. We trust this will be of special benefit to any who may find time hanging heavily on their hands. We hope to be able to provide transport for those who need it *and that this Friday meeting will be a healthful oasis in many a man's week.*

[2006 COMMENT: THIS IS THE MEETING THAT HAS NOW GROWN TO SEE MORE THAN ONE HUNDRED MEN WHO GATHER EACH FRIDAY!
A case of little acorns growing into mighty oaks!]

FEBRUARY WCN 1994.

February WCN looks forward to the visit of JIMMY SMITH, in the hope that it will be as fruitful as the visit of the Woodersons a year earlier.

February WCN is a bumper edition that includes the annual Kirk Session report and reports from our multifarious organisations, including our newest one:
THE FRIDAY MORNING MEN'S GROUP held in 91 Crawfordsburn Road.

"The meeting got off to a good start. The attendance was good. We enjoyed our tea, coffee, scones and pastry nicely prepared and served by Renee Robinson: to Renee we all say a big 'Thank you'.

As it was our first meeting we had an informal discussion on the various aspects of our work experiences up to now, led by Walter McAllister and Billy Hanlon. This enabled us to get to know one another a little better. We were encouraged by a talk given by Rev David Bailie on the ways of helping one another.

If you are free on Friday mornings, we would welcome your company.
OUR CLERK OF SESSION - Mr William McClelland.

At the end of the Kirk Session report, we appended this tribute:
"We thank our Clerk of Session, not only for this thoughtfully prepared report for the Kirk Session, *but for the work he does throughout the year, the care he shows to so many, his presence in the church so faithfully Sunday by Sunday to meet and greet our members, and his guiding hand upon so many aspects of our work.*
Nor do we forget Elizabeth's helping hands preparing for our Communion services, or the distribution network that she runs as she dispenses, month by month the bundles of West Church News to our distributors - quite a work in itself!"

TEACHING OUR CHILDREN.

Through West Church News we have a continual input of material to help us FOCUS ON THE FAMILY in all sectors of life.

We do not forget the youngest children, and we incorporate stories, with pictures to be 'coloured in', month by month.

For some time also our SCOUTING ORGANISATIONS have been giving their regular reports, lavishly illustrated in WCN.
Most of our organisations and groups take real care to inform our whole membership of what they are doing, and for this we are grateful- it means that everyone may have a full knowledge of all being done within the Body of our congregation.

IN THIS MONTH'S WCN there are reports from:
Our Church Committee,
Our Kirk Session,
Mothers & Toddlers, with news of a Coffee Morning for Meningitis Trust;
The Scouting groups, reporting that Venture Scouting got off the ground last year with Gary Thompson taking on the leadership;
The Girls' Brigade;
11th Bangor Girl Guides;
West Church Bowling Club;
The Friday Morning Men's Group;
Rainbow Guides;
Junior Badminton Club;
The Crèche;
PWA;
West Church Young Men;
The Sycamore Club.

Each of these reports was well and informatively written, keeping us abreast of so much labour, inspired within the Body, by Christ our Head.

A PROMISE - 'I GIVE YOU MY PEACE'.

"I remember lying in bed one night, unable to sleep, really being laid low by different worries - family, relationships, health -and by a feeling of helplessness. Seeing no way out, as one tends to do in the early hours of the morning, I felt as if I were wandering in a desolate land, without the friendly touch of a human companion, or even a glimpse of God's hand in nature, on account of the barrenness of the landscape.

*Suddenly I was aware of being lifted up and away from this place, as if on a lightweight rug or sheet. The sheet was gathered up round me as I travelled and I was enclosed in a safe, comforting and light place.
I was gently carried in the air to -I suppose one would call it - an oasis.*

Lovingly, still enclosed in the sheet, I was lowered down and landed on something warm, soft - and liquid! There was a soothing, relaxing smell as the sheet opened up - and it did open up just as a flower does - because I was resting in the middle of a beautiful water-lily, floating in a warm, quietly rippling pool, with flowers and birds and insects all around.
The pool itself was surrounded by greenery - but most of all - the whole place was overflowing with a sense of tranquillity, security and care-less freedom.

I knew without doubt that God's Holy Spirit had visited me with His peace.

The Good News of John says: "Peace I leave with you; my peace I give you. I do not give as the world gives. Do not let your hearts be troubled and do not be afraid," (John 14: 27).

[Note: This was an experience of God's grace and peace given to one of our members.]

MARCH WCN 1994.

MARCH WCN gives news of forthcoming Holy Week Services with these verses for Lenten Pondering:

'Christ paid a debt he didn't owe, to satisfy a debt we couldn't pay'.

'Patience means waiting God's time, without doubting God's love'.

'Prayer is not a way to get what we want, but the way to become what God wants'.

Never be afraid to entrust the unknown future to the all-knowing God.

'It is better to declare the truth and be rejected, than to withhold it just to be accepted'.

'Christ became a curse for us, to remove the curse from us'.

A MATTER OF REJOICING!

Once in the past, and simultaneously, we had 3 people studying to become ministers- David Knox, George Moffett and Ivan Warwick.

More recently, and again simultaneously, three of our members studied at Union Theological College in Belfast - Jim Hunter, Ann Kennedy and Heather Thompson.

Now we rejoice that three men among us, who have a sense of call to the Christian ministry, after a stringent vetting procedure, have had that call corroborated by our PCI -they are ANDREW COLE, CECIL GRANT and BRIAN MARTIN.

Andrew will study at Union College, Belfast; Brian at Regent College, Vancouver and Cecil Grant at Princeton Theological Seminary, New Jersey.

This means leaving paid employment for slender scholarships- **our Easter Special Offering will enable us to give them some monetary encouragement.**

CALLED TO BE A MINISTER! - ANDREW COLE writes:

"God came into my life in a very special way on 20th January 1982, when I was saved by his grace through faith in Jesus.
In recent years the Lord has been gently prompting me with thoughts of becoming a Minister, but I needed a clear call.
On 5th August 1992 I was thanking God for my wife, children and the many ways in which he had blessed me, and I had just thanked him for my job when he put a very strong clear thought into my mind, three

words **"Be a Minister."** At the same time a wonderful peace enveloped me. My wife Florence was the first to know and she was startled to say the least, but she is walking in faith and trusting the Lord for the future. My children are getting used to the thought of their dad becoming a minister, and my training starts this October in Union Theological College.

A BANGOR HIDDEN FROM MANY!

CHRIS WILSON, a member of West, has been working until recently in BANGOR YMCA, in one of the most successful of all S.T.E.P. Schemes. Excerpts from his Final Report, December 1993. (STEP = Support, Training and Enterprise Programme).

A WORLD I NEVER THOUGHT EXISTED!

"Through my involvement with STEP over the last three years I discovered a world which I never thought existed within our affluent town of Bangor.: **a scene of drugs, alcohol and illicit sex, a situation where many young people are living in squalor and being exploited by unscrupulous landlords.** Never by choice, but mostly from rejection, have these young people entered into a world which dulls the pain of their apparent worthlessness and in turn shows itself in all kinds of anti-social behaviour.

A REVELATION - FROM STABLE HOMES.

It has been a revelation to discover that all but a few of our young people have come from stable homes. **The breakdown of the family has been the most destructive element in the lives of young people causing so much hurt and neglect.** In *STEP* it has been our privilege to be inferior substitutes for a loving family, to those who needed our support and encouragement, while we recognised the pain and absorbed the hurt, and gave unconditional support.

SELF-ESTEEM - able to seek employment.

Our brief, in STEP was aimed at the socially disadvantaged between the ages of 18 - 25 (an area sorely neglected by statutory agencies); to help build their self-esteem and possibly give them their last opportunity to find fulfilment in a society that has virtually ignored them. **By building our trainees' self-esteem, where they began to appreciate their worth, they were consequently able to seek employment. Our record of those gaining full-time employment was 46 out of a total of 57 trainees.**

I AM GRATEFUL TO GOD.

Needless to say, we have had disappointments, but taking into account that a considerable number of trainees **spent time in prison or on probation, or have grown up in institutions, it is creditable that our programme has touched so many lives.**
It is ironic that while we received no funding from Social Services, many of our referrals came from that source lending credibility to our more holistic approach.
As I look back over the three years I am grateful to God, without whose help little would have been achieved. Recognising that all young people are precious to God, and that we can do no other than respond to His call to 'feed His sheep', that is the only criterion demanded from us.

THE NEED FOR STEP.

It is not with any self-gratification that I put pen to paper, **but to stress the need for such a programme as STEP.** It is not enough for society to dole-out 'conscience money', no matter how inadequate, yet a fair government must aim to give people self-respect and dignity, in this age of much unemployment and injustice - hence the need for the STEP approach.

A TRAVESTY.

The current lack of funding for STEP is a travesty when one considers the ever-increasing need for such a scheme. While our protestations fall on the deaf ears of bureaucrats who have lost sight of the individual and are content to invest in the easier option of providing facilities for the affluent young person at the expense of the disadvantaged, **we as Christians have no such choice. We cannot stand idly by and ignore those who have been denied, both educationally and socially, the privileges of a so-called civilised society."**

[NOTE BY DGB:
Chris Wilson is grieved by the decision to cease the funding of STEP, but thanks those who have supported him for three and a half years, concluding "Over the years we have striven to bring hope to the hopeless and self-respect to those people whom society has devalued through no fault of their own."

We in West Church are grateful to Chris for giving us eyes to see things in our own locality, to which we could easily have been blind, and are grateful to God for the tender heart and strong spirit that He has inspired in His servant, and our brother and friend.]

A CALL TO FULL-TIME MINISTRY - BRIAN & CHRISTINE MARTIN.

"Christine and I were married in December '86 and over the last three years we have both experienced God directing us towards some form of full-time ministry. My home church (West Church) confirmed my sense of calling and it felt right to apply for the ministry of the Presbyterian Church in Ireland.

In September '93 PCI interviewed me for the ministry. After looking carefully into my family and financial situation, which caused them some concern, **they unanimously accepted me as a candidate for the ministry.**

Following my recent acceptance by Regent College to start study in September '94, we are now making plans to move out to Vancouver in July/August.

REGENT COLLEGE.
Regent College located in Vancouver, British Columbia, Canada is an international graduate school of Christian studies that seeks to educate, nurture and equip Christian men and women from around the world to live and work as mature leaders. While theological and academic training is its primary mission, the College believes that education has to be holistic and life transforming. *To facilitate this educational process, community building has been built into the life of the College."*
Brian continues:
"The goals of the College are ones that I cherish, in particular, the training of all believers to take an active role in the Body of Christ. I have seen to some extent the working out of these goals and the fruit that follows in West Church. This I would see as an important part of my role as a minister of a local church, in the event of ordination."

Included in March WCN is an essay, grappling with the subject of ABORTION, by Robert Adrain, one of our elders doing some study at the Belfast Bible College. I give but one quotation from a substantial presentation:

"I find it impossible to understand how with an 'unwanted pregnancy' a mother and doctor can regard the foetus as nothing more than a growth to be removed. Yet the same mother and doctor in a 'planned pregnancy' cherish the foetus, regarding it as a baby rather than a blob, a life rather than a lump - something real and living - a child. The real difference does not lie in the foetus but in the deceitful hearts and corrupt minds of those involved."

OPERATION MOBILISATION - BARRY McCROSKERY'S WORK. PLANTING A CHURCH IN PARIS.

A letter from Operation Mobilisation sets Barry's work in context:
"Barry is part of the church-planting team at Asnieres. Asnieres is a North Western suburb of Paris which houses 80,000 inhabitants of which 20% are immigrants (a majority of North African Muslims). The area has a dog cemetery! one mosque, one synagogue, seven Catholic churches, a Haitian Church and an evangelical church. The evangelical church was begun 3 years ago. The work has been slow so they have invited an OM team to join them. This considerably shortens the time for establishing a church, from about 10 years to four years.
Do pray for Barry and the team this year. The team consists of 6 other members, of 6 nationalities! **This will make the experience a rich one. But you can imagine the potential for problems!"**

LATER - AN ENTHRALLING LETTER FROM BARRY HIMSELF:
."... I'm the only guy in a team of six girls all of different nationalities and we're living in the headquarters building with office staff, the director and his family.

BACK TO THE BOOKS.
I was quite surprised on coming here to learn that on the Year Programme there's as much time spent on training, teaching and study as on evangelism, which so far has been excellent.
*We learn about all kinds of ministry, relevant both to us and the people we meet. Subjects like forgiveness, counselling, self-image, gifts of the Holy Spirit. There's also a Bible Study programme, for which I have chosen to study the Old Testament history books, and there's a list of topical Christian books to get through as well.
Part of the practical training for me has been learning to cook for 14 once a week (this I need prayer for).
It's no easy task to meet the culinary demands of the ten different cultures represented here.*

PARIS.
PARIS is a mega-city of 12 million, one fifth of the total French population. There are more Jews in Paris than in Jerusalem, more Arabs than in any other European country.

OUR WORK.
"Every afternoon we fly round the Peripherique in our OM Belgium van to Asnieres where we work. The church there is the only evangelical one in the district, run by a Swiss pastor, and there's usually between ten and fifteen people who come on a Sunday.

FRIENDLY MUSLIMS.
Our work is mainly door-to-door in Asnieres. We ask people if they would like to buy a Bible or a New Testament, and then maybe ask a few questions to see what they know of the gospel. This way a conversation is sometimes started. Muslims will usually talk much more readily about religion and are really hospitable.
Over the past couple of weeks we've had a lot of different kinds of Ramadan food.
<u>Up to now there have been about twenty people requesting Home Bible Studies which is a lot for our small team</u>
*We also have a market stall on Thursday mornings and have been building up friendships with some of the other traders there.
The neighbouring stalls are run by Jews who seem to have a great knowledge of the Old Testament. When the weather is good we go to the park which has been a great place for chatting to people.*

VISITING VARIOUS CHURCHES-
we have spent some time visiting churches and youth groups, both to help

evangelism and help the young people take part in mission. We spent a week in Alsace working alongside Christians who want to see an evangelical church started in a nearby town....."

A QUESTION WE MAY ASK ABOUT SUCH WORK - IS IT WORTH IT?

When Barry tells us about 12 million people in Paris, and the few, struggling, tiny evangelical churches, we may question whether any substantial impact for the gospel can be made.
And this situation is typical of much of Europe - is there any realistic hope?
My mind goes back to what I have read of the apparently tiny impact of evangelicals in South and Latin America through their church-planting programmes which began in the early years of the Twentieth century.
*For the first 50 years relatively little seemed to happen -in the second 50 years, fantastic growth! So let's pray for the seeds that Barry and others sow, that they may bear much fruit!
And we are glad that already we have indications of West Church young people who are planning to go on a LOVE EUROPE project in the summer of 1994.*

APRIL WCN 1994.
STAFFING CHANGES IN WEST. DON & HELEN.

Don & Helen Ritchie have been with us for four and a half years. Recently Don has been appointed to **'CHRISTIAN NATIONALS'**, initially on a half-time basis.
*However we have worked out a financial package that will allow Don, at once, to give himself fulltime to this work, while Helen remains with us on a substantial halftime basis.
With a good initial launch our hope is that Don may be able to develop the important work of* 'Christian Nationals' *in a vigorous manner.
Its success will mean many missionaries, evangelists, pastors and teachers taking up work, planting and nurturing churches in many parts of the world. <u>And what a harvest that will produce!</u>*

IAN HART/ THOMAS MULHOLLAND.

As you know, we contracted with IAN HART to work with us on a halftime basis until the end of May 1994 to help bridge the gap between Alvin's departure and Thomas Mulholland's becoming available fulltime as a licentiate, on the completion of his studies in May of this year.
Most realise that we have seen very little of Thomas in West during the past year. His studies have given him very little time to work for us in West, and his work has lain almost entirely in Young West Church. *Even here that has been limited through the fact that since October he has been suffering from M.E. Our hope is that with his examinations completed and full health returning, he will be able to make a substantial contribution to West Church. However we feel it would be unrealistic in the short term to see him filling the gap left by Alvin, though we hope that in the long term he may have a fruitful ministry with us.*

TERRY LAVERTY.

**There is much work, in many sectors, waiting to be done in West and we have been giving thought to future vigorous development.
So we believe that it is in the providence of God that Terry Laverty will be coming to us.**

While he is like Thomas, completing his theological studies at Union, he is a mature student, married with three young children. He has trained as a teacher, been involved in 'Further Education', worked with the YMCA, served as an elder in Hamilton Road Church, and has an accredited and much sought after ministry with young people. **He's a young man of vigour, of character and stature, a good and cheerful communicator of the gospel to young and old alike, a man with ideas and vision, and above all a deep devotion to Christ.**

TO BE ROOTED LOCALLY.

Over the past year he has worked as a student assistant in Comber where his ministry has been much appreciated. It was a felt need to work nearer to his home base in Bangor, for the sake and the good of his family, and to be rooted in the congregation where he works *that opened up the way for him to come to West Church.*
Our Kirk Session, unanimously and warmly issued the invitation for Terry to work with us, and the Assignment Committee in Belfast, after careful consideration and consultations, assigned him to us.

One is grateful for the vision of Kirk Session and Committee and for the generosity of our people. We all look forward to a Team Ministry in West, in which Terry will have a fruitful ministry of substantial duration.

MAY WCN 1994.
'THE TROUBLES':
COULD WE, SHOULD WE PRAY MORE?

The hopes generated a few months ago in respect of new PEACE initiatives for our land, have at the moment well-nigh evaporated, and the incidence of sectarian tit-for-tat killings is escalating bringing grief and loss to many families.

As West Church Editor, I recently received a letter form one of our members, beginning with this observation:
"A Northern Ireland pastor said recently, at the funeral of a young innocent girl, '*There is great evil in this land. It has a Mission Hall*

on almost every corner and a church on every road, yet this is a land of darkness. It is up to God's redeemed people to do something about that darkness'."

Our correspondent continues:
"There have been stages in my life since I sought to follow Jesus, when I have been able to use, with spiritual conviction, His words, **"The time has come."**
After much thought, I know that **"the time has come"** for me to say that I agree wholeheartedly with the pastor's remarks.
Concerning our troubled land should we pray more? Could we pray more?"

Our correspondent continues:
"God pours out so much help and blessing on our land and its people day by day - so much that we never see, hear or read about, so much that we don't therefore acknowledge. *Why should He do more, unless we are prepared to pray to Him, as members of His Church, in a fuller, more committed way, petitioning Him and making our quality concentration a regular sacrifice, showing our faith and trust in Him alone?*
I'm sure God is often disappointed by our lack of attention in prayer to our Troubles; after all, peace in our land is of vital importance to each of us now, and to all coming generations."

COMPLACENCY.
So our correspondent has written, and West Church News Editor and minister acknowledges, *'a certain complacency, especially when the 'troubles' do not affect us directly. We do not take up corporate opportunities for prayer in the congregation in the way that we should. Sometimes prayer for our land is omitted in our main services, or lacks the cutting edge of urgency or faith. We can do better!*

ABSENCE = A PUNCTURE.
There have been times that, preoccupied by many concerns, the priority for public worship has ebbed away
PUNCTURED!
How often good services would have been *great* **services, if all the places had been occupied by alert people, giving themselves ardently to worship!**
ABSENCE is like a puncture that allows spiritual pressure to leak. Don't be lightly absent when you can be positively present, to pray, to sing, to worship, to cause buoyant worship to ascend as a fragrant offering to God.
Absence is a way that tells *worship is no longer a priority to me or to my family. The first 3 Commandments declare that God is to be worshipped wholeheartedly, and the fourth emphasises a day set aside for this very purpose.*

KENNEDY NEWS FROM MINTERBURN & CALEDON.

An excerpt - Ann writing this!
"I am adjusting well to "the country life" and am learning something about farming. So far I have herded straying cattle into a field, hand-milked a cow and observed the Caesarean birth of a calf. Unfortunately I had 'flu over the Christmas period and missed the local turkey plucking party!
I have been very aware of God's blessing and protection throughout the year. Caledon church was damaged by a mortar bomb in November but praise God no one was injured or killed. We began a combined Bible Study and Prayer Meeting in the autumn, following an excellent study course."

LEADERSHIP WEEKEND
FOR YOUNG PEOPLE.
Helen Ritchie reports on a Weekend to take place 30th April - 1st May.
This will comprise Saturday morning and afternoon sessions with Paul & Sharon Reid conducting a Sunday afternoon Praise Workshop.
Helen & Don announce a Life in the Spirit Seminar for young people, and also announce **that the young people are heading off to Caledon to take a young people's Praise Service in Ann Kennedy's church on 8th May!**

MAY WCN 1994
gives us our regular monthly slot on "Building Beginners" for our children;
updates us through the faithful and beautifully presented work of **Graham Dore on Wycliffe Bible Translators**.

gives us news of Maurice & Winnie Sloan in Brazil;

tells us of PCI Summer Outreach teams;

includes an excellent contribution by Elaine Brown, warning us that **Unforgiveness carries a heavy penalty, and showing us how to get free from it;**

gives us comprehensive Scouting news;

tells us of the forthcoming LICENSING of Terry Laverty in Hamilton Road church on Sunday 12th June,
and of Thomas Mulholland in 2nd Kilrea church on Wednesday 15th June;

invites our people who were present at the JIMMY SMITH meetings to put pen to paper to indicate the ways God worked in their lives then, and the outworking of it since then.
JUNE/JULY WCN 1994.

"TEN OUT OF TEN", he said!

Going out after a recent morning service, a relative newcomer said, with an approving smile, "Ten out of ten, I should say." It was his way of saying that he found the service helpful and uplifting throughout.

It set me thinking - in how many departments do we score "Ten out of ten"?
In generosity and vision- World Development Christmas Appeal; Development Fund for additional personnel; Outreach Fund? **Yes!** Recently, our Easter Special raised more than £6000 to be a support to our 3 theological students.
Yes, Ten out of ten!
Over the years in Healing Service and 'Life in the Spirit Seminars' and in a plethora of organisations and groups, that reach **out** with vision and love and reach **in** also to cherish and bless those within our membership.
"Ten out of ten!" - YES!

But places in which we could 'do better'!?
Yes! **Faithful, assured attendance at all our Sunday Services. Committed, sacrificial participation at all our prayer gatherings and projects.**
Yes! Yes!

**JUNE/JULY WCN again gives good coverage of all our Scouting groups; and of "Building Beginners."
It gives notice of "WOMEN'S PRAISE" on Tuesday morning 14th June, promising that everyone will be blessed, where there will be 'Praise, Prayer, Testimony, Friendship, Love, Coffee, Tea", where children are welcome and a Creche available.**

JUNE/JULY WCN has contributions from 2 young men, one about to embark on his training to become a minister and the other in the midst of practical training and experience as an assistant minister.

HELP! I'M BECOMING A MINISTER! - BY CECIL GRANT.

"Some people, as in the parable, are able to "leave their nets immediately" and follow God's call, but I'm afraid that's not for me! **Before I would have followed Jesus that day, I would have calculated the lost revenue of fish sales, considered the poor wages, long hours, and thought about the lack of job security involved in following some strange bloke standing on the beach.**
So when God called me to the ministry, it wasn't through a flash of divine inspiration, after which I jumped up singing, "we're marching to Zion." God had to take his time, and gently show me step by step what his will involved.

GOD WANTED ME TO WORK FOR HIM FULL-TIME.
I first began to feel that God wanted me to work for him full-time, **when I was about 15.** Dr. Moore, a teacher at Bangor Grammar, took some of us to missionary meetings at Belfast Bible College, which I found very challenging. I then went on various outreach teams, such as **Project Evangelism** and **Operation Mobilisation.** Over a time I began to understand that as a Christian, **I could have no claim on my own future, for God had purchased my life through Christ's death, and now I had to acknowledge his lordship over me.**

CAMBRIDGE - TO STUDY LAW.
In 1988 I went up to Cambridge to study Law. I had a wonderful time there, and the course wasn't bad either! I became involved in **the Christian Union and in local churches,** which greatly helped me to assess the gifts that God had given me. Throughout this time, although I didn't know the specifics of God's plan for me, **I was aware that God was moving me at his pace in the direction he wanted.**
It was also at this time that **I became a Presbyterian!** I had been brought up in the Brethren church, but gradually I found that I could no longer remain there. **As I studied Scripture, I realised that the Reformed tradition and the doctrines of Grace, more accurately reflected the Bible's teaching.**

WEST CHURCH- from age of 17.

I first began coming to West Church from the age of 17, but did not feel able to leave the Brethren, where my parents are still members, until I left home for university. It was then that I approached Mr Bailie for membership.
**So I had felt God calling me to fulltime ministry, and now that I was within the Presbyterian Church, the way ahead was gradually becoming clearer...
BUT....**
(and this was a huge "BUT" for me) .....
I had a Master's degree in Law from Cambridge,
my training was leading me towards a job in the Corporate Finance Department of some firm of Solicitors in the City of London.
*How could I give this up?
Was it not God's will that I had read Law?
Had these four years at University been a waste of time?
These were hard questions that really troubled me.
And though it may not sound very holy.... as well as these questions, I so much wanted to be able to afford a nice car, a comfortable house, and clothes from Next!
I wanted all the delights yuppiedom promised.*

SOLICITOR'S TRAINING.
Meanwhile I had applied for solicitor's training in London and Belfast. I was offered a job in London, but I knew that if the way opened back to Belfast, then this was the path God wanted me to take. **One morning in April 1992 I heard that I had been accepted for training in Belfast.**
For the past 2 years, therefore, I have been working as a trainee solicitor in Belfast.
This has been an invaluable experience; working in an office and dealing with the public soon dispels the naivety and idealism of student days!
I have become involved in several

groups in West Church - I have even managed to join the Girls' Brigade! I have learned so much from being part of these groups and seeing the deep love and selflessness shown by the leaders.

THE TIME HAS FINALLY COME.
I now feel that the time has finally come for me to train for the ministry, which the Church has also confirmed. I would like to train in the U.S., and I have been offered places at Harvard and Princeton, but I still have not heard about whether I will receive a scholarship. If the U.S. idea doesn't work out then I hope to go to Edinburgh. It's all so desperately complicated!

This has been a slow journey, but God has graciously taken me along this path at a pace I can cope with, so that, when difficult decisions had to be taken, I was confident that, according to his will, I was making the right choice. *I wouldn't be honest, if I didn't say that the uncertainty of what lies ahead is rather scary, and often I have simply had to go off for a long walk to sort things out. But I suppose we all must trust in God of whom it is said:*
'He tends his flock like a shepherd;
He gathers the lambs in his arms and carries them close to his heart;
He gently leads those that have young.'   Isaiah 40: 11."

NOTE: Cecil received a Scholarship to Princeton.

A SPECIAL SERVICE ON 31st JULY, to make presentations to our 3 theological students, Cecil Grant, Brian Martin and Andrew Cole, as they embark on their studies in September.

ARTHUR YOUNG -
MOVES FROM LEEDS TO CHINGFORD, LONDON.
Arthur writes to West, "Dear Friends,

It has been almost 2 years now since I came to Seacroft Congregational Church Leeds, as Assistant Minister. Many of you know that I've found the work here to be quite difficult and different from the culture and atmosphere of Northern Ireland.

A SWORD OF DARKNESS AND FEAR.
Seacroft has a large population, which brings with it great and increasing problems dominating the lives of so many people, young and old. **People seem to live their lives here very much confined to themselves, with a sword of darkness and fear hanging over them, and a wedge of apathy and indifference between them and the Church.**
Children and teenagers are bombarded at the schools and through TV with ideas and values opposed to the Bible's teachings. All these things alert us as a Church to the serious and vital task of teaching children, teenagers and adults, the most important things of all. The need has never been greater or more urgent. And the power of God's Word remains life-changing and destiny changing.

DOOR-TO-DOOR WORK.
Over the past 2 years door-to-door work has been an important feature of our church work, seeking to establish new contacts and relationships with the people here in Seacroft. **This has been difficult in a climate where many are hostile and ignorant of the Gospel.**
But surely such hardships in the work of God do no harm - God can use even rejection to his glory.
There has been a sense of joy to have some breakthrough and establish contact with six families, whom I visit on a regular basis once a month. One cannot always speak freely about the things of God, but there is the opportunity to express God's Word and Love through action, by showing interest and offering encouragement and hope.

My duties and responsibilities within the church family have been very rewarding. The pleasure of helping people with problems, the privilege of sharing friendship with so many, **and the thrill of leading a congregation in worship - the inestimable honour of preaching and teaching the message of a loving, living Christ - all this is wonderful!**

CALL TO LONDON.
At present I'm entering upon my final 3 months at Seacroft, as my assistantship draws to an end...
I now tell you with joy about my call to South Chingford Congregational Church, London. This was issued by the congregation there on the 13th April - after much thought and prayer I have accepted that call. It will be a shared ministry with the Rev. Malcolm Boulter who has been minister there for the past 4 years...

MY RESPONSIBILITIES.
One aspect of my responsibilities at Chingford will be the pastoral oversight of three small country churches, situated at Shalford Green, Bradwell and Bocking End, all on the outskirts of Essex. The main aim is to come alongside these elderly fellowships, and to use the resources and abilities of the Church at Chingford to support, encourage and build up the work and ministry in those areas.

I would value your prayers that God would continue to guide and lead me during the remaining months at Seacroft and especially in September when I embark on a new chapter in my life and ministry at Chingford.
I thank you from the bottom of my heart for all your regular concern, encouragement, support and your faithfulness in constantly praying for myself and the work here in Seacroft over the past 2 years.
I look forward to sharing fellowship with you soon!"
NOTE: Arthur was to preach at the Ten O'clock service in West on 24th July.

SEPTEMBER WCN 1994.

NURTURING NEW SECTORS OF CONGREGATIONAL LIFE.

Arthur Young has painted a picture of young people alienated from the Church in the 80,000 housing estate in Seacroft, Leeds, and of taking up work in 3 small congregations on the border of Essex that are entirely of elderly people.

LEFT TO FEND FOR THEMSELVES.

In the September issue of West Church News ROGER COOKE draws our attention to the fact, that when young people pass formally into adult life at the age of 18 *we often leave them to fend for themselves spiritually, at the very time when, at college, they are confronted with new philosophies and need to be grounded in their faith.*
BARRY McCROSKERY has given us a similar picture of the great housing estates on the outskirts of Paris.

This edition of WCN paints a picture of our young people, active and working in the Gospel in Ireland and in many countries of the world.

NOT LOSING TOUCH WITH OUR CHILDREN!

We are attempting through our Eleven-Thirty Family Service to maintain contact with our children, as they grow up, within the context of our church services.
"This service needs to have an enthusiastic, buoyant, consistent committed **attendance of parents, with their children, Sunday by Sunday, with both parents and children entering fully into worship.**
To achieve this we need to sharpen the first 20 -25 minute slot of the service *seeking to ensure, in the songs, the prayers and the teaching that the children truly learn to worship.*

TERRY LAVERTY.

We are glad that Terry Laverty, who has a very special gift with children and young people, will be joining us in September and we welcome him and his family wholeheartedly into our midst.

We shall be asking Terry, in his visiting, to concentrate on families where there are Sunday School children; and to go into our Sunday School departments to give encouragement. Terry will lead the service of DEDICATION for Sunday School teachers and leaders of Young West on the evening of the 25th September.

And in the autumn term we are asking him to preach a number of sermons on the FAMILY, which, we realise, needs up building.

SEPTEMBER WCN gives news of re-starting dates for all our Youth organisations and other groups resuming with their autumn programmes.

ROGER COOKE - CRITICAL TRANSITION GAP FOR YOUNG ADULTS.

"Of the many encouraging aspects of the life of West Church, few *are more exciting for me than the work with children and teenagers.* There is such a huge potential in each of the children we have in our church family, *and the sheer numbers that attend should never be taken for granted.*
But this work must continue right up to 'adulthood'.

YOUNG PERSON TO ADULT.

The years of transition from young person to adult are vitally important for us who have been nurtured through our early years in the church.

For all who have left school recently, regardless of what they hope to do next, *they will undoubtedly be open to new pressures and may have their beliefs challenged seriously for the first time.*
Over the last year in Scotland, I have seen many people come to faith in Christ, but I have seen as many, if not more, former schoolmates fall away from their relationship with God.

CONTINUING SUPPORT.

As a congregation, it is vital that we continue to support our young adults.
There seems to be a dangerous tendency to consider 18 as a watershed for adulthood, and often as young people we are pushed into leadership roles before we are ready for it. (It's worth bearing in mind that Jesus' main ministry didn't begin until he was 30 years old.)

Those of us in this transitional age-bracket still need encouragement, support and good teaching.

It is with this in mind that we hope to start a group for all in the 18-23 age range. Our aims:
1. To teach and encourage those who are still at home.
2. To actively support those who are studying away from home and keep them informed concerning the life of the church.
3. To encourage a loving concern and accountability among all our young adults.

There will be Bible Study/ Discussion each Sunday evening in September at 8.30. and a social event on Saturday 10th September.

Finally, it would be brilliant if one or two people in the congregation felt enthused about co-ordinating or leading some sort of student fellowship.

DEREK POLLEY - THE TEENAGE 'SUMMER

SCHEME'.
"What has 220 legs, a voracious appetite and makes a lot of noise? Answer is of course the teenage section of the Summer Scheme which was in action from 15 -19 August.
The varied programme included **Ice Bowl, It's a Knockout, Hot Pursuit, Barbecues, Bangor Leisure Centre, Coffee Bar and a Barn Dance.**

Peter Wilson provided a challenging and often musical message every evening and some of our own young people helped in Drama and Witness.
This year we were able to use 10 - 12 of our University students, who, 3 or 4 years ago were themselves enjoying this week.
Numbers were slightly down since some of the 13/14/15 year olds voted with their feet, hung around but did not come in. They were under a lot of peer pressure, having no firm church connection though associated with the Tuesday group led by Don Ritchie and Alan Cowie. Derek adds:
"They need a lot of prayer over the winter, that the grip which Satan has on them might be loosened and that next year they might want to join the 80/90 regulars who did enjoy themselves and did hear the message which Peter had sowed. In time we look for a harvest from the teenagers who come along."

SEPTEMBER WCN TELLS US STORIES INVOLVING OUR YOUNG PEOPLE IN CHRISTIAN WITNESS OVER THE SUMMER.

If space permitted we would like to give in full how LAURA PERVER spent two fruitful and enthralling weeks with SUMMERSERVE in Portadown; or give the story of Jenni Wilson and many others 'On Fire' with 9 - 11 year olds in our own Summer Scheme, or the story of EMMA HANLON'S 10-week Physiotherapy Elective Placement in Kenya. These speak of the boldness, adventure, compassion, fulfilment, and fruitfulness of our young people in self-giving, and in strenuous and joyful team witness.
All this has been building maturity and Christian character into our young people and for all this we thank God.

WITH 'OPERATION MOBILISATION' IN MOROCCO -VICTORIA STEWART'S STORY!

Salam Walaykoom (Hello).

A WEEK AT THE CONGRESS!
I left Bangor on Friday 22 July at 5.45am and I was on my way to Germany to the Congress. We arrived there the next day at teatime. **I had a week at the Congress and we all enjoyed it thoroughly.** The conditions were like a refugee camp but that was part of the adventure. I met my team and we had meetings throughout the week to learn about Islam and to learn some Arabic. The funniest thing was learning how to greet each other. **We also learnt a song in Arabic.**

At the international meetings we learnt a song about 'Marching in the light of God, living in the love of God, and moving in the power of God.' **On the last night at the Congress at the international meeting we (approximately 3000 people) all sang this song while doing the conga round the large hall.**

ON OUR WAY TO MOROCCO.
On Friday we left at 7.25am and we were on our way to Morocco. I was sad to leave the Congress but I was so excited that I was on my way and scared because I did not know what to expect.
On our way down to Morocco, we stopped at night and slept at the side of the road, but that added to the adventure.

ON TUESDAY WE HAD A DAY OF ORIENTATION. We learnt a song that we had to sing at every mosque on entering a new town or city:
'Jesus has the victory over (Casablanca),
He has set it free, from Satan's slavery, Alleluia. Alleluia.'

At the end of the day we got into our teams and prayed for each other.

THE BOAT TO MOROCCO.
We left Malaga at 10.30am and headed for the boat to Morocco. We arrived at Fes at 11.00pm and stayed at a Missionaries' Home. **At Fes we did prayer walking round the old and new town. We also met a Moroccan who had become a Christian eight years earlier. Some of the team were in tears over his testimony.**

MARRAKECH.
On Monday we arrived at Marrakech. On Wednesday we left for Casablanca early so we could have morning worship at the Park. **We sang and prayed, and then we read the Bible where it said that with God's power everything was possible.** *So we prayed that through God's power miracles would happen. We started to sing more and the crowd that gathered round was unbelievable... In the end we had to stand as there was no room to sit. We used English/Arabic Bibles and one man read the cover that said 'The Book of Life' so he asked to see it, then everyone wanted one, and we handed them out, but the people were so hungry for the truth that they started to take them from our rucksacks.*
The crowd was too great and we were afraid in case the police would come, so we grabbed our belongings and ran for the bus.

A YOUNG GIRL of 8 or 9 years followed us on to the bus and she asked another girl in my team for a Bible. We told her we would give her one when we got off as it was very crowded. When we did get off

I looked up at the bus and there was the girl trapped on the bus with a pleading look on her face which was indescribable, and her hand was sticking out between two men. The bus started to leave and I quickly shouted to Hong Sik, my leader - he grabbed a Bible and ran after the bus and got it into the girl's hand just in time.

THEY TRIED TO CONVERT US TO ISLAM.
On Thursday we went to the famous Mosque in Casablanca. We prayed over it and sang the song, 'Jesus has the Victory'. **On Friday we went to a Muslim's house for lunch and they tried to convert us to Islam but failed. It was then our turn to try to convert him to Christianity.** The girls in my team got their hands painted by the lady at the house. **This is make-up in their culture.**

We arrived at Asilah on Saturday. We had worship time on the beach, and some people passing stopped to listen.

ON SUNDAY WE WENT TO THE TOWN and sang songs, prayed and read the Bible. We did this in the morning and at night. At night time a crowd appeared as it did at Marrakech. This time we didn't have many Bibles left so we handed out as many as we could and exchanged addresses with some people.

WE LEFT MOROCCO ON MONDAY AND HAD A MEETING IN SPAIN, TELLING EVERYONE ELSE OUR STORIES.

On the Tuesday we headed for Germany to meet other O.M'ers going to England and I arrived home on Saturday 20th August.

SEPTEMBER WCN HAS FURTHER NEWS of our young people at work.
There is a substantial contribution from Jill Young in Rostrevor Renewal Centre where she has become involved mainly in the leadership of Youth work.

Then STEPHEN INNIS, who studied Theology in Bangor North Wales and did a Community Course in Birmingham, has just started working as a Development Officer for the London Federation of Clubs for young people.
This involves working with up to forty clubs, from the Islington and Camden area, and London central YMCA to clubs for ethnic minorities.

SEPTEMBER WCN also tells us that PATRICIA FERGIE is back home after a stint of 4 years in Woodstock International School in India.
We are full of admiration for what these young people have done- and are doing! Praise God!

BARRY McCROSKERY MOVES FROM PARIS TO LAVAL.
Like Arthur Young in the vast Seacroft Housing estate in Leeds, so Barry McCroskery, with an OM team worked in a similar estate at Asnieres on the outskirts of Paris, where there were a lot of crime and drug gangs.
Barry writes: "Lately we have been concentrating our evangelism here, sharing the gospel by doing door-to-door questionnaires. **The response on doing questionnaires like this is great and much more natural. The church is doing well.** It's hard to see the fruit of what we have been doing, but there are people, just starting to come to the church now, who received literature or with whom we had good conversation months before. Good news, we heard just yesterday from Arab World Ministries, is that an Egyptian, with whom Stephanie - one of the Team members had contact, *has given his life to Christ.*
Also, yesterday, Dreeze another one of our contacts, a Jew, has expressed an interest in meeting *someone from 'Jews for Jesus'."*
Barry tells us that he is going to be transferred to work in LAVAL a provincial town of 53,000, to assist a pioneering pastor as he starts a new church.

SICKNESS DEEPLY UNDERMINES OUR WEST CHURCH STAFF.
People regularly ask me, "How is Julie (Hamilton)?" They ask with concern as for someone they love. Julie is under a consultant's care, some improvement is affirmed, but return to work is still some time away.
Likewise Thomas Mulholland has been unwell since the middle of the autumn term in 1993.
This has meant that he has been little in evidence in our West Church congregation. From the beginning of 1994 until May '94, he conserved his energies almost entirely for his college studies and examinations.
He began 'fulltime' working with us in July of this year - but his illness still severely dogs him and has drastically reduced any normal working.
This is disappointing for us and clearly also for him.

PRAYING.
Our members obviously want to pray for Julie and Thomas, and some may be glad to undertake a special, daily upholding prayer for them.
We have included here a prayer for each day of the week that may become the basis for praying for them. And one hopes that Julie and Thomas may be able to use such prayers for themselves.

DAY ONE PRAYING.
A Meditation on Psalm 139 allows us to invite the Holy Spirit into our lives, to search us in our inmost being.

DAY TWO PRAYING. A Meditation on Isaiah 53 leads into a prayer of UNLOADING where we may lay all our sins, griefs and sicknesses upon the Lamb of God.

*DAY THREE PRAYING.
A Meditation on Matthew 18: 15-20 and 21-35 enables us to forgive deeply, deeply over every phase, circumstance and incident of our lives.
We pray such a prayer for ourselves, and for others.*

DAY FOUR- USE THE SAME PATTERN OF PRAYER, USING THE LORD'S PRAYER.

DAY FIVE: use Ephesians chapter one, to pray all spiritual blessing, and status in Christ, into one's own life, and for others.

DAY SIX: Similarly use Ephesians 3: 14ff.

DAY SEVEN: Matthew 18: 19-20. Praying is greatly magnified, when, on occasion, we join with one or two others.

HOW GOD USED SADDAM HUSSEIN - THE STORY OF PAUL GRAHAM.

"When the Gulf War began in the latter months of 1990, I along with the rest of the Western world, I suppose, was fascinated by the regular news reports, and followed events with great interest. It all had the elements of a good story; the mad oil-rich dictator of an Islamic state, the big bully annexed the neighbouring, small, oil-rich state and made bold proclamations of emerging as the leader of an Arab super-state, which would obviously attack beleaguered Israel, given half a chance. *The world community may or may not act, what next?*

NOMINALLY CHRISTIANS.
Skipping back to 1986, my wife Beverley and I were both from nominally Christian families and had so little to do with any church that neither of us could claim a particular one as our own. Our first child, Stephanie had been born and we did agree, although not church goers, **that a child should have a Christian type upbringing, just in case.** Although I was never an enthusiast for the hard standards of the gospel, I did accept that it was an ideal to be looked up to, and certainly the way to train a child.

This led us to our nearest Presbyterian Church, Bangor West. So as not to be total hounds about the issue, Beverley and I began to attend Church on a semi-regular basis and were impressed, even moved, by the warmth and fellowship that we felt there. **Three children and three Christenings down the road we were attendees, but not born-again believers - there was just something that kept me from accepting the whole package. I was truly nominal.**

ALONG CAME SADDAM.
Then along came Saddam. I had been at work, where we gossiped with relish about all the build-up and potential consequences of the Gulf War. Beverley had been to church and was trying with difficulty to find a passage in the book of Daniel that might relate to the war, because the minister, (I don't know which one), had made some comment on it. I sat and tried to make sense of it in the King James Version, but found it to be heavy going. I resolved to go to the local Christian bookshop to get something to explain it more clearly.

I went into the bookshop much as someone would enter anywhere that they didn't want anyone they knew to see them there. I was terribly self-conscious. However, on the advice of the assistant, I bought an N.I.V. and two paperbacks written about prophecy in the Bible and the Middle East.

THE BOOK HAD A PROFOUND EFFECT ON ME.
The book that was to have the most profound effect on me was, "THE 1980'S COUNTDOWN TO ARMAGEDDON" by Hal Lindsay. I could not put it down. I had never heard anyone explain how the Bible is crammed with prophecy from start to finish and how much of it was fulfilled in Jesus.
Some had been fulfilled in living memory (formation of the state of Israel, which I visited in April 1993). Much was still to come. **This convinced me of God's awesome power and plan for the earth,** *but it was a 2-page explanation of God's plan for redemption,* <u>that no man is right under the law (something I could relate to) and that Jesus HAD to die, be sacrificed, to fulfil the way of reconciling man to God that did the trick for me.</u>
It was as if my eyes had been opened to this amazing truth that had always escaped me before

GOD SO GRACIOUS.
When I think back, God was so gracious to allow that precious moment of realization in private, so that none of my workmates saw the joyful tears roll down my cheeks.

HUNGER FOR GOD'S WORD.
My hunger for God's Word was now aroused and I had disovered that if there were areas of the Bible that I had difficulty accepting, **the proper response is to beat a path to the Christian bookshop** and get a book which deals with that topic from the view of a believing Christian author. Many of these authors have spent years studying the whole Bible searching out issues of special interest to them, and can smooth the way for those following them.

I HAVE EXPERIENCED MANY CHANGES
Since that night when my eyes were truly opened, I have experienced many changes in my life, too numerous to mention. Different things helped me to grow in faith and knowledge as a born-again believer:

1. Attending a 'Life in the Spirit' seminar in West Church.
2. Reading and studying the Bible, finding assurance in its authority.
3. Membership of a House Group (Fellowship is so important!).
4. Christian books, videos, tapes, lectures. So much is available.

SINCE BECOMING A 'BELIEVER'.
Since becoming a 'believer' I have seen moves of the Holy Spirit and signs and wonders that are truly supernatural and testify to the loving power and grace of God, to those who follow Jesus.

My own calling, I believe, is boldly (but with love) to proclaim the absolute truths of the Bible, contrary to the many false teachings, i.e. evolution, that hold sway in the corrupted minds of so many these days, which I also believe to be frighteningly close to the return of our Lord Jesus, as described in the Book of Revelation. The world may wallow in confusion and unbelief, but God has warned his people.

In closing I want to thank many people for putting me on the narrow path and leading me to become a follower of Jesus, our only Saviour.
These are Saddam Hussein, whose efforts in provoking the Gulf War undoubtedly caused many people to turn to God! My dear wife Beverley, whose fears and insecurity sent me on the search for the truth. Hal Lindsay, the author, for explaining the gospel in terms I could relate to, **and most of all, Jesus Himself, without whom my being enabled to accept Him would not have been possible.**
A minister, with whom I once had a conversation, told me that he had heard many testimonies and that no two were alike. **Now you have heard mine."**

[NOTE: In WCN 2006 we find Paul Graham serving in Iraq as an International **Policing Advisor.**
"It has been very interesting working closely with people of different races, culture and religion and I am much more knowledgeable now about Islam than before. About 80-90% of their beliefs are like a direct lift from Christianity and Judaism, but it is where they stand on who Jesus is, that the real differences show up. Apart from the Muslims and their beliefs, it is a sobering thought that out of a camp of over 1000 souls, only 6 -10 regularly attend any form of Christian worship. One of the English chaps I work with happily declares, 'I have no God'. **I make a point of attending all the meetings I can at St. Paul's in the Desert, and enjoy fellowship with the various eclectic mix who also attend."**]

OCTOBER WCN 1994.

OCTOBER WCN tells us that our **HARVEST SERVICES** will be on 9th October and that the Rev. John Seawright will lead them. But the October issue also deals with a spiritual harvest and asks: "ARE WE ON THE *VERY EDGE* OF REAPING A MASSIVE HARVEST?"

TORONTO.
"Since the beginning of this year a quarter of a million people have visited an unpretentious church in Toronto where God's Spirit has been working in a very strong, persistent and dramatic way. Since January of this year, there have been services at this church, 6 days of each week, without interruption. People are queuing to get in from 4.30pm. The lives of many people have been deeply transformed under the impact of the Holy Spirit.
And people who have gone there, and been steeped in the Holy Spirit, have often returned to their home congregations, *to see a similar work of the Holy Spirit begin.*
PUTTING THINGS IN THE PERSPECTIVE OF

HISTORY.
WINSTON CHURCHILL used to commend the study of history, declaring that the farther you can see BACK, the farther you can see FORWARD!
I thought, therefore, in this issue, that it might be instructive for us to look at **a significant outpouring of the Holy Spirit in Ireland in the last century - the famed '59 Revival.**
I have therefore enclosed in this October WCN an account **by the zealous and respected evangelist-minister, R.A. Torrie about the effects of the '59 Revival in Coleraine.**
As well, **our new minister, TERRY LAVERTY did a substantial essay on the '59 Revival as part of his B.D. degree** while at Union Theological College, Belfast, and our readers will find this interesting and instructive.

Churchill was right - the better we know past history, the more truly we will understand present happenings, and see into the future.

HOLY TRINITY BROMPTON.
In 1994 Holy Trinity Church, Brompton was known as a lively, evangelical Anglican church. At a time of declining church attendances, with many church buildings coming into disuse, Holy Trinity was a vibrant, growing church which was planning its fourth church plant at St. Stephen's, Westbourne Park, disused for 3 years.
Over the years since 1994, Holy Trinity has become known all over the world through the Alpha Courses that issued from it. These have brought incalculable spiritual blessings.

A MIGHTY WIND FROM TORONTO.
"The story begins far from London, at a little church near the end of the runway at Toronto Airport in

Canada. **In January the Holy Spirit began to fall in a new and powerful way upon the members of that Vineyard Church.** Services began to be held each weekday evening as the extraordinary outpouring of the Holy Spirit continued. **Pastors from North America, and then from other parts of the world, began to travel to Toronto to see and experience for themselves what was happening.**

Among the visitors was ELEANOR MUMFORD, wife of the pastor of the south-west London Vineyard church. Back at their home in Kingston, she spoke briefly to several church leaders about her experience and then prayed for them to be filled with the Holy Spirit.
Everyone present was affected in a remarkable way and the session continued unabated throughout lunch.

NICKY GUMBEL.
Among those present were Nicky Gumbel, curate at Holy Trinity, and his wife Pippa.
Nicky suddenly realised that he should have been back at Holy Trinity for a staff business meeting. He hurried there to find the meeting about to break up. He apologised and spoke briefly about what had happened. Everyone was in a hurry to get on with other matters and Nicky Gumbel was asked to say a closing prayer.

HE ASKED THE HOLY SPIRIT TO FILL EVERYONE.
He asked the Holy Spirit to fill everyone in the room. The effect was instantaneous. The Holy Spirit touched all those present in ways that few had ever experienced or seen. **People fell to the ground again and again. Other people walking past the room were also affected.**
The news spread to those in other offices and they too were powerfully touched by the Holy Spirit. Prayer was still continuing at 5pm.

THE FOLLOWING SUNDAY.
On the following Sunday, 29th May, Eleanor Mumford spoke at the morning service at Holy Trinity. At the end she prayed for the Holy Spirit to come.

A TIME OF SILENCE.
There was a time of silence. Then slowly, members of the congregation began to cry quietly, and some to laugh. As the Holy Spirit came, Eleanor asked people to come forward if they wanted prayer. Many did so...
As Eleanor's team and members of the church ministry team started to pray, people began to fall in the power of the Holy Spirit. Soon the whole church was affected. **There were scenes that few had ever seen before.**
The children arrived from their groups, and many of them were deeply touched and began to pray for each other. Prayers went on well past 1.30pm.
AT THE EVENING SERVICE the scenes were repeated and prayers continued for more than an hour and a half.

OTHER LONDON CHURCHES.
By Tuesday news was coming in of other London churches being affected by a similar outpouring of the Holy Spirit, including Holy Trinity's 'plant', St. Paul's, Onslow Square.

TRIP TO TORONTO.
Meanwhile, such was the extent of what was taking place that Sandy Miller, the Holy Trinity vicar, and Jeremy Jennings, pastoral director, decided to fly to Toronto for a 3-day visit.
There they met John Peters, of St. Paul's Onslow Square, some members of St. Stephen's, Twickenham, and pastors from all over the world anxious to see and experience what God was doing.

THE SUNDAY FOLLOWING.
On the following Sunday, 5 June, Sandy Millar asked Nicky Gumbel and members of the congregation who had been touched by the Holy Spirit the previous week to say what had happened to them.
Soon the Holy Spirit was falling upon people all over the church. Such was the impact upon so many people that the planned communion service could not go ahead.
The evening service was packed with some 1,200 people. Sandy Millar again invited people to come forward to say what God had been doing for them.
One young man said that he was suffering from AIDS and had come to the church just recently. He had never experienced such love as he had at Holy Trinity at that time.

SANDY MILLAR WRITES TO HIS MEMBERS.
"We have begun to see an astonishing outpouring of the Spirit of God upon our own church and congregation.
It seems to be a spontaneous work of the Holy Spirit, and there are certainly some very surprising manifestations of the Spirit excitingly reminiscent of accounts of early revivals and movements of God's Spirit.
Some of the manifestations include: **prolonged laughter, totally unselfconscious for the most part, and an inexpressible and glorious joy (1 Peter 1: 8).**
For some it is prolonged weeping and crying and a sense of conviction and desire for forgiveness. purity and peace with God.
For others it seems to be the silent reception of the Spirit of God sometimes leading to falling down and sometimes standing up, sometimes kneeling, sometimes sitting.
LOOKING FOR FRUIT.
The manifestations themselves of course are not as significant as the working of the Spirit of God **in the individual and in the Church.**
Let's above all continue to pray that, through this outpouring of God's Spirit, he will build a church worthy of Him, holy, equipped and full of love and

grace towards him and the outside world."

OCTOBER WCN has also a report by TERRY VIRGO of an outpouring of the Holy Spirit in Columbia, Missouri, where he says that some of the manifestations were strange, but that the continuing impact upon people's lives has been magnificent..
"We have seen so many lives totally transformed. People have a new hunger for God and a new zeal to see him glorified. Bad relationships have been healed and weak marriages have been wonderfully strengthened. Formerly depressed people have been changed beyond recognition. I have never seen such rapid change take place in individual lives and in the whole atmosphere of a church. I am so glad that, from the beginning, I saw substantial spiritual growth in the lives of those affected.

CHRISTIAN NATIONALS.

Our West-sponsored St. Petersburg graduates Fyodor and Elena Dzuba are now pioneer church planting evangelists and teachers among 1,250,000 Muslim Bashkirs who are on the move throughout the Soviet Union.

Marivic Fetizanan, our sponsored student in the Philippines, was encouraged to receive our Christmas card and letter, and tells us that she spent her summer working in San Agustin Gospel Church, *teaching children to know and love the Lord. 'I was really touched and had compassion for these children, most of whom came from a squatters' area, starving for food and for spiritual food. In spite of hardships they continued to attend church and hear God's Word. Now they know how to use the Bible, to recite verses from the Bible, and sing songs to God. and they invite children like themselves to come and hear about Jesus.*

The Lord gives me joy when the young people I have told about Jesus, decide to follow him completely, publicly in baptism. Now it's time to end my letter - I hope we could meet some day!'

CHRISTIAN NATIONALS- "Mindanao, an island in the Philippines, is a staggeringly beautiful place. Clear mountain streams pour through bamboo forest on the slopes of ancient volcanoes. These surroundings are home to 250,000 T'boli people who live poor lives dependent on subsistence farming. Many have one basic meal per day and few possessions.
In 1993 we were able to build a dormitory so that T'boli children could go to school. The impact of this project extended far beyond the children as T'boli people from another area came to view it.
The villagers asked Pastor Mariano Detorio, of the Philippine Missionary Fellowship, to visit them - **so, one February day, he rode his motorcycle over rocky mountain roads, before walking for 2 hours into their remote homeland.**

On his arrival, the people gathered and pleaded that he tell them about God. After dinner, Pastor Detorio and two companions preached until dawn - and a total of 80 persons accepted Christ. *Since then eight new churches have been planted."*

OCTOBER WCN gives us comprehensive Scouting News; "Building Beginners" Jottings from the Church Committee; and sundry other domestic matters.

AND LETTERS from Cecil Grant at Princeton, and Brian & Christine Martin in Regent College, Vancouver.
Cecil tells us that he had been a bit anxious at the prospect of arriving at New York airport late at night having to cross the city and change buses to get to Princeton.

BUT THEN The Sunday before leaving, JENNIFER WILSON tells him that she will be catching the same plane, going to visit relatives just 5 miles from Princeton. So he gets a lift from the airport right to his dormitory door!
He sends greetings to West, with thanks for the generosity of the financial gift received, and is obviously settling well into life at the Princeton Seminary.

BRIAN MARTIN also expresses thanks 'for your most generous monetary gift received at the farewell service.'
The Martin family have been very hospitably received at Regent College, with people supplying all needed furniture for their unfurnished rented accommodation.
"All in all, having been here a month now, our overall impression of Vancouver is favourable, and we feel very much at peace about having made the move."

RONNIE BAIRD -HOW COULD GOD TURN OFF HIS POWER?

A TRADITIONAL CHURCH.
"I was brought up in a traditional Presbyterian church. The pattern was church on Sundays, and Sunday school. My grandfather forbade whistling on Sundays; in the early days my parents forbade TV and Sunday newspapers. Naturally I rebelled, left Sunday School at eleven years and church soon afterwards.
The personality of my modern history teacher influenced me in my formative years. I thought, 'if he is a minister, religion must have something going for it'.

MY GRANDFATHER DIED.
My grandfather died in my early teens. That made me think about death, heaven and hell and God. I prayed to God if he was real and alive, to look after him. I prayed in private for years, but did not go to church, nor read the Bible, had no real relationship with God I was a typical teenager of the swinging 60s.
I started to go to church, seeking God. Church was dull and dead- as were Christians! I became a communicant, as

a precaution, without being born again.

WHY DID GOD TURN OFF HIS POWER?

I met my old history teacher again, whom I liked and respected, and began to attend his church. However, there was no reality. Why had God left us, why turned off his power?

A NEW CHURCH, AND DIFFERENT!

We moved to Bangor, and on the first Sunday decided to go to church. We wanted to thank God for our new home. We were pointed to a church of modern design, West Church. The minute I walked through the door, I knew it was different. - or was it just the design, or the friendly people on the door? Then I heard David Bailie speak- never before had I heard the 'word' like this. It was alive! Going out that morning I found myself asking him to call (never thought I would see the day!) which he did.

TELL US MORE!

On Tuesday he came and talked about the Holy Spirit. We asked him to return and tell us more, (boy, was I interested, hungry!).

GOD HAD *NOT* TURNED OFF HIS POWER!

I joined a 'LIFE IN THE SPIRIT SEMINAR' where I discovered God was alive, and he became real in my life. *He had not turned off his power*. It was still real today. The Bible was no longer dull but vibrant and alive, and now I enjoyed it, rejoiced in it. Why had I never realised this before? *Best of all,* I was able to do and witness the things that the early church did.

I HAVE SEEN SATAN'S HOLD BROKEN AND DESTROYED.

As a Home Group Leader, I have seen the unbelievable become real. I have seen Satan's hold destroyed in people's lives. I see the living God each day, in and around me. I know he has died for me and in that I have seen real love. **The predominating words** in all of this are **real** and **seen**, but I needed **the Holy Spirit to open my eyes,** for now I know he had been always working in my heart.

DON'T HOLD BACK AS I DID!

Don't hold back; seek Him as I did, no matter how naively or secretly, **for He is real and is wanting and willing to** show you.
Ronnie Baird.

NOVEMBER WCN 1994.

SURPRISED BY THE POWER OF THE HOLY SPIRIT.

In last month's issue of West Church News we gave a report of the amazing working of the Holy Spirit at the Airport Church in Toronto, and how this was carried back to Holy Trinity Church, Brompton and other London churches. Sandy Millar, vicar of Holy Trinity wrote to his members about this, saying that while some of the manifestations - like weeping or laughing or falling down - were unusual, yet it was important to focus upon the genuine and wonderful work of the Spirit in people's lives, to remember that such things have often happened in times of revival.

West Church minister, David Bailie, here declares that through a watershed experience of the Holy Spirit, in his own life in 1968, a new stream of life came into West Church and has been flowing fruitfully ever since.

DECENTLY AND IN ORDER.

"Some time ago, I saw a letter in the Times by a disgruntled member of the Church of England, who wanted things to continue as they always had done in his experience, who complained bitterly at the statistic that 30% of the ministers of the Church of England admitted to the practice of speaking in tongues!"

At the present time, where there seems to be a new outpouring of the Holy Spirit and an intensification of prayer, yet while there is some danger of people being alienated or disturbed by unusual manifestations, we must take care not to 'throw out the baby with the bathwater'! We must not miss out on the good that the Spirit would do in our midst. And sometimes this fear is allied to the theological myth that signs and wonders and the supernatural working of the Spirit ceased with the era of the apostles.

Thus we can find those who lay great emphasis on the total veracity and supremacy of the Word of God, yet they affirm alongside this, that miracles, healings and the supernatural dimension *are not for today!*

Therefore we draw special attention to a book by John Deere entitled "SURPRISED BY THE POWER OF THE HOLY SPIRIT."

JACK DEERE'S EMPHASIS UPON THE WORD OF GOD.

For ten years Jack Deere had been Professor of Theology at conservative, evangelical Dallas Theological Seminary. His passion was to preach and teach the Word of God. All our needs God would meet through our studying of His Word.
"*I KNEW* that God no longer gave the miraculous gifts of the Spirit. There was no need for them; *we had the completed Bible now.. The absence of New Testament miracles in my experience didn't bother me, because I thought God was the one who initiated the change. I was confident that I could prove by Scripture, by theology, and by the witness of church history that God had withdrawn the supernatural gifts of the Holy Spirit.
I was also confident that he no longer spoke to us except through his Written Word. Dreams, visions, inner impressions and the like reeked of subjectivity and an ambiguity that nauseated me. I cringed when one of my students came up to me and said, "God spoke to me and...." Hardly anything else could provoke such a stern rebuke from me as rapidly as that statement!*
As you may guess I was not the kind of believer who was looking for 'something more'. I didn't need any healing miracles from God.

SURPRISED BY THE POWER OF THE HOLY SPIRIT.

So when Jack Deere published a book, thus titled, it produced such a reaction in the Theological Seminary where he had been an esteemed professor that he felt obliged to resign his post.

WHAT OTHERS SAID OF THIS BOOK:

"Like many of us, Dr Jack Deere came kicking and screaming from his cessationist position. This is the clearest presentation of a theology of miraculous gifts that I have ever read..."   *Ralph Neighbour.*

'A dramatic turning point came in Jack Deere's life when the Spirit of God took him by surprise. Sovereignty God took charge of him, just as he did of Saul the Pharisee, of Augustine the profligate and of John Calvin the 16th century humanist. Dr Deere's book describes that turning-point *and examines its biblical foundations."*
John White, psychiatrist and author.

' Through fascinating stories, *a fresh look at the Bible and a theology of passion and power, Dr Deere assaults the traditional Protestant position that the miraculous ministry of the Holy Spirit has ceased."*
Bruce Waltke, Regent College.

WHY DID WE RECOMMEND JACK DEERE'S BOOK TO WEST CHURCH READERS?

Because he was a man steeped in the Word of God, with a great love for the Bible and a formidable knowledge of it,

AND

because he had entered into a transforming experience of the Holy Spirit and had come to see and experience the lovely, gracious and often wondrous things He did to set people free and make them whole.

AND

because we did not wish our people to miss out on any fresh working of the Spirit in our midst due to any strange or unusual phenomena that might accompany it, declaring that we wanted everything to be done decently and in order!

JACK DEERE INVITES JOHN WHITE TO LEAD A CONFERENCE AT HIS CHURCH.

It is quite a story how Jack Deere, who was totally convinced that healings and other signs and wonders had ceased in the Church, came to invite John White - an eminent psychiatrist, medical doctor and author of many fine theological books - to speak at a Conference in his church.
During a phone call to Dr. White, Jack Deere was horrified to learn that in dealing with "The Kingdom of God", Dr White proposed to speak on Christ's authority, not only over **temptation and sin** but also over **demonic powers and disease.**

When Jack Deere affirmed that everyone knew that the age of miracles and of healings etc had passed away with the apostles *John White was not impressed.*
Jack Deere challenged him **"Well, have you ever *seen* anyone healed?"**
"Oh yes" he replied but gave no examples.
Taking the offensive, Jack Deere said, **"Tell me your most recent spectacular healing."**
"I'm not sure what you mean by spectacular, but I will tell you two recent healings that have impressed me."
"He then told me about a young child in Malaysia who was covered from head to toe with eczema. The eczema was raw in some places and oozing. The child was in such discomfort that he had kept his parents up for the previous 36 hours. The child was behaving so wildly that they had to catch him in order to pray for him.
As soon as Dr White and his wife, Lorrie, laid their hands upon the child, he fell fast asleep. Within twenty minutes or so of their prayer, the oozing stopped and the redness began to fade. By the next morning the child's skin had returned to normal and was completely healed. Dr White told me of a second spectacular story of bone actually changing under his hands while he prayed with someone with a deformity."

STUDYING THE SCRIPTURES AFRESH.

This phone conversation took place in January 1986 - the church Conference was due in April. Jack Deere relates:
"I spent a good deal of time from January to April studying the Scriptures to discover what they said about healing and the gifts of the Spirit. The first time I had studied the Scriptures on these topics I had not studied them with an open mind. Godly and brilliant men told me that the Bible taught that the gifts of the Spirit had passed out of existence with the death of the last apostle <u>and that God only spoke through his written Word today.</u>
But from January to April 1986 I questioned all my cessationist arguments in the light of scriptural teaching. This time I tried to be as objective as I knew how.
By the time our conference took place in April, a radical reversal had taken place in my thinking. *This shift in my thinking was not the result of an experience with any sort of supernatural phenomena. <u>It was the result of a patient and intense study of the Scriptures.</u>*

THE CONFERENCE ITSELF.

Jack Deere writes that at the end of the final fourth lecture on "Christ's authority over Disease", when John White invited people to come forward who desired prayer, about a third of the three hundred people present came forward.
**"I could not believe what I was seeing. People I knew well, who seemed so in control of their lives, were on their knees crying and asking for prayer. I recall one very wealthy woman confessing that she didn't feel loved by

anyone except her husband. She asked for prayer that the Lord might remove the barriers she felt around her. I remember another very strong man on his knees confessing that he was eaten up by jealousy over some of his friends' successes and his own lack of success. It seemed that people were hurting all around me. I was perplexed and mildly repulsed."

JACK DEERE PRAYED- NOTHING HAPPENED.

Jack Deere then speaks of a very articulate and intelligent lady, standing at the front who asked for prayer. She had an amazing heart for God, spent long hours in prayer, and was a gifted Bible teacher. **Yet for many years she had suffered from fears and depression.**
"Would you pray for me?" she asked Jack Deere.
Jack Deere and another elder prayed for her - **and absolutely nothing happened!** She thanked us and walked away..... A few minutes later, I noticed she was standing in line to talk to Dr White....Since I did not seem to have much success in praying for people, I thought I would listen to Dr. White pray for her to see if I could learn anything.
"O.K., let's pray for you then", he said to my friend.
When she bowed her head, it was more like she hung her head in shame. Despair seemed to be all around her, fuelling her pain... Like a gentle father John White put his hand under her chin and lifted her head. **"Look up"**, he said **"you don't have to do that any more. You are a child of the King."**
I was mesmerized by this. I thought, *that's a nice touch. I have to remember that line - "Look up; you are a child of the King."*
At this point I was still asssuming that technique and formulas were the keys to healing. Mercifully I would be delivered from that assumption shortly.
Then he put his hand gently on her shoulder, and said, **"Lord, I bring your servant Linda into your presence now in the name of Jesus Christ. She doesn't feel the affection of the Lord Jesus Christ for her. Let her feel in her heart how much Jesus loves her and likes her."**

ANY DARKNESS MANIPULATING?

Then Dr White prayed, **"And Lord, if there be any darkness here manipulating this pain, I pray that you would make it leave now."**
When he said these words, Linda's head began to go up and down, and she began wailing. **She could not stop her head or the wailing. I had never seen anything like that before. It was as though those sounds had a physical force in them. When I looked at her, it was as if she had lost consciousness, or at least the control of her body. I sensed a tormenting presence around her.** Almost everyone in the auditorium was shocked by what was happening. I had never seen a demon before, but I was convinced that I was looking at the work of a demon that very minute.
"In the name of Jesus Christ, I command you to be at peace now", Dr White simply said. And when he said that everything stopped immediately. He was not going to allow her to be humiliated before all those people. Later my friend was prayed for in private so that the evil spirit was dealt with and sent away.
Today Linda ministers very powerfully in teaching and healing prayer.
And so Jack Deere was led into a whole new dimension of ministry.
HE WAS SURPRISED BY THE POWER OF THE HOLY SPIRIT.

I HAVE GIVEN THIS SLENDER INTRODUCTION INTO JACK DEERE'S BOOK SO THAT, IN A DEEPLY NEW TESTAMENT MANNER, WE TOO MAY COME TO KNOW AND BE AMAZED AT THE POWER OF THE HOLY SPIRIT AND WELCOME HIM WHEN HE REVEALS HIMSELF TO US IN THESE DAYS!

DECEMBER WCN 1994.

As usual the December edition of WCN begins by highlighting our PCI Christmas World Development Appeal, this time to support the Christian Aid Project for Tigray in Ethiopia, an area that has just emerged from 15 years of war.
They aim to provide 80 water-points, tree nurseries, community health, veterinary services, goat husbandry, supply of livestock food and employment.
If West Church were to top last year's response and give £6000 that would provide 3 water-points, supplying 1500 households and 9000 people.
We have the incentive in knowing that each
£5 would provide clean water for a whole household.
£20 for 25 people.
£50 for ten households.

----

40 YEARS ON, STILL A PILGRIM SEEKING THE *PROMISED LAND!*

ORDINATION OF DAVID BAILIE, 28 NOVEMBER 1954.

I was ordained - now I read on that ancient Order of Service - as a "Missionary Minister" by the Presbytery of Templepatrick, just prior to my departure for India.
In those days it was much more a "God be with you till we meet again" affair - by boat to Liverpool, and then the 3 week journey, through the Bay of Biscay, the Straits of Gibraltar, the Mediterranean, calling in at Port Said, on through the Suez Canal, the Red Sea the Indian Ocean, a call in Karachi, Pakistan before arriving in Bombay; then a journey up to Surat, and warmly welcomed at the Missionary bungalow of the Rev. H.P. & Mrs Cromie, and the washing off of the dust of the 3rd Class railway journey and the sweat of the unspeakably overcrowded compartment.

Of course there was the luxury of a modern bathroom - the cement floor, with a hole to let the water flow out, complete with a bucket of heated water!

DEPARTURE - A COMPLETE BREAK!

Departure to India then was a break of a kind largely unknown today, where you can now be whisked anywhere in the world in a matter of a few hours, and whisked back again if necessary. *It was just a little bit more like the departure of Abraham from Haran! You did not expect to be back home again for 5 years, so one left family - and the fiancee of 2 months! And it would be almost a year before that fiancée would make the same journey, and arrive in India for marriage in Bombay!*

And so began a year, not only of getting acquainted with a vastly different country and culture - but a year of waiting, and pining and language study! *A strange year, where one slowly moved from the confining inability to communicate freely as mind and tongue sought to master the Gujarati language.*

CRAMPED BY LANGUAGE LIMITATION.

I look back on those five years in India, in which we were to learn a great deal, about people and the sharing of the Gospel. We received much kindness and forbearance, **and learnt a lot that was to remain with us.**

By God's grace, no doubt, we were able to contribute something and Indian people have been generous enough to declare that time of service worthwhile!

For my own part, I was always aware of how cramped we were by language limitation, and from the fact that culturally there was a great gap between us.

God's grace did bridge the gap - *and yet one felt that indigenous pastors were better equipped to build up the Church, and indigenous evangelists to carry the Gospel out to society beyond the Church.*

CHRISTIAN NATIONALS.

That's one of the reasons why I think **CHRISTIAN NATIONALS,** *- now that the Church has been planted so widely throughout the world, - is such a good idea. It means that - at a fraction of the cost of sending a missionary family abroad - indigenous people can give themselves in service to people of their own language and culture.*

[DGB in 2007 says "I have recently been delighted to read a book by K.P. Yohannan, entitled **'REVOLUTION in World Missions'**. This tells of the amazing sense of call felt by Christians in South India to carry the Gospel to the world's least evangelised countries. For example there are 500,000 villages in India which have no Gospel witness. In the 10/40 Window there are three billion people unevangelised. This has led to the formation of 'Gospel for Asia', which already has 16,000 missionaries in ten Asian countries, with 54 major Bible Colleges, and nearly 9000 students preparing for pioneer ministry. And amazing to realise that from £500 per year a missionary can be trained and sustained in ministry.]

AN EVER-ALERT CLERK!

Some people are clearly more aware of the passing of my years in Christian ministry than I tend to be: an ever-alert Clerk of Session was obviously able to inform Kirk Session and Committee that the fortieth anniversary of my ordination was coming up; and so the most generous recognition of that fact on Sunday last (27/11/94) gave the congregation the added pleasure of a minister with an unexpectedly interrupted order of service!

Rhoda and I want to thank you, with deepest sincerity for yet another significant token of your accustomed kindness and generosity!

NOW, WHAT OF THE FUTURE?

A couple of months ago in WCN I asked the question:"**Are we on the very edge of reaping a massive harvest?"**

Some people are already asking whether a significant moving of God's Spirit is under way in the UK.

WHAT PETER ROBERSON TELLS US.

Peter Roberson, of Christian Nationals, has visited our home on a number of occasions over the past two years and has kept us up to date with the adventurous work of that organisation throughout the world, and of our own sponsored students in St. Petersburg and the Philippines.

However, on his last visit, he talked almost continuously for about two hours about his own home congregation in Stockton-on-Tees!

A MOVEMENT OF THE HOLY SPIRIT.

Beginning on a particular day in September, there has been a movement of the Holy Spirit in that congregation, such as they have never seen before. Since September until very recently they have found themselves holding two services daily: one in the morning/afternoon, the other in the evening with an attendance of 300/400.

The services have had a pattern of praise/teaching/ministry.
Many people have been deeply refreshed or renewed in their faith by the Holy Spirit. There have been healings and deliverances. And the congregation of 150 members have had 90 people added to it through faith in Christ.

And he has told me that what has taken place in his own church, in various ways and degrees, *has been happening on quite a widespread scale*

It was good to see a man, aglow with the Spirit, and so excited by what God was doing.
*Let it be said, however, that this movement is not just a question of a healing river flowing over everyone. As always must be, it involves hard spiritual warfare, the need for vigilance and the need for

wisdom.

WEST CHURCH- THROUGH A GLASS DARKLY.

No one can foretell exactly what God's future or immediate plans for West Church may be. In prophetic terms we always see through a glass darkly. We are grateful for the intensification of prayer that we see in our midst. In the past we have seen a gracious work that God has done in our midst through our Seminars, where many have come to faith in Christ, both in our own congregation, and from other congregations.

If we should see a new work of the Spirit among us, we shall seek to offer ourselves to God that the Kingdom of God may grow powerfully in our midst, and from this place. Should prove to be so, *we shall adopt the same policy that has been ours in the past: not to take people who come among us from other congregations, but to encourage them to find their future in their own congregations.*

RISING TIDE OF EXPECTATION IN OUR MIDST.

"I am grateful; for the advent of Terry Laverty to our Pastoral Team, for the devoted yeoman service of Heather Thompson, and for the investment of love and prayer of Helen Ritchie among our young people - and others. We look forward with faith and hope. In the immediate term, I feel there is still work for me - with Rhoda - to do in your midst."

DECEMBER WCN 1994 ALSO GIVES DETAILS OF:

Advent services into the New Year;
Update on Finances;
Call of Kirk Session to Terry Laverty for Ordination in January;
A Letter from Cecil Grant at Princeton;
Friday Morning Men's Group;
The news that Frank & Maureen Rea are to be Book Aid organisers for Northern Ireland;
News from the Dores at Wycliffe Bible Translators;
The 'Building Beginners' feature;
Comprehensive news from our Scouting groups;
B.B. Christmas Car Wash and Fair;
Christian Nationals news.

THE BEATITUDES OF ONE WHO IS OLD:

(Found among documents left by the Rev. Joseph McAteer).

BLESSED are those who understand my faltering step and palsied hand.

BLESSED who know my ears today, must strain to catch the things they say.

BLESSED are they who seem to know, that my eyes are dim and my wits are slow.

BLESSED are they who looked away, when coffee spilled at the table today.

BLESSED are they with cheery smile, who stop to chat for a little while.

BLESSED are they who never say: 'you told that story twice today'.

BLESSED are they who know the ways, to bring back memories of yesterdays.
BLESSED are they who make it known that I'm loved, respected and not alone.

BLESSED are they who know I'm at a loss to find more strength to bear my Cross.

BLESSED are they who ease the days on my journey Home in loving ways.

Author Unknown.

JANUARY WCN 1995.

GIVING WHAT WE HAVE RECEIVED!

"A little more than a quarter of a century ago, we entered a charismatic dimension of fullness in the Spirit, and, especially through our Seminars we have shared all that with many others, both within and outside our congregation.
We must not grow slack in this, but continue to invite others, out of hearts warmed by the Holy Spirit."

NOT AS SALESMEN SEEKING TO CLINCH A DEAL, TO OUR ADVANTAGE!

"I believe that when we invite people to come to a Seminar, we should not be like a salesman trying to clinch a deal to our own advantage... It should be as a grateful servant of the Lord Jesus Christ, knowing that in Him **there is immense good and blessing waiting for any who will receive him, in overflowing measure. We want to share the marvellous blessings of Christ,** *who lifts off heavy loads, who releases from stress and disease, who cleanses the conscience, and gives inner joy, peace and life! That's our goal!"*

ENCOURAGEMENT TO REACH OUT - FROM A BIRMINGHAM CHURCH.

Our son-in-law Geoffrey Lanham ministers in St. John's, Harborne, a large and vibrant congregation, that in terms of ethos and fellowship is not unlike West Church. While good at nurturing its young people and bringing them to faith, it came to realise that they were not at all successful in bringing outsiders and adults to faith in Christ. Recently it decided that it must make a real effort to address this unhappy situation.
It decided to attempt this through an ALPHA COURSE that over a

period of 14 weeks, seeks to lead unbelievers to knowledge of the Good News in Jesus.

INDUCEMENT TO COME.

Critical for the success of such a course is the warmth of invitation by members of the congregation to people that they know, and who respect them.

As well church services may be used to tell about the Course, and some services adapted for this purpose. *For example they found that quite a lot of uncommitted people come to the Christmas Carol Service. So into this service they incorporate elements of drama, witness and teaching that encouraged people to seek for that reality that touched them in such a warm, vibrant, spirit-filled service... If people said they enjoyed the service they could be invited to the ALPHA COURSE.*

FIRST COURSE IN AUTUMN OF 1994.

In St.John's their aim was to have 50 uncommitted people attending the first course. They actually just achieved that target, though genuine circumstances meant some loss in numbers. **However, at the time of writing about 30 of those, previously uncommitted people, have come to put their faith in Christ!**
WHAT A CHANGE! for years NO adult conversions, and now 30 in just a few months!

SOME PEOPLE ARE NATURAL EVANGELISTS!

Like our own late Margaret Gibson, so enthusiastic in her love for Jesus and in her care for people. It was no problem for Margaret to invite people to a Seminar or to a Healing Service. She often brought along people that she had met at the bus-stop, or that she happened to meet up with.

But even Margaret would have been hard-pressed to equal the record of one warm-hearted and unpretentious Birmingham lady, who brought thirteen people to the first Alpha Course and she's already ten queued up for the next one!

However, while there are some remarkable evangelists, every one of us, **who have a care for people in our hearts, and a confidence in respect of what Christ can do for them, is able to tell others about the good things that God is doing in our midst!**
AND OUR NEXT SEMINAR BEGINS ON WEDNESDAY 1ST FEBRUARY.

NO JOY EQUAL TO THIS!

"As I was leaving our son-in-law Geoffrey to the Airport for his flight back to Birminghma and to a crowded, awaiting schedule, he said that there is no joy quite like that of assisting a person to put faith in Jesus - and with that I entirely agree!

He mentioned a lady who had come to the Alpha Course, and who on the first night was so terrified that she hid away, for a while, in the toilets, and then, through Mary, our daughter, was pacified and made to feel at home and comfortable in the meeting. At the end of the first evening she asked Geoffrey if there were any Marriage Guidance counsellors in the Church. Geoffrey replied that he would think about it.
Half way through the course she was at the point of walking out on her marriage.
That evening Geoffrey told members in the Course, that if they had any problems, they should really talk seriously to God about them.
This woman went home, opened her Bible, and the first words her eyes landed upon were words of Jesus *that man should not put asunder what God had joined. Then she prayed seriously, and her perspective changed dramatically. In due course she put her faith in Jesus.*
Her husband, who has started to come to church, recently confided that at his work, he had prayed with one of his associates.
His wife has made no further enquiries about Marriage Counselling. Deeper, underlying attitudes have been dealt with and a new dynamic has entered her life.

A HEALING MINISTRY.

In the West Kirk Session Report for 1994, we read:
"We thank God for those involved in the healing ministry every Sunday evening after the evening service and that they do see the power of God at work today.

More spectacularly we witnessed the ministry of Jimmy Smith in West Church during February and again with the very different but powerful ministry of the Rev. John Coles and his wife Anne in October. So we learn that God's promises and God's power are available to the church today, something which we must all take seriously."

In the Kirk Session report our Clerk, William McClelland speaks of the encouragement we find in all who serve God in our congregation - choir and singing groups leading our worship; all who teach in Sunday School, who lead in Young West or in PWA, Tuesday Together, Friendship Group, seminars, Men's Friday Group, the Men's Fellowship; those who lead in all our youth organisations or in the not so young fellowship fun groups; those who work through drama or with difficult youngsters in non-uniformed situations -indeed anyone engaged in any work in the church family and outside like Abba Trust.

PASTORAL TEAM.

Our thanks go to the Pastoral Team whether in full service or recovering from illness, like Thomas and Julie, with our prayer that they may regain full health and vigour.
Heather and Helen have had a particularly demanding year of work and we give thanks for all that they have been able to accomplish as they have worked tirelessly with many groups and individuals, with loving care and deep concern.

The resignation from the Kirk Session of a beloved and dedicated elder, MRS ROSLYN WILSON has been a tremendous loss to us. Roslyn was an exemplary elder who cared for and prayed for the people committed to her care, a care which she exercised with a warm smile and a gracious personality. We thank her for her work and contribution to the life of this congregation over many years.

It is with particular delight that we welcome TERRY LAVERTY, HIS WIFE SANDRA AND THEIR FAMILY into the fellowship of West. Terry has already established himself in the work and in the esteem of the congregation and we look forward to a fruitful ministry in our midst."

In JANUARY WCN 1995 **TERRY LAVERTY** issues a *CALL TO MEN* in the congregation to meet with him on Thursday 26th January for a time of praise, to hear about Men's Fellowships in the church and consider the challenge of a 'March of One Thousand Men' in the autumn, *"so that we may come together to share ideas and dreams, and raise up an army of men who will lift high the Cross of Christ."*

YOUNG CHRISTIANS URGED TO BE ACTIVE IN 1995.

Terry Laverty urges young Christians to realise that they belong to the Body of Christ in West, to be active, not to hide their talents and find a job to do! He challenges them to take the opportunities of **short term mission**, declaring that he has a bulging file of information and ideas: **'Why not spend one or two of your nine summer weeks serving the Lord?'** He adds: 'You can **grow** if you are willing to **go!!   Ask Barry McCroskery!!'**

TERRY ALSO EXPRESSES APPRECIATION of
arrangements made for his Service of Ordination on 29th January, for those who had taken part and for generous gifts given to him and his family.

SHINE JESUS, SHINE!
Pamela Brow writes:
"SHINE JESUS, SHINE!" was so beautifully sung on Sunday evening at Terry's Ordination that I decided to listen to it again...
When I closed my eyes I saw Crumlin Road Belfast (outside the prison) on a very wet day. Cars, lorries etc. were speeding along the road and crowds of people were rushing along the pavement.
A little old lady was trying to cross the road, but no one stopped to help her.
From the prison gates emerged a prisoner, tall, well built, wearing a white tee-shirt and jeans, with tatoos on his arms... Very gently he took the old lady by the arm and led her across the road...

When I got home I decided to meditate on that very clear picture and asked the Lord to show me what it meant.
The people rushing were on their way to church! We all do the same getting the Sunday roast in the oven, dressing the children etc. But what about the old lady next door who would need a lift to Church on a wet Sunday? Is it time for us to 'wise up' and slow down, get our priorities right and give more **time** to people? To be more observant and see their needs and then deal with them, by love, friendship and prayer. We should get off our 'backsides' (me included!) and do this.

Let us all be ordained like Terry and witness for our precious Lord who has done so much for all of us.
'Shine Jesus, shine' *through us* and *let us* fill this land with the Father's glory."

GOD'S LOVE CAN BE SHARED IN SIMPLE WAYS.
Pamela Brow writes about our services in Carnalea Clinic.
"If you are free any Thursday morning between 11.15am and 12.15pm we would be delighted to have you with us.
You could help to turn the hymnbook pages for those residents who find it difficult. You could sit beside them during their short services and offer a smile, a kind listening ear, or just a touch upon a hand, or give a hug, **to be a channel of God's love and comfort and encouragement to these dear folk who are lonely and frail at this time in their lives.** Edna Byers has been helping us faithfully in this way, once a month since we began our services.
We hope, and indeed we feel, *that our presence and singing encourages the residents so much as we worship God together, and is really appreciated by them. In this way, they can receive a measure of God's blessing, love and peace, which ultimately helps to make the work of the nursing staff easier. If you feel you would like to help please ring....."*

OUR OWN "LETTER FROM AMERICA."
Cecil Grant, 24 January 1995.

"Hello everyone!
Well Christmas has come and gone, the Christmas trees have come down, the tinsel is stored away and turkeys everywhere can take a deep sigh of relief! Here in **Princeton** the campus is like a ghost town over the holidays as everyone went home. I had mountains of work to do so that kept me from being bored or lonely. **In addition my mum and dad sent me a big box of presents, so like big kids everywhere on Christmas Day I jumped out of bed, tore open my presents, and feasted on sweets, nuts and chocolate. It was great! And a BIG 'thank you' to everyone who sent me cards and letters, it was extremely kind and

thoughtful of you.

EXAMS!
For the last couple of weeks we have had exams, which meant people beavered away in their rooms all day, only to appear at mealtimes to get some food before scurrying back to their books. **It was surprising how pressurised everyone felt by the exams!**

VISIT TO THE WHITE HOUSE.
The exams finished last Tuesday (Praise the Lord!!), and so a friend and I went down to Washington D.C. for a couple of days. **This was my first week without any work since September so we made the most of it.**
We saw the Capitol and sat in on Congress, we went to see the graves of JFK **and Jackie Onassis, and had a personal tour of the White House by a secret service agent,** who was a friend of the person we were staying with. I got to stand in the Oval Office, and saw the Cabinet Rooms. Of course Bill and Hilary - that's the Clintons you know... they invited us to stay for tea, but we were pushed for time so had to say no - as you can imagine they were very disappointed! **Tomorrow sees the beginning of a new semester: more Greek, more theology, MORE WORK!!** Anyway I hope all is well in Bangor, and that you are having a happy and contented New Year."

ANNE SCOTT TELLS OF THE DISTRESS OF
SUDDEN UNEMPLOYMENT - and testifies to God's Faithfulness.

"Wednesday 28th September, 1994, was a beautiful autumn day. My husband, Brian, who is a Sales Representative, was to go to Omagh on that day, our son Richard was going to Queen's, and I was going to work as a part-time Medical Secretary.

A WEEPING COTONEASTER!
I had arranged on that particular day to meet my friend Heather, and we had lunch at Gillespie's Nursery at Gilnahirk. We enjoyed our lunch, and from there we went to Braeside Nursery at Gilnahirk, where I bought a weeping cotoneaster.
I arrived home about 4.00pm **and was surprised to see Brian's car in the driveway.** I wondered if he was ill, but before I got out of the car he came out to me, to tell me his firm had gone into liquidation and he was out of work. I cannot begin to describe my feelings which were of complete shock and despair. **Here was I home with a beautiful tree, on a beautiful day, only to find I was the sole bread-winner for our family. I deeply regretted having bought that tree.** However, Heather said **"go and plant the tree, as your tree of hope."**
This we did the next day. That Wednesday evening was a nightmare. **Brian is 62 years of age and we felt there was no chance that anyone would give him a job. Our son Richard said 'leave it with God', but it was very difficult not to be fearful for the future. Although I had my job we knew we could not meet all our bills on my salary alone.**
I did however thank God that it was only a job, because I knew how much worse things would have been if Brian had told me he had only a short time to live!
We talked of nothing else that evening. We knew we might have to sell our home if Brian didn't get a job.

CHRISTIAN RADIO.
I normally listen to a Christian Radio Station on my way to work each morning. At 8.30 am. there is a 5 minute talk by the Rev. Bob Gass. Just a few days previously he had been talking about what a **great God** we have. He said that God wants to deal with **all** our problems, not just part of them, and that God wouldn't do anything if we didn't hand **everything** over to Him. I know that God is able to do **'more exceeding abundantly more than we ask or think'**, and so I believed there and then that if we gave this whole problem to God He **would** deal with it.

NOTHING TO OFFER!
The next day we had to go and tell my Mum, and we were very concerned about this as she had had a heart attack in December, 1993. We were worried about this and how she would respond to our news. My Mum also, is a Christian, and although she was very upset for us, thankfully our news did not have any ill-effects on her. We knew she would be praying for us. The next evening was **'job night'** in the Belfast Telegraph, so we carefully examined every advertisement, and we found several jobs for which Brian could apply. He had, of course, already been to Gloucester House, and round many employment agencies to register his name, but they had nothing to offer.

NO REDUNDANCY.
Brian had been with his previous company for 14 years, and only changed his job in May 1994, so, as he had only been with this firm for 5 months there was no redundancy, and no month's notice, just one week's salary.
Brian applied for several jobs, but then we had to wait to see what would happen. We had given the WHOLE problem to God, and we were utterly dependent on Him.

A HIGH WALL OF LOVE.
We had many 'phone calls from our Christian friends, assuring us they were praying for us, and offering us help. **It seemed to us that we were surrounded by a high wall of love, and we knew that through these wonderful people, God Himself was letting us know how much He cared.**
It was amazing that the readings in "Our Daily Bread" were so appropriate to our needs. For instance, on the 29th September, the day after Brian came out of work the title was **"You have not passed this way before"**, and part of the reading states **"We too can become fearful sometimes as we look ahead, because we've never been there before....perhaps right now you are anxious about some new

and untried pathway on which the Lord is leading you. Then listen to God's Word and take courage: 'I will never leave you nor forsake you' (Hebrews 13:5). "Place your hand by faith into your Heavenly Father's hand, and let him lead the way."

"I have promised you My presence,
With you everywhere you go,
I will never leave you,
As you travel here below."

The readings on the 3rd, 4th, 5th October were also most appropriate, and on the 8th October the little verse read:
"When fear and worry test your faith,
And anxious thoughts assail,
Remember God is in control,
And He will never fail."

THE NORTH ANTRIM COAST.
We love the North Antrim coast, and always spend at least part of our holidays there. Some 5 years ago we decided to put an advertisement in the Coleraine Chronicle to see if we could perhaps get a small cottage to rent on a yearly basis. I prayed about this, and asked God to put us in touch with the right people if such a place was available. There were several replies, but a couple of these were for detached bungalows, which we did not want, and there was one for a cottage at Whitepark Bay. However we were unable to go immediately to see it, and when we were free to go a couple of weeks later, we discovered that a mix-up had occurred, and the cottage had already been let to someone else. However, some weeks after that, out of the blue, came a letter offering us a cottage in Ballintoy. We went to see the owner, and when we walked into her house we knew immediately she was a Christian. The cottage she offered was more than we had hoped for - again proving that God is able to do exceeding abundantly more than we ask or think. This started a wonderful friendship with Gretta McClelland. When Brian became unemployed we knew that one of the first things to go would have to be the cottage. We dreaded telling Gretta because she is a widow and she looks forward so much to having our company every week-end during the summer months.

SHE JUST PUT HER ARMS AROUND US.
We went to see her on the Saturday following Brian's news. She was very upset that Brian had lost his job, and just put her arms around us and cried with us. Then, without any hesitation, she said **"this cottage is here for you as long as you want it, and I will be very hurt if you don't come and use it."**
She couldn't afford to lose the rent for the cottage, yet she reached out to us in love, and was totally unconcerned about the money she would lose. We were so deeply moved by her love and concern for us. She also gave us a little book entitled "Comfort for Troubled Christians." It was the most wonderful little book we had ever read, excluding the Bible, of course. That little book instructed us completely to believe on the promises of God, and He *would* fulfil them.

"I WILL SUPPLY ALL YOUR NEEDS."
I constantly held in my mind God's promise **"I will supply all your needs"**, and we trusted He would do just that. We had to believe it because we couldn't continue in our home if we didn't trust God completely.

Brian then had a couple of replies to his job applications, and was to attend for interview at two of the companies. The first interview went very well, but as the Head Office of the company was in England he was told he might have to come back for another interview in a couple of weeks time, when arrangements could be made for Head Office staff to be present. He then went for the second interview, and was offered a job provided he could meet a certain target within a 6 month period. He was given a few days to think about this. The following day he received a letter from the first company requesting him to attend for a second interview 10 days later.

A FLEECE BEFORE GOD.
We were then in a situation where Brian had to decide whether to take the job which had been offered, or wait for the interview which was to take place ten days later, following which he might not even be offered the job. No salary had been discussed for either job, so we really didn't know what to do. **We knew we had to pick the right job, or it could be disastrous. How we wished God could send us a letter to guide us!** *Then I remembered the story of Gideon and the fleece (Judges 6: 36), and we decided to put a fleece before God.*

THE SALARY AND THE FLEECE.
As previously stated, no salary had been discussed, so we chose a figure which was quite a bit less than Brian had been earning previously, and we asked God to confirm that this was the right job for Brian by letting the salary be the amount we had chosen, or above, and that a letter of confirmation would be provided stating that Brian would be permanently employed if he met his required target figure. *We also knew that, although we were extremely anxious for Brian to get a job, that we must turn the job down if the salary offered was even £100 less than the figure we had placed before God. This made us a little nervous but we both knew that if we were placing a figure before God as a 'fleece', then we MUST TURN THE JOB DOWN EVEN IF IT WAS ONLY £5 LESS THAN THE GIVEN FIGURE.*

EXACTLY THE FIGURE.
Brian went for the interview, and when the salary figure was given to him, **he was absolutely amazed that it was exactly the figure we had placed before God- it was neither £1 over or £1 less.** In

addition to this he was told a letter would be sent to him confirming the details of the appointment. God, therefore had responded to the fleece placed before Him, *and we knew this was the job for Brian to accept. He started work again on 31st October, 1994.*

HE DOES KEEP HIS PROMISES.

We are so grateful to God for all He has done for us. We have proved that "He is the same, yesterday, today and forever." If only we would completely trust Him for everything - **He does keep his promises.** He says "**I will never leave you nor forsake you**", and He certainly did not leave us in our trouble. We were surrounded by the love and prayers of all our Christian friends, who kept in constant touch with us, offering support in every possible way. He says "**I will meet all your needs**", and He certainly did that, again through a **wonderful Mum, and Christian friends.**

Our 'weeping cotoneaster' is flourishing in the garden, and will always remind us of the despair we felt on the day it was bought, and how God taught us how much we can trust Him if we give Him all our problems, and trust Him to deal with them."

LETTER FROM REGENT-
BRIAN & CHRISTINE MARTIN.

The Martins, five months into their year at Regent College send Christmas greetings, rejoice in the opportunities and experiences that they have had, the splendour of the North American "Fall"; the multi-cultural experience at Regent, the awareness of God's presence and provision. They report that their young family are well and that 'studies at Regent continue to go well and we both feel quite part of the community; Greek proves to be a continual challenge but one which so far is manageable. We want to express our sincere thanks to those of you who are standing with us both in prayer and financially.'

MISSIONARY RETURNED!
BARRY McCROSKERY.

Barry McCroskery has been returned to us after a two-year stint with Operation Mobilisation in France, and **Marcel Georgel** has given him a good report!
OM team support in Asnieres has helped a congregation of ten to grow to one where 20 -25 people attend regularly and Barry has been a part of the team involved in active evangelism.
He has been involved in a study and training programme; he has grown in boldness and faith and is also a good listener.

Marcel Georgel has also enclosed a pamphlet on "Helping your Missionary to bounce back"
He points out that short-term missionaries often go abroad with **stars in their eyes. They dream of great things happening in the field. They're admired for their dedication. They feel supported by everyone. But usually they are poorly prepared for the task. They're often surprised by what they find,** *and they can be even more surprised by what they find when they return.*

When abroad, short termers tend to assume that life back home remains the same. It's startling then, to return and discover change. Friends have married, purchased homes, changed jobs, moved. Any of these changes can create a feeling of insecurity.
PERSONAL REACTIONS.
Because of his or her own commitment and sacrifice, the returnee may see friends and others as being uncommitted to the priority of sharing the gospel with the entire world. The person may be right. It becomes easy to see usual spending habits as lavish, foolish and unspiritual. The casual £10 date would feed a family for days, maybe weeks. Houses that cost £70,000 would support the entire mission programme. The price of a Christian music tape could support a national missionary for a week. These seeming excesses can cause judgemental reaction, leading to bitterness and disillusionment.
Often the short term missionary returns without a clear vision for the next step in their lives.

These are matters of which the home congregation should be aware, so as to help him to **bounce back!**

MARCH WCN 1995.

IT CAN BE *INTIMIDATING* TO ENTER A CHURCH *FOR THE FIRST TIME!*
TWO EXPERIENCES OF WEST.

1. A person who has been coming to West for the past few months has taken her place, Sunday by Sunday *in different parts of the Church!* **That's unusual for we tend to be creatures of habit! Unusual unless one comes fairly late and it's a question of getting a seat anywhere!**
Well, this person relates **that every time at the end of the service, the people immediately behind, as she turns round, greet** *her and introduce themselves! Isn't that marvellous?* **Maybe not everyone is so fortunate, but it is encouraging for us to hear of such a level of warmth and friendliness.**

2. **On Sunday past, after Terry had pointed out that it can be painful - if you're currently unemployed- to be asked what your job is, a lady at the end of the service told him that her experience in West has been, that while people greet you,** *that has never been a question asked!*

One relates these two incidents, not to give ourselves a pat on the back, *but to help us all to be aware of the need to show sensitive friendliness!*

WEST CHURCH BANGOR ONWARD JOURNEY   WEST CHURCH BANGOR ONWARD

WANTED; BANNERMAKERS!

Wanted: new recruits for the Banner-Making Group.
No pressure. No sewing skills (if you can sew on a button that's good enough!)
Good conversation and a cup of coffee (or two) guaranteed.
Wednesday Mornings, 10.30 - 12.30 in Number '91' during school term time. If you are interested just come along; our production rate needs a boost - perhaps you have noticed that there is nothing to replace the Christmas Banners at the front!
We are working on it, but extra hands would help.

LIZ BAIRD   ANNE ANDERSON.

BOOK AID SAYS "WELL DONE, WEST!"
In response for an appeal for Christian Books, Bibles and Ladybird books, West have brought 1197 such books during the last couple of weeks, and Frank & Maureen Rea say "Well done - and bring more!."

BLASPHEMY (ABOLITION) BILL.

A number of our members, alerted by United Christian Broadcasters inspired our folk in West to pray about this issue and to write to members of the House of Lords. Anne Scott writes:
"Thanks to all those who wrote to the House of Lords in respect of this obnoxious Bill which was before the House of Lords on the 22nd February. As I am sure everyone knows, the Bill was defeated by 25 votes to 14. I make no comment with respect to the fact that only about 40 people were bothered even to attend the debate!"

APRIL WCN 1995.

NEEDS, OPPORTUNITIES, RESOURCES.
AN ANALYSIS OF WEST CHURCH TODAY.

For quite some time we have been painfully aware that, in spite of running, we have sometimes not quite managed to hold our ground!

NOT THE RESOURCES NEEDED!
Many churches complain that they have not the resources in personnel that they require, to do all the work that needs to be done, to grasp the opportunities that plead to be grasped.
IN WEST WE ARE FAVOURED!
We can consider ourselves more fortunate than many!
One could not listen, for example, to the reports given by **Pat McNutt** on Sunday School work and Christian Education,
or by Mervyn Callender on Youth Work involving the uniformed and non-uniformed organisations, to realise that *we have almost one hundred people helping in each of these sectors!*

OUR CONGREGATION GENERATES NEW LIFE!
Our congregation generates new life in Christ- *that is why we have so many helpers! So many prepared to serve Christ in a whole variety of ways!*

FROM THE MINISTER'S PERSPECTIVE.
The minister is well aware of excellent work being done, but not blind to the places where we fall short, of gaping holes in ministry, of situations that need to be retrieved. **And one can be a bit overwhelmed by the awareness of all this!**
Therefore at our Annual Meeting, it was important to pick out nine situations, where over the past year or so, *we still managed to make progress and could rejoice in new, up building developments.*

1. 11.30 am Service. Greater numbers, participation, spiritual buoyancy, *with whole families entering into the singing and worship in a much enhanced manner.*

2. Wednesday Night Prayer Meeting. Increased numbers, and the sense of fellowship and spiritual vitality.

3. Scouting/ Guiding organisations. A new sense of dynamic, additional committed leaders, as evidenced in the recent **Thinking Day service.**

4. Friday Morning's Men's Group. The success of this group led by **Walter McAllister** and **Billy Hanlon**, and the positive input into the lives of retired men.

5. Praise Services for Women - no less than two of these, one morning, one evening scheduled for early April.

6. The notable development of Prayer Counselling and Deliverance ministry.

7. More extensive and intensive times of Prayer.

8. The emergence of Expression of Faith - a young people's group, with the desire to carry the Gospel out beyond the confines of our church buildings, to people who would not normally hear it.

9. The Tape Ministry for the elderly and shut-in. David Baillie spends two and a half days a week visiting homes with these recordings of our services.

Having given these nine examples at the Annual Meeting, I asked if others would like to add to them. Three more examples were given.

10. The coming of Terry Laverty.

**11. The visible improvement in

the health of Thomas Mulholland.

12. Continuing blessing through the Life in the Spirit Seminars and the testimony of people beyond our congregation to their helpfulness.

Apart from this, **there's the vast amount of work that proceeds from year to year, faithfully done by a host of our members, whether individually or through the many groups and organisations within West.**

SITUATIONS THAT NEED SPECIAL NURTURE.

The massive input of Alvin Little among our young people is sorely missed, and while we applaud what others have done, we still have a situation that needs to be addressed.

We long for a spiritual breakthrough among the young people who meet informally on a Tuesday Night.

We endeavour TO REACH OUT through Marriage Preparation Seminars; through Parenting Seminars; through having a strong teaching/ministry team from Ellel Grange come to us in June; through Cross-Fertilisation between congregations- through a brief visit to Iain McNie's church in Girvan; through a large group that will visit us from Arthur Young's church in London.

Of course we know that without the enlivening breath of God's Spirit we can accomplish nothing.

Our Kirk Session has made an evaluation of our situation, and recognises rich opportunities that lie ahead, a massive amount to be undertaken, sufficient to keep us all at full stretch.

JULIE HAMILTON TO LEAVE WEST.

We have been depleted through Pastoral Team illnesses, over the past 18 months as far as Thomas is concerned, and the past year as far as Julie is concerned.
In the circumstances of congregational needs not being met, it has been reluctantly felt necessary to make staff changes, in order to grasp the future.
**Julie has been off work, for almost a year now, and the Kirk Session, very reluctantly, felt it to be right not to call her back into service, but to terminate her employment with us.
In our letter to the Deputy Clerk of Assembly we acknowledge excellent work done in pulpit ministry and in seminars, in time past, while handing her back into the hands of the PWA, who are her ultimate employers, with responsibility for her.**

In our formal letter to Julie, we assured her of the fund of affection felt for her in Kirk Session and in the congregation as a whole, with the prayer that she may find God's purpose for her life in the time ahead.

The Kirk Session believes that we are at a time of rebuilding for the future, and we solicit the prayers of our whole congregation, in changes that are made.

OUR GOD:
**Father to the fatherless,
Brother to the Brotherless,
Prince of Peace!!!
TERRY LAVERTY bears witness.**

STUCK IN A TIME WARP.
"One of the things that seems to hold people back from a total abandonment of their future into the hands of the all-knowing and all-powerful God is **that we carry so much pain from past experiences in our lives...*and that we don't seem to have the ability to let go!!***
The result is that we get stuck in a time warp. We live our lives through the spectacles of the past... *and the result is that we are not really FREE to move on and to grow as people.* Our growth has been stunted by events in the past which hurt so badly!

DISASTER STRUCK OUR FAMILY.
I was born in Ballycastle as the fifth child in a family of seven - four boys and three girls.
Life in our house was always very busy, as you can imagine... and everybody in the town and district knew Jimmy and Jean Laverty very well. **My dad was a hill farmer**, who began a small butcher's shop on the seafront, to supplement their income. **Mum had the Midas touch.** She could turn her hand to anything - and she was renowned for her 'bed and breakfast' provision in the summertime. Disaster struck the family when I was a lad of four. My dad had a massive heart attack at the age of 38, and so my mum was left with 7 children (the youngest only nine months) **and I no longer had a father.**

JUST ENOUGH!
The years that followed were hard but happy. Mum sold the house and the shop... and had just enough to buy a house. **In fact, those words *just enough* would just about describe the first 15 years of my life.** We never wanted anything but there was never a surfeit!! Nevertheless I can testify that God really was a Father to me and a Husband to my dear mother, *whose ingenuity and sheer devotion to the seven in her care has been recognised by all who knew her.* The words of 2 Corinthians 12:9 have always meant a lot to me. In them God says **"My grace is sufficient for you, for my power is made perfect in your weakness."** *I can certainly testify to the truth of these words, over and over again!*

MY BROTHER MURDERED.
But God has not only been a Father to the Fatherless, He has also been a Brother to the brotherless!! I had three brothers. Jimmy is the eldest-

a landscape gardener. Shane is the youngest - a teacher and a father of triplets! I had another brother, who was two years older than me. His name was Robert and he was a really popular guy. He joined the police when he was just 18... and six months after he passed out of the depot in Enniskillen, **he was brutally murdered in an IRA gun attack.**

I can't really describe that experience in this short article. It was a time of great pain and desperate loss, especially for my mother, BUT *the Lord was very gracious to us through it all, not least by the way He put caring people in our paths.*
Terrorist murder was a hard pill for a sixteen year old to swallow ...but I thank God that he delivered me from any bitterness or malice that could so easily have polluted my life from that day onwards.

"It is mine to avenge; I will repay" says the Lord.
These words from Romans 13: 19 ministered to the heart and mind of that broken and confused teenager, and I just thank God that he has given me the desire NOT to be overcome with evil, but to overcome evil with good (v 21)

THE NEARNESS OF GOD.
I didn't become a Christian until I was 22, but I can honestly say that I **knew** the nearness of God in so many ways in the years following that blight on my family. JESUS has never replaced my brother that I loved so dearly, **but He has been very near to me, especially at those times when my heart sank very low, as I relived the *pain of* the past.**

DON'T SUFFER IN SILENCE!
Maybe you're a teenager, who has gone through the mill recently, as your family has been torn apart by death or divorce?? **Please...***don't* **suffer in silence!! Try to find someone to cry with... to get the anger out with. It made all the difference to me when I was a** broken 16-year old. Maybe it could help you?

YOU DON'T HAVE TO GO THROUGH IT ALONE!
Perhaps you're past your teens now, but the pain lives on just the same? It's a sad fact of life that none of us can avoid some kind of pain or suffering. **But I'd just like to say that *you don't have to go through it ALONE!!***
When I lost my father, it was the love of God through **others** that sustained me. When I lost my brother, it was the love and prayers and tears of others that carried me and lifted me up.
When my wife and I lost our third child just 17 weeks after conception, it was the love and casseroles and childminding of others that saw us through, so that somehow we could say *it was all right even when it was all wrong!!*

DEEPER INNER PEACE.
God uses people to pour his love and peace into our troubled lives, but it wasn't until I was 22 that I discovered that deeper, **inner peace that comes from knowing Jesus as my Saviour and Lord.**
He has enabled me in some measure, *to leave the past behind.*
He has promised me a bright future... and so I'm on the move, with expectancy and faith that I know who holds the future.

The past still haunts me sometimes, *but I know it's just a shadow now.*
I can face the Valley of the Shadow now, because **I'm not alone,** *and I'm not burdened down with bitterness or pain from the past.*

MOVING ON WITH JESUS.
I'm free!! and I'm moving on with Jesus. Jesus said "If the Son will set you free, *you shall be free indeed!! (John 8: 36)*

WHY NOT LOOK TO JESUS?
I dare say that you have already tried lots of different things to try to break free from the pain of your past. **Why not look to Jesus?** He's the One they call THE PRINCE OF PEACE!

A CHRISTIAN INITIATIVE IN OUTREACH.
A BOOK/GIFT SHOP.
Brian and Carol Moorhead have recently celebrated their first year at the *Vineyard, The Christian Book and Gift Shop,* which they opened at The Grapevine Restaurant, Conlig, last March.
Apart from having a healthy year financially, they have experienced a great deal of pleasure in serving many, many people with God's Word through books, music and other products.
Unlike most Christian bookshops, a lot of 'non-Christians' use the shop and many items with texts and verses find their way into homes where God's Word might not otherwise be.
Within the last week or so they have received the very encouraging news that a girl's life was dramatically changed as a result of reading a book which was given as a gift just at the right moment!
Although the plan was to open the shop for strictly one year only - 'to see how things went' - Brian and Carol have been so pleased with the results that they have decided to continue with the work for the foreseeable future."

OUR THEOLOGICAL STUDENTS ABROAD.
As in 1994 our Special Easter Offering will be for the support of our three theological students. Here we give excerpts from Easter Greetings from Brian Martin at Regent College and Cecil Grant from Princeton.
BRIAN writes:
"Regent continues to provide for me a very rich and relevant preparation for future ministry and service. The required reading, though the thickness of a telephone directory, **encourages me and causes me to marvel at the reality of Scripture.** With professors like J.I. Packer, James Houston and Gordon Fee, to name but a few, I

am continually challenged and inspired.....

I was recently invited to preach at a Mennonite Brethren Church at Bowen Island (closest place I know to heaven- outstanding beauty), so all the family made the journey over to the island. **The church meets in the local school and consists of approximately 30 members. They expressed great interest in our reasons for being at Regent, so much so, that they pledged to assist us financially in our endeavour. For this we are truly thankful as it brings the possibility of completing the full degree programme at Regent so much closer..."**

CECIL WRITES:

."..I hope you are all well and beginning to enjoy spring. Here in Princeton the birds have returned, the trees are budding, and the temperature is rising! At the minute the weather is very unpredictable, one day it can be wet and cloudy, and then the next day it can be incredibly hot.
We have just begun our Easter "break", the Seminary gave us three days off for Easter, but they also gave us three papers to write as well, just so we wouldn't get rusty!
In one of my papers I have to analyse what the Letter to the Hebrews teaches about Jesus, and in another I have to discuss the state of Christianity in modern Latin America, so we cover a wide variety of topics.

BACK-WOODS WEST VIRGINIA.

In about 4 weeks we finish for the summer. As part of my course I have to work with a church (isn't that a strange thing for a trainee minister to do!), and the Seminary insisted that I do this in the States, so I will be travelling down to a small town called **Welch**, in back-woods West Virginia, where I will be the minister in charge of two small Presbyterian churches. **Welch** is situated in a very poor area, so the churches have been unable to attract a full-time minister.
If you have ever seen the **Waltons** on TV, that will give you some idea of the type of community in which I'll be working; very mountainous, the people are laid-back, and they all love **Country & Western music!** But it's OK - I've bought ear-plugs!! **It is going to be an incredible experience to say the least.**

SECULARISED.

On a different note, over these past few months I have come to realise how much America is secularised. **Religion is very much a private affair to be kept out of the public realm. I think we are increasingly seeing this trend towards a secular society in Northern Ireland, where even a Council decision not to open a leisure centre on Sundays was considered religious discrimination.**
Yet Easter reminds us that *the Gospel can never be reduced to a private affair. The same Lord, who was publicly executed on Good Friday, publicly burst forth from death on Easter Sunday. If this really happened then this is headline news not Chinese Whispers!*
May God help us all to be his "witnesses in Jerusalem, and in all Judea... and to the ends of the earth" (Acts 1: 8)."

PARENTS - DO 'POWER RANGERS' WORRY YOU?

Recently in one of our Seminar groups, a Christian teacher expressed concern over the fact that some of her primary age pupils *seemed to be obsessed by the phantasy world of 'Power Rangers', and that violent attitudes and behaviour seemed to be spilling out of the children: she felt it was related to the morning watching of 'Power Rangers'.*

At our Annual meeting **Mervyn Callender** gave an altogether excellent and challenging report on our young people's work, in the course of which **he mentioned that as he had been going down the Rathmore Road a few nights earlier, he came upon a fracas involving youngish children. He was horrified to see one youngster on the road being kicked on the head!**

It seems that somehow the moral controls that used to inhibit such vicious behaviour that can cripple for life have somehow been removed.
Another lady, in the same group as the Christian teacher mentioned above, told of an incident where a teenage lad was plucked from his fellows, pulled away by a group, *who likewise began to kick him on the head and that without any provocation at all.*

We need to consider what kind of society we are creating.

NOTE: These were new and noteworthy phenomena beginning to emerge in 1995!

MAY WCN 1995.

May WCN tells us of a number of visitors coming to West during May/June.
One of these is a New Zealander, **IAN GRANT**, who comes on Friday 12 May, under the auspices of Youth For Christ. His SEMINAR will be:
PARENTING WITH CONFIDENCE.

LIKE AN AIRPORT.

"The modern family", says Ian Grant "is like an airport, with everyone going in different directions. Research has shown its members spend an average of 30 seconds a day in meaningful conversation.
"We're saying a family needs time."
"We" is Ian Grant and his wife Mary, who have worked with young people for over 30 years, and now have a grand plan to inspire families all over the country"
Ian Grant says that by running **an early parenting seminar in**

Auckland, they discovered *a gaping wound in society.* Requests came in from all parts of the country, and hundreds of such seminars are now planned.

THE BALANCE BETWEEN PARENTS.
Getting the balance right between parents **is essential to good child rearing.**
Men shouldn't expect their wives to do the things their mothers did. Times are different, "She works. My son and I iron our own clothes."
After 30 years of marriage, not always perfect, he says his wife "loves me to listen to her. I have to discipline myself. I'd rather fix things up around the house, or make sure she has the best gear available."

CHILDREN BORN AFTER THE SECOND WORLD WAR.

Such children have an increasingly difficult environment in which to grow up.
Children lost their innocence in the 50s. They had to learn about **sex when they didn't want to know,** but had to know because of the society we were in. **After the age of rock 'n roll, children lost their parents as their controlling authorities and their peers became their controlling authorities.**
Then in the 70s they lost love. Sex became the big thing. Most girls give sex hoping to get love. Boys give the promise of love hoping to get sex. **In the 70s they still hadn't learned you couldn't have love when somebody went off the next day.**
In the 80 s hope was gone. We had the concept that the world might be blown up. **In the 90's you might not have a job.**

Ian Grant has advice for solo parents and "reconstituted families" His aim is to have all parents establishing "self-nurturing and self-governing families. When there is happiness in the family there will be contentment in the community and prosperity in the nation."

One of his personal aims is to maintain his "best pals" relationship with his children.

PARENTING SKILLS CAN BE LEARNT.
Ian Grant says that through his Seminar "Parenting with Confidence" his aim is to raise awareness of the importance of parenting to **the whole health of society.**
He declares that the 2 key elements in a happy family **are humour and communication. He believes many parents take themselves too seriously and being part of a family should be fun, with lots of celebration.**

CELEBRATE!!
Families should use any excuse to celebrate, for example big birthday parties with everyone saying something positive to the birthday person!
COMMUNICATION is also crucial, and parents must take time to talk and listen to their children.
So many parents make sure their children are eating properly and wearing the right clothes, but when did they last make time for conversation?
QUALITY TIME.
He suggests that families designate two nights a week to sit down and have a meal with the whole family present, or that the entire family goes for a walk together.
Good parents should smother their kids with lots of hugs and warm fuzzies, and tell them they're proud of them -*but not to the point where they become self-esteem junkies.*

13-STRONG TEAM FROM LONDON.
The group of young people, led by Arthur Young, and accompanied by the Rev. Malcolm Boulter and his wife Pauline arrived in West on the evening of the Saturday 17th May and brought great warmth and refreshment with them. They led in our Sunday services, and were with us for about a week, mainly on a bed-and-breakfast basis in the homes of West members, going out during each day for excursions.

It was a happy co-incidence that when they arrived on the Saturday evening we were in the midst of a wonderful BELCANTO CONCERT! The music of Belcanto has won appreciation for its vibrant quality and inspired arrangements.
Our party from London were baptised into a veritable atmosphere of heavenly worship in glorious Christian hymns and songs and likewise enjoyed the releasing happiness of captivating secular songs and music!

MAY WCN 1995.
LIFE IN THE SPIRIT SEMINARS. As one turns over the pages of West Church News, one finds frequent notices in respect of the starting of new Seminars. In May 1995 a Seminar that started in September 1994 came to its conclusion. Our records show that 35 people enrolled in that Seminar. We can still read the names of those who enrolled, but it is quite impossible to compute the spiritual effects on all the people involved. Most of them were from West, but a considerable number were from beyond our own congregation. The first two names enrolled were those of RON & RUTH WILSON from Belfast. We do know how it blessed them for they have written about it in WITNESS SHEET 81, under the heading:

"IT'S NEVER TOO LATE TO START AGAIN"

"And the God of all grace.... will Himself restore you and make you strong, firm and steadfast."

A SAD TIME.

"As Ruth and I look back on those days before we came to West, we realise just how spiritually low we had become. There was a time when we had been enthusiastic for the Lord and enjoying the tasks He had called us to do. **But without realising it, a gradual decline came about in our enthusiasm. Tasks became less enjoyable, our vision had become clouded, and our hopes unfulfilled.** It was a sad time for us as we realised we had lost a sense of belonging, and we knew we had to do something about it.

We prayed much about the situation and asked the Lord to show us what we should do. It was some time later that he began to show us the way forward. He chose a former member of West as his signpost."

CHRIS McWILLIAMS.

"I was a patient in the Ulster Hospital, when I met Chris McWilliams, who was also a patient at the time. When I discovered that Chris was a Christian, I shared with him about how we felt spiritually dry, and how we had been praying for a way out of the dryness. **Chris told me about the new "Life in the Spirit" seminars which were held regularly in West, and recommended that we should consider attending a series.**

The following September, Ruth and I came to our first seminar in West. *The Seminar continued until May of the following year and over those eight wonderful months the Lord graciously breathed new life into us. The Scriptures once again became alive for us and we were once more experiencing the warmth of a loving fellowship.*

And so, over a period of some months the Lord has gently led us to come to West and since that time the "God of all grace has restored us and is making us strong, firm and steadfast." We thank Him with all our hearts, for His faithfulness to us, His patience with us, and the opportunity He has given us to start afresh and enjoy the tasks which He has prepared in advance for us to do."

JUNE/JULY WCN 1995.

DELIVERANCE FROM OPPRESSION, WHOLENESS IN CHRIST. WE WELCOME A TEAM FROM ELLEL GRANGE.

On the 14/15 June we shall host a 2-day Conference, primarily for the benefit of our own members.

FREE FROM OPPRESSION.

Even a cursory perusal of the Gospels shows Jesus involved in setting people free from *every kind of oppression*. Likewise He gave his apostles authority over evil spirits of every kind.
Very recently I heard a person say, with awe, gratitude and wonder:
"Now I am free! I had believed Satan's lie" -the lie was that as a Christian he had to bear the tyranny, onslaught and unceasing pressure of lust and perverted thoughts.
But now after ministry in Jesus' Name, HE WAS FREE!

ABUSE, TRAUMA, DRUGS, THE OCCULT.

People in life can undergo much abuse and trauma, many hurtful relationships, damage from drugs or the occult, the fall-out from a society where God and His clean commandments are discarded and despised as antediluvian. **There's a huge harvest to be reaped** *among people who need to be set free.*

"EVERYMAN" PROGRAMME.

"Last Sunday evening A BBC "Everyman" programme drew attention to the fact that there can be crude and unenlightened practioners in deliverance who can do great damage when they venture into this field, and spoke of Peter Horrobin of Ellel Grange in very derogatory terms. Naturally this can raise questions and doubts in the minds of our members, as we invite an Ellel Grange team to lead a conference in our midst.

NO PROFESSION EXEMPT FROM MAKING MISTAKES.

There is no profession exempt from making mistakes, or from having their 'cowboys'; but we do not damn the whole medical profession, or the social services, or the building industry, or anybody else, *by citing some cases of neglect, mis-diagnosis or malpractice. As well, it is true that people grow in knowledge and expertise in the course of time: this also applies to the field of DELIVERANCE.*

EVERYMAN MISSED THE MARK!

EVERYMAN grievously missed the mark when they maligned a college of expertise in this sector at Ellel Grange. **No doubt Ellel Grange has grown in expertise over the past 8 years. They have thousands of people who queue up for their wide range of courses, including deliverance.** Their ministry is carried on without shouting and histrionics, with a quiet sense of authority in the presence of Jesus. We have West Church members who bear witness to that fact. **We confidently invite Ellel Grange to West to teach a broad-based and balanced course on** *Wholeness in Christ* **- and we invite others to join us.** *Come and See!*

KEN SYMINGTON BEARS WITNESS:

"**Having watched the "Everyman" programme on television, I feel that it is important to put the record straight on the ministry of Ellel Grange.**

I have attended three training programmes under their ministry - two at their Ellel Grange headquarters in Lancashire, and one at Glyndley Manor in Kent - and I know of approximately a dozen others within, or closely associated with our church who have also attended.

The founder, Peter Horrobin is a quite remarkable man. In just eight years the Lord has used him to establish a much needed ministry in England, Canada and Hungary. He also organises the Brighton Christian Conferences, *"The Church Ablaze"* and *"The Day of his Power."*

He has just recently purchased a huge property in Sussex, called *Pierpont* at a price of over £2,000,000, which like the other centres, he bought on faith, and is now praying in the money.

The property is virtually a village in size, and will be used to train Christian workers from all over the world, in every aspect of ministry.

He has seen thousands come to faith, and thousands healed and delivered. *All this is from a nil start some eight years ago!*

Our own West ministry team has benefited immeasurably from their input, as many can affirm.

DISGUSTED!

I was 'disgusted' during the EVERYMAN programme to hear one man claim that Peter Horrobin was a 'man obsessed', accusing him of something so outrageous that I wouldn't even mention it again. *That a man with an obvious grudge is allowed to make such unsubstantiated claims on national television without any witnesses or evidence to support his claim seems hardly possible, but it happens.*

Any man of God has to run the gauntlet. Peter, I suspect, has to run it more than most. *Please come and hear the Ellel team when they come to West and decide for yourself. They are special!"*

THOMAS MULHOLLAND
TELLS OF HIS HEALING EXPERIENCES AT ELLEL.

[NOTE: West Church members know that Thomas Mulholland has spent almost two years with us, largely undermined by ill-health, but have seen a substantial change of late. Thomas here bears witness to benefit received at Ellel.]

"This month sees the visit of a group from Ellel Grange to West. Due to a recent television programme, some questions may have been raised as to what exactly is going to happen during that time, and just exactly what kind of people are going to come, expounding what kind of beliefs??? **These are valid questions, ones which should be exercised** *with regard to anyone's ministry.*
However, should we let our opinions be formed by the media portraying Ellel and their ministries in a negative light with unsubstantiated claims?
What has happened in the past I cannot tell. I can merely recount my experience of two Healing Retreats at Ellel.

I WAS ILL.

I was ill for some considerable time and went to their healing retreats **seeking God's face on this issue. When I arrived I was greeted by people who treated me with love, care and tenderness. Their devotion to God and passion for Jesus was clear and obvious.**
They were a people who were there not to expound their own particular beliefs. *They simply desired those who came to meet with God.*
We had times of Praise and Bible Study. The Praise was tremendous, and similar to the Praise in West.
The Bible Studies undertaken while I was there focussed on *forgiveness, the Prodigal Son, and how to move forward with God. They taught the whole counsel of God and not just selected bits.*
It was a healing retreat, but they did not believe that *they* did the healing, **rather it was by God's grace.**
The healing involved healing of every sort, physical, emotional and spiritual. **However the overall concern was to surround the** person (i.e. they did not treat the person as a catalogue of illnesses) **with the love of the Father, and to deal with any issue that prevented the person from knowing Him as such.** *Everything was done in a quiet, orderly, gentle, graceful and tender manner.*

TWO WAYS TO ASSESS THIS MINISTRY.

At the end of the day, there are only two ways to assess what they do. T **The first, by the character of the people involved, and second by the fruit of their ministry.**
They are a humble graceful people who desire to walk ever closer with Jesus, to glorify Him, and to bring the love of Jesus in a real way to all who walk through their doors.
In Galatians 5:22 we read that the fruit of the Spirit is love, joy, peace, patience, kindness, goodness, faithfulness, gentleness and self-control. Against such things there is no law" **This was present in all I met at Ellel.**
Second their fruit. In Matthew 7: 20 Jesus says, "By their fruit you will recognise them."
That, I think you have all seen in me since my return from their healing retreat.
This month, when they come to West, you will have opportunity to see them, hear their teaching and assess the fruit of their ministry."

OTHER WEST WITNESSES:

Other people who bore written witness to Ellel ministry in the June/July WCN are Glenda Eddis, Robin & Sharon Bryans and Linda Cummings.
WCN Editor, David Bailie writes:

A WESTERN, RATIONALISTIC MIND-SET EXCLUDES THE SUPERNATURAL EVEN IN THE CHURCH!

"I remember a time, now more than 25 years ago, when, to speak about the fullness of the Spirit, or the gifts of the Spirit or anything that seemed so irrational as 'speaking in

SENIOR DEPARTMENT OF SUNDAY SCHOOL.
Led by Eleanor Baillie, assisted by John McConnell, Jack Gardiner and Joan McClure.

An inspiration of the Spirit given to Margaret Conroy showing the need to provide Christian education and worship for those with mental disabilities led directly to the formation of the SYCAMORE CLUB.
Top left we have a picture of Margaret with William and to the right her daughter Gillian with Ryan. Beth Myatt and Heather Ennis played the guitar for worship, and fully helped in the work of the Club. Another young helper in the early days was Neil Sinclair. In more recent years the work of the Sycamore Club has greatly expanded, under the leadership of Derek and Tanya Polley and a team of gifted and enthusiastic helpers. For more information see Index.

REV. TOM SMAIL, with his wife Truda, had strategic input into the life of West, see Index. LINDA CUMMINGS, with Renee Robinson provided thousands of Alpha meals. JANET WOOD, veteran deaconess had much to give in West, and takes services in Carnalea Clinic. MAUREEN KENNEDY, great input into West, taught many to play guitar. JILL YOUNG became member of Rostrevor Christian Renewal Centre. John Bingham, Harold McCaughan, Anne Andrews, Sylvia Taggart among those with a welcome ministry in West.

WEST CHURCH PASTORAL TEAM IN THE MID-NINETIES.

Bobby Liddle, Terry Laverty, David & Rhoda Bailie, Heather Thompson, William McClelland, Don & Helen Ritchie, and Julie Hamilton.
Rev. Hemant Parmar from Gujarat spent a year with us and enriched us through his presence.

YOUNG WEST CHURCH.
A snapshot of leaders, including Bobby Liddle and Catherine Bell.
And of members, with small groups led by Catherine Bell and Elaine Jefferson.

MEN'S GROUP -Leader over many years, Mr Robert Crawford. See Index.

Part of the DONEGAL MISSION TEAM, October 1990 at Donoughmore.
Miss Doreen Hayward, of LISTENING POST ministry.
The Walking Group.   Leslie & Roslyn Wilson.
Elaine Ward, the Church office.   Brian Moorhead, a significant ministry through MIME.
Cecil Stewart has kept many young -and older- people active and agile.
The legendary Margaret Gibson - flanked by the Bailies- at son Ian's marriage.
A Prayer triplet: Elizabeth Scullion, Frances Smyth and Glenda Eddis.

OPENING AND DEDICATION OF NEW MINISTRY CENTRE.
Mrs Judith Hamilton (Architect) Rt. Rev. Dr. David Clarke, Rev. Charles McMullan and Rev. David Bailie.
Worship in refurbished Church.

tongues', would, in the eyes of many church people, have put you in a 'Looney' group.

Yet now, even among many churches and ministers in the UK, these things are regarded as quite normal. And when one looks at the global situation, in areas where the Church has grown in a massive way, in China or Korea or the Philippines, in many African and South American lands, these things are regarded as quite normative.

DELIVERANCE.
And so I believe it will be in respect of the ministry of deliverance. A western, rationalist mind-set precludes the possibility of these things. **The gospels** clearly show Jesus delivering people from the oppression of evil spirits, **and some estimate that a third of the healings performed by Him were in this category. To suggest that the incarnate Son of God was not really perceptive in these matters is, in my opinion ludicrous and well-nigh blasphemous. Our Lord was not deceived when He gave this ministry to his followers.** *The deliverance element in the evangelistic ministry of people like Carlos Annacondia of Argentina, who has seen a million people make public decisions for Christ in the last ten years, demonstrates that some at least of his followers, still fruitfully obey His commission.*

A RATIONALISTIC MIND-SET NEUTERS THE CHURCH, LEAVING IT IMPOTENT TO COMBAT THE EVILS IN THE WORLD.
That is why, in WCN we give examples of the Church anointed by the power of the Holy Spirit, so that our members may be open and believing for the power of the Holy Spirit to work in the Church today. Read a remarkable story from Colombia!

AGAINST THE TIDE IN

THE CITY OF DEATH.
Medellin, Colombia, is considered the most violent city in the world. Bella Vista Prison, Medellin, is the most dangerous in Latin Ameica. But now God's power is transforming prisoners' lives and bringing hope to the whole nation. Jeannine Brabon tells the story.

"Medellin is a city *where the death culture reigns. Sometimes the death toll hits 100 in one day. Death is a business and young lads aged 12 begin to earn money by killing. The football player Andres Escobar, was killed for scoring an own goal in the World Cup.*"

BIBLE SEMINARY TEACHER THRUST INTO MURDEROUS SITUATION.
Jeannine Brabon writes: "The situation came close to me early one Monday morning. I teach Biblical Hebrew at the Bible Seminary of Colombia, an International Seminary of 150 students. **One of my students, Margarita came to me** and said **"Jeannine will you please go with me to the morgue?** My brother has been missing for five days."
Well, I know that usually 150 die on a weekend in Medellin.
We went to the large city morgue and as far as I could see there was just body after body, all violent deaths. We didn't find him there so we went to the second morgue. **I will never forget Margarita's cry as she recognised her brother. She grabbed me and wept, and I wept with her.** Gustavo had never responded to the love of Christ. He was only twenty-six, but he got involved in the drug scene and in Medellin it's just a matter of time before you die.

WHERE IS GOD?
We got to the cemetery at dusk. We had a small service there with Margarita and her eight brothers and sisters, and when we were walking away her younger brother said to me, 'Jeannine, why my brother? Where is God? Where is God?'
I said to him, 'What they did to Gustavo is what nailed Jesus to the Cross. He feels your pain'. **And I too felt the pain in the heart of God at Calvary. And my heart cried out, *'Lord what can I do?'***

"I WAS BORN TO DIE."
We had thirteen bombs that night and it was a very hard week. The next day I heard gunshots. I looked up and across the street was a young man who had just been gunned down. I saw him reaching in his pocket as he was dying and handing a card to the two assassins. It was his ID card so they could collect payment because they had gotten the right man.
The young people have a saying: **'I wasn't born to live, I was born to die'. *But Jesus holds the keys of death. Jesus was one man. Can one man make a difference?***

OSCAR.
Well, there was one young man, Oscar, aged 28, and all he had ever known was poverty. At twelve he took to the streets and became a thief just to have something to eat. **Being on the streets led to drugs. He was in and out of prison for the next sixteen years.** He came out of prison and was met by a colleague. Oscar looked at him and said 'You are fat!' meaning he had had enough to eat, he wasn't wasted by drugs. He said 'What's happened to you? **You look different'.**

JESUS HAS CHANGED MY LIFE.
The man said, 'Jesus has changed my life. I have come to know him, and Oscar, he can change your life too', **and he invited him to a small church.** Later Oscar said, '**The Holy Spirit drew me like a magnet. I found myself at the front of the little chapel, weeping my eyes out and asking God to forgive my sins and come into my life. When I stood up I was a new man,** *the 16-year drug habit broken'.*

HE BOUGHT A BIBLE.
Instead of buying drugs, Oscar used the money in his pocket to buy his first Bible. He couldn't read, but he

took it home to his mother and she read it to him. ***This is what the Lord spoke to Oscar on the first day he was a Christian:***
"The Spirit of the sovereign Lord is on me, because he has anointed me to preach the Good News to the poor, he has sent me to bind up the broken hearted, to proclaim freedom for the captives and release for the prisoners..."
THIS PASSAGE WENT RIGHT THROUGH HIM; HE COULDN'T GET AWAY FROM IT.
<u>And so he went back to Bella Vista Prison from which he had just come out, and asked the Governor if he could have a pass to go into the prison.</u>
The Governor said, 'No one wants to go into this prison. Don't you know what the situation is?'
Oscar knew!
There were between 30 and 60 men murdered every month! The administration was ready to send in the army, they didn't know what to do.
Yet Oscar, in obedience to God, one small man, stood before the Governor and said, ' God changed me and he can change any one of these men'.

HE GAVE OSCAR A PASS.
The governor's heart was touched, he gave him a pass, **and Oscar began to go into the prison.** He said, 'I was a criminal, but I had never seen what I saw there. I saw decapitated men. I saw wounds from multiple stabbings, the situation was absolutely infernal.'
He had to take a clean shirt because they would throw things at him and do all kinds of things.
'But I prayed God would give me some of the hardened ones, the top dogs', said Oscar, and one by one men began to come to Christ.
One of these, Orlando, had had a similar experience to Oscar. At twelve he became involved in crime and eventually reached the Mafia.
He became a professional killer, a 'sicario' He had his own offices in several major cities in Colombia with men working under him, and he could earn $15,000 from one assignment.

PRISON- *I WILL COMMIT SUICIDE.*
He landed in prison and thought, 'I'm going to commit suicide. I would rather take my own life than have someone else take it'. But another prisoner said to him, 'That isn't the answer. Jesus is'. He said, 'How can I know more?' The man replied, '**This little man comes in and he will tell you'.**

So the next day when Oscar went in, Orlando found him. He said ' I had everything money could buy, *but I never had happiness. That day I found not a religion but a person, the Lord Jesus Christ.'*

KILLINGS STOP.
With a small group of these men, Oscar had a desire to preach in the wings, and they got permission to hold a campaign. The day before it started thirteen men were wounded and three were murdered, *but that didn't deter Oscar.* He went in the next day and began to share that Jesus was the answer to the conflict that raged within, the answer to the death toll.
The day he began to preach publicly in the prison the killings stopped. The press waited outside for the death toll, and there was none that day, nor the next. One year later in the secular press was the headline: 'One year no homicides in Bella Vista' and *then a full page report of what God was doing inside the most dangerous prison in Latin America.*

YOUR AUDIENCE, MAINLY KILLERS.
Jeannine tells: 'It was at this time that I was crying out to the Lord, *"What can I do?"*
Oscar has never had any schooling but his wife has and she was studying in our seminary. <u>Through her I met Oscar and he invited me to the prison.</u>
The first day I went he asked me to preach and I asked, 'Oscar, who is my audience?' He answered 'They are mostly sicarios (killers), and not Christians.'

About 30 or 40 men came in. Orlando was there: I recognised his face from his testimony in the newspaper and *I just couldn't believe that he was that tremendous killer.*
I took a Bible passage about King David wanting to show God's steadfast love to someone of the house of the enemy, **and as I began to share I felt the Lord's presence there in a real way.**
When Oscar gave the invitation at the end of the message, 23 men stood to their feet with tears streaming down their faces asking Jesus to come into their lives.

Oscar said to me, 'Jeannine, would you help to train leaders?'
Oscar was pastoring over 300 men behind bars, *and from the questions he was asking I knew he needed to be trained.* <u>So in February 1992 the Bella Vista Bible Institute began with 25 men.</u>

300 MEN BAPTISED.
Since then we have baptised close to 300 men. For the men to be baptised they have to really walk the experience in the wing. It is very hard because they are ridiculed. Yet they are respected too, because everyone knows that the peace of the prison is due to the believers, and the other prisoners have been told, 'You don't touch them'. In fact, when delicate situations arise the leaders in the wings come to our men and say, 'Get your men together and pray so there won't be bloodshed.'

RADIO.
God is using what is happening in the prison to reach into homes. **We have a live radio programme inside the prison, put on by the inmates. They sing, one preaches, they give their testimonies and I speak, and** *it's one of the most listened-to programmes.*

At the close the prisoners give greetings to their families, so the families all tune in and you can see the guards up on the walls listening too. *Prisoners' entire families are coming to Christ and the impact upon society has been tremendous.*

THE DIRECTOR OF PUBLIC PROSECUTIONS asked to see me and for an hour I shared with him. *Tears streamed down his face and he said, 'This gives me hope for the country.'*
And so God is reaching from the lowest in society to the very highest.

THE PRISON A PULPIT FOR COLOMBIA.
It's not easy - Colombia is in a life and death struggle and it's spiritual warfare. *We live with death threats. We have six missionaries kidnapped by the guerillas. Oscar's brother was tortured and murdered and when that happens it's a direct threat. But God is building his church. He is working at a time when the violence has opened people's hearts, and the prison has become the pulpit for the rest of Colombia.*

[NOTE:
We have given this story in WCN to demonstrate the reality and power of the Holy Spirit in and through the Church; to help us lay aside a rationalistic mind-set that abhors the supernatural dimension of a living Christ and a dynamic Holy Spirit, so that we may be fully equipped to wage spiritual warfare.]

FROM GOSPEL HALL TO WEST CHURCH - AND TO FAR BEYOND!
SHARON BRYANS tells (2006):

"In 1984 I came to West Church- not my choice! I had got married and my husband's family were very involved in West. Until this point in my life I had gone to a Brethren Gospel Hall and I had invited Jesus into my life as a seven-year-old girl. I had never known a time when I had not known God's love - how much He loved me, how very much! He had given his Son Jesus to die for me. I had a wonderful Christian upbringing in a family with parents who were a shining example of God and His love.

ALL THIS HOLY SPIRIT STUFF WAS NOT FOR TODAY!
I would like to say that I loved West Church from the start, but that was not the case. I went only when I had to and was quite happy to state that it was not friendly. I wondered why people went to it in contrast to the kind of service I was used to. I didn't think anyone could become a Christian by going to West Church. My husband's parents would often ask me to go to a 'Life in the Spirit Seminar', **but I always declined as I knew it was wrong - all this Holy Spirit stuff was not for today!** It was not in the Bible and I didn't want anything to do with it. I suppose really I felt sorry for them and thought they were a bit gullible believing this. Yet at the same time I saw in their lives that Jesus was more real to them in every area of their lives than He was to me. Around this time house-groups from West came to speak in the Richmond Nursing Home. [Note: owned by the Bryans family, where Sharon was Matron] **I saw in these people's lives the real love of Jesus in action with the residents.**

A VEIL LIFTED FROM MY EYES.
In 1991 my mother-in-law asked again if I would like to go to a **'Life in the Spirit Seminar'.** I said 'yes', not because I wanted to, or thought I needed to, but so I could say I had been there, done that and it was wrong! **What a surprise I was in for!** The first few weeks I looked around the large group of people and thought, *there is nobody here I want to get to know!* The Rev. David Bailie took us week by week through the Life in the Spirit booklet with many Bible references. *I looked up these verses knowing that they were quoting them wrongly, because I had learnt many of these chapters off by heart during my childhood.*
To my surprise I discovered that these verses were in my Bible!
It was as if God had lifted a veil from my eyes and for the first time I could see these truths in his Word.
Each week I began to see God's wonderful treasures in his Word. **I began to understand the significance of the Holy Spirit.** This part of the Trinity had been previously passed over, and only occasionally referred to as the Holy Ghost. I had never any appreciation **of the reality of the Holy Spirit in my life, or that there could be a baptism of the Holy Spirit, a filling of the Holy Spirit. I had a 'God compartment' in my life, but God wanted all of my life!** He had plans for my life - plans so much better than my ideas. (Jeremiah 29:11).

COMPASSION INSTEAD OF JUDGEMENT.
I would love to say that I opened my life completely to all God had for me at this time, **but I still had to check out everything** though in a different way. Instead of relying on my own understanding, I would ask God to show me his truth- and He did so in many amazing and very personal ways.
After being prayed with for the baptism of the Holy Spirit I found I had **a new boldness** to talk about Jesus; **the other thing I noticed was a new compassion** - *God's compassion for people instead of my own judgement of people!*

When the Seminar ended we became a House-group led by **Don Ritchie** who made the Bible so alive and real for us as he shared each week. *This group of people whom I did not really even want to get to know had, over the weeks, and with the unity of the Holy Spirit, become some of my dearest friends.*
I looked forward to each week at the home group, but I could never pray aloud during the prayer times which were lovely and very special.

So often I would feel prompted to pray for someone or for a situation, but I could never muster up the courage to pray aloud and would feel relieved when someone else in the group would pray for the same thing. **It did not occur to me that GOD had prompted me to pray, and due to my disobedience he then prompted someone else to pray who had been obedient.**
One day as I was asking my child to do something, and they were busy telling me about something else, God spoke to me and said **'Sharon, that is what you are doing -** *you are telling me what you think I want to hear and you have chosen what you will do for me* **but I am asking you to do, what I want you to do,** *and you are refusing!* From that moment on **I decided I wanted to live my life** *doing what God had planned for me to do. And so as a start to that, I prayed aloud for the first time the next week at the house-group.*
This may seem a small thing but to me at that time it was a very major step of courage. I have no idea why I found it so difficult but I did. *This was the start of a walk of obedience with God.*

A PASSION FOR JESUS.
The Holy Spirit had illuminated Jesus to me and I had a passion for Jesus I had never known before. I wanted to obey God not out of a religious duty. If you love someone you *enjoy doing things for them.*
The house-group was now led by KEN SYMINGTON and each week he shared valuable teaching that I will treasure all my life and probably in eternity.

God asked me to get involved in various ministries and I had the privilege of being part of a ministry team in West Church. **This was awesome: I saw the love and also the power of the precious blood of Jesus. I came to know the freedom we can have in Christ - what it means when God says 'I have come that you may have life and have it in all its fullness'.**
I saw how Satan wants to keep us captive to fear and to so many other things in our lives - to keep us from knowing the power of God in our lives.

LITTLE AFRICAN CHILDREN.
One night in the house-group Ken prayed for me- following this prayer God showed me, among other things, *many little African children and I knew they were orphans.*
All my life I have always known God's love. I have always known as a daughter that I was loved. I always wanted to share that love with others who had never known it. At this time I had no idea how I might share with these African orphans. I myself had a young family and to go to Africa seemed a remote possibility. I had no idea that it could ever happen! But with God nothing is impossible when He has a plan for our lives. We only have, step by step, to walk in obedience to Him and He will open the door.

I WENT TO KENYA.
So, some years later I went to Kenya with **'EDUCATE THE ORPHANS'**, and what an experience that was! I was very fearful about going as it was a remote area, way out in the bush with no electricity or running water. Anyone who knows me would not have sent me there, *but God knows me even better!* I arrived fearful yet with deep excitement in my spirit. **From the first visit I felt like I had been born to be there: although it was so different I felt so at home!** *It became my favourite place on earth!* I received so much more than anything I could give to these dear people. **Basic Health Care Education** is so needed and the most of our time is spent in presenting it in relevant ways. I also run a clinic in the **Marie Wright Centre** and have seen the power of prayer many times. God has always answered prayers in amazing and miraculous ways. I have been involved in teaching women's groups and have wept and prayed with these dear women and they have shared a little of their lives with us. **We have also run Bible Clubs.** These have been busy but so rewarding as so many children have asked Jesus into their lives.

MY FAMILY BECAME INTERESTED.
Listening to me share about **Kaguma in Kenya** my family became very interested and **Simon** was the first that wanted to come with me when he was only ten years old. **God really spoke to him on his first visit there about returning again** and gave him a real heart for these people. They also really embraced him and he loves to be there. He has shared his experiences and raised support for his friends there and wants to visit every year.
When **Peter** reached 17, he and his friend **Richard Best** joined the summer team who went out and both gained valuable experience while there.
Last summer (2006) Jeremy came with me with other young people from West Church. **It was wonderful to have their help at the Bible Clubs and the kids just loved them.**
God has made them a blessing in our lives. **It has been a joy to see my family reach out and care for others as God has touched our hearts. I know that God has so much more for us in the rest of our life here on earth.** *He knows us best and it has been a joy and a blessing to walk in obedience to him thus far. I know there is much more for us all.*

SEPTEMBER WCN 1995.

"HOW CAN I MAKE THE MOST OF THE REST OF MY LIFE?"
- WEST CHURCH TO EXPERIMENT WITH ALPHA."

Many of us want to make the most of the rest of our lives, whether we are under 16 or over 60, or any age in between!
It's important for those **soon to be**

married. It is important for those who have brought a new proud baby into the world, and seek the best environment for the child to grow up in. It may have some urgency for young couples with marriages already under stress and strain. and not unimportant for faithful church members who find life tiring and tedious. It is **certainly important for those who have tried to squeeze the greatest amount of pleasure out of life, yet still feel empty!**
And there are plenty who get urgent signals from body and spirit, that all is not well within them, **who need something more!**

THE KIRK SESSION, at its meeting on the 14th August, gave long, detailed consideration to the whole concept of ALPHA. In the end it decided that in addition to our fruitful 'Life in the Spirit' Seminars, we should make an experiment with Alpha.
Alpha Courses differ from 'Life in the Spirit', not so much in content as in presentation.
They begin each evening with a meal, which of course entails a substantial amount of work. After the meal the teaching on the topic of the evening is given, after which people are allocated to sociable groups of about a dozen, a context in which people quickly make friends and can ask questions and make comment freely.

Alpha Courses have evolved in Holy Trinity, Brompton in London, over the past 17 years, and are the means by which many people are now coming to faith, not only in that church, but all over England, and well beyond it.

TRAINING EVENINGS FOR ALPHA AND FOR HOME GROUP LEADERS.
These will take place on the 5th, 12th and 19th September.

ALPHA TASK FORCE:
To run an Alpha Course for 50 people, who enrol, requires an additional 25 people in terms of leaders and helpers, as well as those involved in cooking and serving the meal.

There will be a bookstall to meet all literature needs run by Brian and Carol Moorhead.

SEPTEMBER WCN also has letters from our three theological students, as well as Emma Hanlon who says 'thanks' for over £800 given for the Kikuyu Hospital in Kenya, and from Jill Young at the Rostrevor Christian Renewal Centre.
We have also news of Jonathan Montgomery who goes to Spain for a year to work with students under the auspices of IFES.

Then there's news of all our organisations who resume for the autumn term, youth groups, uniformed and non-uniformed; our Christian education departments; choir and singing groups; recreation groups, study groups and the whole wide plethora of groups and ministries.

Various people contribute enlightening and encouraging articles: an example is CAROL ASPINALL, a beloved member. She has suffered from debilitating Multiple Sclerosis, but her life had become deeply rooted in Christ. She has sent in an article broadcast on FEBA Radio, by Lindsay Allen.

CAMPING IN THE MOURNES.
"Years ago I went camping for the weekend in the Mournes with my mate and two other friends. We **spent** the first night at the Hare's Gap. Notice the verb. We didn't **sleep** the first night at the Hare's Gap, we only **spent** it there.
For those of you not familiar with the Mournes, the Hare's Gap can be a windy sort of spot.
The other two boys didn't have much experience of camping in the hills and to their delight managed to pitch their tent long before us.
In fact they had their tent half up while we were still looking for a suitable site, and we had to put up with a lot of heavy banter while we struggled to drive the heavy metal pegs into the hard ground on which we decided to pitch our tent.

I suppose the decent thing would have been to take them aside and explain what the weather could be like up there - but *we decided to be less than decent!*

In the middle of the night we got our own back! In the howling gale and driving rain their pegs pulled out of the soft ground and their tent blew away down the hill. The lesson- pegs that go in easily come out easily too! Sometimes people's lives collapse for the same reason

THE SOFT OPTION.
It is tempting to go through life choosing the soft option. I know because on occasion I've done it. **Disciplining the children is one obvious example.** Rather than confront some misdemeanour, we turn a blind eye. We know that confrontation takes time to resolve, and we don't have the time, **so we hammer the peg into the soft ground. Even as we do so, we know the danger. When the going gets tough these pegs will pull out.** If we have taken the easy way out and too often, hammered too many pegs into soft ground, **the child has nothing left to support him when the storm comes, and events bowl him over.**

Jesus never offered easy options and He never took them. The heavy metal spikes hammered through His hands and feet into the rough timber of a Roman cross weren't going to pull out easily, and just as well. They had to hold him there through that dark night while the storm of your sin and mine raged all around Him.

[NOTE: I think we can guess why Carol chose to send this story to us in West Church News! The discerning understand that the tent pegs that held her soul firm and strong, had been driven in by the Holy Spirit in the Name of Christ!].

LETTER FROM ANDREW COLE TO WEST:
"Hello Everyone,
It seems like only a short time since I started to train for the Presbyterian ministry, *and yet the first year of lectures and exams is over already, and what a good year it has been! Florence and I have both been encouraged and blessed.*"
Andrew goes on to speak of pastoral visitation work in the warm and loving fellowship of 1st Holywood church, and of acting as assistant chaplain for 3 months in the prisons at the Maze and Maghaberry.
On return to his final year of study at Union Seminary, he will be gaining 'hands on' experience in the Ballygowan Presbyterian Church.
"Although I have been gaining a wider experience of our Presbyterian Church in Ireland, and will continue to do so by the grace of God, *my roots are still in West Church, and we thank God for all the love and care lavished upon us during the past 17 years. We send a big 'thank you' to all in West for your love and generous support.*"

LETTER FROM CECIL GRANT IN VIRGINIA:

"Hello Everyone!
Well here I am back in the mountains of West Virginia. It was indeed wonderful to be home in Bangor, and to be back with you in West Church, even though I was only able to be at home for one week. It was great to see everyone again and to catch up with all your news. May I thank the congregation for the very generous gift which I received when I was at home. I do sincerely appreciate your thoughtfulness and your interest in my training.

I HAVE SEEN EXTREMES OF POVERTY.
My time in West Virginia is drawing to a close. There are only four Sundays left before I return to Princeton. **I have thoroughly enjoyed working with both churches in Welch: the people have been extremely warm and kind. I have also had my eyes opened to a whole new side of life. I have seen extremes of poverty** which I imagined only to occur in the Third World, scenes such as people living in old wooden shacks which provide no protection in the icy winter months, sewers which run into the local creek six feet from the front door, and towns which have been reduced to ghost towns since the coal pits closed.

THE PRESBYTERIAN CHURCHES have suffered immensely since the coal industry went into decline. They have lost many of their members, and have been without a minister for almost two years. *They wonder what the future holds for them, or even whether they have a future.*

THE FINEST PEOPLE.
Yet in the midst of all this chronic poverty and economic depression can be found some of the finest people one could ever hope to meet, and it is in this context that I have spent my summer. *I have learned much, but I also leave with many difficult issues unresolved. Perhaps the most important thing I have realised is that life throws up many issues that Cecil Grant just can't cope with; but thanks be to God we have One who can cope, One to whom we can turn when we feel so inadequate and helpless.*
"I can do all things through Christ who strengthens me." (Philippians 4: 13).
Thank you all once again, With love, Cecil Grant."

BRIAN & CHRISTINE MARTIN WRITE FROM VANCOUVER.

Christine writes of the visit she had been able to make to Bangor, and speaks with appreciation of **'continued prayer support, 'faithful correspondence'** and of those **'who have made a financial sacrifice on our behalf'**.
"A very sincere thank you to **Carmel and Des Perry** for opening their home in Ballymoney to some West Church ladies on the weekend of Focusfest Carmel did this, unknown to us, as a means of helping us financially. The ladies gave her what they would have spent on B&B accommodation. Brian joins me in thanking both Carmel and the ladies who so willingly contributed."
Brian writes:
"Studies continue through the summer at Regent with an intensive list of courses: Trinitarian theology; Apologetics; Ephesians book study; Spirituality - character study of David; Counselling skills; and The Pastor and self-esteem! These will also keep me busy right through the next semester which starts in September.

September also brings some more changes. As you may be aware from our previous letter, a Brethren Church on Bowen Island is helping support us financially; now a couple in the congregation have offered us their house rent-free from September to December. The house is beautifully situated in a veritable 'paradise'. My daily commute to college will be just under two hours: however the time is not wasted as I enjoy the scenery and work through my reading lists
Blessings on you all!"

OCTOBER WCN 1995.

HARVEST:
ANCIENT PROMISES AND TEACHING- MODERN APPLICATIONS.

We have Harvest Thanksgiving Services on 8th October. We celebrate God's great goodness in the luscious gifts of harvest time, and rejoice in that ancient promise "**as long as the earth endures, seedtime and harvest, cold and heat, summer and winter, day and night,** *will never cease.*"
We also heed the precept to gather together to give thanks to God, Creator and Father. We bear in mind the injunction to bring the best, the first fruits to offer them to God. And we recall how, in the book of Leviticus, farmers were told: "**When you reap the harvest of your land, do not reap to the very edges of your field or gather the gleanings of your harvest. Do not go over your vineyard a second time or pick up the grapes that have fallen. Leave them for the poor and the alien.** *I am the Lord your God.*"

RUTH - DESTITUTE REFUGEE.
In the Bible story of Ruth we see the application of the above instruction towards Ruth, refugee, alien, and immigrant. It was through *gleaning* in Boaz's field that Ruth survived.

HARVEST THANKSGIVING - SPECIAL OFFERING.
We link Harvest Thanksgiving with a special offering for the United Appeal of our PCI, and we have been given a target of £13,415. This is for all the outreach and mission work of our Church, nurturing a widespread network of good causes.
From our *first fruits* and our gleanings *we* seek to build churches, train ministers, send out missionaries, and feed the destitute.

JOTTINGS FROM OUR CHURCH COMMITTEE.

Over the summer the floors in the New Hall and the Major Hall have been restored, and a grand new machine costing £500 has been purchased to enable us to keep them up to standard.

EXTREME NOISE RESONANCES in the Major Hall have disappeared through new panelling on the walls designed to reduce noise reverberation times from 4.9 seconds to 1.5 seconds. We have relocated the growing Junior Department of the Sunday School to the Major Hall, and this should now prove to be a congenial meeting place.

CHURCH COMMITTEE RECORDS ITS GRATITUDE.
to James Smith, George Stevenson and Tom Finn, who do so much to keep our grounds in superb condition.
Our extensive grounds require a lot of maintenance, from the cutting of grass and the pruning of burgeoning trees, to the maintenance of beds and general upkeep. **We are always indebted to Ken Macartney who is forever working on the inside, maintaining and repairing, often prompted by our alert and vigilant Ethel Anderson. We thank all of these people, and others, who take such a pride in our West Church complex, and give themselves unstintingly.**

Our Treasurer, Victor Stephens reported that over the summer we had spent £600 on Sunday School prizes and £653 on glass repairs. **We had also repaid the residue of our debt of £17,500 to the Presbyterian Mutual Society** in respect of our purchase of '91' and '93' Crawfordsburn Road.

ALPHA COURSE GETS OFF TO A GOOD START.

Strenuous effort is often required when launching something new and this applied to the launching of Alpha in West.
Because the time between the launch of literature and the inauguration of the course was short, **it was only in the last week that we came to know how many we were liable to cater for, and the number increased substantially over the last weekend.**

We have approximately *ten groups of twelve enrolled,* making almost 120.
And we provided a hot meal for them on the first night!
That's a tremendous tribute to Linda Cumming, Renee Robinson, Pamela Dobbin, Jean Crichton and a veritable army of industrious, smiling ladies. *In view of our very limited kitchen facilities, this is a miracle!*

Better facilities are highly desirable if ALPHA should be destined to have a long-term future on this scale.
We have made a great start, and we ask you to undergird this whole endeavour with your prayers, *so that we may reap THE FULL HARVEST the Lord intends.*

LIFE IN THE SPIRIT SEMINAR!
If anyone thought that Alpha might kill off our Life in the Spirit Seminars, this fear has so far proved unfounded. 22 people have enrolled in the new Seminar, beginning on Wednesday 27th September, and to be led by Heather Thompson.

LEADING WORSHIP AT MAIN SUNDAY SERVICES - SIGNIFICANT ADJUSTMENTS.

When we began our *additional morning service* about 17 years ago, a *Singing Group* of young people was formed to lead the new service at Ten O'clock, with the *Choir* attending that service *once a month.*
In the course of the years the Ten O'clock service has become the larger service, and, overall *has the more senior composition.*
Some time back we made an adjustment *whereby the Singing Group and the Choir each led the Ten O'clock service (*and therefore also the Eleven-Thirty service)

twice per month.
And over the years, the situation has arisen that the **Choir leads the evening service twice per month** - on the other Sundays we have Praise Services.

FURTHER NEW ADJUSTMENTS.

THE CHOIR will lead the Ten O'clock service on the first 3 Sundays of each month, and the Eleven-Thirty service on the fourth and fifth Sundays, as well as on the second and fourth Sunday evenings.

THE SINGING GROUP will lead the Ten O'clock service on the 4th and 5th Sundays of the month, while their main contribution will be in the Praise services, where they will lead 2 out of 3 services.

THE ELEVEN-THIRTY SERVICE will be led on the first 3 Sundays of the month by the new group led by Paul Shields. During the first part, when the children are in church, we shall endeavour to engage the young people and their parents in lively worship, involving both traditional hymns and modern songs.

Our Organist Maurice McKenzie will be present, and the second part of the service will include the core of the Ten O'clock service *We hope to foster and strongly develop this Service, to cater for our younger families.*

WE MUST NOT FORGET.

Of course, none of us who minister in the leading of worship, should forget *that we are present, dutifully and joyfully, to offer our worship in the songs we sing, <u>to inspire the whole body of people to such worship. Our attitude needs to be one, not of self-pleasing, but of worshipping God with heart and voice.</u>*

NURTURING WORSHIP IN YOUNG WEST.

TERRY LAVERTY is giving his prime energies to our young people, in Young West Church, in our Sunday School departments and all our youth organisations. *We shall be seeking to train musicians among our young people and in the primary age sector.*

ROBERT SINCLAIR. Kirk Session and Committee have made provision for Robert Sinclair to help in such training under Terry's guidance.

Robert will train the Young West Church Group fortnightly on Monday evenings; and Primary age musicians on Tuesdays at 6.30 in the Intermediate Hall, and young musicians from 7.30 - 8.45 in '91'.

Robert, who earns his living from teaching pupils, will receive some modest remuneration for this service with us.

HALLOWE'EN:
HARMLESS OR DANGEROUS?

We quote from an article in Renewal Magazine.

31st OCTOBER.

On 31 October many Christians around the world will celebrate **REFORMATION DAY**. Martin Luther's powerful hymn, 'A Mighty Fortress is our God', will be sung to remember the time in history when the truth of the Gospel was restored to the church.

The same day *many witches around the world also celebrate the reality of the spiritual world. But their festivities will focus on activities expressly forbidden in Scripture and linked to the Kingdom of darkness.*

THE NIGHT OF HALLOWE'EN.

This is the night of Halloween. While it is a tradition more firmly rooted in the United States, primary school children are being confronted by classrooms decked out in black, with witches' hats, masks, pumpkins and candles, along with books about goblins, curses, and the supernatural.

Some people are also beginning to hold Halloween parties **and send their children from door to door to 'trick and treat'.**

These activities put pressure on Christian families. Some maintain that Halloween is just harmless fun, while others see it as dangerous dabbling in the occult.

Before looking at Halloween itself, here are some general comments which can be applied to a range of similar issues.

DOUBTFUL ORIGINS.

When in doubt, don't is usually good advice. But it should not be an excuse for ignorance. **It is a concern when Christians take a strong stance on issues they know little about.**

Halloween cannot be dismissed because of ignorance. Sometimes Christians dismiss something **simply because it has doubtful origins.**

So anything that comes out of Asia is treated with suspicion because Asia is dominated by false religions; artefacts from Africa come under judgement because those countries have witchdoctors, and so on.

The ungodliness of the world around us *is* a constant danger to us. Exposure to t *does* threaten to drag us away from the truth and from God. The unbelief of most of the population *does* affect what they produce, even if unconsciously.

Yet Christians do not need therefore to withdraw totally from society. Our challenge is to be 'in the world, but not of the world', to transform and redeem every area of society in which we live and take our part.

New Testament writers do this frequently. Paul is not afraid to take illustrations from the Games and apply them to the Christian life. John and the writer to the Hebrews take Greek philosophical concepts and use them as vehicles for the Gospel.

Halloween cannot be dismissed just because of its roots.

INHERENT EVIL?

There are few things that are evil in themselves. **It is our sin that poisons and corrupts God's good gifts.** So **sex** remains a good gift even though it is often perverted. **Television and sport** are neither good nor bad in themselves; even **alcohol** is not in itself evil.

THROUGHOUT HISTORY
Christians have condemned some things because of the **associated evil**. For example, **the theatre, card-playing, the pub, and make-up** have been frowned upon because they were associated with immorality, gambling, drunkenness and vanity. But **in themselves** none of these things is wrong (yes, I think Jesus would have spent time in pubs).

So the paraphernalia of Halloween is not evil or dangerous in itself. The colour black is not the devil's colour - it is the association with darkness that gives it its bad reputation.

The witch's hat made in the classroom does not possess some kind of spiritual power which will affect the wearer just because it is in the shape of the traditional witch's hat.

Pumpkins, with cut-out faces and a candle inside have no power in themselves.

It is true that there are some, *and it is a small minority, who will use Halloween as a time to dabble in the occult, but that does not necessarily make Halloween a celebration of the occult.*

Little Johnny's invitation to his friend's party is not an invitation to join in occult activities.

WRONG DIRECTION.
The problem with Halloween is the direction in which it heads. Rather than focusing on "what is noble, pure good" (Philippians 4: 8), Halloween fosters superstition, *and makes light of spiritual realities and witchcraft.*
The motivation behind *'trick or treat'* is unhealthy. Children go from door to door asking for a gift, threatening the householders with some kind of punishment if they do not oblige. *Even if that is done in fun, it is hardly a Christian attitude or one to be fostered.*

Often horror films or movies dealing with the occult will be shown at Halloween. *Some* teenagers and adults will experiment at this time with séances, Ouija boards, and so on, sometimes with disastrous results. Halloween can lead people *in the wrong direction.*

WHAT SHOULD OUR RESPONSE BE?

In October we had two meetings. The first was on Saturday 7th October, entitled: "DEFEATING THE DARKNESS" from 8 -10pm. It was a meeting of prayer, praise and testimony, under the heading "They overcame him (Satan) by the blood of the Lamb, and by the word of their testimony." (Revelation 12: 11).

The second was on Tuesday 31st October from 10.30pm - midnight, entitled VICTORY CELEBRATION, celebrating the Lordship of Jesus in his defeat of the powers of darkness.
"And having disarmed the powers and authorities, He made a public spectacle of them, triumphing over them by the Cross." (Colossians 2: 15).
Both these meetings were held in the Church, and were to become at the Halloween time of the year, an annual event in our West Church calendar, and a declaration of the cosmic lordship of Christ, exulting in his triumph.

BOOKAID - West members have donated 5087 books & Bibles. Demand for Bibles is 'insatiable'. One container load has been despatched to Nigeria, and another to Ghana. Book aid had the opportunity to purchase 215,000 new Bibles at very reduced prices.
These, along with the fine used ones being donated by Christians all over the U.K., will help to make possession of a Bible within the reach of many more Christians in English-speaking Africa.

NOVEMBER WCN 1995.

HOMOSEXUALITY - FINDING THE WAY OF TRUTH AND LOVE.

WHERE ARE WE ON THIS ISSUE?
"Are we tossed back and forward by the waves, blown here and there by every wind of teaching, by the cunning and craftiness of men in their deceitful scheming;
or built on the foundation of the apostles and prophets, with **Christ Jesus Himself as the chief cornerstone?**"

MEDIA OPINION.
If one were to go by opinions almost universally proclaimed on the media - which have an obsessive interest in matters sexual- then one would be swept and carried into the conviction *that to be sexually active is the natural right of everyone, and that to be lesbian or gay is just as natural and normal as to be heterosexual.*

Orthodox Christian theology is regarded as unnatural, uncaring and antediluvian.
ON WHAT BASIS do Christians evaluate and respond to the ideas *which are shaping our society?* Does the Bible have anything constructive to say on the controversial issues being debated today?

THROUGH MY LETTERBOX.
I recently received through my

letterbox, a study entitled "HOMOSEXUALITY: finding the way of truth and love." It has been published by a group of Christian friends and scholars who meet in Cambridge.

The aim of 'Cambridge Papers' is to make clear the relevance of Biblical teaching to a range of contemporary issues, providing material to stimulate further thought and discussion,, and aiming to make a strategic contribution to public debate at a time of rapid social and cultural change.

We want to be rooted and grounded in the truth of Christ, and to grow up in every way into Him who is our Head!

A SUMMARY of the Cambridge Papers:
"Christians today hold divergent views on homosexuality. This paper reviews the key Biblical material on homosexual practice and considers scientific and theological explanations of the origin of homophile attraction. Finally, an indication is given of a multi-faceted response of the gospel to the needs of the homosexual person and the *importance of Christian churches being communities of acceptance and friendship.*

HOMOSEXUALITY DEBATED IN THE CHURCHES.

In the churches homosexuality is debated with increasing intensity and growing division of opinion. **Until the post-war period,** in the long history of the church there were few, if any, dissenting voices, **to the view that Scripture and nature teach us that homosexual behaviour is, without exception, immoral.**

The last few decades **have seen a reappraisal by academic theologians, heated discussion in denominational bodies,** *and the emergence of organisations such as Lesbian and Gay Christian Movement, promoting an active homosexual lifestyle as consistent with Christian teaching.*

FOUR APPROACHES.

Four approaches now represent the wide spectrum of views and attitudes within Christian circles to homosexual behaviour and orientation.

'Rejecting-punitive' stance. **This rejects homosexual behaviour and orientation** as incompatible with Christianity, and is hostile towards people who are homosexual.

'Rejecting -compassionate' stance. This approach regards homosexual behaviour **as contrary to God's creative intent and never permissible for Christians.** However, actions and orientation are distinguished. *The church is to welcome into the community of forgiven sinners all who follow Christ - irrespective of sexual orientation.*

'Qualified acceptance' stance. This amounts to saying that the homosexual person **is rarely, if ever, responsible for his sexual orientation; the prospects of developing a heterosexual orientation are minimal; celibacy is not always possible; stable homosexual unions may offer the prospect of human fulfilment and are obviously better than homosexual promiscuity.** *Homosexuality is never ideal. Because God's intention in creation is heterosexuality, attempts to develop heterosexual desires must be made, but occasionally and reluctantly, one may accept homosexual partnership as the only way for some people to achieve a measure of humanity in their lives.*

'Full acceptance' stance stresses the **'unitive purpose'** of sexuality as central in God's sight and regards the **'procreative purpose'** as, by comparison, incidental. **Same-sex relationships can fully express the central purpose for sexuality, so homophile attraction may be affirmed. All sexual acts should be evaluated by their relational qualities; what matters is whether or not a particular relationship or action will enhance human fulfilment, faithfulness between persons, genuine intimacy and mutuality. The gender of the persons concerned is immaterial.**

THE VIEW REACHED BY CHRISTIANS IS IMPORTANT.

The view reached by Christians on the morality of homosexual behaviour **impinges directly on church life, pastoral care and evangelism.**
Much is at stake when we discuss this subject. **Much unnecessary pain has been caused by divisive and insensitive remarks.**

SOME KEY BIBLICAL TEXTS.

There are relatively few Biblical texts that directly address the issue of homosexual behaviour.
Genesis 19: 1-29. The word **'sodomy'** owes its origin to the incident where the men of Sodom demand that Lot, bring out his guests (angels) that they may **'know'** them. Homosexual violence and rape is the key characteristic of Sodom's sin. **2 Peter 2: 7-8 speaks of the lawless deeds of the people of Sodom. Jude 7** says that the people of Sodom **gave themselves up to perversion.**
Leviticus 18: 22 and 20: 13 prohibit sexual intercourse between two men as 'detestable'.
1 and 2 Samuel depict the friendship between David and Jonathan in intensely emotional terms.
But there is no hint of erotic behaviour in the biblical text.
Romans 1: 18-32 speaks of **homosexual acts as contrary to 'nature'.**
By 'nature' **(phusis)** Paul clearly means **'in accordance with the intention of the Creator. By 'unnatural'** he means contrary to the intention of the creator.

1 Corinthians 6: 9-11.
"Do you not know that the wicked will **not inherit the kingdom of God?** Do not be

deceived: neither the sexually immoral nor idolaters nor adulterers nor male prostitutes nor homosexual offenders nor thieves nor the greedy nor drunkards nor slanderers nor swindlers will inherit the kingdom of God. *And that is what some of you were. But you were washed, you were sanctified, you were justified in the name of the Lord Jesus Christ and by the Spirit of our God."*

Conclusion: *The review of key passages reveals a consistent antipathy towards homosexual behaviour in both Old and New Testaments.*

In the New Testament this involves God's Creation (Romans 1; 26-27.); God's Law (1 Timothy 1: 9-10); and God's Kingdom (1 Corinthians 6: 9-11).

HUMAN SEXUALITY: BIBLICAL FOUNDATIONS.

Sexuality, sexual differentiation, sexual intercourse and human procreation **are woven into the divine plan for humanity** (Genesisis 1: 26-29). However, the relationship between the first man and woman is given for another reason: **'It is not good for the man to be alone'. Marriage, given for companionship, involves leaving, cleaving and becoming' one flesh'. 'One flesh' refers to the personal union of a man and a woman** *at all levels of their lives, expressed and deepened through their sexual relationship. The permanent, exclusive relationship of husband and wife is given as the proper context for sexual intimacy.*

THE LIFE OF CHRIST shows us that neither a committed, exclusive partnership; nor sexual experience is essential to personal fulfilment.

Jesus, who lived the only perfect human life, was single and celibate. The need not to be 'alone' may be met through friendships without sexual intimacy. Indeed while human **sexuality is affirmed in the Bible, its significance is also qualified. Our true humanity does not ultimately rest in our sexuality** *but in fulfilling our capacity for personal communion with God.*

ORIGIN OF HOMOSEXUAL ORIENTATION.

Dr A.C. Kinsey conducted a famous investigation into human sexuality in the 1940's... and concluded that 4% of white Americans have an exclusively homosexual bias.

A recent survey by the Wellcome Trust says that 90% of men and 95% of women who had a partner of the same sex *also had a partner of the opposite sex. Exclusively homosexual behaviour is rare.*

Suggested explanations *of the origin of homosexual orientation suggest either* <u>biological</u> *or* <u>environmental</u> *factors.*

Biological theories point to **genetic or hormonal** factors. **Environmental** theories point to psychological or social factors. For example **the sense of rejection by and loss of the same-sex parent may result in emotional needs. The seeds for longing and closeness with a person of the same sex may thus be created.** However, there is a general, if informal, consensus that no one theory of homosexuality can explain very diverse phenomena.

THEOLOGICAL ACCOUNT.
The theological account of the origin of homosexual attraction does not explain why the attraction is there in particular individuals. Instead it declares that the rejection of God by the human race has led to 'every kind of wickedness'. This has led to a corporate situation where 'there is no health in us'. One of the consequences of rejecting God is that *in some* **there is thus a rejection of God's normal pattern of sexuality for us. In the state of deep disorder within our sinful human nature, it may be 'natural' for people to have same-sex orientation. This is contrary to God's creative purpose - and it is wrong!**

THE CHURCH, THE GOSPEL AND THE HOMOSEXUAL.

The meeting of Jesus with the woman caught in adultery (John 7: 53ff) has much to teach Christians about how to deal with homosexual people.

First Jesus reminds the Pharisees of their own sin and does not tolerate hypocrisy. None of us is without sexual sins and we must not throw stones, we must not judge. Jesus does not condemn the woman, but neither does he condone her sin. **The challenge for the church is to find ways in which to express a similar balance.** *Jesus acts as the woman's friend before he confronts her sin. She is friendless, an outcast in a hostile society, in danger even of her life and Jesus is the person on her side.*

THE GOSPEL.

The Gospel is God's answer to the problems caused by human sin. Full forgiveness for the past, the love of a new heavenly Father, membership in a new family, new resources for living as God intends and a new future are available. These over time, dismiss the spectres of guilt, fear, loneliness and lack of self-respect some homosexual people feel keenly. Sin is present in a homosexual lifestyle and in some form, ultimately lies behind homophile attraction. The Gospel offers 'gay liberation' by breaking the power of sin.

OUTWORKING OF THE GOSPEL.

"Who are you?" If you asked a heterosexual person that question, the person would not normally say: "I am a heterosexual." But if you asked a homosexual person that same question, he might well reply- if he felt free to do so, with "I am a homosexual." That person would see the homosexual orientation as their deepest self-identity image, the most important single fact about themselves.

EVERYONE who hears Christ's call to follow him is confronted with the need for radical repentance, to deny himself and take up the cross. For many, the depth of the repentance may dawn slowly over the years. For the homosexual his whole identity is on the line from the outset. In evangelism we need to be sensitive to this and offer grace - but not cheap grace.

JESUS addresses each one, intimately and personally, by name, yet he gives each believer 'a new name', a new, unique and eternal identity. In spite of grace the redeemed sexuality can still be a struggle, involving loneliness and depression. The Christian battling with homosexuality can however expect, as God works within, **homosexual attractions to become less frequent, less intense, less of a preoccupation. This is an outworking in holiness and healing.**

The heterosexual person, on the other hand, may have chosen singleness, or believe marriage is likely in the future. Singleness may bring advantages not available to the married person. Through prayer and counselling a person may undergo a change from homosexual to heterosexual orientation.

COMMUNITY- many people of homosexual orientation experience a sense of alienation from the church. Yet the church is called to be a 'new community' where people may know and be known, may love and be loved.

We need to review the life of our churches at congregational level, at small-group level, and at one-to-one level to see if we are achieving this ideal. Patterns of church life are often designed **with married couples and their children in mind. Our churches need to be communities of friendship in which the single person may find deep friendship. Friendship can be the answer to 'aloneness', a therapeutic experience, a source of support and human enrichment.** *Barnabas's befriending Paul when he first turned to Christ, was viewed with suspicion, that is an example to us. David and Jonathan, in their intimate and loyal friendship, is another.*

THE CAMBRIDGE PAPERS conclude: **that when Christians accept a created moral order they cannot affirm homosexual behaviour, and can love homosexual people to the full only when they have tender hearts** *and a firm grasp on the searching insights and transforming power of Christian truth.*

[NOTE: We have grappled with this subject to help our members to be informed, strong, and sensitive.]

In November WCN, **TERRY LAVERTY** writes in direct and trenchant manner about our **SUNDAY SCHOOL:**

"I'M PLEASED TO REPORT THAT ALL DEPARTMENTS OF THE SUNDAY SCHOOL ARE THRIVING- and we have the privilege of bringing these children up in THE WAY, as we teach them the Good News about Jesus and seek to make disciples for Him. The same applies to the **Creche** which is now in new premises.

SO! We are blessed in West - BUT privilege brings with it a sense of RESPONSIBILITY, and while we have *a veritable army of helpers and Sunday School teachers there is a very obvious LACK OF MEN!!*

The PRIMARY DEPARTMENT: we are in urgent need of two men to join the rota for November. **Perhaps the Lord would have YOU do this job? It's a golden opportunity to act as a role model, especially for the boys, who might otherwise have little contact with males outside of their own home.** All the necessary resources and support are provided for you. After prayerful consideration, please call Terry Laverty if you wish to find out more.

TUESDAY NIGHT YOUTH CLUB: The Great Commission in Matthew 28 and Mark 16 *isn't limited to mission abroad. We have a mission right on our doorstep, and the Tuesday Club which was pioneered by Don Ritchie, is one of the most exciting aspects of the work of our church at West.*

Unchurched teenagers from our backyard come to an informal youth club from 8.00 - 9.30 on Tuesday nights. They are **'rough diamonds' and the work can be demanding at times, but THEY COME and we have the privilege of getting to know them and sharing our faith with them.** *Here again we desperately need MEN and women! (aged 20+) who will come alongside these young people and give them the gift of TIME.* Please commit this matter to your prayers (or COME!!).

BALLYCASTLE WEEKEND - *A Touch of the Spirit. A 'Paul Graham' Perspective.*

"THE SATURDAY NIGHT SESSION was, I feel, the highlight of the entire trip. **Terry Laverty** ministered to us in a service of praise, worship and communion, (nice crusty bread and Schloer), when the next series of events surprised us all, I think. The first clear sign of the Holy Spirit at work came when one of those present fell gently to the floor. Sensing that there may be some present who had not seen such occurrences, I began

to speak to explain what was going on, and in a declaration of faith that flowed with power, not merely rational thinking, but from the Spirit, we all found ourselves on our knees, many weeping, at our human frailty and weakness.

Whilst we were aware of the presence of the Holy Spirit, and trying to assist with, not hinder His work, it was a gentle loving power, not at all frightening, though it was humbling. After time spent praying with and ministering to one another, we ended the session. *It was an inspired group of visitors that sang in the Sunday service in Ballycastle Presbyterian."*

HATS FOR ROMANIA.

In the early part of the summer we asked ladies of the congregation to knit hats for Romanian children. We had hoped to get 1000! Instead we got 2500! A very big "Thank You" from Betty & Adrian Topping to all the ladies who helped us achieve this wonderful result!

RAJASTHAN BIBLE INSTITUTE, INDIA. Rev. Anand Chaudhari writes:

"As we celebrate the Silver Jubilee of RBI, my heart overflows with gratitude for my Lord **who brought me out of darkness into His marvellous light and called me to serve him.** As I look back I see some significant landmarks:

February 1970: In obedience to the vision the Lord had given us, my wife and I along with our little daughter Pushpanjali arrived in Kota, Rajasthan. **The vision was clear: to establish a multi-faceted ministry - evangelism, training and church planting.**

April 1971: The Lord directed us to move to **Jaipur, the capital city of Rajasthan.** The work began to grow steadily.

May 1975: The Lord enabled us to purchase our present campus. It was just a miracle. August 1976: We became part of the worldwide fellowship of CHRISTIAN NATIONALS. This partnership has helped us to achieve more for the Lord *and has become stronger over the years.*

June 1978: Massive literature distribution, 'Aradhana' (worship) radio broadcasts *five days per week, and residential training courses brought in a tremendous response. The impact was felt all over North India.*

Since then the ministry has been growing and expanding. The Lord has used it to bring thousands of men and women to His feet. At present 624 worship groups have begun. The future is bright. Opportunities are unlimited. We realise there is much land to be possessed. We are confident in the Lord, that in his strength we will possess it to the glory of God."

Marivic Fetizannan - GRADUATED! Our student in the Philippines has graduated from the Bible Training College and is already involved in pioneer ministry. In her place we will now be supporting ROSEMARIE ANGAYON who enters Bible School to be trained in music ministry.

DECEMBER WCN 1995.

PCI WORLD DEVELOPMENT APPEAL - This year it is to send displaced refugees back home, providing them with "Going Home Kits" of bean seeds, grain seeds, pots and pans, blankets, money. £100 is enough for one family. There is also the endeavour to restore education, and to provide basic clothing - *'many people in Southern Sudan are forced to walk about virtually naked'. In that economy a £5 note would go a long way in "clothing the naked."*

How many displaced families can West send back home -30, 40, 60 or even more?

GET SMART FOR CHRISTMAS!! EXAMINE YOUR GOALS!!

TERRY LAVERTY quotes an old adage "If we always do what we always did, we'll always get what we always got!" If we want things to be better, we've got to make decisions to make changes. Terry challenges us to make SMART decisions. Our objectives should be Specific, Measureable, Achievable, Realistic, and Time-related.

He invites us to choose **three** of the following, and give them priority over the next two months.

Read one book of the Bible every fortnight......make my prayer life more effective....have one hour of quality time with my family every day....ensure that I give money back to God as a sign of love.....find a definite role to fulfil in the church before next Easter....invite two people to our next Alpha course....thank leaders of youth organisations for their hard work.....visit my new neighbours, two doors down....learn sign language within the next six months.... keep a prayer journal beginning tomorrow....involve my kids more in making family decisions.....read 4 good Christian books every year....make my home a welcoming place for young and old. .. find out why Joe Bloggs hasn't been at church for a while....give £1 to Tear Fund for every £10 spent on Christmas goodies.

So don't just go with the flow this Christmas! Take control of your lives and of your chequebooks, and get SMART about the way you live your lives!

RUTH WAKELIN SENDS IN A POEM FOR WCN:

"I dreamt death came the other night, And Heaven's gates swung wide, With kindly grace an angel came And ushered me inside. And there to my astonishment Stood folks I'd known on earth, Some I had judged as quite unfit Or of but little worth. Indignant words rose to my lips But never were set free For every face showed stunned surprise NO-ONE EXPECTED *ME!*"

THE MARTINS RETURN FROM REGENT and will be with us before Christmas. Brian writes: ."....when staying over last week with our Danish friends, Henric asked me what had challenged me most from our time in Vancouver..... over the next few days, the answer came...GRACE! Christ accepts us exactly where we are! I simply have to recognise him as Lord and receive him. As Christmas approaches with all the joy and festivity *I want to be able to see the baby Jesus, as one coming into the world, full of GRACE and TRUTH. May you know His unconditional acceptance and love at this joyous time of celebrating his birth.*

A SHORT UPDATE ON MY STUDIES. My return home is not the end of my study at Regent. Under the supervision of Regent College, I will be undertaking guided studies and a ministry research project. I feel very privileged to have as my supervising professors, J.I. Packer and Eugene Peterson, two men who have been a great inspiration to me as I prepare for ministry. The successful completion of these projects will, more or less, complete my studies at Regent. That will then be two complete years of study at Regent, with a further year to do at Union College, Belfast.

Chris and I give thanks to God for the time at Regent College. We've had a lot of fun as well as study for me, and I am sure it is a time we will look back on with very fond memories.

CECIL GRANT AT PRINCETON writes:

"Here in Princeton the autumn leaves are falling, the squirrels are busy storing food for the winter, and this morning the frost was thick on the ground. This year Fall was not as dramatic as last year, perhaps because we had more rain, but nevertheless the trees were very pretty and the colours beautiful.

This semester is going very quickly. Classes as always are providing me with an endless stream of work to keep me out of mischief. **This year I have started to learn a little Hebrew, which is great fun but very difficult.** Not only do they read back-to-front, have a completely different alphabet, but in order to produce any sound at all it seems you have to contort your mouth into the oddest shapes! Not a pretty sight! How on earth did Moses cope?

This year I am also working with a Presbyterian church a few miles north of Princeton. I help lead worship and preach occasionally, **but the main thing I am doing is teaching a class on Revelation. I know very little about Revelation, but I'm learning. FAST! This congregation is very different from the small mountain churches where I worked this summer, in that it is larger, younger, and urban, so it is interesting to see the different challenges and priorities that each congregation has. A good learning experience!**

I hope you are all keeping well and in good heart! Cecil.

BOBBY LIDDLE, STUDENT-ASSISTANT seems to have slipped into West Church rather quietly! But Christmas Holiday time sees him more in evidence, conducting a Praise service on 3rd December and the 11.30 Family Service on 24th December.

The Evening Service of Carols and Lessons are on 17th December, led by the Choir and Heather Thompson.

"JOY TO THE WORLD" is a new service led by West Youth Drama Group on Christmas Eve at 7.00 pm. It's a Celebration of Christ's birth and life through the medium of drama, dance, mime, music and signing. Members are invited to "Come and join us to praise the King of Kings!"

This year the women lead in two Christmas Praise Services, on Tuesday 12th December at 10.00 am and Thursday 14th December at 8.00 pm, with tea/coffee and crèche available.

On Christmas Eve also there is the now traditional Communion service beginning at 11.00pm, with Christmas Day services at 10.00am held simultaneously in Church and New Hall. We note that the Rev. Dr. Andrew Adams takes our Ten O'clock service on 31st December, while the 11.30 Service is a Family Service, and the evening service our traditional annual Student Service with our Youth Singing Group.

At Christmas ABBA TRUST also distributes the gifts placed at the Christmas Tree.

LEONORA SCOTT SAYS "THANK YOU."

"It was through David Bailie's prayer at a Seminar that Sam came to West Church.

One night David asked 'does anyone need prayer?',and I spoke - 'Could we pray that Sam would come to the divine healing service?', as he had a need after an operation for a duodenal ulcer; after much thought David spoke , 'We will pray that God will put the desire within Sam's own heart'. Wow, what a prayer! That was a Tuesday night and I wasn't looking forward to the next few days - I was thrilled and apprehensive at the same time. However, on the Friday night over a meal I spoke to Sam, 'Would you like me to take you to any other Healing service?' I had been asking him for six weeks and suddenly to hear him say, 'No! I am going to West Church after the evening service'. My mouth hung open.

Sam came and God healed him and the following Sunday I found him up and dressed for the Ten O'clock service and through time he asked if I would change churches. He enjoyed David's preaching and got to know the people took part in the collecting of tokens and was proud to do so - he felt he belonged and he was aware of a special love from the members.

Sam had health problems and people from Bangor town, prayer groups in different parts of Northern Ireland, missionaries in other countries, as well as the lovely people of West *prayed for his spiritual healing. God answered those prayers on September 15th 1993, as Julie Hamilton led Sam to the Lord.* I would like you to know how much Sam and I valued your prayers these past two years. They lifted us up to higher ground and enfolded us in the Lord's arms when we felt we couldn't go on.

'Thank You ' to all who enquired after him, to those who met and hugged him, others who visited and prayed with him and everyone who telephoned and cheered him up. Please through this letter may I give my thanks to all who supported me and my family at Sam's funeral service with their presence and many gifts of love. Sam is with the Lord and we give all the glory to God for things well done."

December WCN also tells of the next Alpha Course; West Church Home Groups; Building Beginners; Wycliffe Bible Translators; Jonathan Montgomery in Spain and Book Aid.

JANUARY WCN 1996.

ALPHA 2 - ARE WE ASKING YOUR QUESTIONS?

Before we launched our first Alpha Course in September, I sub-titled it under the heading:

"HOW TO MAKE THE MOST OF THE REST OF YOUR LIFE." One member of our congregation said to me, "When I read that heading, I thought, 'that's fantastic'", then added "but when I read the questions being asked in the Course, I realised they were not the questions I was asking."

We want to address the questions that truly concern people. One young person, **Catherine McQuitty,** who attended our first Alpha Course, has written: **"It was good to be with people who asked the questions I had never dared to ask."**

Another participant, **Norman Hawthorne** has written, "I found Alpha an enjoyable and rewarding experience. The format of each meeting was important for its success. **The group rapidly bonded around the supper table; this helped us to absorb the teaching session, and made later discussion more relaxed, so that questions were freely raised and debated."**

We are eager that people should feel free to ask, and if possible find satisfying answers *to the real questions that rise up within them. No question is considered too simple, or too hostile!*

THE NEEDS OF THIS GENERATION. Sandy Miller of Holy Trinity, Brompton declares that, 'by taking account of literally thousands of questionnaires, *the Alpha Course has been adapted and improved so it is truly moulded to the perceived and experienced needs of this generation'.*

IN OUR FIRST ALPHA COURSE we had an enrolment of almost 120 divided into ten groups. By the time we reached our final Celebration Dinner, there was a strong consensus that the course had been well worthwhile. Some may have entered upon the Course with a measure of TREPIDATION, and a few with real RESERVATION.

Five YOUNG COUPLES. In the first Alpha Course we had five young couples planning to be married within the next year or so. Among these **Denise Wilson and Barry Powell,** needed a little persuasion to join! When asked about this recently they admitted some real reluctance in the beginning, and, especially on Barry's part, a somewhat negative attitude. But it turned out well for them and they would now emphasise the **importance of the meal together that made for free and easy talking with one another, and brought real bonding, firm friendships and the desire for the group to continue together.** Barry and Denise have found a growing ability to express what they think *and would urge other young couples not to turn down an invitation to come to Alpha.*

WELCOMING NEW PEOPLE-Alpha has proved useful for welcoming new people right into the West Church family. **Billy & Mandy Johnston,** for example, speak of a deeper and more meaningful fellowship in the company of brothers and sisters in the Lord, **and the special joy of seeing people come to new life in Christ.**

ALPHA has been effective in bringing people from the edge or periphery of church life into the warm working core of the congregation. Sometimes this involved renewing those whose first love for the Lord had grown cold, or, as Rosemary Strawbridge declares, 'During the Alpha meetings my static Christian life was challenged and God re-awakened my spirit'.

SUCH TESTIMONIES could be multiplied many times over from our first Alpha Course.

THE INFRA-STRUCTURE OF ALPHA: There is a lot of **work involved in launching an Alpha Course - and last time we started big!** At least we thought 120 were quite a lot to have for dinner! But the team of **Linda Cummings, Renee Robinson, Jean Crichton and Pamela Dobbin - the chief cooks-** assisted by quite a little army of helpers and waitresses, were undaunted, **and week after week they produced delicious meals!** There were also those who cleared the church and set up the tables each week, and put things back after the meeting, manfully **led by Bill Walmsley and Andy Robinson;** there was also group who undergirded the whole enterprise in prayer each Tuesday night, and a further group who helped with baby-sitting and child-minding.

AND NOW WE ARE PREPARING FOR ALPHA 2! Carmel Perry is going to come all the way from Ballymoney each week, to head up two catering teams, so that the burden will be a bit less this time round. We would be grateful for further assistance for kitchen staff, table setters and waitresses!

THROUGH THE GENEROSITY OF OUR MEMBERS, 2 new Cookers should be in place for Alpha 2! Subscriptions given have paid in full the dinner expenses of Alpha 1.

VISIONS AND DREAMS FOR 1996?

Last month TERRY LAVERTY challenged us to get SMART for Christmas and choose three objectives to implement. Now in the New Year he asks how we have been getting on, and encourages us to think of 'Visions & Dreams' that might be implemented in 1996. Particularly he speaks of a host of opportunities, for all ages, *in respect of Summer Outreach.*

Youth for Christ are planning **Summerserve and Interserve;** Operation Mobilisation (OM) have issued their **Challenge 1996** leaflets on **Love Europe, Love Latin America, Love Asia, Love London, Love Austria, Love Africa.** Scripture Union is planning a range of camps **and CSSM missions.** PCI are planning missions throughout Ireland and overseas.

TERRY emphasises that the time to plan is NOW. This applies for any of the above projects, or for our own West Church Summer Scheme - or, *for families the PCI FAMILY HOLIDAY at the Share Centre in Fermanagh. In respect of the Family Holiday, Terry reminds us of Ian Grant's Parenting Seminar of last year,* saying, 'Here's a readymade opportunity for your family to create memories!'

FOR MORE DETAILS CONTACT TERRY!

ALPHA WORKS!

"Alpha is spreading like a bush fire all over southern Africa. Michael Cassidy speaks of its 'huge potential' for evangelism for the whole continent.

Three years ago there were fewer than ten Alpha courses throughout Britain. Now there are more than 2500 and dozens more are registering every month.

'THE PRISON OFFICERS CAN TELL THAT THEY HAVE CHANGED' Several prisons and young offenders' institutions are running Alpha courses with considerable success.

RURAL CHURCHES have been thrilled to see that Alpha works, not just in large urban churches, where young people predominate, but in small rural churches with a higher average age.

HOMELESS PROJECTS: Mary Sutherland runs an Alpha course at the SAFE, a homeless project based at St. James the Less Church in Pimlico. 'The honesty of the group is extraordinary. You really meet people face-to-face... we have seen a huge change in these guys over the months'.

HUNDREDS OF ALPHA COURSES start up in Asia, Africa, America, Australia, and Europe.

FRANK REA MINISTERS IN UGANDA.

"Blue skies, temperature around 80/90 degrees, lush countryside, lovely people, beautiful scenery, the adventure of travelling along pot-holed roads in a Land Rover and a one -and-a-half hour flight in a **Missionary Aviation six-seater aircraft** are some of the memories I have of my visit to Uganda!

Although at times it seemed as if I was on holiday, the purpose of this visit was not to holiday, **but to encourage the clergy of Nebbi Diocese in their ministry.** We had been invited by the Bishop, **Rt Rev. Henry Crombi**, to conduct meetings over a two week period in different churches in the Diocese. Many people were struck **by the visible evidence of the unity of the Body of Christ** *in the team, the Rev. Niall Griffin and his wife Geraldine, Church of Ireland, Maria Madden, Roman Catholic and me, Presbyterian.* Although coming from different denominations, we had two things in common. We all had a personal relationship with Jesus and were filled with the Holy Spirit.. We saw and experienced those lovely and powerful words in Psalm 133 - **'How wonderful it is, how pleasant, for God's people to live together in harmony! that is where the Lord has promised the blessing...'**

As a team we met together during the five months before going to Uganda, to pray and wait on the Lord for the ministry we would be involved in, and God spoke directly and encouragingly to us during these times. I thank God for all who were praying for us during our time away and for the financial gifts received that made it possible for me to go on this outreach. Thanks especially to my friends in West Church for such generosity and encouragement. As a Team we were carried along by your prayers and saw **God answer those prayers in wonderful ways.**

During these two weeks of ministry the Holy Spirit moved very gently but powerfully in many lives. We saw God bring people to a personal relationship with Jesus. Many were filled with the Holy Spirit and were healed physically, emotionally and spiritually. We saw the Holy Spirit bring reconciliation between a pastor and a former witch-doctor, something the Archdeacon told us he and his clergy had been trying to do for years. God is good!

I had the privilege of speaking to a group of 121 men and women in a local prison and at the end of the meeting 55 came forward for ministry. I will never forget the expectant look on their faces as they stood before me. At another meeting we saw 25 people come forward in response to a word of knowledge that some were feeling a call from God to be evangelists. We prayed that the Holy Spirit would come and fill them and empower them for this work. What a mighty God we serve!"

PAUL GRAHAM WRITES TO EAMON HOLMES ON "PAST-LIFE" REGRESSION. RE-INCARNATION.

David Bailie writes: In choosing material for our "West Church Journey" discernment about what to include and what to omit is continually involved. For example, is it appropriate to include Paul's letter? Very recently I spoke with a couple, brought up in Christian tradition, who told me that they believed in Re-Incarnation and appear to have imbibed Hindu philosophy. A factor in their acceptance of all this was the compelling evidence of people, who in trance appeared to have regressed into former life and to know things pertaining to life many hundreds of years ago. PAUL'S LETTER.

"Dear Eamon Holmes,

I watched tonight's show involving the "Past-life regression" of Paula Hamilton and saw that it followed the usual pattern of such activities, in that it was not quite conclusive, but yet well nigh impossible to explain by any rational means.. This is so. No rational scientific explanation will satisfactorily explain how Paula knew those obscure historical facts.

We are left, therefore, searching for a supernatural explanation. Basically there are two paths that can be followed in this regard.

1). That Hinduism is correct and re-incarnation is a fact of the cycle of life, or, 2). There is some sinister supernatural force at work intent on showing the likely prospect that statement 1) is to be believed, **bearing in mind that the teaching of the Christian Bible is clearly at odds with this point of theology.**

Today's society seems to be content to dismiss Bible-believing Christians as a lunatic fringe with nothing to offer, *but of course if society has been deceived and the well-read God-fearing Christians are right, society is in BIG trouble.*

Anyway, as a believer who is a Mensa member and a professional person, I am neither mad nor stupid, trust me. I hold to the view that there is more to the world than mere intellect and that the spiritual dimension of our existence is denied at our peril.

So to the phenomena of **"regression"**, which is the topic of prime concern on your show. **Hypnosis** itself is a very dubious practice with its roots in the Eastern pagan religious mysteries of Hinduism and Buddhism and the like. There are many case histories of people being seriously harmed by losing control of their conscious minds. Less well documented, are the numbers of people who, under the latent after-effect of hypnosis, are kept from coming to faith because they have been made resistant to the things of God. These are deep spiritual waters, but such are the issues involved.

The effect of being in a state of **"altered consciousness" be it through meditation, hypnosis or taking drugs,** *can put one in contact with the dark spiritual realms whose mission is to enslave and destroy humans, by deceiving them. These deceits are always made to seem harmless and fun. Not so.*

I'm sure all this sounds very strange, so I will employ some scripture to illustrate my points: - 2 Corinthians 4: 3-4. **"But if our gospel be hid, it is hid to them that are lost: in whom the god of this world (Satan) has blinded the minds of them that believe not, lest the light of the glorious gospel of Christ, who is the image of God, should shine on them."**

People are deceived and blinded in many ways. To put it in a nutshell, Paula Hamilton, while in a state of trance, was fed various bits of information by a demonic entity, or *familiar spirit*. These entities don't always tell the truth, but have access to data, being immortal by nature. Sounds far-fetched? This is what God says on **re-incarnation:** - Hebrews 9:27 "and it is appointed to men *once* to die and after this the judgement."

And as for familiar spirits? Read Leviticus 19: 31 and 20: 6 and Isaiah 8: 19.

I don't get any pleasure from writing harsh letters to celebrities; it is an area I have been called into from a sense of spiritual duty and divine guidance. I think you are a great presenter and very charming. Please don't be employed to promote the cause of those who would deceive and mislead the masses with false gospels. "**Then you will know the truth and the truth will set you free."** (John 8: 32).

Yours in a spirit of love and concern," Paul Graham.

FEBRUARY WCN 1996

FOUR YEARS AGO WE MADE A PLAN - and have fulfilled it!

In 1992 we faced a challenge of buying 2 adjacent properties, which with loan interest and repayment **amounted to about a quarter of a million pounds.** On our somewhat cramped site, with limited room for car-parking or any further development, we felt this was a once-in-a-lifetime opportunity that we should not pass by. **As well we have been able to give away £5000 each year on Outreach projects..** '91' has been well used over the past four years, providing a home for our deaconess Julie Hamilton, and then for Thomas and Lorraine Mulholland, as well as providing accommodation for **seminars, Bible Studies, prayer meetings, and for Sunday School and Young West groups.**

DO WE HAVE AS COMPELLING A PLAN FOR THE NEXT FOUR YEARS? What may we hope to achieve?

HIGHLY ACCELERATED SPEED OF CHANGE- Technological change is taking place at an amazing, if not even an alarming speed: **the computers of yesterday, and all they control and provide, are outdated today!** Social change likewise is rapid, symptomatic in the *manner in which the whole nation may suddenly take part in the lottery, or tune in to satellite TV and radio stations.*

SECULARISATION. After just a few years in New Zealand, a Presbyterian minister back home on a visit, told me he was utterly amazed **at the extent of the secularisation that had taken place in a short time.** As a Church we could readily feel overwhelmed by the great waves of secularisation: for example, **through extended Sunday opening will we see our young people swept out of our churches into part-time jobs as Sunday working becomes more accepted, as we are told has already happened in Scotland?**

IF WE ARE PASSIVE AND DRIFT, we are in danger of being overwhelmed and consumed. However, if we are active and wait upon God's Spirit, **RECEIVING VISION, INSIGHT AND STRATEGY FROM HIM,** we may make huge inroads into a secular society, build up and extend the church and gather an immense harvest. For this we need to plan and set goals that *are specific and realistic.*

1. **PASTORAL CARE.** A visit to every family from a TEAM member every year, and from an elder/church Visitor every quarter. We want to see the drifting and the lapsed restored. We want to have such contact with our members, that we are able to address real needs and questions and to draw them into groups or seminars where they may become active and committed.

2. **MAKING CONTACT WITH THOSE ON THE FRINGE.** We have a large fringe in West, people whose names appear on our West Church Directory, yet seldom if ever come to church. **Some may count themselves as agnostic in respect of faith; some may even see 'religion' as a source of trouble in the world! Likewise among young people, a growing number in our nation appear rootless and disenchanted, some feel themselves unwanted, secondclass may be bitter, destructive, unmotivated.** It is a big task to engage in meaningful and effective dialogue with all these folk, and our TEAM members require energy, insight and wisdom from God to galvanise our whole church body in this endeavour.

3. **WE NEED INPUT** into the plethora of congregational organisations and agencies, so that all are encouraged and work harmoniously together. We want through Jesus' Name *to see a release of love and creativity that will refresh and enrich our whole community.*

HOW MAY THESE GOALS BE ACHIEVED?

These goals cannot be achieved without a warm, buoyant, lively Christian fellowship, or without prayer and the working of the Spirit. BUT key also is PERSONNEL. In the work, witness, fellowship and outreach of a congregation *it takes precedence over buildings and plant. Church Halls, maybe costing millions, do not of themselves bring in the Kingdom of God!*

TEAM PERSONNEL IN WEST. At the moment the Team consists of senior minister, one fulltime ordained assistant minister, Terry Laverty; one student-assistant minister Bobby Liddle due to become a fulltime licentiate minister in June 1996; Heather Thompson who has a pastoral ministry works full-time; and Helen Ritchie on a part-time basis, working mainly with young people.

If we are to have the staffing outlined above, involving 2 fulltime assistant/associate ministers, then over the next two years, we would require an increase of about £12,000 in our **Development Fund, from the present £48,000 to £60,000.** In the past we have had the local incentive to raise **additional monies for personnel and ministry** *that have wonderfully helped our congregation to grow. Without that additional personnel we could not have achieved the growth and richness of ministry that we have, with God's help, achieved.*

IN PCI ADMINISTRATION (CHURCH HOUSE) some fear that <u>additional ministry funds</u> may undermine the Number One or General funds of congregations. It is on these General Funds that other assessments are levied. There is therefore some suspicion in regard to ministry funds, like our Development Fund, through which we endeavour to expand our personnel base.

WHAT IS OUR WEST CHURCH REPLY?

In West Church it has been clearly demonstrated that our Number One/General Account **has continued to grow in a buoyant manner, in spite of the extra monies that have gone into the Development Fund, and, for the purchase of adjacent properties into our Number 6 Property and Outreach Fund. Our Number One Account is now the second highest in the Ards Presbytery.**

In our hearts we are Presbyterian and subscribe willingly to the view that the larger congregations should, through central funds, help the weaker and so we endeavour to keep our Number One Account strong and growing, **and this we have consistently done!**

FEBRUARY WCN 1996 also includes: the Kirk Session Report for 1995; news that the RAINBOWS had won the County Challenge Cup; that Women's Praise were holding a Coffee Morning in aid of the Mizo Choir, India; that the GB are continuing to collect aluminium cans; that the Brownies had split into two packs to cater for huge growth; that the Guide camp was at Dunluce on the north coast; an exhortation "be keen, go green with 12th Bangor BB; a letter from our Christian Nationals' Philippine student; a report from Mums and Toddlers; news of the Women's World Day of Prayer; a letter from Jonathan Montgomery in Spain; the Sycamore Club's thanks for founder member Margaret Conroy - and request for three people to fill the huge gap that this has left, and a guitarist to support Beth Myatt; a PWA report; Julie Hamilton,s thanks for the 'most generous gift' of the congregation; news on Building Beginners; an account of our 'tenacious Scouts' in Mayo, and the sterling part they played in the rescue of two seriously injured Scouts that involved a helicopter rescue; George Coburn's resignation as an elder and the demitting of his work in keeping the Communicants' Roll, to David Baillie.

MIZORAM - An Indian state totally transformed by the gospel! "THE MIZOS ARE COMING!" This cry would have struck terror into the hearts of villagers bordering Mizoram one hundred years ago. At that time the Mizos were **feared head-hunters.** In 1871 one such raid on a tea plantation in Assam ended the life of the British planter, James Winchester, and began a new chapter in the history of the Mizo people.

During the raid six-year old Mary Winchester was kidnapped and the British army was brought out to search for her. The subsequent return of Mary to England caused great excitement in the newspapers of the day. **God soon burdened the heart of a wealthy businessman to send missionaries to these fierce tribesmen. He sponsored JH Lorrain and FW Savage to go to Mizoram and they arrived on 11th January 1894. The Mizos celebrate this day as the 'day of the coming of the Gospel'.**

Although the first Mizos were not converted until 10 years later, **there then followed one of the most remarkable experiences of church growth in missionary history. From two believers in 1903 the church grew to 90 by 1905 and to 7000 by 1915!**

Today Mizoram's population of 600,000 may be considered 100% Christian. It is the only state in India where you will find few, if any, beggars or homeless people. It has the country's highest literacy rate - facts which the Mizos believe are a direct result of the Gospel changing lives. With very limited resources 1000 Mizo missionaries have been sent to serve in other states of India and other parts of the world - <u>a higher proportion of missionaries than any other country in the world.</u>

THE MIZOS LOVE TO SING!
Try to imagine 2000 gathering to sing in harmony half an hour before every service! This is the routine in Mizoram. The churches are large - 1000 to 2400 is typical in Aizawi! **As you hear the choir sing, you will sense the presence of the Holy Spirit who fills the hearts of Mizo Christians.**

VANIAL NGHAKA led a Mizo

Choir to sing in West Church on 25th February 1996 and we were all uplifted by the beauty of the singing and could indeed sense the Holy Spirit's presence.

MARCH WCN 1996.

MILLENNIUM FUND & PROJECTS.

The March Edition of West Church News gives us an overview of all our funds, and how we may strengthen them, providing the *personnel* that we require to expedite our programmes.

BUILDING & OUTREACH FUND: - a plan is laid before our congregation to utilise £40,000 surplus already in this Fund, to increase our Car Parking space from 36 to 85 spaces, and to embark on additional building to link '91' with our main church complex. We would remove the decrepit conservatory buildings from the back of '91' and replace them with 2 rooms, the first 18ft by 14ft, and the second 20ft by 28ft. In addition there would be a new lobby, with toilet facilities, and a new 'legal' stairway to the upper floor. There would be a new thoroughfare to the church entering the Approach Room, through the area where the Prayer Room now is. In addition there would be a Thanksgiving Chapel, 30ft by 19ft to accommodate about 50 people.

THANKSGIVING CHAPEL: this to be a place where the Choir and singing groups could meet for practice and before church services, provide storage for music and equipment, and for the recording of services etc. Where smaller numbers may be involved, it could be used for marriage or funeral services and be an appropriate venue for some Praise and Prayer meetings or for occasional Communion services.

Detailed information was then given to lay before the congregation as to how these goals might be achieved - in a manner similar to when we purchased '91' and '93' in 1992.

ESTIMATE: "It is impossible to give exact or definite figures on the cost of the plans for Car Parking and Building. A rule of thumb might suggest £25,000 for Car Parking and £130,000 for buildings. [*These were to prove optimistic estimates!*]

BELCANTO'S PASSION
MUSIC ON PALM SUNDAY. On the very edge of Holy Week BELCANTO will lead our evening service on Sunday 31st March, in many beautiful Passion songs and hymns, which will deepen our awareness of the Christ, who suffered in our place and made full atonement for our sins. It's a service that some may be tempted to attend for the depth and beauty of music and song, but which, I believe, will enable us *'to watch one hour with Christ'*. This leads into our Holy Week Services: the pattern is a little different this year since the **Wednesday Youth Service and Good Friday Service will be in West Church.**
We'll all rejoice together on Easter morning. Easter Evening will be a Praise Service led by Terry Laverty, and will incorporate **baptism, confirmation and communion.**

"THE QUALITY IS IN THE MUSIC": Robert Sinclair.
Robert announces that his album is now on sale at £5. He plans to use the proceeds from the sale to purchase new sound equipment. Robert is convinced that there is a huge wealth of musical talent in West which he is 'ambitious' to record!

Robert tutors and encourages children (P 4 and upwards) to sing and play a musical instrument each Tuesday Evening at 6.30pm in the Praise Room. As well, anyone from 1st Form Secondary level is welcome to a one-hour session in '91' at 7.30pm on Tuesdays. "You will be given helpful tuition for your instrument and be taught how to follow a band with the help of written music or effective notes. Come along and do your best!"

WEST CHURCH MEN'S FELLOWSHIP WEEKEND will be led by Pastor Bill Foster at Childhaven. and the theme will be: "the Holy Spirit and You." 26th -28th April.

PRAYING FOR PEACE IN OUR LAND
- Terry Laverty, in encouraging us to pray for peace in Ireland cites MARTIN LUTHER KING.
Martin Luther King, who was assassinated because of his fearless campaign for racial equality, spoke of his faith in Jesus Christ using the term 'soul force', by which he meant the Power of God's *agape* love which we read about in 1 Corinthians chapter 13. Love for him was nothing sentimental or anaemic, but a force to be reckoned with. "Somehow we must be able to stand up before our most bitter opponents and say, 'We will match your capacity to inflict suffering by OUR capacity to ENDURE suffering. We will match your PHYSICAL force with SOUL FORCE! Do to us what you will and we will still love you!! But... be assured that we will wear you down by our capacity to suffer, and one day we will win freedom! WE will not only win freedom for ourselves! WE will so appeal to your heart and conscience that we will win YOU in the process and our victory will be a double victory!"

MAY WCN 1996.

WE WANT TO VISIT YOU, BUT IT IS DIFFICULT TO FIND YOU AT HOME!

A couple of months ago we said that with our enlarged pastoral **team** we wanted to provide greater pastoral care. **We hope to have Bobby Liddle working with us full-time from June and living in Bangor. Our aim for each family is an annual visit from a team member and a quarterly visit from an elder/ church visitor.**

Our team members find that *social changes* make their home visits amazingly difficult! Just as we find that people are being despatched from hospitals so quickly, that it is necessary to phone through to the Belfast hospitals to discover if patients are still there, *so something similar appears to be necessary for our ordinary pastoral visiting.* It is no longer possible to do a good stint of visiting of an afternoon or evening. There is so often the frustration of going from one unanswered door to another!

However, we still want to visit you, and we hope you want to see us! So over the next months, we want to make an experiment. We are asking **Heather Thompson** - who has been working hard to renew and enlarge our team of Church Visitors- to phone you, to make arrangements for our Pastoral Team to visit you, so that when they set out for an afternooon or evening's visitation, **they will be sure to find you at home. Over the next few months we plan to visit districts K, L, M, A and B.**

BUILDING & CARPARKING PLANS.

At a meeting of Kirk Session and Church Committee on Monday 15th April, our Property & Outreach Fund Treasurer, John Poole, told us that over a four-year period, **an amount of £123,000 had been promised,** including covenants repayments projected. **This was somewhat less than had been hoped for, but substantial enough to convince Kirk Session and Committee, to recommend to the congregation that we proceed with this plan.** It was decided that our architects employ a Quantity Surveyor on our behalf, so that we may have a more precise figure in respect of the cost of the whole project before we seek approval at a congregational meeting, on the likely date of Sunday 16th June.

KEN MACARTNEY to take over CLEANING AND MAINTENANCE DUTIES IN WEST.

Ken Macartney has already done a vast amount of work, repairing our buildings, decorating, doing electrical work, clearing up after the vandals! Some may not know that a couple of months ago, Ken took early retirement from BP, and our Church Committee has been very happy to make an arrangement by which Ken is coming to work for us in West Church. **He will do the cleaning work in our extensive suite of buildings, and will also work on the repair and decoration of our buildings, keeping our whole complex in good order.** We know that this is not easy in an ethos in which we have break-ins to our property and not a little vandalism. We are hopeful that his presence in West will be helpful to all the people and organisations who come to our buildings, and that he will receive maximum help and encouragement in this work.

We thank Ken for all that he has done so willingly over the years, and believe that it will be great for us to have him on our staff.

TERRY LAVERTY alerts us to

THE MANDATE, A ONE DAY EVENT for Ireland's Christian men in the Assembly Hall, Belfast. Speakers are **FLOYD McCLUNG & GORDON MacDONALD.** As men we **have a mandate from God to stand up and be counted! Saturday 23rd November.**

JUNE WCN 1996.

WEST CHURCH MEMBERS - "WAKE UP!"

Paul also wrote these instructions to the Ephesian Christians: **"Be very careful how you live; Do not be foolish, but understand what the will of the Lord is; Submit to one another out of reverence for Christ."** Spot-on for us today! And Jesus prayed for his people that **"they may be brought to complete unity."**

A HARD, DARK PATCH!

Recently someone going through a hard, dark patch in life, where a number of painful knocks had been sustained, confided in me **that the earlier joy in the Lord had slipped away *and also the sense of sustaining love among God's people. The*** feelings were akin to William Cowper who wrote:
Where is the blessedness I knew
When first I saw the Lord?
Where is the soul-refreshing view
Of Jesus and his word?

What peaceful hours I once enjoyed How sweet their memory still! But they have left an aching void The world can never fill.

FULLNESS OF THE SPIRIT.

Read the whole New Testament and you will discover that this fullness may ebb away, and that people need to be **topped up, to be continually filled with the Spirit.**

A tell-tale sign of this ebbing away of the Spirit, is a loss of **intimacy and the emergence of a judgemental spirit and divisions.** When this happens we need to repent. As well Paul tells the secret of being filled, again and again, with the Spirit; "Speak to one another with psalms, hymns and spiritual songs. Sing and make music in your heart to the Lord, always giving thanks to God the Father for everything, in the name of the Lord Jesus Christ."

Here in West we have **much** for which to give thanks and some **matters** where we need to take care, lest we hurt one another and distress our God!

MOBILISING ALL OUR RESOURCES to offer true worship.

WE ARE RICH, in all the groups we have to lead us into worship, in our Choir, in our Singing Groups, in the Young West Group of singers and musicians; in the new Singing Group led by Paul Shields; and in Belcanto.

Each group has its own particular contribution to make, in enabling the whole Body of the congregation, young and old and middle-aged to enter into a fullness of worship.

YET WE NEED TO TAKE CARE to build one another up, to encourage and highly regard one another. There is STRENGTH in MAGNANIMITY!

"I feel it would bring great joy to our CHOIR MEMBERS, of a Sunday evening, to see the church well filled by members of our various Singing Groups and those who appreciate the services that they lead! Likewise our Singing groups would be greatly encouraged to see the Choir largely represented, when the young are leading to see the older, and the older to see the younger! **We are a Body! We are inter-dependent: we are strengthened by one another's presence; we are discouraged by one another's absence.** *But the main thing is that we are there to worship God with our whole hearts, and blessing one another!*

IT IS AN OPEN SECRET HOW WE MAY RECOVER THE

FLAME OF THE SPIRIT WITHIN US!

NEW BUILDING PROJECT:

We had hoped to have a formal meeting of the congregation on Sunday 16th June to present plans, seeking the approval of the congregation. The Church Committee are still actively giving consideration to these plans and are not yet in a position to present them to the congregation.. So this meeting has been postponed.

PASTORAL VISITATION. This has got off to a good start! It has been a pleasure, through the new arrangements to do a full afternoon's or evening's visiting, knowing that people will be expecting you. We thank Heather Thompson for her telephone ministry, which she has been finding a happy and fruitful experience in itself.

LICENSING: Andrew Cole, at the conclusion of his theological studies is to be licensed 'as a probationer for the Christian ministry' in West Church on Sunday evening the 16th June, and **Bobby Liddle,** likewise in Craigy Hill, Larne on Sunday 23rd June.

USING SGM LEAFLETS ALL OVER THE WORLD: We devoted one page of June WCN to show how other people use Scripture Gift Mission leaflets.

PERU. "Down through the years, as I've travelled by car, I have always given lifts to those who have asked for them. I use the opportunities to speak to my passengers about the Lord. When they arrive at their destinations, I always give them some gospel literature to read. One man had a lift with me several times between Chuquibamba and Aplao.

Not long ago he invited me to visit his house, to talk to his family about the Lord. He, his wife and one grown-up son made professions of faith in Christ. They will be baptised on my next trip that way. On my last visit I was also able to talk to his brother-in-law, who lives on the next farm. He too made a profession of faith'.

ZIMBABWE. 'Tired, upset and hungry was I. I was so confused after all my day's plans had failed. I bought some food and found myself sitting next to a woman under a tree. I offered her my food and surprisingly she joined me. "What kind of woman is she?" I asked myself. Something inside me said, "She is as hungry as you are. Spiritually she is too."
I took out my booklet, "Can I share with you another kind of food?" I asked. "No, I cannot read", she replied. "Don't worry," I said, "I am going to read it to you."
As I was reading, I could see her face changing. She admitted it was the first time in her life that she was hearing the truth that God "cares about my future if I believe."
There, under a tree, she surrendered her life to him. Later she blurted out her story. She was tired and hungry. Divorced the previous day, she was on a long journey on foot to her parents. I gave her the Scripture booklet, and money for her bus.

In June WCN Ronnie Baird gives an account of the Men's Fellowship Weekend in Child haven...... Robert Crawford passed around a bag filled with little 'spills' of paper, each with the name of a man on it. You drew a spill and for the rest of the weekend you prayed for that man, never revealing the name of the person you were praying for..........Pastor Bill Foster was our spiritual leader and teacher... concentrating on the Word of God and keeping the message simple........ on Sunday morning we went to Shore Street Presbyterian, Donaghadee to hear the Rev. Alvin Little preach on divorce and the family - what can one say except that Alvin was his usual well-prepared, thoughtful and hard-hitting self - it spoke to us all!

June WCN also gives us an Annual report from the Dores at Wycliffe Bible Translators; and Pamela Brow's account of the Summer outing to Armagh of the Friday morning Men's group, elegantly and lovingly written!

DEAF/HEARING IMPAIRED.

We also learn that **Midge (Marguerite Hughes), has been 'signing' for the deaf at some recent Sunday morning services.** Quite a few people in West have been attending classes in '91', led by Midge, to learn basic communication skills, and another is to begin. There could be up to 3500 in North Down who are deaf or 'hearing-impaired'. **It is not at all inconceivable that we could have Alpha Courses or 'Life in the Spirit' Seminars or Home Groups for the deaf.**

12th BANGOR B.B. - 'Astonishingly successful' paper recycling scheme- in a short time six skips have been filled, each containing three tons.

Well done, Darren Duncan and Neil Blackmore!

SEPTEMBER WCN 1996.

OUR NEXT ALPHA BEGINS 24th SEPTEMBER.

Recent statistics suggest that on a normal Sunday about 3% of Britons attend Church, and only one in 200 of Londoners! We set that against the commission of Jesus to take the Good News to every person, and we realise that in our own country, we have a long, long way to go!
That, says Sandy Millar, **is why so many people need Alpha. While promising things have been happening over the last few years, in many places there are still declining congregations and crumbling buildings. Yet there is hunger in the hearts of many for a spiritual dimension, and this is reflected in the mushrooming of the Alpha movement: 4000 courses currently taking place.**

In this 40-page edition of West Church News we include some interesting and challenging articles that tell us of encouraging things happening throughout the U.K. and in many other parts of the world. .As well, having now done 2 Alpha Courses in West we include some reports from those who have attended our own Courses.

Do read through the whole of West Church News to update yourself on all that is happening, and to inform yourself of new developments and projects, through which we seek to strengthen the life of our whole congregation, of old and young, of male and female. There are opportunities to learn how to come to faith, to grow in commitment, and to learn to serve and witness in Jesus' Name.

There are whole segments of our society which are almost entirely de-christianised; we give a perhaps unexpected article on "The Church at the Racecourse"! That may challenge you to think of other sectors or segments of society where the Church needs to be planted! GOOD READING! READ ON!

SEPTEMBER WCN

calls all Sunday School teachers to a Training Evening led by the Rev. Ian McKee on Thursday 19th September, and to a Service of Dedication (with other youth Leaders) on Sunday evening 22nd September. It also tells us that **'THE PLACE IS SPARKLING'** since **KEN MACARTNEY** has taken over the duties of Cleaning and maintenance. During the 'fallow' summer months with fewer activities from organisations Ken has repainted the Praise Room, the Minor Hall and the Intermediate Hall, with many repairs effected. Floors and windows shine, outside work has been done while work on the roof over the Vestibule and over the New Hall storeroom will soon be initiated.

THERE'S A LIGHT IN THE WEST CHURCH OFFICE! You may see a light there at unexpected times, with one car in the Car Park! On occasion it may be as late as midnight or as early at 6.00am. In all likelihood it is **Billy Richardson, meeting a harsh deadline we have imposed upon him, so that the collating team may begin work on West Church News on the Friday morning at 9.30am!**

TERRY LAVERTY tells our young people -and all! - that there are great opportunities in Christian Education, and encourages us to learn what God is doing in the big world out there, by attending the Missionary Convention.

He reminds us that we need additional Sunday School teachers and that Young West Church involving praise, drama and Bible-based discussion groups resumes on Sunday 15th September; he also floats 'Saturday Night Live', as a real alternative to 'the High Street', and as a place where teenagers may have fun in a safe and wholesome environment.
ISABELLE NEWELL reports on a two-week Outreach among Gujaratis in Wembley, in company with a group of Irish Presbyterians, while **Alex Nicholls and Emma Hanlon invite West members of all ages to a BARN DANCE with a difference on Saturday 14th September.** This 'Tribal Dance' is to provide educational opportunities for young people in Kenya, giving bursaries to those who cannot afford fees

CHURCH AT THE RACETRACK.

[From time to time in West Church News we include articles that tell of what God is doing in other parts of the world. We do so to inspire and encourage our members *and with the aim that we also may be inspired with the vision of doing unusual and lovely things in Jesus' Name.*]

"God cares about grooms, hot walkers, clockers, exercise riders, and trainers who work behind the scenes at racetracks. That's why He sent 'Assemblies of God' Chaplain, Tino Rodriguez, into this hidden world.

'Racetrack people are a community unto themselves', he says, 'They don't associate too much with others'.

Danger, low pay, long hours, boredom, loneliness, alcohol abuse and drugs are all part of the scene. **'It's a hard life'**, says Laura Rosier, wife of a trainer. 'You work seven days a week. The horses are treated better than people- they are considered more valuable than the people who care for them.'

THE DOWNS. Chaplain Rodriguez's unusual church is San Luis Rey Thoroughbred Training Centre, located 50 miles north of San Diego. On a typical day he arrives at the track at 7.30a.m. He walks through the barns greeting trainers and workers who have been up since 4.00am. 'I'm there to serve people', he says. At any one time the Downs may have some four hundred horses in training and 300 employees. It is close to Del Mar Racetrack which has a six-week racing season in the summer. Employees live at the Downs in trailers, tack rooms, or in nearby apartments. **Many are Hispanic and do not speak English. Some are transients. They feeling rejected often say, 'I'm a nobody. No one cares'.**

At any one time, Rodriguez can be **an evangelist, marriage counsellor, Bible teacher, pastor, labour mediator, or social** worker. He also supervises Alcoholics Anonymous meetings, helps with medical insurance problems, marries couples, and conducts funerals. He even leads devotions with jockeys at Del Mar before the first post time.

He wrestles with trying to help people overcome alcohol or drug addictions. 'It's integrated into the racetrack', he says.

Yet Rodriguez has witnessed many conversions and estimates 40 - 50 decisions for Christ each year. *'I could not be here if it were not for Christ,' he says. 'I wouldn't have a message. Christ has been my sustainer, my life, my everything. He has given me success in my marriage and family. As a result I can share with others that He can give them the same thing.'*

Rodriguez's wife Linda helps with Spanish Bible study, women's activities, and special programmes aimed at families during Christmas and Easter. *'We see lives transformed'*, she says.

MOSSY.
Jospeph 'Mossy' Mosbacher, who clocks horses, experienced the saving grace of Jesus in 1994, when he was 78. Horse racing had been in his blood since he was 14. He has been a jockey, exercise boy, valet, and jockey's agent, and he trained horses for 20 years. Mossy admits, 'I got into a lot of fights and did not respect my fellowman. I missed not having a relationship with God'. Now he says 'Praise be to God! I thank Tino for bringing Jesus into my life. By dying on the cross Jesus forgave me for my sins'. **Mossy eagerly shares what God has done for him through poetry!**

THE ROSIERS. Laura and Tim Rosiers suffered through a stormy relationship before they gave their lives to Jesus. **Ten years ago Laura had decided to leave Tim because of alcohol and drug problems.** They weren't married then, but they were living together with several small children. After she had argued with Tim, Laura recalls her son asking, **'Mom, why doesn't Jesus ever come to our house?'**

At just the right time Tino Rodriguez visited their trailer home. 'I know the Lord sent him' Tim says. **'I accepted Jesus that day'.** Laura was sceptical. She says, 'I was real bitter and thinking, 'Is this some kind of joke? Timmy must have found out I was leaving and, instead of becoming angry, he's going to play this little charade.' Several months, later they were married and Laura became a born-again Christian too. After ten years Laura says,'No matter how much out of line either one of us gets, we always have someone to answer to. **We have Jesus, our hope for the future.'**

PURPOSE.

Tino and Linda Rodriguez serve God in a ministry quite different from the Assembly of God they pastored in Berkeley, California for ten years. **Yet they serve a needy, almost forgotten slice of society that God sent his Son to die for.** Rodriguez sums up his specialised calling with **'I try to be God's representative on the racetrack, that when people see me, they see His love and forgiveness'.** Not surprising, the theme of his ministry is, **'I consider my life worth nothing to me, if only I may finish the race and complete the task the Lord Jesus has given me -the task of testifying to the gospel of God's grace'. (Acts 20: 24).**

CAN *YOU* SEE A NICHE IN THE MARKET?

Having read "Church on the Racetrack" we asked our members to pause, not to rush on, but to ask God, to show any work that needs to be done, that is dear to his heart. Even better to ask God to reveal to YOU any work that He may be calling you to do. When we GENUINELY offer ourselves to God, then He begins to speak to us.

ANNE ANDREWS - In the

context of our own congregation Anne Andrews came to see that there could be a ministry for widows, for women who have suffered the pain of bereavement, and to bring comfort and encouragement into their lives. In terms of the Kingdom of God *there's a niche in the market here!*

MINUS ONE FOR WEST?

Anne Andrews sends "an **invitation to the widows in our West Church family to meet together for mutual support and encouragement as we study God's Word together.** We are planning to begin a support group which will be held bi-weekly over the Winter months beginning mid-October. We will use the material prepared by Feminine Focus and used in their Minus One support groups. For the past ten years I have been involved in Minus One and we have seen God's love reach gently into many hurting hearts with the comfort and healing He alone can bring. Minus One support groups are currently held in several homes in the Greater Belfast area. **For some time now I have felt there is a need for us to reach out to the widows within our own church.** I believe there is a very special place in God's heart for the widow, and as his servants we seek to be instruments of His love. To this end we have planned an informal introductory meeting on Friday September 6th at 8.00pm. All widows will be most welcome. **Come if you feel you need loving support** *and also please come if you feel you could help those more recently bereaved than yourself.* "*For further information contact Anne Andrews.*

ANNE SCOTT, some time back, came to see that there are many **hard-pressed CARERS out there in our community, sometimes at breaking-point.** And that there was a ministry in coming *under their burden to give respite, even for a few hours. To do this in the love of Jesus makes all the difference to them!*

CAN YOU SEE A NICHE IN THE MARKET?

JEREMY & HEATHER EVES saw the value of preparation for young people about to be married!

"LOOKING UP THE AISLE?" Preparing for Marriage.

"Does it ever strike you as odd the amount of time, energy and money which goes into the preparation for a wedding? Every detail is talked over, thought about, decided upon - the clothes, the flowers, the invitations, the reception, the food - **the list goes on!** Nothing odd about that; after all, it's a special day; it needs preparation. **But how long does the wedding last? One day. How long is the marriage intended to last? A lifetime, but how much preparation goes into that? How much time and energy is spent looking at how a marriage relationship really works? Often very little.**

SO HOW CAN A COUPLE PREPARE FOR MARRIAGE? **For the past four years at West we've been developing and using a course which offers a couple a chance to look at how a marriage relationship is built and provides them with a framework to facilitate their communication and understanding.**

WE USUALLY RUN THE COURSE FOR SIX WEEKS, one evening per week. During that time many issues and topics relevant to marriage are looked at, including discovering what God has to say about them and how this can be put into practice in real life. This is not as 'holy' as it neither sounds nor as far removed from everyday living as many imagine. **Real insight and hope is available!**

Here are a few of the subjects we focus on:-

LOVE -probably the most ill-defined and mis-understood word in the English language.
COMMUNICATION - its importance as the life blood of marriage and how it can be improved.
EXPECTATIONS- identifying and maybe adjusting them.
DIFFERENCES-made to be different!
MONEY- often claimed to be the number one marriage-breaker.
RESOLVING CONFICT - without spilling blood.
INTIMACY AND SEX - love is a language to be learned.
FORGIVING EACH OTHER - a daily choice.

After the talk on the evening's subject(s), each person individually goes through a brief work-sheet designed to help them identify their own thoughts on the topic. Each person then swops their work-sheet with their fiancé so that they can then discuss and work through their thoughts and feelings together as a couple. *This work, which the couples do on their own, is where the real value is gained from the course.* **There are no group discussions where couples feel they have to 'bare their souls'.**

Over the four years this course has been running, couples nearly always tell us at the end, that many of the topics raised issues which they needed to talk about and provided a good opportunity to do so. Sometimes they even have a laugh as well!"

CHRIS & CATRIONA RITCHIE - "We are grateful to Jeremy & Heather for their frank, humorous and humble presentation. We had known each other for seven years- five as boyfriend and girlfriend by the time we attended the marriage preparation course at West Church. We were eager to participate, but Catriona was overheard to remark at the outset, 'Frankly, I'll be surprised if they tell me something that I don't

know already!'

Suffice to say that Jeremy and Heather, armed with flipchart and markers surprised us!

After each talk, worksheets were distributed and we had an opportunity as individuals and as couples to respond to what we had learned. We had freedom to be honest because we did not share our answers with the group. **In the busy weeks leading up to our wedding, we grew closer to each other as we learned how the other felt about the issues raised.** We were taught **how to... how to** accept that the other person had a different viewpoint, different family background, and different fears; **how to listen, even how to talk, talk without accusation that is. In our spare time, we tried to practise discussing a contentious subject without saying, 'you make me mad', 'you** *always'*, **'you never'.** *We were speechless for twenty minutes as we struggled to say something in our new loving language!*

We are now married five months and the **course teaching becomes more relevant, not less, everyday.** Forewarned is forearmed and we are grateful to Jeremy and Heather for their frank, humorous and humble presentation. *Since we want our marriage to be happy, it was a very small and pleasant sacrifice to spend seven evenings in preparation."*

ALPHA COURSES.

The September Edition of West Church News reports on the amazing growth of the Alpha movement throughout the UK, and all over the world, and has a number of stories of transformations wrought in individual lives and families that are most impressive. As well, Alpha is being used in churches large and small, urban and rural and found to be effective whatever the place. More than that, it has been reaching out to dark and needy places, such as our prisons, bringing light and liberation. All this is most heartening, often awesomely inspiring.

AS WE BEGIN OUR THIRD ALPHA COURSE IN WEST we feel it right to enlighten our members on the INFRASTRUCTURE to launching an Alpha Course, and the harvest that Alpha has brought us.

RENEE ROBINSON tells the story of the social and catering dimension behind 1600 meals!

"When Mr Bailie asked me about my thoughts on providing food for Alpha, I gave him some ideas that he might consider in respect of such an enterprise. Well, he must have been impressed because I received one of those famous phone calls, asking me to join with **Linda Cummings** to look after the catering for the first Alpha. At this stage I was still thinking about sandwiches and tray bakes. **However, at our first meeting it became obvious that Mr Bailie was looking for a fully prepared evening meal.** *So it was that Linda and I set about considering the implications of having to supply approximately 130 meals each week.* The first step was to enlist the aid of folk from among the congregation to plan for what was ahead. At this stage **Pamela Dobbin and Jean Crichton** joined Linda and me. **From the deliberations of this group, the telephones burned and eventually we built up a team of helpers for a whole variety of tasks that were to be accomplished, to ensure that the food would be prepared and served at the appropriate time.**

READINESS OF MANY.
Without going into all the experiences that occurred such as inadequate cookers etc. **I prefer to think of the many positive events that we witnessed, such as, the readiness of many, many people to carry out their tasks throughout the twelve weeks with grace and good humour.** During the first Alpha approximately 1600 meals were prepared and served, and of course 1600 sets of dishes had to be washed and dried, 24 tablecloths had to be washed and ironed each week, and as I said all this work achieved without any hint of complaint, a testimony of the typical West Church response to carrying out and supporting the Ministry in a very practical way. From a personal point of view I was blessed by meeting and making friends with members of the congregation with whom I was simply on 'nodding' terms, especially the younger women of the Team, and renewing and strengthening existing friendships. As Alpha progressed our group formed its own little prayer circle and was itself blessed and strengthened through our intercessions.

(2) THE PHYSICAL AND FURNITURE-REMOVING DIMENSION.

The Alpha meal took place in the church building itself, which meant the chairs had to stacked each week and placed at the sides to provide space, and then in due course replaced afterwards, a considerable labour! ANDY ROBINSON and a group of men from one of our Home Groups undertook this considerable task and faithfully fulfilled it.

(3) THE SPIRITUAL AND PRAYER DIMENSION.

ANDY ROBINSON relates how in England a Prayer Group was designated to pray for the Alpha programme as it progressed. "So four of us met at 7.45pm each week in '91 to pray for all aspects of the Alpha programme. We prayed for each person attending the course, and all the support groups. In due course we were joined by Ailsa Weir and Hilary Guest. This enabled us to have a time of Praise, thus strengthening the Prayer time. The experience was an enriching one for us all and we know that prayer was answered, and this was specially witnessed at the celebration dinners. Some prayer has not been answered, at least not yet, however seeds have been planted and are being nurtured and will spring forth sometime." Andy Robinson challenges, "For Alpha

Three, if you are not directly involved, why not 'adopt' a group or individual on the course, and undertake to cover them with prayer during the Course?"

RESPONSES FROM SOME WHO ATTENDED ALPHA.

"I WAS AWARE OF GOD'S LOVE; I GAVE MY LIFE TO THE LORD." **Barbara Reaney writes:**

"As another Alpha course will be starting soon, I would like to take this opportunity to share with you my experience of the first Alpha Course. *I was not a Christian when I was first invited to Alpha. I was, however, searching for something new in my life, and increasingly found myself turning to God. I had so many questions but did not know where to find the answers. Then as if from nowhere came an invitation to attend Alpha.*

What happened that night was to change my life. Never having been to West Church before, I was immediately overwhelmed by the welcome I received. No matter who I was, no matter where I had been, **I was welcome.**
For the first time I was aware of God's love. Alpha is open to Christians and non-Christians alike. It is a place you can go and in a relaxed setting learn about the Lord, His works, His word. My group was a mixture of Christians and non-Christians, and the age range was diverse. Therefore, there was a wealth of experience and knowledge to draw upon, and many friendships made.
The teaching received was soundly based on the Bible, questions are encouraged and answered, no matter how silly they may seem. I gave my life to the Lord during that first Alpha Course. I believe the Lord knew I was close to making a commitment to him, and that He led me to Alpha. He knew it was there I would find the answers to my questions. I give thanks to the Lord for being in my life, and also for all those at West involved in Alpha. I would encourage everyone to attend an Alpha course, for me it was a blessing. I know it will for you also! Yours in Christ, Barbara Reaney.

ALPHA: "THANK YOU WEST FOR THE WARMEST OF WELCOMES."

"He leads me beside quiet waters, He restores my soul, and He guides me in paths of righteousness." Psalm 23
"ALPHA was all these wonderful things to us; at the time of coming to West, we had an urgent need for more spiritual food and the Lord guided us to an oasis, namely Alpha. We thought that perhaps it wouldn't be designed for us, but we were wrong. Alpha provided a new fervour for reading the Scriptures, a fellowship that we had not experienced before, and friendships in the Lord that have deepened and developed now into a home group which provides us with much needed regular and meaningful fellowship.
Jesus and his disciples shared many meals together, and it is certain that the most meaningful conversations took place at those times because folk were relaxed and glad to be in one another's company.
Alpha is the same, the atmosphere is relaxed and the company the best you'll find anywhere.
Thank you West for the warmest of welcomes! **Bill & Mandy Johnston.**

ALPHA: GOD NIGGLED AT ME - John Wilson.

"GOD and his meanings, for many years, niggled at me, and I was happy to do nothing about it. After all, I was my own master and was doing my own thing!
I enjoyed a hard working, disciplined career in the Royal Navy. I could do my job. "Work hard and play hard", was my policy in life. **Then I met and married Linda.** I left the sea behind me and moved to Bangor.
Some four years ago, I moved house again, just four doors from West Church. I remember David Bailie saying to me, "I have got you nearer to church John." To which I replied, "And that is as near as you'll get me, sir!" **How wrong was I!**

One evening, prior to the second Alpha course, **I was visited by Terry Laverty. (Big T to some).** I have always enjoyed his company and yarns; after all, we are "Townies" from Ballycastle.
During his visit, Terry took me unawares, *when he asked me to pray with him, but I agreed. Listening to his prayers, I felt a great heat come over me, so much so, that I broke out into a sweat, yet before, I had felt quite comfortable. On leaving me, Terry gave me an invite to Alpha. The next day I committed myself to the Lord.*
SOMETHING MISSING. As days passed by me, it dawned on me that my happy life had something missing from it and my thoughts grew serious about joining the Alpha, *and I had an urge to know more about God.*
I joined the Course and was immediately impressed by the friendliness and sincerity of the members. As the course progressed I soon realised that I had been looking upon God in the wrong direction. Whereas I had looked for FACT, I should have looked for

FAITH. **Once realised, I experienced a fulfilment in every session and Tuesdays would not come round fast enough for me.**

TWO EXPERIENCES: **Two experiences happened to me about the midway period of the course. The first was during a restless night. I got out of bed and started to read the Bible at a random opening of it. I had been confused in my thinking and feeling dubious about the course.
I found I was reading Hebrews chapter 11. "It amazed me."
The second experience was after a pleasant day in the garden. I dozed off for about 10 minutes. I awakened to a very clear thought. "Read Psalm 31" was my thinking.
I had never read this Psalm before or discussed its meaning in the past. I did not even know it existed. "It amazed me."
I now realised I had finally found the right direction to take. Thanks to this course and to all involved in it.** JOHN WILSON.

ALPHA - "YOU MAY MISS MUCH IF YOU DO NOT REFRESH YOURSELF" Harry & Ruth Wakelin, who put a prodigious amount of work into West in its early years, but had slipped out of the warm core of the church's life, write of Alpha:

"Not everyone will know the names appended to this piece, but those who know us will remember us in 1961 as two forty-year olds, playing our part in the formation of West Church. **So we know church life.** From the beginning in the old Carnalea House to our custom-built church on the Rathmore Road, **we have heard many ministers and prayed many prayers. So what had they omitted that Alpha had to give? In our seventies what had we to learn?**

Reading the format of the course it varied little from others we had experienced under the tutelage of our own minister and as I remember the late Rev. Dr. Tom Patterson too. One significant difference was the communal meal each evening where we made new friends. **This is where the ice was broken.**

I thought that many may be zealous evangelicals, and while some were highly committed people, there were many, perhaps the majority, who knew God, had accepted that Jesus died for our sins to be forgiven, but needed a new assurance. **Our faith was in the doldrums and required a kick start to make us sure again. This is what Alpha did. We heard much that we had forgotten; to us, not a lot was new, but we met many who were new to us** *and we would not have missed that!*

You are not expected to know your Bible from back to front, you are not expected to pray aloud alone; no one will touch you and no one is induced to fall about in paroxysms of religious fervour. **You will enjoy these meetings.
You may miss much if you do not refresh your memory of our Living Lord!** Ruth & Harry Wakelin.

**ALPHA- "WE ARE IMMENSELY GRATEFUL."
Harold & Joy McCaughan 'swithered' about whether to join Alpha or not, but in the end decided 'to give it a try'.**
"The warmth of welcome was indeed a lasting impression of all the meetings. We were welcomed each week by Mrs Bailie, by Heather and Anne, our group leaders, and just by everyone.
Next, the food - an absolutely delicious meal, lovingly prepared and smilingly served every week. A real opportunity for people to relax and get to know one another.
After an introduction from David or Terry, music and prayer, followed by a withdrawal to our groups to **discuss a prearranged subject each evening - and so often the subject incorporated questions we** had long wanted to ask.
The people who attended were a mix of young, elderly and those in the middle, bringing with them the experience of many different backgrounds and in our group Heather and Anne demonstrated, by their patience, gentle demeanour and shining faith, many of the gifts bestowed by the Holy Spirit.
They had their work cut out with us as we continually questioned, *but every point made was gently and convincingly dealt with, and at the same time one felt a gradual bonding with many people one might only have greeted in Church with a pleasantry.*

A BEGINNING AND A RETURN.
We feel that Alpha is both a beginning and a return -a beginning for many with a hazy idea of God's word and for many of us who attend Church each Sunday, a return, a brushing up and a reinforcement of the basics we all believe.
God has made us all differently, and as a couple we keep our faith quietly and perhaps too privately. That faith in God has been confirmed and underpinned by Alpha 2.

We are glad we joined and are immensely grateful to those who made it possible." Harold & Joy McCaughan.

This bumper edition of SEPTEMBER WCN 1996 gives other local testimonies in respect of Alpha, and much else besides, like news of our Guides and Scouts, our GB and BB; letters from Jonathan Montgomery in Madrid, and Astrid McElwaine who spent 2 months in India; from Laura Perver's Scripture Union Beach Mission in Port St. Mary; from Astrit Kumnova in Croatia; from the Abba Trust; news from Maurice and Winnie Sloan in Brazil; and a Short Story from Paul Graham.

AND ALL THESE ARE PART OF THE WEST CHURCH STORY!

OCTOBER WCN 1996.

PEOPLE SHOULD BE INVITED! On the front page of October WCN, David Bailie writes: "During this week I visited a man who started coming to West quite recently. He declared that he was astonished when he first went along to the Ten O'clock Service: *'It was just like the chapel - there were so many people!'* And the atmosphere inside truly warmed his heart - a sense of the presence of God and the friendliness of the people!

A couple of days later I visited another man who has recently come to West and seems happy and enthusiastic about what he has found: he described it as a **'Christ-centred church'**, and suggested one or two people he thought should be invited!"

DOES YOUR CHURCH GIVE INVITATIONS?

On page 12 of October WCN, Brian Kingsmore, PCI's Evangelism Promoter asks this question, and tells us that, "*some anecdotal evidence exists that the average PCI member seldom invites someone to their church.*" He goes on to quote Martyn Marty: a recent study shows that in the U.S., the average Episcopalian invites someone to church once every 28 years!. Brian Kingsmore declares, **'I am sure that PCI members are better than that, by perhaps 10 or 12 years!'**

Brian Kingsmore quotes Gallop, as a result of detailed analysis in England and Scotland. **It would appear that non-church attendees would view an invitation to visit church in a positive manner. Indeed 63% of Gallop's GB survey indicated that they would attend church if invited.**

Dr. Kingsmore then goes on to outline the context in which invitations *can most helpfully* be *given!*

DOES WEST CHURCH GIVE SUCH INVITATIONS? YES, BUT NOT ENOUGH! Our **THIRD ALPHA COURSE** got under way on Tuesday last (24/9/96), with an enrolment of more than 140!

Through the INVITATIONS of ONE member, four people came along! Wonderful! But then she had given about 20 invitations!

Korean Christians, where churches have grown amazingly, are dumbfounded, when they come to this country, to find that Christians don't invite others to our church services- **they** do! **Enthusiastically! What about inviting some people to our Harvest Services?**

NOISY SERVICES - AND JUNIOR BEGINNERS!
Recently someone spoke to me, after a particularly noisy 11.30 Family Service. The point was made that the level of noise from the most junior members of the congregation, really made it very difficult for folk to concentrate and enter into worship. The person-herself, a young woman, was surprised to learn that the **Junior Beginners' Department operates from 11.30am, and that three - four year old children may be left there in the competent, caring hands of a waiting staff from 11.15 onwards.**
While we like to emphasise **Family worship,** including our young children, **we want parents to know that this provision is made,** and to have discretion to realise when junior noise levels make it difficult for the main body of worshippers to enter into the service.
A WORD TO THE WISE! THANK YOU!

ALPHA GROUP NUMBER TEN - GIVES RESPITE!

"We were **Alpha group number Ten! When we first came together we did not know one another!** However, as the weeks passed and we had our meal together, and then later the discussion time, *we realised that we really looked forward to being together as a group on a Tuesday evening,* and so when the Alpha course ended, *we decided to stay together and to continue to meet on a Tuesday evening! We took it in turns to be host for the meeting.*

One particular evening, several months ago, we used **Matthew chapter 25 as the basis for our discussion; this really must be one of the most serious and thought-provoking chapters in the Bible!** Next morning, when driving to work, one of our members was suddenly given a picture of the room in which we had been sitting on the previous evening, each person seated exactly as they were at that time, and then Jesus said " **It's lovely that you meet together to talk about Me, and to pray together but what are you** *doing* **for me?** At our next meeting we discussed what had happened and decided to pray about it *and ask the Lord how best we could serve Him, because, as a group, we hadn't any ideas as to what we could do. We therefore prayed and asked the Lord to show us what He wanted us to do.*

Some weeks passed and nothing happened, and then one evening, a member received a telephone call from a friend who is a mother of a severely handicapped child. She said she had a friend, and that this young woman was much stressed at times, as she also had a handicapped child. She asked if anyone in West could visit this young woman who lives in Bangor. Our member took the name and address, thinking she would see if there was a Church Visitor in that area, **but then quickly realised that perhaps this was something the Lord wanted** *us* **to do.**

Three of us went to visit the lady,

and we explained that we were a church group, who would try and help in any way we could. *Basically what she really needed was a little time to herself.* She had a young child in a wheelchair, and felt very cut off and alone. We told her we would try and help her out for an afternoon every second week and she was delighted about that. **AS A GROUP WE WERE SLIGHTLY PUZZLED because** although we believed this to be the Lord's direction for us, *we couldn't all be involved!* We have six women and two men in our group, and while the women could baby-sit and cope, we couldn't use the men in this situation. **Also we felt we were only helping one person in a very slight way.** Nevertheless, we did go ahead and let this girl out on a couple of occasions. However, she herself was concerned about the situation because she felt if the child needed lifted in or out of the wheelchair, this could be awkward for inexperienced women on their own, one of whom suffered from angina. We had been going to look after this child two at a time. **We believed this was the work the Lord wanted us to do,** *because this mother was so appreciative of what we were trying to do to help her, but we didn't know how to improve things.* Then the Lord spoke again to the same member of our group, and this time He said "What about the church?" This was something that hadn't occurred to any of us. We spoke to our friend again and asked her if we could get a room in the church, **would she be willing to leave her child there with us on one Saturday each month.** *Her reply really confirmed for us that this was the Lord's will;* all she said was "**It would be wonderful!**" We therefore approached the Rev. David Bailie and he told us there was no problem whatsoever about having such a room!

WE NOW HAVE A COMPLETE ANSWER FROM THE LORD, and that has thrilled and amazed us- we have the room and the whole group can be involved together, because our men are so valuable and necessary in lifting the children as required, and it will take every ounce of energy from the six women in caring for the children.

We started this service on the 7th of September 1996, but we didn't make it known because we wanted to have only two children on that day so that we could see exactly what was needed, and how best to organise things. **However, the joy on the faces of those two mothers as they set out to enjoy themselves for a couple of hours,** *was worth a thousand pounds to us!*

OUR PLAN THEREFORE, is to be available in Minor Hall B in West Church, on the first Saturday of each month, from 1.30m - 5.00pm to care for handicapped children while their parent/parents have a few hours to themselves. If you have such a child, or know someone else who has a handicapped child, *then please give us the privilege of loving that child so that you can have a well-earned break. All you have to do is to ring one of the undernoted and let us know you are coming. We very much look forward to meeting you and your child.*

Dennis Wilson	Leonora Scott
Anne Scott	Heather McAuley
Peggy Smyth	Susan Wyeth
Irene Marsden	Robert Crawford

THE SUMMER OF 1996 MUST HAVE BEEN ONE OF POLITICAL UNREST AND VIOLENCE. Here is a POEM born in a West member's heart in the context of that bitterness and confrontation:

An illegitimate spawning
The bastard child of
An unholy alliance

Who is it that calls in the night
To its father? But the night is
long. It is filled with unrest.

A sorrowing mother
She too a hurting soul.
She fights to keep her child.

Rejected. I am rejected.
I cry out and no one hears
My voice and so I
Take up bitter arms and

Fight.
My God, where is your hand
To save? My God will fight
With me.

My God and Ulster,
My god is bitterness.
My God, come to my defence,
My god is hatred and

Defiance, Seeds sown   On
a bed of rape and   Plunder.
I know nothing else than my

Marred inheritance
Who will listen to the
Cries of the innocent?

Only one true Father will bring
Healing. Cast out then
the bitter roots of Vengeance.

Forgive the anger of
Rejection and release us from
Deep wounds formed in the womb
before
Evil was birthed, on

This day.
Hear our repentance on behalf of
Blind eyes, deaf ears and

Hardened hearts.
Forgive your Church,
Restore us Lord.

Who will hear? who will hear?
Take off the colours of allegiance
And clothe yourselves forever
In white.

THE SYCAMORE CLUB.

The Sycamore Club meets weekly under the leadership of **Derek and Tanya Polley,** who are assisted by

Harry Fulton, Beth Myatt, Rita Wilson, Colin Patterson, Jenny and Valerie Wilson, Pat McNutt, Heather Ennis, Violet Lowry and Richard Polley.

**During the coming term their subjects are: Olympics, Feeding the 5000, Moses/ Red Sea, Nehemiah, Hezekiah, The Paralysed Man.
In addition they have a Halloween Party with the PWA and a Christmas Party.   Folk come from the Croft Community, Ward House, Blair Lodge and two Barnardo's Homes.**

We rejoice that the Sycamore Club flourishes and ministers to a need in an important segment of our community, and we bless them for the work they do!

VISIT TO KENSINGTON TEMPLE, LONDON.

David Bailie writes: In June 1995 Rhoda and I paid a visit to London, primarily to attend a Conference about ALPHA in Holy Trinity, Brompton. As a consequence of that we began our first Alpha Course in West in September 1995.

While in London, on the Sunday evening we went to a service at the Kensington Temple - a remarkable event! In West Church News we regularly tell the story of what God is doing in other places, to teach us and to inspire us. In this edition of West Church News we include an article on KENSINGTON TEMPLE by its senior minister COLIN DYE, under the title: "A CHURCH REBORN THROUGH PRAYER." In this Colin Dye tells the story of the rise, decline and rise again of Kensington Temple, *which now has Britain's biggest congregation!*

"In the space of a little over 20 years Kensington Temple has **grown from a church of 300 members to around 10,000 people, meeting in up to six different Sunday services and over a hundred satellite churches all across London.**

During this time I have been a church member, a deacon, an elder **and am now the senior minister.** Having witnessed this life and growth at first hand, **I want to pass on to you the spiritual keys that have opened spiritual doors.** Kensington Temple is one of the most cosmopolitan places in Britain, just one mile from London's Hyde Park.
Situated in Notting Hill Gate, we receive people from all over the world. Over a hundred nationalities from every continent crowd into our services every Sunday. But we are just people, more or less like any others, with a complete mixture of traditions, a variety of jobs, interests, sorrows, struggles and joys.

Yes, we have all discovered the reality of Jesus' resurrection and experienced the fullness of his life-giving Spirit, **but so have a vast number of people in other churches. So what accounts for this remarkable expansion that shows no sign of slowing?** *It is undoubtedly God's work. But why has God chosen to bless us so much?*

THERE ARE MANY ASPECTS TO RAPID GROWTH, yet the fundamental reason for it cannot be found in smooth organisation or advertising or social action groups, desirable as all these may be. **There is one master key; behind every successful development, every creative plan and every thrust forward, there has always been one thing -** *earnest, sustained prayer.*
Prayer is the creative powerhouse of God within us. Prayer effects real change. *Prayer transforms lives, churches and communities.*

KENSINGTON TEMPLE BEGAN WITH LESS THAN 50 PEOPLE. But they were 50 people who took hold of God and God took hold of them! All it takes are men and women open to share and respond to the desires of God's heart.
The story begins in the decade after the first world war. The initial jubilation of peace had passed and the coming depression of the thirties **was having a grim impact on the life of everyone in Britain. Churches were struggling too.
TWO WELSH EVANGELISTS.**
Under the anointing of God's Spirit George and Stephen Jeffreys began to blaze a new trail for God across the nation. These men were known as Pentecostals, a new group of Christians who were rediscovering the power of the Holy Spirit.
They were to be tremendously effective evangelists, not because they were special in themselves but **because they had learned a revival secret, the secret of powerful praying.**

**POWER RELEASED.
The events that followed the Jeffreys brothers around the country could have come straight from the Acts of the Apostles. Apostolic power was being released in a new wave of miraculous healings and in thousands of conversions.** Called and set apart by the Lord, these evangelists dedicated their lives totally to the work of spreading the Good News.
This was the vision God had given them - **to set people's hearts on fire for Christ and turn the nation back to God. They abandoned the trappings of the world and lived their vision.**

This was the power released through prayer and evangelism that began the work of Kensington Temple.

'BETHESDA OF THE WEST END' The original name of this Victorian Congregational Church was Horbury Chapel. George's brother Stephen held meetings there. So many people were healed that the papers called the Church, the 'Bethesda of the West End'. **Ten years later, George bought the building, and it continued as a place of prayer and healing. But then war-time conditions, the London blackout, and the evacuation or call-up of many of the congregation seriously eroded their numbers. Disagreements over organisation and structures further sapped their energy.**

Finally, the last surviving trustee was unable to continue, and a small Pentecostal group under the leadership of Eldin Corsie was invited to take the building over.

Corsie was youthful, hopeful and yearning to see a new visitation of the Spirit of God in Notting Hill. As God would have it, *the trustees wanted to sell Kensington Temple and approached the new church group who promptly bought it.*

DAUNTING EXPERIENCE. It must have been a daunting experience for that small congregation of around 60 as they entered Kensington Temple for their first service.
One can imagine their thoughts as they looked around, swamped by a building designed to seat a thousand. **They were well aware of the one-time success of the previous church and the realisation of the enormity of the challenge before them began to dawn.**
'You have done it before, You can do it again. Lord, fulfil your Word. SEND PEOPLE HERE FROM ALL OVER THE WORLD. MAY THIS CHURCH BE LIKE A CITY SET ON A HILL' This was Eldin Corsie's prayer in 1965.

'CHURCH FULL' During a session of spring-cleaning, Eldin and his helpers unearthed a sign that had been set outside the church during the revival. It read **'Church Full'.** In the basement they were astonished to discover among the rubbish, a number of wheelchairs, crutches and other aids discarded by the sick when they had been healed. The sight of these reminders of the earlier revival under the Jeffreys brothers stunned everyone into the realisation of their need for God. **They cried out in desperation, hungry for a new movement of the Spirit's power. An urgency entered into their prayer meetings.**

HARD GROUND.
Outside the building things seemed to be getting worse, not better. Notting Hill saw race riots, drug trafficking and prostitution. It was the swinging Sixties, the era of drugs, sex and rock'n roll. Inside the church the believers were hard at prayer. They felt the spiritual confusion and emptiness all around them **and sought God, pleading with him to act. And He did.**

One by one, lost, hungry and broken people began to come in. Heroin-addicted, sexually disillusioned, lonely and frightened people, alongside the wealthy and secure-in-the-world began to swell the congregation.
At the same time **occult practitioners** were very active in the area. A number of witches' covens were a stone's throw away from the church, **One such follower, Audrey Harper who came 'only for a cup of coffee' received such a warm welcome that she stayed, and later went on to accept Jesus for herself. Other converts followed from all walks of life. Personalities from the media, political and sporting worlds all found their spiritual home. We were now in the Seventies. People from other nations, often rejected elsewhere, found acceptance in the congregation that now numbered over 500.**

PRAYER had begun to break up the hard, unploughed ground of people's hearts. *God was sending his showers. The harvest was ripening rapidly.*

AN OASIS. The Church at Notting Hill Gate was like an oasis in the middle of a wilderness. Week by week a core of 80 faithful people kept up the momentum of prayer and earnestly called upon the Lord. The Spirit of God was powerfully present as, one by one, people stood up in public prayer. Eldin Corsie encouraged us in those days with the words **'Prayer is the powerhouse of the Church'.**

Colin Dye says "That was the Kensington Temple I was introduced to. I took to it like a duck to water. It seemed as if it was what I'd been searching for all my life!'

A CHURCH THAT COULD COPE WITH MY EXCITEMENT.

It was 1972. I was a young student dancer in London, and a new, enthusiastic convert to Christ. I had given my life to the Lord when on holiday, through the ministry of a tiny mission hall in the north of England. Once back in London I started to look for a church that could cope with my excitement, a place where I could grow spiritually and find out more about Jesus. **Until this time I had found most churches boring and dull. As far as I was concerned they were irrelevant, never able to touch me where it mattered most in my life. I APPROACHED KENSINGTON TEMPLE warily, and, happily had my illusions well and truly shattered!**

FREEDOM. **The freedom of expression in the Holy Spirit was enthralling. The services were full of spontaneous praise and worship and I was filled with joy and an inexplicable delight just being among the congregation.**

REAL HEROES.
There were a few people that stood out to me even then as especially radiant members of the church. *Their love for God seemed to shine out from their faces and in*

*their every action. Everything about them spoke of their constant contact with the Lord.
As I got to know them I realised that the secret of this 'oneness' with Jesus was prayer. These people were 'prayer warriors'.*

It wasn't that they held public offices or were known and recognised for great achievements. **In fact most of them lived ordinary, mundane lives. Some worked in factories, others were office workers or cleaners, and a number were elderly or retired. Their spiritual stature was largely unrecognised. Aware of the difficulties standing between ourselves and prayer, I am always deeply impressed by truly prayerful people. To me they are the unsung heroes, the real champions of the faith."**

This is an excerpt from 'Prayer Explosion' by Colin Dye. (Hodder)

NOVEMBER WCN 1996.

**Our front page headline is:
A SHIP IS SAFE IN HARBOUR -** *BUT THAT'S NOT WHAT SHIPS ARE BUILT FOR!*

"There's a temptation in life to play safe! Some folk by temperament, may have that disposition. Others may be more impulsive, more ready to have a go, have more of the gambler instinct in them. *The first may achieve little, the second come to grief!*

It is important that we fulfil the purpose in life that God has for us, lay hold of his destiny for us. Sometimes people attempt too much in their own strength, and experience stress and 'burn-out'. Some folk say: 'better to burn out than rust out'. Others, who have attempted too much, may come to the place in life where they have now withdrawn, hurt and bleeding, and just want to play it safe!

We each need to know that God has endued us with a unique personality with our own special gifts. We need to know that Jesus came to give life in its fullness. Jesus is the One who told stories of the talents: the hero is the person who uses them to the full. The anti-hero is the one who attempts to play safe!

Paul says that WE SHOULD MAKE LOVE OUR AIM AND EARNESTLY DESIRE THE GOOD GIFTS THAT GOD FREELY GIVES. The context in which this should be done is **within the Body of Christ's people, where the whole body should grow, and each one playing his part.**

A QUOTE FROM UCB NOTES
"On the day she died, Miss Jones, an elderly spinster, was the oldest resident of her Midwestern town. In writing her obituary, the editor of the local paper was stomped, after noting her age. Miss Jones had never spent a night in jail or been seen intoxicated in the streets. *Neither had she done anything noteworthy.* While musing what he might write, he went out for coffee. In the local cafe he met the owner of the tombstone company, who was equally perplexed as to what to write about Miss Jones.
The editor returned to his office and assigned both the obituary and the tombstone epitaph to the first reporter he saw, who happened to be the **sports editor.** If you pass that little town, you'll find this on Miss Jones's tombstone:

Here lie the bones of Nancy Jones
For her life held no terrors.
She lived an old maid,
She died an old maid.
No hits, no runs, no errors.

If we don't **try**, we don't **do**. If we don't do, we can't bless others. **We each have a contribution to make to the lives of others. Give your best effort today. It's your best shot at scoring in the game of life!**

IN NOVEMBER WCN ARE CONTRIBUTIONS OF THOSE WHO ARE GIVING THEIR BEST SHOT IN THE CHRISTIAN LIFE!

You'll find BARRY McCROSKERY, intent on fulltime Christian service embarking on a Theology Degree at the Belfast Bible College.

You'll find TERRY LAVERTY calling all in their mid-teens and early Twenties to a YOUTH ALPHA on Sunday nights. YOUTH ALPHA is a 12-week course which will run at West every Sunday Night from 17th November to 23 February with a gap in the middle for Christmas holidays. We invite young people from 4th form upwards to come to tea at 6.00pm on these Sundays. At 7.00pm we will share in an act of Worship followed by a Thought Spot and discussion groups on the theme of the evening. This will be your chance to ask YOUR questions about God and to hear what others think. Typical topics for Thought Spots are - Is there anyone out there at all? What's the big deal about Jesus? How can there be a God in a world of such suffering and evil? Can I really trust the Bible?

TERRY also tells us that SATURDAY NITE LIVE is now alive and kicking as well as the Tuesday Youth Club.

BOBBY LIDDLE writes about the Church in Thessalonica. This is an introduction to a Short Series of 6 Sermons to be preached in West on the basis of 1 Thessalonians.

It is perhaps appropriate to state here in our "West Church Journey" that over the years Biblical exposition has formed the backbone of our teaching in West

Church. We have always been eager to draw our strength from God's Word, so that we may walk securely in his Way.

CHRISTINE MARTIN gives us an update on the Martin family, telling us that Brian is in his final theological year at Union College, and is a student assistant minister in Rathcoole. In this she speaks of the storms in life, of times of feeling overwhelmed and trapped, of times also when Christ drew alongside: "With Christ in the vessel We can smile at the storm, smile at the storm, smile at the storm. With Christ in the vessel we can smile at the storm, As we go sailing by."

KEN SYMINGTON, one of our members, WHO HAS CERTAINLY BEEN A PERSON READY TO DARE FOR CHRIST, declares that he has seen WONDERS in Poland and Lithuania, on a trip where he has travelled 4000 miles and visited eight countries.

ELLEL MINISTRIES; "After serving on their two-week Irish tour in June, Ellel Ministries invited me to lead a team jointly, with Pastor Clive Carr, to Poland and Lithuania from 10th September to 1st October. **INTERCESSION & EVANGELISM.** Ellel had asked me to teach the Polish Church on 'Intercession linked with Evangelism', and this was something of a challenge since I had never actually done this, or taught this! Three years ago, however, the Lord had shown me that He was going to lead me into this area of ministry in the future, **so now was a good time to find out!** Anytime I tried to prepare written notes at home the Lord checked me, and so I set off with **no experience** in this field and **no notes** to lean on! **The plan (in Poland) was that I teach every morning for an hour on Intercession and then, after coffee, Clive Carr teaches the following hour on Evangelism.**

During my Quiet Time on the first morning I was due to teach, **the Lord began to show me what He wanted me to teach,** *and the same thing happened every morning until we left Poland. Although I already knew each piece of the 'model' as an individual teaching fragment, it was only as He showed me the whole picture pieced together that I understood.* **The exciting part was the testing of the teaching,** and the first day we put this teaching method into practice **the Polish team led 17 people to the Lord during a standard hospital visit. Excitement rose!** However the real test came the following day. The Church interceded in their normal manner for an evangelistic team at another hospital in the afternoon, **and then they used the new 'model'** for the same team's visit to the city's drug rehabilitation centre in the evening. **Two extremes in results are hard to find:** one person made a commitment to Christ at the hospital, but it was a heavy atmosphere, and while we were in the hospital two of the van's tyres were stabbed by a sharp instrument, and one of the Polish team had their car broken into and the radio stolen. We were left stranded at the hospital for two hours. **We did not feel more than conquerors! That evening we arrived at the Drug Addiction Centre,** where the Polish Team Leader told us that **the young people would ignore us or mock us. But as soon as we went in, I said to the team, "The covering is in place, watch God surprise us" and He did! It was an open heaven and it seemed as though every addict came forward and made a commitment. I prayed for one lad who had Aids, and nearly, so very nearly got the Centre Manageress to make a commitment. I'm sure she's there by now, it was so close! Only 14 were to be allowed in to the centre, but they suddenly let everyone in and to cap it all, the centre agreed to hold a Bible Study each week from then on. An amazing two hours!**

MODEL PUT TO TEST: The last day saw us put the model to the test in a street in Wroclaw. After only an hour and a half **one lady arrived back breathless at our intercession base to tell us that she alone had personally led three people to the Lord. Clive Carr** told me that it was the first time in his life that someone approached him in the street and asked him how to get right with God. Clive said it was the best day in the streets he could ever recall, **such was the liberty to preach the gospel.** (He said that prior to this trip he would have to go back ten years, to India, to recall when he last saw anyone get saved in the street!)

On the last evening I found it impossible to tear myself away from the people. I shed many tears in the church To cap it all the church's intercession leader gave me a lovely gift for Linda *and said that the teaching had been God's answer to their prayers. Could anyone ask for more?"*

KEN SYMINGTON then goes on to tell of the 'long haul' journey in the van to Lithuania. This, a normally hassled affair often taking eleven hours, was completed in eleven minutes!

EVANGELISTIC SUCCESS. The evangelistic success continued in Vilnius and to the church's astonishment we saw people make a commitment on the streets on every occasion. They told us that when they went out not only were people never saved, *but no one even stopped to listen to them! The pastors said that they had never seen so many new converts in their church.*

Ken Symington concludes, "the way God blessed me most (and Clive Carr too, I think) **was to place us with 'Ela' in Poland. There we witnessed someone with an intimacy with Jesus that I had not experienced before....I will not rest until I have such a relationship with Jesus."**

[DGB COMMENT IN 2006. Most of the material in our "West Church Journey" is pre-1998. But occasionally one is tempted to look beyond that, and for one example we have chosen the case of KEN SYMINGTON, who over the years has entered upon a significant and very fruitful ministry. As an associate of Ellel Ministries he has taught and ministered in the USA, Russia, Poland, Ukraine, Lithuania, Hungary, Australia, England and Scotland.

DRUG ADDICTION. Ken writes, "we have been granted grace and favour to work with men and women coming out of drug addiction backgrounds and this is our favourite area of working right now."

DGB writes: When visiting the Christian Renewal Centre recently, Harry Smith, Director of the Centre, told me that a short time previously a group of young men from Dublin had come to the Centre for ministry by Ken Symington and how powerful and effective that ministry had been, in releasing people and setting them free. It had brought them into an experiential knowledge of the Father-heart of God.

MASSIVE VIRUS ATTACK ON HIS HEART.

On 6th July 2005 Ken suffered a massive virus attack on his heart. To survive was in itself a miracle- in due course to be restored to full health and strength and ministry was a miracle compounded several times!

Ken writes: "We have been doing two weekend Conferences, -one on the Father-heart of God, the second on the Lordship of Christ- in the major cities of Southern Ireland. So far we have done Kilkenny and Cork, with Dublin and Limerick coming up shortly. The final city will be Galway scheduled for 2007."

DGB writes: For many these have been life transforming and equipping, and we rejoice to see this continuing and developing ministry.]

NOVEMBER WCN also draws our attention to PCI CHILD PROTECTION GUIDELINES, which involves vetting and training every leader or helper in Youth work who is over 18 years of age.

Our own Kirk Session with responsibility for providing a training programme for our Youth Leaders, have asked Mr. Lindsay Conway, one of our elders to give a talk to our Kirk Session and our Youth leaders on Monday 11th November 1996.

WCN also gives news of Ron George and of Muslim lands and missions.

DECEMBER WCN 1996. DAKAR, SENEGAL, SMALL BUSINESSES.

In 1995 West Church gave £6365 to PCI's World Development Appeal. Now we are going to take a look at what a similar amount might achieve in 1996.

PCI's 1996 Appeal will be helping Shoe Makers in Brazil; creating employment opportunities for people affected by war in Sierra Leone; revitalising ailing industries in Senegal; and aiding a Nurses' Training programme in Bangladesh.

We have chosen out the Senegal programme to paint a picture of what our money can accomplish.

We look at how we may establish or strengthen small businesses to increase prosperity and employment.

ADPES: PCI PLAN TO GIVE THIS GROUP £20,000 TO HELP 1000 FAMILIES.

That is £20 per family - but in Dakar it is enough to establish a little jewellery business and create three new jobs; or help a fisherman to buy new nets and make his business more productive, giving additional employment also; or create a little tailoring business.

Through these businesses there will be a knock-on effect that benefits many more people and improves the quality of life for hundreds more families. West Church members are encouraged to visualise what gifts between £3 and £200 can accomplish! What a spur to generosity!

DECEMBER WCN gives us full details of Christmas services and invites us 'hit the Dublin sales' with 12th Bangor Boys' Brigade, who are organising a coach for Saturday 4th January 1997; who tell us us of their *Christmas Card delivery service* and their *Recycling efforts which have filled 18 paper skips;* and their Mournes expedition for 12-13 year old boys.

BOBBY LIDDLE ponders the significance of CHRISTMAS for people in other lands and tells us that in West **"YOUTH ALPHA IS UP AND RUNNING!"** He informs us about **Alpha for non-wrinklies!** "Three weeks into the course and things are looking good. Each night there has been about 40 young folk between the ages of 15 and 22ish. Although we have the experience of three Alpha Courses behind us, **the Youth Alpha is new to West Church and a different ball-game.**
More thought has to go into dividing the groups according to age, friendships etc. In many ways we didn't know what the first night was going to be like. We told the young people to 'suck it and see', but the Team had to do the same the first night. Everything went well and so far we have looked at the

topics - **Who is Jesus? Why did Jesus die? and Turning off.. to turn on: repentance and faith!** Sometimes the teenagers, who are thinking through the issues of faith, **don't have their questions clear in their own minds.** Also the pressure of peers can keep them silent in discussion groups. **Thank God that there has been open discussion and pray that this will develop in the groups which are more reserved.** Please remember the Team as they try to show and tell the Good News in a way that is understandable and relevant to youth culture today."

In the context of YOUTH, Bobby Liddle alerts us to *ANGLICAN CONCERN* over the 'deserting' young. A report reveals that since 1987 **Sunday attendance among 14 -17 year-olds has fallen by 35% and the number of 21 year-olds in church has declined by 34%.**
It notes that large numbers of young people still marry in church, but they don't go to Sunday services. **The report's first recommendation is that a greater allocation of resources is paramount.** *However an outspoken leading article in The Times, made the point that it was not 'resources' that would bring the young to God! It says* "The national Church is withering, with a dramatic decline in attendance among the impressionable and spiritually hungry section of the population and the working party is obsessed with 'resources'!
AN UNAPOLOGETIC CHRISTIANITY!
By presenting an unapologetic Christianity, evangelical and Pentecostal churches have attracted and held a growing congregation among the young. The style of worship is accessible but, more importantly, the theology and morality are demanding. By seeking to ape the informality of its rivals, the Church of England has mistakenly attributed its appeal to the style of service and not the substance of the sermons.
A few choruses on the guitar will not satisfy the questing soul in the way that honest engagement with the challenge of Christianity can. The leader writer concludes, **"perhaps the church should recognise that the young will, like the prodigal son, come back to faith anyway after sowing some wild oats.** *But that return will be more likely if the Church remains on firm foundations."*

CECIL GRANT writes his Christmas letter from Princeton- a few excerpts follow. "It was great being home over the summer, and I found my time in Holywood to be a real blessing....... So far this semester has been extremely busy. I have enough papers to keep me typing from now (4th November!) to Christmas. **This past week I had to write a 20-page epic on the 'Judgement of God'** After being cooped up for five days thinking and writing about nothing else I was longing for the Second Coming!! It was interesting to discover than in the last 30 years very little has been written on this subject, **which says something about our modern culture and church where we want all the blessings but none of the accountability.**
I'm also taking a course on Buddhism. Now before you think I've gone crazy, it has been very helpful to study another religion and to see how they view things. If ever you hear someone say that all religions are the same, tell them that they don't know what they are talking about- they aren't! By looking at Buddhism I've become even more aware *of the uniqueness of the Lord Jesus, and the fact that 'there is no other name under heaven by which we must be saved' (Acts 4:12).*

QUOTES THAT IMPRESSED JOHN WILSON DURING ALPHA 2.
In light of what has been written above about the desertion of the young from Church, and in regard to other religions, it may be apposite to give a few of the 'quotes' from Alpha that impressed John Wilson as he did this course.

"The doctrine that decided me to embrace Christianity and make public confession of my faith **was the doctrine of the vicarious death and suffering of Christ."**

"All religions other than Christianity have a kind of points system for obtaining eternal life. **Unlike other religions, we can do absolutely nothing to work for salvation; we must just receive it as a free gift.** These are roads that lead over the precipice. **In Christ we have been shown** *the* **road."**

"Everyone has a dark side which he never shows to anybody. **We have not yet discovered any human answer to the fundamental sickness and selfishness and weakness in our nature. If I wrote down every thought and deed I have ever done, men would call me a monster of depravity."**

"The Church is the only society on Earth that never loses a member through death... The Christian is not preparing for death, he is preparing for life. Eternal life begins as soon as we receive Christ our Saviour."

"Churches may be emptier than yesterday, but when Christians get together for worship, **something inside us urges us to be with God's people."**

DECEMBER WCN also gives us an update from the Dores; news of the couple we support in the Philippines through Christian Nationals, and Christmas greetings from Thomas & Lorraine Mulholland in which they tell us that they are adjusting to life in England, Lorraine teaching R.E. and Thomas doing voluntary work with 'Rugby Youth for Christ'. "Church wise, after much searching we have found a renewed Church of England church, called St. Matthew's... the pastor has a heart and vision for the people of Rugby. The people there are warm and friendly. In fact this has been our general experience of the people of Rugby and most weeks we have been at someone's house for dinner."

JANUARY WCN 1997.

CHALLENGING LIFESTYLES. This course is a follow-up to Alpha. It aims to help us enter into full possession of what is rightfully ours when we have put faith in Christ. Each person has a manual to study at home, and then the opportunity in the context of group worship, to share the topics of the course with others, so that this process is further enriched and fortified.

It is very much a **'HOW TO'** course. There are 19 chapters:
How to live under God's blessing;
How to have influence on society;
How to understand the Old Testament;
How to deal with anger;
How to avoid sexual sin;
How to avoid divorce;
How to live and act with integrity;
How to respond to evil people;
How to love your enemies;
How to give;
How to pray;
How to fast;
How to handle money;
How to stop worrying and start living;
How to handle criticism;
How to get our relationships right;
How to find life;
How to discern false prophets;
How to build a secure future.

We begin this Course on Wednesday 22nd January in the Praise Room at 8.00pm.

OUR *FOURTH* ALPHA COURE begins on Tuesday 21st January at 7.15pm. January WCN pays tribute to all who work so hard to provide delicious food and attend to all the infra-structure arrangements and includes encouraging testimony from some who attended the Third Alpha Course.

REV. ELIZABETH BREZELL WILL LEAD CONFERENCE ON WORSHIP.

Our aim in West is to worship God in spirit and in truth. Mrs Brezell will give encouragement and inspiration to all who are involved in the leading of worship in West - the Choir, Belcanto, the various Singing Groups and those who lead worship in our home groups. Mrs Brezell is well equipped to do so.   Mrs Brezell, whose husband is also a Church of England minister, is well qualified in music; her training has been in classical music, she is an Examiner of the School of Music and has conducted at the Guild Hall. She used to be Director of Music at St. Aldate's in Oxford. **She now teaches on Worship, and with her helpers conducts workshops on the Creative Arts and their place in worship and healing.** With two youthful helpers, Roseanne Bhioyan and Anne Rowley, the Team will conduct workshops on Painting, Banner-making, music, mime, movement, art, drama etc.

The programme will begin with a Buffet Meal on Friday 14th February to which all members of Choir, Belcanto, Singing groups and those involved in leading Home Group worship are invited, to meet Mrs Brezell, to hear from her, and to have the opportunity to worship together. This is followed by a whole weekend programme on the Saturday and Sunday.

PRAYER WORKS - IN SUNDERLAND AND AFRICA!

At our traditional post-Christmas Student Service, **RICHARD POLLEY** told us of the church he is attending in Sunderland, from which he has gained much support. A few years ago a number of Christians had a vision for a church in one of the less salubrious and less favoured districts of Sunderland.

So they began to pray... and pray... and pray! Now a thousand people gather to worship the Lord! The secret in its inception was prayer.... and that's the way they are still continuing.

AND AFRICA! One of the most remarkable features of Church life and growth in Africa has been the evangelistic ministry of Reinhold Bonkke, where hundreds of thousands of people have come together to hear the gospel, tens of thousands of people have come to faith, and many mighty miracles have been performed in Jesus' Name.

PRAYER SUPPORT: A person, who has been much involved in raising the prayer support for these huge rallies, is **RACHEL HICKSON**, now, with her husband, Pentecostal ministers of a growing church in London. **Many reports indicate that there is a real anointing on her teaching on Prayer & Spiritual Warfare. She will lead a Weekend in West on 2 - 4 May. It could be significant indeed!**

FRIDAY MORNING MEN'S FELLOWSHIP -
Walter McAllister encourages faith and tells of growth.

As he looks into the future he reminds us of a Christmas message given by King George: "I said to the man who stood at the gate of the year: **'Give me a light that I may tread safely into the unknown'. And he replied: 'Go into the darkness and put your hand in the hand of God. That shall be to you better than light and safer than a known way'."

Walter continues: "It is now 3 years since we started our Men's Group and there have been some changes during this time..... We have moved from '91' Crawfordsburn Road to the Praise Room because our numbers are continuing to grow and we needed extra space. This has been great for us all, as God is still blessing us when we meet together to praise and worship Him for all his goodness to us. There are many people to whom we owe a great deal for their support and prayers for our work. **We have had the joy of seeing men accepting the Lord Jesus Christ as their Saviour and Lord, and other men who have come into a closer walk with God. I would ask you please to continue to pray for this work.**

And Walter particularly thanks Renee and her helpers for the tea/coffee and scones provided lovingly each week!

INVESTMENT PLAN FOR YOUR FAMILY IN 1997.

TERRY LAVERTY writes: "I want to encourage all you parents *to start an Investment Plan with your kids* - not in the local bank or building society, but in the acquisition of WORDS OF LIFE! Parents, discuss together the possibility of PAYING your children to learn the Scriptures! This is necessary for our children's health and for the future of the church. The Spirit calls us to wake up! We work so hard to provide comfort and education and all mod-cons for our kids - yet just leave their spiritual welfare to chance! **We are willing to invest money and time and energy in their sport, cultural development, travel and leisure and in anything else that will give them a rounded understanding of the world in which they have to find a job - and every parent should do that!**

But surely their spiritual development should have priority. *Many of us have lost our first love, and the Gospel has become only moderately important to us - and our children realise that!*

We need to learn to stand with Joshua, who from the heart exclaimed: *"As for me and my family, we will serve the Lord!" (Joshua 24: 15).*

Terry draws our attention to Deuteronomy 6: 4ff: "Hear, O Israel: 'The Lord your God, the Lord is one. Love the Lord your God with all your heart and with all your soul and with all your strength. These commandments that I give you today are to be upon your hearts. *Impress them upon your children. Talk to them when you sit at home and when you walk along the road, when you lie down and when you get up."*

Terry affirms that this suggests a **structured teaching situation,** and advocates that we teach our kids, all day, every day... living, teaching, and talking. Terry challenges parents to **invest money in their children's knowledge of the Scriptures.**

HE GAVE US MONEY TO LEARN THE SCRIPTURES.

Terry continues: "My reason for the call to invest is that I owe a sincere debt of gratitude to a little man in my Sunday School for investing God's Word in my life in my most formative years. **He gave us money to learn the Scriptures and that was motivation enough to get me started. As I learned more and more of God's Word I began to enjoy it and when I eventually became a Christian at the age of 22 in Armagh Rugby Club,** *it was in response to Words of Life from John 10: 10 which I had learned as a child, and which the Holy Spirit brought to mind at a time when I was searching for the true meaning of life.*

AN INVESTMENT IN ETERNITY. I would be delighted if all the parents in West Church began to give incentives to their children to learn the Word of God. It can be a fun thing, especially if you agree to learn with them. Ten pence a verse and £2 a chapter is the arrangement I have made with my kids. You can sort out your own arrangement according to your means.

Terry goes on to speak of the great value of taking God's Word into mind and heart, with understanding and with reverence, and challenges our families to do this. **'May the Lord grant you success and joy as you live and learn together,'** he commends.

PASTOR JURAS GRINCEVICIUS of Emmanuel Church in Vilnius, Lithuania.

KEN SYMINGTON WRITES: "When on mission to Emmanuel Church in Lithuania, *the Lord laid it on my heart to help this young pastor.* Some years ago he had enough money to build a small home for his family, but during construction the economic situation in the USSR changed overnight and he was unable to proceed further with the home.

LIVING ON A BUILDING SITE. "For 4 years now, he and his wife and children have lived on what is virtually a building site, with rubble, ladders to upstairs and no heating. **While staying in a home in Vilnius in September I had to put on 6 layers of clothing at night in order to sleep, so the situation for him and his young family is difficult to imagine.** His wage is £10 per week and it will take $5-6000 (£3000+) to make his home clean and habitable with heat, and a further $3-4000 to finish the home completely.
During the mission we had a **'Marriage Refreshment'** night which was a real blessing to many exhausted couples in the church. As

I saw the couples at the end holding hands and embracing with newly awakened eyes for each other, **I will never forget seeing Juras' wife as he sat with his arm around her. Where other wives were smiling and laughing with their husbands, *she sat there motionless and wrung out. I was told she had a great ministry, but conditions at home have taken their toll.*** We in West have the economic power to help him. I think we should try. I have written to Juras to tell him that whatever has been raised by February 28th I will send him. **Any monies will help.**

ALAN CUNNINGHAM, well-known local singer is offering his services for AN EVENING OF MUSIC AND WORSHIP and will mobilise West church resources in Belcanto and in other gifted groups and people. A love-offering will be taken up, and the money sent to Juras.

SIMON ROWLAND WRITES: "HE WAS LIKE AN ANGEL."

"My association with West started in 1994 when I began to go to the occasional Praise Service. I was not a Christian then. However as a result of one Praise Night and the work of Alvin Little, now minister of Shore Street, Donaghadee, I gave my life to the Lord.

The love I received in West was wonderful. The Sunday Evening Healing Service undertook to pray for me and did so for a number of years; and Willie Hall's Wednesday night group were very faithful in prayer for me and for my whole family. I gladly acknowledge the work of the Holy Spirit in all this. However, due to my own ignorance and stupid self-will, there were areas of my life that I did not fully surrender to God ... I ended up in the local PNU in a very desperate state. Then **Ken Symington** came into my life, and in the grace of God managed to turn my life around.

However I was still in the PNU and Satan was furious at having his stronghold over my life broken and really attacked me. **He had me convinced that I was of little value and that the world would be better off without me. I was lying on my bed when I rose and turned to get my razor, when right in front of me was Charles McMullen.**

Charles had been taking a funeral in Newtownards and was returning home very tired. He was driving home when the Holy Spirit spoke to him telling him to visit me. *He was not sure about this, he was tired, and I was not a member of his church and therefore he didn't know me. Thankfully he was obedient, and came to see me. I thank God for that; he was like an angel standing in front of me when I needed one most. With seeing him the self-destructive spirit within me left and Charles was able to pray for me.*

I and my family are now members of West and the love and care we have found there has only been surpassed by that of God Himself. **Thanks be to God for His goodness and mercy, the true Shepherd of His flock. And thanks also to the men and women who are obedient to God first and foremost.**

PLANS FOR LINK EXTENSION AND CAR PARK. In this edition of WCN we present our plans for the Development of '91', for the Thanksgiving Chapel and the Cark Park Extension. Peruse them well.

The plan has been carefully thought through, and we trust you will find it a well-integrated one, uniting all our buildings into an organic whole. The sum given or promised within the 4-year period beginning April 1996 is about £120,000. This is unlikely to enable us to implement the whole - an option would be to leave the Thanksgiving Chapel to a later day if sufficient funds were not forthcoming. At any rate the time has come to present the plans to the congregation as a whole, and this we shall do soon.

FEBRUARY WCN 1997.

THIS GIVES DETAILS on the Conference of Worship to be led by Rev. Elizabeth Brezell from the 14th - 16th February. It also tells us a visit from Dr. John Bendor-Samuel, International Director of Wycliffe Bible Translators, and the organisation for which the Dores work.

It tells of the THINKING DAY SERVICE to be held in West on Sunday 23rd March when all our guiding and scouting organisations will be present at 11.30 am for their Annual Service.

RATHMORE SCHOOL will be celebrating 25 years at a special event to be held in West Church on Thursday 6th March. We send our good wishes to the Principal, Mr Alan Kennedy, and his staff, for the positive, up building and valued contribution that the school has had in the Bangor West community over the past quarter of a century.

In February WCN we have also the comprehensive Kirk Session Report for 1996, prepared and presented by our Clerk, Mr Billy McClelland.

The PWA **'mourn deeply the death of two beloved members, Margaret McCurley and Violet Camlin. Margaret was with us for about five years and served as member and Committee member. Violet was a founder member of West Church PWA and served as President from 1970- 1972, and as Treasurer from 1972 until 1989'. A faithful member, she died two weeks ago in her 93rd year.'**

VIOLET CAMLIN: OVER A VIRTUAL LIFETIME Violet inscribed the names of the hundreds baptised in West on to our Cradle Roll and provided a beautiful certificate for each child. A warm-hearted lady, with

a sense of humour, and a rare devotion, beloved by all.

MARCH WCN 1997.

The March edition of West Church News is a mammoth one of 34 pages! So we have to be selective in what we draw out from it!

TERRY LAVERTY writes on **SPRING CLEANING:** A Time to search the heart as we draw near to Easter.
"Every year as we draw near to Easter, I am always amazed at the amount of energy that I see being expended, as people come out of their holes and begin to wash windows and paint fences and plant new flowers in the garden. How we thank God for the brightness of recent and the ever-lengthening days! **Winter is on its way out - and spring has sprung!**

FIRST TIME I SHARED MY FAITH: This time of the year also reminds me of the amazing first time that I shared my faith with another person. It happened in a little church in Belfast, where I had gone for a Good Friday service. **I was very early for the service, as was another guy who sat in the back row, seeming very sad and troubled.** I said "Hello" and sat down in front of him. Both of us picked up the church magazine in the pew and began to read. **To my alarm, about 10 minutes later, the stranger behind me reached his magazine over my shoulder and asked "Does this scripture apply to me? I think it does - and is afraid there is no hope for me with God."**
I swallowed hard and looked at the passage of which he spoke. Then I swallowed harder!! The passage was Hebrews 6: 4ff! What was I to say?

I PRAYED EARNESTLY! God mercifully gave me a reprieve when another member of the church came and sat beside him. I sighed with relief and that was that *until the service was over! Then he came back with his question!* After two hours of conversation, I left him to the bus station and prayed a simple prayer which he repeated after me, with tears and thanksgiving, rededicating his life to the Lord. **This guy had been a Christian for years, yet had grown cold and fallen into a pattern of sin. That day he was utterly miserable, and went to five closed churches on the Lisburn Road, before eventually arriving at that church, which just happened to be open - and that's how I came to meet him.**

WHAT A TRANSFORMATION there was when we parted! The head was high. His eyes were alive and happy and he headed home with a song in his heart. *Here was a man who had been spiritually spring-cleaned. I'll never forget that night! Praise the Lord for his goodness!*

TERRY EXHORTS: It's no bad thing for **all** of us to have a good 'hoke about' in our lives as we draw near to Easter. **All** of us have things that need re-arranged or thrown out; or we need fresh imput from the Lord for the months that lie ahead. **So, GET TO IT! You'll be surprised by the amount of garbage you might need to dump. But there will be encouragements too as you discover the green shoots and flowers which are evidence of the Holy Spirit's lovely work in you.**

Then TERRY proceeds at some length to show people how they may be renewed. Ultimate assurance may involve going right back to the Cross! That's where Jesus died to give you new life. HE will give you assurance.

BOBBY LIDDLE reports on UNIFORMED AND NON-UNIFORMED ORGANISATIONS AT THE ANNUAL MEETING.

In our "WEST CHURCH JOURNEY" it is not possible to give regular updates on all our organisations. However, it is right to give the occasional overall snapshot of this work that involves so many leaders and so many young people, and flows from the faith of the Body of Christ in West. This is what Bobby had to say:

"This report shows just how many young people come in through our doors at West each week. In this day and age we should give thanks for the opportunity to influence them for Christ. **As a congregation we commend and thank all those leaders and helpers who give so consistently and sacrificially of their time to work with our young people.** *They love it - otherwise why would they do it? However, their work in preparation, organisation and leading seldom gets the recognition it deserves. How much more encouraged the leaders (and young folk!) would be if we, the wider congregation, made a point of praying for them, actively supporting their ventures and asking about the organisations.*

GIRLS' BRIGADE
There are 80 girls between 2-18 years on the roll. The girls participate in their four-square programme of badge work covering the areas of **the spiritual, physical, educational and service.**
This year the annual missionary lunch raised £500 for '**Protect a child in Thailand'**. A Table Quiz was held once again and enjoyed by everyone who attended. **The Christmas outing was to the Pantomime.**
Presently the girls are preparing for their annual display on 4/5th April and a Weekend Camp at the Share Centre, Lisraskea for the 11/13th April.

BOYS' BRIGADE.
At present there are approximately 120 boys across all sections, Cabin boys, Anchor boys Junior and Company sections.

The usual range of badge work, drill, sports and spiritual input is ongoing. Three of the senior boys play for the Battalion Football team.
The Junior Section are planning their annual camp from 9/11th May to Glen River YMCA Centre, Newcastle.
This year our Company is responsible for hosting the Bangor District parade and for the Bangor District at the Annual Belfast Battalion parade.

GUIDES.
The Guides have had TWO camps at Lorne in the past year, *after which they were one of only three companies in the district to be presented with the Outdoor Award.* They entered the Ewing Johnston Challenge with a group of girls **performing a unique dance/fitness routine.**
For their GOOD TURNS all sections went carol singing and held a Blue Peter Bring and Buy Sale which raised £120 for leprosy sufferers.
60 Interest Badges have been gained this year and there are a few Guides working for the Baden-Powell Award which is the highest award in Guiding.

STEPHANIE SHIELDS is to be congratulated on her appointment as District Commissioner.

A Sponsored Walk will be held on Saturday 22nd March and a Coffee Morning between services on Sunday 23rd March.
Because of large numbers, the Brownies still meet in two Packs.
In September they had a Pack holiday to Lorne. At the moment the girls are working hard for their journeys and badges and hope to follow the Guides in gaining their Outdoor Award.
The Rainbows presently have 26 girls. Like the other sections their programme is designed to help girls develop physically, creatively, spiritually and emotionally. **The size of the group may require splitting into two. More help is needed to comply with association leader-to-child ratios.**

SCOUTS.
Among all sections, Squirrels, Beavers, Cubs and Scouts there is a total of 104 young people.
The Cubs won the Bangor and District Swimming Gala this year in competition against 13 companies.
The Beavers came third in their Sports Day and the Scouts will take part in their 5-a-side competition on 22nd March.
Together the Scouts and Cubs are planning a camp at Crawfordsburn and there will be a Cake Sale for company funds before Easter.

Chris Miller, in addition to being the sole leader of the Scout section, is also Group Scout Leader. There are only 8 leaders to cover all sections of the Scouts which is not enough to keep the proper leader/child ratio. *Without additional adult help both the Scouts and Guides may have to turn children away. If anyone is willing to help, even on a rota basis, they should contact Chris Miller (or for the Guides, Stephanie Shields).*

TUESDAY NIGHT YOUTH CLUB.
On average about 25-30 teenagers meet on a Tuesday Night. The majority of these young people are from non-church backgrounds. **For most of them the Tuesday Night Club is their only contact with the church.** *Although the work is slow, and at times not easy, it is a valuable outreach to young people who have virtually no other Christian contact.*
The staffing levels have fluctuated but have been better than in previous years.
Before Christmas the group held a sponsored **'Pancake Eating Competition' which raised £140 for Children in Need.**
Many completed a questionnaire about their attitudes to Jesus and the Church. This led to very helpful discussion.
So far we have had 2 outings and plan to have a Table Quiz soon.

SATURDAY NITE LIVE.

Saturday Nite Live started in October with ten leaders but the numbers were disappointing and averaged only ten young people. Although this seemed to be a setback it gave the team an opportunity to bond together and establish control. Even though the average was only ten, new faces were coming each night. **Since the New Year the attendance has grown to 25 per night which has been a great encouragement.**
As we feel it is important that the work has enough leaders each week to ensure the club is well controlled, we are restricted to opening only on 1st and 3rd Saturdays of the month. **We would hope to extend the work to every Saturday as soon as more leaders are available. This is a new outreach in our church and as such needs much prayer and encouragement.**

BACK HOME AGAIN!

IN MARCH WCN we have included an amazing report by the Rev. Dr. Jack Weir, for many years Clerk of our General Assembly and respected senior statesman in our Church. For him "Back Home Again" was a return to China, where he had been born to missionary parents in the region of Manchuria. His father had been a missionary in China from 1899 until his death in 1933.
Jack Weir spent the years of his childhood in China, and returned to that country for his early Christian ministry, involved in student and relief work during war-time conditions. Following the Communist victories he turned to teaching in the Church's North-Eastern Theological College until the withdrawal of the last remaining Scottish and Irish missionaries in 1950.

All are aware of the sometimes savage persecution of the Church in China at the time of the cultural

Revolution and the Red Guards. Jack Weir gives an absorbing account of the Christian scene in China today, and of his return to the Theological College in which he had once taught. This was on the occasion of the opening of a rebuilt College, some eight storeys high. I give a brief excerpt from his attendance at one church service during his trip:

"Soon after arrival, I joined with the crowded Friday-evening congregation for a Testimony meeting, at which we were regaled by the usual lively accounts of how the women had been healed of their ills. *Then I was introduced and invited to speak. Before the sea of faces and overcome by the emotion of the occasion I could only stammer a few sentences.*"

Emotional it must have been for Jack Weir to see such a revival and growth in the Church!

PARENTING - WHAT MUST WE DO? SOME HELPFUL GUIDANCE GIVEN BY MICHAEL PERROT.

In light of the break-up of family life, and the alienation of young people in our society, Michael Perrot's guidance is helpful indeed. It gives insights necessary to grasp, if things are to mend. And that's why, for the enlightenment of our members, we include this in March WCN.

PREPARATION FOR MARRIAGE.

"The evidence is clear - where marriages break down *parents struggle and children suffer.* Therefore let us set high standards for marriage for basically, the better the partners the better the parents. **MY WIFE AND I LEARNED THE HARD WAY.** The wedding wasn't over one hour before the first sparks began to fly. Yes, it was over mother-in-law. The photographs hadn't even been taken. **The honeymoon ended in moody silence. And within seven months** *'I love you'* **had become** *'I hate you'.* It was a stormy and tempestuous beginning. Why? **Well, we went into the marriage blind.** *All the preparation for a wedding of one day and nothing for the marriage designed to last for life. How crazy!*"

PASTORS DO NOT PREPARE PEOPLE FOR MARRIAGE.

"Why not? Many say because they haven't been trained to do so in Theological College." Michael Perrot continues: "I plead with those colleges; teach Hebrews and homiletics if you will, *but don't let your students go out into their ministry without teaching the art and skills of marriage that they may teach others also. Ministers, I plead with you that so far as it lies within your power, do not perform the weddings of any couples who refuse to take their marriage seriously and will not prepare themselves for it.*"
Michael Perrot continues: "I regard as one of the great privileges of my life the opportunity of training young men and women for the great adventure of marriage. **I find that when they realise what is on offer they grasp it with both hands.** *Let the Church take the lead and one day some government will discover that stable homes save billions of pounds.*"

PARENTS INVOLVED WITH THEIR CHILDREN.

"You know the saying that children spell love T-I-M-E. Time to play with them when they are small, time to listen when they are big. The Bible says, 'Fathers, do not exasperate your children'. One exasperated young man said to me 'My father gave me money but not time'. Time for the TV, time for the telephone, time for the pub, time for the Church! *The father is the model of what a boy should become, and if the father is absent or emotionally distant the boy can become confused sexually.* ONE STUDY OF 300 MALE HOMOSEXUALS showed that not one had a close relationship with his father.** Michael Perrot continues "I grew up in a single-parent family. I had no model of maleness. I started on that homosexual road myself - briefly- but then turned from it so that it is but a memory and I would never know that I had felt that way. **But I predict as we gaze into the next century** *that as more families break down and there are more absent or distant fathers, so the practice of homosexuality will spread much further.*"

TOUCH, HUGS!

"Fathers - and mothers - be in touch with your children not only in **time** but also in **touch. Happy the daughter who can hug her dad and be hugged by him, healthily, wholesomely.** And mum too! One woman told me, **"I can never remember being kissed or cuddled or even touched by my mother."** No wonder that in later years, reaching for warm assuring touch, she found it in the wrong arms.

INFORMATION ABOUT SEX.

Where did we learn about sex? From parents? The evidence is that the home is the best place to start and to start the teaching early. Thankfully there are materials published by NavPress to help parents, as appropriate for different ages, 3-5; 5-8; 8-11; 11-14 year olds. Then there are Steve Chalke's videos: **'Lessons in love' for younger teenagers** and **'How to help your child to say 'No' to sexual pressure.** We should work towards the day when it is the norm for parents to inform their children; to inform, and gently to warn of the unwelcome molesting approach and to tell the child that it is OK to say 'No'. If necessary it is OK to shout and scream and run away. **The overwhelming evidence is that when a child does this the would-be abuser backs away.**

PARENTS TOGETHER.

Michael Perrott asks **'Have you read the teenage magazines? Have you?** I am ashamed that for so long I didn't; *but I tell you I* have now and I'm incensed. Here's a message for 11-14 year olds. You can tell because all the letters are (apparently) from kids of that age. **There was sex implicit or explicit in every corner *and never a question as to whether it was right*.** And I'll tell you something that enraged me. *I don't believe for one moment that those letters were written by children but by an adult, the same adult in each case, unable to disguise his or her style.*

NOW HEAR ME!
Most parents love their children, and don't want them into violence and drugs and promiscuity **but we stand helplessly and hopelessly by.** *We don't need to. We can get together. We MUST get together. Christian parents, non-Christian parents, parents from ethnic minorities, all agreed on a few simple things- angry, courageous, united parents!*

'ALPHA COURSE' FOR PARENTS.
Maybe the Evangelical Alliance could devise a kind of Alpha Course for parents, including valiant single parents, **which could be used across the country.** Something simple, not obtrusively Christian, which could be sold in High Street stores and station bookshops. *Let someone here write it!* Is a million copies unthinkable or 2 or 3 million?? Basic stuff that so many parents know so little about - discipline with love, handling conflict, building self-esteem, encouragement.

ENCOURAGEMENT.
There are psychologists who tell us that for every one negative thing said to us we **need four positives. What exasperates children and young people so much? It is when there is correction and condemnation day after day until they feel they can do nothing right and end up doing or becoming what the parents feared most.** *A negative parent does not breed a positive child.*
Of course we have to correct, but let our correction be in the warm embrace of encouragement.
'Thank you, well done, that was a good choice, you look great, your mother and I are looking forward to the day you drive and we can sit in the back'. **Nothing so warms and motivates the young as the proud affirmation of the parent.**
Michael Perrot speaks of Jesus' baptism, when the Father's words were spoken of him and to him: **'This is my son whom I love; I am well pleased with Him'.** And we can learn from that!

A man telling of the early influences upon his life paid tribute to his parents with the words, *"From whose lips I first heard of Jesus and in whose lives I first saw Him."*

APRIL WCN 1997.

SHAPING OUR FUTURE - FORGING A STRATEGY FOR FUTURE GROWTH!

In West we have 35+ years behind us, and the infant sapling of 1961 has burgeoned into a formidable tree in whose branches many find shelter. *We have reached a stage when, while we give thanks for all that has grown in the past, we must set ourselves to discover the ways in which God would lead us in the future.*

ANY ENTERPRISE.
There is a proverb (24: 3-4) that says: "Any enterprise is built by wise planning, becomes strong through common sense, and profits wonderfully by keeping abreast with the facts."
And here are some additional, helpful proverbs. In Proverbs 15: 22: "Plans go wrong with too few counsellors; many counsellors bring success."
16: 3 "Commit your work to the Lord, then it will succeed."
16: 9 "We should make plans - counting on God to direct us."
20: 4 "If you won't plough in the cold, you won't eat in the harvest."

In West, we must plan for our future, bearing in mind the wisdom of the Proverbs: *we must keep abreast with the facts, use common sense, consult widely, commit our work to the Lord, and look to God to guide us.*

IN WEST, GRATEFUL FOR PAST.
In West we are grateful for the quality of love and worship that has been built up, but not so naive as to believe that there is no room for improvement. We are thankful that the congregation has reached out to bring many to faith and to minister to the needs of many - yet the Commission to tell the Good News to all, is still far from fulfilment.

So our Kirk Session wants our members *in various groups to meet together on Monday nights, beginning 28th April, and continuing to mid-June to study for our future development.* We want the whole core of our congregational members to be involved, all who have leadership in our multifarious groups and organisations - **all who are stakeholders in our congregation.** All such are being invited for this series of meetings and to a whole-day conference on Saturday 31st May.

OUR SUBJECT OF STUDY -
Rick Warren's new book **"Purpose Driven Church."** In this book, the minister of Saddleback Church, in Orange County, California, tells the story of a church begun in 1980.
This church aims at *the unchurched*, and during 15 years until 1995, 7000 people have come to faith, the church has now an attendance of 10,000 weekly in four services. *Of these 5000 are committed members and 5000 would-be seekers* - whom the committed members and the reputation of Saddleback church, bring along. In West our intention

is not just to clone, imitate or replicate, **but to study, ponder, gain insight** *and to sharpen our own focus, on how, under God we may develop.*

The aim of this exercise is to set us thinking, to make us aware of important and relevant issues. In the beginning *it is not to make decisions, but to take widespread note, on the basis of which some decisions may be taken later.*

AIMING AT GENUINE, CONVERSION GROWTH.

In a Foreword to Rick Warren's book, W.A. **Criswell** writes that the Saddleback church is rooted and grounded in the Word of God, in Spirit-anointed servant leadership and a genuine love for people. It has not relied on biological growth or transfer growth from other congregations, **but is wholeheartedly committed to conversion growth. Rick Warren understands the mind-set of the unchurched of this world, and encourages local churches to penetrate a materialistic, humanistic society, with the transforming message of Christ.** Church leaders should read the Saddleback story. "I heard a fellow say once, **'Minds are like parachutes; they work best when they are open!'"**

IN WEST WE STUDIED THIS BOOK.

Over a period of six weeks, a core group in West studied 'Purpose Driven Church', and we encouraged our members to immerse themselves in this remarkable story. We gained valuable insights. We can but **mention** a few of the insights gained. One can do no better than give a few quotations!

"SURFING is the art of riding waves that God builds. God makes the waves; surfers just ride them. No surfer tries to create waves. Growth cannot be **produced** by man. Only God makes the church grow. Only God can breathe new life into a valley of dry bones.

As Paul pointed out at Corinth, ' **I planted the seed, Apollos watered it,** *but God made it grow.'*

At Saddleback we **have** tried to recognise the waves God was sending our way, and **the more skilled we became in riding the waves of growth, the more He sends!"**

TWENTY YEARS OBSERVING
Rick Warren writes: "For the past 20 years, I have been a student of growing churches, regardless of their size. In my travels as a Bible teacher, evangelist and later as a trainer of pastors, I have visited hundreds of churches around the world. In each instance, I made notes on why some were healthy and growing, and why others were unhealthy, had plateaued, or were dying. I've talked to thousands of pastors and interviewed hundreds of church leaders, professors and denominational leaders about what they've observed in churches. **Long ago I wrote to one hundred of the largest churches in America** *and spent a year researching their ministries. I've read nearly every book in print on church growth.*

I'VE SPENT EVEN MORE TIME **going through the New Testament.** I've read it over and over, studying it with church-*growth eyes, searching for principles, patterns and procedures.* **The New Testament is the greatest church-growth book ever written. It's the owner's manual for the church!"**

"I'VE ALSO LOVED READING CHURCH HISTORY. It is amusing to me that many concepts currently labelled **innovative** or **contemporary,** are not new ideas at all. **Everything seems new if you are ignorant of history!"**

"MY GREATEST SOURCE OF LEARNING has been watching what God has done in the church I pastor. It has given me an education that no book, no seminar, and no professor could have ever given me.

The principles of this book have been tested over and over, not only at Saddleback church, but in many other purpose-driven churches of all sizes, shapes and locations and denominations."

Rick Warren declares 'Pastors are the most strategic agents of change to deal with the problems of our society'.

Here are a few illuminating headings from Rick Warren:

"**MINISTRY** is a marathon. It's not how you start that matters but how you end.

VISION is the ability to see the opportunities within your current circumstances.

To design the right **STRATEGY** you must ask the right questions.

Most healthy, large churches are led by a pastor WHO HAS BEEN THERE A LONG TIME.

A CHURCH'S HEALTH is measured by its *sending* capacity, not its *seating* capacity.

God always uses imperfect people to accomplish his will.

WHEREVER GOD GUIDES, HE PROVIDES."

RICK WARREN PREPARES FOR HIS FIRST PUBLIC SERVICE IN THE SADDLEBACK VALLEY.

WHAT KIND OF CHURCH?
Some of the best-known pastors in America ministered within driving distance: Chuck Swindoll, Chuck Smith, Robert Schuller, John MacArthur, E.V. Hill, John Wimber, Jack Hayford, Lloyd Ogilvie, Charles Blake, Greg Laurie, Ray Ortlung or John Hoffman.
In addition there were at least two dozen solid Bible-teaching

churches in the Saddleback Valley. *I concluded that all the Christians in the area were already happily involved in a good church or at least had plenty of options.*

"I decided we would make no effort at all to attract Christians from other churches - we would not even borrow workers from other churches in the area. We don't want transfer growth. In every membership class we say 'if you are coming to Saddleback from another church, you need to understand up front that this church is not for you. It is geared towards the unchurched who do not attend anywhere. If you are transferring from another church, **you are welcome only if you are willing to serve and minister. If all you intend to do is to** *attend services,* **we'd rather save your seat for someone who is an unbeliever. The position may sound harsh,** but Jesus defined his ministry by saying "*It is not the healthy who need a doctor but the sick. I have not come to call the righteous, but sinners."*

THE MIND-SET OF UNBELIEVERS.
"I spent the first twelve weeks after moving into the Saddleback Valley going door-to-door talking to people. Even though I knew what these people **really needed** most was a relationship with Christ, **I wanted to listen first to what *they* thought their most pressing needs were.** That's not marketing; it's just being polite. **I've learnt that most people can't hear until they've first been heard.** People don't care how much we know, until they know how much we care. Intelligent, caring conversation opens the door for evangelism with non-believers faster than anything else I've used. The fastest way to build a bridge to the unchurched is to express an interest in them and show that you understand the problems they are facing. Felt needs are a starting point for expressing love to people.

AN OPEN LETTER TO THE UNCHURCHED.

Rick Warren and the fifteen members of his Home Bible Study group -many of whom were unbelievers- addressed 15,000 letters to the unchurched in the community. The first sentence of it was,'At last! A new church for those who've given up on traditional church services.' It went on to explain the kind of church being started. on the coming Easter Sunday. **'I guessed if we could get one percent response from the letter, then 150 might show up'.**

We had a dress rehearsal for the Easter Day service on Palm Sunday- a trial run! We hadn't expected our letter to arrive in homes until a few days before Easter. However, due to an efficient post office some were delivered early - **and sixty people showed up at our dress rehearsal. And five of them gave their lives to Christ that day!**

THE FIRST TASK OF LEADERSHIP IS TO DEFINE MISSION "so I tried to paint, in attractive terms, the picture as clearly as I saw it. Our vision has never really focused on getting big or erecting buildings; *instead our vision has been to produce disciples of Jesus Christ.* I remember how scared I was after sharing the vision at the dress rehearsal service. I was overwhelmed with the fear of failure... It was one thing privately to dream of what I expected God to do; **it was another thing publically to state that dream.**

His first sermon, March 30, 1980 expressed his dream:

It is a dream of a place where the hurting, the depressed, the frustrated, and the confused can find love, acceptance, help, hope, forgiveness, guidance and encouragement.
It is a dream of sharing the Good News of Jesus Christ with the hundreds of thousands of residents of south Orange County.
It is a dream of welcoming 20,000 members into the fellowship of our church family - loving, learning, laughing, and living in harmony together.
It is a dream of developing people to spiritual maturity through Bible Studies, small groups, seminars, retreats, and a Bible School for our members.
It is a dream of equipping every believer for a significant ministry by helping them discover the gifts and talents God gave them.
It is a dream of sending out hundreds of career missionaries all around the world, and empowering every member for a personal life mission in the world. It is the dream of sending our members by the thousands on short-term mission projects to every continent. It is the dream of starting at least one new daughter church every year.

It is the dream of at least 50 acres of land, on which will be built a regional church for south Orange County - with beautiful yet simple facilities, including a worship centre seating thousands, a counselling and prayer centre, classrooms for Bible Studies and training lay ministers, and a recreational area. All of this will be designed to minister to the total person - personally, emotionally, physically, and socially - and set in a peaceful, inspiring garden landscape.

I stand before you today and state in confident assurance that these dreams will become reality. Why? Because they are inspired by God!

FIRST PUBLIC SERVICE -
"Saddleback Church held its first public service the following Sunday, Easter, April 6, 1980. 205 people showed up. **We had caught a wave!** *I will never forget the feeling of watching all those people I'd never seen before walking up the sidewalk to Laguna Hills High School Theatre. ...A mother holding her newborn baby for the first time could not have felt more*

joy.

AN UNUSUAL ASSEMBLY.
It was an unusual assembly for the beginning of a new church. There weren't more than a dozen believers at that first service. It was filled with unchurched southern Californians. Having so many unchurched people at the service actually made it quite comical. When I asked people to open their Bibles, nobody had one. When we tried to sing some songs, nobody sang because they didn't know the tunes. When I said 'Let us pray', some of the people just looked around. I felt as if I was standing before a Rotary meeting. **But to my amazement, the people kept coming back week after week. Each time a few more would commit their lives to Christ. By the tenth week after we began our services, 82 of the unchurched people who had attended at Easter had given their lives to Christ.**

OUR FIRST MEMBERSHIP
CLASS drew 20 people. 18 of them were unbelievers. By the end of the 6-week class, all 18 had accepted Christ, were baptised and welcomed into membership

GROWING PAINS - Saddleback has experienced continuous growing pains throughout its brief history. **To accommodate our continuous growth** *we used 79 different facilities in the first 15 years of Saddleback's history!"*

TURNING SEEKERS INTO SAINTS -
"During Saddleback's first 15 years, over 7000 people gave their lives to Christ through our evangelism efforts. **If you found yourself up to your neck in baby Christians,** *what would you do?* **Our sanity and survival depended upon developing a workable process** *to turn seekers into saints, turn consumers into contributors, turn members into ministers, and turn an audience into an army. Believe me, it is an incredibly difficult task to lead people from self-centred consumerism to being servant-hearted Christians. It is not a task for faint-hearted ministers.... but it is what the Great Commission is all about, and it has been the driving force behind all that has happened so far at Saddleback."*

JUNE/JULY WCN
TELLS US THAT OUR GUIDES celebrate their 30th Anniversary at a special service in West on 16th June; that the congregation is invited on Monday 16th June to make out a call to Mr Bobby Liddle to be Associate minister in West, on the unanimous recommendation of the Kirk Session.

We have also told that a Licensing Service for Mr Brian Martin is to be conducted by the Presbytery of Ards on Sunday 15th June at 7.00 pm, with Rev. Alvin Little as Moderator, and the Rev. Roy Patton giving the charge.

Praise & Prayer meetings will take place throughout the summer on Tuesday evenings, with Rev. Terry Laverty drawing up the programme for these meetings. Details are also given about Family Services throughout July and August.

CECIL GRANT - has completed three years of theological study at Princeton. And he has done so with such academic distinction **that doors have been opened for him to pursue doctoral study at his old alma mater in Cambridge where he has been awarded a scholarship.** *'I am going to be working on the book of Ecclesiastes, and trying to discover how the writer's outlook was shaped by the world in which he lived... it will be both exciting and worthwhile to spend some additional time studying God's Word and allowing my thoughts to mature a little more.'*

SEPTEMBER WCN 1997.

WEST STRATEGY FOR FUTURE GROWTH.
In April our Kirk Session, with core members of the congregation, began to explore the way forward for our congregation, and, to gain further insight and inspiration, studied Rick Warren's book on the Purpose-driven Church.

SURVEY IN BANGOR WEST.
In the month of May, fifteen 2-person teams made a survey in Bangor West *that excluded West Church members.* **We wanted to gain an understanding of how people in the community at large,** *outside our own congregation*, **felt about a number of important issues.** We wanted to discover what people perceived **to be the greatest need in our area;** the reasons **why people do not attend church** *and what proportion do actively attend church;* what qualities in a church people might be seeking for; *and any advice people might give us, about ways in which the Church can serve the community.* Here is the response from 100 Questionnaires.

Q 1. What in your opinion is <u>the greatest need</u> of people in this area.

More activities for the young / children's play areas / leisure facilities / youth drinking	31
Jesus / Salvation / Church	11
Community Centre / Social provision /visitation and care for the elderly	9
Speed limit on Crawfordsburn Road/ bus, road improvements, /better parking at West	6

Q 2. Are you actively attending any Church?

YES	62

N0	39

Q 3. Why do you think most people don't attend Church?

Boring / long, heavy sermons / formal /unfriendly /unwelcoming	24
Society sinful / changed times / lack of spiritual interest/	23
Too busy/ Sunday work	19
See it as irrelevant	18
Habit / Laziness /No one to take you or go with	10
Lives of Christians unappealing /division / hypocrisy / dress code	9
Too many other attractions	8
Materialism	6
Sunday day for relaxing	4

Q 4. If you were looking for a church to go to, what sort of things would you look for?

Friendliness / welcoming / relaxed	22
Family based / youth provision/ young minister	19
More social activities / keep fit/ women's groups/ something for everyone / wide participation/ good community spirit	13
More lively/ informal worship / variety/ modern feel / not regimented or formal	13
Good Bible based teaching/ clear statement of right and wrong/ relevant / preaching God's power /encouraging, not rambling	12
Care for members/ neighbours /fellowhip/ home groups	10
Not denominationally focused/ freedom to move between churches/ broad-minded	5
Other spiritual factors / mission minded/ evangelistic / baptism of Spirit	4
Strong pastoral leadership / contact with ministers/ minister's personality	4

Q 5. Is there anything WE could do for you? What ADVICE would you give members of a church that really wanted to be helpful in the community?

Offer practical help / care for sick and elderly/ companionship / counselling service/ identify ourselves with the needs of the community / advice centre   24
Members to be approachable / make ourselves known to community "

/ avoid cliques /be genuine and accepting / welcoming and friendly / coffee at the end of services.   16
Youth work (teens, twenties and younger) 'go on longer / more in the summer   14
Variety of activities, social events   6
Preach the gospel /more evangelism/ more Christianity than religion / reach out with a positive view of the church   6
Lifts to church /accompany 'seekers' /personal invitation to attend church`   6
Be non-partisan politically / no hypocrisy / greater co-operation between churches   6
Better advertising of activities   4
Make services more interesting and attractive   2
Encourage broad participation   2
Visit schools more.

PERUSE THESE FINDINGS! Members of West are invited to peruse these findings. It is interesting to compare them *with suggestions already made by our own members out of our in-depth study of Rick Warren's book.*

Rather than make a minute analysis of these findings, let us tell you some of the new things we plan to do in the new session beginning in September.

In the survey responses, emphasis was laid on work among children and young people - 31% saw this as *the greatest need.* 19% said they would look for family based youth provision, 14% would like to see youth work continue longer into the summer.
OUR RESPONSE TO THIS:
We already *have hundreds of our members involved in Youth Work, Sunday School departments from Creche through to Young West Church; in uniformed organisations, Scouts, Guides, BB and GB, with Youth Clubs on Tuesday and Saturday nights, drama groups and music groups etc.*

But we realise that THERE IS MORE WE CAN AND SHOULD DO!
In September, **our young minister, Bobby Liddle is to be ordained as an Associate-minister.** He will be in overall charge of Young West Church, giving it his primary attention, in the same manner that Alvin Little did in his last two years in West. Bobby Liddle will also be in charge of **Youth Alpha**, and the Scripture Union "2:7" group on a Sunday evening after church.

We believe it to be quite remarkable that we have produced in West, *so many people to work among the young! YET WE DO NEED MORE!* How do we get them?

Firstly, by harnessing and mobilising the unused gifts and abilities within our members. We often do this by inviting and encouraging people in a personal way to help us! We can inform people about work urgently waiting to be done. For example, at the moment our Scoutmaster, Chris Miller has been coping valiantly but almost singlehandedly with our Scout group. *Already, within our congregation, there may be someone who could help him. And a person can grow into this job receiving training on the job! Where a person feels an attraction for such work, they should let us know.*

We have many opportunities for useful and fruitful service throughout the congregation. Our people are invited TO FILL IN THEIR SHAPE PROFILE! With this copy of West Church News a SHAPE PROFILE form is included.

WEST CHURCH BANGOR ONWARD JOURNEY

We have the conviction **that every member within the Church, the Body of Christ, has a work to do, and an ability that God gives, to do it.**

More than 50 spheres of work and service are listed, some of them needing urgent and immediate help. As well, our members are invited to seek guidance directly from the Holy Spirit in respect of the special abilities that God has given them. These are often indicated by the fact that there is something that people 'would just love to be involved in'.

Folk should know that we are a warm, open inviting fellowship of people. In our Survey in the community, people are telling us of much more that needs to be done - and we in West already know this! We genuinely want the 'unemployed' in our midst to begin work with us!

IN OUR COMMUNITY SURVEY people indicated so much more that the church needs to do, and the caring, healing quality of life that it should have. Many congregations might reply that **they just don't have the personnel resources for all of this. In West, over the years, we have had hundreds of people who have become ready to serve and minister in Jesus' Name.** The truth is that we have brought these people to spiritual life through our **Life in the Spirit Seminars** and, more lately through our **Alpha courses.** Through pondering God's Word, through coming to faith in Christ, through being filled with the Holy Spirit, people grow into their full potential and develop a heart to serve our community. God enriches them with gifts and abilities.

SURVEY: WHY PEOPLE DON'T COME TO CHURCH. 24% felt that long, boring sermons and a formal, unfriendly and unwelcoming atmosphere are responsible. Yes, of course **sin in society** undermines spiritual interest- busyness, Sunday work and laziness are factors... And what might induce people to come to church? **22% cite friendliness, a welcoming and relaxed atmosphere and family-based youth provision, also, more lively worship, with variety and a modern feel, neither formal nor regimented!** There was a call for services to be more interesting and attractive, and the encouraging of broad participation.

Many of these things we have been seeking to develop and implement in West. We know that we must welcome people not only at the door as they enter but in every activity of the congregation, in each Sunday School department, each organisation, each seminar that we run.

Some of the things we plan to do in West to increase this sense of family, of welcome and of worship:

(1). A series on STRENGTHENING THE FAMILY in an age of disintegrating families and crumbling values This series will run from 21st September -14th December at our morning services.

(2) LEADING OF PRAISE by choir and Singing groups - some adjustments.
Ten O'clock Services -The choir will be present at ALL these services. Also, for 5 minutes before this service, the Singing group will also be present to lead us in more informal songs **to add variety and an element of informality.**

Eleven-Thirty Service: our Second Singing Group led by Paul Shields and company will lead, *taking special care to lead in appropriate songs while the children are with us in the first part of the service, and to give us an enriching mix of songs and hymns in the remainder of the service.*

The Eleven-Thirty service has been developing an ethos of its own, congenial to children and parents together. We like children and parents to be able to worship happily together... *However, this happens most readily when parents take their very young children to the Crèche, and their 3 - 4 year old children to Junior Beginners <u>at the start of the service. When small children are noisy or unsettled the concentration, peace and enjoyment of the congregation is undermined.</u>* We aim for the quality of care in the Crèche and in Junior Beginners to be such that the little ones are not deprived. *OUR AIM is to advertise this Family Service to all who have pre-school or primary age children, and we are seeking to encourage a regular attendance of people who may not have worshipped with us often previously. We want the quality of this service to be high and therefore ask parents to make use of our Crèche and of Junior Beginners, as appropriate.*

Young West Church: Bobby Liddle will have overall care to nurture Young West Church, to develop it intensively and to promote greater pastoral care. We treat Young West as a congregation in its own right, to be equally developed with the other two morning congregations.

Evening Services: Praise Services will continue on the first and third Sundays of the month. These services will be led by our Singing Groups and by the Youth Singing group. 2nd and 4th Sundays will be led by the Choir, and where there is a fifth Sunday, by Belcanto.

MORE SOCIAL EVENTS IN OUR CALENDAR - Our Survey indicated a need for more social events, and with us this is a welcome suggestion. Some look back nostalgically to our Church holidays at Kerrykeel in County

Donegal; some remember the amazing annual sales run by the PWA, that helped to bind members of the congregation together, as we raised money to help build and furnish our halls.

NORMAN & ELIZABETH SCULLION, who are themselves the epitome of warmth and friendship, are back with us after a post-retirement stint of work in London, and are eager to help While offering to do ANYTHING to serve Christ in West they are ready - with the help of others- to promote a calendar of social events!

THE GOD WHO CHANGES LIVES!
Our SURVEY showed that 24% thought that the reason people did not attend church was because it was 'boring' and 18% deemed it to be 'irrelevant'.

SEPTEMBER WCN advertised our Fifth Alpha Course in West. Folk are invited to an Introductory Evening, to hear more about Alpha and enjoy a good meal with us. Those who may have doubts about the historicity of the Christian story, or may feel it to be irrelevant will have these beliefs robustly challenged!   "As well as those who want to avoid and evade Christianity because it is morally and spiritually challenging, *there must be many who, deep down, wish it could be true: that there is a Father God who is over all, that Jesus came from Him to help and save us, and that the Holy Spirit's life and power can be actually experienced today. Whatever category you may be in, you could have much to gain by joining us. And this is true, not just for those who have intellectual difficulties about the Christian faith, <u>but for those who need energy to lift them into a new mind-set and life-style."</u>*

You may find it worth procuring the book "THE GOD WHO CHANGES LIVES" that tells the stories of people whose lives have been changed, mostly through Alpha Courses. This book is available on our Bookstall.

IN WEST WE ENCOURAGE PEOPLE TO EXPERIMENT by attending an Alpha Course or a 'Life in the Spirit Seminar', by relating the real-life transformations of people with whom we can readily identify. In this edition of WCN we gave the testimony of Sandy Millar, Vicar of Holy Trinity Brompton, and birthplace of the Alpha Course.

A RESPONSE TO THE SECOND ALPHA COURSE IN WEST IN 1996.

There have been myriads of responses to participation in Alpha courses, in terms of changed lives, the birth of faith, healings, mended relationships, new vocations, a new mind-set. ROBERTA CORBRIDGE found that in each session, the questions under consideration, and the scriptural references given, triggered in her mind and spirit, a response, in writing, each particular piece being given at once and in its entirety. There were eleven such pieces. We give a sample to indicate how, in Alpha, God can give a new mind. The second piece was **"LIFE IN THE FAST LANE"** with this introduction by Roberta, "many people today live life in the fast lane and not always by conscious choice! As human beings we seem to be preoccupied with our own needs.
 Ambitions and greed motivate us and we attempt to preserve our lives in sterile boxes passing for homes. We are often reluctant to share ourselves with God or with our fellowman. Loneliness is the scourge of the twentieth century yet often we inflict this loneliness upon ourselves.
Our sense of community is rapidly disappearing and by and large we have forgotten how to support one another. As Christians we should be building one another up and sharing our joys and sorrows."

The Scripture verses that **triggered** a response in Roberta were:
"Nobody should seek his own good, but the good of others."
1 Corinthians 11: 24.
 "Carry each other's burdens and in this way you will fulfil the law of Christ." Galatians 6: 2.

LIFE IN THE FAST LANE.

Busy people
Furrowed brows
Busy lives.

Sideways glancing
Back watching
Insecure lives.

Smiles which don't engage the soul
Emptiness behind the eyes
Climbing upward
Competitive lives.

Ambition, greed, self-centredness
The value of relationships
Diminished by the lies.

Ever onward, ever upward
Wanting ever more and more
No time to stop or hesitate
Lift a brother, help a friend.

Sterile boxes, privacy preserved
Don't get too close, don't pry too much
Don't get attached it hurts too much
Lonely lives.
INTO THE LOOKING GLASS

Roberta writes, "Many of us face a daily struggle to be the person we would like to be or feel we ought to be. We are often aware that we are falling short of some instinctively recognised standard. So much effort is expended in the striving to be something we simply are not no matter how much we aspire to be!

How comforting to realise that the work of repairing our fallen nature and restoring us to our original condition and rightful relationship with God, belongs to God himself. He has the power to transform us into the likeness of Christ through the ongoing work of the Holy Spirit. What a relief to stop striving and simply allow God to undertake his work!"

These were the Scriptures that **triggered** in Roberta her piece "Into the Looking Glass."
."...so I find this law at work: when I want to do good evil is right there with me.....making me a prisoner of the law of sin" Romans 7: 21-23.

INTO THE LOOKING GLASS

I stare into the glass
Consider what I see
It seems there are two people here
And one of them is me.

But which am I? It's hard to tell
I seem to alternate at will
Between the purer higher self
And that of which I am not proud.

I much prefer my nicer self
I struggle so to keep control
But other self with darker ways
wins the toss on many days.

I wrestle and I wonder why
I lack the strength to keep at bay
Unbidden thoughts, unwholesome deeds
I wish I could fulfil this need
To be transformed.
Reluctantly I admit defeat
I have not power or will indeed
To win this fight.

"Stop striving child and lean on me"
A voice is clear within my head
"Rest on me for I have power
To break the bonds, restore you now.

I have the power and the will
To banish sin and darkness still
And someday in the glass you'll see
A clear reflection child of me."

THE PRODIGAL.

"I will set out and go back to my father... the father saw him and was filled with compassion, threw his arms around him and kissed him" Luke 15: 18-20,

These verses triggered this response in Roberta.

"O what freedom!
To act and think independently
Without reference to any other
No longer compelled to tow the line
Of family or tradition
I am my own person
Great and wonderful adventures lie ahead.

O what enjoyment!
The world is all I dreamed it to be
Full of new experiences, exciting opportunities
Always someone willing to share
A drink or meal when I am host
Why did I wait so long?

O what despair!
Friends now are scarce, my wealth depleted
I who should receive homage by birthright
Forced to pay homage, grovel and beg
Did some unseen hand extinguish the light
Which bathed the world in golden rosy glow?
All seems darker now
I am alone, I am afraid.

My mind replays dim memories of home and family
I struggle to imagine the warmth of an open fire
Freshly baked bread, the love between human kind
Which nourishes - almost tangible.

I long to return to this place of warmth and security
What would they think, how would they react?
I have been wrong, made such foolish mistakes
Dare I admit that
To myself, to them?

I am weary, so weary
The road has seemed so long
Perhaps this too is a mistake
But no, what's this I see?
Surely not- Oh joy it's true!"
As we cover the rough and dusty ground between us
The focus becomes clearer.

I feel I can take not one more step
I am fainting from hunger, exhaustion.....
I am upheld- uplifted, supported
My father's arms encircle me
I am safe - I am home."

IN-DEPTH MINISTRY AND COUNSELLING.

Over and above that, there is the ministry that has grown up over many years with HEATHER THOMPSON, who counsels and prays for people, often one-to-one, in a more extensive way. Heather seeks to do this in a very thorough manner and in a most loving yet professional way.

TRAINING OTHERS - Later in November 2001 Heather writes:

"At present there are 11 women in the Ministry Training Group. I have been teaching them for several years now and there is a great love and support amongst us all.
I have been accredited with the Association of Christian Counsellors for four years now, and Glenda Eddis and I have practically finished a Diploma in Pastoral Counselling.
Eight others have finished a basic counselling course and it looks as if four of these and Glenda would like to go for accreditation also. Another has completed the Relate Course for marriage guidance.

IN PREPARATION - I believe that all this is in preparation for the days ahead when God will be bringing in many more that will be damaged and, perhaps, suffering from drug abuse, sexual abuse and other major problems. I believe that God has told me that West Church, as part of the

Body of Christ, will continue to be a sanctuary for all."

IN - DEPTH MINISTRY.
Heather writes: "The more in-depth ministry / counselling have been very fruitful, *with many dramatic changes in individual lives. It is very exciting to see the chronically depressed become well enough to come off all medication, after being on it for ten or twenty years; to see the abused become free within themselves and able to live abundantly; to see those under addiction released; and to see those who have rejection released to love and be loved again!* There is such a variety of needs and we are learning all the time under God's leading. Sometimes we can hardly believe the mercy and goodness of God as He does mighty things for His people and we celebrate together, release that is real and lasting.

SEPTEMBER WCN ALSO gives us details of many groups and organisations resuming their meetings in September, like the GB and Scouts and Bowlers and PWA - everyone starting again in September!

It tells us of the Ordination and Induction of Bobby Liddle as Associate-Minister in West by the Presbytery of Ards on Wednesday 3rd September;

that there's to be AN ELECTION FOR TEN NEW ELDERS on Sunday 13th October.

It gives news about RICHARD SCOTT's joining an IFES team for the academic year 1997-8 in Slovakia;

about JANE RICHARDSON, having just retired from the demanding work as Head of a Department in Methodist College, Belfast, to become Area Representative of TEAR Fund. We know that, in this voluntary work, she will make a superb contribution. We might say, to use the current jargon, that she has the right SHAPE PROFILE!

Sunday, 18th September is being observed internationally as "SUFFERING CHURCH SUNDAY."
"Remember those in prison as if you were their fellow prisoners and those who are ill-treated as if you yourselves were suffering." Hebrews 13: 3.

GRAHAM & JANET DORE, WYCLIFFE BIBLE TRANSLATORS.
Over many years Graham Dore has informed, interested, inspired and motivated us. Graham has the strategic work of producing **"Take my Word."** Graham's literary and spiritual gifts always make this an inspiration and a delight to read.

In this edition of West Church News we have spoken of *our* endeavours to ensure that the **Praise Input in our services facilitates all our members to worship wholeheartedly.** Therefore we appreciate this story from Ghana:

"For decades **the only music the Vagla Christians of northern Ghana had to praise God with,** *was borrowed from other language groups, so that worship was a foreign experience for them, even after the New Testament was translated.*
But recently the first culturally-appropriate Vagla Christian music was born, as non-readers spontaneously began to praise God in the way that pleases him- from the heart, in a way that was natural to them.
Someone read the Vagla Scriptures, and then the people waited expectantly. Hesitantly at first, but with growing confidence, *one woman began to sing the song in her heart:* 'He who is carrying a heavy load and is getting tired, bring it to Jesus. He will save you. You, who labour hard, come to Jesus because he has peace.'

The two thousand year old words tumbled out of her mouth, carried by her own melody **in traditional Vagla style.** Immediately the others responded with the chorus line. **As the singer moved deeper into worshipping her Lord, she fell to her knees:** *"Let's give him glory because He is our Father." Soon everyone was on their feet dancing in a circle, improvising to the accompaniment of rattles or drums.*

They were so eager to sing and dance, as people who are uniquely both Christians and Vaglas. Now they could use their own music to communicate the gospel in a form that all Vagla people instinctively recognise as their own. It certainly sounds unique to the uninitiated. John 3: 16, accompanied by 7 antelope horns *playing intricate, interlocking patterns, sounds remarkably like a traffic jam, but to Vagla ears it was one of the sweetest sounds on earth especially when coupled with gospel words."*

OCTOBER WCN 1997.

DIANA TOOK THE HAND OF a MAN WITH AIDS - and the whole nation has been acknowledging and applauding this bold act of compassion, and many other ways in which the Princess identified, with obvious feeling, with many vulnerable, rejected, handicapped, needy people.

JESUS TOUCHED -and healed- the leper, *and His people, are reaching out continually to hurting and broken people, the world over.* In many places this is being done, to a remarkable degree, **where the Church is growing and buoyant - among the Pentecostals of Brazil, Argentina and Chile; also in the great house-movement growth of the Church in China or the Philippines, Indonesia, or in parts of Africa.**

OUR PCI HAS A SHARE IN

DOING THIS! It does this through its 'United Appeal'. This year West Church's 'target of honour' is £15,000. We plan, in part, to reach this goal, through our special offering at our Harvest Thanksgiving Services on 12th October.

DID YOU KNOW? that there are 600,000 orphans in Malawi, whose parents have died of Aids? Our PCI is doing something about that! You may have heard about **the fierce persecution of the Church in the Sudan** - PCI is assisting FEBA to broadcast the Gospel to the **Nuer and Dinka peoples there!** **Did you know** that in 20 years Christians in the Indonesian island of **Sumba** have grown from 50,000 to 180,000 and that our PCI Sunday Schools have been providing resources to help the Church there, in providing teaching, training and pastoral support for all these new Christians?

You may read about all this - and much more- in PCI's 'World News'.

When you hand in your United Appeal envelope on Harvest Sunday, **you are making your investment in the Kingdom of God: in this way we may bring comfort to the Aids orphan in Malawi; send a message from Jesus to persecuted Christians in the Sudan; give a trained job to an apprentice in Jamaica; help the church in Sumba; help the 17 seminaries now under the China Christian Council, a country where 25,000 people are becoming Christians daily!**
It is good for us to make profitable investments in the flourishing enterprises of the Kingdom of God! We reap a spiritual harvest in proportion to our generosity.

ADDITIONAL HARVEST GIFTS - Do you remember Astrit Kumnova?
ALAN CRICHTON writes: "A few years ago Astrit Kumnova came to the Worldwide Missionary Convention representing 'World in Need'. From an Albanian Muslim family, he believed in God from childhood and had a deep desire to serve him. He learned Muslim prayers and the Koran in Arabic. He rose to become an elder in his mosque and led in prayers there in Arabic. In May 1986 he first heard about Jesus. After 3 months of intense spiritual warfare in his heart, he asked for a sign that Jesus was real. The Lord appeared to him in a vision, and he heard a voice saying 'you **will find the way - I have died for you, and I love you'.** Subsequently, some years later he studied at a Bible College in Croatia and has now finished his 4-year course.

In Muslim culture, the eldest son is expected to provide for his family's needs if the situation arises. Because of the civil war and break-up of Yugoslavia, there is great hardship with 90% unemployment. Astrit's father has not worked for several years, and the pressure is upon Astrit to support his family.

Mr Ron George, International Director of 'World in Need' has sent this appeal:
"At this Harvest Festival time would it be possible for your congregation to collect *soup powders, sugar, rice, flour, dried beans, oats and used good quality warm clothing for all ages - to be shipped to Astrit Kumnova who will oversee the distribution in Kosovo?"*

So, at Harvest Thanksgiving in West we have a double opportunity to bless others: first through our 'United Appeal' envelopes and also in an immediate personal way, sending food and clothing direct to Astrit Kumnova, to feed the hungry and clothe the shivering.
Alan Crichton, in whose home Astrit stayed, is making the practical arrangements.

ELECTION OF RULING ELDERS. Enclosed in WCN are voting forms, as well as an article on QUALIFICATIONS from a Training Manual on the Eldership.

RICK SCOTT NOW IN BRATISLAVA. Rick writes: 'I believe God has called me to Bratislava, but I am well aware that the call was confirmed through the generosity of so many people in West providing most of the £3500 required for me to answer the call.... pray for me... thank you", Rick.

THANK YOU, IAN GIBSON!
In West Church we have a building lacking in acoustic resonance which makes buoyant praise difficult. Sound amplification is necessary to enhance the endeavours of Choir and Singing Groups and preacher. We are especially dependent on the person who sits behind the Mixing Desk in the Gallery. An alert controller chokes off intrusive 'feed-back', lifts the too quiet voice, and helps to save us when things threaten to become too thunderous!
IAN GIBSON has done this work with meticulous care and great devotion for many years. Ian now feels that it is time for him to hand over this responsibility and we want to thank him wholeheartedly for all that he has done!

BAPTISM, A SIGN AND SEAL OF GRACE.

In the course of the years since 1961 we have had near to a thousand baptisms in West, and I have had the privilege of marrying those that I baptised, and in turn baptising their children. I include here an article on BAPTISM, published by the Rev. David Searle, with his kind permission.

HARRY FULTON LEADS TEAM TO SANDOWN PRIVATE NURSING HOME.
Bobby Liddle reports:
"For some years now members of West have been taking services in local nursing homes for people who

cannot come to Church any longer. Our senior citizens grew up in a time when Sunday attendance at Church was the norm. Not being able to attend can leave feelings of frustration and of spiritual loneliness. **So these services are appreciated by residents and staff. Most recently a team from West, led by Harry Fulton have started a service on the second Sunday of each month in the Sandown Nursing Home.**

JAYNE FULTON PAINTS A PICTURE OF THE SUNDAY SCHOOL SCENE - Crèche, Junior Beginners, Primary, Junior and Senior Departments, and points to a few vacancies in our teaching staff.

LOST IN A WARREN OF ROOMS! "One could be forgiven for getting lost at the best of times in the warren of rooms that make up the West Church suite, but on a Sunday morning after the first part of the Family Service, **when there are upwards of 200 children on the move, plus a considerable number of adults,** *then one could easily be tempted to just try to find the exit door and escape!*
If you are one of the families that are joining us during our **'Strengthening the Family'** series, please don't run away as you seek to take your children to their Sunday School rooms - **there will be people around to guide you to the right place.**

EACH DEPARTMENT HAS A PERSONALITY!
Sunday School is divided into different departments according to the age of the children. Each meets in their respective room during the Family Service. *Each department has a personality of its own and seeks to teach the children in a way that is relevant to their age group.* The older children usually start each week with an 'open' session and then move into smaller groups. The younger ones spend most of their time in the security of a small group *where they get to know the teacher and the teacher is able to build a relationship with them.* For the pre-school children a lot of time is spent in play and of course, in the midst of that, children have lots of time to relax, chat and lose their inhibitions and insecurities.

A ROTA BASIS: most departments work on a rota basis, so don't be surprised if after a month or two your child says they have a new teacher - the other one will return in due course!

A CENTRAL BIBLE STORY - the teaching for each Sunday is normally built around a theme with a central Bible story. Long gone are the days of just sitting quietly and listening, though *it is great when they actually do this!* The children are actively involved through drama, singing, puzzles, drawing, and games or even on special occasions they might celebrate a Passover meal together, as the Primary department did last year. *Every child will have a workbook which they complete each week. They take the relevant page home which gives you, the parents, and the opportunity to talk with them about what they have been learning that morning.*

A LOVELY PROBLEM! *In our Sunday School we have had at times a 'lovely problem' - we have too many children!* This meant that we did not have sufficient space and had to change rooms around, or that we needed more teachers to enable the groups to be small enough to be effective... **This year there are 82 children on the roll of the Junior Department. We are delighted to say that the number of teachers there has increased 100%- from five last year to ten this year.** But we are still one short for the rota in the Primary Department.
Finally I'd like to share with you a lovely thing I witnessed in one of our departments on the first day the children were back after the summer holidays. A child had been hugged and individually welcomed back to Sunday School. He was just about to move off to play at one of the tables when he turned back, looked up at the teacher and said "I missed you." Not many are as expressive as this little boy, but lots of us look back and give thanks for Sunday School teachers who were there for us. **Could God be calling you to be there for the children of our family in West?**

SHAPE PROFILES - COUNSELLING. Heather Thompson writes: **"As part of our response to our study on "The Purpose-Driven Church"** *we encouraged you to fill in "Shape" profiles, to help you focus on what you might like to do, in the service of the Body.* We are now responding to these as opportunity affords and are offering an invitation **to those who expressed an interest in counselling and** to any others who would like to come.

"LEARNING TO CARE" video course produced by CWR is an excellent introduction, not only for those who would like to be counsellors, but for all who would like to be more effective in their care for others. Those of us who attended these training courses in the past, when Selwyn Hughes and his team came over here, would recommend them.
We welcome anyone to come and benefit from this video and the discussion arising from it. The time spent together will also be beneficial in building up relationships of trust and understanding which in turn will facilitate us in this work of caring. First meeting in '91' on Monday 20th October at 7-8 pm.

"IS THERE A FUTURE FOR A MIDDLE-AGED FAILURE?" asks Bill Wamsley.

"When my marriage came to an end, I found myself alone, feeling guilty that, as a Christian, my marriage had failed. It seemed that I had no future or worth. Although attending church on Sunday mornings, it was more from tradition than any desire to get close to God. This continued for about a year, during which time I tried to avoid letting people know about my failure. I would avoid people who would ask after my wife and family and tried to bury myself in my work, where I felt safe.

This continued until September '94 when I decided to go back to another 'Life in the Spirit Seminar'. Little did I know what God had in store for me!

I knew very few members in that Seminar when we started, but it didn't take long before I began to make real friends.

It was not only meeting with other Christians that helped me - God started to work in my life. By the end of the Seminar which actually lasted 9 months - a lot longer than we had expected -, **I had regained a desire to live for and serve Him.** The summer that followed had a great influence on my life.

It started with the Team from **Ellel Ministries** who held a 2-day seminar in West, **in which I was broken and freed before God.** The wonder of this was that I decided to take time off for the seminar, only at the beginning of that week - but **God knew I would be there, to be healed.**

TUESDAY NIGHT PRAISE MEETINGS - During that summer at our Tuesday Night Praise meetings, we studied the Alpha book, "Questions of Life." On the last of these **Ken Symington** called for those who wanted to give themselves completely to God's service, to come forward. Although the Lord was speaking to me, I decided not to go forward. Two girls were standing at the front for prayer when Ken said, "*The Lord says that there is a man that He is speaking to*", and *I just couldn't sit there any longer. By the end of that summer the Lord had put in my heart a hunger to serve Him.*

Since that time the Lord has led me into youth work in the Church which is such a joy. The Lord has blessed us here in West with so many young people who want to live and serve Him and I praise the Lord that I have been given this great privilege of working with them.

So what can I say? The Lord has taken me from being a middle-aged failure to a middle-aged teenager, *but most of all He has given me the honour of being a helper in his Church!*

YOUNG WEST - Bobby Liddle, now in full leadership in Young West, declares that the Young West Team has gelled well together over the summer, and is excited over prospects for the coming year. Their aim is to build strong relationships with the young people and give them a clear presentation of the Gospel. To this end they will use the Youth Alpha material, and while doing this the older teenagers also will break up into small groups in Young West.

Bobby says that he knows of no other church which has a tailor-made service for young people, which keeps our young people with us during their teen years.

BACK-TO-FRONT CHURCH THINKING.
Bobby gives us insight into youth psyche through a quotation from Mike Pilavachi that is worth pondering!

"Mike Pilavachi, leader of Soul Survivor, has said that *young people need first to feel that they belong - they can then believe and finally will behave.*
Too many churches expect young people to behave, so that they can belong and finally (hopefully) believe. **It is back-to-front thinking. THE NEED TO BELONG IS SO INTENSE that young people will fall prey to cults and sects, street gangs or peer groups, friends who are into drugs, drink and sex - anything to feel part of something worthwhile**: *part of a group where they are accepted.* These groups often then abuse their new members, physically, emotionally or spiritually. *The church should be a safe place for young people, where they can be certain of a warm welcome and acceptance of who they are now.*

Young people rarely get enough time from adults who are close to them. We need to open our homes and hearts to youngsters, taking time to listen to them, to love them, to discipline them and to learn from them.
If some people think they are too old to relate to a young person, **look again at the relationship between a grandparent and grandchild - it can be one of the best family relationships going.** The church family should be no different. Giving time to young people means being vulnerable with them, being willing to be hurt by them or even rejected in attempting to share the love of God
They need constant affirmation and building up because so many carry great burdens and unresolved hurts from their past."

BOBBY LIDDLE'S TIME IN WEST.
In May 2001, I asked Bobby to reflect on his time in West. This may be an appropriate place to insert what he has written.

ENCOURAGEMENT - IT SUSTAINED ME.
"What a mixed bag of memories I have carried away with me from West Church! Within my first few weeks at West I told a colleague, '*If you can't preach in West Church you can't preach anywhere!*' Such were the warm expressions of encouragement I received for my preaching right

from the start. *That spirit of encouragement is a prevailing memory.* It sustained me at times when, suffering from a deep sense of my own inadequacy, I felt like handing in my resignation, believing that the work of God might well move forward better in my absence than by my presence! Hugs and handshakes! Words of encouragement delivered with deliberate eye contact! Observing individuals quietly praying for one another at the end of services! Fellowship in Christ Jesus, not as a theoretical concept but as a living reality is a profound and lasting memory.

LAUGHTER! Closely aligned to this was laughter! A strange thing to mention in a history? I think not! While any group of people, not least in a church, **will have their struggles there is something very significant going on if there is much smiling and laughter among them.** It speaks of relaxation in one another's company. *It speaks of acceptance and warmth, sharing and tolerance.* West Church, like any local congregation had its sorrows and tensions but there was much laughter and that in many ways exemplifies the fellowship to me.

CONTINUOUSLY CREATIVE / BODY MINISTRY.
One sunny afternoon I decided to drop in to the Art Class in the Praise Room, expecting to find a small handful of dedicated artists. There were closer to 30 and not a 'Minister' in sight! The wide range and number of activities at West was not accidental. It grew out of two important beliefs. One was the belief that God is continuously creative. **He is always doing a new thing, placing in the hearts and minds of His people the desire to serve Him and others in creative ways.** The other belief is in 'body ministry'. **The belief that every believer is a minister and has the privilege and responsibility to serve. This is to be carried out according to the gifts given to them by the Holy Spirit.**

A church can handle this in one of two ways. It can stifle diversity, with a view towards keeping control (or to work the 'Minister' to death), *or it can celebrate diversity by developing a culture of innovation. West church deliberately chose the latter!*

ACTIVELY OPEN TO THE DYNAMIC OF THE SPIRIT.
Some number of years ago before joining West I moved away from the theological position that the gifts of the Spirit died with the Apostles. Coming to West was my first consistent exposure to a local congregation that was actively open to the dynamic of the Spirit in this way. This was an opportunity to grow in understanding through active involvement in a ministry that was open to the charismata without being either stereotyped or blinkered.
The years during which I was at West had **their struggles in this area. A few felt it necessary to leave and worship elsewhere.** For others, including myself, it was time for discussion, thought, searching the Scripture and prayer.
Two outstanding features of this time were the steady unwillingness of Rev. David Bailie to jump on any passing bandwagon. Rather, his ministry continued as it had been, both Christ-centred and directed towards people in love. This was a great example.

THE MINISTRY TEAM. **The second feature was the attitude of the ministry team. While there were differences of understanding and emphasis, above these, clear and sure, was the desire to glorify Christ Jesus and to honour Him by working together in harmony as an example to the congregation.**
During the vacancy after David retired the Minister's room was 'done up'. It needed a new carpet for it had been worn by much kneeling and walking to and fro to lay on hands and pray or to give a hug.
One of the deeply ingrained lessons I learned from David, **Terry, Heather, Helen, Billy and latterly Charles was to stand in other people's shoes, to sit where they sit and stand where they stand,** *to value the person and maintain the unity of fellowship even when not agreeing on every detail. Come to think of it, didn't Jesus say something about that?*

YOUNG WEST CHURCH - A SPECIAL PLACE IN MY HEART.
There is so much I learned and in which I was involved during my years at West, but Young West Church holds a special place in my heart. I have lost count of the number of Sunday mornings I awoke feeling the fear of facing 70 teenagers! God granted them grace to put up with an old fogey! Graciously God worked through those years in two key areas.
i) In building a strong team with a passion and commitment to the young folk.
ii) In drawing the young folk into a group in which there was a sense of belonging.
The two are inextricably linked and both grew out of two convictions regarding youth work. The first was that young people must be loved and know that they are loved and cherished.
The second conviction was that to come to know and grow in Christ to the point where they could stand on their own two feet, taking responsibility for their spiritual growth, the young folk needed to be solidly grounded in the Word of God. **Only a team dedicated to work and preparation could do this.**

PRAYING, EVALUATING, AND PLANNING.
As a team we met regularly, praying, evaluating and planning... **There were often strong views expressed and the kind of healthy energy that flows from a group who are seeking the best as opposed to the better.** *Keeping accurate records, contacting those missing for a few weeks, class outings, prayer for each child were all encouraged to help the young*

folk know they were loved. Probably the most significant development during the years 1997 - 2000 was the weekly prayer meeting after Young West Church. It provided a solid base on which to carry out our plans to create a net through which young people would less easily slip; to establish the pastoral care of the young folk and to establish a strong Bible-based programme.

PARTICIPATION OF EACH CLASS.
During these years the participation of each class was developed in order to increase a sense of belonging. **Celebrating successes and crying with the hurting increased. Each week the worship was enhanced by a gifted Young West band and the drama skills developed in tandem with the Youth Drama group.**

ANNUAL WEEKEND. The annual West weekend grew and developed as the sense of unity and belonging grew. **A watershed in the work was the weekend held in the Autumn of 1999 in Portrush. More than 60 attended.** For the previous two years the team had been sowing the gospel and watering it in prayer. *It was felt that the weekend should hold a real challenge to the young folk to respond to Christ. Pastor Graham McClelland, a freelance evangelist based in Lisburn was the speaker.* At the weekend 11 young folk responded to the invitation to open their lives to the Lord and others who had earlier become Christians asked for help to rededicate themselves. Praise God!

Leaving Young West Church was difficult as was leaving the congregation. However, God carries on His work and it was simply my privilege to be involved in His work at West Church for over four years.

In May 2001, I also asked HEATHER THOMPSON, who over many years has developed a considerable ministry in West, if she would write something for our "West Church Journey." Her first contribution reached me in August 2001. Heather writes:

'THAT'S WHAT I WANT YOU TO SAY'.
"About a year and a half after I came to N. Ireland and was settled into West Church, I woke one morning with a whole lot of thoughts going through my head. **It was like a replay of the previous year of my life in scripture.** As it came to an end I heard a voice say 'That's what I want you to say'. I puzzled over it and got ready for church. After the service you 'collared' me and asked whether I would like to speak at the 'Praise and Prayer' on the following Tuesday. *I was dumbfounded! And very fearful! I remember that Tuesday night that you stood beside me as we looked at the curved rows of expectant faces and, with your arm around my shoulders, said,* "You are among friends, Heather", and as I looked again all I could see were rows of encouraging faces.

This was my first experience of this sort of thing and perhaps, in a nutshell, was indicative of how I was to find life from then on - <u>challenges that seemed beyond me, followed by confirmation to meet them, followed by sheer grace from God and loads of encouragement from you and all in West.</u>

THE QUIET, RETIRING ME.
As the years have passed by I don't feel that they have passed me by! Life has been exciting, stimulating, scary and full of variety. Never once did I think of church, "Oh, this is so boring!" Just as God's mercies are new every morning, so is life lived with Him. *As I look back I remember a quiet, retiring me, who had very little confidence to start with, and who had lost what she did have, as her world collapsed before her. I remember that very special hug that Rhoda gave me on that first visit to the Manse when I was caught by surprise and had to work very hard not to fall on top of her!*

I remember those times when you both made me feel your love and comfort as I worked my way through the trauma of Stuart leaving.
As I faced those difficult days I had this strange joy within that defied explanation - the joy of the Holy Spirit- and though there were equally traumatic times later on I never lost that Joy. These days it continues to bubble over to such an extent that I look at me and think, "What has happened to you?" But of course we know, don't we?

EVERY RELATIONSHIP IN WEST SPECIAL.
It was not long after I came that you invited me to a Life in the Spirit morning Seminar. Among the group were Rhoda Montgomery and Molly Watson... As so many have witnessed to you, **a strong bond was formed among those in the Seminar, and from then on, whenever I chanced to meet Molly, she would remind me of how special our relationship was.**
As I ponder this, I think to myself, **"Every relationship I have with someone in West is special because each person makes it special and values the others."**
David and Rhoda, I thank you for so much, **but especially for how you taught us all that we are special just for who we are and then, and only then, also special for what we do.**
You encouraged us all to believe that it didn't really matter if we didn't do things perfectly and professionally, as long as we did them to the best of our ability, with love in our hearts and with integrity. You kept a "fatherly" eye on us, to make sure we didn't do damage "

[Over the years from those early days, Heather Thompson has found freedom to develop and encouragement to venture. *One of the ventures in 1997 was the emergence of INTERFLO*].

Heather (2001) continues:
"Because we were allowed to

grow in an atmosphere of encouragement, WE DID GROW AND STILL CONTINUE TO GROW! These days you would hardly recognise people like Flo Coey, Hilary Guest, Beth Myatt, Glenda Eddis, Elizabeth Scullion, Jane Richardson, Rita Wilson, Julie Malcolmson, Gill Montgomery, *all of whom have taken up the challenge of INTERFLO with all its fun, creativity and fellowship.* Interflo continues to meet many needs among women. We usually have around 50 with more at Christmas. They are a mixed group and include many that are not involved in other things. It is pleasing to draw in such. As yet there are not many of the younger mothers who have come but we keep praying. I would love to see all age groups together, including the teenagers! We have involved some of them from time to time in the dramas"

[What is INTERFLO, you may ask, and how did it start?] Heather relates: A word came to me: "Interflo." It suggests life flowing among people in abundance. God had been giving me a vision for women meeting together and this word summed up all that was in my heart. I was seeing women of all ages, enjoying one another's company, and learning together how to live in the freedom that God offers and encouraging one another through difficulties. As the vision continued I saw these women helping one another and having fun together, and drawing others into friendship.. These in turn helped and encouraged others. *And as I watched, the love, fun and freedom of these women touched their own families and those around them.* THE FOCUS OF INTERFLO is Jesus, His relevance to everyday living. There is love; there is teaching; there is support; there is friendship; there is fun; there is variety; there is opportunity. Come and see!

WE WELCOME A MIX!
"Women of all ages are invited. We would welcome a mix of outgoing, chatty people and of quiet, pensive ones. We like to welcome those who brave it alone because they find they are happily included, and we like to welcome those who come as a group because they gladly open their circle to include others. We just love to welcome anyone and want you to know there is a very nice supper waiting for you!"

3 YEARS ON...
"**Consistently those who come, speak of how much they enjoy it and how helpful it is.** We have been encouraging women to think about and discuss very practical topics. Always the focus is upon Jesus, His example, how He related to people and how He was real in His relationships. **Our aim is to help women become free and confident and bold enough to step out for Jesus.** We want all women to feel loved and of great worth and to learn in an enjoyable, friendly, non-threatening environment. **RECENTLY, we have been addressing such issues as confrontation, handling conflict, forgiveness, reconciliation etc. and are about to look at different ways of helping others, including helping in a crisis.**
We tackle these subjects through teaching, drama (home-made sketches, which usually are hilarious, even when unintentionally so!) games and quizzes. We're always looking for new ways of doing things. **All joking apart, I have been deeply thrilled at how the "helpers" have been willing to step out into new territory, and do things that were previously terrifying to them,** *all because they love Jesus and want to help others to love Him too. I think those who attend are getting the message that "to try is fun" and that the Holy Spirit seems to be able to use anything to point the way to Jesus, when the hearts of those who get involved have no hidden agenda - only a desire to love Jesus and His people and encourage them in daily living.,"*

Four women lead the worship. Once they know the theme, they choose the songs and practise every week. They work well together, "each preferring the other." It is lovely for me to be alongside such willingness and cheerfulness, knowing that they are all seeking God on the matter. We always have a lovely supper supplied by enthusiastic helpers.

"PAINTING FOR PLEASURE" BY GEORGE COBURN.

"There were 23 titles suggested for our painting class when it started in the autumn of 1996 but when a secret ballot was conducted **"Painting for Pleasure"** came out tops. It might sound like a haven for hedonists but in fact we occasionally have to recall our purpose when our products of paint and paper disappoint and discourage us. It is so easy to take our pursuits too seriously and to allow them to become a threat when they should really be therapy.

The project was originally the **brainchild of Joan Kennedy.** She and a few friends had an interest in painting and she organised an enjoyable course on the subject. Soon after this she negotiated accommodation in '91' Crawfordsburn Road where we met for a couple of years. Joan, meanwhile got married and went to live in Newcastle, Co. Down and we continued as a d-I-y outfit. Naturally some of Joan's friends came less often and our numbers diminished.

Shortly after this **ALBERT JENNINGS arrived and new members were attracted.** Membership reached the twenties and continued to grow. Some people have come and have found that it is not as satisfactory for them as they had hoped but *we have a steady nucleus, whose regular attendance over the years speaks* *for itself.*

***WHAT DO WE GET OUT OF IT?
The act of drawing and painting answers an instinctive, creative feeling some people possess - something akin to gardening I would imagine.*** Like gardening our efforts are sometimes rewarding and sometimes in vain. **But there is more to our membership than the production of pictures.**

We develop an appreciation of observation. We learn to notice light and shade and to note proportion. We endeavour to differentiate intensities and tones and reflected colour. Kaleidoscopic colour clashes and harmonies of hue are also challenges that we encounter with varying success.

BUT THERE IS STILL MORE. Sometimes we sit silently and sometimes we joke. It is often a time for friendships to flourish and not a few of us benefit from the peaceful experience of being involved with the smooth flow of liquid under the control of a soft brush. **There is delight in the use of colour that is hard to explain.**

HENRI ALEXANER. Albert's wife, Etta had a serious fall last year and this resulted in his retiring from the scene to care for her. His place was very acceptably filled by Henri Alexander until Albert returned in October last.
INDEBTED! We are genuinely indebted to both these tutors who have taught us cheerfully and voluntarily. Their patience must have been tested sometimes but we hope that it has also been rewarded in seeing a measure of progress in their pupils.

We are deeply appreciative of the excellent facilities we enjoy.

"KEEP ON SOWING YOUR SEED, FOR YOU NEVER KNOW WHICH WILL GROW - PERHAPS IT ALL WILL" Ecclesiastes 11: 6.

DGB writes: "Over the decades many seeds have been sown in West Church, and often in fertile soil. Some initiatives have fulfilled a purpose for a time, like 'The Couples' Club' and 'The Young Women's Association', and then have disappeared or been absorbed into some new venture. 'Good News Teams' fulfilled a fruitful purpose for a relatively short time, and could be due for a renaissance! The 'Friday Men's group' grew beyond all initial expectation.

George Coburn has just written about "Painting for Pleasure" which began with a few ladies and over the past ten years has grown into a strong club which has brought blessings to its members.

NURTURED BY ALBERT JENNINGS.

This has in large measure been nurtured by Albert, himself an artist of flair and vision, and with an enthusiastic ability to encourage many others, treating all with equality, and each one as worthy of respect.

Each week 12 tables are set out in the Intermediate Hall by Hugo Simpson and Jack Coey; and though they go early to attend to this duty, they normally find people already gathered and chatting happily. The Club fulfils a social **function, for not a few of the members live alone or have experienced bereavement.**
While over the years Albert has seen standards in painting rise, *and this is gratifying*, **yet the ethos and culture of the meeting is to have an absence of competition - no exams, no failures,** *only painting for pleasure!*
As Albert goes round the tables, from person to person, making suggestions and giving encouragement, he may sometimes take the brush, and with a stroke demonstrate what needs to be done and thus leave the person encouraged and enlightened, and all happily content with what they have been doing!

Albert prays that the whole venture may be therapeutic for all involved -he encourages people to be bold, **to enjoy painting, and to rejoice in the friendship and fellowship of the group, so that as they leave the afternoon session it may be with a lift to the spirit and a smile on the face!**

For Albert the "Painting with Pleasure" club draws in all sorts of people, at every stage, and it is a ministry through Christ and inspired by the Holy Spirit. **This lifts it to higher and broader dimensions of beauty and grace, inspired by the Creator of the Universe, by the Redeemer Christ and guided by the Holy Spirit.**

That each person gains fulfilment is reward enough! And who knows but that some outstanding talent may be encouraged and released! Let God be glorified in all!"

NOVEMBER WCN 1997.

WEST CHURCH HOUR OF PRAYER.

Many triplets organised to pray in 3-month experiment.

How many times one has noticed that when a group meets together to pray for an hour - a large proportion of the time is spent *in talking about what we are going to pray about - and often only a little time is actually spent praying!*

So now, in 'West Church Hour of Prayer' we divide the time into 6 slots of ten minutes, with pre-ordained matters for prayer, **and we seek to pray almost the whole time!** "At the time of writing WCN about 2 dozen little groups, mainly in threes, have organised themselves to pray, and many more are actively engaged in mobilising others to pray.

I met a couple after their first hour of prayer: their faces were shining and they declared that the hour had flown by - we recall how when Jesus was up the mountain with 3 of his disciples, they noted that his face was transfigured as he prayed, with a spiritual radiance.

On the Sunday evening I asked one of our young people, if she had got started with the other members of her trio: 'Oh, yes' she said, 'we have already met twice. It has been wonderful. God has already answered some of our prayers.'. **And we recall the promises of Jesus "Ask and you will receive, seek and you will find, knock and the door shall be opened to you."** Yet another person, (and one who prays a lot!) said it had been hard and wonderful! She had never before prayed FOR Jerry Adams. And now she feels a special calling to pray for him, that Christ may come to dwell in his heart!

WHERE TO PRAY? Hour slots have been set aside each morning in the Prayer Room, and each evening in '91' - and there *is* virtue in praying in church - or you may pray in your own homes.

SUGGESTIONS ON HOW TO USE THE HOUR OF PRAYER.

FIRST 10 MINUTES.
Listen to God's Word in Bible Reading Notes.... be silent....then speak to the God who has spoken to

us.

SECOND TEN MINUTES.
Prayer for the Province and land, its leaders and people. Scripture passages are given. And then a schedule for intercessions, for each of the four weeks in the month. It was in this section that someone, for the first time had prayed for Jerry Adams - but it could also have been for David Trimble, Ian Paisley or others!

THIRD TEN MINUTES.
Pray for the Church and its mission, throughout the world, in our own land, province, town, district, and parish. Helpful Scriptures are given, and a suggested schedule for intercession, for each of the four weeks in the month. No shortage of definite intercessions to make!

FOURTH TEN MINUTES.
A few minutes silence before God, giving Him the opportunity to rest upon our spirits, speak to our minds, and give insight for our praying. The singing of a song or two may be appropriate - or just to read a song together!

FIFTH TEN MINUTES.
This is devoted to prayer for our own congregation, with a definite schedule for each week of the month. The first week for Kirk Session and Church Committee and all the matters that they oversee; the second week for our uniformed organisations; the third week for our Sunday Schools, Young West, Sycamore Club; the fourth week for all our other organisations.

SIXTH TEN MINUTES.
Each week prayer for ministers and Team members, then first week for elders and church visitors; second week for Wednesday Night Witness and Prayer meeting, Friday Morning Men's meeting; Minus One meeting, Bible Study groups; Youth "2/7" group; third week home groups, Alpha, Life in the Spirit, catering teams, Challenging Lifestyle; fourth weeks for those who look after our premises and grounds, Ken McCartney, George Stevenson James Smith; those who publish, print, collate and distribute West Church News.

Our aim is that our ONE HOUR be filled with praying!

THERE'S NOTHING MORE POWERFUL THAN PRAYER.

On the morning of August 13th 1737 a group of people in Moravia were waiting before God in a prayer meeting. Suddenly at 11 am the Holy Spirit came. That prayer meeting lasted 100 years. According to the late Leonard Ravenhall (who did a special research into the phenomenon) **the prayer room in which that great spiritual event took place was occupied by either a praying individual or a praying group for a century.**

----

27 BOXES OF FOOD, 79 CARTONS OF CLOTHING FOR ASTRIT IN KOSOVO.

Alan Crichton writes: "We know that West Church responds warmly and generously when asked, but even knowing this, it did not prepare me for the size of the response which met me when I went to the Church on the Monday morning after Harvest Sunday. The task of sorting and packing was quite daunting at first, but with very timely help from Ken McCartney, the task was completed in good time for the shipping deadline..... We packed 27 banana boxes of food and 79 cartons of clothing. **This will make a real difference to the believers in Kosovo.** A local transport company agreed to deliver the consignment free of charge to WIN headquarters in Crowborough, East Sussex. This means that the £400 given towards transport costs will now be gift aided to WIN funds.

NEW ELDERS - ten of our members have been chosen out by the congregation: Ronnie Beggs, Maureen Bennett, Christine Careleton, Gwen Dodds, Hilary Guest, Harry Fulton, Walter McAllister, Brian Moorhead, Renee Robinson and Ron Wilson

AFRICAN CHILDREN'S CHOIR RETURN TO WEST ON 16th NOVEMBER - and we have the promise of a wonderful worship service/concert. James Dobson (Focus on the Family) has written - "I sat and wept in the church service....I felt the Spirit come through the music."

We'll need at least a dozen families to offer hospitality over that weekend from Friday night to Monday morning - please get in touch with William McClelland.

DECEMBER WCN 1997.

WORLD DEVELOPMENT CHRISTMAS APPEAL OF PCI.

Over the years West Church has had *an outstanding record of generosity in respect of the Christmas Appeal.* This has come about because we have consistently informed our people about specific projects that they can support, and enable them to visualise the great good that their gifts can achieve. And we have done the same in respect of the 1997 Appeal.

SAGULA FORESTRY PROGRAMME, ETHIOPIA.
One hundred years ago 40% of Ethiopia was covered by forests: today just 2.9%. This has had a disastrous effect upon the land. The soil from the bare hillsides has been eroded, fertile land becoming a desert. Not only so, **large stretches of forest encourage the rain to fall, draw it down.** With the land deforested the rains fail to come, and severe droughts are the result. And when rain does come, instead of seeping into the ground, it flows rapidly, destructively, over the bare land, causing still further erosion.
The droughts of recent years have caused severe famines, notably during the years 1983-86.
We all know that it is easier to pull down and destroy, than it is to nurture and build up. **But happily** *the process that has decimated the land, can be reversed,* **though it involves knowledge, ingenuity, patience and hard work.**

One such project is THE SAGULA FORESTRY PROGRAMME, supported by TEAR Fund, and promoted by the Kale Heywet Church. This programme: restores and rehabilitates bare hillsides, so that vegetation grows again, and the land is re-established. This involves **trapping the water, and planting various seeds to give growth vegetation that retains the water; and a skilled programme that,** *with amazing speed, gives a base for trees to grow once more.*
In due course **the trees provide poles for building and fuel for fire.**
A tree nursery has been established, *with 3500 varieties of tree seedlings.*
It is hoped to raise 2 million forest and fruit trees through this programme.
Income for the project is raised from the sale of logs, firewood and poles for construction.
Local people are selected to work on the project, and through their experience, gain a good knowledge of reforestation, soil and water conservation.
The fruit trees will eventually improve the local nutritional standards.

THE PROJECT'S MAIN ACTIVITIES are raising seedlings in the nursery; planting trees in the community forest; and distributing seedlings to local farmers.

WHAT WEST CAN DO.
Last year West gave £6153 to the Christmas Appeal. This year TEAR Fund gives £6800 to the Sagula Forestry Project -**could we take care of this amount?**
To inspire us, we may listen to Isaiah 35: 1ff:
"The desert and the parched land will be glad; the wilderness will rejoice and blossom.
Like the crocus it will burst into bloom; it will rejoice greatly and shout for joy.
The glory of Lebanon will be given to it, the splendour of Carmel and Sharon; they will see the glory of the Lord, the splendour of our God.
Strengthen the feeble hands, steady the knees that give way; say to those with fearful hearts, 'Be strong, do not fear; Your God will come, He will come to save you.'"

IT CAN HAPPEN!
It may take some time for the forests to be restored and have the glory of Lebanon's cedars - *but it can happen! And we can be agents that God uses to make it happen!* Through the Sagula Forestry Programme, we can demonstrate something that can be replicated throughout the land.

On the assumption that the total cost of the Project over a 5-year period will be in the region of £100,000, this would enable 2 million trees to be planted - each £1 planting 20 trees. So £5 plants 100 trees, £10 plants 200 trees; £20 plants 400 trees; £50 plants 1000 trees and £100 plants 2000 trees.
***CAN YOU ENVISAGE YOUR OWN COPSE IN FARAWAY ETHIOPIA,** helping to turn arid desert into well-watered fertile land?*

If West reached the goal of £6800 it would allow us to give a gift of 40 trees to each of the 3000 congregations of the Kale Hewwet Church.
Or an individual giving £175 would be able to give a gift of all 3,500 varieties of tree seedlings.
The beauty of this project is that to a large degree it is self-supporting and self-sustaining - a little bit of outside help enables much to be accomplished through the income generation of the sale of logs.

DECEMBER WCN also tells us of a Presbytery Visitation to West in January.
The Ordination of Elders on 14th December.
It gives details of all our Christmas services and events.
It tells of many additional Church Visitors to help fill the gaps in our Visitation Network. "It is our aim to visit each family in our congregation once a quarter, and to

care for our members according to their pastoral needs. Many of you know just how far short we have fallen in this endeavour, and even with our new elders coming on stream, this has not been greatly helped, since most of them were serving as Church Visitors.
For all our elders, old and new, and for Church Visitors, old and new, we are going to use a study course prepared by Selwyn Hughes on CARING, over a period of six months - once a month, January to June."
DECEMBER WCN tells us that **Bobby Liddle** will lead his first Communion service since ordination, on Sunday 14th December, obviously a very significant service for him.
Also that a **Church Office opens in '91' and that Elaine Ward has been appointed to do secretarial work.** Over the past year a huge amount of data has gone into our West Church computer, which, we hope, will mean much improved administration and service to our members. **Heather Thompson *has put in a phenomenal amount of work,*** over and above her heavy schedule, for which we thank her most warmly.

DON & PAT McNUTT leave for MALAWI. They write:
"It all began when Don retired a year early and wanted to use his talents while he was still fit and able...Terry McMullan, Overseas Board PCI suggested Secondary teaching in Malawi....therefore after months of filling in forms, interviews, a medical examination and injections, **time has rushed past and we need to be ready to leave soon after Christmas. Pray... that we are enabled with our teaching. Don will be taking Science and Religious Education full time while Pat will be teaching English and possibly Maths on a part time basis. Pray that God will protect our family, especially Jane who will have the responsibility of our home as well as doing her medical training.**

'We thank God for giving us this opportunity to serve Him... we also thank our family and others who have supported us, especially Jane and Billy Richardson who took the photographs for us and are sending out our prayer letters. We shall be glad to hear from you, but do not send tapes since we are told they can get 'lost' in the post'.

AFRICAN CHILDREN'S CHOIR - Choir Administrator, Andrew McCombe has written to West thanking us for opening our hearts to the Choir, thanking William & Elizabeth McClelland for their hard work in ensuring that all the details for the visit were in order, and for the gift of £2206.36.

GLOWING FACES of those who offered hospitality led us to ask **Ivan & Diane Hunter** and **Mervyn & Denise Shaw** to write about what the visit of the African children meant to them.
Ivan & Diane write about 'An unforgettable visit from two African choir-girls: ."... when Di & I collected the 2 girls- a 12-year old Kenyan and an 11year-old from Uganda - late on Friday afternoon, we were immediately struck by their courtesy and friendliness. By breakfast time on Saturday we had discovered their love of fried eggs! By bedtime that night they had revealed much more of the depth and richness of their personalities.
For 2 days the girls captivated us with their perfect manners and impeccable behaviour (neither of them even entered a room which they had not been taken into); their gratitude for anything done for them; and their faith in the Lord. This was displayed in many ways, such as the songs of praise which they sang to us at their bedtime.
Di and I feel very privileged and grateful for the opportunity to welcome these wonderful children into our home. If an experience can be both humbling and uplifting, this

was it. To know that we were also helping the great work done by 'Friends in the West' was a bonus. **Yet, while people in the west can provide much needed support to children in various African countries, there is much that *we* can learn from them.** So, if you should be given a similar opportunity, our advice would be to take it, and you will be richly blessed!
All these words of mine convey very inadequately the sense of joy and blessing these young girls imparted. I will finish by sharing with you the words which the 11 year-old penned for us, on a 'Post-it' pad, during breakfast on Sunday:
To Uncle & Auntie **"How are you doing? I hope you are having fun. Thank you for having us here with you. Jesus loves you very much. I will be praying for each of you. Have Jesus in your heart. May the joy be with you in all you do."**

MERVYN & DENISE SHAW, PETER & GARY WILL NOT FORGET THIS WEEKEND IN A HURRY! Denise writes: **"It was a weekend I will not forget in a hurry!** It began on the Friday afternoon when I went to collect "my two children." I didn't know what to expect because I knew very little about the African Children's Choir.- Would I be given boys or girls? What ages would they be? How would they react to me? What would they want to eat? All sorts of questions running through my mind. **Then I met Joseph and Mark and I knew immediately that we were going to have a great weekend.** Joseph is 13 years old and his young brother, Mark, is 9. They are orphans from Rwanda and although we don't know what their background is, we found them to be two cheerful, energetic and Christian young lads.
NOT ALLOWED TO WATCH TV.
When we arrived home the rest of the family came out to greet the boys. After a short period of getting

to know one another Joseph and Mark made themselves very much at home. I had been told beforehand that the children were not allowed to watch TV, so, as a family, we decided to explore the roofspace and retrieve some board games. **Friday night was spent becoming re-acquainted with Connect 4, Ludo, Dizzy Dinosaurs and Dominoes. I can honestly say we all enjoyed being beaten at these games by two young boys on the living room carpet!**
On Saturday the choir rehearsed at West Church for most of the day and we collected our 'charges' at 5pm. With several other host families we then headed off to Dundonald Ice Bowl for Ten Pin Bowling which was great fun. **Back home again for tea when, like all the other meal times, there was an opportunity for chatting, laughing and leaving clean plates.**

THE CHOIR SHOWED THE LOVE OF JESUS IN THEIR HEARTS.
On Sunday at our evening service I was confronted by the reality behind the Choir. We were told of the thousands of children in African countries who have experienced horrors which we can only imagine, **yet the Choir led us in worship in a lively and vibrant way and really showed the love of Jesus in their hearts.**
BEDTIME PRAYERS.
We had a lot of enjoyable times during the weekend, however the highlight for me was probably at bedtime when in the quietness of their bedroom I listened to the boys saying their prayers and we read the Bible together. Although Joseph and Mark came from a completely different background and culture to my own two boys, nevertheless they all love, worship and follow the same Saviour - Jesus Christ.
If the opportunity arises in the future to host members of the African Children's Choir I would have no hesitation in putting my name forward again."

WEST CHURCH BLESSED AND ENRICHED BY SUCH CONTACTS - and by insights that come to us from Christians in other faraway lands and cultures. Over many years, Graham Dore of Wycliffe Bible Translators has amazed us by the stories he has related, for example: HE REVEALS A PAPUAN TEST FOR THE RELIABILITY OF THE SCRIPTURES:
"Des and Sisia had finished translating *Matthew - except for the genealogies at the beginning.* Des had deliberately left them till last, *for fear they would put Sisia off the rest of the book! Surprisingly though Sisia sailed through the long list of names without a murmur.* When he rose to leave, he said with some deliberation: "We're going to have a meeting in my house tonight. *Please come and bring this."* Des wondered what was going on in his mind. *That evening Sisia's house was packed and tension hung in the air. When Sisia asked Des to read the genealogies they had just translated, the room became extraordinarily still. They crowded round him, seemingly grabbing and examining every word.*
"What's going on here?" thought Des. "These people are so volatile, they could erupt with fury so easily." ".. and fourteen generations from the Exile to Christ."
Des raised his eyes and saw, not anger, but incredulity. The room erupted. *"Why didn't you tell us all this before?"*
"No one bothers to write down the ancestors of spirit beings!"
"Jesus must have been a real man on this earth then; not just white man's tales."
"Then all this is real!!"
From then on the Binumarien people never doubted the truth of Scripture.

JANUARY WCN 1998.

STEPPING DOWN AS MINISTER- David Bailie writes: "In 1998 I will be stepping down as minister in West Church. I seek to leave the congregation in as good heart as possible, and well prepared for the 'vacancy' that must intervene before a new minister is called.
FORMIDABLE PASTORAL TEAM.
In June 1997 the congregation called **Bobby Liddle** to be Associate-minister in West. In September he was ordained and installed. With **Terry Laverty** already in place, and with **Heather Thompson, they form a united, visionary and formidable Pastoral Team.** The recent appointment of **Elaine Ward** as part-time Secretary should help ensure that our administration runs with increasing smoothness and efficiency.
And in **Billy McClelland,** now retired from his secular employment, we have one to help ensure continuity, stability and advance into the future.
In **1997, we had 2 Alpha Courses, several Life in the Spirit Seminars, various Bible Study Courses, as well as the work of the Home Groups that** *brought new life and greater commitment to many of our members. We had the study of Rick Warren's book that helped sharpen our focus and our vision,* and led to our autumn series of services on **"Strengthening the Family."**

ADVANCE ON ALL FRONTS...
It is not easy to **sustain the multifarious activities of the congregation and advance on all fronts simultaneously** A major concern is for the *pastoral care of all our families, and in the latter part of 1997 we have given attention to that.*
The congregation has elected **10 new elders** to strengthen our Kirk Session, ordained and installed on 14th December. **In addition we have enlisted more than 30 extra Church Visitors,** so that our schedule of elders and Church Visitors has been brought up to full

strength, **and each family should have an elder or Church Visitor calling at their home.
And in 1998 our Elders and Church Visitors embark on a Course on 'Learning how to Care.'**

In the autumn also we embarked on our PRAYER **TRIPLETS (3 people praying together for an hour a week),** and we provide people with material to help in this praying.
As 1997 ends, we thank so many people, in so many groups and organisations throughout the congregation for all the work they do on behalf of West, and for the sake of the Kingdom of God.

AN APPROPRIATE TIME FOR THE MINISTER TO STEP DOWN!

VISITATION OF PRESBYTERY on 22nd and 29th January.
Every ten years or so, in the Presbytery of Ards, congregations receive a Visitation Commission. Detailed questionnaires are sent to congregations, so as to gain a comprehensive picture of the congregation's life and work. Immediately after their ordination on 14th December, our new elders joined the Kirk Session on Monday 15th December, when we considered our draft-form answers to the Presbytery's questions.
New elders found that a very helpful and enlightening introduction to the work of the Kirk Session, in that, in the course of one evening, *it gave a comprehensive overview of our work in West. And, because many in our WCN readership, may like to have this overview also, we have published our answers in this January Edition of West Church News.*

FEBRUARY WCN 1998.

OVERVIEW OF FINANCES.
Our financial year ends on 31st March, so in this issue of the WCN we publish the givings of our people during the first 3 quarters of the financial year, so that we may manage to fulfil our financial undertaking by the end of the full year. We paint a picture of our various funds, and how they enable us to resource all the work of the congregation, and meet the many commitments laid upon us. Number 1, Number 5, and Number 6 accounts may seem rather distant and abstract. But each of them undergirds important Kingdom work. For example, within our Number 6 - or Building Account - we have an 'Outreach' element. That, for instance, allows us to support the work of Wycliffe Bible Translators.

GRATITUDE FOR PARTNERSHIP - Graham Dore writes: "Dear David and West Church, at the end of December we received the welcome gift of £1300. Once again we are full of gratitude for this annual reminder of your partnership in the task of Bible translation. **You give and pray; we keep on blowing the trumpet on behalf of millions of people who do not know the Gospel, more workers join us to help translate God's Word, more people overseas are saved and God's Kingdom spreads. Thank you for helping us to 'preach the gospel to all peoples before the end comes. (Mattherw 24: 14).**

Graham Dore shows us the sacrifice that some people make to translate the Bible, for example Eddie Mungai in Kenya:

"NOT THERE, SURELY?"
"No way! I am **not** going to work with the Boni people. No sober Kenyan would agree to live in such a remote place!" **I was adament!**
"Listen to God and be obedient,"

Trizzer, my fiancée, advised quietly. "I want to marry a man given to God."
That was in 1991 after we visited the Boni area on the north-east coast with an evangelistic team of Kenyan students. **I was astonished by the remoteness and desolation, and was acutely conscious of immense cultural, linguistic and spiritual barriers as we attempted to communicate the gospel in Swahili.**
On the 600-mile journey back I wrestled within myself, "Why would God bring us all this way and yet we saw no spiritual results?"
BONI ON PRIORITY LIST.
I had contacted the Kenyan organisation Bible Translation and Literacy (BTL) previously, and now learned that the Boni people were top of BTL's priority list! **"Go and spend 2 months with the Boni," Director Micah Amukobole advised, "and then come and tell me what you think."**
So I returned to the Boni area to find out more about them. This was the most spiritually agonizing time of my life. **Each night I wept at their material and spiritual hopelessness. God was speaking. "Eddie, I have given you everything a young person needs, are you willing to sacrifice a little for the sake of the Boni people?"**
That settled it! Now I knew where God wanted us to be.

IN 1995 TRIZZER AND I MOVED TO THE BONI AREA.
We face many challenges: the Boni live in closely-knit communities and treat outsiders with suspicion; their neighbours treat them like slaves; the roads are poor and there are armed bandits around.
Sometimes we wonder if we made the wrong decision, and if it is worth the loneliness, harassment and humiliation. In Nairobi we would earn good money, and our daughter Eva would have a good school and Christian playmates. And yet, what joy it will be to hear a Boni person say, **"If it wasn't for you, I would not have come to know God."** *That will make all*

our efforts worth while.

GIVING- PERSONAL AND IMPERSONAL! In our special Christmas offerings, we gave, through our envelopes, for the Sagula Forestry Programme in Ethiopia. And we have been able to envisage how much good the £6322 given will do!
As well, we were able to send gifts of food and clothing to Astrit in Kosovo. And from cold Kosovo, Alan Crichton has received a letter of warm thanks, to all in West who gave money, food and clothing. Alan writes: "I*n December I received a message from the WIN office in Surrey to say that the journey had been safely completed, the clothing delivered but the food had been removed by the Customs at the border 'for testing'.* As a result many of our House Group leaders were contacted and asked to pray for the quick release of the food, and that it would not be spoiled or interfered with.
You will all be delighted to know that Astrit telephoned in January to say that our prayers had been answered and all the food was received in A1 condition. He asked me to pass on his warmest thanks to all those who contributed and prayed in West Church.

TRIPLETS; WEST CHURCH HOUR OF PRAYER.
In February WCN we have added some new material to encourage and refresh our members, as they pray. For example in the first slot of Ten minutes, we encouraged people to meditate upon the Word of God. Here we have given an apt quote from the Danish philosopher/theologian, Soren Kierkegaard, who once observed;
'**A man prayed, and at first he thought that prayer was** *talking. But he became more and more quiet until in the end he realised that prayer is LISTENING.*
Learning to become still and quiet before God is an art to be mastered: this can be enhanced when we focus, quietly, with growing intensity upon the Word of God, so that we learn to hold that Word steadfastly in the mind, gently, persistently bringing the wandering mind back to the subject of meditation. *This may most readily be done when one is alone.* **But it can be done and the intensity increased, when three or four people do this, in silence, together.**

THE SECOND TEN MINUTES:
In this we pray for our Province, our land, for its leaders and people. **Maybe you have been wondering if the special praying is of any real value!** We give a quote from Packie Hamilton's book "**A Cause Worth Living For." David Hamilton was a hard, loyalist terrorist who became a Christian in prison.** David Hamilton writes: "I didn't know that God had someone praying for my salvation. He had placed me on the heart of an 83-year old lady named Annie Beggs, my uncle's mother-in-law....**on the day I was sentenced to prison she spoke to my mother who was sitting crying about her hopeless son. My mum said I was a hopeless case, that all I lived for was the UVF, and that I would never change.**
Mrs Beggs shook her head and told mum, "**God can change your son."** Mum disagreed and shook her head in despair. Mrs Beggs continued, "**If God could change the heart of John Newton (who**, after his conversion composed the hymn '**Amazing Grace'), he can change the heart of your son. I will put him on my prayer list and pray for him every day, I promise you."** At that time she was in her eighties. An amazing woman for her age, she had all her faculties about her, spending most of her nights in prayer.
Annie Beggs had learnt to pray with persistence and intensity. She did not give up easily. Eventually the miracle occurred, and a man bent on hate and destruction, has become a man through whom God does lovely works of grace.

STRONGHOLDS OF EVIL. David Hamilton's mother believed he could not change because his heart and mind were entirely bound by the destructive ideas of the UVF. But, like the apostle Paul, Annie Beggs had weapons of spiritual warfare able to demolish the strongholds of evil.
THE FOURTH TEN MINUTES.
In respect of INTERCESSION it is important, like Jesus, to pray with compassion. Compassion flows into our hearts when we are caught up in worship and adoration. We are told to be filled with the Spirit, and we are so filled when we sing, psalms, hymns and spiritual songs.

So, in February WCN some additional material is injected into 'The Hour of Prayer', to help us to pray with greater intensity and purity of heart.

WALKING! -want to become fitter, enjoy fresh air, beautiful scenery and good company, then plan to join our WALKING GROUP on the last Saturday of each month. Initially we plan to do local walks and eventually, as the weather improves, venture further afield. A day walking on Rathlin Island has been mentioned. Our next walk will be on Saturday 28th February, meeting at 11am at Ballyeidy on the road to Newtownards past "Clandeboye Lodge" from where we will proceed to Helen's Tower. Further details, about this new venture, from Derek Polley or Jean Crichton.

GETTING IN *SHAPE* **IN 1998 - Terry Laverty reports: "We began our Course on discovering how God has shaped us for service on Wednesday, 21 January, with 27 people, ranging in age from 21 to 50+.** The thing that unites us all is a love for Jesus and a sincere desire to know what His calling is on each one of our

lives.
Each evening begins with a time of praise and prayer, followed by teaching and discussion **on what the Bible says about our unique spiritual make-up. We began by examining the biblical basis for all-member ministry,** *being reminded again that God has made every Christian to be part of a dynamic, growing BODY - the Church of Jesus Christ."*
S H A P E .

S Stands for Spiritual Gifts - looking at what they are and how these gifts enable us to fulfil the purposes of the Church, building up the Body.

H Stands for Heart - God has given us different passions - there are loads of different contexts in which we can learn to exercise our gifts. The aim of this session was to discover what our unique heartbeat is. **We managed to find useful direction as we put our mind to it.**

We still have to consider **A P E - Abilities, Personalities and Experiences.**
No doubt we will be affirmed in what we already do, but also find new challenges, not least in seeking to match people with programmes, *and to help them work out their SHAPE in the family of God.*

THE 'SHAPE' PROFILES were very much Terry's 'baby' in West, and this may be an appropriate time to insert Terry's Reflections on his 5+ years in West. At this point in 1994 West had been moving quietly in the things of the Spirit for a quarter of a century! Terry - and later Bobby- arrived at a time when the *'TORONTO BLESSING' had just erupted and there were questions, excitement, turbulence, wariness within the wider Church. So, for a few years we had to guide our ship through somewhat rougher seas!*

TERRY LAVERTY REFLECTS!

Terry writes: "I have decided to sum up my thoughts under 3 headings: SPECIAL CHALLENGES, SPECIAL OCCASION, And SPECIAL PEOPLE.

SPECIAL CHALLENGES:
"I arrived at West in September 1994, to be faced with a barrage of queries and dilemmas regarding what has become known as the 'Toronto Blessing'. Many of the parishioners were full of curiosity and seemed to bombard me with one theological question after another - **and my response was to encourage them to watch and wait and pray.** The truth was that I had not had the chance to consider what was going on for me - and I had no right to impose my limited views on anyone else. Nonetheless, this was to be the first of many challenges that I was to face during my stay at West Church.   **CONFERENCES-** One of the exciting things was the constant flow of conferences on a vast range of topics, some of which disturbed me and even made me angry - while others were a source of tremendous blessing and encouragement. One thing is for sure, though, all of us were **challenged** to stop and think and pray and *seek to be open to what God might do through His people in the parish of Bangor West.*

FUNERALS/ 'KIDS ON THE BLOCK'.   I can remember being challenged in so many ways at West. **Some of the funerals I had to conduct seemed to drain me both spiritually and physically. And then there was the thorny question of 'the kids on the block' who lived in the vicinity of the church, and yet, in spite of all our attempts to reach and integrate them, we seemed to get so far and** no further. *How I longed for these young people to experience new life in Christ, yet our impotence was so painful!*

YES, WEST CHURCH WAS A CHURCH FULL OF CHALLENGES!

SPECIAL OCCASIONS
"I can recall some very special occasions. I've already referred to the Conferences. *There were also great times of blessing during the all-night Prayer Vigils and in many of the regular services, not least the Evening Praise Services.* **PRAISE.** *Praise was a very special feature of the life of West Church.* In my time **MAURICE** McKenzie was in full flow with such a rich repertoire of material *which we enjoyed at the hands of the CHOIR and of a choral group called 'BEL CANTO'.*   I always enjoyed those times when Maurice forgot about his script and his hands seemed to move like lightning up and down the keyboard, emitting sounds that brought delight to us all.   **WHAT A JOY THAT WAS!**
Then there were the SINGING GROUPS - Carol Moorhead's group; Paul and Beulah's group; and the Young West Band, so ably led by the inimitable Robert Sinclair.
Each of these groups brought its own contribution to our worship, offering a variety of styles and approaches which, *though sometimes a challenge,* were a source of great blessing for all. Add all these components together and the resultant menu of praise was full of variety and vitality.   *I miss that so very much!*

SPECIAL COMMUNION SERVICES.   As I continue to reminisce about Special Occasions, it strikes me that the best of these were the ones that brought me closest to the people. I have such

fond memories of 'special communion' services in the Praise Room for some of our older members, who found the Sunday service too long. **What a joy it was to share bread and wine - and a cup of tea afterwards- before ferrying them homewards with the joy of the Lord in their hearts.** 'Life in the Spirit' Seminars have been a part of the fabric of West Church for many years - *and I have very fond memories of profound moments when people experienced the Presence and Power of the Holy Spirit in ways that transformed their lives. Like them, I, too felt the reality of the Spirit's Presence on several occasions and can testify to the strengthening effect that the seminars had on so many people.*
THE SAME APPLIES TO ALPHA COURSES. When we first got involved we were dealing with over 100 people around beautifully laid tables, **prepared by Linda Cummings, Renee Robinson and their team - but as time went on the Course numbers fell to between 20 and 30.** *Alpha is designed to help people find answers to their deepest questions - and I was both stretched and enriched as I worked with a team who engaged with people of all ages and stages, sharing with them on the Journey of Faith. What a privilege this is!*
I thank God for many lessons learned and many new friendships which were formed during Alpha Courses.

YOUNG WEST was always such a pleasure to me, since I have always been sixteen at heart! One of my fondest memories was of a Weekend in Kesh, Co. Fermanagh. When the Holy Spirit moved so powerfully among the young people that many were in tears and desperate for someone to pray with and for them. Such was the kind of openness that was encouraged in West Church. **That same openness was manifest at Men's Weekends, too - and Robert Crawford was always so pleased to oblige in** organising those events.
I could go on and on describing special events and occasions, but to be honest the most special thing about my time in West *was my engagement with people- many of whom were -and are- so very, very special.*

SPECIAL PEOPLE.

David & Rhoda Bailie always received me with open arms and open hearts. I received so much encouragement from them that I felt it almost an obligation to grow in grace - though it has been such a blessing. I can't really thank them enough for all their love and care which they showered so generously on my family and me. **We had such blessed 'Team Times' - initially involving David, Heather, Helen, Bobby and myself -** *times of prayer, meditation, waiting, expectation and praise. Such blessed times! Latterly, when Charles McMullen took the reins, we maintained that weekly focus on prayer and preparation. I miss that very much! It was a privilege to work with such special people and to receive the support of ELAINE WARD in the office, who never failed to excel, regardless of the challenges we set before her.* **I just loved meeting KEN MACARTNEY in the corridor, or looking down from the roof - always whistling, as he served the Lord and served us all with that broad smile on his face. Thinking of smiles, I dare not forget WALTER McAllister's smile as he welcomed me to the Men's Fellowship or WILLIE HALL'S, as I received such a warm welcome to the Prayer meeting,** *where my needs have always been carried (with everyone else's, both near and far) to the Throne of Grace.*
I TELL YOU, THERE HAVE BEEN SO MANY SPECIAL PEOPLE AT WEST!
Bobby Liddle and Ann became our soul-mates for those few precious years. I thank God for their love and grace and wisdom, as we faced many challenges together, especially during the long months of the vacancy. *I miss my times with Bobby in the same way that David longed for Jonathan. It's a great gift to find a friend like that. I found one at West! - And there are so many other people that I could mention who found friendship too.*
YOU'LL BE AWARE THAT SO MANY MINISTRIES INVOLVES CONFIDENTIALITY, and so I am in honour bound not to disclose many of the most profound experiences that I had at West. Nevertheless, I want to mention just a few, which are examples of the kind of highs and lows that ministry involves.
DEATH presents such a challenge to us all, and yet I will never forget the deaths of several of our members which, though painful to the family **brought times of great bonding between family members and myself or other members of our team. God was just so gracious in guiding us through the troubled waters - and his grace was always sufficient- no doubt about it!**

THERE WERE SO MANY TIMES WHEN WE PRAYED FOR HEALING for one thing or another! Sometimes the answer came almost before we asked. Sometimes we had to persist for weeks before relief came. In many cases God's answer seemed to be very different from what we asked for- **but there was so much blessing in the asking- and always a great sense of peace and the presence of God, as we sought His face together.** One of my most joyful moments at West was when JOHN SMITH was able to swallow a piece of bread as we shared the Lord's Supper in his home, with Brian Scott and myself. *This man's one plea to the Lord was to be able to swallow again, following the onset of a* *medical complication.* After months of fervent prayer, God mercifully gave him his heart's desire- and whereas in previous services he had to eat and drink 'in spirit', *at last the day came when he could swallow. What a lasting joy that brought!*

IT SEEMS UNFAIR TO MENTION SOME NAMES AND LEAVE OTHERS OUT- *but there are so many people from West Church whom I will cherish forever in my heart, because West Church was always about caring for people. I beg forgiveness of any readers whom I have overlooked. As you know my heart, you know that you all meant so much to me. Your hugs and letters of encouragement were a constant source of strength. Please continue to pray for us!*

WHEN I LEFT WEST CHURCH IN APRIL 2000, *I knew that I had gained much more than I had given. The nature of the place is that there is a constant flow of grace for those who can reach out and lay hold of it. My prayer is that grace may flow in abundance for generations to come -and that the Church which stands on the hill will be a beacon and a place of refuge for many, many souls who need a touch of the Saviour's hand and a fresh breath of his Spirit to spur them on to love and service.* **THANK YOU WEST CHURCH, FOR SO MANY RICH BLESSINGS.** *Affectionately in Christ,* TERRY.

FEBRUARY WCN ALSO REPORTS A NEW 'LIFE IN THE SPIRIT' SEMINAR to be led by Heather Thompson. [Heather Thompson had been leading these Seminars for a number of years and after my retirement in May 1998 was to continue this fruitful ministry. Below we show how Heather introduces a 'Life in the Spirit' seminar in September 2001].

"WHO ARE THEY FOR?
Have you a desire to go deeper with God -to experience afresh or for the first time, the reality of His love for you, to know without a shadow of a doubt that God really does know you, guiding and protecting, teaching and encouraging?
Do you long to know Jesus with deeper certainty as your Saviour and Lord, your friend and comforter? **Do you want to nurture your relationship with Him** through spending unhurried, quality time in His presence, worshipping, meditating and sharing with others as together you grow spiritually? **Do you hunger for a greater freedom** and sense of joy in your relationship with Jesus?
Do you long for peace to fill your mind and heart and spirit even in the midst of grievous or troubled times? **Have you a burning passion** to help the needy and the sick, the outcast and the forlorn with the loving power of Jesus through the Holy Spirit?
Do you just want to explore what it's all about without being pressurised?
FOR ANYONE WHO IS SEEKING TO KNOW JESUS MORE I'D SAY, "Come to the Life in the Spirit Seminar."

WHAT DO WE DO IN THE SEMINAR?

We encourage and help all to know and experience the love of God the Father; the joy of forgiveness and release into freedom and peace through entering into a trusting relationship with Jesus as Saviour and Lord; a growing confidence in being able to call upon the gifts that the Spirit gives, to bring hope, healing and encouragement to others.
All are encouraged to learn to recognise God's voice for themselves and to walk step by step in the Spirit as He leads.
Over the years many, many people have entered into a living, loving relationship with Jesus for the first time, while others who may have trusted Him for 5, 10, or even 50 years *find a new exciting depth to their relationship to Him."*

HEALING... "Many people have been healed **or begun the process of healing** in the course of seminars. **Such an encounter with Jesus** brings hope in the One who loves them and who gives peace in the face of difficulties. There have been those who have been freed from chronic painful conditions such as arthritis and back problems, from emotional stresses such as fear and anxiety, doubt and depression and from spiritual negativity and heaviness. In the last seminar, a two year old boy whom the doctors had declared was dying was healed. *It is good to be with God's people when circumstances are fraught and it is good to be with God and His people when all seems fine, for whether it rain or shine we can know His joy, His peace, His strengthening, and, most important, His love."*

MARCH WCN 1998.
CANON TOM SMAIL TO VISIT WEST.
As I draw closer to the end of my active ministry in West, it is a matter of great happiness that we are to have a visit from **Tom Smail.** Most of you know that in February 1968, a visit by Tom Smail to West was, in God's grace, a means by which we entered upon a new dimension of the Holy Spirit that has had a profound and continuing influence upon the life of our congregation. A few months ago Tom phoned to ask if he could stay with us on the weekend of 27-29 March, as he had been asked by his friend, Bishop Harold Miller, to lead a Diocesan meeting for the Church of Ireland. **And so Tom is available to be with us on Passion Sunday 29 March. And this fits admirably with our programme on the Passion of Christ, entitled**

THE CRUX OF THE MATTER. Tom Smail has been making a special study of the atonement and will soon be publishing a substantial new book "ONCE AND FOR ALL." So on 29 March he will be speaking on "The Cross and the Atonement." At our Sunday evening service, we will continue on this theme in a service that expresses **in appropriate hymns and music,** *the awesome wonder of what the Saviour of the World has done for us all.* **It's the fifth Sunday of the month, and happily Belcanto's time to lead our worship.**

HOLY WEEK SERVICES: The theme of our United Services will be PERSPECTIVES OF THE PASSION distinctively perceived through the eyes of the evangelists, Matthew, Mark, Luke and John.

YOUR MINISTER, DUE TO RETIRE AT THE END OF MAY, EXPRESSES THANKS TO THE PRESBYTERY OF ARDS.
"Moderator, First of all, may I also personally wish you well {just installed as Moderator of Presbytery} as you begin your work as Moderator.
It is exactly 30 years ago that I sat where you now sit, with people like JT Carson, my former and much respected boss in Trinity, WAA Park, David Burke, and many others of a former generation in front of me.
In West I have served under 4 Clerks of Presbytery, Bertie Spence, James Lorimer, Charles Kerr and Donald Watts. I have held them all in the highest regard, and from each have received courteous, affectionate Christian support, with wisdom with grace.
I was installed **as minister of the Church Extension charge at Bangor West in October 1961, after 5 years missionary service in India, for which experience I have always been grateful, in terms of** insights gained, the lasting friendships of colleagues, and a perception of the Church that lifts it beyond local or provincial perspectives. The work that this Presbytery installed me to do in West Church has satisfied all my ambitions and required my total energy, Never once during the years have I been tempted to look for ministry elsewhere, and never once, may I add, has anyone from outside made any overture towards me! **Looking back over the years, an experience of the Holy Spirit in 1968 gave me an additional dynamic in my ministry** *and greatly enlarged my confidence in the Gospel of Jesus Christ as the power of God for salvation, for all sorts of people, seeing them built into the active Body of the Church. We found a well then that has not run dry over the years.*

DIFFERENT - At times our path may have been somewhat different from others, but I want to pay tribute to the Presbytery for allowing us to develop as we did; and express gratitude to my fellow-ministers for the warmth of their friendship.
At the latter part of my time in West, **a Team Ministry** has gradually been established, and I want to pay tribute to what **John Seawright** and **Alvin Little** have done in times past, and what **Terry Laverty** and **Bobby Liddle** are now doing, as well as other lay helpers. I have felt deeply indebted to **George Eagleson, Financial Convener of the Presbytery for many years,** for his sympathetic and substantial support as we sought to expand our ministry. **Over the years we have always had a Team Ministry, for my wife Rhoda has been totally involved with me throughout, winning the affection of our people.** I cannot speak highly enough of our congregation in West, whose support and love have been wonderful. **I do not hide the fact that it will be a severe wrench to leave them,** *while one has still appetite and vision to work alongside them;* but the time has come to do this, and I do so with gratitude and faith.
I thank Presbytery for making arrangements for the vacancy, and know that the Convener will find in our Clerk of Session, William McClelland, and in our Kirk Session, people well equipped in helping him to find, under God, my successor."

OUR ORGANIST - MAURICE McKenzie.
Maurice McKenzie has been our organist and choirmaster over the entire second half of my tenure as minister in West Church.

PERIOD OF DRAMATIC CHANGE.
During this period, a dramatic change has developed in terms of congregational and choral singing and West Church was in the vanguard. **Until this time, his predecessors like Mrs Elizabeth Jamison trained the choir to lead the congregation in hymns and psalms from our Church Hymnary, and through well-known anthems, with special renderings of Christmas, Passion, Easter and Harvest music.**

The Renewal Movement sent a flood of new songs our way, and there was a time when crowds filled West Church for our Praise Services.
Maurice McKenzie was with us in this time of transition and development which he admits to being 'something of a culture shock'.
Of course our chief diet of worship for our main services still consisted of wonderful substantial, glorious hymns which lifted heart, mind and soul to God. **One cannot fail to regret, for example in our Communion services, that now one seldom hears hymns like,** "And now, O Father, mindful of the love, that brought us once for all on Calvary's Tree" or "Lord enthroned in heavenly splendour,

First-begotten from the dead" or "Let all mortal flesh keep silence."

YET A PLACE FOR NEW SONGS, with a grateful welcome for the best of them! Who, in all conscience would want to exclude Kendrick's 'Meekness and Majesty" ; 'My Lord what love is this that pays so dearly'; 'Make way, make way for Christ the King'; 'Lord the light of your love is shining" 'O Lord the clouds are gathering'?

GRATEFUL!
As minister, with the whole congregation, I was ever grateful for the manner in which Maurice presided at organ and piano, and for the full hearted energy with which he lifted choir and congregation in worship, *whether in triumphant exultation or in holy solemnity, or in gentle trusting devotion; whether in capturing the mood and music for times of funeral grief or liberated nuptial joy.* With Maurice, minister and congregation could be totally assured that everything would be exactly right.

And if the minister's choice of hymns should be tardy in arriving there was never a difficulty - *there was nothing Maurice could not or would not do!*

When there was a vacancy in the leadership of our Singing/Praise Group, Maurice responded to our request for help, and we appreciated his readiness to work within a genre somewhat foreign to him.   AN

INSPIRATION!   As minister I would sometimes drop in to a Choir or Praise Group practice, and always found this an inspiration, a joy and refreshment to the spirit! How happy we are to drink from various fountains where the Fountain is Christ.

GIVING SACRIFICIALLY.
I like to think that Maurice's willingness to give of himself sacrificially, as a servant to different groups, *opened up the way for the remarkable contribution that he made through the music of Bel Canto, where he took the best of the new songs, and enriched them with his own wonderful, creative arrangements. Those deserve to live on, and bless future generations of Christian worshippers.*

"ONE THING I DON'T UNDERSTAND, DAD....."
(Adam Harbinson, on Daphne's Death).
[Adam had been doing a short series of articles for West Church News. The last in February WCN had been on 'Suffering Saints'.]

"I told someone recently that the love affair that Daphne and I shared, lasting a third of a century, made EdwardV111 and Mrs Simpson's relationship look like a one-night stand. But it's over. After all the praying, the anointing with oil, the fasting and the pleading, all the believing and the laying on of hands. Daphne's dead.

I could pontificate about the peace of her death-bed, I could say that her race was run, or 'God gave us another two great years together after her grim prognosis', all of which may be true, but when it has all been said, she's gone. *I can only be honest and say that my overwhelming emotion is one of profound disappointment. She was so full of life and vitality, and there were so many things she still wanted to do.*

MY YOUNGEST SON.
My youngest son and I were chatting the other evening when suddenly he said, **'Dad, there is just one thing I don't understand. Why did our wee Mum die?'**
How do you answer that one to a 14-year old Down's Syndrome boy who has just lost the Mum he adored? The answer is, with the truth. And what is the truth? *'The truth, Jonny, is that I don't understand either.'*

The best I can manage for now is that while it would be lovely to believe that good people like your Mum shouldn't die young, Christians shouldn't die at only forty-eight (she doesn't care now that you know her age), *that is not living in the real world. As Solomon discovered, good things happen to bad people, and bad things happen to good people. The simple truth is this, our Mum got cancer and she died. So did 150,000 others in U.K. last year, so let's not complicate the issue.*

I DO NOT BUY INTO NICE PLATITUDES such as **"God wanted her home with Him"**, or that **"She has now received her perfect healing."** Death is a fact of life, a sad fact of life. We must all face the reality that we all must die, and there is never a right time. Let me share with you something of the **last conversation that Daff and I had, just** a couple of days before she died. We were talking about that lovely Scripture in Philippians 4: 6-9. It speaks of the **peace of God** and **the God of peace.**

DOES IT REALLY MATTER?
She was extremely weak and struggling for breath, and after we had talked for about an hour, I said to her, "*Here you are pet, not feeling great, fully believing that God can heal you, but not sure that He will. But if we have the peace of God in our hearts, and the God of peace at the centre of our lives, does it really matter?"* Well of course it does, but doesn't it take on a completely different complexion? *There's no fear, none.* We have come to believe that the peace that we have, which is so great as to be beyond human comprehension, *and the intimate love we can experience in this three-fold cord, is not conditional on our understanding all that He does. He is not accountable to us. He does not have to explain His actions to be assured of our loyalty.*

DAPHNE AND I LOVED HIM, because He first loved us, and that's the way it still stands for me and mine. As Job said, "The

Lord gave and the Lord has taken away; may the Name of the Lord be praised!" (Job 1).
Like Daniel's friends (Daniel 3) we prayed often, "Lord, we know that you can heal, up to the last minute, beyond the last minute. But even if you don't, we'll serve no other."

WHY AM I WRITING PUBLICLY TO THE CONGREGATION?
Because you, by your prayers, your visits, letters, phone calls, and your invitations to dinner, have taken my four kids and me to your heart, and made us your own. Thank you!
Four words will appear on Daphne's headstone, to sum her up, if that is possible. And they can be applied to many in West Church.
MUCH LOVED MUCH LOVED.

MAY CONFERENCE.
When I look back over the years I see clearly how the visits of outside speakers at Conferences in West, **have brought people to faith and vision.**
I have already mentioned the visit of Tom Smail in February 1968. Therefore, before demitting my charge in West, *I desire to leave the congregation with something to sharpen the vision, enrich devotion to Christ, and prepare our hearts to grasp the future.* So, from Friday 15 May to Sunday 17 May, all are invited to a Conference led by Rev. Teddy Saunders and his wife Margaret, and by the Rev. Bruce Collins.
Teddy Saunders has had a wonderful ministry in the ten years since his retirement, running HENSOL Courses for the benefit of ministers and church leaders, ably assisted by his wife; and Bruce Collins has a prophetic ministry, that has made him a sought-after speaker in many parts of the world

----

PRAYER TRIPLETS- REPORT.

Or, in this case, Prayer Quadruplet!
Glenda Eddis, Elizabeth Scullion, Nan Faulkner, Frances Smyth.
"Since our group started a few months ago, we have found that the desire to intercede on behalf of our land and our church has increased. **Parallel with this, our love and joy for one another has deepened.**
As we were obedient to God's call from 2 Chronicles 7: 14 -16, to humble ourselves before him and repent of our own sins, before we pray or intercede on behalf of others in our Province, **we started to be challenged in our minds and hearts in areas we would not at first have given much thought to.**
Praying on our knees is now a regular position for us, and through it we have learned much of what really lies on our own hearts.
The GUIDELINES and EVENING SERMONS have been a wonderful help and incentive to us all each week, *while still allowing us freedom to be open to the guidance of the Holy Spirit in other areas or situations in need of prayer.*
Bob Gass of UCB enables us to pray for others in practical ways while the Scriptures provided each week are taken and prayed into specific situations or troubles in people's lives. **Weekly we are finding new ways to praise and pray to God. Whether it is praying in silence, praying for each other, singing or listening for his still, quiet voice,** *we know we are growing in our ability to pray for and love God's people.*
WE LOOK FORWARD TO THE NEXT THREE MONTHS!

PRAYER: Over the years in West, there have been many initiatives to develop and intensify prayer within the congregation. Unlike John Seawright, Alvin Little, Terry Laverty, Bobby Liddle and myself who have all moved on, Heather Thompson continues on in West, so when she writes about PRAYER in the congregation, she goes beyond my departure in May 1998. Heather writes, in 2001:
"For 3 months, starting on September 24th 1994, 24-hour prayer was begun in West. We met *weekly* from midnight Friday until midnight Saturday.
Now, seven years on, we continue to meet on Friday evenings from 8.00pm to 10.00pm. in the Ministers' Room. *Our primary desire is to use this time to worship Jesus for who He is, and to seek to pray for what is on His heart.*
WE LISTEN! Over the years God has been teaching us how to pray about issues that concerned Him. *We listen, and pray on the basis of what we hear Him telling us.*

RENOUNCE SIN, BREAK ITS POWER. For example, we have been led to repent of, and renounce, un-forgiveness, bitterness, jealousy, pride, gossip, fear, anger etc, first of all in our own lives, then on behalf of the church.
Then, following His instruction, we have broken the power of these things over West in Jesus' Name and commanded them to go *and prayed that we would live all our lives in the love and forbearance of God, in His peace and joy, with His understanding and patience, and so on.*
AMAZED: *As we did this week by week we were amazed at the variety and depth of prayers, covering a wide range of issues, under each heading.* As time has gone on we have had a sense of battles won in the heavenlies in these areas and of consequent lessening of the grip of wrong attitudes amongst us, and a growing and deepening love and encouragement and understanding, the one for the other.

RECENTLY Deuteronomy 6: 4-5 was brought to our attention:
"Hear, O Israel: The Lord our

God, the Lord is one. Love the Lord your God with all your heart and with all your soul and with all your strength."

AS WE WAITED BEFORE GOD, we were led to pray that all idolatry be brought to nothing in the church: that we would no longer live as though independent of God, *following our own desires and leadings nor worship in any half hearted way.* We prayed for all, that we would be able to see God in all His sovereignty and loving power, as the God who created us, and who loves us as His children, and that we would no longer allow the limitations of our understanding to reduce Him to someone smaller than He is.

SIGNIFICANTLY IMPORTANT. We believe that such prayers as these are significantly important *in preparing us as a people to be ready for a new move of God. It is important that we, as a church, are enabled more and more to open ourselves to the fullness of Jesus, and so be willing and able to move with Him in whatever He is doing.*

SPECIFIC GROUPS. Sometimes we are led to pray for specific groups, for example children, and we can easily spend a couple of hours exploring all sorts of avenues in prayer in a way that is informed by the Holy Spirit, **and is lively and creatively spontaneous, so much so that we scarcely notice the time.**

WORSHIPPING HIM. At times God leads us to spend a whole evening, worshipping Him and enjoying His presence as we sing, read scripture and sit quietly before Him. **In times like these we grow in our knowledge of Him and of His desire to enjoy us, and we, Him, in undisturbed communion. We often don't want to leave!** We encourage those who feel they would like to participate in this prayer time to come any Friday that suits them.

NEW WEST CHURCH DIRECTORY FOR 1998 - to produce this is a considerable undertaking, and its publication have awaited the completion of our network of elders and Church Visitors to cover the whole congregation. This has now been achieved!

CAR PARK DEVELOPMENTS. You may have noticed that Ken Macartney and James Smith have been hard at work in our grounds, preparing the way for our projected new Car Park: some trees, bushes, briars have disappeared **and quotations are being sought. We still await the detailed plans for '91' development and extension.**

MARCH WCN also gives reports from our Brownies and Guides, and our Annual Kirk Session Report, as well as Financial Accounts for 1997. There is also news of the Men's Fellowship Weekend where the speakers are Bobby Liddle and Adam Harbinson.

DON & PAT McNUTT IN MALAWI. 2nd January 1998.
"Dear David & Rhoda,
We were delaying writing to you until we had settled into teaching in Livingstonia and could assess the situation *However,* the news in a fax from Maureen Bennett that you are going to step down in June has prompted us to communicate and we wish you a happy -though we are sure- active retirement. You will probably agree from your own missionary experience *that one goes through phases.* First, wonder and excitement with the new experiences, then a certain amount of disillusionment as one faces frustrations and a different culture, and finally - hopefully- a more balanced attitude. Although we may be at the second stage, **we have no regrets about coming to Malawi, and with a certain amount of humour can cope with most situations.**

LIVINGSTONIA - BEAUTIFUL. Firstly, Livingstonia is a most beautiful place, reasonably cool at night, and our house is roomy with both running water and electricity. It looks out on a constantly changing mountain scene to the south and west and to the east there is Lake Malawi with the Livingstonia Mountains on the far side.

THE ROAD TO LIVINGSTONIA. The big obstacle is the road to Livingstonia, which is off the main route to Tanzania along the lake shore. **This climbs 3,000 feet in 10 miles and has 21 hairpin bends.** To illustrate the difficulties, we came the 80 miles from Mzuzu, the Northern Province capital, by minibus with the headmaster Saturday a week ago. We reached the bottom at about 5.30pm, and the Head had phoned for some transport to meet us, since the school lorry had been broken down for some time. Apparently a Landover did come earlier but had returned to Livingstonia with a load of students. We therefore had to spend the night at a local 'hotel' - basic but clean and cheap. **It gave Don the opportunity to swim in the lake the next morning. OUR BREAK!** Our break came when a lorry arrived about 10.30am to **transport maize up to the plateau, so about 30 of us piled on top of the bags. Great for views but a bit unnerving when the lorry had to reverse to a precipice to negotiate some of the bends!** The first bit is very rocky, we got stuck once but there was plenty of people-power to push! On the top it can be very muddy, but the weather stayed dry.

SCHOOL STAFF AND STUDENTS.
You are probably more interested on how we are getting on with the school staff, students and locals generally. **They have been most welcoming and helpful, English being widely spoken.** We had two weeks to settle in since the start of the term was postponed. Even now there are only years 2 and 4 present, since 1 and 3 are awaiting exam results. **Pat therefore has still to**

start her Maths teaching. The Secondary School buildings are most impressive, obviously the Scottish missionaries majored on brickwork, but are getting run down due to lack of funds, and the same applies to equipment. Classes are boy/girl mixed about 3 to 1, some quite adult, and total about 45. **You will therefore recognise the difficulties of getting to know the students and of practical work in Don's Physical Science.**

CHRISTIANWISE we have been to three Tumbuku services in Livingstonia Church, an impressively large brick building. The locals would like Synod Headquarters transferred here from Mzuzu, but we think that is unrealistic. **We are now attending an English service, catering mainly for the students, and will have to take our turn in organising it as well as taking school assembly.** Pat is the patron of SCOM (Student Christian Organisation of Malawi) but this is run mainly by the pupils.
PAT HAS MADE THE HOME COMFORTABLE and we have an excellent cook whose latest treat was lemon marmalade. We have had some backpackers for lunch and hope to have school staff later on when we get more fellowship with them. **We met Northern Ireland (and Scottish) missionaries when we stayed a night at Ekwendeni Hospital near Mzuzu. Dr Gaston, who attended Ballymena Academy and his wife moved next door for 2 weeks to allow Mr Mbeya of Livingstonia Hospital to go on a course.** Don is attempting to start vegetables in the clay soil but germination is poor. This being the wet season, we have plenty of rain and thunder, often at night. **Please pass on our thanks to the congregation for the generous gift of £300. We felt obliged to send this to PCI Church House since we were grossly overweight in airfreight. Remember us to the other West Church staff. We hear Bobby had the job of reading our faxes from Mzuzu. Your in** Christ, D & P.

APRIL WCN 1998.
ANGUISH AND JOY IN FIERCE JUXTAPOSITION - GOOD FRIDAY/ EASTER.
We have the ultimate extremities in human emotion and experience, in Good Friday's torrid, unspeakable suffering and in Easter dawn's intense, laser joy. *And in our heart of hearts we know that we cannot have the one without the other!*
Paul said that **He, who knew no sin,** *became sin for us, that in Him we might have the righteousness of God.*
Jesus hung on the cross in our place, and on Him was laid the sins, griefs, sorrows and pains of the whole world.
That is exactly what He experienced when He cried out *'My God, my God, why have you forsaken me?'* He experienced for real **dereliction and sin-bearing:** *in his own human person he made* **ATONEMENT.** *In his own person he has gained resurrection for all mankind.*

Within two days humanity is raised from ultimate depths of judgement to the very heights of heaven! In some real measure we must enter into **all of that**, the sorrow and the joy, if we are to identify fully in heart and spirit, with all that has been gained for us through the events of Holy Week, culminating in Good Friday and Easter Day. **And so our members were encouraged to enter fully into our united Holy Week and Easter services.**

JOYS AND SORROWS TOUCH ALL OUR LIVES.
As you read through this edition of West Church News, you will find ample testimony to the fact that joys and sorrows do touch all our lives and are woven into our experiences . **Our lives are a tapestry where the dark threads and the bright ones can make a beautiful picture, creating character.**

More and more we talk with people who hurt, because the very fabric of family life is torn, broken, fragmented, and where the pain is intensified because of poisoned and angry relationships that continue, even after separation and divorce!
GRANDPARENTS. Some time ago, we quoted statistics that showed tens of thousands of children in Malawi, *who are orphaned because both parents have died, often of AIDS.* The burden of bringing them up often falls upon grandparents. **In this country too,** grandparents often assume a considerable responsibility in the family: sometimes because both parents are working, sometimes because of family fragmentation. **We pay tribute to the work done by grandparents and in this issue of WCN, Alma Boal's eleven-year old granddaughter has written about an exciting adventure when on holiday at the West Church Holiday Caravan in Kilkeel, with her much-loved and intrepid gran!**
Again, on the JOY side of things, don't pass over the story written by the theological student we sponsor in St. Petersburg! It will make you smile!
ON THE HARDER SIDE -two of our members tell of testing experiences, one where a marriage crumbled, and another where Christian vocation plans were painfully frustrated.

"I WOULD HAVE BEEN POORER SPIRITUALLY WITHOUT THIS EXPERIENCE" JANET DERRAUGH writes:

"But as for me, I trust you, O Lord, I say. 'You are my God'. My times are in your hands."

Dear Friends, This verse was fastened to the wall of my room at the Missionary Training College in Birmingham. **For someone embarking on a new career overseas those words were timely, and I made them into my prayer. Beside this was a map of Nepal - my destination in January 1998.** My arrival at the Training College was the culmination of months of waiting and wondering, medicals, visas, interviews. Many potential obstacles had been removed by God to bring me to this place. My old life was disappearing and I was looking forward to what lay ahead. **How easy it was to say the verse above, then, and really mean it!**

A BATTERING! My hopes and dreams then took a battering. Within hours of arriving at the college **I felt unwell, after a week I felt worse (viral infection) and after six weeks of struggling, I had to abandon the course and return to Bangor. United Missions Nepal** were contacted and agreed to wait until April 1998 for my arrival. However, by Christmas I was still unwell and not able to return to College in January. Following a medical report in January I was informed in March, that I had not been given medical clearance to go to Nepal. The job reserved for me in Kathmandu will be filled by someone else. When I am fully recovered from this illness I can re-apply - but it would mean starting the whole process again.

THE CLOSING OF THIS 'DOOR' took place over a number of months, *so I saw my future plans slowly dissolving.* I had time to adjust, but when I finally heard in March that it was all over *I still hurt inside. My heart felt deeply wounded.* Before and after Christmas I had many questions and no answers (and still have). **Why? Why? Why? I felt 'let down' by God because He allowed this to happen, and because He did not stop me from going to Nepal** *before I gave up my job!* (Many of you will have heard me say that). **My pride was hurt too - what will people think? Then, of course, Satan taunted me with 'You're a failure, everything you try to do goes wrong, just give up,'** When I looked at Psalm 31: 14 (which I had brought back with me) *I could no longer say it! I was ill and spiritually wounded. I didn't want to talk to God - it was all his fault!*

But I knew in my head that He was my hope, my life. When I was well enough to venture out, I forced myself to go to the Healing Service. I did not want to explain the situation to lots of people, (I was too ill), so the small group was less intimidating and from past experience of attending a Healing Service, **I expected to meet with God** (rather than hiding and sulking). **God used the Healing Service to reach out to me. He reminded me of His love for me through the group's compassion and love, and gradually I opened the communication lines with God again.** *I was bruised and hurt but being bound up by love.*

I WANT TO THANK YOU FOR BEARING MY BURDEN.
At a time when I was in danger of labelling myself a failure, (among many other negatives) or becoming depressed because of illness, the prayers of so many in West enabled me to cope. God always sent someone to me when I felt low - a surprise caller, a phone call, a 'chance' meeting in the street, a letter, an encouraging word after a Sunday Service - all were important to me. **I have been truly moved by your kindness and love towards me. I want to thank you for 'bearing my burden'. I know many people have been praying for me over the last few months and God has used your prayers to strengthen me spiritually and physically. I can honestly say I feel enriched by your care in ways I cannot quite describe,** *but I would have been poorer, spiritually, without this experience.*

LET GOD BE GOD!
I don't know why what happened, happened, but for now I am trying not to question and just let God be God. I thank God for the recovery I have made so far and pray it will continue. As to the future, thank God I can say once more: "But as for me, I trust in You, O Lord, I say, 'You are my God!' My times are in your hands." Psalm 31: 14-15.

MY BEST FRIEND SAID: "IT MUST BE GOD'S DOING!" Elaine Jefferson writes.
"A compassionate and gracious God, slow to anger, abounding in love and faithfulness."

"Asked to write a Witness Sheet I had to think what to say that could in some way convey what God has done in my life - what I have learned from Him and what I have had to *unlearn*. The quote above from the Psalmist, sums it all up. I have discovered a God of **compassion** who has never failed, especially when I have most spectacularly failed Him; whose **grace** is so far reaching that I know I have not understood a fraction of it; His **love** so extravagant that it is beyond my wildest hopes; but most especially for me, His **faithfulness** has been the lifebelt that has kept me afloat through some rough seas. **WHEN LIFE IS HARD and we face failure, disillusionment and disappointment, in whatever guise they come to us as individuals, we discover then if God is real and what He is really like.**
THROUGH A DIFFICULT MARRIAGE AND A LOT OF MISTAKES I discovered God was there for me, not to take the problems away but to give me the strength and courage to carry on and especially to reassure me of His love *when I began to realise how much the problems were my own fault.*

HE IS A VERY PRACTICAL GOD. At low ebb about eight years ago, I called out to Him in desperation that I couldn't carry on; I was emotionally and mentally at the end of myself. *If I expected a reply from Him at all, it would have been an admonition to try harder, pray more or join another Bible Study. But to my amazement He said quite clearly to me two words, 'Open University'. So for the next five years I spent my free time studying all sorts of weird and wonderful things - God took me out of a cesspool of self-pity and gave me what He knew I needed at that time.*

HE HAS PROVIDED FOR MY *REAL* NEEDS.
During the last three years my marriage has broken up and my two sons have left home. God provided for me during this time. He hasn't given me everything I wanted but I can see how He has provided for my real needs. **I think I have at last learnt the lesson that He knows what is best for me and, however much I want something, I have learned to offer it up to Him to give or withhold as He wills.** He brought me to West Church just before this period of my life and here I have been accepted and welcomed by people of God in a way that has been truly food to a hungry soul.

MAKING PEOPLE WHOLE. I believe God is in the business of making people whole. **There is a lot of healing needed in all our lives.** *Often the symptoms of our pain and heartache are the things God is using to call our attention to things that He wants to change. It could be resentment, unforgiveness or self-centredness.* It could be lack of real trust in Him. After all the purpose of this life for us is to become like Jesus so, whatever eternity holds, we are fitted for it.

LOVE RELATIONSHIP WITH GOD. I read in David Watson's book, 'Fear no Evil', something which encouraged me very much. ***David Watson knew he was dying and the prayers for his healing had not been answered.*** His question was, "Why have you, God, given me such a successful and far reaching ministry if I am now to die and it will all come to nothing?" He was sure that God's reply was, that the most important thing in God's eyes was David's love relationship with Him, not the successful ministry. The love relationship between us and God *is more important than any achievement or ambition,* however, 'Christian' or mission-orientated it may be. This is in the grasp of all of us. *We are all qualified and able to enter into a closer relationship with Him and learn to love Him with all our hearts, minds and strength.*

ON THE JOURNEY STILL!
So I am very much on the journey still, *but God is continually surprising me,* showing me that He cares for me and He can do anything. **He is God.** My best friend is not a Christian (so impressed with what she sees in me!). However, even she said, 'It must be God's doing' when she saw, how last month I sold my house and every single item of furniture, carpets and curtains that I didn't want, (even down to the lawnmower) without an estate agent or advertising. *I was just a spectator and watched it all happen!*

HIS FAITHFULNESS.
It has been in the small things that make up everyday life that God has shown me his faithfulness. I find it a battle to believe that God, this amazing God who created the universe and is in control of all things, *is a God who cares about me and wants a relationship with me.* But through joys and successes, as well as the hard times, God has shown over and over that this is indeed the kind of God He is. The challenge for me is to know more of His presence, of Emmanuel, God with us, day by day."

MY WEDDING- EXCITING!
Oleg Morohovets, one of the theological students we support, writes from St. Petersburg. "Peace to you, dear brothers and sisters! I, Oleg Morohovets address you with words of gratitude! I want to share some of the events in my life that have taken place in recent weeks. During the Christmas holidays, many events, and meetings with various people, took place... It was a period of preparation for my wedding, one of the greatest events of my life! The person with whom I now share my life, Ruth, is a second year student at St. Petersburg Christian University, where I am in the third year. **The time of preparation for the wedding, and the wedding itself, were very exciting! Many friends from our College were present, as well as some who had graduated and were working in distant places.**
For example, Michael and Olga who work in a Christian Education Network in the city of Sevestopole, Ukraine. Paul and Inna came from Tumen, Siberia, where they are starting a new church and running an orphanage. **It was interesting to hear about their work and how they are settling down after graduation from our college.** And it was a time of meeting and talking with relatives!
Even though the Christmas holidays were longer than normal, they passed as in a moment for us, for me and my wife! Now again we are back at college, back at classes, at exams, tests - though now it is different for us!
We sincerely thank you for your prayers - we feel them strongly in our lives. **Thank you very much for your support and helping us**

through college. *We ask from the Lord, blessings upon you and your church."*

ON HOLIDAY WITH NANNIE!

Alma Boal's 11 year old grand-daughter tells of a holiday in the West Church Caravan, in Sandilands, Kilkeel.

"My Nannie is very special to me. She looked after me through my childhood when my parents were out working, especially in the summer. My Nannie comes to our house every Sunday for dinner. I find it hard to accept that she is slow on her feet, and needs the support of crutches to be able to walk. *Years ago my Nannie could have walked anywhere she wanted, without these props. During the summer months, she used to walk for miles with my cousins, sister and me.*

THE MOST VIVID MEMORY of a special time with my Nannie was when she took my four cousins, my younger sister and me on holiday. Being the eldest of the brood, along with my cousin, Paul, at the grand old age of eleven, *we were second in charge! My Nannie must have been mad, taking six young children on holiday, without any support from parents! Though that was my Nannie, she could cope with anything and she wanted to make this holiday special for her grandchildren!*

ADVENTURE WITH A RAM!

On the second day of our holiday, we decided to begin to explore around the country roads. We walked along singing, and laughing, even my Nannie joined in! One of our favourite songs was one we made up ourselves. It was called, ' We're all going on a mud hunt." As we walked along, we passed a farmhouse, **which had a ram in its front garden.** We stopped a while and made fun of the ram, saying that it was out playing football, or going to get on the skateboard! As we left the ram and went on, I remember saying to my Nannie, **"Imagine if the ram chased us!"**

Little did we know that a few seconds later, just that would happen! I remember looking back to the farmhouse and nearly died when I saw the ram come hurtling towards us. **I screamed in a state of panic. Everyone else looked around to see what the matter with me was. Then they saw for themselves what had shocked me so much.** We all ran to try to increase the gap between the ram and us. My younger cousin, Suzanne, who was in the buggy, willed my Nannie to run to try and escape the ram. Paul and I ran into a bend in the road, my sister and the others followed. I remember running into a clump of nettles and weeds, while everyone else ran on. **Just when I had nowhere else to hide, the ram came charging round into the bend and went head first into a farm gate.** *This was my time to escape and I ran as fast as I could to reach the others. I was relieved to know that the ram had passed my Nannie without hurting her.* We were all in stitches laughing after the ordeal, but knew that it was not funny at the time. We carried on walking, hoping that the ram would not make another attempt to scare us.

AT LEAST 6 MILES!

When a caravan site came into view, we thought we were home, as we had walked about 4 miles that day. Though as we got closer to the site, *we realised it was not our caravan site!* Nannie asked a lady nearby if we were far from Sandilands. She looked in amazement and said, **"You've miles to go - at least 6 miles along the beach."** I wondered if we would get home before dark. Though Nannie reassured me that everything would be fine and that we would be home in time for dinner. *We then began our long journey home along the beach. The tide was coming in and my cousin, Andrew, asked Nannie if we would be safe or if we would drown!* Again Nannie put on a strong face and said that the Lord would keep us safe.

We kept on over sand and rocks. We came to a grassy bank that we had to climb. All I could think of was how would my Nannie be able to get up this bank. For her it was not a problem. She put her trust in the Lord. Although I didn't know how He would help her this time. *But He did!*

WE FELT RELIEVED as we came to the end of our tremendous journey - we saw the caravan site

Come into view. *We were back in time for dinner and home before dark, just as Nannie had promised. There was laughter in the caravan that night, recalling the day's events!*

I am so glad I can remember this special time that I had with Nannie. *Nannie made our holidays brilliant for all of us. Most of my holiday memories recall the days all of us spent together, such as exploring and going to the beach, though my memory of this holiday will stick in my mind forever!*

FAREWELL EDITION MAY WCN 1998.

FARE WELL!

This is the last time I sit at my desk to write West Church News! It's a long span of years since I hammered out the first editions of "West Church News-Sheet" on the old wax stencils! And now we stand on the edge of what the new computer age will provide! A wide span of years, and aeons in terms of the new technology, now upon us! *Yet the purpose remains the same: to make sure that no West Church member be ignorant of all that goes on in West Church! We have also sought to present new ideas about what it means to share the Gospel, and to help the Church grow, in our own local situation.*

IN THE BEGINNING I sometimes turned the handle of the old Gestetner duplicator myself, but then others soon came to help, like George Coburn's father! *Over the years West Church members owe an immense debt to those who have done the duplicating, down to Billy Richardson of the present time; and likewise the collating, down to Maureen Blackmore and her helpers of today.*
<u>I want to thank all of these, faithful, willing and normally cheerful folk for often prodigious endeavours on behalf of us all.</u>

WHAT AM I TO WRITE TODAY?

I simply pray the blessings below upon you! And invite you to receive them into your hearts and lives! Some final words or greetings from the New Testament:

"The grace of the Lord Jesus Christ be with you. **My love to all of you in Christ Jesus. Amen.**" (1 Corinthians 16: 23).
"Finally, brothers, good-bye. Aim for perfection, listen to my appeal, be of one mind, live in peace. And the God of love and peace will be with you.
Greet one another with a holy kiss. **May the grace of the Lord Jesus Christ, and the love of God, and the fellowship of the Holy Spirit be with you all.**" (2 Corinthians 13: 11).
"Be joyful always; pray continually; give thanks in all circumstances, for this is God's will for you in Christ Jesus. **Do not put out the Spirit's fire, do not treat prophecies with contempt. Test everything. Hold on to the good. Avoid every kind of evil.
MAY GOD HIMSELF, THE GOD OF PEACE, SANCTIFY YOU THROUGH AND THROUGH. MAY YOUR WHOLE SPIRIT, SOUL AND BODY BE KEPT BLAMELESS AT THE COMING OF OUR LORD JESUS CHRIST. THE ONE WHO CALLS YOU IS FAITHFUL AND HE WILL DO IT."** (1 Thessalonians 5: 16).
"To Him who is able to keep you from falling and to present you before his glorious throne without fault and with great joy - to the only God and Saviour be glory, majesty, power and authority, through Jesus Christ our Lord, before all ages, and evermore! Amen. (Jude 24).

"THE GOSPEL AND THE SPIRIT." On the eve of 'the vacancy' an important Conference to strengthen and sustain us.
This Conference will be led by the Rev. Bruce Collins, accompanied by Dick Westerkemp, Richard Scott and Helen Goldenberg. There will be three main sessions Friday 14 May at 7.30; Saturday Morning at 9.00, a double session until lunch; and an evening session at 7.30. **Bruce will preach at both our Sunday morning services, and Teddy and Margaret Saunders at our evening service.**

Appropriate, perhaps, in this Farewell edition, to give a quote from the Presbyterian Herald's "Wit & Wisdom"!

"YESTERDAY IS HISTORY, TOMORROW IS MYSTERY, TODAY IS A GIFT, AND WE CALL IT THE PRESENT!"

YESTERDAY IS HISTORY!
But not dead history, not history to be forgotten, not history to be dumped, as though worn out and useless!
From among the West Church files of yesteryear, I picked out, from 1986, the West Church Silver Jubilee edition, *and found it entrancing!* There were skeletal pictures of the 'New Church' under construction in 1962-3, as well as a picture of Carnalea House on the day when it was dedicated for use as a church in October 1961. And there were reminders of the plans, projects, endeavours of the first 25 years, **and the people who filled and enriched our lives, fellow-labourers in the cause of Christ. And hard to believe that since then,** *we have covered half the distance that carries us from silver to gold!*

GRADUATED! We cannot think back, without realising that many of our dear friends have 'graduated', *and of how many friends we have, above and beyond, in the presence of Christ!*

At our Service of Thanksgiving in October 1986, we sang:

"Mercies new and never-failing Brightly shine through all the past....Shadows deep have crossed our pathway, we have trembled in the storm....
Many that we loved have left us, Reaching first their journey's end; Now they wait to give us welcome - Brother, sister, child and friend. When at last our journey's over, And we pass away from sight, Father, take us through the darkness Into everlasting light."

THE PAST: History peopled with friends - friends who have matured, or grown older with us, or who have passed on ahead of us.
Beyond our own natural family that we love, Rhoda and I count the people of West Church *our family, dearly beloved. You may miss us, but you maybe cannot envisage how much we will miss you. YOU ARE IN OUR VERY HEARTS, PART OF OUR LIVES, and we bless and thank you for all that we have shared together.*
HISTORY! LIVING HISTORY!

TOMORROW IS MYSTERY!

WHAT WILL YOU DO WHEN YOU RETIRE?" is one of the commonest questions we are asked these days. It wouldn't be entirely true to say that we give no thought for tomorrow!
But it would be true to say that our main pre-occupation is to follow the task in hand until our final Sunday on the 31 May. Then our first main task will be to prepare to change house, a formidable endeavour since we have lived in West Church Manse since April 1962.
As many of you know, we are moving to 18 Bryansburn Road, an old, large semi-detached house. With two daughters living in England, who, with their families desire to visit us as often as they can manage, **a commodious house will allow them to continue to visit us.** And now that both Elizabeth and Mary have children of school-going age, and they are constrained by school holidays, their visits may coincide or at least overlap. So we are glad to have a house on the west side of Bangor, convenient to the shore, and to the well-loved locality of their youth.

And may we say that while, on retirement, formal, institutional links are severed, and that it is right that we leave space for our successors to carry forward the work in West unhindered, that we rejoice that all the informal links of friendship remain. And our door at 18 Bryansburn Road will be open!

"What will you do when you retire?"
Obviously we shall have more time with our family, and their needs will claim priority on our time.
Beyond that we have no immediate plans.
We shall desire to make ourselves available to God. And we have no doubt that as we do that wholeheartedly and sincerely, **God will have useful work for us to do!**
I have never worn a pair of carpet-slippers, and it's not my first ambition to go out and purchase a pair now!
While not having an ambition to be a workaholic, **we would prefer to be a Caleb or a Joshua, people useful in the Kingdom of God, rather than fill our lives with synthetic activities!**
None of us have any special purchase or grip upon life, so best to take each day as a gift from God, to be lived under his control and, enthusiastically, for his glory.

TODAY IS A GIFT AND WE CALL IT THE PRESENT.

We enter the last month before retirement. I look forward to taking part in the following services:
Evening Praise Service on 3 May.
Main morning services on 10 May.
Ten O'clock service on 17 May when Bruce Collins will preach.
Main morning services on 24 May.
Farewell Services on 31 May. I plan for the final evening service to be an informal Communion service, at which people will come forward for communion. If anyone present should not be a communicant, there is no difficulty. Still come!
At this service I am inviting all our music groups to play a part, Choir and Belcanto and our various Singing Groups.
We want it to be a service filled with rich, diverse praise of God, at which we know ourselves to be a family, eating at the one Table, serving the one Lord!

AT PEACE ABOUT RETIRING-

May I say that I feel at peace about retiring at this time: I'm in my seventieth year, and a compulsory retirement date looms early in 1999. At the present we have a strong pastoral team, with administration well ordered - so the time is ripe!

DISCOVERING THE NEW MINISTER OF GOD'S CHOOSING.

A Study presented by your Minister at a Kirk Session "Away Day" on 24th April, and now included in May WCN. A summary:

GOD GIVES LEADERS with differing gifts and abilities. God is rich in the amazing diversity of people He has created and equipped for ministry in His Church. There are people of widely differing temperaments, like the impulsive, warmhearted Simon, apt to buckle under pressure; or the thrusting, domineering, single focussed Saul of Tarsus. But imbued and transformed by the Holy Spirit, Peter became bold and fearless, and Paul became a father-figure to the churches he founded, tender and as a nursing-mother towards young and immature Christians.

OPENNESS TO THE SPIRIT GIVES DYNAMIC FOR MINISTRY. In looking for a minister equipped to serve in West, you will be open in heart and spirit, to people who, whatever their natural abilities, **are themselves open to the transforming and enabling power of the Holy Spirit,** *to give dynamic for ministry.*
Jesus chose the Twelve from people He had already come to know and after a night of prayer to his Father.
When the prophets and teachers in Antioch were fasting and worshipping the Lord, the Lord said 'Set apart for me Barnabas and Saul for the work to which I have called them'.
Before choosing someone to be a minister for West, there should be an endeavour to know the candidates well, with some real knowledge of their track-record, an assessment of abilities in respect of the work to be done,

and a waiting upon God's Spirit to know whom He is calling.

THE NATURE OF THE CHURCH AS A BODY
determines the qualities and character that the minister should have. God gives some to be apostles, prophets, evangelists, pastors and teachers. While we cannot make an exact transference between these offices and the church of today, there must be some real endowment of the Spirit so that the Body of the Church may be built up.

THE MINISTER MUST BE AN ENCOURAGER.
Barnabas was an Encourager, who sought out Saul of Tarsus, Paul, and brought him to Antioch to help in the developing work of the Church where Gentiles were coming to faith in Jesus. Paul had many apostolic qualities, but he also was, pre-eminently an encourager, perceiving the church to be a body of many members, each and all to be encouraged to use their unique and specific gifts up building the whole body and making it dynamic.

MINISTERS SHOULD HAVE A FERVENT GRASP OF THE GOSPEL.
Paul said: "I am not ashamed of the Gospel because it is the power of God for salvation for **everyone who believes**, first the Jew, then the Gentile." To Corinth he wrote; "*Christ's love compels us, because we are convinced that one has died for all, therefore all have died.....from now on we regard no one from a human point of view..... If anyone is in Christ he is a new creation: the old has gone, the new has come. All this is from God, who reconciled us to himself, and gave us the ministry of reconciliation.*" Ministers need that conviction at the heart of their ministry, however expressed, from the pulpit, in Bible studies and seminars and in person-to-person relationships. To the Thessalonians Paul said: "**We were gentle among you, like a mother caring for her little children. We loved you so much that we were delighted to share with you, not only the Gospel of God, but our lives as well, because you were so dear to us.**"

MINISTERS NEED A GOOD GRASP OF THE WHOLE WORD OF GOD.
In the Reformed tradition, emphasis is laid upon the minister as teacher and preacher of the Word of God. Remember how the apostles said that they were not to neglect their study of the Word of God in order to serve at tables. The study of the Word of God and praying over and through it must have priority, so that they are fully acquainted **with the whole Word of God.** It is easy for Christians to latch on to one or two particular doctrines or themes from the Scriptures, to have hobbyhorses, only one or two strings to their bow. This can lead to a dangerous lack of balance. In his letter to the Colossians, Paul said his aim was that people **grow in the knowledge of God, being strengthened with all power, so that they might have great endurance and patience.** *A minister must be well equipped theologically.*

MINISTERS NEED TO BE SELFESSLY HARD WORKERS.
The apostle Paul spoke of how tirelessly he laboured in the cause of bringing people to faith in Christ, and of nurturing them in that faith, and the extent to which he was ready to sacrifice himself. Jesus spoke of the fact that when talents were given, they need to be wholeheartedly exercised - and there were hard words for those who were indolent and unbelieving. I remember **Jean Darnall saying that when she appears before God, her hope is that she will have many sheaves harvested, to present to Him!**

These are some thoughts and insights to guide you. You must look not just for a superhuman Christian who combines every virtue, gift and ability: that's impossible to find! But a person of faith and love who will work with you, and alongside whom you will work, giving allegiance, respect and love, so that TOGETHER, you do the work of Christ in West. And the person who comes, open to the Spirit, WILL GROW WITH YOU, in the knowledge of Christ, in fruitful service to Him, and there will be new initiatives, inspired by the Spirit.

DOES GOD GUIDE US?
Jane Richardson discovers that God does guide us as individuals- evident in all the little details.

Does God guide us as individuals? I wonder what our answer is to that question. Some of us think perhaps that God is too remote to be interested in our individual lives. Others believe it in theory, but there are times when it seems much more difficult in practice. *Our church family faces a situation where we will have to make a decision about a new minister, which will affect the lives of many people, in many different ways, for years to come. Do we really believe that God can make his way known to us as individuals?*
When David asked me to write a Witness Sheet I thought I had nothing really out of the ordinary to say. **However, as I look back over my life I know there have been many instances when I was convinced that** *God had guided in a very clear way.* I hope that as I share some of these that you too, will be convinced that God does

take a real interest in our lives, and that when we ask, **He does show us the way He wants us to go.**

MY MOTHER DIED WHEN I WAS JUST 14.

I became a Christian when I was quite a young child, through the witness of my Sunday School teacher. My faith was very real to me even as a child. It was this trust in God, as Someone who was concerned about my life, that helped me to cope when my Mother died when I was just four **I remember being very angry with God for letting this happen, yet in all that difficult time I had an underlying awareness that He was there for me. This was confirmed in so many ways as I saw how He guided even my choice of subjects through the wisdom of good teachers.**

I HAD ALWAYS WANTED TO TEACH.

I finished school and went to university. I had always wanted to teach and planned that after my degree, I would do a teacher training course. However, just a couple of months before my finals my Father took ill. He was diagnosed as having lung cancer (he had always been a very heavy smoker) and he died that summer. He did not even get to my graduation. I was in a real dilemma then. I had not applied for any jobs as I thought I was going back to study but, as I now had no one to support me; I had to get a job quickly. **I really prayed that something would materialise. but in August there are not many teaching jobs to be filled.** Then I saw an advertisement in the paper for a Physics teacher in Methody. I had always vowed that this was one school I never wanted to teach in as I felt it was much too big. **So although I was desperate for a job, I decided not to apply.**

GOD HAD OTHER PLANS!

God however had other plans! About a week after seeing the advert I received a letter from the Headmaster asking me to come and see him as he had heard that I was looking for a job. To my great surprise, he offered me the position as a Physics teacher to start in September. **I saw that as a very powerful indication of God's guidance, as I had no idea how the Headmaster even knew that I was looking for a job.**

I taught in Methody for 4 years **and then felt very strongly that I should go to Malawi to teach there. I resigned my post and went to Malawi on a three-year contract.**

About six months before this was due to end I had to decide whether to renew my contract or come home **and I really did not know what to do. I loved the work in Malawi and would have been quite happy to stay but wasn't sure whether it was the right thing to do. I prayed that God would make it clear and I asked Him that if He wanted me to come home then someone at home would offer me a job. Imagine my surprise when that week I had three letters from various people in Methody telling me that they would need a Physics teacher in September. The last one was from the Headmaster offering me a job. *I took it that God was guiding me back to Ireland. I stayed in Methody for the rest of my teaching career until the way opened up for me to take early retirement last year.***

IN ALL THE LITTLE DETAILS.

I could relate how God guided me to come to Bangor and to West Church. Both stories would take too long, but it was very evident in all the little details **that God was in those decisions and it was exciting to see it all unfolding at the time. He brought Billy and me together and we have had 12 really good years of marriage. I think I have discovered that God can guide us as we step out in faith.**

All these things have convinced me that God really does care about the details of our lives. If we seek his guidance sincerely He will not let us down. *That helps me to be sure that He will guide us as a congregation in the decision we have to make, if we take time to ask Him.*

God has used many people in my life to be His instruments in His guidance. I would like to say a very big 'thank you' to Rhoda and David for all the help and encouragement they have been to me over all the years I have been at West, and for the time they have given so generously in so many ways.

LIFE IN THE SPIRIT SEMINARS? "NEVER IN MY LIFE WAS I INTERESTED IN ANY CHURCHY STUFF...... I HATED IT!" Ronelle Watson.

"I am Ronelle Watson, born and bred in South Africa. From a very early age I knew there was a God and a Jesus, *but never did I know there was a Holy Spirit, (just like the people in Acts 19 who had not heard about the Holy Spirit), someone to help us and teach us the right way of living.*

At the age of ten I bought myself a Bible, knowing in my heart that I must read it and say a prayer. My parents were ordinary, everyday people. They went to church on a Sunday because it was tradition. So for years I went to Church and read the Word. **As I became older and temptation was everywhere I still read the Word of God,** *but it was just like reading something I did not understand.*

My husband is from Londonderry. It is strange how God works, because I had always wanted to live in the UK. Through coming to Northern Ireland for visits to my in-laws, God started to

WEST CHURCH BANGOR ONWARD JOURNEY

pull my heart towards this country. For nine years we remained in South Africa. I started living wild and falling into the darkness of sin. *I became so blind it was only me and nobody else. My kids and my husband were pushed aside; I was lying and it just got worse.* **Thanks to God, He stepped in.**

MY HUSBAND DECIDED TO LEAVE SOUTH AFRICA.
He left us to stay at his parents' home until he found work. After only 3 weeks he found employment in Scotland. *Looking back now, it was all in God's timing, not mine nor his.* So while he was away I liked what I was doing, and decided to stay and not go back to him. *Things in my life became so bad that I reached a point where I had to leave South Africa and join my husband in Scotland.*
We decided to go to church. I found it very difficult to understand the accent in Church but was determined to go with it, and so we settled in Scotland. We lived in Scotland for only nine months when God moved us on. **My husband was offered a job in Northern Ireland but we decided to stay in Scotland because we were tired of moving.** My husband turned the offer down. But God had other plans. The company phoned him again and persuaded him to take the job. **So we packed up again with a lot of tears, not knowing what waited for us on the other side.**

A NEW HOUSE, A NEW CHURCH!
We were concerned about paying a mortgage as well as rent, as we could not afford it. But God provided for us on this side. The company paid our rent for two years until we got a house. In Bangor we enquired about a Church and school. My husband's cousin told him to try **West Church. The love, the warm welcome we received and the joy on people's faces was great. We sat at the back. Terry was preaching that day. It had** been comfortable to be in a church where you could almost fall asleep! *And now suddenly to hear someone so clear and full of life! It was wonderful to be able to understand what the minister was saying. Even my husband commented on this also!*

HEATHER THOMPSON STOOD AT MY DOOR!
So time went on. One morning Heather Thompson stood at my door. I welcomed her in and all I could speak about was 'the weather'. *Today after five years I think how true it is that when you are in the world you talk only 'worldly', but when you are a new creation in Christ and you sit in the company of other Christians, you talk only about the one you love - JESUS!*

LIFE IN THE SPIRIT.
Heather invited me to a 'Life in the Spirit Seminar'. I decided to go. (Never in my life had I been interested in any churchy stuff! I felt very uncomfortable. I hated it). But by now I had had enough of being lonely with nobody to talk to. I wanted somebody or someone to fill the lonely gap.

THAT MORNING AT WEST I MET LOVELY PEOPLE - friendly and welcoming me into their 'world'. Sitting in a circle singing songs, I thought they sang too long and it was boring! Then Heather asked us why we were there. Everybody answered and there was one woman who said she was thirsty. So I thought 'Wow' I am in the right place! **She has come for a cup of coffee because she said she was thirsty. Now I can laugh at this, because now I know what she meant.**
I went every Wednesday to the Seminar and it was great and today I am a totally new person in Christ.

I THANK GOD for saving my life and choosing me to be His child. I *still have to fight with myself but He is right by my side. I love Him with all my heart, and looking back He was with me all of my life. It is great when the blindness disappears and you see Jesus in your life.* **THANK YOU, MY LORD!**

ANOTHER WITNESS TO "LIFE IN THE SPIRIT."
Lorna McQuitty invites us to read Galatians 4 4-7 and Romans 8: 13-17.

"One September Sunday evening in West Church David Bailie said 'This is your last chance to join the Life in the Spirit Seminar'. For me, it seemed that it would be my last chance ever *to find an answer to the burning questions in my heart and head...*
I had been to several of the Bangor churches, to Christian meetings and even to Capernwray but no one gave me the help I needed! I really wanted to be a witness for Jesus. I had given my heart and life to him when I was a teenager but I was too afraid to speak to anyone about him. A friend and I joined the Seminar and were in John Seawright's group.

EMPOWERED TO BE A WITNESS. On 21st November thirteen years ago God, by his grace, filled me with His Holy Spirit and empowered me to be a witness for Jesus *All the fears were gone and I just delighted in talking about Jesus. In all situations He is there with me and often gives me the right words to open a conversation.*
When the Seminar ended, two years later, I had been taught so much about the gifts of the Spirit. The Bible had become relevant to my life and I had fellowship with the Father through the Son in a new and much deeper way.

ASKED TO HELP WITH A

SEMINAR.
Some time later David Bailie asked several of us to help him with a seminar he was leading. All he asked me to do, he said, was to smile - not too difficult, I thought! Wrong! Smiling was easy - **keeping quiet** and only speaking when David asked me was, for me, a hard but important lesson to learn. For a later seminar David asked me to lead the worship time. *Truly the Lord uses us in our weakness!*

FROM MANY PLACES: People have come to seminars from Dungannon, Portglenone, Antrim, Belfast, Newtownards, Groomsport, from many areas in Bangor, and from West Church. They represent various denominations, were at different stages in their Christian lives **but all were wanting more of Jesus in their lives.**

To see people gradually experiencing new things in their lives, leading them to witness for the Lord they love, and to being of service to Him in so many ways was wonderful.

To get to know people on a deep spiritual level and yet know little about their everyday life and work amazed me - but knowing them on this deeper level was much better.

SOME OF THESE DEAR FRIENDS HAVE GONE TO BE WITH JESUS. Harry McCaul and Lorna Sinclair who were in my first Seminar group, both died too early and too tragically and I miss them; Harry Graham's quiet witness to his new life in Christ was such a powerful one; Margaret Gibson, that remarkable Christian lady and dear Phil Dornan helped in Seminars.

In the Life in the Spirit Seminars people have become new creations in Christ; they have developed and started to use the gifts of the Spirit; they have started to take part in the work of West Church, in a new way.

With so many others, I have experienced the gentle, wise, God-inspired teaching given by David Bailie who has discipled us with such loving care over many months, and **I have been there when God, by His Holy Spirit and through His Son, Jesus has moved in our hearts and minds and spirits to help us to worship and praise Him in a way that is beyond words.**
Thank you, David.

A 'RISKY' INVITATION TO THE LORD! Tanya Polley writes in May 2001.
"While on a camping holiday in France in August 1997, I unexpectedly (and most unusually) found myself alone for a period of time. I decided to have a Quiet Time during which I found myself saying to the Lord: *'If there is anything extra you would like me to do in the Church will you make it clear to me.'* As the words were coming out of my mouth the thought, 'This is a bit risky' was running through my head! I led and still lead, a busy life as a lecturer in North Down College, a Sunday School teacher, wife and mother to two energetic boys (three if you count Derek!) *so I was not looking for something to occupy my time. The family returned, the thoughts went to the back of my head, and I resumed my holiday.* **FIRST SUNDAY IN SEPTEMBER.**
Back from holiday, refreshed, relaxed, and looking forward to returning to my own church, I walked in through the door *and was suddenly made very much aware of the reality of my faith.* A lady, Maureen Blackmore, who at that time I didn't know very well, approached me. This is what she said: **"Margaret Conroy (who leads the Sycamore Club) asked me to speak to you about helping with the club. I was very reluctant to do so because I hardly know you, so while praying before I came to church this morning, I promised the Lord that if you walked past me I would speak to you about it. What else could I do!!"**

GOBSMACKED! GAVE IN!
"The only person I knew with learning difficulties was the small son of my best friend. I was, and am, a Maths teacher. I even had limited experience of teaching my own subject at a basic level, let alone something as important as my faith. Let's say I was gobsmacked - but then I remembered my prayer. I also remembered previous occasions when the Lord had confirmed my firm belief that He has a sense of humour and takes us at our word, **so I gracefully, reluctantly and fearfully gave in.**
THE SYCAMORE CLUB. At that time the Sycamore Club membership was mainly made up of young people who were in the care of the Barnardo's organisation. It met weekly and could probably best be described as a Sunday School. We did a lot of singing, prayed and sometimes had a short talk. Every Halloween the PWA gave us a party, we had another at Easter, and a barbeque in June to finish the session. **Margaret Conroy** was in charge, with me and various other people from the church and elsewhere as helpers. **To my surprise and relief I found myself really enjoying the meetings.** Shortly after I joined, **Margaret Conroy took really ill with a virus. She was in hospital for quite a long period of time, *so I was suddenly in charge.***
The dynamics of the group were changing. **There were now adults coming, so it was decided to divide into two groups meeting on alternate weeks. Helen Hanlon and Iris Elliott who knew the young people, continued with them, and another adult group came into being.**

GROWTH EXPLOSION.
Throughout the years since then the Sycamore Club has continued to evolve. We experienced what could

be described as a growth explosion when **The Croft Community joined our numbers.** The original group grew up and re-joined the other group, *so at present we have one group of approximately forty members meeting on alternate Tuesdays.*

MANY COMMITTED AND TALENTED HELPERS.
Having been joined by many committed and talented helpers our programme has been able to expand to include artwork, drama and dance to reinforce the talks. One of our members teaches us proper signing, so members who have difficulty with speech can worship in this way during our time of praise. We concentrate mainly on Bible stories which show us how much God loves us and wants to be involved in our ordinary lives. **We talk about how we can respond to Him in practical ways by our care of and for one another. We, the leaders,** *are frequently humbled by the way in which our members do show this care for us and for each other.*

PROSPECTS. We have joined forces with the **PROSPECTS** organisation, which is a UK-wide Christian group working with people with severe learning difficulties. "Prospects" provide us with support and material which we can use in our meetings, and also has regular get-togethers when the various NI groups can meet with one another. It is good to be able to compare notes and learn from one another since very little specialist material is available. **It also helps us to realise that we are no longer ploughing a lonely furrow!**

ALWAYS REFRESHED!
At the beginning I spoke of my reluctance and self-doubts about helping with the Sycamore Club. Now I know that I am refreshed by my time there. At the end of a meeting **we all agree that we have benefited from being present, that we are less tired than we were when we arrived and we thank God for allowing us to help with this special group of people** At one of our Halloween parties hosted by the PWA, we were pairing off members of the two groups, giving out photographs, and committing to pray for our partner. There being more members of the PWA than there were of us. **I was approached by an elderly lady, who had yet to find a partner. One of our young helpers who was home from University at the time piped up:** *'I'm a member of the Sycamore Club and I haven't got a partner yet to pray for me.'* <u>To me that says it all!</u>

BORN AND BRED IN THE CHRISTIAN FAITH... yet

Jean McCormick never stops wondering about life's mysteries.

"Always be ready" writes Peter, "to give an answer... if asked for a reason, for the hope that is in you." *Although my pilgrimage in faith has nothing spectacular to report,* my conviction that Jesus Christ is Lord of Creation, Lord of me and all men, has grown deeper and stronger through the years. Always I have been *"compassed about by so great a crowd of witnesses"*, from childhood to a ripe old age, that I would like to pay tribute to those who have nurtured me and smoothed my path in faith. *Certain of the essentials, I never cease to wonder about life's problems and mysteries.*

BORN IN A LOVING HOME, where devout Christian parents accepted their faith without question, and practised it in every area of their relationships, it is natural that I should not remember a time when I was not a Christian. My parents had been schooled in suffering. My mother lost both parents, as a child, my father lost his father, as a boy. My only surviving grand-parent must have taught me the 23rd Psalm at three years, for she died around my fourth birthday.

My parents would be amused to have moral precepts of St Paul pinned on them. My father abhorred conceit. No child of his dare think of herself **"more highly than she ought to think."** My mother frequently quoted a command from Paul (sometimes to my father!) which we in N. Ireland should have graven on our hearts **"As far as in you lies, live peaceably with all men."**

AS A FAMILY we were sent to two Sunday Schools. The saintly Church of Ireland rector taught us "Our duty to God", "Our duty to our neighbour", and many collects. In the Presbyterian Sunday School we learned by heart the Shorter Catechism without understanding the big words of the doctrine, *but what a wonderful body of theology to have available in later life.*
AT UNIVERSITY, where the academic teaching was abysmal, **the spiritual guidance from intellectual giants in the faith through the Student Christian Movement marked me indelibly at a time when we were questing and impressionable. It was like the early Christian Church after Pentecost. We were fired by sound Christian teaching and warm inspiring Christian fellowship.** *I have been fortunate too, in my Church congregations, and have been nurtured in the faith, in Bangor West since its foundation.*

WE LIVE IN AN INCREASINGLY SECULAR AND SINFUL WORLD. Is it true, this Christian faith? Is it relevant to the world where people live and work? The older one grows, the more one reads the newspapers, and observes the world

- in business, in politics, in social life, the more distressing, the more frightening, *and the more overwhelming evil seems. It is a cruel, callous world, where dog eats dog.*

THE SOUND TEACHING OF JESUS AND PAUL ON HUMAN SINFULNESS.
One of the strongest planks in the defence of Christianity, *when set against the diverse clever scientific philosophies of life is the sound teaching of Jesus and Paul on human sinfulness.*
Scientific thinkers from Darwin to Dawkins; computer experts dazzled by their ingenuity in inventing "smart chips" for the internet to govern our lives in 2020, think they have outgrown Christianity. **They may explain our biological evolution and our genes, but they fail to acknowledge the perpetual battle between Good and Evil in the realm of human relations.** *They refuse to see the self-love - the original sin- at the heart of every one of us, destroying our relations with fellow human-beings.*
Paul summed it up neatly. **"The good that I would, that I do not. The evil that I would not, that I do."** The taint of selfishness and pride vitiates every impulse of the human heart to some degree. But Paul puts the solution just as neatly. He cries, **"Who shall rescue me from my slavery to this deadly nature? Thank God! Jesus Christ, our Lord, has set me free."**

THE HEART OF CHRISTIANITY.
After his blinding insight on the Damascus Road, Paul, the proud Jew, did a roundabout turn, and ever afterwards spent his life and energy **pointing people to the Living Lord who can transform the sinfulness that besets us, and who invites us into his Kingdom of love,** *where He lives in human hearts, and provides the enabling power to live in loving communion.*

I consider myself privileged to have entered this fellowship early and to have been guided and enriched as I have explored its many-faceted splendour by countless saints from our own age and all ages belonging to that "blest communion fellowship divine"

Battered, bruised, broken, in agony on the cross, He prayed, "Father, forgive them." **Such forgiveness is beyond human power.** That is enough for me. I leave the mysteries of his incarnation with God. It was the same Lord, now risen who left the message, **"Tell the disciples, and Peter, I go before them into Galilee."** Such tender concern for His mortified heart-broken friend demands my total allegiance.
FOLLY? OUT-MODED NONSENSE? Always we must test our faith, and explore its truth for every situation, and keep our spiritual antennae alert for the Spirit's prompting.

SEEING ONLY THE PHYSICAL WORLD.
Those who see only the physical world **fail to see God ever-active in His universe.** John claims that the cosmic Christ, the Creative Love, there from the beginning made everything that was made. **Job uses wonderful poetry to express the Creator's power.** *We need to translate it for today to "Gee! What a brilliant mathematician! Gee! What an exciting scientist!"* It is He who makes the "smart chips" and the internet possible. He created the wonders of the universe on a mathematical basis, and made us in his image, so that our little brains could fathom some of its secrets.

FREE TO RESPOND TO HIS LOVE.
What is more, He created us free to respond to His love. Being holy, the source of all goodness, He searches people out. When they respond with answering goodness, they are in touch with Him. When questing spirits reach insight into the truths of life, **Jesus, the Truth, the Light that lightens every man, meets them.** When their hearts leap for Joy *at the glimpse of beauty in a rose, a laughing child, or a moonlit sea,* **the Creator of all beauty touches them with his wings. God is love, and whoever loves is born of God, and knows God. So He reaches out to the hearts of His children everywhere.** <u>The Christian imperative</u> **is to tell men that this God, whom they encounter, came to earth to draw them into the divine family.** It is our responsibility to help them to reach the fullness of understanding. Perplexed by the sin, the suffering and misery everywhere, when they cry to God in despair, He says, "I *was* there; I *am* there. My love will support you. I have overcome the sin, the suffering and death. **I will share my Risen Power."**

GRATEFUL! I am grateful to a long list of Christian mentors like CS Lewis, David Watson, Jean Vannier who guided me, and to the Italian painters and sculptors of the Renaissance who nourished my emotions; and to poets like Donne and Herbert and Hopkins who have given me many insights into God's relation with us. **I love especially the lines where Hopkins describes the myriad host of saints in-dwelt by Christ:-**
"Christ plays in ten thousand places,
Lovely in limbs, and lovely in eyes, not His, to the Father, through the features of men's faces."
PRO TANTO.... QUID? What return do I make? To my shame I have never done enough. I yearn to share my faith with those who find it difficult or impossible. I yearn for better community relations. Since God is Father of us all, there can be no room for bigotry, hatred, self-seeking, cruelty or violence. We can all pray without ceasing; and every moment of our lives, *we are faced with the challenge to love more fully, especially those in need of*

love, and to serve men where we can.

PAUL PUTS THE GOAL OF OUR STRIVING MEMORABLY. "Till we all come in the unity of the faith, and in the knowledge of the Son of God, unto a perfect man, unto the measure of the stature of the fullness of Christ" and are ready for the Kingdom of Love, living in love with God and our fellow men, here and hereafter.

MIKE & LORRAINE CAHOON- each came to West in 1995, and in due course were married in West. They write (2001):
"Hello David and Rhoda. Thank you very much for your letter regarding the history of West. We are both so grateful for your ongoing care for us as a family and to know that God continues to use you mightily in the work of the Kingdom. We thought that we might share our individual experiences.
LORRAINE says....
MOST CHALLENGING EXPERIENCES OF LIFE.
"By a wonderful "God-incidence" I came with the intention of making a one-service visit to West Church in 1995 and ended up staying and making my fellowship there!
My previous Minister released me with his blessing when I shared that I believed God was moving me on to a new place both physically and spiritually.
In West I found that my most challenging experiences of life were able to be shared and received in a spirit of compassion and understanding. After I received prayer ministry I found a freedom to enjoy the Lord in a brand new way. From that point I was encouraged to seek God's will in using the gifts He had given me and found that God uses ANYONE who earnestly seeks his Kingdom to be brought in. I've been involved in 'Life in the Spirit' seminars, Alpha courses and prayer ministry to others. **These were areas in which God placed me and allowed me to grow.**

BRUCE COLLINS. One of the greatest encouragements was the visit of Bruce Collins in May 1998. *His prophetic teaching was so personal to us as a family that we look back and see that as a major milestone in our journey with the Lord...... David and Rhoda, I bless you so much for enabling such a variety of special godly teachers to come to West and for loving your flock so much."*

MY TURN NOW, Mike says.....
"I came to West around 1995, fairly raw in the ways of the Lord. I had become a Christian in my late teens and really hadn't taken my side of the Christian journey all that seriously. However, in coming to West all that was to change. Though I had not kept my side of the relationship with God all that well, **He most definitely had kept His. He knew what was best for me!** It was at a 'Shape' course run by Terry Laverty that I realised how much I actually didn't know about the Christian life. *I was out of Christian shape!!*
BASIC GROUNDING NEEDED! I needed basic grounding in the Christian faith and so in early 2000 I joined an **'Alpha'** course, enjoyed it so much that I did a second and then went on to do a **'Life in the Spirit'** seminar. **Through the love of friendships made at these I then received prayer and counselling from the ministry team.** *All of this I completed in one year!*
ANY INDIVIDUAL! It is my experience that West Church is dedicated to the whole ministry of any individual entering through its doors. I have found friends that I know genuinely supported and cared for me and my family. *I have had the opportunities to experience the real life-changing power of God working gently yet firmly in my life. Life is for living, this is not a dress rehearsal, and our lives are a precious gift from God.*

WHAT THE FUTURE HOLDS. Now I am excited at what the future holds because I know that God really does have the best mapped out for me. New and exciting challenges are on the horizon that before were dreams, but are now becoming reality. *Church is all the people in it!* We need each other to help us, to support us, to laugh and cry with us. No man or woman was ever meant to be an island. **At West you can be assured that you really do belong to a family, the Christian family, and the greatest family in the world!!**
Thank you David, for the opportunity to jot down these thoughts. We hope they will be of support and encouragement to other readers in **'West Church Journey'**.

"EVERYDAY SOME MORE OF ME CRUMBLED." Gill Montgomery writes:
"Lost, hurt and worthless are words which describe how I felt as a fairly recent single mum of three young children. I was trying to convince myself and others that I was coping and yet everyday some more of me crumbled.
IF YOU COULD RUB YOURSELF OUT AND START ALL OVER AGAIN!
That was 18 months ago, before the Lord Jesus came into my life in a very gentle and special way and I have been amazed at the way **He has taken the tangled mess and straightened it out.** I once said it would be nice if you could rub yourself out and start all over again, leaving out the bits that were no good... Well, that's more or less what Jesus has done for me. *I have to be perfectly honest and say I haven't always liked*

what had to be done or the way it had to be done. But I have come to learn that our God is a big God. He can shoulder our grievances as He gently shows us it can work out for our own good.

I have been truly blessed many times over, at times when I've least expected and in ways which I never imagined. All the time God is showing me that *I can trust Him and He won't let me down.*

TOGETHER AS A FAMILY.

I have been blessed through prayers being answered. **One of the first prayers I prayed was that God would bring us together as a family. Within two months of my being saved each of my children gave their lives to the Lord. One of the most beautiful things about having a relationship with Jesus is the Love, the perfect love that casts out fear, the everlasting and unconditional love.**

It took a while for me to be convinced that God could really love me. But love me He does, for if it were not for His love, grace and mercy *I could not have come through the last eighteen months.* They have been the most difficult time for me, but I have had Jesus with me, carrying me, guiding me, encouraging me every step of the way. **I have learnt that God is faithful and will fulfil His promises to us in a way that only He can. It's exciting when something happens that has GOD stamped all over it.**

USEFUL AGAIN!

It is a privilege to be His child, to think that the Creator of heaven and earth loves me and has called me for His own. There is **contentment and security** in knowing He will never leave me nor forsake me. (Hebrews 13: 5). I thank God that He came looking for His lost sheep and searched until He found me. **He is healing the hurt; He has given me a purpose and makes me feel useful again.**

So if you are going to reach out and touch somebody's hand, make sure that hand belongs to Jesus.

He will bring you from the darkness into the light of eternal life.
May His Name be Glorified!"

"THE GRACE OF GOD IN WEST." HENRI ALEXANDER.

[Henri Alexander was one of those from outside our congregation, who joined a Life in the Spirit Seminar in 1986].

"I am delighted to write of my experience of the grace of God in West Church. I came to a 'Life in the Spirit Seminar'. By God's grace it was provided for me at a point of need and spiritual thirst. This was not the first time that God had provided for me dramatically - as a child of nine years, in a remote hall outside Armoy, I came to experience the joy of the Lord through two Faith Mission ladies who brought a knowing of God beyond what was being offered in the traditional church I attended. I marvel at the way God provides - through people like yourself, who help and guide and lead by the Holy Spirit.

INCREASINGLY WORRIED!

I had had the benefit of two godly assistant minsters **in John Seawright and David Cupples,** *but had become increasingly worried about world disasters, earthquakes, famines, wars, the Chernobyl nuclear accident and a brother-in-law getting leukemia. I also had not been able to forgive my mother fully for past hurts.*
At the time of joining the Seminar, I had a very good friend (Mairi Wright) and we prayed together and decided to join.

OBSTACLES.

Like many others I felt that Satan was trying to stop me continuing - **fear of speaking in tongues, fear of total commitment etc.** At that time there were two sessions and we were led by John Seawright initially, and as the main song which he played and we sang was

'Jesus is Lord, Creation's voice proclaims it', my anxieties started to melt away. I became all too aware that I had been a part of the groaning of the world.
You, David, prayed with me regarding forgiving my mother and a great new love was released between us; in fact, in short, I was able to love people more.

THE SAD PART OF THAT TIME

was a strong sense of loss as if God was telling me that there would be sorrow as well as boundless joy.
Mairi Wright became ill and died, and two other members of our small group also: Heather Armstrong I will also remember for *singing so beautifully as we received Communion in church, and, most tragically Lorna Sinclair.*
I remember an old lady, Evelyn McMath who declared that she had 'a heart of stone', and how she was changed beautifully!
I remember the joy of being able to bring Carol Aspinall to Jesus *(Carol suffered badly from Multiple Sclerosis),* **and how West Church provided for her.**

MANY ENRICHED.

Many churches have been enriched by the teaching and preaching at West. I had a brother, a sister, a cousin and friends **who have been blessed by the Holy Spirit in West,** *and who have subsequently been used more powerfully in their own churches.*

DAVID - THINGS YOU DID!

It is difficult not to be personal in this. so David a few things that you did at West which **showed God's love and helped us.**
1. Telling us to speak to one another, and especially to strangers at church. (Rhoda was and is brilliant at this).
2. Your dedication in learning names and knowing about people.
3. Emphasis on prayer and encouraging us to tell out to one another how God has been good to us.
4. Willingness to share your pulpit with others.

5. Great teaching and preaching each Sunday.
6. Setting up the House Group system, where we grew together to share spiritually on a weekly basis, and the answers to prayer we have had have been wonderful.

I BECAME A MEMBER OF WEST.
As you know I became a member of West just a few years before you retired - **it is to your credit that you encouraged us stay in our own congregations** and in your good wisdom you did not press me for details of why I left First.

I QUICKLY FOUND ACCEPTANCE.
Once a member of West I quickly found acceptance. **I had often heard other preachers complaining that only a few people help,** *but you phoned or for example asked directly, to help with the catering at Alpha.* Once there the Holy Spirit bound us together. *It was good to be useful and it was fun!*
I experienced some health problems and then found it too tiring so I rested from that - got prayers, got tablets -and I was ready to go again when Terry Laverty preached on finding our SHAPE.

SYCAMORE CLUB: I went along to the Sycamore Club Barbeque - **our interdenominational club for mentally handicapped adults -** *and felt immediately that this was where I wanted to help.*
The leadership (Tanya and Derek Polley) were open and welcoming, encouraging any new helpers to do what they could. *The members were friendly, loving and obviously enjoying themselves. It is good to have the opportunity to bring them the gospel, as simply as possible.*

THE MEETINGS. We begin with singing, with much signing and any actions; we have simple musical instruments - mostly percussion and it is a happy time. We then have a prayer time with requests for prayer and thanks to God for good things.

Next follows the 'Bible Interpretation'; five of us take it in turn to present this, so it is not a big burden for one to have to do it and prepare every week. This session we are talking about **Roads in the Bible - to Bethlehem, to Egypt, from the Temple at Jerusalem, to Jerusalem, to Calvary, to Heaven. I have been an artist all my life and have always thanked God for my talent; on many occasions I have felt that it is a selfish indulgence** *but I am delighted to share this gift with the Sycamore Club.* **I have also had a theoretical interest in Art Therapy,** *so now I have the opportunity to put it into practice. To see Campbell (aged 66) in the club painting away - just colour and pure enjoyment!* It is so different from teaching art where the finished result was all-important. **Please pray that we find ways of reaching 'into' those who are very handicapped.**

"The Lord gives, the Lord takes away." "As I have been with Moses, so I will be with you." David, we have been so blessed with Charles your successor and his wife Barbara: - you must be happy to see God's work continuing 'in the Spirit' at West Church.
CHURCH VISITOR -my other involvement is as a Church Visitor and I hope and pray that I am being useful in this too- thank you for your trust in asking me to do this.
MATT, (my husband) is well and happy in West now; for some time he felt disloyal in leaving First Bangor.
Although he refused your request to go to Alpha I can see that his faith and dependence on God has strengthened **and we are a good spiritual support to each other.**

I am so pleased you are able to share with the wider church now. God bless you both and all your family.

BANNER SEWING GROUP. ANNE ANDERSON.

"After joining West Church in 1969 as a new bride and a newly qualified artist, I quickly became involved in various aspects of church life including some creative activities such as illustrations and designs for magazines and Sunday School classes.

INNOVATIVE IDEAS.
One of the refreshing things about West Church has always been an openess to new and innovative ideas and the infectious enthusiasm of David Bailie and the pastoral team for implementing them. **When the Family Service was introduced I was part of the team, my main role being to produce story illustrations for the newly acquired overhead projector.** This was right up my street and I enjoyed being part of a creative group of Christians. I soon learned, like many others, that when I answered the phone and heard David Bailie's voice, **it usually meant that he'd had another "idea"!**

4 DECORATIVE BANNERS.
In 1983 when the new hall was completed, **I had one such call asking me to consider making four decorative banners to enhance the sense of worship in the hall when it was used for services rather than recreation. Although banners were becoming popular in some churches in England, I had never seen any, and while I was excited about this new creative opportunity I felt I needed help.** The obvious choice was **Liz Baird** who had recently joined the church and had been at Art College with me where she studied textiles.
Liz readily agreed to join me and we started meeting in the mornings surrounded by our babies and a growing mound of fabric and scraps. *We prayed for guidance about the wording and designs for the banners and quickly found that we were very much in tune with each other; the ideas came fairly easily and we both enjoyed this*

new creative outlet at a time when we were almost entirely taken up with our young families.

A SMALL GROUP. We got together a small group to sew every week and soon the four banners were made. "Could you make four more so that we can ring the changes?" - OK - and so we did...."people feel it's a shame they only see the banners in the hall, so could you make some for the church itself and here are ten (very long) verses I think would be suitable" We *just kept making them, one by one at our own pace until the walls were lined with the words of Jesus.*

THEN ON TO THE FRONT OF THE CHURCH AND SO WE CONTINUE....
We had a regular, weekly sewing group *and soon discovered that there were very positive side benefits.* The friendship and fellowship became almost as important to us as the work we were doing -*it is amazing how easy it is to talk freely and share worries and problems when our hands are busy.*
We have all gained great satisfaction from making the banners, and when we get feedback from members and visitors telling us that they have been blessed by the banners, *we feel doubly blessed!*

COLOURFUL BANNERS FOR CHURCHES OVERSEAS.
Our group has made banners for several other churches including some in kit form and for many organizations within our church. *Recently we had fun making colourful banners for churches overseas - one for Sumba, Indonesia and two for a new church in Kenya.*
Liz and I have also been invited to show and speak about our banners in various women's groups all over the Province. This has been very fulfilling too, **especially when these groups have been inspired to make their own banners.**

NOT SELF-INDULGENT!
I don't think I am the only Christian artist who has sometimes felt guilty because what I do seems self-indulgent - less useful to society than a job like nursing or social work where God could really use me.
However some time ago **I was quite surprised to hear the banner making referred to as a 'ministry'** and it made me think of it in a new light. I suppose on reflection it is in the same sort of category as music or any other creative activity in the context of our Christian lives.
Many have helped with the banners over the years including: **Helen Stevenson, Edna Byers Doreen Hayward, Margaret Mottram, Margaret Webb, Ingeborg McElwaine, Valerie Wilson, Margaret McMullan, Jean Crichton, Jayne Fulton, Roberta Hagan, Barbara Stewart.**

" I THOUGHT I WAS FINE - JUST AS I WAS."
Denise Redpath writes:
"Although I'd always gone to church and believed in God, **it wasn't until a service in West Church** *that I realised God really knew me!*

A few years before Mum had been to a "Life in the Spirit" Seminar And it really changed her. She seemed to have a peace about her that I couldn't really describe. She talked about praying about this and that and thanking God for so many blessings.
IT WILL BE FINE!
I found myself thinking that if Mum prayed about something it would be fine; and *sometimes asking her to pray about something for us.*
She suggested I go to a seminar but I thought I was fine, just as I was.

RACHEL HICKSON.
A friend asked me to come to West Church one Sunday evening when Rachel Hickson was speaking. At the end she said she was going up for prayer and would I go with her. Very reluctantly, I did, thinking I'd just stay near the back. God had other plans and Rachel Hickson asked me what I would like to pray about. **I told her I'd like peace and security (thinking of what Mum appeared to have).**

GOD KNEW ABOUT ME!
She suddenly dashed off and got her Bible saying she had a reading for me. She came back and read the 121st Psalm. *I couldn't believe my ears!* How on earth could this complete stranger know this was my favourite chapter in the Bible (I'd even had it sung at our wedding). I'd heard of people "seeing the Light" and all those phrases, *but I just realised that God was alive and He knew about me.*

'LIFE IN SPIRIT'.
A few months later Mr Bailie called at the house. The minute I saw him at the door, I knew he'd ask me to a 'Life in the Spirit' seminar. **This time I didn't think I was just fine.** I said I would go, although when the evening came, *I'd have done anything rather than go to that seminar, but it was very different from what I expected.* Mr Bailie and Lorna McQuitty put us all at our ease. If you didn't want to speak you didn't have to; little did I think a few months later I'd be biting my tongue because I felt I was talking too much.
Mr Bailie's ability to make so many stories from the Bible relate to everyday life has been a real revelation as has the power of prayer. *I am really learning that God is interested in all the little things in our lives as well as the big things.*

"WORD FOR TODAY"
As well as reading the Bible, I started to read the "Word for Today" notes written by Bob Gass **and found they were another revelation. They deal with everyday problems and really show how relevant the teachings of the Bible are.** *Some days I feel they are really directed at me.*

In fact, recently, 'My Psalm' was quoted and Bob (I feel I know him!) said <u>sometimes he asks God to speak to him or he'll have nothing to say to help anyone. If God had actually written me a letter that day it couldn't have been any clearer or more relevant than what those notes said!</u>

A LEARNER!
I am very much a learner and every morning I put my day, my family and all I have been given, into God's hands and ask Him to guide me. *Even if things don't work out as I would want them, I have this wonderful reassurance that it's all in God's plan for me and as it says in 'My Psalm':* "The Lord will keep you from all harm; He will watch over your life.... both now and forever more." Psalm 121: 7-8.

"SEEK FIRST HIS KINGDOM AND RIGHTEOUSNESS - AND ALL OTHER THINGS WILL BE GIVEN AS WELL." Denise Redpath (in 2001) writes: "When I think of the person I was when I came to the 'Life in the Spirit' seminar four years ago **I am awestruck at what the Holy Spirit has shown me and how patient and gracious God is. I realise that when I received the Spirit, HE began to work in my life to translate me from the Kingdom of darkness into the Kingdom of Light.**
God says 'As the heavens are higher than the earth, *so are my ways higher than your ways and my thoughts than your thoughts'.*

I HAVE LEARNT that God is able to supply, exceeding abundantly above and beyond anything I could ever ask or hope- *but that is through His power working in me!*

HE HAS SHOWN ME TO SPEAK ACCORDING TO HIS WORD.
God has given me Scriptures to stand on, which in the beginning made no real sense to me. However, as I have come to trust His words, *they have changed my life.*
And my attitude to God's words have changed -**'the old me' would have reasoned, questioned, demanded answers.** I am learning to say '**I don't understand, but I trust you, Lord!'**
The Holy Spirit shows me what to do in my life, and when I seek to obey with a good attitude, He provides everything I need to carry it through.
In my experience so far, it has been awesome **when God has guided me to give a word of Scripture, or something specific, to someone, and I have wrestled, and said, "Not me, Lord! I'd be so embarrassed!" Yet, when I have done it and seen how significant it is for them, I STAND AMAZED AT THE FATHER'S LOVE FOR US, and how my pride could stop or delay someone else's blessing.**

TO LEARN WHO I AM 'IN CHRIST'. I really am a new creation, filled with the Spirit, I live and move and have my being in Him. And when I bring anything to the Cross, and give it to the Lord, *He will show me the truth* -though that may take a lot of Scripture searching, and a lot of time seeking the Lord; then that truth will set me free. Though there are times when things change very quickly, there are times when other people change in a wonderful way. And there are times when, in the Lord's presence, **I change, and am given a completely different perspective.**
I HAVE LEARNED TO ASK GOD TO SHOW ME TRUE HUMILITY, because it is only when I am truly humble before Him that I can receive from Him. Then He can show me where I am judgemental, negative and fearful.
HE HAS SHOWN ME 'that fear of man is a snare', and that learning a holy, reverential fear of the Lord brings a wonderful freedom.
Psalm 25 teaches me to keep my eyes for ever on the Lord.

'Show me your ways, O Lord,
Teach me your paths,
guide me in your truth,
and teach me that You are my God and Saviour, and my hope is in You all day long'.

What peace and security to know my part is to seek the Lord in everything, and He will take care of everything else.

LOOKING BACK AND LOOKING FORWARD!

DAVID BAILIE WRITES, October 2006.

The names of many appear in our "West Church Journey" thus far. The last who has just made a contribution (prior to the Addendum!) is Denise Redpath who happened to be a member in the final 'Life in the Spirit' Seminar that I led in West!
But there are many who shone brightly- and some of them over all the years from the first day until now- whose names do not appear at all. Their names are known to the Good Shepherd, who has seen their labours and rejoiced in their witness, and in their embracing, outreaching love, and who rates them highly in His Kingdom.
Though, by whatever lottery or providence may be involved, their names do not appear in our little tome, yet, far more importantly, their names are written in the Book of Life, and they will receive the highest accolade of all, "Well done, good and faithful servant."

PRIVILEGED AND BLESSED!

I was privileged to be minister of West from the beginning, and whatever *success* the congregation may be judged to have achieved, I attribute it all to the grace of God and the sovereign power of the Holy Spirit. And I am ever conscious of *the great cloud of witnesses*- those who were brothers and sisters through Jesus ' Name - who laboured with me, so *that we ran together with perseverance, the race marked out for us. Together we fixed our eyes on Jesus, the author and perfecter of our faith.*

I rejoice in them all, relied upon all, and invited -compelled!- service from all- and received it in full measure!
Thank you, again and again!

ONE NAME SELDOM APPEARS!

In terms of love, encouragement, support, devotion, unstinting service, the name of my wife RHODA seldom appears in our official writings. Yet all in West know how unceasingly and sacrificially she gave herself in the love of Christ, with a word of warm encouragement for all - and especially for those who needed it most.

There was always reassurance and welcome on the Manse telephone, and so, so regularly a place at the Manse table. Especially in the early years, supper at the Manse on a Sunday evening, was a regular feature for new members finding their way into our congregation.

Folk in West know how freely I gave myself to the work of the congregation - *but only I know that this was possible through the prodigious labours and enabling of my wife, for which I thank her, with my family, with all my heart!*

LOOKING BACK to the May 1998 edition of West Church News, we find that we were actively preparing the ground for our New Car Park, which was completed in 1998.

We were also awaiting our final plans for our new building extension, renovating and extending '91' and providing additional halls to link it with our main church building.

These plans were NOT then implemented and it was not until September 2006 that new buildings were opened, and then on a far grander and more visionary scale than was earlier envisaged.

The magnificent new buildings, together with the church building, totally and beautifully refurbished, and the original halls upgraded, provide a suite of buildings, and an admirable platform for the fulfilment of many ventures and initiatives for the extension of the Kingdom of God, in and from West.

In all this I, now as minister emeritus in West, heartily rejoice. No doubt many of the ambitions we had when we purchased '91' and '93' (see pages 387 ff) will be fulfilled and much, much more. And for any further development, it is good to realise we still retain '93' and spacious grounds around it!!

MY SUCCESSOR THE REV CHARLES McMULLEN,

has now been leading the congregation since 1999. The new buildings are an index to the generosity and vision of the congregation under his leadership. Much more important is the fact that the congregation is growing in numbers, in its ability to draw in young families, to bring many to faith, to have a hungry vision to reach out into the community for Christ, and to be a resource of inspiration and blessing for the whole Church.

It is a comfort and cause of gratitude for me to know that my successor has been anointed of God to lead the West Church congregation- and to realise that he himself has this knowledge and conviction.

I leave it to Charles to tell you about this in the last chapter of "West Church Journey"; pray that the Lord's blessing will remain with him and his family, realising that there are many more chapters of "West Church Journey" yet to be written.

My Call to West Church, Bangor

My journey West proved to be one of the most challenging and rewarding spiritual experiences of my life. It all began in the month of June, 1998 at Union Theological College, Belfast, where I had just finished leading devotions at a Summer School. During coffee I was approached by a tall, debonair and well-spoken gentleman who announced that he was Session Clerk of West Church, Bangor. According to Billy McClelland the congregation had just become vacant and he wanted to ascertain if I would be interested.

There comes a certain stage in your first congregation when you receive seemingly endless calls from vacancy converters, the assumption being that you are ready for a move. I had always been able to shrug off all these offers, but this time my reaction was completely different. In fact, my mind was thrown into such a state of turmoil that I never heard a word of the ensuing lecture. With hindsight a little ironically, I recall it was based on Psalm 103 – "as far as the east is from the *west*, so far has he removed our transgressions from us."

There were no further developments during the summer apart from having coffee with ministerial friends who mooted possible candidates for West. Much to my relief and even bemusement my name wasn't even included!

Day-trip to Bangor
At the beginning of September we had a family outing to Bangor. En route there was an urgent toilet call in the vicinity of Crawfordsburn and we found ourselves parking outside West where a scout car wash was taking place. We were totally incognito and disappeared as quickly as possible once the emergency had been successfully sorted out.

It was a strange feeling returning to Legcurry later that Saturday afternoon. After glorious weather in the Pickie Pool area with excited trips on the puffer train and adventures in the play park, now as I stood in the front lawn at home the sun disappeared momentarily behind the clouds. You might well smile, but it was an uncanny feeling in a spiritual sense of change being somehow in the air.

The next evening Barbara and I had a detailed conversation about Bangor in the front room of our home. We had just come to the conclusion about 10.30pm that the matter was totally unsettling and should not be pursued any further when the phone rang. It was Rev. Alistair Kennedy, who was in charge of West, asking me formally to consider the church and if he could send me an application form and profile. Our topic for the evening had not finished after all.

A Harvest that went West
Again with ongoing ministry in Legacurry the matter was slowly but surely tucked away in the most extreme recesses of my mind! As Harvest Thanksgiving services were taking place I went into the gallery area of the church to pray. You have no idea how stunningly beautiful and extravagantly decorated the place was. We had developed a Flower Club which gave itself totally to creating breathtaking works of art. I looked around and blessed by name all those involved. The fragrance, the endless displays of colour and the overall feeling of God's fullness and contentment confirmed for me that I wasn't moving anywhere. Suddenly I heard a voice in my spirit asking the question: "Will you come over West?" Subsequently a friend explained this to me as a Macedonian call (Acts 16:6-10), a totally new experience to me I can assure you! There was such an awareness of people praying and when I finally came to have a look around West I was startled to recognise the room where I had seen those people praying in my vision. That was in the larger of the two sitting rooms in the old bungalow at 91 Crawfordsburn Road. Never do I go seeking the dramatic and the unusual, but this was turning out to be totally amazing.

Mixed Feelings
The interview took place at the beginning of November. I was invited to do a ten minute presentation on my view of ministry and to answer several questions. There is absolutely no doubt in my mind that my performance was appalling. I found it excruciatingly painful having to sell myself in front of so many elders and terribly difficult to find immediate answers to what seemed to be endless questions. To compound the matter, I refused to give any presentation, stating very categorically that I was very happy where I was in Legacurry but nonetheless felt it was right to be seeking God's will for my future. In spite of my nervousness and reticence I left that meeting feeling on such an incredible high with Barbara being taken completely aback by the radiance of my countenance as I returned home. That evening I would have moved mountains to be called to West.

The next morning, however, as I sat at my desk in the cold light of day everything seemed different. I have never remotely contemplated adultery, but there was the awful reality of betraying people I loved dearly, should I receive a call. A terrible, agonising struggle began! Legacurry was where we had settled together and where our children were born and baptised. We had seen the place grow by one hundred families and there was endless potential for growth. We had numerous friends and our roots had gone down very deeply. It hadn't occurred to me that after eight years it was slowly but surely becoming much more difficult to get less done and that a wave of the Spirit had been completed.

At the end of the interviewing process I discovered I had been one of three names to be shortlisted and was given several days to make a decision. I had no peace about pulling out, and felt that I had to allow my name to go forward. The saving grace, by my assessment was that the two other men on the list stood a much better chance than me of being called and I could hide in their shadow!

God's perfect peace
I went to Portballintrae for a day of prayer and studied the application form which I had filled out. For the first time I saw a marriage between questions and answers and later, as I walked along the beach watching the waves crash against the shore, I realised that whatever the outcome I had to correspond to the rhythms of God's grace.

Informing my Kirk Session at Legacurry of what was happening was painful and then came the unnerving pleas of many folk in the congregation for us to stay! Early in January I went to see two dear friends for prayer – Derek McKelvey and George Grindle. They confirmed for me what I already knew in my heart of hearts which was that I would have to be stripped bare and lay my life totally on the altar of God's love. The day before the final congregational meeting at West was a Sunday and for the one and only time in my life I wasn't well enough to conduct worship. The Lord has a delightful sense of humour as I realised how prayer had been answered quite literally with me lying naked in a hot bath rather than in the pulpit!

You are becoming aware that this entire process was remarkably intense, much more so than it needed to be, but I was genuinely struggling to be in God's will and to know His peace. Again to quote Psalm 103, God is always compassionate and gracious. As a ten year old I had heard His audible voice and now again as I needed reassurance I heard Him speak resoundingly. The message is too personal to share in its entirety, but it did underline the importance of trust.

Barbara was definitely concerned by the depth of feeling I was experiencing and I cannot speak highly enough of her unconditional love and support throughout this tortuous process. Her conviction not in any arrogant sense was one of inevitability. I didn't realise at the time the extent of her personal emotion and the tears she shed as the call came. I was also extremely indebted to friends who gave themselves totally as confidants. One of them was the late Harold Graham of the Christian Training Centre. Another gave me such release when he prayed, "Blessing if you go, blessing if you stay."

First time in the pulpit of West
I do not remember very much about the Sunday I came to preach for the vacancy. My sermon was based on 1 John 4 and the theme was "God is love." It was West's first introduction to a quote by Selwyn Hughes which is my own personal manifesto or mission statement: "A church can be orthodox in doctrine, efficient in service, blameless in character, beautiful in ritual, rich in culture, eloquent in preaching –yet all these things are but ashes on a rusty altar if it knows nothing of a burning, blazing love for the Lord Jesus Christ." My children's address was based on a bedtime routine with my children when I asked them to guess how much I loved them. There was always great hilarity as it climaxed with my hands stretched out as far as they could be in love – in the shape of a cross!

After the services I knew that I had to stay in the process until the end. Barbara finally broke the silence in the car as we made our way to have lunch together, "You were yourself!"

My call came on Monday, 1st February 1999. My final fleece was that it would be totally unanimous and although the "white smoke" signals were initially slightly confusing, I now knew God's perfect will. Nevertheless the next twenty-four hours were spent in floods of tears and I did not know how I was going to face Presbytery where my call would be presented and sustained the following day. Just as I was about to leave the house I had a phone call from Heather Thompson which was timely encouragement and gave me deep peace.

Our arrival
The following eight weeks were of Challenge Anneka style proportions as we made endless decisions about our new home. A new school had to be found for Lydia who was in P1 and we went no further than Grange where there was just one place left. God reassured me that if He called us, He would provide for our family, and that has proved to be an extraordinary testimony in itself!

When we finally arrived in our beautifully decorated new home at 37 Kensington Park the grass had been freshly cut, and casseroles and sandwiches left for us in the kitchen. Immediately, I revelled in my most luxurious, donnish study with views across Belfast Lough. On the day of my installation on 16th April 1999 I can remember feeling God's presence in a remarkable way. Mind you, as I shook hands at the door when the Legacurry contingent kidnapped me and carried me off to their bus, I felt terribly torn!

My first Sunday morning I was given such a special, spontaneous welcome absolutely typical of West and preached on the subject of "All for Jesus." Robin Mark's famous chorus of that title was sung at all the services that weekend. I have no doubt that my call to West was absolute. I still stand on that call with total conviction and complete assurance. Now after a similar number of years to my time spent in Legacurry I love West in equal measure. And I have no doubt that God's plans for West are immeasurably more than all we can ask or imagine!

A window of grace
On 24th September 2006 we marked our return to the sanctuary after extensive renovations. For me it was special that David Bailie conducted communion with such beautiful, meaningful and special prayers that resonated totally with me and underlined continuity with the past. As I soaked in the presence of God I smiled as I viewed the ten small windows in the now greatly enhanced rear wall of the gallery. One of them has always had special significance. I had always interpreted it as the sword of the Spirit representing the Word of the Lord. Apparently the scene is the expulsion from the garden, the Flaming Sword barring re-entry!

I used to be a member of a prayer triplet in Legacurry. Gordon Dickson, Ruth Bryans and I met weekly and even now such is the bond between us that we still know when to pray for each other! One day in the autumn of 1998 before I had even mentioned West as a prayer topic, Ruth shared a picture of a flaming sword. The night of my installation, never having been in West before, she came over to me with tears in her eyes: "Charles, there's the window!" I struggled with this wanting God to tell me why He hadn't given her the more obvious windows at the front of the Church. One Sunday night a few weeks later when Terry Laverty was preaching, again I felt God nudging me: "Those are the windows you see from the from the pulpit. They're for your encouragement."

And just one further story to complete the picture. The second time Barbara and I ever met was at Ann Kennedy's service of licensing here in West in June 1990....

To God be the glory!

INDEX.

ABBA TRUST is born   344, 349

ABORTION
'Child of my heart'   200
Robert Adrain writes   409

ABUNDANCE of life in West   84

ABUSE
How to gain freedom from   288
6-week seminar on sexual abuse   369

ACOUSTICS
cause difficulties for singing   25
a wet blanket, a 'sound-system'
as a radical solution   245

AFTER-LIFE!   240
Judgement, heaven, hell?
Pragmatic evidence? 2 books:
Dr Maurice Rawlings, 'Beyond Death's Door'; and Dr. George Ritchie, 'Return from Tomorrow'.
4 sermons in West: Judgement; Death & Resurrection; Heaven; Hell.   240

AFRICAN CHILDREN'S CHOIR
joyful, released singing   370, 498
the choir showed the love of Jesus
'an unforgettable visit' say Ivan & Diane Hunter who took 2 choir-girls into their home.   498
'a weekend we shall not forget in a hurry' say Mervyn a& Denise Shaw.   498

AIDS   345
Ian & Roberta Clarke in Uganda;
a Christian, died from AIDS -   382

Terry ALLEN
no true sobriety until...   354

Pauline ALLEN   392
suggests home for 'Good News' team

ALPHA Courses
West to experiment with Alpha   442
120 enrolled for first Alpha   442
answering **your** questions?   452
various responses to Alpha   452
what one 'young couple' found   452
infra-structure to Alpha   453
new Alpha course in West   460
Alpha mushrooms, 4000 courses in UK; only 1 in 200 Londoners attend church. Great need/ hunger   460
Responses from some who attended Alpha in West: 463
Barbara Rearey- 'I was aware of God's love, I gave my life to the Lord, for me Alpha was a blessing.'
Bill & Mandy Johnston 'the most meaningful conversations took place at those meal times'..   464
John Wilson 'God niggled at me; my thoughts grew serious about joining the Alpha, and I had an urge to know more about God, I experienced a fulfilment in every session'.   464, 473
Harry & Ruth Wakelin 'one significant difference was the communal meal where we made new friends. This is where the ice was broken'   465
Of Alpha, Harold & Joy   465
McCaughan say 'we are immensely grateful, every point was gently and convincingly dealt with, one felt a gradual bonding'.
Alpha Group Number Ten gives respite care   466
TL calls folk to Youth Alpha   470
Alpha inspires Roberta Corbridge to write in response to Alpha   486

Chris ANNETTE
God works a miracle, miracles! 101

ANNIVERSARIES
we celebrate first anniversary   13
our tenth anniversary   107
Silver Jubilee   **267**

ANOREXIA NERVOSA AND ME.
Heather Ennis tells the story   308
terminal illness - diary kept   **403**

Where APOSTLES lived and laboured - modern Turkey
The Bailies visit Laodicea, Ephesus, Cappodocia   314

ARMISTICE DAY
to help you meditate worthily   87

Ethel ANDERSON
felt impelled to go to Jean Darnall's
meeting, profound effect   91

Hugh ANDERSON
reflections   104
visits all homes of young people
181

ANGELS
only one set of footprints   143
an angel intervenes to save   220

Heather ARMSTRONG   405
enriched choir   405, 523

Carol ASPINALL   361, 442
MS, but life rooted in Christ   522

David BAILIE
installed as minister of West   2
goal to nurture caring fellowship
and realise potential of all   3
insights from Church in India   5
must discard negative mindset   6
key role of 'layman'   6
A personal testimony   99- 101
off-duty, rest needed   136
gratitude to many   137
40th anniversary of ordination   423
stepping down as minister-
pastoral team & congregation
strong.   499
on retiring David Bailie expresses
appreciation to Presbytery   505
and to Maurice McKenzie   505
'looking back and forward'   525
'my successor, Charles McMullan'
526/528

Rhoda BAILIE   526
one name that seldom appears in
'West Church Journey"!

Elizabeth BAILIE
A Manse Childhood   118
teaches in Jagadhri, India   182
intriguing glimpse of Delhi   183
impressions of school, principal   183
shopping with my friend, Rani   184
first experience of an Indian bus
184
top-knots & plaits, fun!   186
schizophrenic Elizabeth Bailie!
186
Chauvinism   188
reputation as hard-bargainer!   188
'stay another year' - but no!   189
off to Delhi for library books
192

a horrid day!   192
motor-bike, in sari, side-saddle   193
Hegelian sequence   193
seated on throne-like chairs   193
beggars obsequiously kissing feet
204ff

David BAILLIE
1971 Clerk of Session   115
leads SS for many years
takes service recordings to shut-ins

Eleanor BAILLIE
Holy Spirit gives energy and
purpose   103

Ronnie BAIRD   420, 459

BANNERMAKERS   431, 523
Anne Anderson tells story of
Banner Sewing Group
'Liz Baird readily agreed to join
me.'
Decorative banners for New Hall,
then for church- and for others   523

Reg BATES
from Healing service to various
ministries   155, 395

Ronnie & Doreen BEGGS
give their experience of West after
ten years.   259

BELCANTO   352
inspirational music group
an alternative Praise service   366
Passion music on Palm Sunday
1996   457

Sore BEREAVEMENT
Margaret Davidson finds help   175
coping with bereavement/loss   369

BIBLES
commemorative bibles for young
people, new church opening   17
Billy Graham commends
'Living New Testament'   80
Like Augustine: take, read!   95
full 'Living Bible' commended   130
expository teaching from John &
Acts at Sunday services   164
1984, Bibles for use in church   233

BIBLE-BUSTERS
7- 11 years, 61 present   202

Junior BIBLE CLASS   214

Men's BIBLE Group   31

BIBLE TEXTS
blue velvet bag in church   107, 304

BIRTHDAY BLESSINGS
introduction of   70
'a turning point'

Count your BLESSINGS   34

BLOOD   Anne Anderson   342
dark red splashes   342
many questions, painful truth   343

BODY ministry   493ff
creative, open to dynamic of Spirit

BOOKSTALL
cheaper paperbacks a boon   37
many books recommended   37
20 paperback books added- £5!   65
3 books on Suffering   67
provides holiday reading   68
recent additions   79, 116
revolving bookstand, new books
    130; 136, 165
elders peruse books to commend
in homes visited   136, 152
books & music cassettes   162
books on bereavement, etc   175
3 books on tramps! and others   189
201, 205, 237, 249, 268, 306, 323
Massive bookstall in Approach
Room, for books, cassettes and
for lending   313

BOWLING CLUB
generates 1980 friendships!   34
a solitary figure   123; 287

BOYS' BRIGADE   176
Derick Ridddell - early days   177
First annual display   191
Review in 1982   215
Junior BB Castlewellan holiday
243
Bugle Band at Omagh   337

Nervous BREAKDOWN   355
couldn't live with the guilt
now blessed and a blessing!
355

Rev. Elizabeth BREZELL
to lead West conference   474

BROTHER'S KEEPER? Yes!
say Eileen Scott & Jean
McCormick! 165

REV. JAMES BROWN
American minister tells how
'the Spirit fell' on his church 76

REV. ROLAND BROWN
a divided congregation- an amazing
change takes place 71, 277

BROWN OWL
Sallie Rees hands over to
Gwyneth Bayly 27

Sharon BRYANS 440
'this Holy Spirit stuff not for today.'
a veil lifted, compassion, not
judgement, passion for Jesus 440
little African children, Kenya 441

"BUILDING BEGINNERS"
May 1994- a monthly feature for
children begins in WCN.
411

Walter BURRELL 360
always an inspiration to us 361

BUS STOP
providing a seat by the bus-stop 50

Mike & Lorraine CAHOON 521
Lorraine- freedom to enjoy the Lord
in a brand new way
Mike- West dedicated to the whole
ministry of any individual entering
through its doors.

Elsie CAMPBELL
Jesus my Lord; danced in Spirit 133

Adeline CAMPBELL
Tuesday Together 150

Violet CAMLIN
inscribed Cradle Roll certificates
for hundreds of our children 476

Hugh CAMPBELL
becomes Clerk of Session 124, 150
becomes 'assistant' to the minister
162
resigns as Clerk of Session,
'moving on', in peace 210

CARERS
for those at breaking-point 462

CARING
Seminar by Selwyn Hughes 251

Christine CARLETON
love poured out, arthritis healed 264

Edward CARLETON
I went along just to please John 264

CARNALEA
wooden buildings in old,
closeknit community 12

CELL groups
overseeing 13,000 adult cells 211
avoiding 'fellowshipitis',
discerning, motivating leaders 212

Rev. J.T. CARSON
many new churches being built 4.

Margaret CATHCART
sees amazing Christian Aid projects
in India. 385

CESSATIONIST theology-
patient and intense study of
Scripture leads Jack Deere to reject
it. 422

CHALLENGING LIFESTYLES
474
post-Alpha course, January 1997

CHARISMATIC services:
Ethel Anderson recalls 91
European charismatic conference
128
CONFERENCES at Bangor,
Portrush and Rostrevor 126
Presbyterian ministers lead 126
1974 Dublin - received Spirit
just like us! 135
West, host role in conferences 135
1975 Dublin meeting, 4000 present
140
Ten + years later - 2 amazing
testimonies of earlier fruitfulness
141

CHILDREN'S CHURCH
began with first service 11

CHINA -PCI mission work 478
Rev. Jack Weir 'back home' visit

CHOIR
in operation from early days 11
Palm Sunday service enhanced
when congregation has the words
54
Harry Wakein's visit to choir 84
1993 rebuilding in progress 375,381

CHRISTIANITY
intellectually discredited? 46
Dr. Mulligan robustly denies 46-48
how to become a Christian 85

CHRISTIAN AID
plants great forests in Algeria 40
money well spent, fine projects 94
Margaret Cathcart, trip to India 384

CHRISTIAN NATIONALS
trains indigenous believers to share
gospel with 2000 millions 378
harvesting in storm, China 382
our first student, St. Petersburg 383
our second student, Philippines 383
visit of "Men of Vision" choir,
Indonesian Seminary 384
600 village churches planted 384
our Filopino student, India 402
8 new churches planted 420
Rajasthan Bible Institute 450
Filopino graduates, another enrolled
450.

CHRISTIAN ENDEAVOUR
group for young people to be started
led by George Coburn & Elsie
Campbell 125
Junior C.E. started 134
C.E. in 1982 213

CHRISTMAS
truly historical and genuine 109
angel messenger, virgin birth 109
Magi guided by star 109, 111
events more than folklore, fable 109

CHRISTMAS DAY
1965 offering plants trees 42
not for indulgence, but worship 62
invite some lonely person 87
WCN Editor contrasts 1666 & 1970
88
secret formula for special party 144
Jesus comes to Strangeways,
Prison- a cell filled with light 281
Terry Laverty- smart goals for
Christmas 450

CHRISTMAS FAIR
run by Women's Guild 14, 41
women worth more than rubies
1966, £700 raised! 50

1969, £800 raised 79
1970, £800 raised 89
1976 superb market, diverse goods
glorious meeting-place 156

CHURCH
a church at the crossroads 3

CHURCH ALIVE 245
amazingly alive in China after
communist attempt to crush it.
In 1985, possibly 50 million who
believe in Christ.
Secrets of its survival and
amazing growth 245-246

CHURCH ATTENDANCE
a good habit 83

CHURCH BUILDING
Women's Guild raise money for
furnishing 11
steelwork erected 12
good progress in furnishings 16
features of new church 24
Church Lounge refurbished 30
to be left open during weekdays 37
Major Hall, 30
Intermediate Hall 49
Plans for Courtyard Hall 123
church under-floor heating fails 163
leaking Praise Room roof needs
replacement 170
sought to be frugal, but pressure
mounts on halls 203
let's build a new hall 221
church cedar shingles cleaned,
Praise Room repairs 228
February 1984 New Hall for
£96,400 233
2 stained glass windows 237
in China lay people witness
effectively without a church
building
refurbished church Lounge to be
used for Sunday Creche 286
1992 purchase of 2 bungalows 363
inauguration of visionary seminars
369
'91' fully integrated 372

CHURCH COMMITTEE
election of church committee 53
report on 1967 a deficit 74, 92, 115
1979 election a vote for **deacons**
172; 1983 new committee 228
1995 jottings 444

CHURCH DECLINE
because of affluence, secularisation
39, 46

PCI CHURCH EXTENSION
4 new buildings in 1965 39
Centenary Appeal, West response
45

CHURCH GROUNDS
let's set our church in a garden 50,
layout of 'garden' 51
1984: grounds laid out in memory
of Cecil and Eileen Scott 238

CHURCH HOLIDAYS
glorious weather at Kerrykeel 229

CHURCH GROWTH
Bishop Newbigin promotes 7
need to maintain intimacy 31
greet by name 32
or is **decline** inevitable? 39
we have population explosion 44
West to be erected? 43
additional chairs needed, 1966
church growth model, Korea 208
Yonggi Cho, perpetual growth 210
1994 West plan for growth
involved increased personnel
455
1997 forging a strategy for future
growth- 6 weeks study of Rick
Warren's 'Purpose-driven church'.
to reach the un-churched.
481
intense study of growing churches
and of the New Testament 481
not interested in **transfer** growth
open letter to the un-churched 482
turning seekers into saints 483
members asked to use their 484
talents through SHAPE profiles-
50 spheres of service offered!

CHURCH SERVICES
something for us to learn? 40
leading our young to pray aloud 52
voluntaries, prelude to worship 52
expository study of Bible 77, 237
use of Proverbs & Psalms 77
extra morning service 159
200+ regularly present 160
attempt to energise **evening** service
163
fruitful **Guest services** 212, 260
'I felt critical' 263
**3 morning services from
September 1984** 237
significant adjustments 445

CHURCH STATISTICS
why numbers are inflated 90

CHURCH neighbours
gift from St. Gall's 25
consecration of St. Gall's 43
help from a good neighbour 78
practical care for those in need 243
our 3 churches produce
brochure to welcome newcomers
251

CHURCH UNITY
by 1980? 32

CHURCH UNLEASHED 239
that the gifts of the Spirit be
released to reach out to people in
every kind of need. Vignettes given
of various churches that have done
this -that we may learn! 239

Glenn CLARK
Quotes from 'I will lift up mine
eyes' 110ff
sees lives transformed, meets man
of mystery, hinds' feet praying
112ff

CLIQUE 94
no clique in West, you **are** wanted!

George COBURN Sr. 140
totally available to God - and us!

George COBURN
"Our beloved Mrs Jameson" 222
"Painting for Pleasure" 495

Joan COCHRANE
spends year in Falklands with forces
344

Andrew COLE 265
Healing - born again -Life in Spirit
'be a minister!' 407
Union, Maghaberry, Ballygowan
443
licensing 459

Florence COLE
'a saving grace' 266

'COME TOGETHER' CHOIRS
songs of Jimmy Owens, promoting
openness to God and one another.

Belfast choir crosses divide   126

Advisory COMMITTEE, formed,
set to work and proceed with hall-
building plans   14

COMMUNION
Sacrament on our first Easter Day   11
Communion Table, font, pulpit   16
last communion in Carnalea House   16
eating worthily, agape love   55
Presbyterian communion service
National Dublin charismatic   141
beautiful cloth given by Mrs
Elizabeth Jameson   157
Sunday evening communion   179
20+ come for first time
15 young people come forward   228
first Christmas Eve Communion
service, 1983, 8 young people   233
a beautiful communion cloth for
the New Hall worship   244
evening communion with sung
elements of liturgy   269, 343

COMPASSION
never to lose it!   14

CONSTITUTION
of congregation, January 1967   51

CONVERTS
caring for, counselling and
discipling, making witnesses   286
must be nurtured in the Body   378

Yvonne COOKE
appointed for pastoral work,
especially among women   125
Yvonne (Cooke) now ADAMS,
now writes of her time in West
as a peak and a highlight   161

COUNSELLING   485
Heather Thompson tells of
extensive, in-depth ministry,
in which she has trained others.

Roberta CORBRIDGE
a northern Protestant in
Dublin Rally, 15000+   386
Alpha triggers response in
writings   486

COUPLES' CLUB

early, vigorous life   12
"African Night"   14

COVENANTING
Harry Wakelin prepares booklet   27
gives 50% increase, so needed!   170
a covenants' breakthrough   172
1983 covenants yield £10,000.

Alan COWIE
'prove to me that Jesus existed'   326
the documentation   326
agnostic finds faith through
revelation of Jesus   329

Alison COWIE
'happy as atheist'   327
Alan's long illness
Life in the Spirit seminar   327
sheer magnitude of God's love   328

CRIME
and imprisonment   400
huge increase in imprisoned   400
Charles Colson 'Crime & Morality'

Visit of Jean DARNALL   90
tells 'angel' story to our children   91

Joan D'ARCY
a story of grace   105

DAWN SERVICES, Ballywalter 92
Ethel Anderson recalls
1983 Dawn service, 200+ present   224

DEATH   338
Evelyn **would not** accept her
husband's death,, anger, depression,
she wanted nothing to do with God.
Wrapped in a cloak of depression.
Lost her eye from cancer.
A healing seminar brings life.
Life that conquers death, a gateway
into his presence.   340
death deals us heavy blows   404
terminal illness- a diary kept   403
reflections on Daphne's death   506
'dear friends gone to be with Jesus'   518
sorrow as well as boundless joy-
'two other members of our small
roup died'   522

DEDICATION

of Carnalea House   3
of new church   23
of Major Hall   30
of Praise Room Suite, 1975   135
of new organ, Moderator   160
of '91' by Moderator   368

DELIVERANCE   436
Ellel Grange team visit West
Ken Symington bears witness   461
deliverance ministry widespread
in revivals in Korea, China,
South America etc   438
ministry of Carlos Annacondia,
e.g. Olmos High Security prison   438

DEPRESSION
'I lost my baby'   168
14 years, enough on drugs   357
lost job, new opportunity   368
Janet DERRAUGH   509
I would have been spiritually poorer

DISCIPLESHIP
disciple one person, win the world
in 32 years!   223

Ken & Pamela DOBBIN
give their experience of West after
15 years.   258
And, in 2006, update us on their
kindfund for Kenya   259

Lillias DODDS
and the American church   73

Gwen DODDS
special place, special people   199

Irwin DONAGHY
a remarkable young man   35

DONEGAL
invitation for week of renewal   334
'the Seventy returned with joy'   335
some lessons learnt   334
not one evangelist, many involved   335

The DORES
in Japan   267, 269
the Dores paint a picture   273
in Japan - one year on!   282
great news from Dores   283; 290
live link   292
agonising decision -return UK   303
back in England   307, 315
Graham joins Wycliffe BT   318,

330, 361
exquisite treasure - New Testament
translation in Obolo language   373
Vagla Christians of Ghana find
culturally appropriate music   488
gratitude for partnership, gift 529
call to translate Bible in remote
and desolate area   500

Ken & Sandra DOUGLAS   310
first Sandra, hurt, rejects God- then
Ken desires what Sandra receives .

DRAMA CLUB
started   55; 66
Jack & Beanstalk   85
Diary of Anne Frank   75
Laburnum Grove   93
The heiress   93

DRAMA,
an absorbing interest   93
a ministry in drama   238 242

Edna DREW
a big umbrella of love and a
fulfilling task   104

Florence DUNLOP
gives thanks and trusts!   98

ELDER/S
as pastor, Rev. D.P.Thomson
challenges us.   36
taking work to heart   123
in 1967 70% qualified vote   52
in 1979 33% qualified vote   172

ELECTRICITY
crippling strikes in 1973   123
1976 huge jump in charges   152

ELLEL GRANGE visit West   436
'I was broken and freed before God'
490

ENCOURAGEMENT
it sustained me   493

ENEMIES
Starr Daily's 'mental portrait
gallery of all my enemies'.
69

ENVISAGING
"Wouldn't it be fine if..."   63
seeing the harvest Jesus sees, 272
helping people to have 'Jesus eyes',
learning from para-church groups
let's **start** the ministry   272

EVANGELISM
intensive training in China   271
Manual **for Evangelism &
Outreach,** prepared in West   274
street evangelism in Chile   285
church-centred evangelism   285
by members of local church   374
in run-down, desolate estate   376
some are natural evangelists   426

EVELYN'S STORY, as told by her
daughter, Roberta Corbridge   338

Major EXPANSION   362
opportunity not to be missed   362
financial package quickly in place
Heather EVES
becomes involved with **Life**,
care for the unborn   323
Heather & Jeremy EVES
marriage preparation   381

God's FAITHFULNESS   141
healed boy, now Methodist minister

FAMILY SERVICES
testimony and other elements   159
singing in whispers lest discovered
by communist authorities   169
Christmas, good news for families
209
1984 Dobson Family video series
and Bible Studies   232
Dobson video led by Brian &
Christine Martin   372

FAMILY viewing safeguarded   267
devotions in the family   405

FANNER BEES
the skills of concentrated, corporate
praying   70, 84,
Manual of Prayer   277
How might a Fanner Bee pray?   278

FAREWELL!   512
David & Rhoda Bailie give thanks
and bless!
Yesterday is history, tomorrow is
mystery, today is a gift and we call.,
it the present!   513
"Away Day" with Kirk Session:
discovering the new minister of
God's choosing   514

Patricia FERGIE in India   330
writes from Woodstock School
333, 335, 381

PCI's FLAME '74   127
West promotes this endeavour   127
fruitful meetings in homes   127-129
AILEEN JERVIS testifies
'Jesus radically changed my life'
129
fulltime involvement & ministry
129

FLITTING
move into new church   23

FORGIVENESS
the joy of   197
strength to forgive   289
Forgive? No! Stunned! I will!   289
In political & personal terms.
a soft option?   399
Wiesenthal, Polish Jew, 89 relatives
murdered by Nazis, refuses plea
of dying German officer, for
forgiveness. Was he right?   399
marchers chant 'we forgive you' 399

FOUNDATION STONES   7
unveiled September 1962   13

George and Jean FRAME
ardent workers for the Lord   137

Barbara FRAZER
from rejection to heaven!   116

FREEWILL OFFERINGS
recorded by number, not name   14
5 levels of giving   66

FRIENDSHIP GROUP formed   360

FRIENDSHIPS
TL speaks eloquently of many
friendships. 'I cherish so many'
504

Very Rev. A. A. FULTON   4
missionary service of new minister

FUNERALS
that drained spiritually and
physically   502

Doris GALBRAITH
the story of James, profoundly
handicapped child, 'I loved this
little 'broken' boy deeply'   324
A song to James, with love   325

GALLIPOLI visited   61

a moving story of an elderly lady

GARDENING CLUB
started 55; 65

Eileen GARRETT
divorce, despair, peace 196

Tom GARRETT
missionary call, sidetracked 197
drift away,, broken marriage,
poorer, wiser disciple 198

GENTLENESS
God orders all with gentleness 32

Ian GIBSON 189, 489
Ian has done a prodigious amount
of printing work in West, and most
recently in sound amplification 489

Margaret GIBSON
wheelchair prospect yet healed
and transformed 153
servant heart- goes **home** 319

Shelagh GIBSON
set free to be loving and fruitful 168

Spiritual GIFTS
emerge when offered
wholeheartedly to the Lord 249

Lenore GILMORE
ardently distributes Herald 29, 44

GIRLS' BRIGADE 178, 179, 181
First annual display 192
Review in 1982 215

GOD
can we truly come to know Him?
Experiment 57
Does God speak to you? 105
a very practical God! provided for
my *real* needs 511

GODPARENTS
congregational godparents for
children baptised in West 35

GODLESS = RUTHLESS
violence released among young
in our own community 434

Sharing GOOD NEWS
notable successes in Java and
Romania to encourage us 252

GOOD NEWS TEAMS 391
in 1993 twenty homes in West
received these teams 391
Paul Shields led such a team 392
Reg Bates led 2 teams 395
Hilary Guest led a team 396

GRACE   Henri Alexander 522
the grace of God - in West!
met spiritual thirst in Life in Spirit
seminar; many enriched 523
bringing others to Jesus 523

Harry GRAHAM 312
shortly before he died Harry felt led
to write this letter to his minister

Lyla GRAHAM
God gives healing, a caring heart 103

Paul GRAHAM - his story
how God used Saddam Hussein 417
writes about Men's Weekend -Holy
Spirit's presence in Ballycastle 449
writes to Eamon Holmes on
re-incarnation 454

GRANDPARENTS 509
role in AIDS-stricken Africa and
in our western society 509
the story of an intrepid gran 512

Cecil GRANT
help! I'm becoming a minister! 412
letter from America 427
in back-woods of W. Virginia 434
'extremes of poverty' 443
new placement, Revelation study 451
study on 'Judgement', Buddhism 473
to study for doctorate at Cambridge 483

GUIDES
at camp with Deirdre Morton 59
we form a BUNNY pack 78
review in 1982 214
new Guide leaders 287
all guides attend Family service 319

The GUITAR group
nurturing a ministry of praise 366

GULF WAR
fear leads 2 sisters to Christ 347

William HALL
was drifting, was restored and
trained for service, with still
growing mid-week ministry 155

HALLOWE'EN
Harmless or dangerous? 445
our response in West 446

Julie HAMILTON
Joins West team 321
place in West team 380
installed as deaconess 380
Julie leaves West 432

Rev. David HANNA
visits elderly in West 46

Visit of Michael HARPER 69

Adam HAREINSON
reflections on Daphne's death 506

Rev. Ian HART to help us 396

Pat HAWTHORNE
something missing, despair 357
other religions - Life in Spirit 357

Divine HEALING
'The Forgotten Talent'; 'I believe
in miracles' - books to be read 92
West service each Sunday evening
92, 122, 153, 311
Hinds' feet healing, remarkable 120
Seminar on divine healing 169
George Moffett's experience 179
at Praise services - experiment
Seminar to equip for Healing
service 251
my injured back healed 266
dying uncle's faith renewed 297
holiday experience of sickness
and healing 311
migraines of 30 years healed 330
healing through prayer/fasting 332
I felt a movement in my injured
back 358
I had never seen a demon before 423
'Bethesda of West End' 468

HEAVEN
we meet in heaven 118
the music of heaven 139

Rev HEMANT PARMAR 349
spends year in West, describes

church life in Ahmedabad 350

Rachel HICKSON 524

HOLIDAY CLUB
Elizabeth Kearney, 1977 159
Alvin's Summer Scheme 304, 333

On HOLIDAY
Go to church, worship
and learn from others : 235
the Kennedys in Oxford 235
Poo Choo Lee in London.
On holiday, go to church 236
'On holiday with Nannie' 512

Renee & Sam HOLLINGER,
married in West, living in England,
Renee attends Seminar while 'on
holiday' with mum 218-220
'the worst year' becomes the best
year - how Sam and 2 sons come to
faith in Christ 220

HOLY SPIRIT
baptism in Spirit, in Timor 67
and breaking of addictions
praying 'in the Spirit' 217
baptism in Spirit - fear! 296
'my husband could see such a
difference' 296

HOLY WEEK SERVICES
united services - Easter joy 66
131, 242
ultimate depths of judgement to
the very heights of heaven 509

HOME GROUPS
need for small groups and large 82
springing up spontaneously
plans to have a dozen 206
'Expressing His Life' course 206
"Goals & Guidelines" 234
Evangelism Manual produced
for use in West 274
"Celebration of Discipline" course:
may not become spiritual giants
but we all may learn something!
310

HOMOSEXUALITY 446
finding the way of truth and love -
4 approaches in churches 447
human sexuality, biblical base
448
outworking of gospel 448
alienation and inclusion 449

study of 300 male homosexuals-
no close relationship to fathers 479

HOSPITALITY
Ann & Maureen Kennedy
drew a group in 20's & 30's 166,
397
Hugh & Anne Anderson decided to
invite a few people to their home,
now 2 groups meet! **173**
Hugh was asked to share his
experience with other elders -from
which grew Willie Hall's
Wednesday Night Prayer meeting.
Margaret Bailie asked to promote
hospitality: ambitious plans 173
meat-loaf recipes for lunches! 188
Hospitality to **Christians** from 396
overseas, gives encouragement
and forges new links with Croatia.

HOUSE COMMITTEE
to ensure good use of halls 56
well-ordered use of halls 209

HOUSING ESTATES
Anne Wooderson's experience 376
Arthur Young in Leeds 413
Barry McCroskery in Paris 416

HUMILIATING OTHERS
dire consequences, breeds sickness,
must relinquish ill feelings 56

Jim & Maureen HUNTER
visit- Jim Hunter, BMMF 175
Jim joins West team 151
healing of myasthenia gravis 152
trains for presbyterian ministry 151
visit to Pakistan 272
Meditation - sickness of a child 299
On Afghan refugees 300
Farewell to Jim Hunter 312

HUSBANDS
give your wife a treat! 87

IMPERATIVE 520
The Christian imperative is to tell
men that this God whom they
encounter, came to earth to draw
them into the divine family

INDIA
Visit of Rev. Suleman Parmar 26
welcome and profitable visit of
Ernest Christian 195
Electric fans for Ahmedabad 240

Bailie links renewed in 1988
and in 2000 301
Bishop Paul visits us for 150th
anniversary of our missionaries
going to India 326
welcome to Rev Hemant Parmar
349

INTERCESSIONS FOR IRELAND
Ten-Point plan for prayer 119

INTERFLO
love, teaching, support, fun 494
bold enough to step out for Jesus

INVITATIONS 466
does your church give invitations?
Gallup says 63% would attend
if invited 466
140 enrolled in Third Alpha 466
'a risky invitation' 518

ISOLATION
deafness isolates 85
church and social integration 87
'get out and do', enrich your life 87
'signing' for the deaf 460

JESUS CHRIST
the Lord Jesus appeared to me 117

Betty JACKSON
muses! 98

Ingeborg JAMESON
Migraine attacks - God's great
mercy 330

Elaine JEFFERSON 510
God's faithfulness, making
people whole 511

Albert JENNINGS
nurtures "Painting for Pleasure" 494

Noel & Janet JOHNSTON
receive a Good News team with
life-changing results 392-394

Our own JOYSTRINGS 124
anointed singing by 5 young women

Silver JUBILEE
Substantial debt reduction 252
our Jubilee tapestry 253, 256
Silver Jubilee magazine 257
Silver Jubilee Thanksgiving 257-90
Visit to India for the Bailies! 257

JUSTICE
only forgiveness halts juggernaut
of 'justice' 399

Ann KENNEDY
news of Minterburn & Caledon 411

KENNEDY
death of President K. 26

KENSINGTON TEMPLE
grows rapidly in secular London,
principles behind this growth 468-70

KIRK SESSION
election of our first Session 52
impressive ordination service 54
Hard at work; many meetings 58
appoints Board of Christian
Education 60
certificate award scheme 75
and Board for Pastoral Care 60
32 meetings in just over a year 66
Kirk Session report for 1968
1969 Election of elders, includes
4 women 75
1972 18 new elders 114
1975 election of 11 elders 147
1977 Retreat on Praise. Rev. David
McKee 160
elder in harmonious Kirk Session 167
1979 18 extra elders needed 171-2
decision to start BB and GB 176/7
statistics that prompted this 177
1980 was year of growth 202
1983 election for 20 elders - 226
principles for selection 227
tribute to Norman Blair, 233
sympathy expressed to Mary 230
KS asks Alvin to prioritise the
youth scene 276
KS appoints Noel Boyd as BB
captain, and Chris Wilson as Youth
Club Leader 299
KS spend day to consider wider
ministries in enlarged premises 366
overview of work of pastoral team 379
1993 election of elders 383, 386
ambitious training programme
for elders and church Visitors 391
KS report on 1995 456
1997 election of elders 488/9, 497

KITCHEN
facilities strained 13

David KNOX
memories and reflections 21
youth scene in 1971, Beatles,
Rolling Stones, Bob Dylan etc 95
tells of vibrant family service in
David Watson's church, York 142
licensing, thanks 165
call to Downpatrick 202

The Church in KOREA
picture of a praying church 317
'organise massive prayer for
great outpouring', says Cho 317

Astrit KUMNOVA 489
Alan Crichton tells of our harvest
gifts for Astrit in Croatia. 489, 496

VOLUNTARY LABOUR
1970 our halls painted for £100 86

LAUGHTER
much smiling and laughter 492

TERRY LAVERTY
to join us in West 410
licensing 411
focus on families with young 414
urges men, young Christians
to become involved, find a job 427
personal testimony to faithfulness
of God - dad's early death, brother's
murder, moving on with Jesus 432
TL suggests smart goals in life 450
on physical force & soul force 457
TL alerts: Mandate event for men 458
TL: pay your children to learn Bible,
a worthwhile investment 475
TL on spiritual spring-cleaning 477
TL reflects on his time in West 502

John LAWSON
contribution to building projects 28
battling inflation in 1975 146

LEAFLETS
how to use SGM leaflets 459

LEAGUE OF CHURCH
LOYALTY formed 15

LIBRARY.
'Give & Take' Library 29

Bobby LIDDLE
slips quietly into West 451
licensing 459
youth Alpha, unapologetic 472
reports on youth work at our
annual meeting 1997 477
ordination as associate-minister 488
in full leadership of Young West
a tailor-made service for the young
the need to **belong intense** **491**
they need **constant** affirmation 491
BL's time in West 491

LIFE IN SPIRIT SEMINARS 148
50 enrolled at Praise & Prayer 150
you could ask anything 166
desire to serve God led to C.E. 166
the turning point in my life 168
a 'gulf stream' in West 216
saved Renee's marriage 219
2 new Seminars, May 1984 235
'the seminar was an education' 262
seminars lead to Open Nights 388
Alvin leads for 16-17 year olds 292
'I saw the power of God at work
in my group' 294
firm, gentle progression 308
seminar evokes poem of trust 331
Junior Life in Spirit, 9-11 years
and Teens & Twenties 333
'the lovely gift of tongues' 354
record numbers enlisting, 1992 363
Don & Helen, young people's 412
impossible to compute spiritual
benefits - 8 wonderful months! 435
TL: presence & power of Holy
Spirit 503
how Heather Thompson introduces
these seminars 504
that morning I met lovely people 517
your last chance to join seminar 517

LISTENING POST -
A confidential service offered by
Doreen Hayward, for individuals to
talk, listen, pray, with Doreen
Hayward. 311

Rev. ALVIN LITTLE
our new minister 269
1989 plans for young people 304
coffee bar outreach 305
place in West team 379
called to Donaghadee 382

LONELINESS

'she produced 3 £5 notes' -
'sit down and talk!' 172
young mum -creche a lifeline 178
'but then you come'! 282

LOVE
A vacuum of love in secularist
China- unprecedented power
through Jesus Christ 246
LOVE LOST-no longer weep 319

William LYNN
to play organ at **first** a.m. service
159; 359

Ken MACARTNEY
takes on cleaning and maintenance
duties in West, 1996 458

MANSE FELLOWSHIP 115, 121

A MANSE childhood
Elizabeth Bailie's recollections 118

MARCH FOR JESUS,
Dublin, 1990 325

MARRIAGE
how love may be engendered 145
my marriage broke up 168
'that Scripture not for you, Renee'
219
'after the wedding' 322
marriage vows renewed at
Childhaven conference 351
'looking up the aisle" 381, 462,
Chris & Catriona Ritchie express
appreciation 462
Christian wife/ unbelieving
husband, how to cope 388
problems? talk directly to God! 426
Michael Perrot's plea for marriage
preparation; pastors please note 479
marriage at an end, myself alone
490
Oleg Morohovets: wedding exciting
511

Brian & Christine MARTIN 408
train for fulltime ministry at
Regent College, Vancouver 433
443 Return from Regent 451

Walter MacALLISTER
leads Friday Men's group 406

William McCLELLAND
1982, new Clerk of Session 213
359; tribute to our Clerk 406

Jean McCORMICK
early years, third world, Eileen
Scott, healing, prayer 19
'never stops wondering about life's
Mysteries' 519

Barry McCROSKERY
with Operation Mobilisation
in France - is it worth it?
406, 409, 410.

Geoff McELWAINE 345
Spring Harvest: 'shaken but not
stirred' 345

Irene McILRATH
God's love - wonderful force 212

Rev. Charles McMULLAN 526/28
'My call to West Church, Bangor'.

DON & PAT McNUTT
leave for Malawi 498
letter from Malawi 508

Lorna McQUITTY
'to find an answer to the burning
question in my heart and head' 517

Christopher McWILLIAMS
wonderful weekend for couples
351

Sharon McWILLIAMS 350
'a brutal tragedy set me searching'

MEN'S GROUP
Weekend at Rostrevor, know
'soul-quickening Presence'
292
Ronnie Baird on Men's Weekend
at Childhaven 459

Friday Morning's Men's group
starts February 1994 406
Walter McAllister reports 474

MILLENNIUM FUND &
PROJECTS 457
Link building & car parking 476

MINISTER
is there to serve you! 42
new minister for West 184

25th Anniversary of DGB
ordination 185
second minister aids growth 202
full work throughout summer 204
Indian minister for West? 301

"MINUS ONE' - for the bereaved
Anne Andrews- invitation to
widows. 462

MIRACLES
'I have seen miracles' 263

MISSIONARY COMMITTEE
254, 255, 322
care for missionary who returns
- Barry. 430

MIZOS are coming to West! 456
Mizoram transformed by gospel

George MOFFETT
licensing of, in West 178
Moffetts speak of West 178/79
call to Cloughey & Portavogie 202

Gill MONTGOMERY 521
"Every day some more of me
crumbled"
If you are going to reach out and
touch somebody's hand, make sure
that hand belongs to Jesus.

The new MORALITY
Dr.Mulligan's critique of 38

MOTHERS & TODDLERS.
start March 1989 318

Thomas MULHOLLAND 385
we welcome Thomas & Lorraine
licensing 411
tells of healing at Ellel Grange 437

Rev. Dr Graham MULLIGAN
veteran Indian missionary 29
and the Mormon Church 36

Bishop Lesslie NEWBIGIN
church growth principles 7

OLD AGE
the beatitudes of one who is old 425

OPERATION MOBILISATION
Chris Ritchie goes to Israel 275

ORGANISTS
1961 Josephine Patterson, Douglas Todd. 4
1966 Adrian Holmes 49, 52
Mrs Jameson: fond farewell 190
June 1980 Maurice McKenzie 194
Our beloved Mrs Jamison, by George Coburn 222
Maurice- his hands seemed to 502 move like lightning - brought delight
David Bailie expresses appreciation of Maurice 505

A new ORGAN
Allen Computer £7300, 1977 158

A heart for OUTREACH 325
June 1990, 50+ come to wait upon God to show us his heart for this.
Christian initiative- bookshop 433

1963 59/60
A momentous year 28
1964 a year of growth 30
1965, heavy influx 33, 35
1967 a new era 52
1969 72, 74
1970 81
1971 7 new developments 89. 92
1972 18 new elders 114
1973 4 questions before Kirk Session 123
1974 Flame '74 127
1975 Week of special meetings 136
1976 Help for troubled Marriages 144
1977 a fluid society, 156
1979 strength-in-depth, elders 172
1979 annual statistics for year 190
1980 2 ministers in partnership 186
1981 for focus, we study 'Acts' 207
1982 'moving on', no recession 210
1984 emphasis on Family 232
1984 January: The after-life 240
1984 The 10 Commandments 241
1988 sustained endeavour after growth, evangelism lifestyle 282
1990 prayer mobilisation 317
1992 major expansion 363

PARENTING with confidence 434
Ian Grant, N.Z. on reconstituted families, skills can be learnt 435
Michael Perrot gives guidance 479
children need encouragement 480
'devout parents, accepted and practised faith in everything' 519

PASTORAL CARE
difficult to find you at home! 458

Dr. W.A.A. PARK.
gives charge to new minister 2
'join new church when small' 4

Jim PATTERSON
reviews impact of YWAM at the end of 25 years on young people 157

PEACE
tangibly imparted 407

PERMISSION granted?!
to invite people home to sing? 326
Desmond PERRY
proof beyond reasonable doubt 357

PERSONNEL
shift from plant to personnel 185
enables additional ministry 267
1989 more personnel enables 7 things:
better pastoral care, open nights, enlarged lending library, enlarged range of seminars, increased training for elders and church visitors; further nurturing of home groups, better Sunday services. 306.

PLAYGROUP established 91

Victor PLENTY
leads team of men to refurbish a home. 30

POLLUTION
physical pollution reduced by 80%
ways to cleanse psychic... 89

Derek POLLEY
1994 teenage Summer Scheme 414

John POOLE
"A Treasurer's Tale" 364

The PRAISE of God.
reformers taught fullness of congregational worship 132

PRAISE & PRAYER MEETINGS
report on first meetings 121
50 enrolled for Life in Spirit 150
Sam Wright describes ethos 151
and clear answers to prayer 151

Jim Hunter refreshed at P&P 151

PRAISE SERVICES
large crowds, brought students 166
each month 182, 201
'it was bliss!' loved, touched! 244

PRAYER
a way to pray Ruth Wakelin 20
5 minutes silence in church before each service begins 25
West Church booklet on 27, 32
We make 'Diary of Private Prayer' available to our members 27
Booklets for SS departments 38
'A Closer Walk' prayers by our members, related to New Testament 39, 42, 53
swift arrow prayers 63
problem-solving prayer 65
'the most meaningful activity' 65
Francis de Sales on 'how'.. 69
spiritual 'fanner bees' - breakthrough 71
a spiritual exercise to release grudges 73
whole church - called to day of special prayer 78
Hudson Taylor, amazing answers 83
George Mueller's secret 84
John Donne - how badly we pray 87
sincerest prayer of Cyrus Brown 89
children conceived:
co-incidence or God-incidence? 108
prayer as 'on hinds' feet' 113, 114
"ten fingers" prayer exercise, early to church 115
pray for young people to be drawn into church fellowship 115
Intercession for Ireland 119
'pray about it 147
prayer & fasting in Korea 208
Jackie Pullinger's way of 216
School of Prayer, Europa, Belfast 224
10 early significant minutes 230
prayer brings growth in China 246
early morning prayer in West 271
late night prayer in West 316
all members in church at once 317
Korea, organised prayer in great numbers 332
in 1945, 27 Christian refugees gathered for prayer- now Seoul Choog Hyun Presbyterian church, with 25,000 members 335
Julie Hamilton New Year prayer 338

dramatic recovery after prayer 347
5-week seminar on Praying 352
4-week seminar on Contemplative
prayer, Doreen Hayward 369
listening to his prayers I felt a
great heat come over me' 464
real heroes of prayer often
lived mundane lives 469
prayer in Sunderland, Africa
474
Heather Thompson and 24-hour
praying 507
Hour of PRAYER 495
hour= 6 slots of 10 minutes 496
guidance for triplets in praying 501
guidelines a wonderful help 507

PRAYER FELLOWSHIP
led by Rev. Tom Patterson 53
learns principles of praying 54

PRESBYTERY Visitation 87, 89
1979 visitation - re-decoration 174
finding 176
1998 visitation 500

The Lord's PRESENCE
'I fell on my knees' 262

PRIDE
pride hurt, a failure 510

PRINCESS DIANA
Pamela Brow writes to Diana 375
Diana took hand of a man with
AIDS 488

Visiting those in PRISON 130
sharing Good News by books 130
more Christian books 156. 162, 165
men in prison praise God 181
Andrew Baillie visits Belfast
prison 188
Men's group at Maghaberry prison
366
imprisonment begets bitterness 400
restitution works! 401
45% of Argentinian prison
inmates become Christian 402
killings stop in Bella Vista Prison,
Medellin, Colombia-
300 men baptised 438
DPP: this gives me hope 440
Packie Hamilton- I will pray for
him everyday 501

PRISON FELLOWSHIP
Frank Rea new Director 288, 292
ministers in Uganda 453

PROBLEMS?
talk directly to God! 426

Special PROJECTS 173/5
Mission Box gifts for these
Easter, Children's Day, Harvest 175
First project: Malawi Book kiosk
Overseas Convener applauds 180
Scholarship to Kenya 185
Convener praises this vision &
support 186, 201
Shankill Rd Mission, 90%
unchurched 190
Bicycles - pastors in Malawi 191,
194, 201
Prantij Leper rehabilitation 203
Missionary Aviation Fellowship
206
project to train 12 village pastors
221
Outreach element of New Hall fund
aids projects 268

PROMISCUITY
private morality, public service 405

PROPHETIC WORDS for today?
Valid and real? 164
a prophecy finding fulfilment? 345

QUESTIONNAIRES
to elicit service from members 51
a 'Good Samaritan' uncovered! 53

QUOTATIONS
worth pondering 70
Hugh Campbell contributes 130,
148.
Unjoltable? 236
about someone who buried her
talent 470

RACETRACK 460
Vision for Church in racetrack
community- chaplain tells story
can you see a niche for the gospel?
461

RATHMORE SCHOOL 476
celebrates 25 years at event in West.

Frank REA
ministers in Uganda 453

Tape RECORDERS
now aid devotion 131

Denise REDPATH 525

I thought I was just fine
God knew about me!
He has shown me how to speak
according to his word, and who I
am in Christ. 525

Duncan REID 102
experiment leads out of agnosticism
Jean REID
from churchgoer to Christian 103

RELEASE
'I released my ex-husband to God'
168

On REMAND
Leslie WILSON ministers hope and
life to such men & boys 156

RESIDENTIAL HOMES
West groups visit 333
God's love shared in simple ways
427
Harry Fulton leads team to
Sandown 489

The glory of RESURRECTION 137
Jesus, resurrection and life 138
2 examples of recall from death 138
Jean Darnall: 'Heaven here I come'
139

REST
well earned and granted! 94

Jane RICHARDSON (Hewton)
Her first visit to West impressed.
She paints a picture of a large and
lively congregation. 165
on Malawi- warm heart of Africa
301
becomes area representative of
TEAR Fund 488
"God does guide us" 515

Chris RITCHIE
with Palestinians on West Bank 300

Don & Helen RITCHIE
to help in West team 314, 333
Don, teaches in West what he
learns at Belfast Bible College 345
Helen with young people in
witness in Bangor 346, 380
Don at Rostrevor youth week 352
Ritchie home burnt down 365
Don, a very merry sinner! 372

Andy ROBINSON
physical and prayer dimension of
Alpha 463

Renee ROBINSON
dimension behind 1600 meals!
463

ROMAN CATHOLICS
friendship and co-operation 36

SANCTUARY
25 new chairs, 1970 88

Albert SCHWEITZER
express appreciation/ gratitude 28
we **express appreciation** for so
many within the body of West
341

Anne SCOTT
distress, sudden unemployment 428
high wall of love 428
'I will supply all needs' 429
the salary and the fleece 429
Brian SCOTT 358
free from pain 359
Richard SCOTT
1997/8 IFES year in Slovakia
488/89

Cecil SCOTT
early days in Carnalea House 8
demits office as Clerk 62
ultimate promotion 163

Eileen SCOTT
death: grief and consolation 217
God's sovereign mysteries 218

SCOUTS
Loch Lomond camp with George
Larmour, Jack Darrah 59
we form a BEAVER pack 77
Scouts in Lake District 97
Squirrels, new group, boys
4-6years,, Winnie Moffett, Lora
Carse 97, 178
Scouts win County Flag 181
1980 camp, Norman Montgomery
194
Review in 1982 215
Our Scouts in Poland
George Stevenson- Chris Miller 372

John SEAWRIGHT
Profile of new minister 184
'walking, leaping, praising God' 200

Saturday 7.30am leaders' meetings
261
tributes to minister 262, 269, 271

SECULARISM
may explain biological evolution,
but fails to acknowledge the
perpetual battle between good and
evil in human relations 519
those who see only the physical
world **fail to see God ever-active
in his universe** 520

Information about SEX 479
Helpful material published by
NavPress. 480
Steve Chalke's videos 'Lessons in
love'. 480
Teen magazines with adult agenda!
480
Farewell to Bob & Mae SHANES
59

Beulah SHIELDS 343
stillborn -'safe in the arms of Jesus'
receives boldness for witness 395

Paul SHIELDS
with some doubt, and under
personal pressure leads a
Good News team 392
a remarkable story unfolds 392/94

Debbie SHAW
Gulf War frightens, love of God
draws. 347

Profound SHOCK
Deaths of Sinclair parents 360
Robert expresses his thoughts 360

SHUT-IN people
tapes of services, poor substitutes,
must take living worship to them
302

SICKNESS
in our West Church staff 416

Rev. Tom SMAIL
forthcoming visit, Pentecostal 66
24th March 1968- significant! 66
installed in Whiteabbey 68
in 1971 speaks to Dublin students
about Renewal 135
visits West, some perceptive
quotations 320
West celebrates 30 years- Tom 352
Smail speaks on Trinitarian

Renewal
Passion Sunday 1998 Tom Smail
speaks on 'the crux of the matter'
504

Violet SIMPSON
key role in Beginners S.S. 30

John SLOAN
in building plans and funding 15
much work done 115

Jimmy SMITH,
American evangelist 395

SMOKING- stopping it 80
Glenda Eddis stops 80
SORROWS
strengthening comfort in 70
3 funerals, 3 days, unprecedented
186

SOCIAL get-togethers 11

SOVEREIGNTY OF GOD
over church history and all 245

SPEAKING IN TONGUES
John Sherrill s book 65
Jackie Pullinger's 'Chasing the
Dragon' 216

Victor STEPHENS
takes over from Mary Blair as
congregational treasurer, 1978
162, 201, 359

Muriel STEPHENSON
'the Lord gave faith to believe' 294
'I bring everything to the Lord'

Helen STEVENSON
a great character 167

Alan & Barbara STEWART 260
Experience related after 5 years in
West. 260/1

Victoria STEWART
with OM in Morocco 415

Caring for STRANGERS.
something to learn 40
speak! to one person! 50

STUDENTS
keeping in contact with them 61

Christmas Conference for them 64
transition gap for young adults 414

SUNDAY
how a Christian family should
spend this day; a gift from God
57, 90
Sunday trading, fractured families
402

SUNDAY SCHOOL
began January 1962 11
radical change in timing, growth,
families attending together 1966 49
irregular attendance, augmenting
staff to improve quality 81
double rota of teachers 108
large numbers, extra teachers 149
111 pupils present in Primary 152
marvellous times, great people 178
June 1980, massed SS choirs 193
needs largely met 200
review in 1982 214
SS teaching for you? 254
Terry Laverty - lack of men! 449
1997 Jayne Fulton paints a picture
of the Sunday School scene 490
standing room only! 491

SURVEY IN BANGOR WEST
100 questionnaires to elicit
attitudes in respect of church 483
analysis of survey, and response
484/5
we offer ' the God who changes
lives' - next Alpha course. 486

SYCAMORE CLUB
for mentally handicapped 251
Margaret Conroy needs help 254
beatitudes for special children 280
13-yearold boy needs a **friend** 286
SC guests of PWA - much fun! 287

Also: could you foster a family?
285
work expands- more helpers 321
God speaks to SC members 322
membership doubles 341
1996 SC flourishes Derek &
Tanya Polley and team 467
how Tanya becomes involved 518
'always refreshed' 519
Henri describes meetings 523

Ken SYMINGTON
to accept the **whole** Jesus 354
successful - but the poorest man;

visits Poland & Lithuania teaching
on Intercession linked with
evangelism- amazing fruit 471
ministry to drug addicts 471
massive virus attack on heart 472
ministry throughout Ireland 472
a Lithuanian pastor in penury 475

TEAR FUND / TRADECRAFT
1976 Hilary Simms runs Tradecraft
crafts' initiative. 149, 153
TEENAGE CHILDREN
Seminar for parents of 369
TERMINALLY ILL
visiting 369

TIMETABLE for groups
timetable in 1979, jigsaw 180

Heather THOMPSON 379
extensive counselling ministry
with training of others 487
HT's ministry in West 493
'you are among friends, Heather'
every relationship in West special!'
"Interflo" 494

Norman THOMPSON
begins to write! 96

Maria TRAPP
upbuilding quotation from 122

Union **THEOLOGICAL** College
3 West students enrolled 275
Jim Hunter, Ann Kennedy, Heather
Lewis.
Gary Wilton, Oxford theological
student - placement in West 276
July 1994, presentations to
Cecil Grant, Brian Martin, Andrew
Cole as they begin theological
courses 413
Become a student at Regent
College, Vancouver with Brian 420

THREE O'CLOCK CLUB 41
their good suggestions implemented
54

TORONTO
a mighty wind from 418
and Holy Trinity, Brompton 418
strange manifestations, yet 419
Jack Deere, surprised by power
of Holy Spirit 421
Peter Roberson (Christian
Nationals) tells of outpouring of

Spirit in his
own local church 424

TROUBLES in Province
that bring despair 73, 115
in 1973 Luke's gospel left in every
home in Ireland 124
Ulster in agony 156
bad news keeps flooding in 209
God's army beats terrorists 230
West issue call for prayer 250
Optimist or Pessimist? 322
1991, murder/destruction 337
GPO Dublin Rally, West member
on platform party 386
'put them in prison and throw
away the key' sentiment! 400
should we pray more? 410
praying for peace: TL cites
Martin Luther King as exemplar
457
1996 bitterness and unrest- a poem
467
83-yearold prays-terrorist converted
501
Prayer Triplets intercede for
province and politicians by name.
507

TUESDAY TOGETHER
Adeline Campbell starts TT 150

'My TURMOIL was constant' 295

Where TWO OR THREE 246
not only for individuals but for
families. Demonstration in China

UNFORGIVENESS
root of immense ill 248

VISION
revelation of Jesus 329
vision, given in prayer in 1992
of greatly enlarged ministry 366
TL visions & dreams for 1996 453
Rick Warren's vision of the church
that should be - a dream! 483
dreams & visions took a
battering 510

VISITING our homes
1988 summer visiting of all homes
with books, news of God's working
and invitations 290
our theological students to help
witness sheets produced & shared
we encourage one another in the

words of Paul, 1 Thessalonians 5
290/291

Sick, you VISITED me!
Robert Crawford + group visits
Bangor Hospital   133

WAITING upon God
conceiving, envisaging, realising
365

WALKING GROUP   501

WJM disillusioned, yet renewal
brought JOY IN THE LORD   167

Harry WAKELIN
a district coming to life   9
Building Fund treasurer   15
the Carnalea House era   17
retires as Church Treasurer   44
becomes Clerk, profile   63, 93
becomes Editor of WCN   81, 93
remembers 'a defining moment'   98

Ruth WAKELIN
a way to pray   20
a poem!   450

Bill WAMSLEY   490
a future for a middle-aged failure?
the honour of being a helper in
his church.

WATERSHED event, 1968   1

Mollie WATSON,
free from arthritis, swims freely
205
a new wavelength, with husband
293

Ronelle WATSON   516
'never interested in churchy stuff -
I hated it!'

Corry WARWICK
tribute to   234
New Hall windows in memory   237

Ivan WARWICK
'the family of God's people'   106
licensing of, in St. Giles   176, 182
'preaching Ivan in'   195

Herbert WEIMANN
redundancy to opportunity   368

WELCOME
we try to give better welcome   174

WIDOWS/ WIDOWERS
12-week Bible Study seminars   369

Doreen WILSON   22
pre-1975 memories, youth,
elder, bible study - with Catholics!

Superintendent of Young People   63

Brian WILSON
early years in West   18

Chris WILSON
-a Bangor hidden from many   408

WITNESS
I went to school and proclaimed the
fact   263
Christian young people should
reach the hundreds of needy young
people on the streets of Bangor   286
credible witness, not platitudes
377

WITNESS BOX
many write of God's grace   292

WOLFCUBS /CUBSCOUTS
WOLFCUBS, pack formed   13
holiday in Newcastle   17
fabulous holiday, Akela Wilson   59

WOMEN'S GUILD/ PWA
began December 1961   11
Review in 1982   216
instead of **taking** an outing,
give an outing   221

God's WORD
hidden in heart brings harvest   34
Jesus' Word pondered brings
life, freedom, undercuts satan's
lies. Experiment and see   146

WORD OF KNOWLEDGE
Wimber relates how dramatic 'word
of knowledge' brings conviction
and salvation   247
Jimmy Smith and...   395

PCI WORLD DEVELOPMENT 79
1969 Christmas Appeal Indonesia
79
1970 transform 50 villages, India 89
1976 Indian Cities,   153

PCI 1982 project for Mataco   223
Indians, Upper Volta farmers   239
South Indian Farming Co-op   231
West raise £3142.
PCI 1984, Food for work, Ethiopia,
forests being restored   240
PCI 1985 domestic water tanks for
Kenya. West response £4178.   249
1987 to help poor farmers, Andhra
Pradesh, India   279
1989 restoring children, freeing
'bonded labourers'   316
1990 literacy programme, Peru   336
1992 Grinding Mill for Tanzania
374
1993 Forestry project in India   402
1994 Tigray, Ethiopia project   423
1995 "Going Home Kits", Sudan
450
1996 for small businesses, Senegal
472
1997 Sagula Forestry project   497
West aims to give 40 trees to each
of 3000 congregations   497

WORLD CULTURE
1971 anti-Christ?   96

WORRY
Dr. Boreham's antidote   29

WORSHIP
intense worship in church   16
Sunday morning miracle   25
whole family should worship
in church together   28
service transformed by worship   36

WORSHIP groups
Junior worship group   303

WEST CHURCH NEWS
to inform and inspire   1
Harry Wakelin, Editor1970/1   81
to inspire us towards outreach   281
gives examples, inspire vision   282
David Bailie's farewell edition
512

Arthur YOUNG
a call to ministry   369, 382
work in Leeds, call to London   413

Jill YOUNG
living in community -difficult!   371
involvement in youth work

YOUNG WOMEN'S
ASSOCIATION, 1966

Margaret Davidson, president 45
provide 100 chairs for New Hall 76

Hugh McCracken trains YWA choir 120
Review in 1982 216

Rev. Michael WOODERSON 376
Good News down the Street 377

Thursday a.m. YOUNG WOMEN
head for Rostrevor CRC 229, 254
urge other groups to have weekend retreats - and men do! 292

Tuesday Night YOUTH 318
Jill Young reports on 50 young people 341
Alan Cowie - their visit to Open Night 346
20 accompany other young people from West to Rostrevor 373
Terry Laverty - men, women! make time for 'rough diamonds' 449
pancake eating competition 478

YOUTH CLUB
Andrew Bailie on "Little Red Riding Hood". 187
Youth Club mania, opportunities, problems, challenges 336

YOUTH DRAMA GROUP 318
lead in Praise service 337
go to Harmony Hill, Lisburn 344

YOUTH GUILD
formed in 1962
junior group, 1965 39

YOUNG WEST CHURCH 268
Young West Weekend, Guysmere
Don Ritchie reports 316
BL: a special place in my heart 491
a watershed weekend 493

YOUTH WITH A MISSION 133
West provide base for YWAM 134
Jim Patterson to lead 134
training weekend for Morocco mission 136
YWAM's Ken WRIGHT visits West, meets our Kirk Session 142
tells remarkable story of Montana minister 143
key strategy of YWAM 144
leads Jayne Ferguson (Fulton) to Olympic Games outreach in Montreal 148
YWAM in Bangor, heartening account of work after perspective of 25 years 157

YOUNG PEOPLE
1971 'what has got into them?' 96
1976 over 100 junior teenagers (12-14 years) in West 148
YWAM joy in Monkstown 149
minister meets young people in homes 164
large, large number in uniformed organisations 206

A YOUNG PERSON
suggests we eat together 54

1985 YOUTH SCENE 254
the Third service with 70,
Senior Youth Fellowship with 40,
Junior Youth Fellowship with 40.
1987 - 150 people involved in youth work. 270
1988 Youth Scene, much buzzing:
Alvin tells of Youth Fellowships, Bible-Busters, Home groups for boys and girls, training conference for Sunday School teachers. 298

YOUTH OUTREACH
1993 prolific youth outreach 397

ACKNOWLEDGEMENTS.

"WEST CHURCH JOURNEY" contains excerpts and quotations from many writers. Through reading and pondering these our members have been enlightened and enriched. We gratefully acknowledge these and have given the sources, as far as possible, within the text, where they occur.

In preparing **"WEST CHURCH JOURNEY"** for publication I acknowledge the help freely and frequently given by **Harry Fulton** to a slow-learning novice on the computer. Harry possesses patience and good cheer in equal and abounding measure!

My thanks are also due to those who eliminated many errors through careful and extensive proof-reading: **Rhoda Bailie, David Bailie, Maureen Bennett, Etta Jennings, Lorna McQuitty, David Thompson, Billy Thompson, Sam Wright.**

Thanks are also due to those who made arrangements for printing, **Ronnie Baird, Bob Johnston.**

PHOTOGRPHS.
It has not been possible to include photographs in "West Church Journey" but these may be found in the West Church website.

[IMPORTANT INSERT].

At page 424 you will find reference to Gospel For Asia. It humbles and thrills me to consider that what I write here about GFA may help reap a far greater harvest into the Kingdom of Christ than all I have accomplished in my total ministry up to this point!
GFA have currently more than 16,000 indigenous missionaries in India and adjacent lands- each one likely to establish more than one church in the course of a year. Currently they have 67 Bible Colleges giving thorough training to thousands of young ministers/ evangelists.
Read about it in www.gfauk.org
Or wwwinfoukgfa.org
Or phone 0800 032 8717
and get a free copy of KP Yohannan's book: Revolution for Mission - so enlightening!
Or talk to me, David Bailie about it (028 91459902) and I will secure a copy for you.
It is amazing to realise that with our support additional indigenous missionaries can be released for fruitful work- at little cost to us! Millions of 'untouchables' may come to receive the transforming touch of Jesus and true life within his fast- growing Church!